THE
ESSENCE
OF
CHINESE
CIVILIZATION

EDITED BY

Dun J. Li

PATERSON STATE COLLEGE

D. VAN NOSTRAND COMPANY, INC.
PRINCETON, NEW JERSEY
TORONTO   LONDON

VAN NOSTRAND REGIONAL OFFICES: *New York, Chicago, San Francisco*

D. VAN NOSTRAND COMPANY, LTD., *London*

D. VAN NOSTRAND COMPANY (Canada), LTD., *Toronto*

Library of Congress Catalog Card No. 67–25328

PRINTED IN THE UNITED STATES OF AMERICA

To June

Preface

This is a book about traditional China, presented in translations of Chinese authors. All the translations are original, and more than eighty percent of them appear in the English language for the first time. The authors range from such famous men as Confucius and Lao-tzu to the comparatively more obscure.

I feel that there is a need for a book of this kind in view of the increasing interest shown by the general public in Chinese culture and the need of a source book in courses on traditional China. Though many books on China have been published in recent years, to my knowledge there is no source book that covers the broad perspective of the entire Chinese cultural system in one convenient volume. To attempt to prepare a book of this nature is obviously an adventurous undertaking due to the potential pitfalls involved in such an ambitious project—pitfalls that are particularly inherent since there is no precedent to follow and no guide to point out directions to the author. But someone must make the first attempt and it is hoped that any mistakes that are made may help authors of subsequent volumes in the same area of concern. For any major undertaking, some humble worker must "move the first stone."

There are three problems involved in preparing a volume of this kind. First, what materials are to be included? Second, are these materials to be arranged topically or chronologically? Third, how are these materials to be rendered into effective English?

The first problem is essentially a problem of choice. Of the millions of pieces of literature that range from imperial decrees to personal diaries, what are the two hundred that are most appropriate for our purpose? The question is not an easy one, and the answer depends largely upon individual propensity or judgement. To me, civilization is not only ideas and ideals that can be argued and debated in abstract terms but, perhaps more importantly, how these ideas and ideals actually influence and effect a way of life. The proper theme of this book is not "the glory that was China," but "traditional China as it really was." To present this panorama, I include in this book a wide variety of materials: sketches, casual observations, personal letters, and short stories as well as the more "respectable" materials translated from the Confucian classics and the dynastic histories. These range from a much-involved, metaphysical discussion of human nature by the Ch'ing scholar Tai Chen to an easy-to-understand contemporary description of a brothel of T'ang China. They depict the shocking reality of famine and war as well as the elegance and ease of a better life during a more prosperous period. It is hoped that by having this broad range of contrasts presented in the selections, the reader may acquire a more balanced view of traditional China.

Since this book covers the entire span of Chinese history prior to the Western impact, generally speaking, only those materials that have a perennial interest, transcending the change of dynasties, have been included among those chosen. Whenever a selection of a more limited application does appear, its transient nature is either implied in the text itself or clearly explained in the introduction or footnotes. It is chosen not for its own merit but because it sheds light on and helps to explain the broader picture as a whole.

The comparative merit of topical *versus* chronological arrangement is an old controversy, and it has been debated in China for many centuries. This does not pose a difficult problem for this volume, however, since we, to achieve our intended purpose, are interested in the "universality" rather than the "particularity" of the Chinese cultural system. Such materials as those showing the difficulties of obtaining a satisfactory livelihood in an agrarian society and the emphasis on the correct relationships among men are indicative of the Chinese culture throughout centuries. Selections written in any historical period certainly pertain to that period, but in most cases they are actually applicable to the entire course of Chinese history. The problems that a Chinese farmer faced in the second century B.C. are described in great detail by such Han scholars as Ch'ao Ts'o and Tung Chung-shu; these are the same problems that a Chinese farmer in the modern period has to face. This does not mean that China has been changeless throughout history; it only means that, by and large, the changes have been made within the broad framework of a sedentary, agricultural life and the ancient Confucian heritage. It is in this broad framework that we are particularly interested.

Since a chronological arrangement poses almost insurmountable problems in a one-volume book and presents perhaps more confusion than clarification with regard to traditional China, to classify selected materials according to topics seems to be the only good choice. This is not a novel approach by any means; books organized in this manner have appeared in the past. However, insofar as popular collections are concerned, almost without exception the traditional historians in China use rhetoric rather than content as the criterion for their selections. They classify the selected materials according to either literary form (imperial decrees, memorials, biographies, poems, etc.) or chronology (Han writings, T'ang writings, etc.). Two of the most popular collections, *Ku-wen tz'u-lei-tsuan* by Yao Nai and *Ku-wen kuan-chih* by Wu Ch'u-ts'ai, both of which were compiled in the eighteenth century, can be cited as pertinent examples. The former classifies its selections according to literary form and the latter according to chronology. While these methods of classification are useful to a student brought up in the Chinese culture, they certainly will not serve our purpose. Instead, four main areas were chosen for the organization of this book: Philosophy and Religion; Government; Economics; and finally, Family and Society—divisions with which a student in Europe or America is more familiar. The literary quality of the Chinese original is not our major concern, though all the materials in this volume have passed the rigorous test of time. A good translator can make even a mediocre work readable, while a poor translator only succeeds in making a literary masterpiece sound ridiculous. This is especially true in translations of Chinese into English, and *vice versa*.

The problem as to how these selected materials can be rendered into effective English is much more difficult than it may appear on the surface. This is so because of the great dissimilarity between the English and the Chinese languages. Practically all of the materials in this book were written in a classical or literary style; and, from the point of view of those who have known a more precise language,

The Essence

of

Chinese Civilization

丁未孟春

華文薈萃

廣德李敦仁譯著

THE
ESSENCE
OF
CHINESE
CIVILIZATION

EDITED BY

Dun J. Li

PATERSON STATE COLLEGE

D. VAN NOSTRAND COMPANY, INC.
PRINCETON, NEW JERSEY
TORONTO   LONDON

Van Nostrand Regional Offices: *New York, Chicago, San Francisco*

D. Van Nostrand Company, Ltd., *London*

D. Van Nostrand Company (Canada), Ltd., *Toronto*

Library of Congress Catalog Card No. 67–25328

PRINTED IN THE UNITED STATES OF AMERICA

To June

Preface

This is a book about traditional China, presented in translations of Chinese authors. All the translations are original, and more than eighty percent of them appear in the English language for the first time. The authors range from such famous men as Confucius and Lao-tzu to the comparatively more obscure.

I feel that there is a need for a book of this kind in view of the increasing interest shown by the general public in Chinese culture and the need of a source book in courses on traditional China. Though many books on China have been published in recent years, to my knowledge there is no source book that covers the broad perspective of the entire Chinese cultural system in one convenient volume. To attempt to prepare a book of this nature is obviously an adventurous undertaking due to the potential pitfalls involved in such an ambitious project—pitfalls that are particularly inherent since there is no precedent to follow and no guide to point out directions to the author. But someone must make the first attempt and it is hoped that any mistakes that are made may help authors of subsequent volumes in the same area of concern. For any major undertaking, some humble worker must "move the first stone."

There are three problems involved in preparing a volume of this kind. First, what materials are to be included? Second, are these materials to be arranged topically or chronologically? Third, how are these materials to be rendered into effective English?

The first problem is essentially a problem of choice. Of the millions of pieces of literature that range from imperial decrees to personal diaries, what are the two hundred that are most appropriate for our purpose? The question is not an easy one, and the answer depends largely upon individual propensity or judgement. To me, civilization is not only ideas and ideals that can be argued and debated in abstract terms but, perhaps more importantly, how these ideas and ideals actually influence and effect a way of life. The proper theme of this book is not "the glory that was China," but "traditional China as it really was." To present this panorama, I include in this book a wide variety of materials: sketches, casual observations, personal letters, and short stories as well as the more "respectable" materials translated from the Confucian classics and the dynastic histories. These range from a much-involved, metaphysical discussion of human nature by the Ch'ing scholar Tai Chen to an easy-to-understand contemporary description of a brothel of T'ang China. They depict the shocking reality of famine and war as well as the elegance and ease of a better life during a more prosperous period. It is hoped that by having this broad range of contrasts presented in the selections, the reader may acquire a more balanced view of traditional China.

Since this book covers the entire span of Chinese history prior to the Western impact, generally speaking, only those materials that have a perennial interest, transcending the change of dynasties, have been included among those chosen. Whenever a selection of a more limited application does appear, its transient nature is either implied in the text itself or clearly explained in the introduction or footnotes. It is chosen not for its own merit but because it sheds light on and helps to explain the broader picture as a whole.

The comparative merit of topical *versus* chronological arrangement is an old controversy, and it has been debated in China for many centuries. This does not pose a difficult problem for this volume, however, since we, to achieve our intended purpose, are interested in the "universality" rather than the "particularity" of the Chinese cultural system. Such materials as those showing the difficulties of obtaining a satisfactory livelihood in an agrarian society and the emphasis on the correct relationships among men are indicative of the Chinese culture throughout centuries. Selections written in any historical period certainly pertain to that period, but in most cases they are actually applicable to the entire course of Chinese history. The problems that a Chinese farmer faced in the second century B.C. are described in great detail by such Han scholars as Ch'ao Ts'o and Tung Chung-shu; these are the same problems that a Chinese farmer in the modern period has to face. This does not mean that China has been changeless throughout history; it only means that, by and large, the changes have been made within the broad framework of a sedentary, agricultural life and the ancient Confucian heritage. It is in this broad framework that we are particularly interested.

Since a chronological arrangement poses almost insurmountable problems in a one-volume book and presents perhaps more confusion than clarification with regard to traditional China, to classify selected materials according to topics seems to be the only good choice. This is not a novel approach by any means; books organized in this manner have appeared in the past. However, insofar as popular collections are concerned, almost without exception the traditional historians in China use rhetoric rather than content as the criterion for their selections. They classify the selected materials according to either literary form (imperial decrees, memorials, biographies, poems, etc.) or chronology (Han writings, T'ang writings, etc.). Two of the most popular collections, *Ku-wen tz'u-lei-tsuan* by Yao Nai and *Ku-wen kuan-chih* by Wu Ch'u-ts'ai, both of which were compiled in the eighteenth century, can be cited as pertinent examples. The former classifies its selections according to literary form and the latter according to chronology. While these methods of classification are useful to a student brought up in the Chinese culture, they certainly will not serve our purpose. Instead, four main areas were chosen for the organization of this book: Philosophy and Religion; Government; Economics; and finally, Family and Society—divisions with which a student in Europe or America is more familiar. The literary quality of the Chinese original is not our major concern, though all the materials in this volume have passed the rigorous test of time. A good translator can make even a mediocre work readable, while a poor translator only succeeds in making a literary masterpiece sound ridiculous. This is especially true in translations of Chinese into English, and *vice versa*.

The problem as to how these selected materials can be rendered into effective English is much more difficult than it may appear on the surface. This is so because of the great dissimilarity between the English and the Chinese languages. Practically all of the materials in this book were written in a classical or literary style; and, from the point of view of those who have known a more precise language, these materials are as terse as they are sometimes ambiguous. To play his role more effectively, a translator would have to be several people simultaneously: a researcher, an interpreter, an editor, and sometimes, unfortunately, an elaborator. Some of the materials were written more than two thousand years ago, and scholars have debated for centuries as to the exact meaning or meanings contained in many of these ancient passages. Whenever faced with different interpretations, the translator must make his own judgement as to which of the interpretations he is going to follow. Extensive footnotes have been added to each of the selections, to make sure that the reader will not encounter insurmountable obstacles in comprehending a particular phrase or term that needs elaboration.

I wish to express my thanks to Professor Robert J. Gowen of the University of Toledo who examined an early draft of the manuscript on behalf of the publishers and provided a number of helpful suggestions. My wife June not only read the entire manuscript and made many valuable suggestions but also made my work easier by keeping the children away from the study room (though unsuccessfully at times) and by freeing me from many household chores that normally belong to a husband. Without her understanding and generous assistance, this work would not have been completed as early as it was. I alone, however, am responsible for any errors that may be found in this book.

DUN J. LI

Contents

PART III. ECONOMICS

The Essence

of

Chinese Civilization

CHINA
(1967)

★ Capital   • Cities

──·── National boundaries   ──── Provincial boundaries

0   200   400   600   800
Scale of Miles

Soviet Union

Lake
Balkhash

Mongolian

Urumchi

Turfan

Hami

Afg.

Tarim R.   SINKIANG UIGHUR

AUTONOMOUS   REGION

Yumen

KANSU

JAMMU
AND
KASHMIR

CHINGHAI

Pak.
(West)

Yellow

Chinsha River

TIBETAN

AUTONOMOUS REGION

Salween R.

Mekong R.

Tsangpo   River   • Lhasa

Shigatse

Nepal

Bhutan

Brahmaputra R.

India

India

Pakistan
(East)

Burma

Bay of Bengal

Thai
land

90°

100°

40°

30°

20°

80°

90°

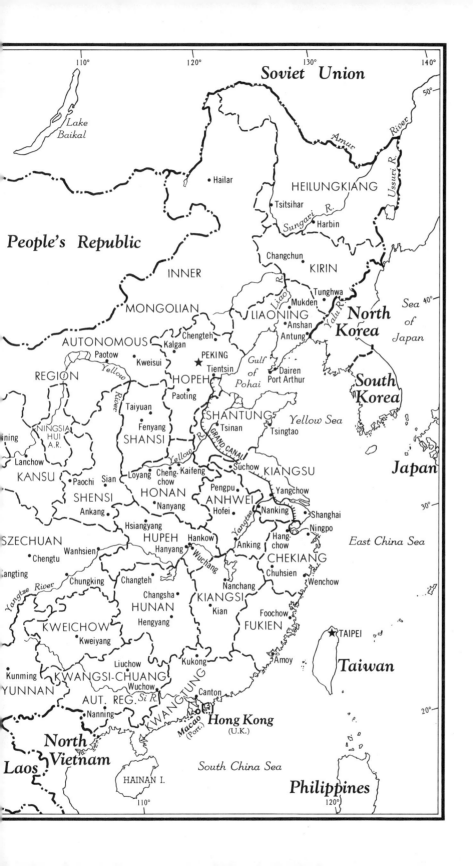

Part I

Philosophy and Religion

CHAPTER ONE

Confucianism

O F ALL ideologies that influenced the thinking and life of traditional China none was more important than Confucianism. In fact, prior to the twentieth century the word "Confucianism" was almost synonymous with the word "Chinese." Confucianism was named after Confucius (551?–479 B.C.), a native of the state of Lu which was located in modern Shantung province. Throughout the centuries there have been so many words and deeds attributed to him that it is often difficult to differentiate facts from mere legends. For a better understanding of this man a more cautious historian relies heavily on the book *Lun-yü* or *Analects* which was compiled by Confucius' disciples shortly after their master's death.

In the *Analects* time and again one encounters the word *jen,* the virtue most emphasized by Confucius. *Jen* has been variously translated as innate goodness, love, human-heartedness, benevolence, etc. Since Confucius never defined it in clear-cut terms (Selection 1), later Confucians freely made their own interpretations. As one might expect, each of them backed up his own judgement by citing a particular statement or statements by Confucius.

Confucianism was not widespread during Confucius' lifetime. The man most responsible for popularizing his beliefs was Mencius (372–289 B.C.) who, considering himself a devoted follower of Confucius, was nevertheless an original thinker in his own right. Among his contributions were the theories about the natural goodness of man and the "innate knowledge" ("All things are complete within me"). Next to Confucius he was regarded as the most important philosopher in the development of Confucian ideology (Selection 2).

Despite Mencius' efforts, Confucianism continued to face competition from rival schools. But time was in its favor. By the second century B.C. when Ssu-ma Ch'ien (d. *c.*87 B.C) wrote the *Historical Records* (*Shih chi*), its ascendancy had been clearly established (Selection 3). When Tung Chung-shu, an expert on the Confucian classic *Spring and Autumn Annals,* suggested to the reigning emperor Han Wu-ti (r. 140–87 B.C.) that Confucianism should be made a state philosophy, the latter was only too happy to comply (Selection 4).

1 · CONFUCIUS: *The Meaning of* Jen [1]

CONFUCIUS SAYS, Those who know how to flatter and those who look pleasant but are insincere inside cannot be said to have possessed *jen.*

Confucius says, What good can rites do if a man does not possess *jen*? What good can music do if a man does not possess *jen*?

Confucius says, A neighborhood where people possess *jen* is a good neighborhood. How can a person be regarded as wise if he is not selective in choosing a place to live?

Confucius says, You cannot share either hardship or happiness with a man who does not possess *jen.* Those who possess *jen* live in it without knowing its existence. The wise will of course use *jen* to benefit others as well as himself.

Confucius says, Only a person who possesses *jen* can love good men and detest bad men.

Confucius says, Those who embrace *jen* do not hate.

Confucius says, Wealth and honor are the things desired by every man. But I shall not have them if I have to obtain them in an improper way. Poverty and humiliation are what people detest. If I cannot eliminate them by proper means, I shall not try to do so. How can a gentleman be called a gentleman if he no longer follows the principle of *jen*? A true gentleman will not violate the principle of *jen* even for the briefest moment. He follows it when he is occupied; he follows it even in adversity.

Confucius says, I have not met a person who really loves *jen* and abhors *jen's* opposite. No one is better than the man who loves *jen.* As to those who abhor *jen's* opposite, they are already on their way to *jen.* They will not do anything which violates the principle of *jen.* If a person devotes his energy to the practice of *jen* for a single day, I cannot see any reason why he should fail. There might have been such a person, but I have not seen him.

Confucius says, People's faults can be classified into different categories. Looking at the particular faults of an individual, I know whether he possesses *jen.*

Some one said to Confucius that Jung [2] possessed *jen* but unfortunately did not have the talent of speech. Confucius replied: "What is the use of the talent of speech? A person who argues well to defend himself will be a source of irritation to others. I do not know whether Jung possesses *jen.* But I do know that he does not need the talent of speech."

Confucius says, Hui [3] does not violate the principle of *jen* for as long as a three-month period. As for the rest,[4] it is a matter of days or at most a month.

Fan Chih [5] asked about *jen.* Confucius said: "Work earlier than others and harder. Enjoy the fruit of labor only after others have done so. A man who follows these principles may be described as a man of *jen.*"

Confucius says, Those who possess wisdom may be compared to water; those who possess *jen* may be compared to mountains. The former are active; the latter are quiet. The former are cheerful; the latter live longer.

---

[1] Passages in this selection are arranged in the order they originally appear in the *Analects.*

[2] Yüan Jung; a disciple of Confucius.

[3] Yen Hui, also known as Yen Yüan; a disciple of Confucius.

[4] The rest of Confucius' disciples.

[5] A native of Lu and a disciple of Confucius.

Tzu-kung [6] asked Confucius: "Suppose a ruler is generous with his people and helps them whenever they are in difficulties. Would you say that he is a man of *jen*?" "Certainly," replied Confucius. "He is not only a man of *jen;* he is a sage. He is even better than Yao and Shun.[7] A man of *jen* wishes to establish others as well as himself. He wishes to understand others to the same extent as he understands himself. The way of *jen* is to work first among people in your immediate environment."

Confucius says, How can *jen* be too far away? If I wish to have it, it will be there.

Confucius says, How dare I say that I am a sage or a man of *jen*? But I enjoy working towards that goal, and I teach what I believe without ever feeling tired. This is all I believe.

Confucius says, The wise do not confuse. The brave do not fear. Those who possess *jen* do not worry.

Yen Yüan asked about *jen*. Confucius replied: "To control and channel your desires through propriety is *jen*. If you can do it for a single day, the world will follow the principle of *jen*. *Jen* comes as a result of individual efforts; others cannot help." Yen Yüan asked for more details. Confucius replied: "Do not see the improper; do not hear the improper; do not talk about the improper; and do not act improperly." Yen Yüan said: "Untalented though I am, I shall abide by this advice."

Chung-kung [8] asked about *jen*. Confucius replied: "When you meet a person outside of your house, greet him as if he were a great noble. If as a government official you have to impose corvée duties, you should approach your task with the same seriousness that you would use in performing a religious ritual. Do not do to others what you yourself would not desire. In this way you will have no complaints against you either as a citizen or as a member of a household." Chung-kung said: "Untalented though I am, I shall abide by these statements."

Ssu-ma Niu [9] asked about *jen*. Confucius replied: "A person who possesses *jen* speaks with hesitation." "Do you mean, sir, that a person who speaks hesitantly will be regarded as a person of *jen*?" "Realizing the difficulty of keeping promises," replied Confucius, "would a person not be hesitant to make them?"

Fan Chih asked about *jen*. Confucius replied: "Love people."

Confucius says, A sage king must rule for one generation before people are converted to the principle of *jen*.

Fan Chih asked about *jen*. Confucius replied: "Be respectful when you are at home. Be diligent and sincere in whatever you do. Be loyal in your relationships with your fellow men. These are such basic principles that you cannot discard them even if you live among the barbarians."

Confucius says, The meanings of endurance, fortitude, simplicity, and inarticulateness are close to the meaning of *jen*.

Hsien [10] asked Confucius: "Could a person be described as a man of *jen* if he is not aggressive, conceited, resentful, or avaricious?" Confucius replied: "Such a person is unusual indeed. But I still do not know whether he can be regarded as a man of *jen*."

[6] His real name was Tuan-mu Tz'u; a native of Wei and a disciple of Confucius.
[7] Two of China's ancient sage kings.
[8] Chung-kung was Yüan Jung's courtesy name.
[9] A native of Sung and a disciple of Confucius.
[10] Yüan Hsien.

Confucius says, A virtuous man has something to say, but a person who has something to say is not necessarily virtuous. A man who possesses *jen* is brave, but a brave man does not necessarily possess *jen*.

Confucius says, A gentleman may sometimes violate the principle of *jen*. A mean [11] man does not have *jen* within him in the first place.

Confucius said: "A gentleman possesses three virtues of which I have none. He possesses *jen,* and he is therefore not sorrowful. He possesses wisdom, and he is therefore not confused. He possesses courage, and he is therefore not afraid." Tzu-kung said: "Sir, you are speaking about yourself."

Confucius says, Men of will and men of *jen* will not value life higher than *jen.* Some of them may choose to die rather than to surrender the principle of *jen.*

Tzu-kung asked about *jen.* Confucius replied: "If a craftsman wishes to make a good product, he first must sharpen his tools. In whatever country you happen to be, serve its virtuous ministers and make friends with those citizens who possess *jen.*"

"If there were one word that should guide our conduct throughout our lives, what word can it be?" Tzu-kung asked. "Can that word be *'shu'* which means 'Do not do to others what you yourself do not desire'?" Confucius replied.

Confucius says, *Jen* is more important than fire or water. I have seen people who died in fire and water. But I have not seen any person who died in *jen.*

Confucius says, When *jen* is involved, you should not hesitate even to disagree with your teacher.

Tzu-chang [12] asked about *jen.* Confucius replied: "A person who possesses five virtues may be said to have possessed *jen.*" "Please tell me about the five virtues." "They are," said Confucius, "reverence, kindness, sincerity, sagacity, and generosity. A respectful man will not be insulted. A kind man will win sympathy and support. A man who is sincere will be trusted in return. A sagacious man is more likely to succeed. Only a generous man can command the service of others."

2 · MENCIUS: *On the Nature of Man* [13]

Every man has the sense of compassion. The ancient kings had it, and they adopted and carried out a policy of compassion. When compassion is coupled with a policy inspired by such compassion, a ruler can govern the world with ease.

What do we mean by the sense of compassion? When a man sees a child about to fall into a well, he is frightened and distressed. When he rushes to save the child, he does not mean that by doing so he is going to build up a friendship with the child's parents, or that he is going to receive praise from his neighbors and friends, or that he hates the child's crying and decides to put a stop to it.

A man who does not have the sense of sympathy is not really a man. Nor is a man a man who does not have the sense of shame. The same can be said with regard to a person who does not have the sense of modesty or that of right and wrong.

---

[11] *Hsiao;* literally, small.
[12] His real name was Chuan-sun Shih; a disciple of Confucius.
[13] Translated from the *Book of Mencius.*

The sense of sympathy is the beginning of love (*jen*), as the sense of shame is the beginning of righteousness (*yi*). Propriety (*li*) does not exist, has there been no sense of modesty, and wisdom is meaningless when people cannot tell the right from the wrong.

These four senses—sympathy, shame, modesty, and the ability to distinguish the right from the wrong—are so important that they are like man's four limbs. When a man possesses these four senses and yet does not wish to do anything with them, he is cutting his body with his own hands. When he says that his king is unable to do anything with the four senses which the king possesses, it is as if he were cutting the body of his king.

Knowing the existence of the four senses within himself, a wise king strengthens and extends them so that they will glow like the flame of a torch and rush out like the fountain of a spring. If he can do this, he can keep his kingdom; if he cannot, he may not be able to care for even his own parents.

* * * * *

If I love other people and my love is not returned, I shall ask myself whether my love has been unconditional and true. If as an official I wish to bring the best kind of government to the people and yet the people refuse to respond, I shall ask myself whether my intelligence and ability have measured up to the task. If I pay my respect to other people and my courtesy is not acknowledged, I shall ask myself whether I have been truly respectful. In short, whenever I fail to receive what I have expected to receive, I shall examine myself with the purpose of finding out my own defects. To rectify the world, I first must rectify myself.

* * * * *

A truly great man has the heart of a small child.

* * * * *

"Human nature is like a water current," said Kao-tzu.[14] "If it is led to the east, it flows eastward; if it is led to the west, it flows westward. Like water which can be led to either of the two directions, human nature is neither good nor bad. It depends upon the direction towards which it is led."

"While it is true that water can be led eastward or westward, is it also true that it knows no difference between 'upward' and 'downward'?" asked Mencius. "The goodness of human nature is like water's natural inclination to move downward. As water is inevitably moving downward, there is no man in the world who is not good. If you beat water hard, it jumps up and can rise higher than your forehead. If you channel it and push it upward, it might even reach the top of a mountain. But, is this the nature of water? It acts contrary to its nature because it is given no other choice. If a man does bad things, he, like water, has been forced to do them and has not been given a better choice. His wrongdoing has nothing to do with his inherent nature which is good."

* * * * *

[14] A contemporary of Mencius.

To examine my mind is to understand the nature of man. The nature of man is the same as the nature of Heaven, and to know the nature of man is to know the way of Heaven. To rectify my mind and to preserve my basic nature (which is good) are the ways of serving Heaven. I will do these regardless of whether I shall die old or young. I shall remain good and upright, whatever fate has prescribed for me.

While I do not deny the existence of fate, I shall only do those things which I regard as proper and right. Those who understand the meaning of fate will not stand beside a sloping wall which can collapse at any moment. To die a natural death at the end of a long, virtuous life is more compatible with the true meaning of fate than to die a sudden, unnatural death in a prison.

Only those who seek can find; not to seek is to lose by default. To seek is to seek what is within me or what will benefit myself. I shall do it in a proper way regardless of whether I may or may not succeed. To seek what is outside of me, on the other hand, is fruitless and useless.

All things are complete within me. Nothing can give me more pleasure than to find sincerity within me after a thorough examination of myself. Strive diligently to carry out the maxim: "Do not do to others what you yourself do not desire." If you do this, you are taking the shortest route to the domain of *jen*.

3 · SSU-MA CH'IEN: *Confucius* [15]

As for Confucius, the Grand Historian [16] comments as follows:
The *Book of Odes* [17] says:

> As I look upward to admire the mountains high,
> I strive to follow the virtuous path of the great,
> Ever so diligently!

It is impossible for everyone to reach this lofty goal; no one, however, fails to admire a man who does. I can visualize what kind of man Confucius was when I read his books.

While in Lu,[18] I visited the temple of Confucius where the Master's chariot, clothing, and ceremonial vessels were carefully preserved and where his modern disciples learned and practiced Confucian rituals from time to time. I walked about silently and could not tear myself from that place.

Since history began there have been many great princes and virtuous men. They enjoyed glory while they lived; but who would remember them after they died? Confucius was a commoner, and yet his influence has been felt for more than ten generations. All scholars have followed his teachings. From kings and princes downward, those in China who speak of the *Six Classics* [19] rely on Confucius as the final authority. He was indeed a sage in perfection.

[15] This comment on Confucius appears at the end of "Biography of Confucius," *Historical Records,* roll 47.

[16] Ssu-ma Ch'ien.

[17] One of the oldest writings of ancient China, dated from 1000 B.C.

[18] The state where Confucius was born.

[19] *Book of Odes, Book of History, Book of Changes, Book of Rites, Book of Music,* and *Spring and Autumn Annals.*

4 · TUNG CHUNG-SHU: *Confucianism as a Universal Ideology* [20]

The emperor [21] decided to issue him [22] another order which reads as follows:

"I have heard that those who speak well about Heaven should have their words proved among men and those who speak well about the ancient times should have their statements tested in the present. I am now asking you to enlighten me with regard to the mutual reactions between Heaven and man; the reason why such emperors as T'ang and Yü [23] should be praised and such emperors as Chieh and Chou [24] should be pitied; and finally, the way or ways in which a nation gradually becomes great or degenerate, prosperous or extinguished. I am open-minded in this matter, and I wish to correct whatever mistakes I have already made.

"You, my minister, are versed in the knowledge of *yin* and *yang* [25] and of the things they create; you have also studied the great deeds of our ancient sages. But in the memorials which you have submitted, the language is short of what it should be. Is this because you have been too much occupied by affairs of the present? Your ideas are not properly arranged; nor are the conclusions adequately revealed. May it also be true that I have not been talented enough to understand or that I have read wrong meanings into them?

"The teachings of the Three Kings [26] are different, and each of them has its own defects. However, there is also the opinion that the correct way of governing is unchangeable and should not be changing. Why do people differ in this matter? You, my minister, have acquired the most profound knowledge in the matter of governing, and you are thoroughly familiar with the causes of order and chaos. Will you study this matter further and report to me directly? The *Book of Odes* says:

> Oh, King,
> Rest Not!
> The gods are watching.
> They will bring thee great fortunes,
> Should thou be not complacent.

"I shall read it personally, whatever you have to say. May you be encouraged in this undertaking!"

Tung Chung-shu replied to the emperor as follows:

"I, your minister, would like to quote a sentence from the *Analects* which says: 'Is he not a sage indeed who finishes what he has begun?' Now Your Majesty has bestowed upon me a great favor by allowing yourself to listen to a man who can

[20] This selection appears in "Biography of Tung Chung-shu," *Han shu (History of the Han)* by Pan Ku (d. A.D. 92), roll 56. This was the last of a series of exchanges between the emperor Han Wu-ti and Tung Chung-shu which led directly to the declaration of Confucianism as the state philosophy.

[21] Han Wu-ti.

[22] Tung Chung-shu.

[23] T'ang means T'ang-yao or Yao; Yü means Yü-shun or Shun. They were two of the most idealized rulers in Confucian ideology.

[24] Chieh and Chou were the last rulers of the Hsia and Shang dynasties respectively.

[25] *Yin* and *yang,* or the negative and the positive, were the two opposite but complementary forces whose interactions created the universe and all things in it.

[26] The founders of the Three Dynasties, Hsia, Shang, and Chou.

do no more than to express what he has learned from his teachers. I am especially honored by Your Majesty's order in which you encourage me to study further the virtues of our ancient sages, in the hope that their full meanings can be thoroughly understood. How can I, an ignorant man, be ever equipped with enough talent to undertake so important a task?

"In the memorials previously submitted my ideas were improperly arranged and my conclusions were inadequately revealed. My language lacked clarity, and my emphasis was ambiguous and obscure. All of these resulted from my own shallowness.

"Your Majesty has correctly stated that those who speak well about Heaven should have their words proved among men and those who speak well about the ancient times should have their statements tested in the present. I have heard that Heaven is the creator of all things in the universe, and it embraces everything with love and without partiality. It makes the universe harmonious by creating such things as wind and rain together with the sun and the moon. It makes the universe complete through the interactions between the *yin* and the *yang* and between the hot and the cold. Following the ways of Heaven to govern men, a sage king is likewise selfless and impartial in his love. He induces the best from men by being virtuous himself; he leads them to a moral life by teaching them righteousness and propriety (*li*) which he himself possesses. As spring is the season Heaven chooses to give birth to all things on earth, a king follows the principle of *jen* to love all of his subjects. As summer is designed by Heaven for things to grow, he likewise cultivates the growth of his own virtue. Frost is the weapon with which Heaven kills; execution is the means whereby a king punishes. To harmonize man's affairs with those of Heaven is the basic principle of all times.

"When writing the *Spring and Autumn Annals,* Confucius incorporated the ways of Heaven and gave equal emphasis to the nature of man. He tested his findings against both ancient and modern evidences and found them unquestionably valid. When disaster occurred, his book satirized; [27] it showed his displeasure when strange and uncanny events were reported.[28] It recorded natural disasters as well as the mistakes made by men. It attempted to show that the doings of man, good or bad, were related to the circulation of Heaven and Earth and that they were mutually responsive. In short, Heaven and man were merely two aspects of the same thing.

"In the ancient times there were the teaching officials whose sole purpose was to transform people toward the good by the example of their own conduct. After the people had been thus transformed, none of them ever committed any crime, and consequently, jails were empty throughout the empire. Later abolished, this teaching institution no longer exists today, and there is no way to transform the people toward the good. Consequently they abandon the way of righteous conduct and risk their lives only for material profit. More and more people violate the law and commit crimes, and thousands of persons are put in jail each year. In view of this situation it seems necessary that we should restore our ancient institutions. The *Spring and Autumn Annals* criticized whenever efforts were made to change the ways of the old.

"The command of Heaven is called fate, and only sages can carry out such a

[27] Satirized the king for his lack of virtue.
[28] Confucius was skeptical of supernatural phenomena.

command. Simple honesty is the basic nature of man, but only education can translate the inherent honesty into action. Human desires are expressed through emotions, and emotions without restraint are bound to be excessive. Therefore, a sage king obeys the command of Heaven to fulfill the fate of man; concentrates his efforts on education to preserve our inherent goodness; and formulates the rules of law and the principle of precedence in order to control our desires. When a king has done all of these, he has completed his basic functions as a king.

"As man alone receives his commands from Heaven, he differs from other creatures and stands above all of them. At home he is related to his father, offspring, and brothers; outside he observes the correct relationships between a king and his subjects and between superiors and inferiors. Whenever he gathers with other people, he follows the principle of precedence: that the old are superior to the young. Moreover, there are rites and rituals to embellish these relationships, and a genuine, joyous love pervades and underlies all of them. This is why man alone is the most valuable creature on earth.

"Furthermore, man raises grain for his food, grows mulberry and hemp to make his clothes, and domesticates animals to enrich his nourishment. He rides horses, and he impresses oxen into his service. He snares leopards, and he cages tigers. These show that man alone is endowed with the spirit of Heaven and is so much above other creatures. Confucius said: 'The statement that man is the most valuable of all creatures indicates the very nature of Heaven and Earth.' Knowing the nature of Heaven, man realizes that he is superior to other beings. Knowing that he is superior, he discovers such virtues as love (*jen*) and righteousness. Knowing the value of such virtues, he emphasizes the importance of rites and rituals. Having acknowledged the importance of rites and rituals, he enjoys goodness and lives in it. Enjoying goodness and living in it, he is happy to regulate his life in accordance with reason. He is a gentleman indeed when he lives a life of reason. This is what Confucius meant when he said: 'A man is not a gentleman if he does not know the meaning of fate.'

"Your Majesty wishes to know why T'ang and Yü should be praised and Chieh and Chou should be pitied; and the way or ways in which a nation gradually becomes great or degenerate, prosperous or extinguished. You have mentioned your open-mindedness and your desire to correct what should be corrected. I, your minister, have heard that 'many' is merely an assemblage of numerous 'fews' and that 'large' results from an accumulation of numerous 'smalls.' All sage kings were obscure in the beginning and became famous and great in the end. Yao was merely one of the numerous rulers in the beginning, and Shun, another sage king, was once a tiller of fields deep in the mountains. They did not achieve fame and greatness overnight. Only slowly and gradually did they become what they were.

"Words, once spoken, cannot be taken back; action, when committed, cannot be concealed. Words and action are two of the most important instruments in the administration of a government, and are the means whereby a gentleman can move Heaven and Earth. Those who devote themselves to small tasks are preparing themselves for the great ones, and those who do not ignore trifles are on their way to undertaking the most important assignments. The *Book of Odes* says:

Only the King of Wen [29]

29 A founder of the Chou dynasty.

Is careful and reverent.

"Thus Yao cautiously cultivated his virtue each day, and Shun performed his filial duties attentively without complaint. With the accumulated goodness they eventually became known; when their virtues were too obvious to be concealed, glory went to them as their due. This is the principle of gradualism: from obscurity to fame and from smallness to being truly great. The accumulation of goodness is like the slow growth of a child: the body grows but the child is unconscious of his own growth. The accumulation of evils, on the other hand, is like the burning of a candle: the candle is so slowly consumed by the flame that one barely notices that it is being consumed. A man cannot appreciate this truism unless he understands the nature of man and has studied the customs commonly practiced among the people. Knowing this truism, he also knows the reason why T'ang and Yü could acquire honor and fame and why Chieh and Chou are examples to be aggrieved and feared.

"One goodness inspires another, and all evils have their corollaries. Like good deeds, evils follow one another, as inevitably as shadows follow objects and as sound follows music. Only when Chieh and Chou became complacent and brutal did slandering thieves emerge and men of virtue and wisdom retreat. As their evils became more evident, the country became more and more anarchic. Meanwhile they were as undisturbed and unconcerned as if they were the sun in the sky which could never fall. The situation continued to deteriorate until it became irreparable. Thus, even the worst sovereigns do not fall overnight; it takes time before causes combine to make their effect felt. Chieh and Chou kept their countries for more than ten years after they had already lost their virtue. This is what I mean by the principle of gradualism: a bad regime begins with slow deterioration and ends finally in extinction.

"Your Majesty states that 'the teachings of the Three Kings are different and each of them has its own defects.' You wish to know whether this statement is incompatible with the opinion that 'the correct way of governing is unchangeable and should not be changing.'

"The essential element of virtue is to love and enjoy life without in the meantime making it anarchic, and to put into practice, repeatedly and tirelessly, what one truly believes. Whenever it is found, true virtue causes no ill effects; ill effects come about when virtue itself has become defective. The teachings of the ancient kings, great as they were, must have contained the biases of their authors, and consequently not all of their policies can be profitably carried out. The proper thing for their successors to do is to discover these biases and then to correct them. The teachings of the Three Kings are different, but they are not contradictory. Each of these kings, acting under a different, changed environment, made necessary adjustments to eliminate the areas regarded as excessive and added new, remedial ideas that had not been emphasized in the past.

"Confucius said: 'If there were a person who governed well without doing too much himself, would that person not be Shun? After his accession he changed only the calendar and the color of official attires in observance of the wishes of Heaven. As for the rest, he followed Yao's practices. There was no need for any change.' Nominally there were institutional changes after one ruler had replaced another; nevertheless the basic way of governing remained the same. Hsia emphasized the virtue of loyalty, whereas Yin [30] attached great importance to the virtues of respect and reverence. Chou, on the other hand, gave priority to cultural refinement. Confucius said: 'Yin inherited its rites from Hsia; what was added and subtracted from them is not difficult to discern. Chou inherited its rites from Yin; its own additions or subtractions are equally known. As to the rites of the regime that will succeed Chou, they too are easy to know; they will remain substantially the same one hundred generations after the establishment of the regime.' This means that all regimes, past or present, cannot deviate much from the Three Dynasties in the matter of governmental institutions.

"Why is it that Confucius did not mention additions or subtractions in the rites which Hsia inherited from Yü? [31] This is because the rites of Hsia were the same as those of Yü. The basic principle of governing comes from Heaven; as Heaven does not change, the basic principle of governing does not change either. Yü [32] succeeded Shun, and Shun succeeded Yao. Though there was a change of ruler in each case, none of the three sages changed the basic form of government. They did not change it because there were no defects in it. That is why Confucius did not mention additions or subtractions in connection with these three sages. In conclusion, it may be said that a regime that succeeds a successful regime does not change the ways of its predecessor. On the other hand, if the preceding regime is a bad one, its successor would have to make necessary changes.

"The Han dynasty was established after a long period of disorder and chaos. It is my humble opinion that it should reduce the excessiveness of the cultural refinement of the Chou dynasty and emphasize more the virtue of loyalty as practiced during the Hsia dynasty. Your Majesty has elevated the virtuous and honored the truthful. You are disturbed by the increasing superficiality of our customs and are grieved over the loss of our ancient virtues. You have therefore selected virtuous and upright scholars, to be examined and observed so that they may become good, conscientious officials. You wish to revive the virtue of love (jen) and righteousness, reestablish the institutions of the ancient sage kings, and in short, regenerate the eternal Way of Great Peace. I, your ignorant and worthless minister, can merely write down what I have heard and recite what I have learned. I can barely follow the words of my teachers without committing too many errors. As for the discussion of the merits or failings of certain policies and the rendering of judgement in connection with the empire's economic affairs, they are within the jurisdiction of the ministers and their deputies, and they are far beyond my ability and talent. However, there are certain things at which I have been often amazed.

"The China today is the same China as that of the ancient times. Why is it that the China today lags so much behind the China of the ancient times? In the ancient times the governing was perfect, and there was a sense of harmony and love between the governing and the governed. The customs were healthy and good, and the government did not need to force people to do what it encouraged and not to do what it prohibited. There were no wicked, corrupt officials; nor were there robbers and thieves. The jails were consequently empty. Even plants and grass felt the benign atmosphere; every man benefited from the rule of an

[30] The Shang dynasty.
[31] Shun, not the Yü who was the founder of the Hsia dynasty.
[32] Yü (d. 2205? B.C.), founder of the Hsia dynasty.

enlightened king. Phoenixes arrived; so did unicorns.[33] What are the mistakes of ours which reduce the world to a state of deterioration which presently exists? Is it not true that we have lost the good ways of our ancestors and have violated the principle of Heaven? Is it not correct to say that to regain what we have lost and thus to win, once again, the approval of Heaven, we shall have to trace the ways of the ancient kings and observe them?

"For Heaven is impartial in its distribution of favors. Endowed with teeth on the upper as well as the lower gums, certain animals do not have horns. With wings on their backs, fowls and birds are equipped with only two legs. Those who have been given a great deal should not seek small profits. Thus the salaried officials of the ancient times did not earn a livelihood by manual work and were not engaged in the non-essential professions.[34] No individual should have too much at the expense of others; that is the wish of Heaven! Even Heaven does not have an unlimited amount of resources; how can man, its inferior, be any different? Since this principle of equity is no longer followed today, people have complained about their inability to make a tolerable livelihood.

"The fact is, the high officials of influence and wealth, while receiving large salaries, are using their positions to compete with common people for making profits. How can the common people compete with them? Since the common people cannot compete with them, these officials continue to increase their private holdings: slaves, livestock, farms, houses, and a variety of other assets. The more they accumulate their wealth, the less likely they will stop accumulating it. While they become more and more wealthy, the hard-pressed common men become poorer and poorer each day; eventually they become destitute. The wealthy spend their wealth on excessive luxuries; the poor, on the other hand, suffer keenly from their extreme poverty. If the government does not come to help them, the poor will not think life worthwhile. If they do not value life, how can they possibly fear death? When life or death means nothing to them, they are not afraid of committing crimes. This is why wrongdoings have continued to increase despite the severity of penalties.

"Thus it seems clear that only when government officials derive their income solely from their salaries without in the meantime competing with common people in the various occupations can the material wealth of the country be equitably distributed among the people. Then every household will be financially sufficient. To prohibit government officials from engaging in such occupations is in compliance with the principle of Heaven and the sage ways of ancient kings. The emperor should make the prohibition a law, to be observed by all of his officials. When Kung-yi Hsiu, the premier of Lu, went home and saw silk-weaving in his house, he was so angry that he chased his wife out of the house. When he noticed that the vegetables he had eaten came from his own garden, he was wrathful enough to pull out the vegetable plants himself. "Since I have been salaried," he said, "how can I appropriate for myself the profits which rightly belong to the gardeners and the weavers?" Virtuous officials of ancient times all thought and acted according to the example cited above. Respecting these officials for their righteous conduct, the common people were more than willing to follow their teachings. As these officials were incorruptible, the people were also non-avaricious.

[33] Phoenixes and unicorns were believed to be auspicious animals sent by Heaven to show its approval of an emperor's rule.

[34] Agriculture, industry, commerce, etc.

"After the Chou dynasty had begun to decline, government officials were more concerned with the pursuit of material profit than that of righteousness. They had abandoned the virtue of modesty; lawsuits involving land titles multipled. The poets disliked this situation and satirized as follows: [35]

> High and steep are the Nan Mountains,
> Where rocks assemble, one upon another.
> August and serene is our prime minister,
> Whom all people look up to,
> As a model of virtue.

"When government officials love righteousness, the common people will follow the principle of *jen,* and their customs will be good. If on the other hand these officials pursue material profit, the common people will become wicked, and their good customs will deteriorate. The emperor and his ministers set examples for the common people to follow, as if they were sitting in the center of a square, with people all around who watch them constantly. All people, whether they are far or near, look at them and follow their examples. Such being the case, how is it possible that those who occupy the position of virtue are engaged in the activities of the common men? To cultivate actively one's own virtue and yet be fearful of one's inability to influence the common people towards the good should be the basic attitude of all government officials. Says the *Book of Changes:*

> Riding a chariot
> With a burden on the back
> Is to invite robbers, certainly.

"Riding a chariot indicates the position of a gentleman, and carrying burdens is the assigned function of a 'mean' person. This quotation means that disasters will come about when those who occupy the position of a gentleman are engaged in the activities of the common people. Like Kung-yi Hsiu, the premier of Lu, a gentleman should confine himself to the activities of a gentleman; the consequence will be grave if this maxim is not observed.

"The principle of grand unity [36] as expressed in the *Spring and Autumn Annals* is the constant, unchangeable principle of Heaven and Earth. It is also the principle which underlies all sound institutions, past and present. Nowadays different teachers have different orientations; people express a variety of opinions. Various philosophies differ among themselves, and each emphasizes the importance of its own beliefs. As a result, the government does not have a basic principle to unify all ideas. Laws and institutions have been subject to frequent changes, and the people do not know which law or institution to abide by. It is the opinion of your ignorant minister that those teachings that lie outside of the Six Arts [37] or Confucian learning should not be allowed to advance and, in fact, should be abolished. Only when heretical ideas are eliminated can a unifying principle be established. It is only then that laws and institutions can be made clear and people will know what to follow."

[35] This poem appears in the *Book of Odes.*
[36] This is the principle that all things in the universe originate from the same source.
[37] Same as Six Classics; see p. 8, Footnote 19.

CHAPTER TWO

"A Hundred Schools"

A S FAR as philosophy was concerned, the five hundred years prior to the establishment of Confucianism as the state philosophy in the second century B.C. were the most productive in Chinese history. This was the time when "thousands of flowers blossom and a hundred schools contend." Aside from Confucianism, there were Taoism, Moism, Legalism, Dialecticism, Agrarianism, and many others.

The two most important works in Taoism are the *Book of Taoist Virtue* (*Tao-te ching*) and the *Book of Chuang-tzu*. The former, though attributed to a mystic figure named Lao-tzu (sixth century (?) B.C.), is a work of anonymous authorship, perhaps of the fourth century B.C. (Selection 5). Chuang Chou, who wrote *Chung-tzu*, also lived in the fourth century B.C. (Selection 6). *Huai-nan-tzu,* another Taoist work, bears the authorship of Duke Huainan or Liu An who lived during the first half of the second century B.C., but it was actually written by a group of scholars under his patronage (Selection 7).

The extant version of *Mo-tzu,* the most important work in Moism, has sixty-one essays. Its author, Mo Ti, is believed to have lived towards the end of the fifth century B.C. (Selection 8).

There are several works generally regarded as Legalist, including *Kuan-tzu* and *Book of Lord Shang.* However, none exceeds *Han-fei-tzu* in importance (Selection 9). Its author, Han Fei (d. 233 B.C.), was a contemporary of Li Ssu (d. 208 B.C.) who, after becoming Ch'in's chief minister, attempted to put Legalism into practice (Selection 10).

The most representative work in Dialecticism is a brief book entitled *Kung-sun-lung-tzu.* Of the six essays contained in its present version, the best known is "A White Horse Is Not a Horse" (Selection 11). It is written in such a terse and ambiguous style that the exact meaning of some of the sentences has been debated among scholars for the past two thousand years. The author, Kung-sun Lung, is believed to have lived in the fourth century B.C.

There are other schools whose representative works have long since been lost and whose teachings are only briefly described in some of the works of their rivals. For instance, we learn something about the beliefs of the Agriculturists by reading the *Book of Mencius.* We should keep in mind, however, that whenever Mencius mentioned other schools besides his own, his primary purpose was to attack them (Selection 12).

16

To a historian who is more interested in an objective appraisal of different ideologies than in engaging in partisan debates, each ideology has its merits as well as demerits, though, like every other intellectual, he has his own preference. In the case of Ssu-ma T'an, the father of Ssu-ma Ch'ien, such a preference was Taoism (Selection 13).

5 · LAO-TZU: *Taoist Virtue* [1]

The concept of ugliness comes into being only after there has been the concept of beauty. The concept of wickedness is impossible without the concept of goodness.

Existence and non-existence follow each other in succession; being and non-being produce and reproduce each other without cessation. Without difficulty there cannot be ease; the concepts of long and short or high and low are but relative terms. Different sounds make harmony; how can there be precedence without sequence?

Knowing the relativity of values, a sage can do a great deal by doing nothing in particular and teach a great deal by remaining silent. Things multiply themselves without his interference. Yet it is he who inspires their growth, though he appropriates nothing for himself. He does not take pride in these things; nor does he take credit for their growth. As he takes no credit for himself, credit will never leave him.

*   *   *   *   *

Contention will cease if no man is singled out as the most valuable to receive praise. Robbers and bandits will disappear if no special value is attached to goods that are difficult to obtain. People's minds will not be disturbed if they have never seen things that are desirable.

When a sage becomes a ruler, he empties people's minds but fills their stomachs. He weakens their will but strengthens their frames. He keeps them ignorant and undesirous. When this goal has been achieved, the knowledgeable few will not dare to act to institute changes. When no one does anything, the best kind of government ensues.

*   *   *   *   *

If you wish to stretch something, shrink it first. If you wish to weaken it, strengthen it first. How can you destroy unless you have constructed? If you wish to take, first you have to give. To succeed, you have to do the least expected.

The gentle and the humble can always win against the hard and the inflexible. In the long run the weak will overcome the strong. A fish which does not wish to be caught hides itself deep in the river. A ruler who wishes to survive does not teach others how to run a government.

*   *   *   *   *

[1] Passages in this selection are arranged in the order they appear in the *Book of Taoist Virtue*.

To do nothing so that everything will be done is the secret of Tao. If a ruler has learned this secret and kept it, all things in the world will be transformed towards the good by themselves. Those who wish to act will be stopped, not by force but by a simplicity, honest and pure. A person who possesses this simplicity will have no desire. If desire is eliminated and all people in the world abide by the principle of quietude, the world will rectify itself, however perverted it might have been.

*　　*　　*　　*　　*

Without leaving my house, I know all about the world. I see the Way of Heaven without ever peeping through the window. The more a man travels, the less he knows.

A sage knows everything without moving himself by one inch; sees everything without seeing anything; accomplishes a great deal by doing nothing.

*　　*　　*　　*　　*

A sage thinks as the people think. He loves what they love. But when they stop loving, he continues to love. That is true love. He trusts what the people trust. But when they stop trusting, he continues to trust. That is true trust.

He sees no difference between himself and the outside world; he and the outside world share one mind and are in fact inseparable. All people look up to him as a model.

In short, the mind of a great sage is the mind of a small child.

*　　*　　*　　*　　*

A child whose body is weak and soft grows. An old man whose body is hard and unbending decays. Trees and grass are soft and pliant while growing, but will become dry and hard after they die. Hardness signals death, while softness and weakness are a symbol of life.

Therefore the stiffest tree will be felled first, and the mighty and the powerful eventually must topple. The strong and the proud should be condemned. Glory to those who are weak and humble.

*　　*　　*　　*　　*

Nothing is softer than water; yet it is stronger than anything when it attacks the hardest and the most resistant. Gentleness prevails over hardness; weakness conquers strength. Everyone knows this; yet, how many have acted in accordance with this truism?

One of our sages says that he who can bear his nation's shame can be its lord, and he who can take its evils upon himself will be its king.

What is not, is what is, and *vice versa*.

6 · CHUANG CHOU: *Sages and Thieves* [2]

To prevent theft, a man locks his chests and ties his boxes. He thinks that he is wise; so does the world. But is he really wise? He may be able to outwit small burglars, but he is helpless against big robbers. When big robbers come in, they carry away his chests and boxes. The stronger the locks and the tighter the bindings, the more convenient they are for the robbers. The so-called wisdom is really wisdom on behalf of the robbers.

This same reasoning, I believe, also holds true regarding many other matters. Our worldly wisdom is really a wisdom for those who rob and steal. And our sages—how many of them are not accomplices to wrongdoings?

How do I prove my point?

Formerly, the kingdom of Ch'i [3] was peaceful and prosperous. It had a large population with many towns and cities. Its agriculture and its fishing industry were profitable and flourishing. It had a territory of more than 2,000 square *li*,[4] and within its boundaries people worshipped and managed their own affairs in accordance with the laws of the sages. What, then, happened to this kingdom? When T'ien Ch'eng-tzu killed the king and usurped the throne, he not only stole the kingdom, but also inherited the laws of the sages that had been used to govern the kingdom. He was in fact a thief; yet he was as safe as the ancient sage kings. Small countries dared not criticize; nor dared large countries send a military expedition against him. Thus for twelve generations his family controlled the Ch'i kingdom. Is it not true that he stole not only the kingdom but also the laws of the sages which he used successfully to protect his own person, a person who was in fact a thief?

I shall use another example to illustrate my point.

Ling-feng, Pi-kan, Ch'ang-hung, and Tzu-hsü were four virtuous ministers of ancient China. Yet they were all killed by their kings, in one way or another. Chih, on the other hand, was a notorious thief who was once asked by his followers whether a thief had any virtues. "How is it possible that a thief does not have any virtues?" said Chih. "To know where the valuables are hidden indicates high intelligence. To enter into the house first shows bravery. To leave the house last is an act of righteousness. To know whether to enter a house or not is wisdom. To divide spoils according to merit is justice. It is impossible to become a great thief without possessing all of these five virtues." Thus, while a sage cannot be considered a sage without having saintly virtues, Chih cannot become a great thief without possessing the same virtues. Since there are more bad than good people in the world, the presence of sages does mankind more harm than good.

Therefore, "teeth suffer from cold without the protection of lips," and "Hantan was besieged when wine was not strong enough." [5] As long as there are sages,

[2] *Book of Chuang-tzu*, roll 10.
[3] Located in modern Shantung province.
[4] One *li* is equal to approximately one-third of a mile.
[5] The first analogy means that people will suffer when their innocence is taken away from them. The second analogy refers to an incident which occurred early in the fourth century B.C. Hantan, the capital of Chao, was besieged by Liang at a time when Chao's ally, Ch'u, was busy attacking Lu and could not send an army to help its protectorate, Chao. Ch'u attacked Lu on the ground that the wine which the Prince of Lu had sent to Ch'u as a tribute was not strong enough. This analogy means that evil consequences

there are bound to be notorious thieves. Only when sages are eliminated and bandits and thieves are turned loose can there be peace and security in the world. Valleys become empty only after rivers have dried up; rivers can be filled up only after mountains have been obliterated. Therefore, not until all sages are dead can banditry be eliminated. Peace will then prevail, as the issues that have divided men can no longer exist. As long as there are sages, there will be bandits. To honor the sages as a way of governing the world is in fact to honor and reward thieves like Chih.

Sages invented weights and measures to forestall cheating; introduced seals and stamps to make sure that people would keep their promises; taught such virtues as "love" and "righteousness" to rectify people's conduct. When a master thief arrives, he steals all the sage inventions and techniques for his own benefit.

How is this so? The fact is, while a small thief who steals a fishing hook will be punished by death, those who steal entire countries become kings and dukes. The kings and dukes are always "loving" and "righteous." Is it not true that by stealing a country a master thief also steals the wisdom and virtues of the sages?

A man who follows the ways of the master thieves will steal a country and the virtues of the sages, together with the weights and measures and seals and stamps which the sages have invented. Once he decides on this course, even the most generous reward or the most severe punishment will not deter him. Why? This is because stealing of this nature is too profitable to be resisted. Since what the thieves covet are the things invented by sages, is it not true that the sages are really at fault?

It is said that as a fish cannot remain alive out of water, a nation's "sharp tools," once revealed to the populace, will cause the nation to suffer from evil consequences. The ways of sages are a nation's "sharp tools" and should never be made known to the general public. Only by abandoning virtue and eliminating wisdom can banditry be stopped. Only when there are no jades and pearls will there be no theft. Only when seals and stamps no longer exist will people be honest. Only by eliminating the system of weights and measures will feuds and strifes cease to divide people. In short, people can be led to a virtuous path only when all the laws invented by the sages are totally dispensed with.

What pleases the ears is harmful to hearing, and what attracts the eyes is dangerous to sight. Only by abandoning music and destroying what is beautiful can ears become alert and eyes become clear. Liner and curve; compass and square— all of these instruments should be destroyed. All men become skillful only when there are no skillful artisans. The most skillful are in fact the most clumsy. Eliminate all virtues—filial piety, loyalty, eloquence, love, righteousness—and people will become truly virtuous. Only when everyone becomes stupid can all men become clever and intelligent. Throw away your wisdow so that people will not be misled. All the great sages of the past, by revealing their own virtues, contributed nothing but confusion to the world. Their way of doing things has not brought any benefit to mankind.

In the remote times when true virtues prevailed and when truly great men like Fu-hsi and Shen-nung ruled the world,[6] people used knotted cords for reckoning and recording. They were satisfied with poor food, and they wore simple,

---

can ensue even though they are not intended by their originator. In other words, sages bring harmful results to a society even though such results are not intended by the sages.

[6] Fu-hsi and Shen-nung were two of the legendary kings of ancient China.

homely clothes. They lived in rude dwellings, and were happy with whatever they had. While neighboring villages were so close that people could hear the crowing of cocks and the barking of dogs in another village, they would not communicate with one another for the entire duration of their lives. It was then that the governing of people reached its most perfect stage.

Today the situation is different. People expect the emergence of virtuous men and, whenever one such man is found, they travel a long distance to meet him, often passing across state boundaries. By doing so they desert their parents and rulers. Why do they do this? The fault lies with the rulers who themselves place a high priority on knowledge and intelligence. When rulers have knowledge and intelligence while remaining wicked, the world will of course become chaotic and unmanageable.

Why? When people become more skillful in catching birds, birds become fearful. The better our fishing equipment becomes, the more confused the fish will be. As hunting instruments become intricate and efficient, animals run wild in the forest. When more and more people are engaged in clever but deceptive arguments, they will be misled by their own falsehood which damages good customs. The result is confusion and anarchy, and the blame should be placed squarely on the love of knowledge.

As the importance of knowledge is unnecessarily overemphasized, intelligent people seek to know what they do not know, while the less intelligent seek to know what they know already. Those who think they know condemn what they do not like, and those who do not think that they know denounce what they themselves really like. How can a state of affairs be more confused? This artificiality is in sharp contrast to the natural brightness of the sun and the moon, the unadorned truthfulness of mountains and rivers, and the dependability of the seasonal cycle. Even the tiniest insect or the smallest plant follows its natural way of growth; how can man love knowledge and thus violate Nature's rule without misleading himself as well as the world?

Since the passing of the Three Dynasties,[7] simple and honest people are despised, while the cunning and the artificially eloquent are honored. Quiet and dignified people are looked down upon, while those who are only too anxious to teach others are hailed as great heroes. The world has in fact been turned upside down.

7 · LIU AN: *A Man Loses His Horse* [8]

In the northern frontier across the Tartar territory, there lived a man who knew how to look at life stoically. One day his horse ran to the north and was lost to the Tartars. His neighbors came to his house and expressed their sympathy.

"Do not feel sorry for me, gentlemen," said he. "How do you know that this loss will not become a gain?"

Several months later, the man's horse came back with a beautiful Tartar horse. All of his neighbors came to congratulate him for his good fortune.

[7] Hsia, Shang, and West Chou.
[8] This fable appears in an essay entitled "The People" *(Jen-chien); Huai-nan-tzu,* roll 18.

"How do you know, gentlemen, that this horse will not bring me bad luck?" said the man.

Being wealthy, this man had many horses, and his son loved riding. One day, while riding the Tartar horse, his son was thrown to the ground, broke his hips, and became crippled.

The man's neighbors came to express their sorrow and tried to console him.

"How do you know that this misfortune will not turn out to be a blessing in disguise?" said the man.

One year later the Tartars launched a massive attack along the frontier. All young men in the border areas were drafted into the army. The battle was so ferociously fought that nine out of every ten draftees were killed on the battlefield. The man's son was not called to service because he was crippled, and his life was therefore spared. Both father and son went through the war without suffering any personal damage.

A fortune is a misfortune, and *vice versa*. The mystery of nature is so deep that no man can really fathom it.

8 · Mo Ti: *Universal Love* [9]

In ruling a country an enlightened monarch must know the basic cause of disorder and chaos. If he does not know it, his regime will fail.

A doctor, attempting to cure a disease, must find out the cause of the disease, and he cannot restore the sick man to health if he fails to find it. Likewise those who know the basic cause of disorder and chaos will succeed as rulers, and those who do not will fail.

What is the basic cause of disorder and chaos? It is the absence of love.

Disloyalty towards one's father or king, for instance, is a matter of disorder. It comes about when a person loves himself rather than his father, elder brothers, or king, at whose expense he works to advance his own interests. Disorder also results when a father does not treat his son as a son, an elder brother does not treat his younger brother as a younger brother, or a king does not treat his minister as a minister. When a father loves himself but not his son, he works for his own advantage at the latter's expense. The same thing can be said about the relationship between elder and younger brothers and between a king and his ministers. All these difficulties arise because people do not love each other.

Another case in point is the repeated occurrence of robbery or thievery. Since a robber loves his own house but not others', he robs other people's houses to enhance the wealth of his own. Since a thief loves himself but not others, he steals from other persons to his own benefit. It is clear that robbery and thievery come about because people do not love each other.

Nobles try to destroy each other's families; kings try to conquer each other's territories. These nobles love their own families but not others'; therefore they try to destroy other families to enhance their own interests. These kings love their own kingdoms but not the kingdoms of others; therefore they attack other kingdoms to enlarge their own. Nothing is more harmful than warfare. What is its cause? It is the absence of love.

[9] This translation consists of selected passages from "Universal Love" *(Chien-ai); Mo-tzu,* rolls 14–16.

If people in the world love each other as they love themselves, there will be no such thing as disloyalty. Disloyalty will not exist if everyone loves his father or king to the same extent that he loves himself. On the other hand, if a king, father, or elder brother loves his subjects, son, or younger brother in the same way that he loves himself, there will not be any tyranny or oppression. If disloyalty and oppression do not exist, how can there be robbers and thieves? If everyone loves others' houses as if they were his own, who will rob? If everyone loves other people as much as he loves himself, who will steal? If the concept of robbery and thievery does not exist, how is it possible for one nobleman to try to destroy the family of another nobleman, or for one kingdom to attack another kingdom? How can one even think of destroying others' families if he loves them as if they were his own? How can one even think of attacking other kingdoms if he loves them as if they were his own? When love prevails, these things do not happen.

Only when love becomes universal can there be peace and order. The alternative is chaos and mutual destruction.

* * * * *

A man of gentle character loves his friend as if his friend were he himself, and treats his friend's relatives as well as if they were his own relatives.

A good prince places the welfare of his subjects above his own. He feeds them when they are hungry, clothes them when they are cold, nurses them when they are sick, and buries them when they are dead.

* * * * *

To love others is in fact to love oneself. The *Book of Odes* says:

> Do not scold me;
> I shall be your friend.
> Be good to me;
> To you I shall also be good.
> Give me a peach;
> A plum you shall receive.

This poem indicates that those who love others will be loved in return. A hater will be hated by those whom he hates.

9 · HAN FEI: *The Importance of Severe Punishment* [10]

A person who is cowardly and fearful of death is likely to surrender himself to the enemy when placed on the battlefield; yet the world honors him and calls him a gentleman who values life. A person who studies different philosophies and advances ideas of his own is likely to violate the law; yet the world honors him and calls him a gentleman of learning and literature. A person who lives well

[10] The Chinese title for this selection is *Liu fan* which literally means "Six Reversals." It appears in *Han-fei-tzu,* roll 18.

and travels a great deal is in fact a parasite; yet the world honors him and calls him a gentleman of ability. A person who is learned and knows how to play with words is likely to be a hypocrite; yet the world honors him and calls him a gentleman of wisdom proficient in the art of debate. A person who is expert in swordplay and loves to attack and kill is a man of uncontrollable violence; yet the world honors him and calls him a gentleman of bravery and courage. A person who has saved the life of a thief or hidden a violator of the law deserves no better fate than the death sentence; yet the world honors him and calls him a knight-errant, or a gentleman of magnanimity. All of these—six kinds altogether—are the people whom the world glorifies.

On the other hand, a person who defies danger and risks his life for a principle in which he believes is likely to be a man of righteousness and integrity; yet the world criticizes him and calls him a man of temerity and indiscretion. A person who knows little about academic learning but obeys the government's orders is likely a law-abiding citizen; yet the world criticizes him and calls him a shallow rustic. A person who grows food by his own labor is a true producer; yet the world criticizes him and calls him a man of meager ability. A person who is innocent and sincere is likely to be a man of uprightness; yet the world criticizes him and calls him a man of ignorance and stupidity. A person who views seriously the government's orders and is fearful when performing his duties is likely to be a loyal subject; yet the world criticizes him and calls him a coward. A person who helps the government to check wrongdoing and prevent conspiracy is an upright citizen; yet the world criticizes him and calls him a man of defamation and slander. All of these—six kinds altogether—are the people the world criticizes.

In summary, the world honors the six kinds of people who, being conspiratorial and hypocritical in nature, are worse than useless, while criticizing the six other kinds who till the fields, fight for their country, and are in fact extremely useful. This is what I call "six reversals." People honor a person in accordance with what he can do in the fulfillment of their own selfish ends, and the monarch, accepting the popular but false evaluation, shows his consideration too, which is usually followed by material rewards. Likewise they criticize a person for their own selfish reasons, and the monarch, unable to rise above the prejudice of the world, looks down upon him too. Contempt on the part of a monarch usually means harm to the person involved. As a result, honor and reward are bestowed upon those who, evil and selfish, should be in fact punished, while harm is brought upon those who, being upright and public-spirited, should be in fact rewarded. When the public has a set of values as that described above, how can a country become wealthy and strong?

An ancient proverb compares the governing of the people to the washing of one's hair. It is true that some hair will fall off as a result of washing; this, however, does not mean that we should not wash our hair. How can hair grow without being washed? He who grudges the loss of a few hairs does not understand the meaning of power.

Cutting off a carbuncle causes pain, and taking medicine is by no means a pleasant experience. However, if a patient refuses either to undergo an operation or take medicine on account of the accompanying pain, he cannot recover from his illness, and in fact he may even die.

The relationship between a king and his subjects is not so close as that between parents and children. Such being the case, it is obvious that a policy of "love and righteousness" cannot be adopted in connection with the governing of the people. When a newly born baby happens to be of the male sex, its parents congratulate each other; if it happens to be a female, they kill her in many cases. Both babies are the children of their parents; yet, one is the cause of jubilation and the other meets death soon after its birth. Why? This is because the parents are thinking in terms of the potential advantages that their male children can bring to them. Since even parents measure their relationships with their children in terms of self-interest, how can one expect that a relationship based upon love and righteousness can exist between a king and his subjects?

However, the scholars today continue to advise our rulers to replace "profit" with "love" as the proper attitude towards their subjects. This advice amounts to a demand that a king should be more loving towards his subjects than a parent is towards his children. Mistaking hypocrisy for genuine gratitude, these scholars have committed a very serious error indeed. It is no wonder that a wise monarch will not accept their advice.

When a sage rules a country, he emphasizes the importance of law and the prohibitions prescribed under it. Only then can a successful government be established. Emphasizing the importance of law, he likewise stresses the usefulness of reward and punishment. Only when reward or punishment is impartially and strictly administered can the people's energy be fully utilized and will the officials faithfully perform their duties. The country will become wealthy and its military power will become strong. Then it will be easy for its ruler to achieve the deeds of a great arbitrator.

Nothing can be more advantageous to a ruler than to possess the omnipotent power of a great arbitrator. Holding this power in his hands, he can bring about the best kind of government. He appoints officials in accordance with their ability, and punishes or rewards without showing the slightest partiality. He makes it clear to his subjects that if they do their best or even defy death to achieve worthy deeds, they will be rewarded with rank and salary, and that with rank and salary they will enjoy honor and wealth. Honor and wealth are foremost in the mind of every citizen since they are as advantageous to him as the omnipotent power is to a great prince. Hoping to obtain them, he will risk danger to do what the ruler desires and will not regret even if he dies in the attempt. To become a great arbitrator does not require the ruler's "love" and the subjects' "loyalty" in the ordinary sense of these terms.

Before a conspiracy can be quelled, a ruler must know of its existence. To stop it from re-occurring, he should execute the conspirators once they are found. An unlocated conspiracy will spread, and an unexecuted conspirator will carry out his conspiracy. Even the most virtuous man will be tempted to steal if he knows that he can get away with his thievery. On the other hand, the most notorious bandit will not touch a bag containing as much as one hundred pieces of gold that is displayed in the marketplace, conspicuous for all to see. This shows that if the government does not make its penalty clear and immediate, even the most virtuous man will be tempted to steal; if it does, even the worst bandit will not touch a bag of gold. To rule a country, a wise ruler stresses the importance of preventing crimes before they occur and inflicts heavy penalties upon those who have committed them. It is the strict enforcement of the law rather than the teaching of moralities that deters people from lawless activities.

A son is twice as much loved by his mother as by his father. Yet he obeys his father's order ten times better than he does his mother's. A government official does not love his people nor is he loved in return, but his people obey his order ten thousand times better than they do their parents'. The more the parents' love accumulates, the less their son will listen to them. On the other hand, the harsher a government official is, the more the people will be obedient to him. It does not require great intelligence to know whether "love" or "harshness" is the more effective.

Moreover, what does a parent want for his son? He wants him to be secure, prosperous, and far away from any crime that may take place. What does a ruler want from his subjects? He wants them to work hard for him in time of peace and die for him in time of war. Yet a man turns a deaf ear towards his parents who love him, but obeys every word of his ruler who has no affection for him whatsoever. Knowing this truism, a wise ruler does not cultivate a sentiment of love or gratitude between him and his subjects; he merely increases his power and influence, so that his subjects will have no choice but to be obedient to him. A mother who piles love upon her child only ruins him; a father who is less loving and beats the child often is a better parent because it is he who commands the respect of the child and can influence him towards the good.

Consider the management of a household. If its members compete with one another in enduring cold and hunger and emulate one another in performing the hardest labor, they will have good food to eat and warm clothes to wear even in time of famine or war. On the other hand, if habitually its members provide each other with food and clothing and concede to each other the moments of pleasure, they will be the kind of family that sells its wives and children during the time of natural disaster or famine. The Legalists teach people to suffer first and then enjoy the fruits of labor for a long time to come. The Confucians, on the other hand, teach people to enjoy the moment, showing little concern for the evil consequences in the long run. Recognizing the difference between the significant and the unessential and the importance of producing the greatest good, a sage prefers the harshness exemplified in the enforcement of law to the womanly sympathy as expounded by the Confucians.

Today practically all scholars advocate a policy of leniency in punishment, not realizing that this policy, if implemented, will bring about chaos or even destruction of the country as a whole. The purpose of reward or punishment is to encourage what the government wishes the people to do or prohibit what it does not want them to venture. Only when the reward is generous will there be quick response; only when the penalty is severe can the prohibition become absolute and inviolable.

Those who wish to reap advantages naturally detest what is disadvantageous, because the word "advantage" is the opposite of the word "disadvantage." How can they not detest disadvantage when it is the opposite of what they truly desire? Likewise a ruler who wishes to establish an orderly government naturally detests chaos, because the word "chaos" is the opposite of the word "order." The more he wishes his government to be orderly, the more generous his rewards will be; the more he detests chaos, the more severe his penalties are. Those who advocate leniency in punishment neither detest chaos as they should nor love good government as they profess. What they advocate is not only theoretically unsound but also physically impractical.

In fact, generous reward and severe punishment are the two most reliable standards to measure a person's virtue or lack of it, his wisdom or ignorance. Severe punishment is not aimed at the person who has committed a crime, rather, it is a restitutive act aimed at the crime for which he receives the death sentence in accordance with the law as enacted by an enlightened prince. Thus to punish a thief is not to punish the thief as a person, but theft as a violation of the law. Since a thief will be executed anyway, to punish him is in fact to punish a dead person, an act that makes no sense. Likewise the execution of a robber is not intended as a mere punishment of the robber as a person; rather, it is a redemption of robbery as a violation of the law. Otherwise it would not have made any sense to kill a person who, already in chains, cannot commit any more crimes. In short, the purpose of punishment is to stop punishment: to make the punishment for one crime so severe that other crimes will not occur. This is the principle of good government.

Those who receive severe punishment are criminals; those who are fearful of it and consequently will not commit any crime are the law-abiding citizens. Such being the case, what is wrong with severe punishment? The purpose of generous rewards is not merely to provide compensation for a particular deserving deed; more important, it is to encourage all the people in the nation to do likewise. While the rewarded person benefits materialistically, all the unrewarded persons wish to emulate his performance. Thus by rewarding one person, the whole nation is encouraged to duplicate his good deeds. Such being the case, what is wrong with generous rewards? There are people who contend that severe punishment brings harm to the people while light penalties can stop crimes. Their contention indicates that they not only do not understand the meaning of good government but also have failed to look carefully into the issue involved. If a crime cannot be stopped by severe punishment, it is unlikely that it can be stopped by a lighter one; if a crime can be stopped by a light punishment, it can be certainly stopped by a more severe one.

Thus only when the government is willing to impose heavy penalties upon the wrongdoers can it stop all crimes. How can the people be harmed when all crimes cease to exist? Severe punishment reduces whatever advantage there is in violating the law and brings great advantage to the government that administers it. Since no man will risk severe punishment for small gain, crime will cease by itself. Light punishment, on the other hand, is of great advantage to the violators of the law while bringing little benefit to the government that enforces it. The people, seeing the benefit that accompanies the committing of crimes and belittling the small punishment if they were ever caught, will continue to commit crimes which in fact can never be stopped.

As one of our ancient sages says, "It is more frequent to stumble on a mound than on a mountain." Since a mountain is large and dangerous, the climbers are more careful. Since a mound is small and seemingly harmless, the climbers are inclined to be inattentive and reckless. If the severity of punishment is reduced, the people will be careless enough to violate the law. If a violator of the law is not executed, the whole country will be encouraged to follow his example. Moreover, to execute a person without warning him of severe punishment in advance amounts to an act of entrapment which a government should not do. Light punishment is in fact like a mound to a climber. It not only brings chaos to the country but also entices people towards their death without their knowledge. It is absurd to say that it is beneficial.

The scholars today quote the beautiful words from the ancient writings while ignoring the reality of the present. They say that the government should love the people but does not, that taxes are too heavy, and that the people are complaining against the government because of the insufficient means of maintaining their livelihood. They suggest that the country can be successfully governed without invoking severe punishment if the rulers love their subjects enough and if the people are economically sufficient. Nothing can be further from the truth. A person who is most fearful of severe punishment is usually a man of sufficient means. However, he, like others, will be tempted to violate the law if the severity of punishment is reduced, no matter how economically sufficient he is or how much his rulers love him.

Suppose, say, that a wealthy family has a son who is well loved by his parents. Since he has all the money he can spend, he attaches little importance to it and lives a life of great extravagance. Meanwhile his parents, because of the fact that they love him, let him do whatever he pleases, and such liberalism on the part of his parents makes him arrogant and reckless. Eventually his extravagant habits reduce him to the position of poverty, and his arrogant and reckless conduct leads him to the act of violence. Love and money bring him nothing but disaster in the end.

Our human nature is such that we do not wish to work hard if we have sufficient means already and that we tend to be indolent if our superiors are weak and lenient. Only a man like Shen-nung will remain industrious long after he has become wealthy, and only a sage like Tseng Shih can preserve his virtue even though the rulers are weak and lenient. Since ordinary people are inferior to these two men, it is obvious that love and economic sufficiency cannot bring about good citizenship.

Lao-tzu once said: "A man who is content will not incur shame; a man who knows when to stop will not invite danger." Only a man like Lao-tzu is morally self-sufficient and does not require outward coercion to make him good. To say that people can be well-governed without the use of severe punishment is to regard all men as inherently virtuous as Lao-tzu was. How is this possible? Although occupying a position as lofty as that of the Son of Heaven and having the wealth of the whole nation under his control, Chieh [11] still was not satisfied with what he had. Such being the case, how can one expect that ordinary people can be governed easily by merely making them economically self-sufficient?

An enlightened monarch encourages people to follow the seasons so as to produce the material goods they need. He taxes in such a way as to level the income between the rich and the poor. He is generous with ranks and salaries so that the virtuous and the able can serve to the best of their ability. He imposes severe penalties upon the wrongdoers so as to put an end to illegal activities. He makes sure that people become wealthy only through their own efforts and acquire fame via worthy deeds. As far as he is concerned, a bad man should be punished and a good man should be rewarded; and there are no such things as favor, love, or partiality. This, I believe, is the true principle underlying a good government.

People do not know that a blind man is among them if all of them are soundly asleep. Nor can they recognize a mute if they themselves remain silent. In the former case, the blind man will be discovered when other people wake up and find out that only he cannot see. In the latter case, the mute will be known when

[11] See p. 9, Footnote 24.

others begin to ask him questions. Likewise a man will not be known for his paucity in ideas if his words are not scrutinized, and an able man cannot be differentiated from an imbecile unless he has been tested in the performance of duties. If words alone are the standard to measure a man's worth, there is no way of telling the difference between a Wu-huo [12] and an ordinary person. Ask them to lift up a heavy tripod,[13] and the difference will be immediately revealed. Governmental positions to an able scholar are like a heavy tripod to a muscled man. Give him an official position to hold, and one can immediately tell whether he is wise or ignorant.[14] Through the test of performance will the degenerate and the useless be eliminated from the position of power and influence.

Though their words are not taken seriously and they themselves have no official positions to hold, the degenerate and the useless continue to write to advance their arguments and conduct themselves in such an artificial and adorned manner so as to convey to others their sense of superiority.[15] Our rulers of today, bewildered by the arguments of these people and wrongly impressed with their superiority, provide them with honor and prestige. This is equivalent to crediting a man with sound vision without testing him in advance and considering him logically sound even before he opens his mouth. We cannot discover a mute or a blind man this way. A wise ruler, on the other hand, tests a man's words against their practicability and measures his performance by the degree of his success in achieving results. It is only in this way that false, outdated ideas can be discredited and done away with and hypocritical conduct will be denied refuge and be exposed for what it truly is.

10 · LI SSU: *The Importance of Thought Control* [16]

The Five Emperors [17] did not imitate one another; nor did the Three Dynasties inherit each other's institutions. Each emperor or dynasty had his or its own ways of governing people. This was not because they differed for the sake of differing; it was because time had changed. Now Your Majesty has achieved the Great Deed, a deed which can be achieved only once in thousands of generations and whose significance ordinary scholars cannot understand. Yet these scholars are insolent enough to ask Your Majesty to follow the models of the Three Dynasties. But we know that the models of the Three Dynasties are not good enough to be repeated.

In the recent past numerous princes in the country competed with one another

[12] A legendary character famous for his physical strength; a Chinese version of the American Paul Bunyan.

[13] A sacrificial vessel (*ting*) made of iron or sometimes bronze, usually found in religious establishments.

[14] Han Fei, like other scholars of his time, was interested in securing a position with the government. This essay, together with others, did reach the Ch'in emperor, Shih Huang-ti. Before Han Fei could be summoned for an interview, however, he was murdered by Li Ssu, supposedly his friend. Li Ssu was afraid that once an interview took place, the emperor might elevate Han Fei at his own expense. A memorial written by Li Ssu appears in this book as Selection 10.

[15] The author had in mind primarily the Confucians.

[16] This selection appears in "Biography of Ch'in Shih Huang-ti"; *Historical Records*, roll 6.

[17] According to Ssu-ma Ch'ien, the Five Emperors were Huang-ti (Yellow Emperor, d. 2698? B.C.); Chuan-hsü (2513–2435? B.C.); Ti-k'u; T'ang-yao (or Yao, 2357–2255? B.C.); and Yü-shun (or Shun, 2255–2205? B.C.).

in extending patronage to the country's roaming scholars. Now that the country has been unified and all laws emanate from one central source, it is only proper that all people should be diligent in their respective professions, whether they be agriculture or handicraft, and that all scholars should study the law in order to learn what is legally forbidden. Instead of trying to learn about the present, the scholars today want us to model our government after those of the remote years. They criticize the institutions we have today, and their criticisms have confused and bewildered the common people.

Risking his life, Your Majesty's minister, Li Ssu, proposes as follows:

In the ancient times the country was divided, and none was able to unify it. As a result, numerous principalities existed independently side by side. People spoke highly of the past to the detriment of the present; they adored falsehood so as to confuse reality. Each person pursued his own school of ideas which was not established by the authority above.

Now Your Majesty has unified the country, and a single authority has been established over all divergences. However, individual schools of philosophy continue to teach in violation of the law; and whenever an imperial decree is handed down, each of them criticizes the decree in accordance with its own beliefs. The followers of these schools not only harbor criticism in their minds but also openly express it in the streets. They seek fame by bragging about the virtue of their beliefs, and they consider themselves superior on account of the strange ideas they hold. All of them take the leadership in slandering the government. If this slandering is not prohibited, the power of the emperor will deteriorate and political factions will emerge from the people. To prohibit it is absolutely necessary.

Therefore I, your minister, propose that all histories, except the official history of the Ch'in state, should be burned. With the exception of the imperial professors who are authorized to keep books in their respective fields, all others who have in their possession the *Book of Odes,* the *Book of History,* and other works of the various philosophies should report to local authorities and hand to them their holdings, all of which would be subsequently burned. Those who dare to discuss among themselves the contents of the *Book of Odes* and the *Book of History* should be executed in public. Those who dare to criticize the present regime by invoking the ancient writings should be likewise put to death, together with all members of their families. Government officials who know that violations have occurred but choose not to prosecute would be regarded as having committed the same crime as that committed by the offenders. If books are not burned thirty days after the order has been issued, the offenders should have their faces branded and should be exiled to the northern frontier to build the Great Wall.

Books not to be burned are books of medicine, divination, and forestation. Those who wish to study law could do so under the guidance of government officials.

11 · KUNG-SUN LUNG: *A White Horse Is Not a Horse* [18]

"Is this statement true that a white horse is not a horse?"
"Yes, it is."
"Why?"

---

[18] *Kung-sun-lung-tzu,* roll 1.

"When you speak of 'horse,' you have in mind a form that is shaped like a horse. When you say 'white,' you have in mind a certain kind of color. You cannot use 'color' to describe 'form.' Therefore a white horse is not a horse."

"If there is a white horse, you cannot say that there is no horse. Since you cannot say that there is no horse, the white horse must be a horse."

"When you say 'horse,' all horses will answer that description, yellow or black. When you ask for a white horse, however, a yellow or black horse will not do. If a white horse is a horse, to ask for a white horse would be the same as to ask for a horse. In that case there would be no difference between a white horse and any horse, and presumably you could give a man either a yellow or a black horse when he asks for a white horse. Since such difference does exist, you cannot do what you presumably could do if it did not exist. In summary, since you *can* answer a man's request for a horse by providing him with either a yellow or a black horse and since you *cannot* answer his request for a white horse by providing him with either a yellow or a black horse, it is obvious that a white horse is not a horse."

"If you say that a horse is not a horse simply because it has a color, the logical conclusion would be that there are no horses in the world, because all horses have one kind of color or another. But you know that there are horses in the world."

"Of course, every horse has a color. Otherwise there would be no such thing as a white horse. If horses, to be horses, cannot have any kind of color, there *would be* only 'horses' in the world and there *would not be* any 'white horses.' Since 'being white' is not the same thing as 'being horse,' how can you still say that a white horse is a horse? Moreover, when you say 'white horse,' you have in mind 'white' and 'horse'; when you say 'horse,' you have in mind not only white horses but also other kinds of horses. Therefore a white horse is not a horse."

" 'Horse' can still be 'horse' without being 'white.' 'White' can still be 'white' without being the color of a horse. You combine 'white' and 'horse,' and you have 'white horse.' Since you cannot deny the validity of naming a 'combination' by one of its components,[19] you cannot deny the validity that a white horse is a horse."

"You equate 'white horse' with 'horse.' Can you also equate 'white horse' with 'yellow or black horse'?"

"Of course not."

"When you admit that 'being a horse' is different from 'being a yellow horse,' you will also have to admit that 'being a yellow horse' is different from 'being a horse.' Once you admit that a 'yellow horse' is different from a 'horse,' you have to conclude logically that a yellow horse is not a horse. If a yellow horse is not a horse, how can a white horse be still a horse? How can you maintain the same name for an object which has materially changed and is now entirely different? When you do, you are advancing an argument that is as false as the saying that a bird can live in the water or that the cart should be placed before the horse. This is a kind of argument that generates falsehood and confuses the world."

"When there are no white horses, you cannot say that there are no horses. In other words, 'horse' can exist independent of 'white.' On the other hand, when there are white horses, you cannot say that all kinds of horses are there. Therefore, when we say that a horse exists, we mean exactly what we say, regardless

---

[19] By this the author means that a "white horse" (a combination of "white" and "horse") is both "white" (one component) and "horse" (another component).

of whether a white horse exists or not. When you say that a white horse is not a horse, you have in fact transformed that horse into two horses: the horse that is a horse independent of the fact that it happens to be white, and the horse that *is* white. You cannot do that."

" 'White' is an adjective transferable, since it can be used to describe other items besides a horse. It is not an essential attribute insofar as a horse is concerned. When you say 'white horse,' the adjective 'white' has become an integral part of the horse and is no longer transferable. Since what is transferable is not what is not transferable, the 'white' in 'white horse' is different from 'white' *as such*. When you say 'horse,' you are not conditioning it with any kind of color, and therefore you can answer it with yellow or black horse. When you say 'white horse,' you have conditioned it with the color 'white,' and you can answer it *only* with 'white horse.' Nothing else can do. Since 'to condition an object' is the direct opposite of 'not to condition it,' a white horse is not a horse."

12 • MENCIUS: *The Agriculturists* [20]

Hsü Hsing, an advocate for the teachings of Shen-nung,[21] arrived at T'eng [22] from the state of Ch'u.[23] He called upon Duke Wen at the latter's residence. "I, who came from afar, have heard that you, sir, wish to carry out the policy of love," said he to the Duke. "I would like very much to receive a house from you and become your subject." Hearing this, the Duke gave him a house. Hsü had with him several tens of his followers all of whom wore coarse garbs and tight straw shoes. They earned their livelihood by weaving mats.

Meanwhile Ch'en Hsiang (a disciple of Ch'en Liang [24]) and his younger brother Hsin, carrying their farm implements with them, also arrived at T'eng from the state of Sung.[25] "I have heard that you, sir, wish to carry out the policies of our ancient sages. You must be a sage yourself. I want to become a subject of a sage," said Ch'en Hsiang to Duke Wen.

Ch'en Hsiang met Hsü Hsing and was immensely impressed with the latter's teachings. He decided to discard what he had learned [26] and follow Hsü Hsin instead.

Seeing Mencius, Ch'en Hsiang related to him Hsü Hsin's words as follows: "Though the prince of T'eng is a good ruler, he has not learned the truth. A virtuous ruler should till the fields side by side with his subjects and should in fact cook his own food. Since the prince of T'eng has granaries filled up with grain and treasuries full of money, he is in fact exploiting the people for his own benefit. How can he be considered virtuous?"

"Does Mr. Hsü eat food other than what he himself has grown?" asked Mencius.

"Yes," Ch'en Hsiang replied.

[20] *Book of Mencius,* roll 3.
[21] Shen-nung, or "Divine Farmer," was the legendary hero who, in the remote past, taught the Chinese the art of farming.
[22] A small principality located in modern Shantung province.
[23] Located in the middle Yangtze valley.
[24] A Confucian.
[25] Located in modern Honan province.
[26] Confucianism.

"Is it true that Mr. Hsü wears no other clothing except that made from cloth which he himself has woven?"

"No. Mr. Hsü wears only coarse garments, however."

"Does Mr. Hsü wear a hat?"

"Yes, he does."

"What kind of hat?"

"Hat made of white silk."

"Did he himself weave the silk that was used to make his hat?"

"No. He obtained it by parting with his grain."

"Why did Mr. Hsü not weave the silk himself?"

"This is because to weave silk would have an adverse effect on his work in farming."

"Does Mr. Hsü use an iron saucepan and an earthen stove to cook his food? Does he use an iron plow to till his fields?"

"Yes, he does."

"Did he make all of those things himself?"

"No. He exchanged his grain for them."

"If exchanging grain for equipment does not harm potters and smiths, how is it possible that exchanging equipment for grain would be harmful to the farmers? Why is Mr. Hsü not also engaged in the work of potters and smiths so that everything he uses will be produced inside his own household? Why does he go through so much trouble to trade with the artisans? Is he a man who does not mind trouble?"

"A farmer cannot do all the work that the artisans do."

"Since what you have said is obviously true, how can we rely on farming alone for the successful governing of the world?" said Mencius. "There are two kinds of work in the world, the work of a gentleman and the work of a mean man. A person, to maintain his life, needs the products of all other people in the society. If we have to make everything we use with our own hands, our society will become a society of strangers. It has been correctly stated that some should work with their minds and some should work with their hands. Those who work with their minds form the governing class, and those who work with their hands are the governed. It is a general principle throughout the world that the duty of the governed is to produce goods while the governing, who do not produce any goods, are supported by the governed. . . ."

13 · SSU-MA T'AN: *A Summary of the Six Schools*[27]

"A hundred schools are only variations of one theme," says the *Great Commentary on the Book of Changes*,[28] "and all try to reach the same destination, though by different roads." All of the six schools, Dualism,[29] Confucianism, Moism, Dialecticism, Legalism, and Taoism, are concerned with the establishment of an orderly society. Their difference is a difference in methods whereby such a goal can be achieved. Some of these methods are sound, while others are not.

[27] This selection is taken from "Autobiography of the Grand Historian" *(T'ai-shih-kung tzu-hsü); Historical Records,* roll 130.

[28] *Yi ta-chuan.*

[29] *Yin-yang chia.*

I have seen the Dualists practicing divination. If they predict an inauspicious outcome, people become fearful and constrained and will abstain from doing what they normally would. On the other hand, the Dualists advocate the conduct of our lives in accordance with the change of seasons, an advocacy which is unquestionably sound. The teachings of Confucians are too broad in scope for one to grasp their essentials: dilegent work yields only negligible result. It is practically impossible to follow all of them. However, the emphasis they lay on the proper relationships between king and ministers, father and son, husband and wife, and elder and younger brothers is certainly a correct emphasis, not to be changed with the change of time. The Moists advocate an extreme form of frugality, so extreme that few can really abide by it. Yet no one can deny the merit of promoting basic industry and of practicing thrift, which they have also advocated. The Legalists are harsh and unfeeling, but their belief in elevating the king above his ministers and the superiors above the inferiors is doubtless valid. The Dialecticians simplify matter to the extent of making it untruthful and unreal. Yet their advocacy of differentiating "name" from "reality" is as interesting as it is plausible.

The Taoists teach people the concentration of mind and the attainment of a status whereby a man can move about without making physical movement and can be self-sufficient without acquiring anything material. As for their technique, they adopt the theory of seasonal adaptibility from the Dualists and the best and the most essential from the four other schools. They change their technique in accordance with the change of time and circumstances. They do whatever they please without doing anything improper, whether it be the establishment of a new custom or the management of a specific affair. Their general directives are broad and therefore easy to follow, and they achieve a great deal with comparatively small effort. In this respect they are completely different from the Confucians. Regarding the king as the model and the example for everyone to follow, the Confucians have maintained that the king should take the initiative and the ministers have only to echo; i.e., the ministers take the path which the king has opened up. Under this theory the ministers have a comparatively leisurely task at the expense of the king who has to toil. The Taoists, on the other hand, incorporate the essence of the Great Way by eliminating desires and abandoning wisdom, thus elevating the virtue of the meek and the humble. Disregarding the Taoist teachings, a person would have to toil in vain against the ponderousness of nature's might and would not reap anything except frustration and despair. When the harmony between "spirit" and "form" ceases to exist and anarchy results, how can man expect to live a life as eternal as Heaven and Earth?

The Dualists teach us the positive and negative forces, the four seasons, the eight positions, the twelve months, and finally, the twenty-four divisions. For each occasion there are definite rules to follow; those who abide by them will prosper and those who do not will perish. The facts, however, do not always correspond with the Dualists' contention, and often they make people unnecessarily constrained and fearful. However, they teach people the most essential of the ways of Heaven: birth in the spring, growth in the summer, maturity in the autumn, and hibernation in the winter; and it is impossible to speak of the ways of the world without in the meantime observing the wishes of Heaven. This is what I mean when I say that their advocacy of following seasonal changes in the conduct of our lives has unquestionable merit.

The basic teachings of the Confucians are contained in the *Six Classics,* and thousands of volumes have been written on them in the form of commentaries. They cannot be mastered even if a person were to devote a lifetime to them, and it would take years before he could be familiar with all of the Confucian rituals. This is what I mean when I say that the teachings of Confucians are too broad in scope for one to grasp their essentials and that diligent work yields only negligible results. Yet their emphasis on the proper relationships between king and ministers, father and son, husband and wife, and elder and younger brother is a correct emphasis whose merit cannot be denied by any of the other schools.

Like the Confucians, the Moists glorify Yao and Shun and speak constantly of their virtuous deeds. Moreover, they prescribe a life of frugality for a gentleman to follow. The main room of his house, say they, should not be more than three feet above the ground; the terrace, made of earth, should not be more than three-layered; the thatch used for roofing should never be trimmed; and finally, the beams and pillars should be made of unprocessed raw wood. He should eat and drink from earthenware, and relish the crudest food. He should wear hemp clothes in the summer and deer skins in the winter. When he dies, his coffin should be made of tung wood no more than three inches thick, and the mourning be conducted in a quiet, dignified manner. This is the kind of life the Moists prescribe for everyone to follow, regardless of his position in the society, high or low. They make no allowance for difference in time or circumstances: all men under Heaven lead the same kind of life. But a life of this kind is frugal to such an extreme that few can abide by it, as previously stated. However, because they emphasize the importance of promoting the basic industries and of practicing thrift, the Moists enable every household to be economically self-sufficient. This is a contribution not to be denied by any other school.

Using the law as the ultimate standard to measure a person's conduct, the Legalists take no cognizance of the difference between friends and strangers, or between nobility and common people. They put to an end the natural affection which a person feels towards those whom he respects or loves. The disregard of natural affection may be proper at a particular time and under a special circumstance, but to make it universal and permanent will inevitably bring about evil consequences. This is what I mean when I say that the Legalists are harsh and unfeeling. Yet their emphasis on the superiority of the king to his ministers and the importance of delegating authority so that no official will overstep his jurisdictional boundaries is a correct emphasis whose merit cannot be denied by any of the other schools.

The Dialecticians scrutinize minute details while ignoring the broad picture of which the details are mere parts. To their listeners the meaning is lost during the reasoning process. Truth or falsehood is determined by what they call dialectics without reference to feelings or emotions. They simplify matter to the extent of making it untruthful and unreal as previously stated. However, they check "name" against "reality" and vice versa, and make each factor in the reasoning process appear in its proper place. Their contribution in this respect should not be lightly dismissed.

The Taoists speak of all-activity as well as non-activity; their teachings are easy to follow. The essence of Taoism is "voidness" which, when applied to the conduct of our daily life, becomes naturalism. It is neither rigid in position nor definite in form. Being flexible and indefinite, a Taoist can study all things without being enchained or imprisoned in return. He, in fact, is the master of all things in the universe. As far as he is concerned, there is no law except that most befitting the circumstances and no rule except that most appropriate for the occasion. As a Taoist saying goes, "Immortal is the sage who abides by the law of change."

As "voidness" is the constant of Tao, naturalness should be the rule by which a king governs his subjects. The ministers are encouraged to express freely their opinions, some of which will be sound and others will of course not be. By turning a deaf ear to the latter, the king not only can forestall treachery which will doubtless occur otherwise, but is also enabled to differentiate the vile from the virtuous, the black from the white. All he needs is a simple technique which, once mastered, will make him successful in every task he attempts. He is incorporated with the Great Way which, shapeless and nameless, shines brightly throughout the universe.

What makes a man is his spirit which, to be physically existing, is embodied in a human form. As his spirit can be exhausted when constantly in use, his physical form will deteriorate if unnecessarily abused. When his spirit is separated from his body, he dies. The spirit that has left will never return; a man, once dead, cannot live again. This is a basic fact that a sage keeps constantly in mind. The spirit is the essence of life, and the form only its embodiment. How can a person say that he can rule the world if he does not even know how to stabilize his own spirit?

CHAPTER THREE

Skepticism and Neo-Taoism

T HE ascendency of Confucianism was followed by its abuse and subsequent decline. A good example of such abuse was provided by the Han states-man Wang Mang (d. A.D. 23) who murdered his sons and grandson on the ground that "when 'righteousness' is involved, one should not hesitate to kill one's closest relatives." While his wife was losing her eyesight "as a result of too much crying," his reputation as a Confucian scholar and virtuous man soared. Hypocritical behaviors like this prompted such people as Wang Ch'ung (c. 27–100) not only to raise the question as to whether Confucianism was the universal truth, but also to subject to scrutiny all popular beliefs, including that on "ghosts" (Selection 14).

Other intellectuals went further than Wang Ch'ung. To Ko Hung who lived in the first half of the fourth century, all political institutions, including that of kingship, were instruments of oppression; he advocated their abolition and the return of mankind to a primitive Taoist "natural" state (Selection 15). By this time Confucianism was in full retreat, and Taoism claimed as its adherents some of the most outstanding members of China's intellectual elite. A treatise of anonymous authorship entitled *Yang Chu,* perhaps written during the first century B.C., enjoyed a sudden popularity because its author assured his readers that life was short and most uncertain and that it had no other goal besides avoidance of pain and the pursuit of pleasure (Selection 16). To prolong one's enjoyment of pleasure, one obviously had to live a long life. Thus the preservation of life became a repeated theme in many of the Neo-Taoist writings (Selection 17).

The question arose as to what the word "pleasure" really meant. To many it meant "drinking"—a desire to escape from an extremely unpleasant reality in a turbulent age (Selections 18 and 19). To others it meant a life of peace and serenity, completely detached from the immediate environment. The difficulty of pursuing such a life within the existing social framework made the longing for it all the greater. This longing prompted T'ao Ch'ien (376–427) to write his short but memorable essay *T'ao-hua-yüan chi,* here translated as "A Peaceful Village" (see Selection 20).

14 · WANG CH'UNG: *On Death* [1]

People say that after death a person becomes a ghost and that a ghost is a conscious being and can harm man if he chooses to do so. I say that these people are wrong and that their belief in ghosts is nothing but falsehood.

How do I prove my point?

Man, like other things in the world, is composed of matter. If all other things cannot become ghosts after their death, how is man alone able to do so? If a person is not certain that all other things will become ghosts after their deaths, how can he be so certain with regard to man?

What makes a person live is his vitality.[2] Once he dies, his vitality disappears. The element that creates and then maintains his vitality is the blood in his veins. Upon death his supply of blood is immediately cut off, and his vitality disappears. What is left is a decomposed body which will be reduced to dust in due course. Where does the ghost come from? . . .

Since the beginning of the world the number of people who have died, either of old age or of disease, must have been hundreds of millions. The number of people who are living today is smaller than the number of people who have died. If every person who died has become a ghost, ghosts must be everywhere. Our streets, our alleys, and even our houses and yards must be full of ghosts. Why is it that those who claim that they have seen ghosts say that have seen only one or two ghosts? . . .

Fire can be rekindled, but the rekindled fire is not the same fire. Once extinguished, a fire cannot continue to burn. Nature can produce man, but it cannot make a dead man reappear in a visible form. If some one can show me that burned ashes can be rekindled to make a blazing flame, I shall believe his story that a dead man can reappear in a different form. Inasmuch as burned ashes cannot be rekindled, a dead man cannot become a ghost. . . .

I am certain that a man, once dead, is unaware of his identity. His situation is the same as that before he was born, *i.e.*, before he acquired consciousness. Before he was born, he was part of the universal spirit. After he dies, he returns to the universal spirit to be merged in it. Since the universal spirit itself is insensible and unfeeling, how can the human spirit, one of its constitutent parts, alone be conscious of its separate existence? . . .

When a man is asleep, he is unaware of what he did while he was awake. How can a dead man possibly be aware of what he did while he was alive? If a man soundly asleep cannot hear the conversation that takes place beside his bed, how can a dead man know the happenings beside his coffin? In the case of the sleeping man, he is unaware of his environment even though he still possesses the vitality as well as the physical form of a living being. How can a dead man be aware of it after his vitality has disappeared and his body has been decomposed?

A man, beaten and wounded by another man, reports this incident to the police. He can do so because he remains conscious or has regained his consciousness. A man who has been killed does not know his killer; nor does his family know where his dead body is. If he were conscious after his death, hating the man who has

---

[1] This selection appears in *Critique of Opinions (Lun heng),* roll 20.
[2] *Ching-ch'i.*

killed him, he would have reported the name of the killer to the police and would have informed his family where his body is. Since he does not do either of these things, it is obvious that he loses the consciousness which he once possessed. . . .

Death is like a fire extinguished, and an extinguished fire can no longer burn. Likewise a man, once dead, can no longer feel or comprehend. Those who say otherwise have been greatly misled. A man who is seriously ill is like a fire about to flicker out, and a dead body without vitality in it is like a candle whose flame has been put out. To say that a man continues to possess consciousness after he has died is to say that a fire continues to glow after it has been extinguished. . . .

Suppose, say, that a jealous husband is married to an adulterous wife. Though living together under the same roof, they are angry with each other, quarrel, fight, and even bring their arguments to the attention of the court. After the death of one of the parties, the other remarries. If the dead person still possesses consciousness, he or she would become angry and would cause harm to the other party who has remarried. The fact that the dead person remains silent and does not harm the party against whom he or she has reasons to hold grudges indicates clearly that he or she does not possess consciousness.

If a man cannot become a ghost and remain conscious after his death (as we have proved that he cannot), it is obvious that a dead man cannot do harm to the living beings. . . .

15 · KO HUNG: *The Abolition of Kingship* [3]

The Confucians say that Heaven creates people and then installs kings to rule them. Can it also be true that the Confucians invoke Heaven to speak out what they themselves wish to believe?

The strong oppress the weak who have no choice except to submit. The clever play tricks upon the ignorant who are forced to be obedient. Involuntary servitude characterizes the relationship between a king and his subjects, and the enforcement of obedience is the way whereby the weak—the people—are effectively controlled. In fact, the very relationship between superiors and inferiors results from the successful contest on the part of the strong against the weak and the clever against the ignorant. . . .

The masses, nameless and thankless, work hard to support the ruling officials. The higher the salary these officials receive, the harder the life the masses have to endure.

A man who has been sentenced to death and then receives clemency greatly rejoices; would it not have been better had the death sentence not been imposed in the first place? A hypocrite acquires the reputation of modesty and humbleness by declining the rank and salary bestowed upon him by his superiors; would he not have been more honest had he accepted the honors?

Loyalty and righteousness become outstanding virtues only in a turbulent and degenerate society. Filial obedience and parental love become conspicuous and praiseworthy only after harmony has been lost among the members of a household.

[3] Ko Hung, who lived in the first half of the fourth century A.D., was the author of *Pao-p'o-tzu,* from which this selection is made.

In ancient times there were neither kings nor ministers. People dug wells to obtain their drink and tilled fields to grow their food. They began to work when the sun rose and rested when the sun set. Being unfettered and carefree, they were happy and content. Knowing no such things as competition and aggressiveness, they neither coveted honor nor incurred any shame. It was then that mountains had no trails and rivers carried no boats; even bridges did not exist. Since transportation was impossible via land or by water, people could not annex each other's territories. Warfare became a matter of unfeasibility because there was no concentration of people in any area.

Then people had no such concepts as power and profit; consequently they had neither strifes nor calamities therefrom. Weapons did not exist; fortifications were meaningless. All things were incorporeal and yet inseparable; they were lost and yet embodied in The Way.

Epidemics and pestilences did not appear then; people died only of old age. Because his heart was untarnished and pure, a person of those days did not harbor evil intentions against his neighbors. Well-fed and carefree, he was happy with himself and harmonious with others. Whatever he chose to do, he moved about with a light heart. The words he spoke were simple and unadorned; his conduct was natural and unpretentious. Since every person felt and acted the way he did, how was it possible for people to hoard goods and amass fortunes to the detriment of others? Was it necessary then to introduce means of punishment to oppress the masses?

It was only in the later years that cleverness was popularized and craft became the fashion. As the precedence of superiors over inferiors became an established rule, true virtues deteriorated. . . .

The further we are away from the days of this unadulterated beginning, the more we become base and dishonest. Now people make better and more effective weapons: the more they do so, the longer they prolong the evil of war and conquest. As far as they are concerned, cross-bows can never be too powerful, armor can never be too strong, spears can never be too sharp, and shields can never be too thick. All of these weapons could be easily dispensed with had there been no oppression of one group of people by another.

How can a jade tally [4] be made if a piece of raw jade is not cut? By the same token, how can true love and righteousness come about if false values are not abandoned? Evil men like Chieh and Chou [5] did such terrible things as burning their subjects alive, torturing imperial counselors, quartering feudal lords, carving out people's hearts, and breaking men's shinbones. Their arrogance and insolence reached the maximum when they put people to death through the use of hot pillars.[6] Had they been commoners, they would not have been able to commit these wanton crimes even though they might be satanic and sadistic by nature. Why could they do these evil things at the expense of the whole world? It was because they happened to be kings.

Evils multiply themselves as soon as the institution of kingship is established. By then it is too late even to be angry. What purpose can anger serve when a person has already been put behind bars and when he has to endure his sorrow and weariness under the worst possible circumstances? While the people suffer

[4] A jade tally was a symbol of authority when carried by a minister or an envoy.
[5] See p. 9, Footnote 24.
[6] Hot pillars or *p'ao-lo* were an instrument of torture, presumably by burning.

below, their ruler trembles above, because every ruler is fearful of his own subjects. He teaches them rites and propriety; he regulates their conduct by the enactment of laws and the imposition of punishment. He tries to stop a great flood with his hands after he has inadvertently broken the dyke. He is bound to fail.

16 · ANONYMOUS: *Yang Chu* [7]

A life span of one hundred years is about the maximum a man can hope to reach. Those who have achieved this goal are less than one in a thousand. Suppose that a person has lived to such an advanced age. Childhood and old age constitute almost one-half of the hundred years. Of the remaining years another one-half is taken up by sleeping. Moreover, there are sickness, disease, distress, and misery, not to mention the mental agonies caused by deaths, misfortunes, worries, and fears. These physical and mental pains take up one-half of his wakeful years. All in all, the total amount of time during which he can enjoy himself is about a dozen or so years. During this short period the occasion upon which he is completely carefree and happily contented occurs only once in a long time.

What is the purpose of life? What makes life worth while? Is it material comfort? Is it sensual enjoyment? Material comfort can never be completely satisfactory because there is no limit to it. Nor can sensual enjoyment be continued forever. Furthermore, there are customs and traditions as well as legal statutes that impose limitations on these types of enjoyment.

There are people who work and compete for worldly fame so that their names will be remembered by posterity. There are others who refuse to see or hear anything improper and conduct themselves in such a way that they are always mindful of the difference between the right and the wrong. Are these people really wise? They forfeit what they could enjoy and lose the opportunity which, once lost, will be lost forever. They are like prisoners in solitary confinement, hands cuffed and feet in chains.

Realizing the brevity of life and the unpredictability of death, the men of ancient times did what their hearts desired and what their nature dictated. They enjoyed the present; worldly fame played no part in their behavior or conduct. They moved about according to their natural inclinations: they did not attempt the extraordinary or the unusual. They never wished to cultivate a good reputation for posterity to remember; nor did they behave in such a way as to incur the wrath of the law. Fame and honor were not their values; they did not even care how long they might live.

Men are endowed differently when they are born, but they all share one thing in common: death. They are different in the sense that some are wise and others are stupid; some are born as nobles and others are not. Yet all of them, once dead, will decompose and disappear. We cannot change our natural endowments: the fact that we are wise or stupid, noble or common, is totally beyond our control. Nor can we change our fate; after we die, we all decompose and disappear. Birth and death; wisdom and stupidity; nobility and commonality—these are the things that we cannot change. But we are the same in the sense that we all belong to

---

[7] This translation consists of the opening passages of the title article. This article appears in *Lieh-tzu,* roll 7.

nature and in the end we all have to die. Death may come at the end of ten years or at the end of one hundred years; nevertheless it is the same death. While living, some are like Yao and Shun, and others are like Chieh and Chou. But virtuous or wicked, they become the same skeletons after their death. Who can tell the difference between the skeletons of the virtuous and those of the wicked?

Let us live! Why should we be concerned with what will happen to us after we die? . . .

17 · CHI K'ANG: *On the Preservation of Life* [8]

Some people say that earthly immortality is a matter of effort; others, on the other hand, have maintained that the maximum age one can reach is one hundred and twenty years and that it is absurd to say that a person can live beyond this maximum. I believe that both opinions are wrong to some extent. Here is my argument.

Though no man has seen an immortal, there is no doubt that he has existed in view of the fact that his presence has been described in written records. It seems that these immortals are endowed differently by nature and that they can defy death indefinitely because of this natural endowment rather than by conscientious efforts. For most of us this goal cannot be achieved. If, however, we conduct our lives in a rational manner so that we can live as long as nature permits it, it is possible that we can prolong our lives to as long as one thousand years or at least several hundred years. Since most people do not understand this and act accordingly, they cannot achieve the goal which they wish to achieve. Let me elaborate on this point.

A person who takes drugs to induce perspiration sometimes fails to achieve his purpose. Yet, the moment he feels nervous or shameful, he perspires profusely. A man who has not had his breakfast is anxious for food. Yet Tseng-tzu,[9] in mourning for his parents, did not feel hungry even though he had not eaten anything for seven days. At midnight a man is eager to go to sleep. Yet, if he has deep worries, he may not be able to close his eyes throughout the night. Even with a strong brush, a man may fail to place his hair in order; drinking strong wine, he may not succeed in reddening his own face. Yet, the moment he is angry, his hair stands up and his face reddens as if touched by magic.

All these tend to prove that our spirit controls our body to the same extent that a king controls his subjects. If the spirit is damaged inside, the body will deteriorate outside. This is the same as saying that if a king is not virtuous, his nation will become chaotic. It is true that one pail of water cannot make a plant grow which, without successive watering, will die eventually. It cannot be denied, however, that this watering, inadequate though it is, does have a beneficial effect on the plant. People say that an occasional loss of temper or an infrequent occurrence of sorrow will not bring any harm; and because of this misconception, they indulge in them only too often. They are like the people who, while belittling the benefit of watering a plant by one pail of water, still hope that the plant will grow to its full length in a waterless field. A wise man, knowing that body and spirit are interdependent and that his body can be damaged by even the smallest negligence,

---

[8] The Chinese title for this selection is *Yang-sheng lun*. Chi K'ang, the author, died by execution on a trumped-up charge of treason at the age of forty.

[9] A disciple of Confucius.

cultivates his spirit and rests his mind, so that the soundness of his body can be constantly preserved. To him there are no such things as "love" and "hate" or "sorrow" and "joy." Devoid of feelings, he is only interested in maintaining the harmony between his body and spirit. He disciplines his breathing and eats only those foods that bring him bodily nourishment. The purpose is to cultivate a close, complementary relationship between the body and the spirit so that one exists for the benefit of the other. A farmer knows that a tract of good land yields ten pecks of grain per *mou;* what he does not know is that its real capacity is one hundred piculs per *mou.* Cultivating fields is like growing trees; the amount of yield varies with the extent of care given to it. People say that there are no such things as a profit of one thousand percent for merchants or a yield of one hundred pecks of grain per *mou* for farmers. They speak of what they have observed rather than the potentials. . . .

Shen-nung [10] once said that the best medicine preserves our life potential and the next best cultivates our natural endowments. Knowing the basic law of life, a wise man conducts his life in such a way that he helps rather than damages his natural self. Most people, however, do not understand this truism. They are tempted by delicious but fattening foods, seductive scenery, and licentious music, and they indulge themselves in these dissipations without restraint. They do not know that delicious food is harmful to the bowels, tasty wine is injurious to the intestines, and spices, fragrant though they smell, are corrosive to the marrow of our bones. Moreover, the stirring of emotion, whether it be anger or joy, disrupts the normal functionings of our vital self, and worries and cares slowly but steadily erode our living spirit. How long can our body, small, fragile, and easily exhaustible, stand these attacks, from within as well as without? We incur illness through our unrestrained and unregulated eating habit; we invite physical exhaustion through our sensual indulgence. We laugh at or feel sorry for a man who dies at his prime as a result of illness or physical injury, and we say that he should have been more careful with himself. Yet we consider natural and unavoidable the accumulation of small damages and the slow but steady deterioration of our vitality until we age and die. When we finally realize that this deterioration process is no more natural than sudden death at the prime of our life, it is already too late. We sigh with regret that we have not been careful at the beginning; but what good does regret do?

While in his death bed, Duke Huan of Ch'i was angry with Pien Ch'üeh [11] because the latter had anticipated his death, instead of blaming himself for having failed to listen to the physician's advice. People like Duke Huan think that illness begins when pain begins; they do not realize that an illness slowly develops and that the best way of curing an illness is to prevent it from developing. Living among mortals and being accustomed to the quick disappearance of life, we reach the conclusion that a man's life span has been and will be as short as it is. We insist that this is the law of nature, and comfort ourselves by saying that there is nothing we can do about it.

[10] A legendary culture-hero who, among other things, invented the art of prescribing herb medicine, "after tasting hundreds of herbs himself." See also p. 32, Footnote 21.
[11] Pien Ch'üeh was a famous physician who lived in the seventh century B.C. Each time he visited Duke Huan, according to tradition, he advised the latter to undergo treatment because of an internal disease. The Duke, looking healthy and feeling well, thought that the physician only wished to cure a non-existent illness so as to collect fees, laughed loudly, and refused the advice. Without treatment, the illness eventually reached the incurable stage. Lying in his death bed, the Duke ordered the physician's immediate presence. But Pien Ch'üeh had already fled.

Some of us who have heard about the preservation of life through careful cultivation do not believe it and dismiss it outright. There are others who, though dubious, lend their ears to it; but they do not know how to go about it. Still others take concrete steps by taking drugs, only to give them up when, after a period of six months to one year, they find no noticeable good result. This is like pouring water into the field at one end and letting it leak out at the other; how can there be good result? Many people pledge themselves to control their emotions and suppress their desires. Yet surrounded by things truly desirable and not knowing whether their restraint will bring any beneficial result tens of years later, they become increasingly skeptical as time goes on. Meanwhile the worldly desirable continue to tempt them from outside. Attacked from within as well as without, they eventually have to concede defeat. . . .

A man who knows how to cultivate life is detached in his mind and peaceful in his conduct. He attaches no importance to personal gains; he indulges in few desires. Knowing that fame and position are detrimental to true virtue, he pays no heed to them, not because he has succeeded in suppressing his desire for them, but because he has no such desire. Knowing that delicious food and tasty wine are injurious to his health, he dismisses them as if they had never existed. Since they have never existed as far as he is concerned, there is no need to suppress his desire for them. In fact, outward things do not exist as long as they constitute a burden to his inner mind; the only thing that is constantly in his mind is his spiritual vitality, pure and incorruptible. His mind is broad and detached enough not to have worries and sorrows; it is peaceful and serene enough not to be disturbed by sentiments or emotions. He carefully preserves this "oneness" within himself; he strengthens it further by harmonizing it with his environment. While he marches closer and closer towards "reason," he becomes identified with and is in agreement to the "grand unity" which is the essence of the universe. Only after he has reached a mental level like this can he draw benefit from such practices as eating the *lingtzu* herb,[12] drinking water from a sweet spring, bodily exposure to the morning sun, and finally, relaxation of body and spirit via the finest music.[13] He is non-active, and he takes pride in his non-activity. His body is as beautiful as his mind is abstruse. He knows no joy; yet he is happy and content. He abandons life; yet life is always with him. If a man follows all of these principles, how can you still say that he cannot live as long a life as Hsien-men or Wang Ch'iao [14] once did?

18 · FANG CH'IAO: *A Short Biography of Liu Ling* [15]

Liu Ling, whose courtesy name was Pai-lun, was a native of P'eikuo.[16] Six *ch'ih* [17] in height, he was extremely unattractive in appearance. He was uncon-

[12] An herb medicine which, according to the Taoists, possessed the power of rejuvenation and prolonging life.

[13] These were the popular Taoist practices aimed at the preservation of life.

[14] Hsien-men and Wang Ch'iao (also known as Wang Tzu-ch'iao) were two legendary Taoist immortals.

[15] Liu Ling was a contemporary of Chi K'ang, the author of the preceding selection. This brief biography appears in the *History of the Tsin (Tsin shu),* roll 49, by Fang Ch'iao who lived during the first half of the seventh century.

[16] Located in the northern section of modern Anhwei province.

[17] The length of a *ch'ih* (Chinese foot) in ancient times was much shorter than its modern counterpart (14.1 inches).

ventional and naturalistic: defying the limitations imposed by our physical environment, he considered his life goal the harmonizing of all things in it. Placid and tranquil, he spoke little; and in choosing friends he was extremely careful. Whenever he met Yüan Chi and Chi K'ang,[18] however, he lost all restraints, and happily he held their hands and repaired to the Bamboo Grove.[19] From the very beginning he cared little about property or worldly fortunes.

Oftentimes he rode a small carriage and carried a jug of wine with him. He told his servant to follow him with a shovel and to bury him whenever he should drop and die. With such an abandon he viewed life!

Once he was very thirsty and asked wine from his wife. Breaking his jugs, his wife threw away the wine. "You have drunk too much, and over-drinking is harmful to your health," she pleaded in tears. "You should put a stop to it."

"That is a good idea," Liu Ling replied. "But I cannot stop by my own efforts. I need to take an oath before the gods. Get meat and wine ready and we shall use them as sacrifices." His wife agreed and complied with his request. Then he knelt down and prayed as follows:

> Heaven gave me my life
> And designated me a drunkard.
> A jug I can consume by one swallow;
> Fifty jugs later I still remain sober.
> An ignorant woman my wife is;
> Oh, gods,
> Please do not listen to her!

After the prayer, he ate the meat and drank the wine. Once again he was deadly drunk.

One day he had an argument with a vulgar man who was anything but a philosopher. The man rolled up his sleeves and raised his arms, ready to strike him. "Why should you, sir, disgrace your honorable fist by striking a chicken rib?" Liu inquired. The man laughed loudly and stopped what he was about to do.

Though living a perverse life of almost constant intoxication and caring little about others' opinions, he rarely erred when quick responses were required and did not make a single mistake in his relations with the government. As far as writing was concerned, he had only one short essay entitled "May the Virtue of Wine be Praised." It reads as follows:

A gentleman there is who considers Heaven and Earth existing in a single day and eternity only a fraction of a second. The sun and the moon are his window and door, and all the land on earth his front and backyard. He moves freely without leaving any traces, and never settles down inside a house. The sky is his ceiling and the earth his mat: he does whatever he wishes inside his own mansion. When he stops moving, he drinks; when he moves, he carries his wine jug with him. Since drinking is his only business, why should he care about the rest?

There comes a nobleman who is a respectable member of the gentry class.

---

[18] Both Yüan Chi (d. A.D. 223) and Chi K'ang belonged to the group popularly known as the Seven Sages of the Bamboo Grove.

[19] A place where these Taoist philosophers discussed ideas and drank wine.

He has heard about the peculiar behavior of our friend and wishes to admonish and criticize him. He rolls up his sleeves, grinds his teeth, and stares at our friend with fierce eyes. He gives a lecture on proper conduct and presents a long list of rights and wrongs.

Our friend is then sitting cross-legged on his couch and, holding a huge jug with both hands, is pouring its content happily through the standing whiskers. All around him there is nothing except wine jugs. He neither thinks nor worries; he is pleased with himself and equally with others. He is sometimes drunk and sometimes sober. Drunk or sober, he cannot hear anything even though it is as loud as a thunder, or see anything even though it is as large as the T'ai Mountains,[20] trying hard as he can. He does not feel any heat or cold that inflicts penalty upon his body; nor is he affected by profit or desire. He looks at all things from far above, and these things to him are as insignificant and small as duckweeds drifting about on the surface of a huge ocean. . . .

At one time Liu Ling served as a secretary-adviser to the government. Early during the T'ai-shih period [21] he, in response to a government's request, wrote a memorial in which he emphasized the importance of using the doctrine of non-activity to transform the nation towards the good. Many scholars like him rose high in the government, but Liu Ling, considered useless, was soon dismissed. Consequently he was able to die a natural death.

19 · T'AO CH'IEN: *The Gentleman of the Five Willows* [22]

We know neither his name nor the place from which he originally came. Since there are five willow trees beside his house, we call him "the Gentleman of the Five Willows."

The Gentleman of the Five Willows loves solitude and speaks little; he does not aspire to either fame or wealth. He likes to read, however; when he reads, he does not care whether he understands or not. When he does understand, he is so happy with himself that he even forgets to eat. He loves to drink; but, since he is extremely poor, he cannot have all the wine he wants. Knowing his financial condition, his friends or relatives sometimes invite him to indulge himself; and in such cases he will not stop drinking until he is completely intoxicated. Then he will not care whether he stays overnight at the host's house or is sent home immediately.

As for his home, it consists of four walls and a roof that cannot protect him from the elements. His clothes are short and worn out, having been mended and patched time and again. Without a steady supply of provisions, his eating and drinking wares are usually empty. Despite all this, he is as happy and content as a man can possibly be.

He writes often to amuse as well as to express himself. He is not concerned with gains or losses, and he intends to abide by this philosophy for the rest of his life.

Ch'ien-lou [23] once said: "He who is wise is neither distressed by poverty nor

[20] Located in modern Shantung province.
[21] A.D. 265–274.
[22] T'ao Ch'ien is also known for his pastoral poems.
[23] A hermit and philosopher of ancient China.

active in seeking fortunes." Does the Gentleman of the Five Willows not fit well this description? All he loves and cares for is drinking wine and writing poems. Can he not be properly regarded as a man of Wu-huai or Ko-t'ien of ancient times? [24]

20 · T'AO CH'IEN: *A Peaceful Village*

During the T'ai-yüan period [25] of the Tsin dynasty a fisherman from Wuling [26] lost his way while peddling his boat along a small stream. Suddenly he saw a forest which extended several hundred paces from both sides of the stream. The forest contained nothing but peach trees; the grass was fresh and fragrant; and fallen flowers of various colors covered the entire ground. Immensely impressed with the sight, the fisherman continued peddling along the stream, hoping to reach the end of the forest. At the end of the forest where the stream originated, he saw a mountain and a small opening in it. There seemed to be light emitting from the opening, and the fisherman, curiosity aroused, abandoned his boat and entered the opening. The opening was very narrow at the beginning and could barely allow his body to pass through. Several scores of paces later, it ended; and a flat, wide plain suddenly emerged before his eyes.

On the plain were neatly arranged, well-built houses, fertile fields and clear ponds, mulberry groves and bamboo forests. Numerous paths crisscrossed the fields; here and there one heard the barking of a dog or the crowing of a cock that disturbed the otherwise tranquil air. Men and women were busy with their work, but surprisingly, were dressed as if they were all foreigners. The old and the young—all of them looked happy and content.

The villagers were surprised to see the fisherman and asked him where he came from. One of them invited him to dinner and treated him with chicken and wine. Soon other villagers learned of his arrival, and they all came to see him. "Our ancestors came to this isolated place during the Ch'in dynasty in order to escape from the fury of a civil war," said the villagers. "They came with their relatives and neighbors and never left this place for the rest of their lives. Neither did any of their descendents, and the village, consequently, has been completely cut off from the outside world." The villagers did not know the existence of the Han dynasty, let alone the Wei and the Tsin dynasties. The fisherman told them all he knew about what had happened since the Ch'in dynasty, and all of them sighed with disbelief. One after another these villagers invited him to their homes and entertained him with wine and meat.

The fisherman stayed in this village for several days before he bid it farewell. "Please do not tell anyone that you have seen us," said one of the villagers. Emerging from the mountain opening, the fisherman found his boat and journeyed home along the same path as he had arrived. He made marks along the entire route.

He went to the city of his district to report to the magistrate his strange experience. The magistrate ordered an official to go with him to locate this isolated

[24] Wu-huai and Ko-t'ien were two legendary emperors of the remote past.
[25] A.D. 376–396.
[26] Located in the northern section of modern Hunan province, near Lake Tungting.

village. But the marks were no longer visible; they lost their way and finally had to return home.

Liu Tzu-yi, an upright scholar in Nanyang,[27] heard about this village and volunteered to locate it. He died, however, before the attempt was made. Since then nobody has shown a similar interest.

[27] Located in the southern section of modern Honan province.

CHAPTER FOUR

Taoist Religion

Taoist religion (*Tao chiao*) developed independently of the Taoist philosophy (*Tao chia*). The oracle priests of the Shang dynasty, the magicians who frequented the court of Ch'in Shih Huang-ti, and the sorcerer who had allegedly arranged a meeting between Han Wu-ti and his long deceased concubine were the true forerunners of Taoism as a religion. Lao-tzu who was hailed by the Taoists as one of their leading deities, would perhaps have preferred not to associate himself with their religion had he lived at the time when the religion was founded.

Though such Taoist practices as alchemy, sorcery, faith-healing, and the worship of natural objects had existed at the beginning of recorded history, Taoism as an organized religion did not come about until the second century A.D. Its inception was attributed to a man named Chang Ling or Chang Tao-ling (fl. A.D. 120's) whose grandson, Chang Lu, established the first known Taoist theocracy in China (Selection 21). The theocracy did not last long, however; it was conquered by Ts'ao Ts'ao (d. A.D. 220), founder of the Wei dynasty, in A.D. 215.

The ultimate goal of every Taoist was to become an immortal (*hsien*; literally, fairy), and the Taoists believed that many in the past had achieved this important goal. One of these fortunate ones was Ko Hung, the author of *Pao-p'o-tzu* (Selection 15). We know little about the procedure or method of Ko Hung's achieving immortality except on heresay: it was said that he had successfully extracted elixir from mercury. In the case of K'ou Ch'ien-chih (fl. A.D. 410's), however, there are more elaborate details, recorded in one of the dynastic histories (Selection 23).

Important though it was, the pursuance of an earthly immortality was definitely confined to a devoted few, because most Chinese were either downright dubious or too busy making a livelihood to be seriously concerned with it. In the popular mind a Taoist priest was primarily known for his great power of exorcising evil spirits. Since misfortunes such as illness were often thought to be caused by the haunting of evil spirits, the Taoist priest played a very important role in dispelling unfounded fears and in bringing peace and tranquility to an otherwise disturbed household. How he went about with his task is vividly described by the eighteenth century novelist Ts'ao Hsüeh-ch'in, the author of *The Dream of the Red Chamber* (Selection 24).

Aside from the regular Taoist priests, there were the less respectable Taoist alchemists who, claiming the ability of transforming ordinary metals into gold or silver, were actually swindlers. The story that appears as Selection 25 may serve as a warning to all those who believe that there is a quick, easy way to become fabulously wealthy.

21 · FAN YEH: *A Taoist Theocracy in Hanchung* [1]

Chang Lu was also known as Chang Kung-ch'i. His grandfather was Chang Ling who learned the ways of the Taoists in the Homing mountains when he visited Shu [2] during the reign of Han Shun-ti. [3] Emerging from the mountains, Chang Ling claimed that he knew the magical way of producing charms and spells, and many people, being ignorant and superstitious, believed in him. Since the initiation to the Taoist membership cost five pecks of rice, the members were derogatorily addressed as "rice thieves."

Chang Ling transmitted his secrets to his son Chang Heng who in turn handed them down to his son Chang Lu. Lu called himself the teacher-king of the Taoist religion, and those who had learned and mastered the secrets of this new faith were called "ghost soldiers," later known as "priests." Each priest ruled the congregation he controlled; if the congregation was unusually large, he would be called a chief priest.

The Taoist adherents were taught the virtue of honesty and sincerity, and they were not allowed to engage in deceit or falsehood. If a person was sick, he was told to repent for whatever sin he might have committed.

Each priest built and maintained rest houses along the roads in the area under his jurisdiction, an idea which the Taoists borrowed from the postal stations. Rice and meat were provided in each of these rest houses and were made available to travellers free of charge. Each traveller was allowed to eat as much as he could take. If he ate more than necessary, the ghosts would make him sick, or so the Taoists believed.

Those who violated the Taoist law would not be punished for the first three offenses. After the fourth time, however, the law violator would be severely punished.

In the territories under the Taoist control, there were no government officials. The priests were political as well as religious leaders.

The religion was very popular with the people.

22 · FAN YEH: *The Magic of Tso Tz'u* [4]

Tso Tz'u, whose courtesy name was Yüan-fang, was a native of Yükiang. [5] He had been recognized for his knowledge of magical power since his boyhood.

---

[1] This article appears in the "Biography of Liu Yen"; *History of the Later Han*, roll 150, by Fan Yeh who lived during the first half of the fifth century A.D. Hanchung is located in the southern section of modern Shensi province.

[2] Modern Szechuan province.

[3] Han Shun-ti (r. A.D. 126–144).

[4] This selection is taken from "Biographies of Magicians"; *History of the Later Han*, roll 112b.

[5] Located in modern Anhwei province.

One day he was invited to a banquet by the then Minister of Public Works Ts'ao Ts'ao. "I am glad to announce that we have prepared some fine food for this wonderful gathering," said the host in a dignified, unruffled manner. "But I deeply regret that we do not have carps from the Wusung River." [6]

"It is easy to procure them," announced Tso Tz'u who was then sitting at the lower end of the banquet table.[7] He requested a bronze basin to be filled with water and, upon receiving it, proceeded to fish in it with the usual fishing equipment: a bamboo pole, a hook, and a bait. Seconds later a carp emerged from the water. Ts'ao Ts'ao clapped his hands and laughed loudly, while all of his guests were astonished beyond belief.

"One fish is obviously not enough to feed all the people at this table. Can we have more?" Ts'ao Ts'ao inquired.

Tso Tz'u fished again. Moments later several fish emerged from the water, and all of them looked alive and fresh. Ts'ao Ts'ao ordered the fish to be cut into small pieces before his eyes and then passed them around among his guests.

"Even though we have the fish, it is still regrettable that we do not have the Shu [8] ginger to go along with it," Ts'ao Ts'ao spoke again.

"It is easy to get that, too," Tso Tz'u replied.

Lest Tso might obtain the Shu ginger in a nearby place, Ts'ao Ts'ao added: "The other day I sent a man to Shu to buy some silk. While you are in Shu, please tell the buyer to purchase two lengths more than the original order." Hardly had Ts'ao finished his words before the Shu ginger was already on the table. Besides, Tso notified his host that his order of purchasing more silk had already been transmitted to the buyer. Later, when the buyer returned from Shu, he reported the manner in which he received the message of the increased order and the exact time that he received it, precisely as Tso had described at the banquet table.

One day Ts'ao Ts'ao, accompanied by a hundred or so scholar-officials, went to the suburb for a picnic. Tso took with him one jug of wine and one pound of dried meat. He fed the picnickers with what he held in his hands, and all of them ate and drank to the full and had a hearty meal. Astonished that he could feed so many with so little, Ts'ao Ts'ao investigated and found out that all of the picnic jars that had been filled up with meat and wine were now completely empty.

Ts'ao Ts'ao was far from pleased with this kind of antic and decided to put Tso to death. Hardly had he made his decision known before Tso disappeared into a wall and could no longer be located.

Later, hearing the report that Tso had been seen in the market place, Ts'ao Ts'ao issued an order for his arrest. However, as soon as the soldiers arrived, all the people in the market place were suddenly transformed and looked exactly like Tso. Needless to say, the soldiers could not find him.

Still later, some one encountered Tso Tz'u in the Yangch'eng Mountains,[9] and again orders were issued for his arrest. As the soldiers chased him, Tso Tz'u disappeared among a herd of sheep. Realizing the difficulty of locating him, Ts'ao Ts'ao ordered the soldiers to adopt a different approach. "We have no intention of killing you, Tso Tz'u," said the soldiers; "we merely wish to find out how much magic power you really possess."

[6] Located in modern Kiangsu province.
[7] A less honorable position.
[8] Modern Szechuan province.
[9] Located in modern Honan province.

Suddenly an old ram stepped out, bent its two front knees, and stood up on its two hind legs like a man. "Why are you in such a hurry?" the ram asked in a human voice. The soldiers rushed towards it; before they could reach it, however, all the sheep had transformed themselves into rams. They bent their front knees, stood on their hind legs, and asked the same question: "Why are you in such a hurry?" The soldiers were so confused that they could not locate the specific ram who was in fact Tso Tz'u.

23 · WEI SHOU: *How K'ou Ch'ien-chih Became a Taoist Immortal* [10]

After Chang Ling had mastered the mystery of Tao at Homing,[11] he transmitted to his disciples the book as revealed by the Lord of Heaven.[12] The book, totalling 1,200 rolls, was in turn transmitted to his disciples' disciples. As the book spread far and wide, so did the Taoist religion. The faithful built Taoist temples where they worshipped their gods: the Three Lords,[13] the Gods of the Nine Directions,[14] and the One Hundred Twenty Deities. Each of these gods was in charge of a particular area or event.

The Taoist believed in the inevitability of calamities that would fall upon man, a pessimism that was also shared by the Buddhists. . . . When the last and most fatal calamity occurred, the whole universe would break into pieces.

The Taoist literature contained many forbidden secrets that were to be revealed to no one but the staunch adherents. These secrets included the transformation of unworthy materials into gold, the magic way of melting jade, the drawing of charms and spells, the making of rain through divine help, and thousands of other magic formulas. The Taoist priests claimed that the mastery of these secrets would enable the believers to rise bodily to Heaven, or at least free them from disaster or calamity while on earth. The credulous believed in them. . . .

During the reign of Emperor Shih-tsu [15] there was a Taoist priest named K'ou Ch'ien-chih, also known as Fu-chen, a younger brother of K'ou Tsan-chih who was once the governor of Yung.[16] K'ou himself claimed that he was the thirteenth descendant of K'ou Hsün.[17] His interest in the ways of the immortals began early in his boyhood when he expressed his desire to cut off his relations with this world. Later he studied diligently the magical formula of Chang Lu [18] and took elixirs of life. For several years he continued his efforts, but achieve immortality he did not.

---

[10] This selection appears in "Buddhism and Taoism"; *(Shih lao chih); History of the (North) Wei (Wei shu),* roll 114, by Wei Shou who lived during the first half of the sixth century.

[11] Located in modern Szechuan province.

[12] *T'ien kuan.*

[13] The Lords of Heaven, Earth, and Water.

[14] The Gods of the East, the Southeast, the South, the Southwest, the West, the Northwest, the North, the Northeast, and the Center.

[15] Wei Shih-tsu (r. A.D. 409–423).

[16] Modern Shensi province.

[17] An upright, incorruptible official who once served under Han Kuang-wu (r. A.D. 25–55), founder of the Later Han dynasty.

[18] See Selection 21, p. 50.

K'ou's sincerity and diligence eventually moved Heaven to intervene on his behalf. One day a stranger named Ch'eng Kung-hsing came to visit K'ou's aunt, hoping to be hired as a servant. K'ou visited his aunt often and had the opportunity of observing this man after he had been hired. Impressed with Ch'eng's unusually muscular body and ceaseless and tireless work, K'ou requested his aunt's permission to borrow the stranger to work on his own farm. His aunt agreed.

Ch'eng was ordered to open up the fields to the east of the K'ou house. Always a diligent worker, he worked even harder whenever K'ou arrived with his book of mathematics which he studied under a tree in the field. Often Ch'eng came to the tree and watched K'ou doing his mathematical work. "You should concentrate your efforts in the field," said K'ou; "let me take care of my mathematics." Though temporarily discouraged, the farm hand came to watch him again two or three days later.

One day K'ou was computing the distance between the Seven Illuminaries; [19] it was then that he realized his inability of ever becoming a mathematician.

"Why do you look so unhappy?" asked Ch'eng.

"I have studied mathematics for many years," K'ou replied. "But my computation of the Seven Illuminaries does not coincide with the result that is given in the *Chou-pi Mathematics*.[20] I feel ashamed of myself. Since you obviously know nothing about mathematics, why did you ask this question?"

"Please follow my directions, sir, and I shall show you the correct way of computing the Seven Illuminaries," Ch'eng replied.

It took only a short moment before Ch'eng reached the correct answer. K'ou was greatly impressed. Thinking that Ch'eng must be a great master of mathematics, K'ou requested the honor of being his student. Ch'eng refused, saying that he would be happy to be K'ou's student instead.[21]

Not long afterwards Ch'eng asked K'ou whether he was interested in learning the ways of the Taoists. If he were, said Ch'eng, they could travel together to a remote place for such a purpose. After K'ou had happily given his consent, Ch'eng ordered him to fast for three days before they started their journey to Mount Hua.[22] At Mount Hua, K'ou was ordered to stay in a stone house where he subsisted on drugs that were gathered in the mountains by Ch'eng. From then on K'ou never felt hungry.

After a brief stay at Mount Hua the two friends moved to Mount Sung [23] where Ch'eng ordered K'ou to stay on the second floor of a three-storied stone house. One year later, Ch'eng said that after he left the house a stranger would come to present K'ou with wonder drugs, and that without any suspicion or hesitation K'ou should eat these drugs. Surely enough, the stranger soon arrived, and the wonder drugs he presented were nothing but poisonous insects that were as repulsive as they were malodorous. Greatly frightened, K'ou fled from the house.

[19] The sun, the moon, Mars, Mercury, Jupiter, Venus, and Saturn.

[20] One of the greatest mathematical works China ever produced, written perhaps in the third century B.C.

[21] In China the relationship between a teacher and a student was not only an intellectual relationship but also a relationship between a superior and an inferior.

[22] Located in modern Shensi province.

[23] Located in modern Honan province.

After Ch'eng returned, K'ou told him what had happened. "It is regretable that you have missed the opportunity to become an immortal," Ch'eng sighed. "However, with the Taoist deeds that you have so far accumulated, you still could be a great minister to a good king."

Seven years had elapsed since the time that the two friends made their acquaintance. "I cannot stay here any longer," Ch'eng remarked one day. "I shall leave here at noon tomorrow. Please wash my body clean after I die. There are people who will come here to fetch me." Upon finishing these words, Ch'eng went to the third story of the stone house, and there he died. Following his friend's instruction, K'ou washed and cleansed the dead body.

The next day at noon K'ou heard some one knocking at the door of his stone house. Opening the door, he saw two boys, one holding a Taoist robe and the other a bowl and a staff made of tin. He led the boys to the room where Ch'eng's body was. Upon seeing the boys, Ch'eng suddenly became alive. He rose to put on the robe, took the bowl and the tin staff, walked away, and then disappeared.

Many years after the above event took place, there was a man named Wang Hu-erh who lived in the city of Pa in the Capital Province. After the death of his uncle, Wang found himself being led by the dead man's spirit to pay a visit to Mount Sung. At a place called Kaopi Cliff they saw house after house made of gold and jade. One house, with the words "The Residence of Ch'eng Kung-hsing" on the front, was particularly elegant. But there was not a single soul inside the house. Being impressed with what he saw, Hu asked his uncle the story in connection with this house.

"This is the residence of the Taoist immortal Ch'eng Kung-hsing," said his uncle. "At one time there was a great fire, and seven houses were destroyed as a result. Ch'eng Kung-hsing was judged responsible for this fire and was then banished from Heaven to earth where he served as a student to K'ou Ch'ien-chih for seven years. It was then that he was convinced of K'ou's sincerity and perseverance to become a Taoist immortal. He left the earth after he had served his term of banishment, but K'ou, who was left behind, continued his efforts towards Taoist immortality with a single-minded diligence. He remained at Mount Sung until the second year of Shen-shui.[24]

"On the Yi-mo day of the tenth month of that year K'ou saw a great god who rode on a dragon passing through the clouds, accompanied by hundreds of male and female retainers. When the great god landed on the peak of a mountain, these immortal retainers lined up on both sides to serve as guards. The great god identified himself as the Supreme Lord of Heaven[25] and remarked to K'ou Ch'ien-chih as follows:

'In the year of Hsin-hai[26] the gods of Mount Sung gathered at the Temple of Assemblage where they decided to send a memorial to the Supreme Lord of Heaven. The memorial stated that since the departure of Chang Ling from the earth, there was not a single man in the world persistent and sincere in the cultivation of Taoist virtues. That was why the position of Heavenly Teacher, once held by Chang Ling, had been until this day unfilled. The memorial continued by saying that K'ou Ch'ien-chih, the Taoist priest at Mount Sung, was upright in his conduct, logical in his reasoning, naturalistic in his behavior, and exemplary in

[24] A.D. 415.
[25] T'ai-shang lao-chün.
[26] A.D. 411.

his ability, and that the title, Heavenly Teacher, should therefore be conferred upon him. Reading this memorial, I decided to come here to examine you in person, and it is my decision that the title should be conferred upon you as requested. I am giving unto you the *New Commandments* totalling twenty rolls. This book has never appeared on earth, and fate alone is the cause of its appearance on earth at this time. I hereby command you to purify the Taoist faith and eliminate the false teachings of the Three Changs.[27] The Changs collected from their followers rice as rent and money as taxes; they even taught people the technique of sexual intercourse. How could they say that they were Taoists when they knew that the basic Taoist virtues were those of humility and seclusion? As the new Heavenly Teacher, you should emphasize the rule of propriety as the most important virtue among your followers. Only by observing this rule can the taking of wonder drugs and the concentration of mind become useful.'

"Then the Supreme Lord of Heaven ordered twelve of its retainers to teach K'ou the technique of building vitality,[28] breathing exercises, and oral incantations. After he had mastered this technique, K'ou found that his vitality continued to increase despite the fact that he did not eat any food. His body became lighter, and he looked many years younger.

"More than a dozen of K'ou's disciples, all of whom looked unusually handsome, also mastered the same technique."

24 · TS'AO HSÜEH-CH'IN: *Taoist Priests in Action* [29]

All members of the Chia household were restive: they were sure that the entire residential compound was haunted. Additional night watchmen were hired, which meant extra expenses for the household. Chia She, however, was dubious. "The garden is as good as it has always been," said he; "how, for goodness' sake, can there be any ghost?" He selected a warm, beautiful day to go to the garden to take a look himself. He was accompanied by several servants, all of whom were armed with fighting equipment. People asked him not to go, but he insisted.

Entering the garden, Chia She found a ghoulish atmosphere, permeative and pressing. He struggled his way forward, but those who followed him were even more hesitant, sticking out their heads and looking carefully around. One of the younger servants, already panic-stricken, heard a "hu-hu" sound and, turning his head, saw a bright and many-colored "thing" jump by, run, and then disappear. He cried "Ah-yo"; suddenly he felt that his legs could no longer support him and collapsed on the ground. Chia She turned around and asked the young fellow what had happened. "I saw with my own eyes a strange ghost with a yellow-colored face and a red-colored goatee but dressed in green-colored clothes," said the young man, still out of breath. "He disappeared into a mountain chasm behind that forest."

Hearing the young man's story, Chia She was also somewhat frightened. "Did

---

[27] This refers to Chang Chüeh and his two younger brothers who led the Yellow Turbans Rebellion. This rebellion was suppressed in A.D. 190.

[28] *Ch'i.*

[29] This selection is taken from *The Dream of the Red Chamber (Hung-lou meng)*, Chapter 102.

all of you see that 'thing'?" he asked. Several of the servants, who were only too willing to follow the lead, replied: "Of course, we did. Since the honorable lord was walking in the front at that time, we did not wish to bother and frighten you. But we are all right."

If Chia She were not fearful before, he was now. Instead of searching further, he returned to his house in a hurry. He gave the order that none of the servants should again talk about the ghost and that, if asked, they should say that no ghost was found after a careful search had been made. But inside himself he was frightened. He thought that he might send for the Taoist priests in the Chen-jen Temple to exorcise this evil spirit.

The servants would normally manufacture rumors when there were none. Now, seeing that Chia She was really frightened of ghosts, they, instead of keeping quiet as they were told, added so many details to the ghost story that even the most unbelieving, when hearing it, was terrified. When the entire household became fearful and nervous, Chia She finally decided to invite the priests to the garden, so they could invoke their magic formula to chase out the evil spirits.

A propitious day was selected, and a ceremonial altar was erected in the main hall which previously had been used for the imperial concubine [30] to visit her parents. On the center of the altar were placed the images of the Three Supreme Lords,[31] flanked by the Twenty-eight Constellations and the images of the Four Generals. Below them were the likenesses of the Thirty-six Heavenly Marshals. The hall was decorated with a multitude of flowers, candles, and oil lamps, and along its left and right sides were neatly arranged the priests' bells, drums, and other religious instruments. Banners signifying each of the "five directions" [32] were also planted in the proper places. The altar was purified for a whole day before the service officially began.

On the assigned day, three chief priests burned incense and fetched holy water [33] before beating their drums—the ritual to exorcise the evil spirits was thus begun. All of them wore the hats of the "Seven Stars," the robes of "the Nine Constellations and the Eight Diagrams," and shoes that enabled their wearers to "ride up in the clouds." Holding ivory tablets [34] before their breasts, they requested the arrival of the Taoist divinities. For a whole day they chanted the scriptures of the Heavenly Abode,[35] which were meant not only to chase out evil spirits and eliminate disasters, but also to induce the arrival of good fortunes. This being done, they summoned all local deities to come before the altar to be assigned for duties. On a huge banner they wrote the following words: "The High Priest of the Three Abodes, the Beginning, the Undivided, and the Infinitely

[30] Chia She's niece, the eldest daughter of his brother Chia Cheng, who was then a concubine of the reigning emperor.

[31] The Three Supreme Lords (San ch'ing) were the Heavenly Lord of the Beginning (Yüan-shih t'ien-tsun); the Taoist Lord of the Supreme (T'ai-shang tao-chün); and the Supreme Lord of Heaven (T'ai-shang lao-chün).

[32] East, west, north, south, and center.

[33] The water is usually taken from a nearby river or well, and becomes holy after it has been blessed by a priest. It is brought to the altar in a flower vase or some other container.

[34] The Chinese name of this kind of tablet is ya-hu which is about three feet in length and three inches in width, slightly tapering at the end. During the imperial days, an official held it before his breast when given an audience with the emperor. A Taoist priest did likewise before his deities.

[35] Tung-t'ien, the place where the Taoist divinities were supposed to have lived.

Pure,[36] with spiritual power duly authorized, hereby orders all local deities to repair to this altar for assignment of duties."

Fully convinced of the priests' ability to capture the evil spirits, all members of the Chia household arrived at the garden to see the performance. "What a decree!" they said. "With the kind of noise they are making in summoning the gods and calling upon the Heavenly Marshals, the evil spirits will be frightened away before the gods can even get here." They pushed themselves towards the altar where they saw the priests' assistants, with their banners raised high, standing on each of the five directions, waiting for the order of the chief priests. The three chief priests—the first holding a sword in one hand and the holy water in the other, the second upholding a banner of the "Seven Stars" with both hands, and the third raising up in the air the devil-flogging whip which, in fact, was made of a peach branch—stood solemnly before the altar. As soon as the music stopped, they threw to the floor three commanding tablets [37] in quick succession. While they were sprouting out incantations, the "flags of five directions" were scattered about all over the place.

Then the chief priests stepped down from the altar and asked the stewards of the Chia household to lead them to all the buildings, hills, and streams within the residential compound. In each place they visited, they sprinkled the holy water and drew lines in the air with the points of their sacred swords. After returning to the altar, time and again they pounded the commanding tablets against the table. When finally the banner of the "Seven Stars" was raised, all of the lesser priests put together the banners which they themselves had hitherto held. One of the chief priests lashed into the air three times with the devil-flogging whip, and the spectators in the crowd said to one another that the evil spirit had already been captured. They surged forward to see what the evil spirit looked like but saw nothing in particular. The chief priests ordered one of their assistants to fetch a bottle which was then sealed; presumably the evil spirit had been sealed inside. To assure that it would not escape, the priests wrapped the bottle with charms written in vermilion. The bottle, with the evil spirit in it, was subsequently taken to the Taoist temple, to be stored away forever.

After the chief priests had dismissed the local deities with thanks, all the images and religious instruments were removed from the altar. To express his gratitude, Chia She kowtowed to the chief priests.

Behind their elders the younger generation like Chia Yung [38] and his cousins could not help laughing. "I thought that after making such a great show as this, they at least should show us what the evil spirit really looked like," they commented. "Who would expect an ending like this? Have they really captured the evil spirit?"

"You stupid!" Chia Chen [39] scolded when he heard their remarks. "The evil spirit acquires a form when it condenses, and evaporates into the air when it diffuses. With so many Heavenly Marshals around, how dare it acquire a form? All we need to know is that the priests have successfully captured the spirit of

[36] *T'ai-yi, Hun-yüan,* and *Shang-ch'ing.*

[37] They are about five inches in length and three inches at their widest width. Usually made of wood, they are hollow on one side and buldging on the other. Flat at one end, they taper off gradually towards the other, beginning at the middle point.

[38] Chia She's grandson.

[39] Chia She's son.

the devil which from now on can never harm us again." Others, however, were not so sure as he was.

Hearing that the evil spirit had been captured, the servants were no longer frightened and in fact did not even mention it any more. Chia Chen and others eventually recovered from their illness, and all of them spoke highly of the magic power of the Taoist priests.

There was one servant, however, who continued to remain dubious. "Of course, I cannot explain all the noises we heard the day we followed the honorable lord to the garden," he remarked. "But the ghost which Shuan-erh thought he saw and which frightened him out of his wits was clearly a wild turkey which happened to fly over our path. Since Shuan-erh gave such a vivid description of this alleged ghost, we all decided not to contradict him. Moreover, how did we know that the honorable lord would take it so seriously? Anyway, we should be grateful: without this incident we would not have had such an enjoyable Taoist show."

Nobody, really, wished to believe his words.

25 • PAO-WEN LAO-JEN AND LI DUN-JEN: *The Alchemist* [40]

During the Ming dynasty (1368–1644) there were few districts richer than Sungkiang [41] where the people produced more rice and silk than those of any other district in the whole empire. As one of our ancient proverbs says, "there are more rich men in Sungkiang than there are carps in the Yangtze"; some of the Sungkiang people, being so proud of their district, would go even further by saying that "there are more carps in Sungkiang than there are in the Yangtze." Among the rich people in Sungkiang was a man named Pan; he was so rich that he was often referred to as Pan the Rich or Rich Man Pan.

All rich men suffer a common disease: the richer they are, the richer they wish to become. Rich Man Pan, a charter member of this club, was certainly not an exception. Though as a former university student he had presumably read Confucius' admonition against accumulation for the sake of accumulation, he was so seriously afflicted with this rich men's disease that he could no longer follow the sage's advice. He wanted to become richer, richer than any other man in Sungkiang. In Sungkiang there were two ways of enhancing one's wealth: either by purchasing more land in the countryside or by buying more shops in the city, and preferably both. But either way was costly and time-consuming; in Sungkiang as well as in many other parts of China there were simply not enough land and shops to go around among so many rich people. What was the easiest way to accumulate a large fortune in the shortest possible time? Pan asked himself. "It is alchemy," he answered his own question.

In fact, Rich Man Pan had been practicing alchemy for a long time, but un-

---

[40] Technically this selection is not a translation; it is a rewriting of a story that originally appears in *Strange Spectacles of Ancient and Modern Times (Chin-ku ch'i-kuan)*, compiled by a man with a pseudonym of Pao-wen Lao-jen who perhaps lived in the sixteenth century. Though generally following the original theme, I have made such additions and subtractions as to render the story more interesting. The original is dull, repetitious, and uninspiring.

[41] Located in modern Kiangsu province.

fortunately he failed in each of his attempts. The Taoist magicians went in and came out through his front door at considerable expense to him, but there were no positive results. One might think that he would be awakened from his folly by then; no, he became more addicted to it. He blamed his failure on the lack of luck and was confident that when the right moment arrived, he would certainly succeed. "Let them laugh at me then," he said to himself. Meanwhile the knowledge of his addiction had spread far and wide; few alchemists in the nation did not know of the existence of Rich Man Pan, a potential good customer.

In the spring of a wonderful year Rich Man Pan decided to visit Hangchow [42] and rent a villa on the shore of the West Lake outside of the city. Hangchow is popularly known as "paradise on earth," but without the West Lake it would have been as dull and vulgar as most cities in China. Around the lake are numerous villas with their golden roofs and white walls, plus numerous temples, monuments, and historical sites. These villas cater to the need of the rich tourists and are expected to earn in one season what normally takes one year. The less affluent tourists, on the other hand, have to be satisfied with cheap hotels further away from the lake. This is the situation today; it was also true during the Ming dynasty.

Next to Pan's villa was a villa of even larger size, occupied by a tourist who seemed to have come from a different part of the country in view of his accent. Since there was only a low fence separating these two estates, Pan had no difficulty observing what occurred on the other side. His neighbor brought not only several servants with him but a young woman as well. Each day he hired a large boat equipped with musicians and cruised on the lake as if he did not have a worry in the world. Wherever he went, he took with him this young woman who seemed to be very attractive from a distance and, judging from the way she walked, was certainly a lady of good breeding. Rarely would the two return to their villa until late in the evening; even then the lights were not out until after the midnight. The two seemed to be very fond of each other, much to the envy of their next door neighbor.

Pan was naturally curious about this man: he was impressed with the elegance of his style, the beauty of his young companion, and most important, his immense wealth. One day Pan decided to send one of his servants to the next door to express his admiration for his neighbor and his desire to meet him. To his happy surprise, the servant came back with the word that his neighbor had as much admiration for him as he had for his neighbor and that he, the neighbor, would like very much to make Pan's acquaintance.

There is no better link between two rich men than wealth, and Pan and his neighbor soon became great friends. His friend's name was Chia Wu-chih, a native of Hupeh, who, admiring the beauty of the West Lake, had come a long distance to visit this scenic place. The woman was his youngest concubine whom he had taken with him so as to make the trip more enjoyable.

"It must have cost you a great deal to travel such a long distance in such a luxurious manner," said Pan one day.

"It is not very much really," said Chia; "it could not be more than a few thousand taels."

Pan was astonished at the cited figure, but somehow managed to conceal his

[42] Capital of modern Chekiang province.

astonishment. A few thousand taels were a large sum even for the richest man in Sungkiang, and yet this man talked about it in a manner as if it were only a few copper coins.

"You must be the largest landowner in Hupeh," said Pan.

"I am not; in fact, I do not even own one *mou* of land," Chia laughed heartily.

"You must own a chain of stores."

Chia laughed even louder as if Pan had said something really funny.

"Well, I give up," said Pan helplessly.

"Someday when I know you better, I will tell you where my money comes from."

"Is this man engaged in some lawless activities?" Pan said to himself. A dark shadow passed across his face despite his efforts not to show his suspicion.

Chia immediately sensed what Pan had in mind. "If you think that I am the head of a group of bandits and thus enjoy unaccountable wealth, you are, I am afraid, very mistaken."

Pan felt guilty for having given thought to this dreadful possibility; he denied, however, that he had ever harbored such a terrible thought.

"I guess I cannot blame you for being suspicious," said Chia calmly. "Where does he obtain this seemingly inexhaustible supply of wealth since he does not own a business any man is aware of? The suspicion is really very natural. I have the feeling that our friendship will not last long if I do not tell you who I really am. Since I do value our friendship, the moment has arrived that I should tell you the truth, reluctant though I am. I am wealthy because I am an alchemist."

"An alchemist?" Pan shouted as if he could not believe his ears.

"What is the matter?"

"I have experimented with alchemy myself, but I have had no luck with it. Some people say that it is merely a form of superstition."

"A form of superstition?" Chia seemed to be annoyed by Pan's remarks.

"I do not believe that it is, but it is difficult to convince others."

"Despite what you have said, I can sense that you have doubts about my profession. Since my honor is involved, I am compelled to give you a demonstration, to clear up whatever doubts you might have in your mind."

Pan quickly agreed to Chia's suggestion since he had never seen a successful demonstration of alchemy despite his long practice. "I shall be happy to see one if it does not cause you too much inconvenience," said he.

"No inconvenience at all," said the alchemist; "it is a simple procedure."

Chia ordered a boy servant to bring in a tripod with charcoal in it. He placed a porcelain bowl containing some lead on the charcoal which he subsequently lit. While the charcoal was burning red hot, he took a paper bag from his pocket and opened it. Inside the bag was some dark powder which, he announced, was the magic transformer that could turn ordinary metal into silver. Using his small finger nail, he shoveled out a tiny amount of this powder and poured it into the bowl. The powder, true to its reputation, transformed the dull-looking lead into white, sparkling silver in less than a minute. Pan was greatly impressed. For the first time in his life he had seen magic translated into science. Whatever doubts he might have had about alchemy were then completely dispelled.

"How do you make the magic transformer?" Pan asked.

"The proper name for the magic transformer you referred to is 'silver breeder' whose function is to transform ordinary metal into high-priced silver," said Chia.

"Once you have it, you can have an unlimited supply of silver because the same breeder can be used again and again for an infinite number of times. Now you can see why I am wealthy without owning one *mou* of land or a single store."

"But you have not told me how you make this breeder."

"The process is long, arduous, and extremely costly," said the alchemist. "It is what we alchemists call 'alchemistic refining' that requires special equipment."

"I have this equipment in my own house since I have been an amateur alchemist myself," said Pan. "May I ask how much you need for making this breeder?"

"A few thousand taels of silver will be good enough to make a half-tael breeder. Since the breeder will not deteriorate or be reduced in size no matter how many times you use it, a half-tael breeder will make a person one of the wealthiest men in the world."

"Poor though I am," said Pan, "I believe I can afford a few thousand taels. Do you mind teaching me how to make it? You know I will be very grateful."

Upon hearing these words, the alchemist looked startled. After staring at Pan for a moment, he replied: "Since you have been an amateur alchemist yourself, you must know that a true alchemist does not reveal his secrets to others. He reveals them only to those who are destined by Heaven to receive them."

"How do you know that I am not destined by Heaven to receive them? I have been very devoted to the trade myself."

With his eyes wide open, the alchemist examined Pan from head to toe without uttering a word. Pan would have resented this kind of examination had he not known that it had something to do with his friend's forthcoming decision as to whether he was qualified to be taught the alchemist's secrets.

"I am not sure," Chia finally announced.

Pan was disappointed. "How can you be sure?" he asked.

"I cannot be sure until I have examined your bone structure."

Pan's eyes once again sparkled with hope. "I shall be happy to have such an examination," said he.

"But you would have to suffer some indignities during the examination process."

"I do not mind them at all," Pan replied with a firm voice.

The alchemist escorted Pan to a side room and immediately shut the door behind him. He closed all the windows, making the room completely dark. He asked Pan to strip off all his clothes, including his underwear. Pan was reluctant at the beginning but finally agreed when he thought of the unlimited amount of money he could have. He then lay on the floor as he had been ordered, not knowing what the alchemist intended to do with his naked body. The alchemist rolled up his sleeves and began to feel Pan's bones. With both hands, he worked from head down, not sparing even the most private parts. Finally he reached the examinee's ankle bones, and Pan was happy that the ordeal was about to be over. "How does it look to you?" Pan asked. "There are several bones hidden so deep under layer after layer of fat that, with your permission, I have to examine them with instruments," the alchemist replied. "There will be a little pain, but I hope that you will not mind." Having been well-fed throughout his life, Pan was somewhat on the plump side.

Coming back with his instruments, the alchemist asked Rich Man Pan to turn over so as to lie on his stomach. He placed a paperboard on Pan's buttocks and began to hit them with a wooden hammer. "Take it easy," Pan yelled with pain. "I am sorry," the alchemist apologized; "but I have to hear the echo of your buttock bones." Having said this, he hit even harder, while Pan was groaning like a pig in a slaughter house. Finally when he finished, he asked Pan to put his clothes on. He left the room while Pan was still dressing himself.

When Pan emerged from the side room, he saw a smiling, jubilant alchemist. "Congratulation!" said Chia. "I have examined many aspiring alchemists in my life, but your bone structure is the best I have encountered."

"Do you mean that I am good enough to be taught?"

"Yes, certainly."

"When should we begin?"

"Well, you can tell me where you live," said the alchemist. "Next time when I come to this part of the country, I shall visit you at your honorable residence, and we can discuss it then."

"My home Sungkiang is only two days away from here by boat," said Pan. "I shall be honored if you would agree to come to my humble homestead so as to begin the lesson as early as possible. Once you leave here, I should never know when you would return."

"Thank you for your invitation, but I am afraid that I cannot accept it," said the alchemist. "I took my woman here for a brief visit, but the beauty of this place has detained us longer than we originally planned. I shall bring her home and also visit my old mother before I can come back to accept your hospitality."

"If the honorable lady is what you are worried about, why do you not bring her with you? My home is not the best place in the world, but I can assure you that it is very comfortable."

Having thought for a while, the alchemist said: "Let me speak with her; perhaps she would not mind staying a little longer."

"The whole thing is settled then?"

"It is settled," the alchemist replied.

In the middle of the West Lake is an island known as the Reflection of the Moon,[43] one of the most popular of the tourist attractions. The next day Pan the Rich invited Chia the Alchemist to dine at the Reflection; and the day after that the alchemist returned the invitation by giving a banquet in the largest boat in the lake. It was then that Pan realized how wealthy Chia really was; for one thing, all dishes and plates were made of solid gold. He also discovered that the alchemist was not only versed in Taoist ideology which after all was his familiar ground but also spoke authoritatively on Confucianism and Buddhism. "If he were not an alchemist, he would certainly have been a professor in the Hanlin Academy," [44] Pan said to himself.

Since Pan was anxious to make the magic transformer at the earliest moment, the two friends decided to leave for Sungkiang the very next day. Pan hired two large boats, one for the alchemist and his concubine and one for himself. When the boats were about to leave their anchorage, he happened to look at a pink curtain across the water. The curtain began to move; and when it was pushed half aside, it revealed a beautiful face. The woman gave him a smile and then quickly lowered her head. That smile struck his mind as a giant wave would strike a helpless boat; it rocked uncontrollably. When he finally regained his composure, the curtain was already drawn and the boat began to move. "What a lucky dog this dirty magician is!" he cursed.

[43] *San-t'an Yin-yüeh.*

[44] The Hanlin Academy was the highest academic institution during the Ming-Ch'ing period.

Instead of taking the magician's party to his regular residence where he would have to introduce them to his family who did not approve of his alchemistic adventure, he escorted them to his country villa where only the care-takers were residing at the moment. The villa consisted of several houses scattered inside a huge garden that was decorated with ponds, pavilions, man-made hills, and a variety of trees. The time being spring, the flower trees were in full blossom, and numerous birds jumped from one tree to another, chirping as they went. "What a beautiful place!" the alchemist commented. "I cannot think of a better place for our purpose."

The alchemist and his concubine were accommodated in the main house, while Pan himself took a side apartment. The alchemist was very pleased with the arrangement and remarked that since he and his family were going to stay at the villa for a while, he would like to introduce Pan to his concubine. He sent for his woman, and shortly afterwards the woman, flanked by two slave girls, emerged from the inner room. This was the first time that Pan had the opportunity of taking a close look at this rare creature who was even more alluring than he had thought possible. The woman saluted and immediately withdrew before Pan had time to utter a single word.

After the woman left, Pan excused himself and went to his own apartment. When he returned, he had in his hands two hairpins and two bracelets, all made of solid gold. "This is a little gift for Mrs. Chia whom I have had the privilege to meet," said he to the alchemist. "Please accept it on her behalf."

"I do not believe that she needs these things since she has too many of them already," said the alchemist. "Anyway, thank you for your kind thought."

"I know that gold and silver do not mean anything to you," said Pan. "But I would like you to think that this little gift is only a token of my respect."

"Since you put it that way, I guess that I do not have much choice." The alchemist took the golden ornaments and then handed them to one of his concubine's maids.

"When should we begin to make the magic transformer—the silver breeder, I mean?" Pan asked the alchemist when the conversation was resumed.

"Any time," Chia replied; "as soon as you have the silver ready."

"How much silver do we need?"

"The more the better," said the alchemist. "A larger amount will insure a better result."

"I shall bring four thousand taels here tomorrow together with the refining equipment," said Rich Man Pan. "If you need anything else, just let me know."

The next day Pan made a trip to his regular residence in the city and brought the silver and the refining equipment as he had promised. The refining equipment consisted of a furnace and a saucepan which he had used on previous occasions. The alchemist chose one room facing the garden as the "abode of purity" where the equipment was subsequently placed. He said that both he and his host should fast one day and wash their bodies clean before the refining would begin. Under no circumstances, he added, should anyone other than the purified persons enter the "abode of purity" to attend to the furnace. In case of emergency which he did not believe would arise, only his woman who had been purified for this purpose could substitute for either him or Pan for their respective duties.

On the scheduled hour early in the morning the alchemist and his friend were dressed up in Taoist robes to perform the purification ritual prior to the firing of the furnace. They burned incense and chanted hymns, invoking the help of

Heaven and Earth to make their undertaking a success. With a horsewhisk in his hand, the alchemist chased the evil spirits from one end of the room to the other, and Pan, watching his thoroughness with awe, was greatly impressed. "Now I know why I have failed in the past," the rich man said to himself. It was not until all evil spirits were chased out that the alchemist began to place the four thousand taels of silver in the saucepan which he sprinkled with some dark powder. This dark powder, he explained, was a unique catalyst which he had acquired from his master in the most sacred of all Taoist mountains, Mountain O-mei at Szechuan. He covered the saucepan with great care and then ordered the firing of the furnace.

After the ritual was over, the alchemist explained to Pan his formula for making the magic transformer, or "silver breeder" as he called it. "Mine is called the nine-nine formula," he said. "The furnace should be fired for nine days and be cooled off for a same length of time. This firing and cooling alternate for a total of eighty-one days before the refining is completed. At no time during this period of eighty-one days should anyone open this saucepan, and the firing should be continuous during each of the firing periods, day or night. No profanity is allowed in the refining room, either of acts or of words. No one except the purified personnel—you, my concubine, and me—should enter the refining room. If we carefully observe these regulations, I can guarantee that at the end of the eighty-one days we will have the silver breeder and you, my friend, will become one of the most wealthy men in the world."

The next day the alchemist dismissed all except two of his servants and sent them back to Hupeh where his home was. "Since I have to stay here for a three-month period, there is no need for so many of you around here," said he. "Tell my mother that I am well and that I will be home as soon as I have completed my mission here." The servants took off for home as he had ordered.

Other than attending the furnace the two friends spent a great deal of time together. They played chess, drank wine, and exchanged poems; they thoroughly enjoyed each other. One day while appreciating a Sung painting, they saw a man rush towards them from the garden and prostrate himself before the alchemist as soon as he arrived. Pan immediately recognized him as one of the servants whom the alchemist had previously sent home. "Please go home quickly," said the servant. "The honorable dowager has passed away."

The alchemist cried and collapsed on the floor the moment he heard the sad news. "Please spare yourself," Pan bent down to comfort him. "Over-grief will bring harm to your health." When he finally calmed down, the alchemist apologized for the unfortunate turn of events and the fact that he had to leave in the midst of their efforts. "But my concubine has been thoroughly trained for attending the furnace," he added. "I would not mind leaving her here to continue our undertaking were it not for the fact that she is too young and naïve and that she might cause inconvenience. I hope that you will understand."

Pan had had his eyes on this woman since the day when he saw her behind the boat curtain. He had been hoping for a chance to convey to her his thoughts, and the departure of her husband would certainly provide him with a wonderful opportunity. Moreover, he would not let the making of the magic transformer stop if he could help it. "There will be no inconvenience to us at all," said Pan. "She will be well taken care of during your absence."

The alchemist was silent as if he did not know how to make up his mind. "My mind is confused, and I cannot think clearly," said he finally. "Maybe she should stay. I will feel very guilty indeed if I cannot help you to complete the task. I promise you that I will be back as soon as the funeral is over."

Pan was very pleased with the alchemist's decision, but somehow managed not to show his jubilation. "What should I do in case you are delayed and cannot return at the end of the eighty-first day?" he asked.

"There is no problem at all," the alchemist replied. "Just leave the furnace the way it is until I return. Be sure that you do not open the saucepan unless I am there." Then he went to the inner room to give his concubine some last-minute instruction with regard to the furnace, said good-bye, and left in a hurry.

After the alchemist's departure, Pan made an arrangement with the Chia woman that she would attend the furnace in the daytime while he would do so in the evening. Since the furnace was to be checked only once in a while, this arrangement did not cause any undue hardship to either of them. Through regular contacts Pan's infatuation with the young woman became daily greater, and the woman, from Pan's point of view, was not altogether unresponsive. One day when he asked her whether she was lonely, she smiled, saying that loneliness was a common fate for all women in the world. He said that a beautiful woman like her need not to be lonely; she flattered him by saying that few men could be as understanding as he was. It was then that he concluded that she would cooperate with his scheme if an opportunity presented itself because, had she been uninterested, she would not have answered the way she did, knowing fully his intentions.

One night while making one of his periodic checks at the furnace, he noticed through the window an elegant figure dressed in white walking in the garden. "Why does she walk so late in the garden? Why should she be dressed in white in a night of darkness?" He immediately reached the conclusion he had wanted to reach: it was an invitation. He left the furnace room and walked towards the garden as if he, too, were taking a walk.

The woman saluted when she saw him. "How is the furnace?" she asked.

"The saucepan is making some sizzling sound," he replied. "I am wondering whether you can take a look and see what the matter is with it."

"I do not believe that there is anything wrong with it, but I shall take a look as you have suggested."

The woman walked in front of him without a word; to all intents and purposes it was a business trip as far as she was concerned. By the time she arrived at the furnace room the sizzling sound seemed to have stopped. The furnace needed some charcoal, and Pan, trying to make up his mind about his next step, fed the charcoal slowly into the furnace. The added charcoal, burning brightly, cast a red glow throughout the room and made the candles on the table dim by comparison. He felt hot under the heat and was about to stand up when he saw the most alluring thing on this side of the Taoist paradise. It was a pair of shapely legs completed with their upper attachments, clearly visible behind a sheet of white chiffon. He grabbed them like a drowning man grabbing a rolling log, and both he and the woman were on the floor.

"Please, not here," the woman protested.

"Why not?"

"We are beside the furnace; it will ruin the magic transformer."

"The hell with the furnace; the hell with the magic transformer!"

Love is a mysterious thing. The more secretive it is, the more enjoyable it seems to be. As far as Pan was concerned, no one knew of this clandestine affair since nobody except him and his lover was allowed to enter the refining room. Days passed by, and their love became greater with the passage of time. All good things had to come to an end, however, and on the eighty-second day after the refining began, the woman's husband returned. He apologized for not being able to return earlier and suggested that he and his host should open the saucepan the very next day. He was glad, he added, that with the help of his concubine, he had not failed his gracious host.

The next day the alchemist and his friend, dressed in their Taoist robes, burned incense and chanted hymns, thanking Heaven and Earth for having made their undertaking a great success. Then they walked into the room together and saluted the furnace. Finally the crucial moment arrived, and the alchemist was about to open the saucepan. No sooner did he open it, however, than his facial expression changed: it was an expression of frustration and anger which Pan had never seen in him before. "The silver breeder is gone; what has happened?" he shouted. "Has anybody done anything in this room which he should not have done?"

Pan's face was as frozen as a sheet of ice; he did not utter a word.

The alchemist called in his two servants and asked them whether any unpurified person had entered the room. The servants replied that no one except Pan and the Chia woman had entered the room.

The alchemist paused for a moment as if in serious thought. "Bring my woman here immediately," he ordered.

"Did you do anything in this room which you should not have done?" he asked in a stern voice.

"I did not," the woman replied calmly.

"I guess that you will not tell me the truth unless I can show you that I mean business." He went out and picked up a horsewhip, proposing to beat her up. The woman lost her composure and began to cry. "I told him that he should not do it, but he would not listen to me." She cried again.

If she thought that her crying could win her husband's sympathy, she completely failed. In fact, the alchemist began to chase her with his whip, beating the air as he went. The woman ran all the way to her own room and quickly closed the door behind her. "I will take care of you later," he yelled from outside.

Returning to the furnace room, he found Pan the Rich standing motionless like a wooden block. "Are you a man or a dog?" he cursed. "You can buy all the beautiful women in the world once you have obtained the silver breeder, and yet you chose to abuse the woman of your benefactor. Tomorrow I will report your dirty deed to the magistrate, and I can assure you that he will put you behind the bars for the rest of your life."

Just imagine Pan the Rich, a leading member of the gentry in Sungkiang, being put behind the bars for the rest of his life! Dear reader, you might think that this was the fate he well deserved, and no doubt you are right. But Pan the Rich obviously did not think so.

So he knelt down before the alchemist and kowtowed like a woodpecker. "It is all my fault," he pleaded. "I seek your forgiveness."

"I should have my head examined if I forgive a dirty dog like you."

"I will do anything you want me to do, but please do not sue me in the court."

"A rich man has his responsibility, and he should always remind himself that people look to him for exemplary conduct," the alchemist lectured. "What kind of example are you? I believe that you will not be taught a lesson unless you are punished in a way which hurts. You are a rich man, and you want to become richer. I believe that it is my duty to make you poorer."

Pan was relieved that the alchemist no longer talked about sending him to jail. "I shall be happy to present you with one thousand taels to redeem my guilt," said Pan.

"I do not need your money, and I guess you understand that," said the alchemist, still angry. "But there are thousands of poor people who do. I will take five thousand taels from you and distribute them among the poor. This is my last offer; take it or leave it."

"But I do not have so much cash at home."

Upon hearing this, the alchemist stood up and was ready to leave. "All right, I will pay," Pan pleaded again. "I will go home and speak with my wife. I imagine that you will not mind taking jewels as a substitute."

"I will give you one hour," said the alchemist. "I will not be here if you are one minute late."

Pan the Rich jumped up to the back of his horse and galloped off. How he explained the whole episode to his wife we can only guess. Anyhow he did come back with the jewels one hour later. Upon receiving the jewels, the alchemist and his entourage left in a hurry. He kept on murmuring "dirty dog" while on his way out.

Thus Pan the Rich not only did not become one of the wealthiest men in the nation but also lost a total of ten thousand taels of silver, a huge fortune even in a city like Sungkiang. For a two-year period he was a cheerless man, constantly blaming himself for having surrendered to a moment's desire. What would have happened if he had not done it or had done it in a place other than the furnace room—the carpet-like lawn in his garden or a comfortable bed instead of that hard floor? He would have caught two birds by one stone: a beautiful woman as well as unaccountable wealth. Everytime he thought about this, he cursed himself. Moreover, where could he meet another alchemist who was so proficient in his trade that he could guarantee success? Chia would not come again; that was for sure.

When spring arrived, Pan decided to visit the West Lake again, not for the purpose of meeting another expert alchemist which he had long given up, but to bury the sorrows which he had nourished for a two-year period. This time he took a moderate villa, having been reduced to a more limited circumstance. One day while taking a walk on the lake shore, he saw a large boat anchored nearby. The boat was apparently hired by a rich man, as rich as he once was. At one end of the boat was a row of small windows, all draped in pink silk. Suddenly one of the curtains began to move, and a beautiful face appeared. "This woman looks very familiar," he said to himself. But he could not figure out where he had seen her.

"Are you Pan the Rich?" the woman called him.

Now he recognized the voice. She was none other than the alchemist's concubine. He moved towards the window.

"Where is your husband?" he asked.

The woman smiled. "I do not have any husband," she replied. "Two years ago

I was hired by my so-called husband for only a four-month period. At present I am in the employment of another alchemist who is now speaking with one of his clients in the front part of this boat."

Pan was stunned in total disbelief. As he turned around and began to walk away, the woman spoke again: "Keep away from the alchemists; I should know."

CHAPTER FIVE

Buddhism

O NE of the earliest writings on the development of Chinese Buddhism is a treatise entitled "Buddhism and Taoism" (*Shih lao chih*) that appears in the *History of the (North) Wei (Wei shu)* (Selection 26). The author, Wei Shou (sixth century), wrote it at a time when Buddhism was enjoying its greatest popularity.

The popularity of the Buddhist faith was manifested in the building of temples on an unprecedented scale. Early in the sixth century there were more than one thousand Buddhist temples in the city of Loyang (then the capital) alone. One of the most magnificent was the Yungning Temple built in A.D. 516. Eighteen years later, there was a civil war, and this temple, together with hundreds of others, was reduced to ashes. Yang Hsüan-chih, who saw this temple at the time of its glory, lived long enough to visit the site where once this magnificent building had stood. It is not surprising that he should write about it with nostalgia (Selection 27).

The popularity of Buddhism did not make Confucians and Taoists happier. Instigated by a Taoist priest, the T'ang emperor Wu-tsung (r. 841–847) ordered the reduction in the number of Buddhist temples and monasteries and the forced return to civilian life of Buddhist monks and nuns (Selection 28). Fortunately the persecution lasted only two years (845–847). Buddhism remained one of the popular faiths in the succeeding centuries, though it had lost official patronage.

One of the Buddhist sects that emerged from this persecution stronger than before was Ch'an, known in Japan as Zen. It remained one of the most influential Buddhist groups throughout the eighth, ninth, and tenth centuries. The man who provided most of the inspiration for its continuous growth was the Sixth Patriarch Hui-neng (638–713). How he received the mandate as the Patriarch is one of the most interesting stories in the tradition of Chinese Buddhism (Selection 29).

In due course Ch'an split into many rival groups. One of these was Yün-men, founded by a man named Yün-men Wen-yen (d. 949). The emphasis of this group on "instant enlightenment" led to the so-called "One Word Gate"; *i.e.*, the understanding of all realities (or The Reality) through the utterance of a single word. But for most of us who are perhaps too rational-minded, the conversation between Ch'an Buddhists sounds not only irrational but also incomprehensible (Selection 30).

As one would expect, the Confucians continued to fight an ideological battle

69

against the Buddhist throughout the centuries. To people like Ou-yang Hsiu (1007–1072) the popularity of Buddhism was not due to the inherent merits of this imported faith, but to the insufficient awareness of Confucian virtues on the part of the Chinese people (Selection 31). His idea may be said to be typical of the Confucian reaction to all alien beliefs, including Buddhism.

26 · WEI SHOU: *The Introduction of Buddhism to China* [1]

During the Yüan-shou period [2] Emperor Han Wu-ti sent Ho Ch'ü-ping as the head of an expeditionary force against the Hsiung-nu.[3] General Ho went as far as Kao-lan and then Chu-yen [4] where he inflicted heavy casualties upon the enemy. One of the Hsiung-nu chiefs, Kun-hsieh, after killing another Hsiung-nu chief named Hsiu-t'u, surrendered fifty thousand of his own followers to the Han authority. It was then that the Han authority obtained from him a golden statue which the emperor called Great Divinity.[5] The statue, one *chang* [6] in height, was later placed in the Kanchüan Temple. No sacrifices were offered to this divinity. However, people could burn incense and worship him if they chose to do so. This marked the beginning of Buddhism in China.

Later, when the Han government opened up the Western regions,[7] Chang Ch'ien was sent as an envoy to Ta-hsia. On his return he heard that there was a country named Chüan-tu next to it. (Chüan-tu was also called T'ien-chu.[8]) This was the first time that a Chinese had heard about Buddhist teachings.

In the first year of Yüan-shou [9] during the reign of Emperor Han Ai-ti, a university student named Ch'in Ching-hsien learned Buddhist scriptures orally from Yi-ts'un, an emissary from Ta-yüeh-chih.[10] Though the Chinese people had by then heard about Buddhism, they did not believe in it.

Still later, Emperor Han Hsiao-ming-ti [11] saw a golden statue in his dream one night. The statue had over its head a white halo which flew around the emperor's palace and yard. The emperor inquired about the meaning of his dream among his ministers and was told by Fu Yi, one of his ministers, that the golden statue was of Buddha. Upon hearing this, the emperor sent a government official named Ts'ai Yin and a university student named Ch'in Ching as his envoys to T'ien-chu where they copied Buddhist scriptures. Ts'ai Yin returned to Loyang [12] with two Buddhist monks, She-mo-t'eng and Chu-fa-lan. This was the first time that China had Buddhist monks and their ways of worship.

---

[1] This selection is taken from "Buddhism and Taoism"; *History of the (North) Wei,* roll 114.
[2] 122–116 B.C.
[3] A Mongolian tribe; for more details, see pp. 210–220.
[4] Both places were located in modern Kansu province.
[5] *Ta shen.*
[6] About 10 feet.
[7] Modern Turkestan.
[8] India.
[9] 2 B.C.
[10] Located in modern Russian Turkestan.
[11] Han Hsiao-ming-ti (r. A.D. 58–76).
[12] The then Chinese capital, located in modern Honan province.

Besides, Ts'ai Yin obtained forty-two books of Buddhist scriptures and a copy of the standing image of Buddha. Emperor Hsiso-ming-ti ordered his artists to paint pictures of Buddha which subsequently were placed in the Tower of Ch'ingliang and the Mound of Hsienchieh. The scriptures, on the other hand, were stored in the stone house of Lant'ai. Since these scriptures had been transported to China on the backs of white horses when Ts'ai Yin returned to Loyang, the emperor ordered the construction of the Temple of White Horses west of the Yang Gate outside the capital. Both She-mo-t'eng and Chu-fa-lan died in this temple. . . .

The essential teaching of Buddhism can be summarized in one statement: *i.e.,* the sufferings inherent in the endless cycle of births and rebirths are caused by man's attachment to this world. There are three worlds altogether, the past, the present, and the future. The important thing is to understand that despite his transmission from one world to another a person's spiritual self [13] cannot be obliterated. Those who do good things will be rewarded; those who do bad things will be punished. A great deed is the gradual accumulation of many small deeds: a coarse, rustic nature can be refined through constant effort. Whatever forms life may take, the ultimate goal of all lives is the attainment of enlightenment, an enlightenment which can be achieved only through hard, diligent work. By then there will be no more births and rebirths, and the Way of Buddha will be finally attained.

Before the final goal becomes a reality, there are many ascending stages involving both the mind and the outward conduct. In general it is a matter of ascending from the superficial to the profound and from the obscure to the apparent. Efforts should be made in the accumulation of loving deeds, the elimination of worldly desires, and the pursuance of a humble, quiet life, so that a man may be able finally to understand himself. The first step is of course to rectify the mind. The rectification of the mind is followed by the observation of the Three Obediences: obediences to Buddha, Buddhist scriptures, and Buddhist monks. The Three Obediences are similar to the Three Fears in Confucian teachings.[14] Besides, there are Five Prohibitions, prohibitions against killing, stealing, adultery, falsehood, and the drinking of liquor. The Five Prohibitions are the same as the Confucian love, righteousness, propriety, wisdom, and faith; only the names are different. It is said that those who follow the Buddhist principles will go to Heaven and those who violate them will fall underneath as ghosts and will suffer all forms of penalties. . . .

People who have been converted to Buddhism shave their heads and beards. They discard worldly burdens and leave home. They attach themselves to a teacher for their own benefit and swear to obey his rules and regulations. They live harmoniously together; concentrate their minds; and maintain pure their bodies. They beg for food and whatever supplies they need. They are called *sha-men* or *sang-men*, as these two sounds are really similar. They are also called *seng* [monks] as a common practice. All these are translated foreign names. . . . As to the laity who follow and believe in Buddhist teachings, all men are called *yu-p'o se* and all women are called *yu-p'o yi*. . . .

---

[13] *Shen.*
[14] The Three Fears are fears of the wishes of Heaven, virtuous men, and the words of sages. Source: *Analects of Confucius.*

27 · Yang Hsüan-chih: *The Yungning Temple* [15]

The Yunging Temple was built by Empress Dowager Hu in the first year of Hsi-p'ing.[16] It was located about one *li* south of the Ch'angho Gate on the western side of the Royal Boulevard. To the east stood the official residence of the Grand Duke in charge of military affairs. . . .

Within the temple compound was a nine-storied pagoda which rose ninety *chang* [17] in height. Above the pagoda was a banner tower which added ten *chang* more. Thus the height of the pagoda structure, from the ground to the roof of the banner tower, was one hundred *chang* in total. The pagoda was so tall that people could see it as far as one hundred *li* [18] away from the capital.[19]

Previously, when the workmen dug the ground for building its foundation, they found thirty golden statues hidden deep within the earth. Believing that the discovery of these statues was a confirmation of her faith in Buddha, the Empress Dowager built the temple even more elaborately than she had originally planned.

On the roof of the banner tower was a golden vessel with a capacity of twenty-five gallons. Below the vessel were thirty golden plates designed to serve as dew receivers in the evening. Golden bells hung from the circumference of each of these plates.

There were four iron chains to lead a visitor from the pagoda to the four corners of the banner tower. Golden bells were suspended from these chains, and each of them was as large as a stone jar. Each story of the pagoda had a roof of nine corners, and a golden bell was hanging from each of these corners. Altogether there were one hundred twenty of these gleaming bells.

The pagoda was four-sided, and each side had three doors and six windows. Each door, painted with red lacquer, had golden rings with numerous small golden bells attached to them; all told, there were 5,400 of these golden bells. The building was so costly and elaborate that only a profound, unshakable faith in Buddhism could inspire such efforts. Those who had seen its sculptured columns and its golden lavishness could not fail to be immensely impressed. At night when the wind blew, thousands of bells gently swung, to and fro, to make a continuous, melodious sound which could be heard more a dozen *li* [20] away.

North of the pagoda was a building that housed the hall of worship. This hall was similar in shape to the Hall of the Absolute [21] generally found in a Taoist temple. Inside this hall resided many Buddhist statues: one huge golden statue of 1.8 *chang* [22] in height, ten golden statues of medium height, three statues inlaid intricately with pearls, and five statues fashioned from silk. The workmanship was unsurpassed in the contemporary world.

The monks' dormitory consisted of more than one thousand rooms. Its beams

[15] *A Story of Buddhist Temples in Loyang (Lo-yang chia-lan chi),* roll 1.
[16] A.D. 516.
[17] About 900 feet.
[18] About 33 miles.
[19] Loyang.
[20] About 4 miles.
[21] *T'ai-chi Tien.*
[22] About 18 feet.

were sculptured; its walls were painted pure white. All of these rooms were so lavishly and beautifully decorated that words are inadequate to describe them.

On the temple ground stood a variety of trees: juniper, cypress, pine, and many others. They grew so profusely and tall that their branches gently swept the eaves. Green bamboo and fragrant grass—they spead far and wide to protect the walking terraces. Could there be another temple in the world which matched this one in quietude and serenity! In fact, this temple housed all of the Buddhist images and statues that were sent to China by foreign countries.

The wall that surrounded the temple compound was protected by a long, narrow roof that was made of earthen tiles supported by wooden beams. This was the same kind of wall that was used in the imperial palaces. The wall of the Yungning Temple formed a square, and each of its four sides faced a different direction. On each side of the wall there was a gate-opening with a gate tower above it. The Tower of the Southern Gate was a three-storied building of twenty *chang* [23] in height, and three separate roads led to it. . . . It was painted with gods and clouds in full color, and inside it the decorations were equally rich, beautiful, and elegant. Outside of the gate were four warriors and four lions serving as guards, all of which were impressive sculpture inlaid with gold, silver, pearls, and jade. They looked serene, dignified, and radiant; their beauty was unsurpassed in the whole world.

The towers on the eastern and southern gates were built and embellished in the same way as the Tower of the Southern Gate; the only difference was that they had two rather than three stories. There was only one road leading to the northern gate above which there was no tower.

Outside the temple wall was a public park where trees grew and streams crisscrossed; it was a popular resort place for the people in the capital. There they could gaze at the drifting clouds without being annoyed by the flying dust. When they felt the gentle, caressing breeze, they knew that there was no better place to meet their friends for merriment.

28 · Liu Hsü: *The Persecution of Buddhism* [24]

On the seventh lunar month of the fifth year of Hui-ch'ang [25] the Secretary-General of the Imperial Office reported to the emperor as follows:

"In connection with the elimination of Buddhist temples it is hereby suggested that the Board of Salt and Iron should have jurisdiction over bronze statues, bells, and chimes confiscated from the dispossessed temples. These articles are to be melted to make coins. As for Buddhist statues made of iron, they should be handed over to each of the provincial authorities within whose jurisdiction they are found, and they should be melted down to make farm implements. Buddhist statues made of gold, silver, and other precious metals should likewise be melted and then handed over to the Board of Revenue and Finance. Within one month after the imperial decree is issued all Buddhist statues, whether they are made of gold, silver, bronze, or iron, should have been voluntarily surrendered to

[23] About 200 feet.
[24] This selection appears in "Biography of T'ang Wu-tsung"; *Old History of the T'ang (Chiu T'ang shu)*, roll 18a, by Liu Hsü who lived in the tenth century.
[25] A.D. 845.

appropriate authorities. If this order is not obeyed, the Board of Salt and Iron should have jurisdiction over the offenders and punish them in accordance with the Copper Prohibition Act. As for Buddhist statues that are made of wood, earth, or stone, they are to remain in the temples where they are presently located."

The Secretary-General Office again reported to the emperor as follows:

"It is hereby suggested that the Board of Protocol [26] should have jurisdiction over Buddhist monks and nuns, instead of the Board of Temples to which they have hitherto improperly belonged. Since radical reformation has been imposed upon Buddhist temples, it is only proper that similar measures should also be taken with regard to Nestorian and Manichaean churches. It is hereby suggested that all Nestorian and Manichaean clergymen be ordered to return to civilian life and be expatriated to their native cities or towns where they will be registered as tax-payers. If they happen to be foreigners, they should be put under the custody of this office."

On the eighth lunar month of the same year [27] the emperor [28] issued a decree which reads as follows:

"I have heard that there was no Buddhism before the Three Dynasties and that it began to spread only after the Han and Wei dynasties. Slowly and gradually it spread; its adherents multiplied with the passage of time. It corrupted and undermined our way of life; the process was so slow that we hardly noticed it ourselves. It seduced people with its beguiling, and the masses fell increasingly into its deceiving traps. As a result, over the mountains and plains, in all the nine provinces, and in cities and towns, including our two capitals,[29] Buddhist monks flourished, and their temples rose higher and higher each day. Manpower was wasted in temple building, and gold and other valuables which should have been people's private wealth were taken away to decorate Buddhist temples. Disregarding their duty towards their king and their parents, the monks and nuns pledged loyalty and obedience only to their Buddhist superiors. They violated the vow of matrimony by deserting their spouses so that they could abide by the so-called rules of discipline. Nothing in the world was so harmful to man and his good customs as this alien belief called Buddhism.

"The plain fact is that for every man who chooses not to till there are several who will suffer from hunger. For every woman who refuses to make silk there are others who will suffer from cold. Now there is a large number of monks and nuns in this country, all of whom, while not doing any work themselves, have to be clothed and fed. Temples and monasteries have multiplied as if there could be no limit. They rise high above in the clouds and are all lavishly decorated, overstepping the limit by making themselves as large and elegant as the imperial palaces. This is why natural resources were exhausted and good customs deteriorated during the Tsin, Sung, Ch'i, and Liang dynasties.[30]

"My ancestors, Kao-tsu and T'ai-tsung,[31] unified the country through the use of military might and governed it by cultural refinement. These two alone—

26 *Hung-lu ssu;* in charge of mourning, funerals, and festivities as part of its normal duties.
27 A.D. 845.
28 T'ang Wu-tsung.
29 Ch'angan and Loyang.
30 These dynasties cover the period from A.D. 265 to 557.
31 The first and second emperors of the T'ang dynasty respectively.

military might and cultural refinement—are adequate to govern a country successfully; how does this small faith from the West [32] dare to challenge our cultural superiority?

"During the Chen-kuan and K'ai-yüan periods [33] efforts were made to rectify Buddhist temples; but, before they could be eliminated, they multiplied and spread at an even greater speed. I have read extensively the old documents relating to this matter, and I have carefully consulted public opinion. It is my conclusion that the curse of Buddhism can be eliminated: let there be no doubt on this score. It is gratifying to me that my upright ministers, both here and abroad, have supported me in this matter. Their petitions are proper and correct, as they have agreed that the proposed measure should take effect as a matter of absolute necessity. In this way a curse of one thousand years will be dispelled, and the eternal law of all kings will be finally reestablished. Since this measure is beneficial to all people, how can I shirk my own responsibility?

"When this measure takes effect, more than 4,600 temples will be demolished, and more than 260,500 monks and nuns will be returned to civilian life and registered as taxpayers. No less than 40,000 monasteries are also scheduled to be demolished. Moreover, good land amounting to hundreds of thousands of *ching* [34] will be appropriated by the government, together with 150,000 male and female slaves, all of whom will be reclassified as taxpaying citizens. It has been clearly established that these slaves belong to monks and nuns.

"As for other alien religions such as Nestorianism, Manichaeanism, and Zoroastrianism, more than 3,000 of their clergymen will be returned to civilian life. These people have never accepted the Chinese way of life, and it is a great pity that this measure of banning their religions was not taken many years ago. This measure has been long overdue, and it should be carried out immediately."

29 · HUI-NENG: *An Autobiography* [35]

The home of Hui-neng's forebears was Fanyang.[36] Demoted as a government official, his father was subsequently exiled to Lingnan [37] where he lived as a commoner in the Hsinchou district.

Hui-neng was born with misfortunes. His father died when he was still a child, and he lived with his widowed mother in the South Street. The family was so poor and life so difficult that as a boy he used to sell firewood to support his mother and himself.

One day while selling firewood in the market, he met a man who ordered the firewood be delivered to his home. Having received the money after the firewood was delivered, he saw a stranger reciting a book outside of the customer's house. As soon as he heard the words from this stranger's mouth, a flash of insight passed

---

[32] Buddhism.

[33] The first period covers the years from 627 to 650 and the second from 713 to 742.

[34] One *ching* is equal to approximately 15.13 acres.

[35] This selection is taken from "Autobiography" *(Tzu-hsü); Scriptures of the Sixth Patriarch (Liu-tsu t'an-ching),* roll 1. According to tradition, it was part of a sermon delivered by Hui-neng and recorded by his disciple Fa-hai.

[36] Located in modern Hopeh province.

[37] Modern Kwangtung province.

through his mind, and he sensed that he had acquired an experience which he had never had before. He asked the stranger what he was reading, and the stranger said that it was the *Diamond Sutra*. Asked again where he had acquired this book, the stranger replied: "I came from the Temple of East Ch'an that is located in the Huangmei subprefecture of the Ch'i district.[38] His Holiness the Fifth Patriarch Jen [39] is preaching in this temple where he has more than one thousand disciples. I myself worshipped in this temple, listened to the sermons, and subsequently received this book. The Patriarch told all laymen as well as monks that one needed only to recite the *Diamond Sutra* to discover his native self and thus become a Buddha."

Right then Hui-neng knew that fate had provided him with a definite course to follow. A friend gave him ten taels of silver to be left at home to support his old mother and instructed him to leave home immediately for Huangmei where he could pay his homage to the Fifth Patriarch.

After he had duly taken care of his mother, Hui-neng left home, and in less than thirty days, arrived at his destination: Huangmei. Seeing the Fifth Patriarch, he saluted and paid his respect.

"Where do you come from? What do you want?" asked the Patriarch.

"I, your student, come from the Hsinchou district of the Lingnan province. I have come a long way to pay my respect to you, Master. I desire nothing except to learn the way to become a Buddha," Hui-neng replied.

"How can you, a monkey from Lingnan, possibly hope to become a Buddha?" said the Patriarch.

"Though there are such things as 'northerners' and 'southerners'," said Hui-neng, "the Buddhist spirit does not recognize the difference between them. Physically there is a difference between a monk and a monkey, but the same spirit permeates both of them."

The Fifth Patriarch wished to continue his conversation with Hui-neng; but seeing so many disciples around him, decided to postpone it for the time being. He gave order that Hui-neng be assigned to work with others.

"Wisdom often springs from your student's mind," said Hui-neng. "As long as I do not deviate from my native self, I shall always live in paradise. Pray, Master, what do you wish me to do?"

"This monkey has something good inside himself," said the Patriarch. "Speak no more! You are assigned to work in the mill."

Hui-neng retreated to the backyard where a visiting monk informed him that his work consisted of chopping firewood and pounding rice. He worked in the mill for more than eight months.

One day the Patriarch walked into the mill and met Hui-neng as if by accident. "I knew that you possess some rare insight," said the Patriarch. "I was afraid that there might be evil men who wished to harm you. That is why I have chosen not to talk with you in the past. Do you understand?" "I do, Master," Hui-neng replied; "that is why I have not dared to venture my presence in the front hall."

Many days later the Patriarch called all of his disciples together and addressed them as follows: "There is no problem larger than the problem of life and death. Now that all of you are seeking diligently for heavenly bliss, do you realize that this goal cannot be achieved as long as you fail to understand your

[38] Located in modern Hupeh province.
[39] Hung-jen.

native self and do not seek ways to escape from the painful cycle of life and death? I am asking you to look inward at your own wisdom, a wisdom that springs from your inner mind. When you find it, express it in a poem and present it to me for examination. Any of you who has shown some understanding of the problem of life and death will receive from me the robe and the mandate whereby he will succeed me and become the Sixth Patriarch. Leave here immediately and do not delay in presenting your findings. Hard thinking has nothing to do with this matter and will not bring about good results. A person who knows his native self knows the truth without thinking about it. He would know it even if he were fighting a war on the battlefield."

The disciples talked among themselves after they left the Fifth Patriarch. "What is the use for us to write poems?" they said. "Shen-hsiu, who is our professor, is bound to receive the nod no matter how diligently we try to write ours. To try to compete with him would be a waste of time and energy." They all agreed and decided not to try.

Meanwhile Shen-hsiu was caught in a dilemma. "They decided not to write any poems because they thought that they would not be able to surpass me," he said to himself. "I, of course, should write. If I do not, how can the Patriarch know whether I am profound or shallow in my understanding? If on the other hand I do, I have no inkling as to how my action in this respect will be interpreted. If it is interpreted as a means to seek truth, that would be fine. If it is interpreted as a means whereby I can succeed His Holiness as the Sixth Patriarch, that would be very bad indeed. In such a case I would not be different from other immortals who use every means at their disposal to acquire a high position which they desire. If on the other hand I do not write the poem, how can the truth as I see it be ever revealed? I am confused."

In front of the Fifth Patriarch's residence hall there was a walking corridor which consisted of three separate chambers. In these chambers were housed Buddhist images, including a portrait of the Fifth Patriarch that showed the circulation of his blood. To these images sacrifices had been regularly offered. After Shen-hsiu had written his poem, time and again he went to the corridor with the intended purpose of presenting it to the Patriarch. Being nervous, he perspired profusely. In a period of four days he tried to present it for a total of thirteen times, but each time he decided not to do it in the last minute. Having thought over this matter again, he finally decided to write it on a wall underneath the corridor. If the Patriarch accidentally saw it and said that it was good, he, Shen-hsiu, would come forward to acknowledge its authorship. If on the other hand the Patriarch said that it was not good, he, Shen-hsiu, would have to write off the efforts of several years and leave the temple for good. At midnight, holding a lamp by one hand, he wrote the following poem on a wall in the southern corridor:

> My body is the *bodhi* tree;
> My mind is a shining mirror.[40]
>
> The mirror I dust constantly,
> Lest dust would it accumulate.

[40] The Chinese original is *ming-ching t'ai* which, literally, means "a shining mirror stand."

Shen-hsiu returned to his room quietly after he finished the writing, confident that nobody had seen him. "If the Patriarch likes my poem," he said to himself, "it must be because fate has destined me to receive the mandate. If he says that it is not good, it must be because I am being punished for the multiple sins that I committed during my previous life. In such a case I have obviously lived a life of self-deception. How much I wish to know His Holiness' reaction to my poem!" The more he thought about this, the more he became restive. He was unable to sleep until early in the morning.

Little did he know that the Fifth Patriarch had long concluded that he, Shen-hsiu, was not the man to receive the mandate because he did not understand himself and could in no way enter the realm of Buddhism. Early in the morning, on his way to the southern corridor to paint holy images, the Patriarch saw the poem that had been written on the wall. He gave the order that only sacrifices be offered from now on and that he was not going to do any more paintings. "What is the use of images?" he said. "Does not the scripture say that images are nothing but self-deceptions? All you people need to do is to recite the poem that is written on this wall; by following its precepts you will not fall into evil ways and in fact can reap great benefits." He ordered his disciples to chant this poem when performing the ritual of worship and burning incense, so that they, like the author of this poem, could truly understand their selves. All the disciples chanted it and were greatly impressed with its truthfulness.

At midnight the Patriarch summoned Shen-hsiu to his private chamber.

"Did you write that poem?" the Patriarch asked.

"May Your Holiness have mercy on me! I did. Who am I who dare to wish to occupy the position of Your Holiness? I only want to know for myself whether I have any wisdom within me," Shen-hsiu replied.

"From this poem I know that you have not understood your native self," said the Patriarch. "You have gone a long way to reach the door, but you have not entered it. With an understanding such as that which you have, a person cannot enter the upper realm of enlightenment, a realm that can only be reached through the recognition of one's inner mind and the awareness of one's true self. Once reaching that realm, a person knows no birth or death because, as far as he is concerned, existence has become eternal. He understands himself in every thought he conceives; and, rising above all hindrances, he is unfettered and free. Knowing one truth, he knows all truths because there is no truth except that which exists in his own mind. The mind, in fact, is the reality, the center of all truths. If you can comprehend this truism, you can also understand the true nature of enlightenment. Now return to your own quarters, and write another poem after thinking about it for a day or two. If you can write one indicating that you have already entered the door, the robe and the mandate will be then yours."

Shen-hsiu saluted the Patriarch and then left. For several days afterwards he tried to write another poem but did not succeed. He was confused, restless, and unhappy. He acted as if he were in a dream.

Two more days later, Hui-neng heard a boy chanting a poem while passing by the mill. Immediately after he heard the poem, he knew that the man who composed it did not understand his native self. Though he had never been taught the Buddhist ideology, he had nevertheless a general idea. "What poem are you chanting?" he asked the boy.

"How can I expect you, a monkey, to understand this poem?" the boy replied.

"The Patriarch says that the problem of life and death is extremely important and that the person who understands its meaning will receive the robe and the mandate and succeed him as the Sixth Patriarch. He has asked all of his disciples to write poems for him to read, and he would judge from these poems as to whom has understood the meaning of existence. Professor Shen-hsiu wrote a poem on a wall in the southern corridor, and it was so good that the Patriarch asked all of us to chant it. We will not fall into evil ways and will reap great benefits instead, said the Patriarch, if we follow the precepts contained in this poem."

"Sir," said Hui-neng to the boy, "I have worked in this mill for eight months, but I have never been in the front hall. Will you kindly lead me to the wall where the poem is so that I can pay my homage in person?" The boy led him to the wall where he performed the ritual of homage. "I am an illiterate," said Hui-neng; "will you please read the poem for me?"

At this time a man named Chang Yüeh-yung, who was the deputy magistrate of Kiangchou,[41] happened to stand by, and he volunteered to recite this poem. After Hui-neng heard the poem that had been recited in a clear, loud voice, he told Chang that he had also a poem in mind and that he would appreciate if the government official would be kind enough to write it down for him. "It would be a rare thing indeed that you also know how to write a poem," said Chang.

"A man who wishes to enter the upper realm of enlightenment should not belittle a person who is determined to learn," said Hui-neng. "It is possible that an inferior man has a superior wisdom while a superior man may not have any at all."

"Well, you speak aloud, and I will write down your poem for you," said Chang. "If by chance you do receive the mandate, you should first bestow upon me your infinite grace. Please do not forget." Hui-neng then recited his poem as follows:

> *Bodhi* is not a tree;
> Nor is a mirror a mirror.
> Since none of these exists,
> How can dust accumulate?

All of the Patriarch's disciples were truly amazed when they saw this poem. "How strange this is!" they said among themselves. "We should never judge a person by his physical appearance. Why did we let a Buddha in flesh work so hard for such a long time?" The Patriarch, seeing the amazement expressed by his disciples, was fearful that they, out of jealousy, might do Hui-neng physical harm. Consequently he erased the poem on the wall with his shoe, saying that the man who wrote it did not understand his native self either. All of his disciples agreed. Seeing that Hui-neng was still pounding rice as usual, the Patriarch said to him: "Does a man who seeks The Way still do such things as this? How is the rice that you are pounding?" "I have finished pounding," Hui-neng replied; "the rice needs only sifting." The Patriarch raised his cane, beat the mortar three times, and then left. Hui-neng knew exactly what the Patriarch meant.

When the drum beat for the third time at midnight, Hui-neng went to the Patriarch's private chamber. The Patriarch covered him with his Buddhist robe so that nobody outside the window would know who Hui-neng was. Then he began

---

[41] Located in modern Hupeh province.

to preach on the meaning of the *Diamond Sutra*. When he came down to the sentence "A thing is where the mind is," Hui-neng became for the first time truly enlightened. There was no truth outside of what was in one's native self. "The native self is pure and unshakable; it is the source of all truths," Hui-neng volunteered. By then the Patriarch knew that Hui-neng had understood the true self.

"It is useless to learn about Buddhism," said the Patriarch, "if the learner does not know his own mind. Knowing his own mind, he will know his native self. In such a case he is a man, a teacher, and a Buddha: all three in one person. At this moment and in the middle of the night I am transmitting to you the Buddhist mandate, a transmission that is not witnessed by anyone except you and myself. I am giving you my robe and my alms-bowl, and from now on you will be the Sixth Patriarch. Please take care of yourself and save those who deserve to be saved. May the truth expounded by us last forever! Make sure that it does. Now listen to my poem:

> A seed has been sown
>   In a spot where it should be;
> It will grow and grow
>   And yield a multitude of fruits.
> No, there is no such thing as seed;
>   Nor is there a place most ideal for its growth.
> Since 'self' is non-existent,
>   How can there be 'birth' or 'growth'?"

"When the great master Bodhidharma [42] came to this land," the Fifth Patriarch continued, "people did not believe in him. He used this robe as a symbol of faith, to be handed down from one generation to the next, so that the Buddhist truth would last forever. The real meaning, however, was to transmit the mind of one generation to that of the next, and each successor to the Buddhist mandate had to reach enlightenment by his own efforts before he was so designated. In ancient times the transmission of Buddhist mandate centered on the transmission of mandate *per se,* without being accompanied by outward symbols such as the robe. It was a communication of mind, private and secretive, between the master of one generation and the master next in line. Since then the robe—the outward symbol—has become a center of contention among the prospective successors, and it is my hope that from your generation on the transfer of the robe will cease to be a part of the transmission of the mandate. Whoever possess this robe is endangering his own life. I beg you to leave this place immediately so that your own life will not be endangered."

"Where should I go?" asked Hui-neng.

"Stop when you meet friends; hide when you encounter enemies," replied the Patriarch.

At midnight Hui-neng received the robe and the alms-bowl from the Patriarch who subsequently escorted him to the Chiukiang Harbor. After both went aboard a boat, Hui-neng took the scull.

---

[42] The Indian missionary who came to China in A.D. 526 (variant 520). He was credited with the founding of Ch'an Buddism in China.

"I should ferry you," said the Patriarch.

"You ferried me when I was in darkness," said Hui-neng. "Since I have already seen the light, I can ferry myself. Though 'ferry' is a common word, it carries different meanings in different areas. I was born in a remote area and could not speak a language commonly understood.[43] However, since I received the mandate from Your Holiness, I have been greatly enlightened. I know my self and therefore shall 'ferry' myself."

"You speak well," said the Patriarch. "I am sure that Buddhism will spread far and wide under your direction. Go southward and have a pleasant trip. The spread of our faith does not depend upon making good speeches."

Hui-neng bid farewell to the Patriarch and journeyed southward. He arrived at the Tayü Mountains [44] in two months.

After his return to the temple, the Patriarch did not attend the worship session for several days.

"Is His Holiness indisposed?" inquired the disciples.

"I am not ill," the Patriarch replied. "Both the robe and the mandate have gone southward."

"Who has received them?"

"The person who should receive them has received them," the Patriarch replied.

It was then that the disciples knew who had received them.

30 · TAO-YÜAN: *A Conversation in Yün-men* [45]

"What is the basic teaching of Buddhism?" asked one of the monks.

"With the coming of spring the grass will become green by itself," the Master [46] replied.

The Master then turned towards a monk from Hsin-lo [47] and asked him: "What means did you use to pass across the sea?" "The bandits have been defeated," the monk replied.

The Master grabbed the monk's hand and asked: "Why are you now in my hands?" "That is the way it should be," said the monk. "You have made another jump," commented the Master.

"How was Niu-t'ou before he saw the Fourth Patriarch?" [48] asked another monk.

"There is a Goddess of Mercy in every household," the Master replied.

"How was he after he had seen the Fouth Patriarch?"

"A moth in the fire has swallowed a tiger," the Master replied.

"What is the Song of Yün-men?"

"On the twenty-fifth day of the twelfth lunar month."

---

[43] Hui-neng was born in modern Kwangtung province and spoke Cantonese which the northerners had a difficult time to understand.
[44] Located between modern Hunan and Kwangtung provinces.
[45] This selection is taken from *The Transmission of the Lamp (Ching-te ch'uan-teng lu,* roll 19. The author, a monk named Tao-yüan, completed this book in 1004.
[46] Yün-men Wen-yen.
[47] Located in the southern section of Korea.
[48] Tao-hsin (580–651).

"How does an ox yell when it is trapped in mud on top of a snowy mountain?"
"It is darkness everywhere."
"How does a wooden horse of Yün-men neigh?"
"Mountains and river are moving by themselves."
"Please tell me, Master, the most basic of all your teachings."
"Face the southeast in the morning and the northwest in the evening."
"What will the situation be when a person fully understands your teachings?"
"Light a lamp in the eastern chamber, but sit in darkness in the western chamber."
"What should a person do at noon if he does not wish to waste his time?"
"Why do you ask this question?" the Master retorted.
"I am ignorant, Master. Please tell me."
"Bring me the writing equipment," said the Master. After the writing equipment was brought in, the Master wrote the following poem:

> I have pointed out the direction
>   Which you fail to heed.
> That is the difference!
> Thinking and reasoning—
> This path if you follow,
> Enlightened you will not be.

"How can I understand myself?"
"Visit mountains and rivers and enjoy yourself," said the Master.
"How do I understand the monk within myself?"
"I cannot find him anywhere."
"How does a person feel when he swallows something in one gulp?"
"I am inside your stomach," the Master replied.
"Why should you be in my stomach?"
"Let us go back where we started."
"What should I say?"
"Get out of here!"
"I really don't know what to say, Master. Please lead the way."
"What has been said is clear enough. Why should I repeat it?"
"How can we rise above the problem of life and death?"
The Master opened his hands and replied: "Life and death—where are they?"
"Why cannot a man join the monastic rank if his parents do not allow him?"
"What a shallow question this is!"
"But I really don't understand."
"Now you are more profound."
"What is the self within me?"
"Are you afraid that I do not know?" the Master retorted.
"What should a person do when all possibilities are gone?"
"Bring me the Buddha Hall and I will discuss this matter with you."
"What has the Buddha Hall to do with this?"
"You liar!" the Master scolded aloud.
"What is the statement handed down outside of the Buddhist tradition?"
"Ask others when you see them."

"What will their answer be if I do?"

"Ask yourself where you should stand when you want to see your own reflection."

"Tell me what the Buddhist spirit is."

"There are scholars in front of the door."

"What is the statement that summarizes the essence of our physical being?"

"Hide yourself in the Great Dipper."

"What is the meaning that comes from the West?"

"It has been cloudy and raining for a long time," said the Master. "It smells like rice gruel."

"People have discussed enlightenment in a variety of ways, but they are not able to advance one step further. How can we achieve what they have failed?"

"The eastern peak of the Western Mountains is always green," the Master replied.

"What is the meaning that comes from the West?"

"If you have lost money in a river, it is only in that river you can find it." . . .

31 · OU-YANG HSIU: *Our Basic Beliefs* [49]

Buddhism has been a curse to China for more than one thousand years. The upright and undeceived, including those who enjoy power and prestige, all wish to eliminate it. It was once eliminated, only to come back with increasing strength. The more it is attacked, the stronger it becomes. Hardly has its fire been extinguished before it is rekindled; it spreads far and wide with great speed. People say that there is nothing we can do about it.

Is it really true that Buddhism cannot be eliminated? It is only true so long as we have not found the right method to combat it.

To cure an illness, a doctor has to find its cause. Only then can he prescribe remedies to eliminate the cause. Illness comes into being when a man's vitality has been weakened; the weakening of his vitality is the real cause of his illness. Therefore, instead of attempting to cure the symptoms, a good doctor concentrates his energy in cultivating the vitality of his charge. Once the vitality of the sick person is strengthened, his illness will automatically disappear.

This is also true with regard to the elimination of a nation's curse. To eliminate it, first we have to find its cause.

Buddhism originated from a barbarian land, a land which is far away from China. It has been in existence for a long time. During the times of Yao, Shun, and the Three Dynasties when the government was just and when the people abided by their good customs, Buddhism could not enter China even though it had been in existence.[50] It was more than two hundred years after the passing of the Three Dynasties that Buddhism made its entry into China at a time when the government was no longer just and when the people ceased to follow the good customs of the ancient times. It is obvious that Buddhism succeeded only after we

[49] The Chinese title for this essay is *Pen lun*. A copy of the original can be found in *A Collection of Essays Written in the Ancient Style (Ku-wen tz'u-lei tsuan)*, roll 3, compiled by Yao Nai who lived in the eighteenth century.

[50] The author obviously regarded Hinduism and Buddism as the same thing.

had failed. If we restore what we have lost so that our government will be just and our good customs will again prevail, Buddhism cannot influence our people despite its existence in China.

Yao, Shun, and the Three Dynasties put into practice the well-field system in which every man in the nation was duly registered and then granted land to till: [51] all those who were able to work had land to till. Taxes amounted to ten percent of the produce. Other requisitions varied, however; and the purpose of these variations was to encourage the laggards to be more diligent. When all men worked hard to attend their fields, they had no time to engage in other activities.

Lest the people should be either too industrious or too indolent and thus become an easy prey to evil influences, the ancient government introduced many good customs such as the consumption of wine and sacrificial animals to strengthen their bodily strength and the performance of religious rituals to please their eyes and ears. Moreover, during the leisure time when work was not performed in the fields, it taught the people appropriate rites for different occasions: rites for hunting, wedding, funeral, archery, and so on. To prevent people from engaging in disorderly conduct, it educated them in the maintenance of correct relationships: the precedence of the superiors over the inferiors and of the elders over the young. All matters regarding births and deaths were carefully prescribed, prescribed in such a way as to be in conformity with the natural desires of man. These rituals were embellished with elegance and grace not merely to please the eyes but also to cultivate genuine and healthful interests. People's conduct was regulated not against but in accordance with their basic desires, in the hope that excessiveness, in whatever form, might be avoided. Fearing that even these measures were not adequate, the ancient government established schools, from those in the capital to those in the countryside; the talented were chosen from among the people to be enrolled as students. These students not only emulated one another in the pursuance of goodness but also encouraged towards the same goal those who were less talented and diligent but who might decide to follow their example. How perfect this ancient system was!

The policies of Yao, Shun, and the Three Dynasties were sound; they took into consideration every detail of people's need. Moreover, they had efficient administrative organs to govern the people, effective methods to prevent people from going morally astray, and persuasive ways to lead them to a life of goodness and honesty. So diligently did they pursue their goals that slowly and gradually their good influence was felt by the people as a whole. It was not a superficial influence; it went deep and became a part of the receivers.

When the people did not work in the field, they were occupied with rites and music. When they were not at home, they could be found in schools. They could not see or hear anything except that which was right and proper. They labored for goodness with gladness and were not tired of the strife throughout their lives.

The Ch'in regime unified China after the Chou dynasty had declined. It abolished the institutions of the Three Dynasties and, as a result, the way of the ancient kings came to an end. After the Ch'in, no government was able to restore the ancient system. Its ways of governing were not effective, nor were its methods of preventing people from being influenced by alien ideas. Buddhism took advantage of this situation and came to China at this time. For more than one

---

[51] For more details about the well-field system, see pp. 264–287.

thousand years, while we continued to bungle, more and more Buddhists came to China. The abolition of the well-field system resulted in land concentration and the rise of rural unemployment. Later, the instruments which the ancient kings had used effectively to teach and govern people, including the rites and rituals in hunting, wedding, funeral, and archery, were all abolished, one after another. As a result, the wicked found time to engage in undesirable activities, while the best among the people were at a loss to know where "propriety" or "righteousness" was. With plenty of unused energy the wicked devoted themselves to the pursuance of heretical ideas; without knowing what was right or proper, the innocent were lost while looking for a correct path to follow.

Then the Buddhists took advantage of our weaknesses and presented forcibly their specious arguments. People followed them as if they had been led by a leash. The elite in our society frequently sponsored Buddhist causes; they maintained that Buddhism was a true faith and that there was no reason why our people should not be converted to it. A few who had not been bewitched by this kind of reasoning would say that they were going to chase Buddhism out of China and that they could do so through the presentation of sound arguments. Can a few people eliminate a curse which has plagued China for more than one thousand years? It is obvious that a poison which has penetrated deep into the marrow of people's bones cannot be eradicated by making speeches.

What should we do? I say that a sure way to win against this alien faith is to cultivate and strengthen our basic beliefs.

During the period of Warring-States [52] the philosophies of Yang Chu and Mo Ti brought about confusion and chaos.[53] Mencius deplored this situation and concentrated his energy in preaching the doctrine of love and righteousness. His doctrine prevailed, and the philosophies of Yang Chu and Mo Ti died by themselves. During the Han dynasty many schools of philosophy flourished side by side. Deploring this situation, Tung Chung-shu worked diligently on the teachings of Confucius. The meaning of Confucianism became clear, and all other schools receded as a result. This is what I mean when I say that a sure way to win against unorthodox ideas is to strengthen our basic beliefs.

Nowadays even a veteran soldier of great courage will worship Buddha whenever he sees his image; he will express admiration and fear whenever he listens to Buddhist teachings. He is strong in appearance, but he is lost inside because he has nothing within himself which he can trust and hold. On the other hand, a physically weak scholar, who may be afraid of every step he takes, will express openly his indigation whenever he hears people discussing Buddhism. Not only will he not surrender himself to this alien belief; he would like to chase it out of China and put an end to it. Why does he react differently? He is intelligent and informed and is thoroughly familiar with Confucian teachings. He has something within himself which he can trust and hold. To learn and then be thoroughly familiar with Confucian teachings is therefore the surest way to combat and win against Buddhism. If it is true that an individual will not surrender himself to Buddhism once he knows about Confucianism, the battle against this alien ideology can be won if all people in China have learned about our basic beliefs.

[52] The period of Warring-States (403–221 B.C.).
[53] Yang Chu advocated an extreme form of selfishness; Mo Ti advocated universal love.

CHAPTER SIX

Neo-Confucianism and Its Aftermath

THE steady decline of Confucianism after the third century A.D. came to an end during the T'ang dynasty (618–906) whose early rulers prided themselves on being the patrons of all ideologies. It was not until the Sung dynasty (960–1279), however, that a revived Confucianism began to dominate the intellectual scene. This revived Confucianism is sometimes called "Neo-Confucianism" by Western scholars, though this term rarely appears in Chinese literature because none of the "Neo-Confucians" ever regarded their philosophy as original or "new."

In terms of influence exercised on posterity the greatest Neo-Confucian was unquestionably Chu Hsi (1130–1200). It was he who took two chapters from the *Book of Rites* and elevated them to the same position as that of the *Analects of Confucius* and the *Book of Mencius*. These two chapters were *Great Learning* and *Doctrine of the Mean*. Together they were called the *Four Books*. Subsequently the true meanings of some of the key phrases in the *Great Learning,* such as "sincerity in intentions" (*ch'eng yi*), "rectification of mind" (*cheng hsin*), "acquirement of knowledge" (*chih chih*), and "observation and investigation of objects and things" (*ke wu*), caused much controversy among the Neo-Confucians (Selection 32).

If we have to use familiar terms to describe the difference between Chu Hsi and his academic opponents, we may say that Chu Hsi emphasized the inductive method ("to know my mind by observing and investigating things outside of myself") while his opponents such as Lu Chiu-yüan (1139–1192) and Wang Shou-jen (1472–1528?) relied exclusively on the deductive method ("there is no truth outside of my mind" and "all truth is complete within me"). To Chu Hsi the investigation of objects or things meant the ascertaining of the "reasons" (*li*) behind the existence of the objects or things (Selections 33, 34, and 35). To all Neo-Confucians, including Chu Hsi, the ultimate purpose was the perfection of a person as an ethical being (Selections 36, 37, 38, 39, 40, and 41).

The emphasis on the inward movement towards oneself gave birth to criticisms by other scholars. To people like Yen Yüan (also known as Yen Hsi-chai, 1635–1704) and Tai Chen (also known as Tai Tung-yüan, 1723–1777) the emphasis on such intangible things as "native self" (*pen hsing*) or "inner mind" was not only Buddhist and un-Confucian but also futile and useless (Selections 43 and 44). To others like Ku Yen-wu (1613–1682) such emphasis served no other purpose than to distract a gentleman from his true task; *i.e.*, "to regard the social well-being of the whole nation as his own private end to strive for" (Selection 42). All of these critics advised people to read the Han and pre-Han writings to ascertain the true meanings of Confucianism, bypassing the philosophy of the Sung-Ming interregnum which they claimed had been corrupted by Buddhist and Taoist influences.

While orthodox Confucians denounced Buddhism and Taoism whenever they had the opportunity, most Chinese were unorthodox and consequently more tolerant. They believed that all religions or philosophies wanted to achieve basically the same purpose and that the society was better off if they were allowed to coexist and compete peacefully among themselves. This kind of attitude was reflected by Liu Oh, a novelist who died early in the twentieth century (Selection 45).

32 · ANONYMOUS: *Great Learning* [1]

The purpose of Great Learning is first, to know and make clear the meanings of true virtues; second, to educate and reform people so that they can acquire these virtues; and third, to attain a state of moral perfection for all people as the ultimate end.

Knowing what moral perfection is, a man will be steadfast in his will. His will stabilized, he will not be distracted from his goal by outward influences. He thus enjoys peace. With peace secure in his mind, he can think thoroughly about each matter he encounters. Thinking thoroughly before he acts, rarely will he make mistakes.

An object has its essential and non-essential aspects. Likewise an event has a beginning and an end. A man is close to the truth if he knows the relative position between the important and the insignificant.

According to an ancient adage, if a man wishes to make true virtues prevail throughout the world, he should first learn to govern his country well. To learn to govern his country well, he should first learn how to manage his household. To learn how to manage his household, he should first learn how to cultivate himself as an ethical being. To learn how to cultivate himself as an ethical being, he should first learn how to rectify his mind. To learn how to rectify his mind, he should be sincere in his intentions. He cannot be sincere in his intentions unless he possesses knowledge. To acquire knowledge, he has to observe and investigate objects and things.

The observation and investigation of objects and things are the beginning of knowledge. Only after knowledge has been acquired can intentions be sincere. Only after intentions have become sincere can the mind be rectified. Only after the mind has been rectified can a person cultivate himself as an ethical being. Only after a person has successfully cultivated himself as an ethical being will he know how to manage a household. Only after every household has successfully been managed can the country be said to have been governed well. When every country is well governed, peace will prevail throughout the world.

[1] According to Chu Hsi, the author of the 'Great Learning* was Tseng-tzu, a disciple of Confucius. Modern historians have generally discounted this assertion.

For every person in the society, whether he is the Son of Heaven or an ordinary citizen, the most important thing is the cultivation of himself as an ethical being. Without this basic achievement it is futile to speak of the successful management of a household, the governing of a country, or peace in the world. It is wrong to be distant to those whom one should love while loving those to whom one should be distant. . . .

For a person to be sincere in his intentions means that he should not be engaged in self-deception. He detests evil to the same extent that he detests bad odor; he loves virtue to the same extent that he loves a thing of beauty. Whether it is love or detestation, it comes from his inner self. A gentleman is careful with what he does, even though he is all by himself. . . .

A person's mind cannot be rectified if he is angry, fearful, pleasure-seeking, or sorrowful. If the mind is not there, he cannot see or hear anything; he does not even know what food tastes like even though he is eating it. Only when his mind is rectified can he know how to cultivate himself as an ethical being. . . .

33 · CHU HSI: *On Reason* [2]

During the stage of The Infinite [3] and later The Absolute, [4] concrete objects did not exist. There was, however, The Reason. . . . As there are many reasons in the universe, there are therefore many concrete objects.

*   *   *   *   *

There is a reason in everything we do. There is a reason in every object that is created by Heaven and Earth.

*   *   *   *   *

A particular reason exists before the existence of a particular phenomenon. For instance, the reason that governs the relationship between a king and his ministers exists before there are such things as kings and ministers. The reason that governs the relationship between father and son exists before there are such things as fathers and sons.

*   *   *   *   *

The reason of an object exists before there is such an object. In many cases the reason of an object exists even though there is no such object.

*   *   *   *   *

Question: What were the things in the universe before the creation of Heaven and Earth?

Answer: There was The Reason or there were reasons in the universe. What

[2] This collection of random ideas on reason appears in *Sample Opinions (Yü lei)*, rolls 1, 4, 94, 95, and 101.

[3] *Wu chi.*

[4] *T'ai chi.*

Heaven and Earth have created during the past millions of years are merely objects.

* * * * *

Question: Man and all objects receive reason from Heaven. Do inanimate objects also possess reason?

Answer: Yes. The reason of a boat is its navigability in the water; the reason of a vehicle is its mobility on the ground.

* * * * *

Question: What is the nature of an inanimate object?

Answer: The nature of an inanimate object is the reason that underlies its existence. That is why we say that there is no object in the universe that is outside the sphere of "nature." When you walk on a terrace made of bricks, the nature of the bricks that enable you to walk on the terrace is the reason of these bricks. When you sit in a bamboo chair, the nature of the bamboo chair that enables you to sit in it is the reason of this bamboo chair.

* * * * *

Everything or object has its "absolute." By absolute is meant the absolute reason. Chiang Yüan-chin [5] asked Chu Hsi: "Can love on the part of a king and reverence on the part of a minister be regarded as 'absolutes'?" The teacher [6] replied: "There are merely individual 'absolutes,' covering particular things or objects. The synthesis of all reasons which underlie all things and objects in the universe is The Absolute. . . ."

34 · CHU HSI: *The Investigation of Objects* [7]

When Heaven creates men, he also creates objects and the rules that govern them. An object is known by its form, and a rule is the reason which underlies the form. Forms are concrete, while reasons are abstract. Man cannot live without the objects that exist around him.

Because of the importance of the objects that exist around him, a man has to understand the reasons that govern these objects if, for instance, he wishes to live a correct life or handle properly his daily affairs. As these reasons exist within the objects, to understand them is to understand these objects. In other words, to understand the inherent reasons of an object and thus complete our knowledge about it, we should be thoroughly familiar with every aspect of the object. Only when all aspects of an object are thoroughly investigated can its inherent reasons be revealed to us. By then our knowledge about it will be

[5] A student of Chu Hsi.
[6] Chu Hsi.
[7] The Chinese original appears in "A Letter to Chiang Te-kung"; *Important Messages from Chu Hsi on the Matter of Learning (Chu-tzu lun-hsüeh ch'ieh-yao yü)*, roll 1, compiled by Wang Mou-hung who lived in the eighteenth century.

thorough and complete. Our intentions will be sincere and our minds will be rectified. . . .

There are people who believe that to discover the reasons of the physical world we have to find the knowledge within ourselves first. This is obviously wrong because it reverses the logical order of affairs. There are others who interpret the investigation of objects to mean the physical contact or handling of these objects. This is also wrong because the reasons within an object cannot be found unless the object itself is *thoroughly* investigated. Their interpretation is not only illogical; it is also incompatible with the meaning as revealed in the text.[8] Moreover, it is contrary to common sense. When our sage [9] wrote about the investigation of objects, he could not have been so careless as to confuse later scholars intentionally.

Some people raise the argument that according to Buddhist and Taoist teachings knowledge can be acquired outside of the investigation of objects. Their argument does not make the Buddhist or Taoist teachings any more correct. As only food can quench hunger, knowledge can only be acquired through the investigation of objects. It is a false knowledge that is not acquired this way. A man is sick indeed when he says that his stomach is full even though he has not eaten anything for a long time. The Buddhists and Taoists who claim that they have acquired knowledge without ever engaging in the investigation of objects commit the error of narrow-mindedness. Their knowledge is not really knowledge.

35 · CHU HSI: *The Importance of Book Learning* [10]

The purpose of learning is to find the reason that underlies all things in the universe. The most important method for discovering these reasons is the study of written works. In studying written works one should follow a gradual, orderly procedure, beginning with the elementary and proceeding towards the most profound. How can we eventually acquire the most profound? The unfailing method is to be respectful in our attitude and steadfast in our will.

As I have said previously, there is a reason which governs each of the things in the universe. There are reasons that govern the relationships between a king and his subjects, father and son, husband and wife, elder and younger brothers, and friends and friends.[11] There are also reasons that govern our daily lives. If we have discovered and understood these reasons, we should be able to know, clearly and exactly, why things stand the way they do and in what ways they can be improved. This is true not only in such important things as the relationship between a king and his ministers but also true in such small things as the study of physical objects. We should follow what is good and reject what is bad; we should be completely objective and impartial in this matter.

Each of the universal reasons is as beautiful as it is exact; it is right and proper for the function to which it is assigned. It has been the same from the ancient

---

[8] The text of the *Great Learning*.

[9] The author of the *Great Learning*.

[10] The Chinese original appears in a memorial written to the reigning emperor Sung Ning-tsung (r. 1195–1224). See Wang Mou-hung, *A Chronology of Chu Hsi (Chu-tzu lien-pu)*, roll 4a.

[11] In Confucian ideology these relationships are called *wu-lum* or five cardinal relationships.

times to our day; it is unchanging and unchangeable. However, only the ancient sages were thoroughly familiar with all of these reasons, and what they said and did set the example for posterity to follow. Those who follow this example are called gentlemen and will be rewarded with good fortune, and those who violate it are called "mean" people [12] and will suffer distress and even calamity. For a king the best fortune is his ability to preserve continuously his own country, and the worst of all calamities is his inability to preserve even his own person. The former is an example to follow, and the latter is a lesson to learn. The evidence of this truism—the inevitable consequences following the presence of certain causes—can be found in all classics and histories. If we do not seek universal reasons from these written records, it is as if we were standing before and facing a blank wall; we can never find them. In short, to discover universal reasons, we must study books.

As for books, there are those we like and those we do not like. With regard to those books that we do not like, our natural tendency is to be indolent and we study them only intermittently. Obviously we cannot achieve very much this way. On the other hand, we want to read as much as we can those books that we do like. Hardly have we opened a book before we wish to know about all of its conclusions. Before we have time to digest one point, we find ourselves pursuing another. As we work day and night and have no time even to take a rest, we feel that we are always in a hurry, pursuing something that is forever elusive. We deny ourselves the joy of leisure and repose. How can we really learn anything this way? Boredom will be the eventual result. As far as achievements are concerned, are we really different from those who are indolent by nature and who apply themselves only intermittently to their studies?

Confucius mentioned the incompatibility between success and speed. Mencius said that those who advance fast will also retreat fast. Realizing the wisdom of these remarks and wishing to benefit from them, we should concentrate our minds on one subject at a time and work steadily at it without switching to other subjects. In such a case the books we read will be related in their contents, and the ideas they convey will be like the blood which circulates freely within our veins. Gradually and slowly we are taken over by the benign influence which the reading of these books creates, and our minds and the above-mentioned universal reasons will be merged to become one single entity. By then we will be greatly impressed with the importance of following the good and avoiding the evil.

How can we acquire the most profound in our learning process? The key to open the most profound is one's mind. As to this thing called mind, it is as ingenious as it is mysterious. It is the governor of our body and controls everything we do. It has to be within ourselves at all times. However, it can fly away from us during a brief moment of carelessness when, for instance, we find ourselves pursuing the satisfaction of our physical or material desires. Then our body loses its governor and all the things we do are no longer correctly controlled. Though our body can still move, we have unconsciously abdicated our authority in the control of its moment. When this happens, it is senseless to talk about the words of the sages, the study of objects and things, and the correct interpretation of "righteous reasons." [13]

[12] *Hsiao jen.*
[13] *Yi li.*

Confucius said: "A gentleman who does not have pride in himself will not command respect from others; moreover, he cannot be persistent in pursuing his studies." Mencius said: "There is no other way to knowledge except to free one's own mind." If a person is respectful and fearful in his attitude and serious and serene in his appearance and if his mind is free from the temptation of physical or material desires, he has certainly acquired the right approach, in the matter of discovering universal reasons as well as in the study of books. He will be at home in whatever he undertakes, and he is proper and correct in his relationships with others. This is what I call "respectful in our attitude and steadfast in our will" which, I believe, is the basic principle underlying the study of all books. This is what I have learned in my life, and it has proven sound in all adversities. I have the feeling that even if the ancient sages were living today, they could not have taught more than what I have indicated. If sincerely adhered to, it will be beneficial to monarchs as well as scholars of the humblest origin. . . .

36 · LU CHIU-YÜAN: *The Key to Knowledge Is the Freedom of Mind* [14]

All people in China are seeking knowledge and yet nobody knows what knowledge really means. This situation should not have occurred, but it did. Is it not proper that we should examine the real meaning of knowledge?

The ordinary concepts of knowledge are as vague as they are confused. People have argued about them, but they cannot reach an agreement among themselves. Those of us who have studied the ancient concept of knowledge are at a loss to understand them.

Jen does not exist outside of one's mind. Mind makes a man a man, and the presence of mind makes man different from other living creatures. You do not seek your mind; it is already there. All you need to do is to free it from its shackles.

As far as the ancient people were concerned, to seek a free mind was as important as to seek food when they were hungry, water when they were thirsty, help when their bodies caught fire, and rescue when they were drowning. To seek knowledge is to seek the freedom of one's mind. The ignorant, careless about what they see and indifferent to what they hear, are immovable as far as their minds are concerned. The so-called knowledge of theirs is no more than a literature of inflated style, superficially ornate and excessively adorned. They use it to satisfy their own selfish desires; its importance is so exaggerated that it harms the good and corrupts the virtuous. What a pity it is!

"There is no other way to knowledge except to free one's mind," said Mencius. Who will not be impressed with these words?

14 The Chinese original appears in "Miscellaneous Articles" *(Shih yi); Complete Works of Lu Hsiang-shan (Lu Hsiang-shan ch'üan-chi),* roll 32, compiled and edited by Wang Tsung-mu who lived in the sixteenth century.

37 · Lu Chiu-yüan: *To Cultivate Mind Is to Eliminate Desires* [15]

If I wish to preserve my goodness, I have to eliminate what can harm it. The goodness within me is an innate goodness that is born with me. If by chance I cannot preserve it, it is because it has been damaged by harmful elements. It can be preserved if I know how to eliminate these harmful elements. When they are eliminated, it can preserve itself without my efforts.

What are the elements that are harmful to my innate goodness? They are desires. The more numerous my desires are, the less I can preserve my innate goodness; the less numerous they are, the more I can. A gentleman is not afraid that his innate goodness cannot be preserved; he is afraid that his desires cannot be as few as they should be. When desires are eliminated, his innate goodness will be preserved by itself. Is it not true that the way to preserve my innate goodness is to eliminate the elements that can harm it?

38 · Lu Chiu-yüan: *Only Those Who Seek Can Find* [16]

Even though it can be temporarily concealed, a man's conscience can never be completely obliterated. Those who have cast themselves outside of the sphere of virtue deny themselves what they inherently possess; they do not seek what is inside themselves. If they do, the difference between right and wrong—and good and evil—will be immediately clear to them. They will avoid evil and work for the good. They will do this voluntarily, and they need no coercion. They will abandon the ways of the ignorant and the wicked and follow the path of the virtuous. When they do so, they are like water in the river rushing towards the sea, and nobody can stop them. How can they change themselves from persons of one type to persons of the opposite type? The answer: they have found themselves. If a person seeks goodness within himself, he cannot fail to find it. "Only those who seek can find," said Mencius.

39 · Wang Shou-jen: *On Human Nature* [17]

Question: The ancient philosophers differed when discussing human nature. What is the final word in this matter?

Answer: Human nature has no fixed form; opinion about it can vary. Some people look at human nature in its basic form; others look at its outward manifestations. Some emphasize human nature as it exists in its original state; others emphasize its derivative forms. Yet it is the same human nature. There are many ways to interpret it—some are profound and others are not. We are in error if we insist that there is only one way of interpreting it.

[15] *Lu Hsiang-shan ch'üan-chi,* roll 32.
[16] *Lu Hsiang-shan ch'üan-chi,* roll 32.
[17] The Chinese original appears in *Messages for Study from Wang Yang-ming (Yang-ming ch'uan-hsi lu),* roll 3, compiled and edited by Hsü Ai, a disciple of Wang Shou-jen.

Human nature, in its original state, is neither good nor bad. Its outward manisfestations, however, can be good or bad. Let us use our eyes as an example. Sometimes they look cheerful; sometimes they look angry. Sometimes they look straight ahead; sometimes they look sideways. Yet they are the same pair of eyes. We are wrong if we say that there are no cheerful eyes at a time when we see only angry eyes; we are equally wrong if we say that eyes cannot look sideways only because, at the moment of speaking, eyes happen to look ahead. We are merely stubborn. When Mencius says that human nature is good, he is talking about human nature in its original state; he speaks only in general terms. When Hsün-tzu [18] says that human nature is bad, he is talking about human nature in its derivative forms. We cannot say that he is absolutely wrong; it is a matter of being unable to see human nature in a more profound or precise way. As these philosophers argue among themselves, the masses are lost as to the basic nature of man's mind.[19]

Question: Mencius looks at human nature as it appears in its original state; he hopes that people will apply themselves to the enlightening of what is basic. Hsün-tzu, on the other hand, sees human nature only in its derivative forms. When you try to correct human nature in its derivative forms, you certainly have to double your efforts.

Answer: That is correct.

40 · WANG SHOU-JEN: *On Innate Knowledge* [20]

Innate knowledge does not come about as a result of investigating the outside world. The information acquired through the use of our senses is merely a manifestation of the innate knowledge which we have already possessed. Innate knowledge does not depend upon such acquired information for its existence; nor should it be confused with it. Confucius said: "When I think that I have knowledge, I do not have it." Outside of innate knowledge there is no knowledge.

Innate knowledge is the font of all possible knowledge and is the most important subject taught by the ancient sages. When people today devote themselves to the investigation of the outside world, they are in fact seeking the nonessentials; they have lost what is really basic. Even if they succeed in what they have set out to do, their accomplishment is only of secondary importance. Lately almost all of my friends have heard about the theory of innate knowledge; yet, despite their efforts, none of them has completely succeeded in achieving the goal of knowledge. Why? This is because they do not know the difference between information and knowledge.

Thus, in the pursuance of knowledge, we should keep in mind what is the most important and basic. Only then can the information we acquire through the use of our sense organs be helpful in the enhancement of our innate knowledge. In carrying on our daily lives we see, hear, and do a variety of things, and everything we do cannot be anything other than the manisfestation of our innate

---

[18] Hsün-tzu, or Hsün Ch'ing, was a Confucian philosopher who lived in the third century B.C.

[19] To Wang Shou-jen the nature of man's mind was more important as a subject of discussion than the goodness or badness of human nature.

[20] *Yang-ming ch'uan-hsi lu*, roll 2.

knowledge. It is one thing to say that our innate knowledge cannot be expressed any other way except in the context of our daily lives; it is another thing to say that innate knowledge can be acquired through the investigation of the outside world. Though the latter statement is somewhat different from the statement that knowledge can only be acquired through the investigation of the outside world, it is nevertheless equally erroneous.

People say that one should see and hear as much as possible in order to recognize or select the best to follow. One's innate knowledge is by no means totally absent so long as one "recognizes" or "selects" the best to follow. On the other hand, to use one's eyes and ears to "recognize" or "select" is definitely to place the cart before the horse. . . .

41 · WANG SHOU-JEN: *Knowledge and Action* [21]

Knowledge, when expressed in a true, honest manner, leads to action. Action when it is of an instructive and discriminative nature, is the basis of knowledge. These two cannot be separated. Later scholars,[22] applying themselves to both fields as if they could be separated, fail to understand the true meaning of either knowledge or action. They have what they call the theory of parallelism in which both knowledge and action advance side by side at the same speed. They do not understand that the purpose of knowledge is action and that knowledge, without being followed by action, is not really knowledge. What I have said here is the same thing as the remark you made in your letter that "the purpose of acquiring knowledge about food is to know what to eat and what not to eat."

Though my statements about the basic nature of knowledge-action sound like a remedial measure at a time of crisis, their basic validity cannot be denied. I do not make these statements for rhetorical or oratorical purposes; nor are they intended merely to correct certain abuses during a particular period.

To concentrate my mind while ignoring the physical world is a sure way to lose my mind. The important thing to remember is that the physical world does not exist outside of my mind. To seek knowledge within my mind while ignoring the existence of the physical world is to reduce my mind to an unknown and inconceivable entity.

The basis of "mind" is "nature," [23] and "nature" constitutes "reason." [24] Since there is an inherent filial mind, there is the "reason" of filial piety. If such a mind did not exist, there could not have been the aforesaid "reason." By the same token, the "mind" of loyalty toward one's king exists prior to the existence of the "reason" of such loyalty. Without the "mind" of being loyal, there could not have been the "reason" of being loyal. In short, "reason" does not exist outside of one's mind.

Chu Hsi said that what one can and should learn is twofold: "mind" and

21 This is a letter which Wang Shou-jen wrote to one of his friends. See *Yang-ming ch'uan-hsi lu,* roll 2.

22 The term "later scholars" (*hou ju*) was often used derogatively to describe those who, in the author's opinion, did not understand, or had misinterpreted, the meaning of Confucianism. It is almost synonymous with the term "my academic opponents." It appears often in philosophical writings from the Sung dynasty on.

23 *Hsing.*

24 *Li.*

"reason." Though "mind" exists within an individual, it is the controlling organ of all reasons in the universe. "Reasons" are scattered in all things, but they do not exist outside the "mind" of an individual. Outwardly "mind" and "reason" are separated; they are in fact united. Their outward separation leads scholars to the belief that they are two different entities. . . . Their misconception arises from the fact that they do not understand that "mind" is in fact "reason" itself.

42 · KU YEN-WU: *A Letter to a Friend* [25]

Lately, as I have travelled between the North and the South, my friends have been generous enough to speak kindly of whatever knowledge or understanding I might have. They honored me by asking me many questions. This was like asking a blind man to give road directions; how could he possibly give the right answers?

For more than one hundred years scholars have spoken frequently of "mind" and "nature," but none of them has been able to give these words clear definitions. We know that Confucius seldom spoke of "fate" and "benevolence" [26] and that Tzu-kung never heard the Master [27] discussing the meanings of "nature" or "the way of Heaven." . . . Yen Yüan, who was almost as sage as Confucius himself, maintained that extensive reading was the key to knowledge and, in replying to an inquiry from Duke Ai,[28] said that "the prerequisite to the performance of good deeds is the broadening of knowledge." Next to Tseng-tzu no man among Confucius' disciples was more honest and sincere than Tzu-hsia. Yet, when he was asked to define *jen,* he said that "a man of *jen* should be broad in knowledge in order to strengthen his will and should be inquisitive in order to refine his own thought."

The gentlemen of our day are notably different. They gather around themselves scores or even hundreds of scholars and students in the same manner as grass and trees of similar species have congregated. They all talk about "mind" and "nature." They hope to find an all-embracing theory to substitute for knowledge and experience. They discuss among themselves such things as the theory of all truths concentrating in a single, small "oneness," while ignoring the grinding poverty around them and throughout the empire. They seem to think that their minds are superior to that of Confucius and that their disciples are more virtuous than Tzu-kung. They are obviously convinced that they can by-pass the Sage of Eastern Lu [29] and receive their inspirations directly from the Two Emperors.[30] What can I say of people like these?

Confucius seldom talked about "nature," "fate," and "heaven"; yet these words are constantly on the lips of our scholars today. Confucius and Mencius spoke constantly of proper conduct; our scholars today rarely mention them. Modern scholars say that "loyalty" and "purity" [31] cannot be said to be close to *jen;* they

---

[25] The Chinese original appears in *A Collection of Writings of Ancient and Modern Times (Ku chin wen tsung),* vol. 8.
[26] *Jen.*
[27] Confucius.
[28] The ruler of the state of Lu at the time of Confucius.
[29] Confucius.
[30] Yao and Shun.
[31] *Chung* and *ch'ing.*

do not know that *jen* cannot exist in a person who does not possess these two virtues. What can I say of people like these?

What, then, is my concept of the way of the sage? A gentleman who follows this concept is broad in knowledge and righteous in conduct. His field of learning covers all that is needed to be known: from knowledge related to him as a person to that beneficial to the nation and the world. Everything that deals with social relationships and personal conduct is the field of his learning. You may also call it a field of learning that centers around the word "shamefulness." How important this word "shamefulness" is! A gentleman should not be ashamed of the poor food which he has to eat or the poor clothing which he has to wear; he should be ashamed of the fact that people do not benefit from his existence in this world. When our ancient sage says that "All truths are complete within me" and "Sincerity comes about as a result of self-examination and self-criticism," [32] this is exactly what he means.

A scholar who does not have a strong sense of shamefulness is a man without principles. Likewise, a field of learning which is unrelated to the ancient classics and is not based upon broad experience is empty and meaningless. Nowadays we have unprincipled scholars engaged in meaningless pursuit. The more they continue their pursuit, the further will they be away from the teachings of our sages.

I may have been too pretentious by saying what I have said. But this is my humble opinion, and I submit it to my friends for whatever it is worth.

43 · YEN YÜAN: *Flowers in the Mirror* [33]

Acquiring knowledge about the worldly phenomena has been cleverly described as acquiring knowledge about "flowers in the mirror and the moon in the water." The so-called enlightenment entertained by the Sung-Ming School [34] is really an enlightenment of this sort. I do not mean that there is no enlightenment like this in Buddhism; nor do I mean that only Buddhists can achieve this type of enlightenment. The idea I try to convey is that the "water and mirror" which people say they understand are really useless, and the "flowers and the moon" which they compare to the worldly phenomena are also useless. Many scholars do not realize this uselessness and, like withered Ch'an Buddhists,[35] spend half their lifetime laboriously pursuing it. Why is it that these people continue to deceive themselves?

Man's mind is like water. As long as it is not muddled by earth and sand and is not disturbed by wind and stone, water can reflect all things in the world. Clean and settled water can reflect whether it is collected in such small places as a gutter or a basin, or in such large places as mountains and seas. It is said that to see the worldly phenomena in terms of "flowers in the mirror and the moon in the water," a person needs to be respectful and serene, and his mind should be neither disturbed by worldly affairs nor sidetracked by unrelated thoughts. In this way, we are told, he can achieve his purpose in less than one hundred days if he is talented, and in a period of three to five years if he is not. When the final

[32] These two remarks come from Mencius.
[33] This selection is taken from a treatise entitled "The Preservation of Man" *(Ts'un jen)*.
[34] Neo-Confucianism.
[35] See pp. 75–83.

goal is supposed to have been achieved after long, arduous work, he happily congratulates himself. He claims that he can foretell the future or conduct telepathy. Once in a while his claims might be verified, and he becomes more boastful in using his magic power to impress others. His reputation begins to spread, and people say that he has acquired "The Way."

Before I was thirty-four I used to follow the teachings of the Sung School, learning to sit and meditate. I am fully aware of the experience that has been described above. From my personal experience I know that this knowledge through "sitting and meditating" is false and absurd. It is totally unreliable.

Is there such a thing in the world as an unmoving water? Is there such a water which does not attach itself to the ground, is completely clear of earth and sand, and is immune from the disturbance caused by wind? As long as it is attached to the ground, it cannot reflect correctly the physical world because, at one time or another, it is bound to make some kind of movement. . . . Those who play with flowers in the mirror or the moon in the water might be able to amuse their eyes or minds. But where would be the moon and the flowers, had the water and the mirror been taken away from them? The life of "mirror and water" which they pursue is really a life of self-deception. Is it possible that they can use the moon in the water for the purpose of illumination or take the flowers from the mirror to make a corsage? The more people talk about the state of abstraction, the more confused they become. As their contemplation and meditation become more profound and consequently less comprehensible, their pretensions also become more absurd.

44 · TAI CHEN: *A Letter to P'eng Yung-ch'u* [36]

The basic motive of the Taoists for achieving an earthly immortality is selfishness; so is the Buddhist motive for attaining an eternal life after death. In each case they deplore their own extinction and strive to achieve their selfish ends through the so-called elimination of desires. Mencius said: "A large territory and a large population are a gentleman's true desires." [37] He also said that to achieve distinction in life is the common desire of all men. "I desire fish, but I also desire bear's palm," [38] he remarked in another occasion; "I love life, but I also love righteousness." We do not find these concepts in Taoist or Buddhist ideology. On the contrary, the Taoists and Buddhists are only concerned with their spirits after they die and take precautions in life to make sure that their spirits will live forever.

The Sung scholars, subject to the unhealthy influence of Taoism and Buddhism, have advocated the so-called elimination of desires. They contend that righteousness, though desirable, is really the essence of Tao or Heavenly reason, and that besides the essence of Tao or Heavenly reason there is the essence of man which

---

[36] Yung-ch'u was the courtesy name of P'eng Shao-sheng, a brilliant scholar in eighteenth-century China. Though an expert on the Sung-Ming philosophy ("Neo-Confucianism"), he was formally converted to Buddism at the age of twenty-nine. This letter from Tai Chen appears in *Works of Tai Tung-yüan (Tai Tung-yüan chi),* roll 8.

[37] By this, Mencius means that a gentleman desires a large kingdom to put into practice Confucian precepts so as to bring about a moral commonwealth on earth.

[38] Bear's palm was an ancient Chinese delicacy.

is interpreted as human desires. They believe that there is an inherent incompatibility between Tao or Heavenly reason on the one hand and human desires on the other.

What is a human desire? It is a means whereby life can continue to propagate life and whereby life can become more beautiful and complete. What is a human emotion? It originates from the naturalness of man which, expressed in its outward forms, becomes, among other things, the recognition of differences between those to whom we are close and those from whom we are remote, between the elders and the young, and between the superiors and the inferiors. What is reason? It is a means to differentiate the sphere of desire and the sphere of emotion so that both can be successfully fulfilled without one infringing upon the other and so that, subtle though the difference between these two is, it is made clear and distinct.

In this matter of human desires, our fault lies more often in their over-indulgence than in their under-fulfillment. A man who over-indulges in fulfilling his desires becomes a captive of his own selfishness and neglects to take into consideration the harm such over-indulgence causes to others. His mind becomes insensitive, and his action is subject to error. That is why Mencius said that "There is no better way of cultivating mind than the reduction of desires."

As for human emotions, our fault lies in the fact that they are often inadequately expressed, though we should keep in mind that over-expressing them is equally bad. When they are expressed in an improper manner, not only should we be concerned with the possibility that they might have been over-expressed, but should also make a thorough examination of ourselves so that whatever errors we have made, in either of the two directions, will be corrected.

Desires, when they are not confounded with selfishness, are compatible with the concept of *jen*. By no means are they an antithesis of righteousness as long as their fulfillment is not that of a perverted nature which brings harm to others. Emotions, when properly expressed, are an indication of harmony, within oneself as well as in one's relationships with others. In short, the fulfillment of desires and the expression of emotions are Heavenly reasons as long as they are done in a proper manner. What is the nature of Heaven [39] then? It is a state of infallibility within oneself before desires and emotions are outwardly expressed. We cannot make a clear distinction between the nature of Heaven and Heavenly reasons on the one hand and desires and emotions on the other. They are in fact inseparable.

You, sir, quoted Ch'eng Hao [40] by saying that the constant and unchangeable emotion of all sages is the lack of emotions towards all things around them, and that the learning purpose of every gentleman is to be broad in mind and selfless in attitude, so that he can face with ease and magnanimity whatever is coming to him. You said that this is the real meaning of the elimination of desires. If you allow me, sir, I would like to quote Wang Yang-ming [41] to prove to you to what school of thought your idea really belongs.

"The substance of innate knowledge can be compared to a bright, dustless mirror," says Wang Yang-ming. "It reflects all objects before it, whether they are beautiful or ugly, good or bad. After these objects have been moved away from it, no traces are left behind on the mirror which remains as bright as ever. This

[39] *T'ien hsing.*
[40] Ch'eng Hao (1031–1085) was a philosopher of the Sung dynasty.
[41] Yang-ming was the courtesy name of Wang Shou-jen.

is what I mean when I say that a gentleman is capable of facing whatever is coming to him with ease and magnanimity and is totally devoid of emotions." The Buddhists say that the mind arises from a detached ground. The mirror which reflects all objects exactly as they are is a Buddhist mind, and the concept of "leaving no traces behind on the mirror" is the same as that of the Buddhist "detached ground." Ch'eng Hao talks about the sages, and Wang Yang-ming, on the other hand, speaks of Buddhism. That is the reason, I believe, why you quoted the former instead of the latter. But permit me to say, sir, that your basic ideas are closer to Wang's than to Ch'eng's.

Wang Yang-ming turned Chu Hsi's chronology upside down by saying that Chu Hsi's ideas were different from those of Lu Chiu-yüan at the beginning but became the same towards the end. Lu Chiu-yüan and Wang Yang-ming honored Taoist and Buddhist ideologies, while Ch'eng Hao and Chu Hsi refuted them. Now, sir, you are honoring not only the Lu-Wang School but Taoism and Buddhism as well. Moreover, you combine them with the teachings of Confucius, Mencius, Ch'eng Hao, and Chu Hsi as if they were the same. I would like to remind you, sir, that not only should Confucius and Mencius not be slandered but Ch'eng Hao and Chu Hsi also deserve a better treatment. Furthermore, as you continue to misinterpret Taoist and Buddhist teachings, I submit that the Taoists and Buddhists will protest too, since they might consider themselves equally slandered.

"How much difference is there between 'ah' and 'chih'?" [42] said Lao-tzu; "how much difference is there between good and evil?" "Human nature is neither good nor bad," said Kao-tzu; "righteousness is not inherent with man; it is an acquired attribute." "Think of neither good nor evil," said the Buddhists; "what one should do is to look at one's native self." "Evil can harm one's mind; so can goodness," said Lu Chiu-yüan. "Mind by itself is neither good nor evil," said Wang Yang-ming. All of these people do not emphasize the importance of goodness.

You, sir, have gone even further than the gentlemen whose words are quoted above. You said that only the form of a thing can live and die and that its spirit never will. Consequently it is sheer nonsense to talk about births and deaths, and the most wonderful thing about all objects in the universe is, as you have stated, that they neither emerge into nor pass away from existence. You further stated that there are no such things as "arrival" and "departure," or "appearance" and "reality." You quoted Ch'eng Hao by saying that Heaven and man are really one inseparable reality and that it is senseless to talk about the harmony of these two. You called this reality "essence" [43] which is as voiceless as it is odorless. It is also the wish of Heaven in its eternal state, you added, which becomes more substantial through the ceaseless, total sincerity on the part of man. It is the way of Heaven in its never-ending evolution towards the absolute good, you concluded, that is being pushed forward by man's complete, unconditional goodness.

If you allow me, sir, I would like to quote Wang Yang-ming to show you to which of the schools your ideas really belong.

"The concept of innate knowledge is indivisible," said Wang Yang-ming. "It can be characterized as godly insofar as its application is concerned. It can be

---

[42] "Ah" and "chih" are particles used at the beginning or end of a sentence. They are not translatable.
[43] Pen.

called vitality [44] if we take into consideration the freedom with which it circulates." "The concept of original truth [45] in Buddhist ideology is the same as that of innate knowledge in Confucian teachings," he continued. "Knowledge in the Confucian teachings arises from the investigation of objects or things as they appear. The Buddhists, on the other hand, emphasize the importance of constant vigilance as a means to preserve their original truth. The goal is the same, though the means to achieve it are somewhat different."

The investigation of objects comes to mean, in the mind of Wang Yang-ming, the building of a defensive wall against outward objects, and the "investigation of objects as they appear" is interpreted to mean constant vigilance in the elimination of desires. The so-called constant vigilance is also invoked by Chu Hsi as the means to preserve Heavenly reasons. Furthermore, he uses it to interpret such terms as "precautions" [46] and "fearfulness," [47] which appear in the *Doctrine of the Mean*. But he completely misunderstood the true meanings of these terms. Wang Yang-ming, following the same path, quoted the *Doctrine of the Mean* to elaborate his "original truth." "To cultivate our virtues and to cultivate our bodies are really the same thing," he said. "If we are precautious enough not to see and fearful enough not to hear and concentrate all of our energy on one purpose and one purpose alone, we can preserve all goodness within ourselves—godliness, vitality, and spirit.[48] The Taoist concept of eternal life cannot be more than this."

Chuang-tzu's advocacy of "returning to the beginning," the Buddhist concept of original truth, and Wang Yang-ming's idea of innate knowledge are basically the same thing: the attainment of self-preservation as well as self-sufficiency. When a person thinks in terms of self-sufficiency, he cannot help being egoistic. There are miles of difference between this egoistic self-sufficiency and the ideas advanced in the *Doctrine of the Mean,* such as "holding goodness tight whenever it is found," "broad learning followed by inquisitiveness and inquiry," and "careful reasoning, discriminating judgements, and finally, energetic and ceaseless action."

"There is no greater joy than to find sincerity within me after I have thoroughly examined myself," said Mencius; "I cannot please even my own parents if there is a lack of sincerity with me." Thus both Mencius and the author of the *Doctrine of the Mean* [49] emphasized the point that without knowing where goodness is, one cannot be sincere with himself. It is totally absurd to suggest that the elimination of desires can be a substitute for the knowledge of goodness as a source of sincerity. It is permissible, however, that those who emphasize the inner mind as a source of knowledge should interpret "original truth" to mean the ability of discerning goodness, though such an interpretation may have deviated a little from its original meaning. Both Lao-tzu and Kao-tzu, while belittling goodness as something beneath their serious concern, still recognized that there was such a word as "goodness." The later scholars corrupt this word to such an extent that

[44] *Ch'i.*
[45] *Pen-lai mien-mu.*
[46] *Chiai-shen.*
[47] *K'ung-chü.*
[48] *Shen, ch'i,* and *ching.*
[49] Tradition attributes the authorship of the *Doctrine of the Mean* to Tzu-ssu, a grandson of Confucius.

they in fact do not even recognize its existence. This is particularly true today. The virtue of theirs is not virtue in its truest sense. They corrupt other terms besides, such as "nature," "Heavenly ways," "sagehood," "wisdom," "love," "righteousness," "sincerity," "goodness," "fate," and "knowledge." They use the same words but change their meanings.

What is meant by "the lack of sincerity after one has thoroughly examined oneself?" It means that the person in question has not exhausted his ways of serving his parents. What is meant by "the possession of sincerity after one has thoroughly examined oneself?" It means that after relentless self-criticisms he finds that he has exhausted his ways of serving his parents. Mencius said: "Yao and Shun were the embodiment of nature; T'ang and Wu [50] expressed it; and the Five Autocrats [51] only corrupted it. The Five Autocrats disguised themselves under its name for such a long time that even they themselves did not know that they did not possess it. Nature is expressed in loving and righteous conduct, and our physical body should be the very embodiment of love and righteousness. Those who use the names of love and righteousness in a dishonest manner for the simple purpose of winning arguments tend to blame others for the lack of these two virtues, while forgetting it is they themselves who do not possess them." "Yao and Shun were the true embodiment of nature, while T'ang and Wu were just the opposite," said he on another occasion. "There is no higher virtue than to speak and conduct oneself in the most proper manner." This is what Mencius meant by nature.

He further stated that the purpose of sorrowful mourning is not to impress the living; that the cultivation of virtue is not to serve as a convenient stepstone to officialdom; and that the purpose of keeping promises is not merely to rectify personal conduct, important though it is. A gentleman follows all of these rules simply because he wishes to observe the law of nature while waiting for his own fate to materialize. He examines his own person regardless of the situation outside of himself, and he does whatever he should do without an ulterior motive or purpose. Moreover, he strengthens himself by constant self-criticism. From these statements it is obvious that Mencius was not interested in discussing human nature in its original state. If he were, he would not have said such things as "not to impress the living," "not to serve as a convenient stepstone to officialdom," "not merely to rectify personal conduct," and finally, "waiting for his own fate to materialize." Throughout these statements one thing that was foremost in his mind was self-examination or self-criticism. It serves no purpose to misuse his words for one's own ends. Permit me to say, sir, that your ideas come from Lao-tzu, Chuang-tzu, Buddha, Lu Chiu-yüan, and Wang Yang-ming; yet you quote copiously from the *Six Classics,* Confucius, Mencius, the Ch'eng brothers,[52] and Chu Hsi.

If you love truth as obviously you do, the truth is far from what you have stated. If you regard the teachings of Lao-tzu, Chuang-tzu, Buddha, Lu Chiu-yüan, and Wang Yang-ming as the truth, why do you not specifically say so since their words and meanings have been clearly recorded for all to see? If you only wish

[50] Founders of Shang and Chou dynasties respectively.
[51] The Five Autocrats (*wu pa*) were Duke Huan of Ch'i, Duke Wen of Tsin, Duke Mu of Ch'in, Duke Hsiang of Sung, and King Chuang of Ch'u, all of whom lived during the Spring and Autumn period (722–481 B.C.).
[52] Ch'eng Hao and Ch'eng Yi (1032–1107).

to use their names for your own purpose, I shall understand because others have done this before. I think that you will agree with me on this point when you read Chu Hsi's letter to Ho Shu-ching.

I have noticed in your writings that you refute the Ch'eng brothers and Chu Hsi whenever they dispute the teachings of Taoism and Buddhism. On the other hand, you do not hesitate to quote them whenever they agree with you. Their ideas with which you have expressed agreement are those in their early writings when, for the time being, they were enchanted with Buddhism. Their words which you have invoked to support your own case are either those in their early writings or those which, though written in a later period, resemble, though remotely, those of yours. The truth which you really love is the Buddhist truth; yet you do not wish to use the name of Buddhism, a name which you detest. Tell me, sir, which of the two men is less sincere, the man who loves the content of an ideology while detesting its name or the man who uses its name while disagreeing with its content.

You have stated that the purpose of knowledge is to recognize the difference between good and evil and to differentiate sincerity from falsehood. I, for one, sincerely hope that you will follow your own advice. If, in seeking truth, you work as diligently as the Ch'eng brothers and Chu Hsi and entertain no selfish motive that inspires such an effort, you will find that the ideas which these gentlemen have advocated are entirely different from those of Taoism and Buddhism or those of Lu Chiu-yüan and Wang Yang-ming, even though at the present moment you believe that there is great similarity between the first and the latter two groups. My real hope for you, sir, goes even beyond this.

The Ch'eng brothers and Chu Hsi stated that "reason" comes from Heaven but is embodied in the mind of man; they spoke as if "reason" were a concrete object. They paved the way for all those in later years who consider every opinion of theirs "reason," however prejudicial it really is, and use their "reason" as a weapon to bring harm to others. As their "reason" is further mixed up with the so-called elimination of desires, it moves further away from the true "reason." The more they adhere to their private opinion which they call "reason," the more harmful it will be to others. "Reason" per se is not a bad thing; the harm arises from the fact that people mistake their private opinion for "reason." In fact, a private opinion that comes from the mind of an individual and is totally divorced from good common sense should be regarded and treated as such. The doctrinaire scholars, following the dictate of their own minds, not only fail to know that the change of names connotes the change of contents but also fight over the use of certain semantics at the expense of contents. An alert person cannot fail to see that while using different names, these scholars really teach the same thing. A man whose eyesight is failing can see only the broad outline of an object in front of him. Since the object resembles what he believes it is, he calls that object by a wrong name. As far as he is concerned, the name corresponds correctly to the object, even though it does not.

A man who imitates another man's appearance inevitably winds up embracing his beliefs as well. If we are humble enough to study diligently the *Six Classics* and the teachings of Confucius and Mencius, in due course when progress is being made, we will find that Confucianism is entirely different from Taoism and Buddhism not only in content but in appearance as well. One simply cannot be mistaken for the other. Scholars who try to camouflage Taoism and Buddhism under a cloak of Confucianism cannot and will not deceive us. I hope that you, sir, will make the effort to differentiate them. . . .

45 · LIU OH: *All Religions Teach the Same Thing* [53]

"As for this Mr. Huang whom I have just met," said Tzu-p'ing, "is he a Taoist or a Buddhist? He talks like a Taoist, and yet he quotes Buddhist scriptures."

"Mr. Huang is neither a Taoist nor a Buddhist," replied the girl. "He dresses the way as he pleases. He often says that the three major religions, Confucianism, Buddhism, and Taoism, are like three separate stores selling the same products, and the only difference between them is that Confucianism, being a much larger store, sells some products which the other two stores do not sell. He also says that every religion has two facets, the ritualistic and the real, and that the basic teachings of the three religions are the same, even though they look different in appearance. Mr. Huang believes in all three of them."

"This is very interesting," said Tzu-p'ing. "If the three religions teach the same thing as you have just stated, what is this 'same thing'? Is or is there not any difference between them? Why did you say that Confucianism is more broadly based than either of the other two religions?"

"Insofar as all of these three religions teach people to be good and just, they are the same," the girl replied. "If all of us are just and selfless, there will be peace on earth, otherwise chaos will rule the world. Of all religions in the world, Confucianism is the most selfless. Look at Confucius. Throughout his life there were many people who criticized him on ideological grounds. Yet he praised them highly because, as a result of their criticisms, they, Confucius believed, had enlightened him. Confucianism is great precisely because it does not believe in religious bigotry. 'To attack others who do not agree with you is to bring harm to yourself,' says Confucius. The Buddhists or Taoists, on the other hand, are bigoted and selfish. Fearful that other people will not follow their religion, they invented such things as paradise and hell to intimidate them. You might say that end justifies means: since the purpose of their invention is to induce people to be good, they can be still regarded as selfless. However, when they go beyond this point (as they do) and announce to the world that a person will be automatically cleansed of his sins when converted to their faith, or that he will be forever condemned and will inevitably go to hell if he refuses conversion, they become bigoted and selfish. Nowadays there are the Western religions that have gone further in bigotry than Buddhism and Taoism. They not only intimidate people with such nonsense as heaven and hell; they also teach their followers to hate people of other religions and urge them to declare war on what they call pagans. The more they kill, the more they will become religious. How low a man can sink! As for the Muslims, they say that the blood shed by the faithful in waging holy wars against the infidels is as beautiful as a purple jewel. They probably think that all people in the world are simply fools."

"The true meaning of Confucianism has been lost for a long time," the girl continued. "The Han scholars were so occupied with the syntax of the *Classics* [54] that they forgot the true meaning of the *Classics*. During the T'ang dynasty people

[53] This selection is taken from *The Travels of Lao-ts'an (Lao-ts'an yu-chi)*, Chapter 9.
[54] Confucian Classics.

did not even care for the syntax, let alone the meanings of the *Classics*. As far as understanding Confucianism was concerned, Han Yü was really an illiterate. The more he wrote, the more confused he became. Some of the things he said were absolutely nonsense. He said, for instance, that 'the primary function of a king is to give orders' and that 'if people do not produce things to support their king, they should be executed.' Even the worst tyrants know how to give orders and kill people. According to Han Yü, these tyrants would be always right and the people would be always wrong. Black to him was white, and white was really black. He denounced Buddhism and Taoism, and yet some of his best friends were Buddhist monks.

"After Han Yü the situation became even worse. Instead of searching for the true meaning of Confucianism, the later scholars only shouted slogans. They cried aloud 'Down with Buddhism and Taoism' and considered themselves good Confucians. Even a man like Chu Hsi did not succeed in freeing himself from this narrow-mindedness. He interpreted Confucianism according to Han Yü instead of Confucius. The more he twisted, the less consistent he became. After the Sung scholars' interpretations, Confucianism was as good as dead."

Tzu-p'ing was immensely impressed. "One conversation with you, young lady, is worth more than ten years of study. Frankly, I have never heard a presentation like this before. Tell me, who are more heretical from the Confucian point of view, Confucius' contemporary critics or modern Taoists and Buddhists?"

"They are all heretical," the girl replied. "The word 'heretics' [55] literally means 'strange extremes.' A heretic is a person who only sees the virtue of his own extremist point of view and is completely blind to other people's ideas. A Confucian does not object to heretical points of view, let alone denouncing them. He only suggests that to know the truth, a person should take into full consideration the points of view at both ends of the ideological spectrum. In fact, there is nothing wrong with heresey at all, as long as its goal is to induce people to be just and good. There are different roads leading to one destination, and one is perhaps as good as the other. This is what our sages meant when they said that the 'great virtue' should be the same while the 'small virtue' could be different. It is wrong to attack other ideologies simply because they are different. The later Confucians first attacked Buddhism and Taoism, and then, during the ideological debate between Chu Hsi and Lu Chiu-yüan, they also attacked their fellow Confucians. How could they attack each other since both sides claimed that they were the disciples of Confucius and Mencius? They had lost their true selves and consequently, to quote Confucius, had brought damage to themselves."

While the girl was speaking, Tzu-p'ing repeatedly expressed his approval. "I am extremely fortunate to have met you, young lady," said he, "and you are one of the best teachers I have ever had. It is doubtless true that the Sung scholars misinterpreted Confucius in some respects. Do you not think that they made great contributions in clarifying some of the hitherto obscure points? For instance, though the words 'reason,' 'desire,' 'reverence,' and 'sincerity' had been mentioned by our ancient sages, it was they, the Sung scholars, who clarified their meanings for us and consequently brought benefit to us in a moral as well as ideological sense. In fact, we know better how to conduct our personal lives as a result of these contributions."

[55] *Yi-tuan.*

The girl smiled and, turning to Tzu-p'ing, cast an inviting glance. Suddenly he saw in her long, narrow eyebrows thousands of charms and in her thin, red lips millions of enchantments. A faint fragrance that seemed to have only possibly come from a flower garden penetrated into his skin and then his bones. He could not control himself, and his spirit had left his body, wafting away into the air. He saw her beautiful arm, white as jade, and her delicate hand, soft as fresh cotton, which was then stretching out to reach his. Holding his hand, the girl said: "Dear sir, how do you compare my holding of your hand with that of your teacher before he proceeds to beat you for your failure to complete your working assignment?"

Tzu-p'ing was silent. "At this moment, dear sir, please tell me which one you really love: your teacher who teaches you how to live a moral life or me, a girl. Our sage is correct when he says that the prerequisite to sincerity is the elimination of self-deception. Love what you really want to love, and detest what you should detest. Confucius says: 'Love virtue to the same extent as you would love a beautiful woman.' Mencius says: 'Food and sex are the two basic desires of man.' Since the love of sex is a basic desire of man, the Sung scholars only deceived themselves when they said that man should love virtue and virtue alone. They tried to deceive others; they only succeeded in deceiving themselves. They were hypocritical; yet they repeatedly emphasized the importance of sincerity. Our sages talked about 'emotions' and 'propriety'; the Sung scholars, on the other hand, spoke constantly of 'reason' and 'desires.' In fact, the very first passage in the *Book of Odes* deals with sex. It says:

> Beautiful is the young lass
> Whom a gentleman truly desires.
> Reach her he cannot;
> Tossing to and fro,
> Sleepless he is throughout the night.

"What does this poem speak of: 'heavenly reason' or 'human desire'? All that the sages want us to do is to satisfy our emotions through proper channels. Emotions are natural with man, and it would be foolish to try to eliminate them. Today, sir, you have had a long day's journey and should have been very tired at this moment. Yet, you are as full of spirit and energy as a man can possibly be. I do not have to be a very intelligent person to know that at this moment you are as pleased with me as I am pleased with you. How can we expect anything otherwise since the attraction of the opposite sex is part of our human emotion that is born with us? Here we are, a young man and a young woman who sit and face each other in the middle of the night. Yet we do not say anything that can be characterized as indecent, and we conduct ourselves within the sphere of propriety. This, I believe, is what our sages want us to do. The Sung scholars made too many ridiculous remarks to be enunciated here; and yet they are right sometimes. Today's scholars who try to follow their path are much worse. If Confucius and Mencius were living today, they would certainly condemn and disown these hypocrites."

At this moment a servant came in with tea. The conversation was temporarily interrupted. . . .

Part II

Government

CHAPTER SEVEN

Government in Theory

THE term that is often used to express the political ideal of a Confucian society is *Ta-t'ung,* variously translated as Great Commonwealth or Great Society. A brief description of this society appears in the *Book of Rites,* one of the Confucian classics (Selection 46).

To the ancient Chinese the establishment of a good government meant the employment of virtuous officials, rather than sound institutions or good laws. Since the emperor was the Son of Heaven ultimately responsible for the welfare of the nation, the Confucians believed that he should be the most virtuous of all the virtuous, setting a personal example for all of his subjects to follow. As a sovereign, one of his most important duties was to recruit virtuous officials to help him to rule (Selection 47). In recruiting government officials or administering justice, he should be absolutely impartial (Selection 48).

Believing that he was installed by Heaven to rule on its behalf, a conscientious emperor such as Han Wen-ti (r. 179–157 B.C.) considered himself personally responsible when a natural disaster struck or an unusual natural phenomenon occurred (Selections 49 and 50). In either case, he should examine himself to see what mistakes he had made that caused Heaven to be wrathful with him.

Most emperors in Chinese history, however, were not so conscientious as to take seriously the theory of the mandate of Heaven. During the later periods one of the monarchs who came close to the ancient ideal was T'ang T'ai-tsung (r. 650–683) who, more than anyone else, was responsible for the founding of the T'ang dynasty, one of the golden ages in Chinese history (Selection 52). Monarchs like T'ang T'ai-tsung were more an exception than a rule, and most Chinese monarchs were primarily interested in maintaining the security of their crown and the continuance of their personal comfort.

This backsliding from the ancient ideals prompted a scholar like Huang Tsung-hsi (1610–1695) to reassert the theory that the primary function of the king was to serve the people and that no king in the world had the right to exploit his subjects for his personal benefit (Selection 53). A minister was to be the king's teacher or friend, and he lost his usefulness as a public official once he was treated like (or regarded himself as) a personal servant (Selection 54). Though there was nothing new in what he said, Huang Tsung-hsi was hailed as a courageous man by his contemporaries because, living in an age of despotism, he could easily have been thrown into jail for his "treasonable" remarks.

The absolutism of Chinese monarchy resulted partly from the necessity of maintaining effective control over all parts of China through a highly centralized administrative system. From time to time people raised questions regarding the soundness of this system, but to a scholar like Liu Tsung-yüan (773–819) whatever disadvantages it might have had were more than offset by its advantages (Selection 55).

Did a Chinese owe loyalty to a ruler who was not a Chinese? Twice in its history China was completely conquered by foreigners, first by the Mongols in the thirteenth century and again by the Manchus in the seventeenth century. In 1727 a group of Chinese, who did not believe that an alien ruler had any right to rule China, engineered a plot ostensibly aimed at the overthrow of the Manchu regime. Upon the discovery of the plot and the arrest of the conspirators, the reigning emperor Yung-cheng issued a decree that was meant to be a final answer to this question (Selection 56).

Other Chinese, however, continued to disagree. During the Taiping Rebellion (1851–1864) the question was again raised and the Taipings, as expected, answered it with an emphatic "no" (Selection 57). But to Tseng Kuo-fan (1811–1872), a Confucian scholar who was then charged with the responsibility of suppressing the rebellion, the word "Chinese" was more a cultural than a racial term and the Taipings, by embracing an alien religion called Christianity, were definitely "barbarian" (Selection 58). Most Chinese tended to agree with him, and the Taiping Rebellion was suppressed.

46 · ANONYMOUS: *Greater and Lesser Ideals* [1]

When the Great Way permeates the world, the world belongs to all of its members. The government is in the hands of the virtuous and the able, and the people maintain friendly and faithful relationships among themselves. A man loves not only his own parents and children but others' as well. The aged are cared for, the able-bodied have work, and the young are properly raised. Widows, widowers, orphans, the incurably ill, and the crippled—all of them are adequately supported. All men have wives, and all women have husbands. Viewing goods as if they were worthless, people do not hoard them for profit. Viewing their own ability as if it did not belong to them, they use it to the benefit of others. Plotting and scheming do not arise, and there are no such things as thievery and robbery. The front door need not be closed, day or night. This is the Great Society.

When the Great Way does not prevail, each man considers only his own relatives his family. He loves his own parents and children and works only for his own benefit. Rulers are hereditary; walls and moats are constructed to strengthen defense. Such virtues as propriety and righteousness are introduced as the ideal to follow, so that the relationship between king and ministers will be proper, that

---

[1] This selection, entitled *Ta-t'ung hsiao-k'ang* in Chinese, appears in the *Book of Rites.*

between father and sons will be sincere, that among brothers and sisters will be amiable, and that between husband and wife will be harmonious. The same virtues also underlie the organization of political institutions, the governing of land tenure, and the management of a neighborhood. A man will be recognized for his achievements and receive credit which is his due. Plotting and scheming arise; so does warfare. A society of this kind produces men like Yü, T'ang, King Wen, King Wu, and Duke Chou, all of whom were extremely careful in observing proper rules. A good man enjoys fame for his righteous conduct, and no man is regarded as trustworthy unless his truthfulness has been proven. A wrongdoing is made known for people to avoid, and all people are taught the virtue of love and modesty as a normal course to follow. Those who do not follow this course will be dismissed if they are government officials, and will be severely punished if they are common people. This is the Lesser Society.

47 · Tzu-ssu: *The Essence of Government* [2]

Duke Ai [3] asked about government, and Confucius replied to him as follows:

"As for the policies of King Wen and King Wu, they have been clearly recorded for all to see. A good policy continues as long as its originator lives; once he dies, his policy goes out with him. As fertile soil grows healthy trees, only good men can make good government. A good government is like a reed; it is easy to establish.

"The prerequisite to the establishment of a good government is the presence of good men. A good man follows certain rules in conducting his personal life, and one of these rules is *jen*. *Jen* deals with man's relationships with other men, and the most important of these relationships is that between parents and children. There is also the rule of righteousness in which one does what is regarded as proper and right. Of all things that one should do, none is more important than honoring the virtuous. To love in accordance with the closeness of the receiving person and to honor in accordance with the amount of virtue the honored possess—therein is the origin from which rites result.

"A gentleman should devote himself to the refinement of his character. To refine his character, he cannot but serve well his parents. To learn to serve his parents well, he has to know the nature of man. To know the nature of man, he has to know the way of Heaven.

"There are five forms in which the way of Heaven expresses itself, namely, the five relationships among men: relationships between king and subjects, father and son, husband and wife, elder and younger brothers, and finally, among friends. There are three virtues whereby these relationships can be correctly observed: wisdom, love, and courage. In short, action, or the lack of it, is the criterion upon which a man's success or failure in observing these relationships can be judged.

"There are three kinds of people in the world: those who are born with knowledge, those who acquire it through their own initiative, and those who acquire it through compulsion. Yet all of them acquire knowledge in the end. When knowledge is translated into action, again we see three kinds of people in the world:

[2] Translated from a section in the *Doctrine of the Mean*.
[3] Duke Ai, a contemporary of Confucius, was the ruler of the state of Lu.

those who act in a spontaneous, leisurely manner, those who act according to a well-planned procedure, and those who act under compulsion. It matters little how they proceed towards their goal; the important thing is that the goal be achieved."

"The love of learning is the beginning of knowledge," Confucius continued. "To act in vigor to implement what one believes is close to the meaning of love, and to feel a sense of shame is an act of courage. Understanding the truism of these statements, a man knows how to refine his own character. Knowing how to refine his own character, he knows how to govern other people. Knowing how to govern the people, he knows how to govern the nation and the world.

"There are nine virtues a king must possess if he wishes to run a successful government for the nation and the world. They are refinement of personal character, honoring the virtuous, love for parents, respect for high-ranking ministers, courtesy to all officials, treatment of all subjects as if they were the king's own children, encouraging artisans from every field of endeavor to come to his kingdom, winning the friendship of foreigners through kindness, and finally, commanding the vassals' fealty via gentleness and magnanimity.

"His character refined, a king will act according to accepted rules. Because he honors the virtuous, he will receive the best counsels and consequently will not be confused. Since he loves his parents, he will not become a target of complaints from his elders or younger brothers. Showing respect for high-ranking ministers, he will be wisely advised and will know what to do when an emergency arises. Being courteous to all officials, he will receive in return not only courtesy but also gratitude. Treating his subjects as if they were his own children, he will indirectly encourage more people to become his subjects. Encouraging artisans from every field of endeavor to come to his kingdom, he will have articles of all kinds and thus ensure his own economic sufficiency. When kindness is used as a weapon to win the friendship of foreigners, all foreigners will be happy to submit. Finally, when he treats his vassals with gentleness and magnanimity, his authority will be not only feared but also respected.

"To be dressed in a dignified manner and act properly is one of the ways to refine a king's character. To be distant from scandalmongers and beautiful women is as important as to honor virtues and minimize the importance of material goods, insofar as the encouragement of the virtuous is concerned. To inspire others to love their parents, a king should set an example by sharing his parents' likes and dislikes and by placing them on an elevated position where they will receive adequate financial support. A high-ranking official should be allowed to recruit his own personnel, however large it may be, and the best way of winning scholars is to provide them with a good salary, besides the trust and faith that are placed in them. Corvée duties are imposed only when people are not busy in the field; tax rates should be kept low at all times. As for the artisans, their products should be inspected daily and tested monthly: let them be well paid so that they can concentrate on and perform well their assigned tasks. To win foreigners with kindness, a king should see to it that they be treated with decorum when they arrive at or depart from his capital; they are to be commended when they conduct themselves well and to be denounced when they do not. As for the vassals, their lines of succession should be maintained, and their territories, if lost, should be returned to them. If chaos and anarchy threaten the position of a vassal in his state, the king should take the initiative to restore order. Besides, tribute missions to the capital and the king's inspection tours among the feudal domains should be conducted according to a definite schedule, and in all cases the gifts which the king gives to his vassals should be larger in value than the tribute which he has received from them. If the king does all of these things, it will be easy for him to win loyalty from his feudal subordinates.

"In short, it is the king's responsibility to translate these nine virtues into beneficial results.

"A task, to be successful, calls for planning. A speech, to be convincing, requires thoughtful reflection. Few difficulties will be encountered in carrying out a plan that has been scrupulously thought out, and no action will yield good results unless it has been thoughtfully begun. Before beginning a journey, make sure that you know where you are going.

"Those who do not enjoy the confidence of their superiors cannot successfully govern the people. Those who enjoy the confidence of their superiors but not that of their friends will cause their superiors to lose confidence in them. Those who enjoy the confidence of their friends but not that of their parents will cause their friends to lose confidence in them. Those who serve their parents well and enjoy their confidence will have to examine themselves as to whether they are truly sincere in their endeavor. If they are not, they will lose the confidence of their parents. No man can be truly sincere if he does not know the difference between good and evil, or right and wrong.

"Sincerity is the way of Heaven as well as that of man. With a sage who is born morally superior, it is expressed in the attainment of the Golden Mean, effortlessly and spontaneously achieved without premeditation. As for the rest of us, it means a constant search for moral goodness which, once found, should be held tightly for the rest of our lives.

"Learning, inquiry, reasoning, distinguishing, and finally, action—this is the procedure to be followed by a gentleman of moral persuasion. Learning should be as continuous as it is broad because by definition it has no end. Inquiry, once begun, generates more inquiries; the inquirer should not stop until he finds what he has set out to achieve. Likewise, reasoning is a continuous process, and distinguishing—the process whereby good can be differentiated from evil and right from wrong—serves no purpose until the answer that is sought becomes definite and clear. Knowing the answer, a gentleman applies it to the conduct of his life and will not cease doing so as long as he lives. A superior man may be able to achieve his goal the first time he attempts it; a less endowed person may have to try ten or more times before the same goal is achieved. It is through constant efforts that an ignorant person becomes wise and a weak man becomes strong."

48 · Lü Pu-wei: *Impartiality* [4]

Impartiality was the principle upon which our ancient sages successfully governed the country. Only when the principle of impartiality is carefully observed can there be peace and harmony among all citizens.

Looking at the *Book of Priorities*,[5] we find that numerous rulers have won or

[4] Translated from *Mr. Lü's Annals (Lü-shih ch'un-ch'iu)*, roll 1, written and compiled under the patronage of Lü Pu-wei. For more details about Lü Pu-wei, see pp. 138–141.
[5] *Book of Priorities* or *Shang-chih* was an ancient classic which has been long lost.

lost their countries. Without an exception, they won because of their belief in impartiality and lost because of their practice of the opposite. When Heaven installs a ruler, it chooses from those who are fair and just. Thus the *Grand Model* [6] says:

> Partiality the king does not have;
> Nor to any faction will he belong.
> The Way of Kings—
> How vast it is!
>
> The king being impartial,
> His wishes we shall observe.
> The king being unselfish,
> His ways we shall cherish.
> The king being merciful,
> His road we shall follow.

The world is not the world of any one person; it belongs to all of its members. The *yin* and the *yang* create all things in the universe with equal magnanimity; dews and rains, when they arrive, are impartial in bringing benefits to all plants on earth. Therefore, the king of all people should not show partiality for any particular person.

When Pai-ch'in [7] was about to leave the capital [8] to rule Lu,[9] he sought Duke Chou's advice. The Duke said: "The most important thing to remember is that you rule for the benefit of the people rather than for yourself."

A man in Ch'u lost his bow, but he chose not to search for it. When queried, he said: "A man of Ch'u lost it; a man of Ch'u will find it. Why should I search for it?" "This man is virtuous indeed," commented Confucius after he had heard this story; "would he be even more virtuous if he did not qualify the finder with the word 'Ch'u'?" "Would the story itself be improved further," commented Lao-tzu, "if the man did not insist that the finder had to be a member of the human species?" Lao-tzu was the most impartial of them all.

The greatness of Heaven and Earth lies in the fact that they create everything in the universe, and yet they appropriate nothing for themselves. Everything receives benefit from them and yet does not know where the benefit comes from. The virtue of the Three Emperors and Five Kings [10] was so great that every man received benefit from them and yet did not know where the benefit came from.

Kuan Chung [11] was ill, and Duke Huan went to see him.

"Sir, you are seriously ill," said the Duke. "Since the possibility of death has to be faced in a frank manner, I hope that you will not mind if I ask you whom you would recommend as your successor."

---

[6] *Grand Model* or *Hung-fan* is a chapter in the *Book of History*.

[7] A son of Duke Chou.

[8] Hao, the capital of West Chou, was located in modern Shensi province.

[9] Modern Shantung province.

[10] Ancient Chinese disagreed as to who the Three Emperors (*San huang*) were. One source says that they were Sui-jen, Fu-hsi, and Shen-nung. As for the Five Kings (*Wu ti* or Five Emperors), see Footnote 17, p. 29.

[11] The chief minister under Duke Huan of Ch'i (686–643 B.C.).

"I did not know enough about people even when I was hale. Now that I might die at any moment, what can I say?" Kuan Chung replied.

"The matter of deciding your successor is of great importance to me. Please help me with your advice," said the Duke.

Kuan Chung said "yes" with great respect.

"Whom would you recommend as your successor? Will Pao Shu-ya do?" asked the Duke.

"Pao Shu-ya and I have been great friends," said Kuan Chung, "but I will not recommend him.[12] He is upright and incorruptible, but he has no patience with those who are not so good as he is. He can never forgive a person who by chance has committed an error. If you cannot find anyone better, may I suggest Hsi P'eng? Hsi P'eng is humble enough to imitate others more virtuous than he is and to learn from those less knowledgeable than he is. Knowing that he is not so good as Huang-ti,[13] he is sympathetic towards those who are not so good as he is. There are many things which he has neither heard nor understood. There are men of talent in this country whom he does not even know. Yet, if you cannot find anyone better, may I still suggest that Hsi P'eng be my successor?"

The chief minister is the most important official in the nation. An official who has an important position does not concern himself with every detail; nor does he attempt to compete with others in small wisdom. A great carpenter does not cut wood himself; [14] nor does a great chef busy himself in the kitchen.[15] A brave man does not fight; a great army does not pillage.

At the beginning Duke Huan was impartial and forgiving; he did not allow his likes and dislikes to influence his judgement in matters of public concern. With Kuan Chung as his chief minister, he became the most powerful of the Five Autocrats.[16] Later in his life he let his personal feelings prevail over sound judgement; he trusted only those who knew how to flatter him. After he died and before he was even buried, his five sons fought over the vacated throne.

A man is ignorant when he is young. He becomes wise after he has become advanced in age. Yet it is preferable to be ignorant and impartial than to be wise and prejudiced. A drunkard cannot distinguish colors; a selfish man is too occupied with his own interest to know where justice is. Wearing a crown does not necessarily make one a king. A king is not a king if he is avaricious and cruel. . . .

Yao had ten sons; yet he designated Shun as his successor. Shun had nine sons; yet he designated Yü as his successor. Both emperors were extremely impartial because they chose virtuous men, instead of their children, as heirs apparent.

Duke P'ing of Tsin asked Ch'i Huang-yang: "The post of magistrate at Nan-yang [17] is vacant. Whom will you recommend to occupy it?"

"I would recommend Chieh Hu," Ch'i Huang-yang replied.

"Is it not true that Chieh Hu is a personal enemy of yours?"

"Sir, you asked me who was qualified to occupy the post at Nanyang. You did not ask me who my enemy was."

[12] For more details about the friendship between these two men, see pp. 369–370.
[13] Huang-ti or Yellow Emperor was a legendary ruler of China's remote past.
[14] He only designs.
[15] He only prepares the recipes.
[16] See Footnote 51, p. 102.
[17] Located in modern Shansi province.

Duke P'ing appointed Chieh Hu as the magistrate of Nanyang, and all people in the country were happy with the appointment.

Shortly afterwards, Duke P'ing asked Ch'i Huang-yang again: "We need a captain in charge of the palace guards. Whom would you recommend?"

"Wu is the right man for this position," Ch'i Huang-yang replied.

"Is it not true that Wu is your own son?"

"Your Excellency asked me who was the best qualified for the position. You did not ask me who my son was."

Duke P'ing appointed Wu as the captain of the palace guards, and all people in the country were happy with the appointment.

After Confucius heard this story, he commented: "Ch'i Huang-yang served well as the Duke's adviser. He recommended the best men for the posts, regardless of whether they were his sons or enemies. He was impartial indeed!"

Fu T'un, a disciple of Mo Ti, lived in Ch'in. One day his son committed murder, "Sir, being advanced in age, you have only one son and he is now in trouble," said King Hui of Ch'in. "Consequently I have already issued an order that he will not be executed."

"According to the law of the Moists, the penalty for murder is death, and the penalty for injuring others is to be injured in return," Fu T'un protested. "The purpose of these penalties is to prevent crimes, and the prevention of crimes is one of the most important principles that govern a nation. Though Your Majesty has shown love for me by ordering the cancellation of my son's death sentence, I, as a Moist, cannot violate the law of Mo Ti."

In complying with Fu T'un's wish, the king ordered the son's execution.

Every man loves his son. Yet Fu T'un placed a higher priority on the principle he believed in than the life of an offspring whom he loved. He was impartial indeed.

A chef prepares food, but he does not eat the food which he has personally prepared. If he does, he cannot be a good chef. Likewise a king should not allow his personal feelings to influence his decisions. He is a great king indeed if he punishes the wicked while inviting the most virtuous to help him to govern. He cannot be great, however, if, when punishing the wicked, he harbors selfish motives in his mind.

49 · HAN WEN-TI: *On the Eclipse of the Sun* [18]

I have heard that Heaven installs rulers to govern the people it creates and that it will warn a ruler with natural disasters if he has lost virtue or if his rule has become unjust.

On the eleventh month of this year there was an eclipse of the sun. No natural disaster can be more serious than this: Heaven has reproached me!

I have inherited the duty of protecting the temples of our imperial ancestors. A simple and insignificant person though I was, I was called to become the king of all people and scholars. I am solely responsible for all occurrences on earth, be they good or evil. In administering the vast empire, I am assisted by some of my closest minister-advisers.

[18] This decree was issued in 178 B.C. The Chinese original appears in "Biography of Wen-ti" *(Wen-ti chi); History of the Han,* roll 4, by Pan Ku (A.D. 32–92).

I have lost my virtue indeed as my inability to take care of my people has aroused the wrath of the sun, the moon, and the stars. Let it be known that immediately after this decree is issued, all of you should think seriously about my shortcomings and inform me on happenings that I have not been able to hear and see myself. Report your findings to me directly! Moreover, you are urged to recommend to me the virtuous, the upright, the honest, and the outspoken so that I can benefit from their counsel and advice. Be it also decreed that all of you are to be diligent at your tasks and that you are to reduce taxes and corvée duties among my subjects.

My inability to influence foreigners with my goodness necessitates the continuous fortification of the frontier, having in mind that the foreigners may at times decide to engage in improper activities. Not only have I been unable to eliminate altogether the necessity of stationing garrisons along the frontier; I have increased the number of soldiers and strengthened the defense instead. Let it be known that the Office of the Defense General is to be abolished. The General of the Stables should see to it that only a small, necessary number of horses is to be maintained along the frontier. The rest should be transferred for uses in postal stations.

50 · HAN WEN-TI: *The Meaning of Natural Disasters* [19]

For several years we have not had good harvests. Now there are such disasters as flood, drought, and pestilence. All of these grieve me greatly. Untalented and benighted as I am, I do not know where the blame should be placed.

Do these disasters come about because my government has erred in its policies and I, as a person, have not been so virtuous as I should have been? Is it also true that Heaven and Earth are unpredictable by nature and that they inevitably cause hardships to man from time to time? Could these disasters result from the lack of harmony among men or from man's negligence in offering sacrifices to gods and spirits? Why has this sad state of affairs deteriorated to such an extent?

Is it true that there have been wastes in the payment of salaries and allowances to government officials? Is it also true that there have been too many useless projects undertaken by the government? If it is not, how is it possible that the supply of food has become inadequate? The amount of arable land has not decreased; nor has the population increased. In fact, compared with the situation in ancient times, the amount of land per capita has somewhat increased. What is the cause of this inadequate supply of food?

Could the cause be the increase of the number of people engaging in nonessential occupations at the expense of agriculture? Could it also be the use, and consequently the waste, of a large amount of grain in making wine? Is it possible that people have raised too many domestic animals that consume a large amount of food? I do not know all the details.

Let the prime minister, the dukes, the governors, and the imperial professors [20] discuss this matter among themselves, in the hope that something useful to the people will emerge from their deliberations. Concentrate and think carefully about this matter. Do not hide whatever you have in your mind.

[19] This decree was issued in 163 B.C. Source: *History of the Han (Han shu),* roll 4.
[20] *Po-shih.*

51 · HAN CHING-TI: *On Being Good Officials* [21]

Emphasis on such non-essential work as jade and gold craftsmanship is harmful to farming. Likewise preoccupation with luxuries like silk embroidery is detrimental to the cause of cloth-making. The depreciation of farming is the beginning of hunger, and the deterioration of cloth-making foretells suffering from cold. He is a rare person indeed if he does not engage in wrongdoings when suffering from hunger or cold.

I personally till the fields, and my wife, the empress, raises silkworms. Because of our efforts we have been able to provide food and clothing as sacrifices in our family temple and also, hopefully, set an example to the rest of the nation. I do not accept tribute from my subjects; moreover, I have reduced the number of officials serving the royal household and eliminated unnecessary taxation and corvée duties. My purpose is to promote agriculture and cloth-making so that all of my people will have adequate savings to meet whatever emergencies that might arise.

The strong should not take things away from the weak, and the numerous should not oppress the few. The old should live their natural span of life; the young and the orphaned should have the care that enable them to grow to adulthood.

The harvest has not been good this year, and there is a shortage of food. Where should the blame be placed? Are some of our officials so corrupt that they act like merchants, cheating and robbing the people? The magistrate is the most important official in a district; he loses his usefulness if he himself violates the law or fails to bring the law violators to justice.

I hereby order all governors and magistrates to be diligent in the performance of their duties. The prime minister is responsible for bringing all delinquent officials to my attention, to be punished in accordance with their offense. Let this decree be made public throughout the empire so that all will know my intentions in this matter.

52 · WU CHING: *T'ang T'ai-tsung* [22]

One day in the first year of Chen-kuan,[23] T'ai-tsung remarked to his ministers in attendance as follows: "The first principle in kingship is to preserve the people. A king who exploits the people for his personal gains is like a man who cuts his own thighs to feed himself. He quenches his hunger for the time being but will die eventually. To secure peace in the world, the king must rectify and cultivate himself as an ethical being. As there is no such thing as a crooked shadow following a straight object, it is inconceivable that the people can be disloyal when their rulers are virtuous. What harms the body is not the objects outside of oneself, however tempting they are; rather, it is the unlimited desire for them that

[21] This decree was issued by Emperor Han Ching-ti in 142 B.C. Source: "Biography of Ching-ti" *(Ching-ti chi); Han shu,* roll 5.
[22] Translated from *Government of the Chen-kuan Period (Chen-kuan cheng-yao).* The author was a famous historian of the eighth century.
[23] A.D. 627.

brings us disasters. People love good food and like to be amused with music and sex. The stronger the desire for them is, the more harmful the result will be. For a king such a desire will not only interfere with his duty of running the government but also cause disturbances among his subjects. One irrational remark from the king will make thousands lose confidence in him. Complaints will arise; so will revolts. Every time I think of this, I dare not indulge in idleness."

"All the sage kings·in the past learned from the near in order to project the distant," replied Wei Cheng, the imperial counselor. "Formerly when Chan Ho arrived at the state of Ch'u as an official, he was asked about the principle of good government. In reply, he elaborated on the technique of cultivating oneself as an ethical being. When the king of Ch'u reiterated his question, Chan Ho replied: 'I have never heard a case in which the country is not well governed when the king is virtuous.' The statements that Your Majesty has made conform well to the ancient teachings."

* * * * *

One day in the tenth year of Chen-kuan,[24] T'ai-tsung asked his ministers this question: "From the point of view of an emperor, which one of the two tasks is more difficult, the establishment of a dynasty or the preservation of it?"

"During the period of civil war numerous leaders raise the standard of revolt and compete with one another for the throne," replied Fang Hsüan-ling.[25] "A city has to be taken by force before it will surrender, and a battle cannot be won until the enemy is vanquished. I would say that the establishment of a dynasty is more difficult."

"A dynastic founder arises at the time of political weakness and social disorder," replied Wei Cheng. "When he launches his attack against a degenerate monarch, the people are only too happy to support him. With the approval of both Heaven and man, it is not too difficult for him to found a new dynasty. After the dynasty has been established, however, he tends to become egoistic and indolent. While the people are longing for a rest, he imposes one corvée duty after another. While the people are tired and exhausted, he is ceaselessly engaged in extravagant projects. When all of these occur, the deterioration of a regime begins. I would say that to preserve a dynasty is more difficult."

"Hsüan-ling followed me in waging battles to unify the country, underwent all kinds of difficulties, and barely managed to survive," said T'ai-tsung. "It is easy to see why he regards the establishment of a dynasty as being more difficult. Wei Chung, on the other hand, helps me to govern the country after peace has been secured. Being concerned that egoism and indolence will pave the way for disaster or even physical extinction, he believes that it is more difficult to preserve a regime. However difficult it was, the establishment of our dynasty has been a matter of the past. Since the preservation of a dynasty is acknowledged to be difficult too, I hope that both you gentlemen and I will think carefully about it."

[24] A.D. 636.
[25] The then prime minister.

53 · HUANG TSUNG-HSI: *On Kingship* [26]

In the remote years of human life every man was selfish and worked only to benefit himself. It was necessary to promote the common good, but none took the leadership in promoting it. It was necessary to eliminate the common evil, but none took the leadership in eliminating it. With the passage of time eventually a man appeared who forsook his personal gains in order to work for the benefit of all, and ignored the danger to himself in order to eliminate the danger common to all. To achieve such a difficult goal, he must have worked thousands of times harder than ordinary persons. Yet, when the goal was finally achieved, he did not wish to appropriate anything for himself. This seems to be contrary to common sense, but people like him did exist in ancient times.

Hsü Yu and Wu Kuang were two of such people who, knowing what kingship involved, refused to accept it when it was offered to them.[27] Yao and Shun, however, took the kingship that was offered to them, but relinquished it as soon as they could find qualified successors. Yü did not wish to become a king in the beginning; yet, having reluctantly accepted the throne, he was unable to find a worthy successor and consequently remained a king for the rest of his life. Why did these people act so differently in view of the fact that the love of an easy life and the abhorrence of strenuous labor is the common nature of all men?

The monarchs of later periods were entirely different from the examples cited above. Since they believed that they were the ultimate source of all power, they appropriated for themselves all the benefits that power could bring, leaving to their subjects all the evils that resulted from the exercise of an unchecked omnipotence. No man dared to work for his own interest; instead, he was forced to work for the interest of the king who, in fact, regarded the satisfaction of his selfish desires as the common end for all of his subjects. If a king had doubts about this in the beginning, these doubts disappeared with the passage of time. As far as he was concerned, the whole world was his private possession, to be handed to his descendants from generation to generation. This selfish attitude was well illustrated by Han Kao-ti [28] who, after unifying the country, said to his father: "Between me and my older brother, who, sir, is richer?"

There is a vast difference in the concept of kingship between ancient and modern times. In ancient times the people were more important than the king who worked diligently throughout his life for the benefit of his subjects. In modern times the king is regarded as more important than the people who, while working diligently for the king, find neither peace nor security anywhere in the world. When engaged in the enlargement of his empire (which he considers his private possession), the king is not the least concerned with the death of millions of people and the break-up of thousands of families in the process.

[26] This selection, entitled *Yüan-chün* in Chinese, is the first essay in *A Ming Barbarian Waiting for a Visitor (Ming-yi tai-fang lu)*. The author, a Ming loyalist, called himself a barbarian (*yi*) because the government to which he had pledged allegiance was then replaced by the alien Ch'ing regime.

[27] According to Chinese legend, Hsü Yu refused the kingship offered by Emperor Yao who wished to abdicate on his behalf. Wu Kuang likewise refused the kingship offered by T'ang, founder of the Shang dynasty.

[28] Han Kao-ti (Han Kao-tsu or Liu Pang, r.206–195 B.C.) was the founder of the Han dynasty.

Without showing any sense of compassion, he justifies his doings by saying that he is merely creating an estate for his descendents. Once he has brought the country under his control, he takes it for granted that all the sufferings and deaths of his subjects matter little as long as they can contribute to the enhancement of his pleasure. The enhancement of his pleasure, says he, is merely the interest he derives from his estate, i.e., the empire. When a king entertains a thought like this, he has become the true enemy of the people. His existence deprives his subjects of the opportunity of working towards their own advancement. The institution of kingship has been grossly abused.

It is no exaggeration to say that people of ancient times loved their king, likened him to a father, and compared him to Heaven. Nor is it a surprise that people today hate their king, regard him as their mortal enemy, and call him a tyrant. Yet some of our half-educated scholars continue to maintain the specious argument that a subject's loyalty towards his king is the most important and unchanging virtue in the world, and that, despotic as Chieh and Chou were, T'ang and King Wu should not have killed them.[29] To substantiate this argument, these same scholars have also invented the incredible story of Pai-yi and Shu-ch'i.[30] They attach no importance to the lives of millions of men who, if we follow their theory to its logical conclusion, should toil to death in order to satisfy the desire of one man, namely, the king. . . .

We could understand the king's selfish desire to preserve his empire for his descendants until eternity to come, had it been possible for him to do so. But a problem derives from the fact that once a king regards the empire as his private possession, he arouses the envy and jealousy of others who are as anxious to take it away from him as he is to preserve it for himself and his descendants. No matter how carefully he guards his crown, he will lose it in the long run because one man's power and ingenuity, however great, are definitely inferior to those that can be mustered by millions of others. He may lose it in his lifetime or, at best, during one of the coming generations. In the latter case, it is his descendants, instead of himself, who may be slaughtered without mercy. As an ancient saying goes, he who is born as a prince is unfortunate indeed. Before he committed suicide, Ming Yi-tsung said to his daughter: "Why did you have to be born as a princess?"[31] How pathetic this remark is!

When the true meaning of a kingship is understood, a king would not hestitate to follow the example of Yao and Shun to abdicate on another man's behalf, and

[29] Chieh and Chou were the last monarch of the Hsia and Shang dynasties respectively. T'ang and King Wu were the founders of Shang and Chou dynasties respectively.

[30] According to Chinese legend, Pai-yi and Shu-ch'i were the sons of a petty prince towards the end of the Shang dynasty. The prince designated Shu-ch'i as his successor, but Shu-ch'i left the principality shortly after his father's death so that his brother Pai-yi could become the reigning prince. Pai-yi likewise refused the crown and left the principality too, on the ground that he could not violate his father's specific wish to name his brother as the successor. When King Wu revolted against the last monarch of the Shang dynasty, both brothers remonstrated with the king against such a revolt, stating that one's loyalty towards his lord was not subject to change no matter how despotic the lord had become. After King Wu had overthrown the Shang regime, unified China, and established the Chou dynasty, the two brothers refused to eat any food that was grown within the Chou territory, repaired to a desolate mountain, and died of starvation.

[31] Ming Yi-tsung, also known as Ch'ung-chen, was the last monarch of the Ming dynasty. He committed suicide in 1644 after a group of rebels had captured his capital Peking.

in such a case, the selflessness of Hsü Yu and Wu Kuang would not be regarded as rare and unique. When it is not understood, everyone would be happy to wear a crown, and it is virtually impossible to find a person who would turn down the offer of becoming a king.

While it is difficult to ascertain the various functions of a king, it does not require great intelligence to know that a moment of pleasure is no substitute for an eternity of sorrows.

54 · HUANG TSUNG-HSI: *On Ministership* [32]

Should a minister serve his king with blind obedience? The answer is no. Should he sacrifice his own life in order to serve the king? Again the answer is no.

Blind obedience may be regarded as proper in serving one's father, but not one's king. To sacrifice one's life for a cause is very noble indeed; but, insofar as being a good minister is concerned, it is still inadequate.

Our country being so large, a king cannot possibly govern it all by himself. Consequently he has to share his governing task with others. When a man becomes an official, his duty is to serve all the people—not any particular family and certainly not the king. If the king is despotic and forces him to do things harmful to the people, he has the right not to obey. In fact, he should not have become an official to a king of this sort in the first place, let alone die for him. Otherwise he would not have been different from a eunuch or imperial concubine who strives to satisfy every whim of his or her master's desire regardless of whether such desire is compatible with sound principle. If a king dies because of his own fault, there is no reason why anyone should follow him unless he is the king's personal servant or intimate, which a good official should not be.

Modern officials, however, do not understand the principle described above. Maintaining that an official is created for the purpose of serving the king, they believe that they, being officials, merely govern part of the territory and some of the people solely on his behalf. In other words, they think that all people in the empire are the king's private possessions.

The king's position is being threatened whenever social disturbances occur on a large scale or people suffer from a poverty so grinding that they have no way to escape. Whether we like it or not, the art of governing is a field which simply cannot be ignored. If no importance is attached to it on the ground that it has no bearing on the survival or fall of a regime, even an unright minister tends to minimize wrongly the implications of social disturbances and people's sufferings. Then the nation is really in danger.

Thus one must make his own choice as to what a good minister really means. He must keep in mind, however, that the nation's welfare has nothing to do with the rise or fall of a particular royal house; rather, it has a great deal to do with the happiness or sorrows of the people. It was good for the people that Chieh and Chou were overthrown; it was bad for the people that the Ch'in and Mongol dynasties were established. By the same token, the rise and fall of such dynasties as Tsin, Liu Sung, Ch'i, and Liang mattered little as far as the people were con-

[32] Entitled *Yüan-ch'en* in Chinese, this selection is the second essay in *Ming-yi tai-fang lu*.

cerned. A good minister is not one who assists his king to establish a dynasty or joins him in death whenever the dynasty is overthrown if, meanwhile, he sees the plight of the people around him and does nothing about it.

To govern a country is like hauling a huge log; it requires close cooperation between the king and his ministers if the log is to be moved. If one of the two parties does not take seriously his assigned task, the other will follow suit, and the log will remain where it is.

The insolent monarchs of the later periods are only interested in the satisfaction of their selfish desires, and they pay no attention to the welfare of their subjects. What they seek in their ministers is servility, and those who have been chosen as ministers naturally regard themselves as the king's personal servants. Once chosen as ministers and thus, temporarily at least, free from cold and hunger, they are extremely grateful, even though they may not have been accorded proper respect when they were selected. They consider themselves the king's servants and are treated as such. During the early years of the Wan-li period [33] when Chang Chü-cheng was treated with courtesy by Emperor Ming Shen-tsung, many people were shocked; they criticized Chang for receiving such courtesy with equanimity, even though the so-called courtesy was merely a fraction of what used to be shown to imperial counselors of ancient times.[34] If Chang had to be criticized at all, he should be criticized for his inability to maintain his dignity as an imperial counselor rather than his refusal to be treated like a servile servant. Yet his critics blamed him for the latter. Why? They took for granted the long-held popular but degenerate notion that a minister was a personal servant of the king. They did not understand that though a king and a minister differed in titles, their goal was nevertheless the same, namely, to serve the people.

Some people may ask this question: Is it not true that a minister's position in relation to his king is the same as a son's in relation to his father? The answer is no. The relationship between father and son is a relationship in blood, since the latter's physical being is derived from that of the former. Though maintaining his separate identity as a physical being, a filial son, being so close to his father each and every day, can understand his father without conscientiously trying to do so. An unfilial son, on the other hand, becomes more and more alienated from his father until eventually they cannot even communicate with each other. Contrary to the father-son relationship, the relationship between a king and his ministers comes about only after the king has brought the country under his control. Yet, as long as he remains a private citizen and does not share with the king the responsibility of governing the country, a person may well consider himself a stranger as far as the king is concerned. Once becoming a government official, however, he will have to make one of the two choices. He either serves the people and, in such a case, he becomes the king's teacher or friend; or, preferring not to serve the people so as to serve the king and the king alone, he becomes a personal servant of the king and nothing else. Though the word "minister" remains the same, its definition can change in accordance with the change in circumstances. The relationship between father and son, on the other hand, cannot and will not change.

[33] 1573–1619.

[34] Chang Chü-cheng, who died in 1582, was then the Grand Counselor, a position equivalent to that of a prime minister.

55 · LIU TSUNG-YÜAN: *On Feudalism* [35]

I do not know whether the universe or mankind has a beginning. But I do know that things that have beginnings are closer to us in terms of time than those that do not have beginnings. The validity of this statement can be proven via the discussion of feudalism.

The fact that the ancient sage kings—Yao, Shun, Yü, T'ang, Wen, and Wu—did not abolish feudalism was not because they did not wish to abolish it, but because they were compelled by circumstances to continue it. These circumstances that existed independently of individual will came into being as early as there were human beings. Since it was these circumstances that gave birth to the rise of feudalism, it might be said that feudalism came into existence as early as the arrival on earth of the human race. It was not an invention of the ancient sages.

What were these circumstances? At the very beginning of mankind, men lived and died in the same manner as the wild plants and untamed beasts which lived side by side with human beings. In competition with the wild beasts men were at a disadvantage because they had neither strong claws and sharp teeth for the purpose of attack nor hair and feathers for the purpose of defense. Relying on physical strength alone, they would not have been able to defend or maintain themselves. Under the circumstances, said the philosopher Hsün Ch'ing, men had to utilize objects outside of themselves to achieve their purposes. The utilization of physical objects led to competitions for such objects and consequently strifes among men. As competitions and strifes continued, men had to resort to a common authority for the arbitration of their disputes and, in doing so, they agreed in advance to abide by his decisions. The wiser and the more enlightened this common authority was, the more numerous would be the people willing to subject themselves to his control. If he told the people what was correct to do and was then ignored, he punished them so that they would be fearful of him and would from then on abide by his orders. This was how the institution of kingship came into being, side by side with the penal code.

Those who lived together became a group. The existence of separate and diverse groups entailed disputes and strifes between them; the intensity of such strifes was usually in proportion to the sizes of the groups concerned. When the issues involved were considered important enough, warfare was restorted to as a means to resolve them. Those who possessed certain virtues to command respect and who had gathered themselves a large following were hailed as leaders over a large number of people. The people elected to obey their leaders so that the latter could maintain peace and order within their respective groups. We may call these leaders princes. As principalities became larger in size, the disputes between them also became more serious. To resolve these disputes, they had to choose among themselves a common leader whose orders they pledged to obey, so that each principality would be able to keep its respective territory. This leader may be described as the head of a confederation. Conceivably the disputes between confederations were even larger, and there must be a man of great virtues who could command obedience from them in order to arbitrate or resolve these disputes. It was only

---

[35] Entitled *Feng-chien lun,* the Chinese original can be found in *Ku-wen tz'u-lei tsuan,* roll 2.

in this way that people could live in peace. This man, with whom the ultimate power of the world finally rested, was of course the Son of Heaven.

Thus above village officials were magistrates in charge of districts. Above district magistrates stood princes who in turn were under the jurisdiction of a confederal chief. Above the chiefs was the final authority, the Son of Heaven. Whether a person occupied as high a position as that of the Son of Heaven or as low as that of a village official, his natural tendency was to secure his heir as his successor in view of the good deeds that he had performed for the people under his jurisdiction. It is clear that feudalism did not come about as a result of some sage's invention; rather, it was an outgrowth of objective conditions over which the sages had no control.

The feudalism of the remote years—the times of Yao, Shun, Yü, and T'ang—was too distant to be known in details. But we have considerable information about the feudalism which existed during the Chou dynasty. After the Chou regime had unified China, it divided the conquered territories among the newly created feudal states each of whom belonged to one of the five feudal ranks.[36] As a result its vassals spread far and wide over all parts of China. Via land or water they came to the Chou capital to pay their homage; returning home, they defended their cities against the invasions or threats of invasions so as to safeguard the security of the Chou kingdom.

This state of affairs took a turn towards the worse during the reign of King Yi [37] when the royal authority was so eroded that the king found it necessary to step down from his royal palace to receive personally those lords who had come to the capital to pay their homage. A regeneration occurred during the reign of King Hsüan [38] who, through the use of military might, punished those lords who had refused to obey orders. Powerful as he was, he was nevertheless unable to place a legitimate heir as the crown prince of Lu. The royal authority deteriorated further during the reigns of King Yu and King Li.[39] After the passing of King Yu the Chou capital moved to Loyang, and the succeeding Chou kings, with their power greatly reduced, were no different from other feudal lords. As the royal power steadily declined, it was repeatedly challenged by the king's nominal vassals. One feudal lord was so impudent as to "ask the weight of the sacrificial vessel of the imperial household," [40] while another actually shot the king and wounded him on his shoulder. Fan-pai [41] was attacked by a powerful lord, and the king could do nothing about this unwarranted invasion. In another instance, the king had to kill Ch'ang Hung [42] simply because a powerful lord demanded him to do so. Rebellious at heart, these lords no longer regarded the king as their sovereign. The royal power continued to deteriorate for a long time, though

36 The five feudal ranks were: *kung, hou, pai, tzu,* and *nan,* comparable to the English duke, marquis, earl, viscount, and baron.

37 King Yi of Chou (Chou Yi-wang, ?894–?879 B.C.).

38 King Hsüan of Chou (Chou Hsüan-wang, 827?–782? B.C.).

39 King Yu of Chou (781–771 B.C.) and King Li of Chou (878–828? B.C.).

40 The vessel of the imperial household symbolized the imperial authority. By asking its weight, this feudal lord was challenging the imperial authority.

41 Fan-pai, whose fief was located in modern Honan province, was regarded as a loyal vassal, having paid homage to the king of Chou in 716 B.C. Source: *Spring and Autumn Annals,* the seventh year of Duke Yin of Lu.

42 Ch'ang Hung, a minister during the reign of King Ling (571–545 B.C.), was killed in 549 B.C.

nominally the king was still the first among the princes. Meanwhile the power of the feudal lords steadily increased until eventually "the tail becomes too large for the head to control."

While ignoring the authority above, the feudal lords conquered and annexed each other's territories with impunity. After a period of elimination their number was reduced to twelve. Then it became seven. Meanwhile the domain of the king was reduced to that of a small vassalage which was eventually swallowed up by the state of Ch'in. Ch'in, incidentally, had been one of the last states given an investiture by the Chou regime.

After Ch'in had unified China, it replaced feudal domains with administrative provinces and replaced dukes and counts with governors and magistrates. It held sway over all parts of China and located its capital at the most strategic point. How triumphant it must have felt! Yet in a few years its empire began to collapse. Why? It was so brutal as to put thousands of men into slave labor and so avaricious as to take away the material wealth of its subjects. The masses—ordinary farmers as well as convicted exiles—rose up in anger; together they formed alliances for the overthrow of the Ch'in regime. However, it should be recalled that the appointed officials remained loyal during this period of rebellion: it was the people who revolted. While the people were complaining below, these officials were afraid of punishments from above. Caught in the middle, they were either killed or kidnapped in numerous cases. The downfall of the Ch'in regime did not in any way result from defects on the part of a centralized administrative system; rather, it came about as a result of adopting harsh and inhuman policies which caused grievances among the people.

After its establishment, the Han dynasty decided to correct what it believed to be the defects of the Ch'in system and to follow partially the Chou idea. It installed as feudal lords the members of the royal family as well as those generals and statesmen who had helped in the establishment of the new regime. For several years these feudal lords were busy consolidating their domains, and when the emperor was in distress and needed help—for instance, when he was besieged by the Hsiung-nu at P'ingch'eng [43]—they could not come to his rescue. Three generations later, the reigning emperor, acting upon the recommendation of his advisers, decided to reduce the sizes of the feudal domains so as to safeguard the security of the central government. This precipitated a rebellion.[44] It should be noted that at the time of the rebellion one half of China was feudal and the other half administrative, and that while some of the feudal lords participated in the rebellion, not a single administrative province revolted. The superiority of Ch'in's central administration to Chou's feudal system was abundantly clear. Such a lesson was not lost to the dynasties that followed the Han.

When the T'ang dynasty was established, rightly and expectedly it divided China into administrative provinces and districts and appointed officials to govern them. From time to time there were cruel and unprincipled men who brought great harms to the territories of which they were in charge. This, however, did not result from any defects of the provisional system itself which

[43] Han Kao-tsu, founder of the Han dynasty, was besieged by the Hsiung-nu at P'ingch'eng (modern Shansi province) and was almost captured.
[44] This was the Seven States' Rebellion during the reign of Han Ching-ti which was suppressed in 154 B.C.

in fact remained sound; it resulted from the use of wrong personnel, especially military personnel. From time to time there were rebellious generals, but there were never any rebellious provinces. It is my opinion that the provincial and district system should not be changed.

Some people say that feudalism possesses great advantages in the sense that a feudal lord in charge will have strong attachment to the territory which is his private domain; that he will treat his people as well as if they were his own children; that he understands better the customs and mores of his people and can adjust himself easily to their needs; and that finally, because of the reasons stated above, it is comparatively easy for him to educate as well as govern his people. An appointed official, they argue, does not possess these advantages. While he is staying in one post, he is thinking of being promoted to another. Such being the case, how can he do a good job in his present assignment?

To refute this argument, I shall cite the situation as it existed during the Chou dynasty. Then the feudal lords were arrogant and conceited, and they enriched themselves by trading and fraternizing with the barbarians. They brought chaos and disorder to their domains; only a small portion of them can be said to have governed well. Their feudal superiors could not change their policies; nor could the Son of Heaven depose them. Those who felt a loving attachment to their domains and treated their subjects well were less than one in a hundred. The fault lay more with the system itself than the policies of individual lords.

In the case of Ch'in, while the administrative system itself was sound and correct, the central government nevertheless chose not to entrust the provincial and district officials with enough authority to enable them to discharge their assigned functions successfully. As the authority was centralized in the hands of the ministers in the capital, local officials were helpless in putting into effect what they believed were good policies. Having lost touch with the people, the central government imposed upon them harsh punishments and excessive corvée which caused grievances and resentments. In short, the fault of the Ch'in regime did not lie with its administrative system which was sound; it had simply adopted bad policies.

During the early years of the Han dynasty the central government could easily carry out its policies in the administrative provinces, but never in the feudal domains. It effectively controlled its appointed governors, but not the hereditary lords whom it could not depose even though they had been proven disloyal. Moreover, it could not eradicate whatever abuse there was in the feudal domains which afflicted the people. Only when a feudal lord was in open rebellion could the central government send troops to eliminate him. But as long as he was not openly defiant, he could continue to amass his ill-gotten fortune, abuse his power, and exploit the people for his own benefit. There was nothing the central government could do.

The situation described above cannot come about under a centralized administrative system. During the Han dynasty when this system was in effect, the government was able to recruit such able officials as Meng Shu and Wei Shang upon the recommendation of T'ien Shu and Feng T'ang respectively. Once it learned about Huang Pa's talent as a judge and Chi An's ability as an administrator, it immediately appointed them to high positions proportional to their talent. Thus, under a centralized administrative system, a good man can easily be appointed to a responsible position whenever he is found. Given the necessary authority, he can be relied on to govern an assigned area successfully. He can easily be dismissed if he has committed an offense and quickly rewarded if he has shown his worth. Appointed in the morning, he can be dismissed in the evening, and *vice versa*. Had the Han empire consisted entirely of feudal domains ruled by hereditary lords, the central government could have done nothing except express sorrow whenever these lords mistreated or misused their own people. Even had there been such able administrators as Meng Shu, Wei Shang, Huang Pa, and Chi An, the government would not have been able to take advantage of their special talents. The past shows that reprimanding or criticizing feudal lords for their misconduct is not an effective means to correct it. Outwardly they would accept whatever advice given to them, but would ignore it shortly afterwards. Were an order issued to reduce the sizes of their feudal domains as a form of punishment, they would soon form alliances among themselves and revolt in anger because, in such a case, they would doubtless feel that their common interest was threatened by the central government. Suppose, say, that the central government is successful in reducing each of the feudal domains by one-half. Who are the sufferers? The people, of course. Would it not have been better had there been no feudal domains in the first place? What happened during the Han dynasty is a lesson to be remembered.

The present administrative system, which comprises provinces and districts on the local level and under which appointed officials are held responsible for administering territorial units, is wise and sound. It should not be changed. The government will function well so long as governing personnel, military as well as civilian, is of the highest caliber.

Some people say that each of the four dynasties adopting a feudal system—Hsia, Shang, Chou, and Han—lasted a long time, whereas the Ch'in dynasty, with a centralized administrative system, survived for only a brief period. This, in my opinion, is a specious argument. The Wei dynasty that succeeded the Han and the Tsin dynasty that succeeded the Wei both adopted a feudal system; yet none of these dynasties lasted a long time. The present administrative system has served the country well for almost two hundred years. Why should we suddenly think of replacing it with a feudal system whose merits are dubious at best?

Other people might say that feudalism must possess some undisputable merits in view of the fact that the founders of the Yin and Chou dynasties—all of whom were sage kings—did not abolish it when they founded their respective regimes. Replying to this argument, I would say that the reason they failed to abolish it was not because they did not wish to do so but because they did not have any choice except to continue it. When T'ang fought to overthrow the Hsia regime, three thousand feudal lords rallied to his support. How could he eliminate his supporters who had helped him to become the king? When King Wu fought against the Shang regime and won, eight hundred feudal lords gave him material support. It was only natural that he should continue the existing feudal system. Under these circumstances, both T'ang and Wu did not have much choice.

The fact that these sage kings did not have any choice except to continue feudalism does not mean that feudalism is sound as a political system. A monarch who adopts feudalism is motivated by his desire to reward those who have helped him in establishing his regime as well as his desire to safeguard the kingdom for his descendants. Nevertheless this is a selfish desire that has nothing to do with the welfare of the people a a whole. The administrative system which the Ch'in dynasty introduced to replace feudalism was fair and impartial, though the motive behind its introduction was a selfish one because, by adopting this system, Ch'in Shih-huang merely wished to concentrate all power in his own hands and thus establish firm control over all of his subjects. Nevertheless Shih-huang was the man who, for the first time in history, introduced and put into practice an administrative apparatus so just and impartial that all men, if qualified, could participate in it.

The operation of a successful government depends upon the availability of qualified personnel. If the rulers are virtuous and wise, good government will come about, however degenerate the people are. Under feudalism in which the rulers are hereditary, it is inconceivable that the rulers can always be virtuous and wise and the people, on the other hand, will always be degenerate. In other words, there is no guarantee that there can always be good government. No matter how well-intentioned he is, a king without bureaucratic support cannot obtain all the information necessary to make the best kind of judgement. Meanwhile his ministers, being hereditary, are merely interested in enjoying the material benefits derived from their fiefs. Under the circumstances even the best among the sages will remain unknown and cannot make any contribution to the betterment of their government. How can people say that feudalism is a sage system? In conclusion, let me repeat that feudalism was not regarded as inherently sound by the ancient sages; it was a product of circumstances over which they had no control.

56 · YUNG-CHENG: *Chinese and Foreigners Are Members of One Family* [45]

Among the attributes that enable a king to rule successfully are his ability to protect all of his subjects and his desire to extend his benevolence to all of mankind. He responds to the wishes of Heaven to love his subjects and provides reasons for millions to rejoice in his rule. It is only in this way that he can unify the country and that his name will be remembered with gratitude until eternity to come.

It cannot be overemphasized that only the most virtuous are entitled to rule and that geography should not be a factor in determining who can or cannot be China's ruler. . . .

Our nation rose from the Eastern Land [46] and was endowed with great rulers generation after generation. It brought under its protection numerous states, and it alone received from Heaven its infinite grace. It delivered people from their sufferings and, because of the benevolent influence it spread, was able to induce all people, foreigners as well as Chinese, to respect their parents. We have been diligent in our task for the past one hundred years.

Since our dynasty has received the mandate of Heaven to rule and since it has proved its worth by extending its love and protection to all men without discrimination, why should it be discriminated against simply because it is not Chinese? You, my subjects here and abroad, have pledged your allegiance to our dynasty as your sovereign, and we expect nothing less than absolute loyalty and obedience from

[45] A copy of the Chinese original appears in Hsiao Yi-shan, *A History of the Ch'ing Dynasty (Ch'ing-tai t'ung-shih),* vol. I, pp. 928–930.
[46] Manchuria.

you as good citizens. Under no circumstances are you allowed to harbor treasonable thoughts on the ground that your rulers are not Chinese.

Here is this rebellious thief Lü Liu-liang who loves anarchy and rejoices in calamities. He wrote in secret, stating that the world had been turned upside down twice in history, first in the year of Te-yu [47] and again in our own time.[48] Other rebellious thieves like Yen Hung-k'uei echoed this falsehood and joined a seditious movement. The movement spread until it eventually affected such a man as Tseng Ching. All of them competed with one another in voicing strange, deceptive ideas and indulged themselves in slanderous attacks upon the government. They went so far as saying that neither the sun nor the moon had shone during the past eighty years, entailing complete darkness in Heaven as well as on earth.

The message of these rebellious thieves is clear. They base their slanderous attack on the specious theory that a clear distinction exists between China and Manchuria and that a Manchu king cannot become an emperor of China. They do not understand that Manchuria to us is the same as a native province to a Chinese. Shun was a foreigner from the east; King Wen was an alien from the west.[49] Yet both of them were great, saintly rulers of China. . . . If all foreigners were dismissed as barbarians, how can we explain the fact that when Confucius traveled throughout China, he accepted the invitation of King Chao of Ch'u to be the latter's guest? [50] How can we explain the fact that when he edited the *Book of History,* he placed the "Proclamation of Duke Mao of Ch'in" immediately after the "Chou History"? [51]

The theory of uncompromising differences between Chinese and foreigners did not come about until the Six Dynasties [52] when the Chinese regimes, then ruling the southern half of China, maintained a precarious existence. They and their northern counterparts shared one thing in common: lack of virtue and achievement. The northerners called the southerners "barbarous islanders," [53] and the southerners retaliated by calling the northerners "pigtailed slaves." [54] Instead of cultivating their virtues and loving their fellow men, both sides busied themselves with a despicable game of name-calling and satirizing.

Now that the world has been unified and that all people, foreigners as well as Chinese, have become members of one family, how dare these rebellious thieves continue to advocate the false theory of differentiating foreigners from Chinese, sowing the seeds of hatred and dissension when there should be none? They want to return China to a state of anarchy when people do not acknowledge either their sovereign or their own parents. . . .

---

[47] A.D. 1275.

[48] This refers to the conquest of China by the Mongols in the thirteenth century and the Manchu conquest of China in the seventeenth century, respectively.

[49] Shun was a legendary Chinese ruler, said to have ruled North China from 2255 to 2205 B.C. King Wen was a founder of the Chou dynasty (c.1122–249 B.C.).

[50] Ch'u, the state that covered the middle Yangtze valley during the time of Confucius, was regarded by the northern states as non-Chinese and "barbarian."

[51] Duke Mao of Ch'in or Ch'in Mao-kung lived in the seventh century B.C. and was responsible for making Ch'in a strong state. The more advanced eastern states, however, still regarded him and his state as semi-barbarian. Yung-cheng, the Ch'ing emperor, did not believe that Confucius had shown such a prejudice.

[52] A.D. 222–589.

[53] *Tao-yi.*

[54] *So-lu.*

In ancient times the territory of China was small even when the country was unified, and people outside of China were looked down upon as barbarians. Before the Three Dynasties such peoples as Miao, Ching, Ch'u, and Hsien-yün were characterized as barbarians, but today they live in the Hunan, Hupeh, and Shansi provinces. Can we still consider them barbarian? . . .

Our dynasty has become the sovereign of not only the Chinese but also of all the people in the world. For instance, we have brought under our jurisdiction the tribes located in the remotest areas of Mongolia. This extension of Chinese territory is one of the greatest fortunes that has even befallen the Chinese. How is it possible still to maintain the difference between Chinese and barbarians or China and alien lands? . . .

57 · YANG HSIU-CH'ING AND HSIAO CH'AO-KUEI: A Public Denunciation Against the Manchus [55]

In observation of the order of Heaven who has authorized them to combat barbarians,[56] the Prince of the East Yang [57] and the Prince of the West Hsiao [58] of the Heavenly Kingdom of Great Peace, who hold the posts of commander and vice commander of all-armed-forces respectively, wish to make the following proclamation known to all people in the world:

The world is God's world; the barbarians have no place in it. Food and clothing belong to God; they are not the barbarians' exclusive possessions. All people are God's children; they are not the barbarians' slaves. We hope that all of you will bear this in mind.

It is strange indeed that since the Manchu occupation of China the Chinese, with their vast territory and large population, continue to condone the occupiers' wanton activities. Is it true that there are no men in China? While these barbarians continue to emit poison and intensify their wickedness, all that we Chinese have been doing is bowing our heads low and humiliating ourselves by willingly remaining their servants. Why is it that no man has offered any resistance?

China is like a head to a man, whereas the barbarian territories are only his feet. China is called territory divine, whereas the barbarians can only be characterized as devils. Why is China called territory divine? When God—the true God—created Heaven and Earth, mountains and seas, He named China territory divine. Why is it that the barbarians are called devils? This is because the barbarians worship only Satan and other evil spirits. Has it ever occurred to you that the Manchu devils, by robbing us of our territory divine, have forcibly transformed all Chinese into monstrous devils like themselves? All the paper in the world is inadequate to record their immorality, and all water in the East Sea [59] is insufficient to wash off their sins. Here we shall enumerate only a few of their most notorious crimes.

The Chinese have their own customs; yet the Manchus forced them to shave part of their heads and to grow long pigtails hanging on their backs, so as to make all

[55] A copy of the Chinese original appears in Ch'ing-tai t'ung-shih, vol. III, p. 70 ff.
[56] The Manchus.
[57] Yang Hsiu-ch'ing.
[58] Hsiao Ch'ao-kuei.
[59] East China Sea.

of them look like animals. The Chinese have their own costumes; yet the Manchus ordered them to discard the attire of their ancestors and wear instead clothes and hats fashioned in the barbarian style, in the hope that all Chinese will forget about their ancestral origins. The Chinese have their own ethical code; yet K'ang-hsi,[60] the late chieftain of the devils, issued a secret order that a Manchu be put in charge of every ten Chinese households, thus providing him with a licence to satisfy his lustful desire with every woman within his jurisdiction. As this mongrelization continues, eventually every Chinese will wind up as a barbarian. Chinese should marry Chinese; yet the Manchu devils continue to collect Chinese beauties as concubines or slaves. How can the Chinese not be infuriated when they stop to think that millions of their beautiful women are sleeping daily with those stinking dogs? Obviously the Manchus will not be satisfied until they have raped every Chinese woman in the nation. The Chinese have their own laws and institutions; yet the Manchus enacted a different type of statutes to make sure that no Chinese could ever escape from their control. The Chinese have their own language; yet the Manchus invented the so-called capital dialect [61] so as to corrupt the pronunciation of Chinese words.

Moreover, the Manchu government shows no sense of compassion whenever there is a drought or flood, watching people starve, wander, and then die without offering a helping hand: it doubtless hopes to reduce the Chinese population. It sends its corrupt officials throughout the empire to exact every penny from the poverty-stricken Chinese. While people weep loudly in the streets, it rejoices at the prospect of imposing poverty on every man in the nation. A criminal is immediately turned loose when and if he pays, and only by bribery can a man acquire a governmental post. The power of the government is concentrated in the hands of the wealthy; the talented and the able are passed by simply because they cannot offer any money. The government doubtless hopes that all Chinese of talent will die of frustration and despair. Those who want to restore China to its former grandeur are denounced as rebels or traitors and are summarily executed together with their relatives. By this cruel device the government maintains the hope that no Chinese patriots will ever dare to challenge its authority. In short, it goes to the greatest extreme to insult and humiliate us Chinese.

Yao Yi-chung was a barbarian; yet he advised his son Hsiang that obedience to China was a righteous path to follow.[62] Fu Yung was also a barbarian; yet time and again he remonstrated with his brother Chien not to attack China.[63] In our times the Manchus forgot their unsavory origin and, taking advantage of Wu San-kuei's invitation, occupied all of China.[64] Ever since then they have been

[60] Emperor K'ang-hsi (r.1661–1722).

[61] This refers to the Peking dialect which was spoken by the Pekingese long before the arrival of the Manchus. It has been the official dialect since the establishment of the Chinese Republic in 1912. It is incorrect to say that it was invented by the Manchus.

[62] Yao Yi-chung (fourth century A.D.) was a ruler of the Ch'iang tribe, racially related to modern Tibetans. His son Yao Hsiang later became the founder of the Later Ch'in regime (384–417) in North China.

[63] Fu Chien came from the Ti tribe which was related to modern Tibetans. He founded the Former Ch'in regime (351–394) and unified North China in the 370's. He attempted to annex South China, then under the Chinese regime East Tsin (317–420), but was defeated in a crucial battle fought in 383. His regime disintegrated after this defeat.

[64] Towards the end of the Ming dynasty Wu San-kuei was the garrison commander at Shanhaikuan, the gateway to Peking. In 1644 he surrendered himself to the Manchus and invited them to enter China proper. The Ming dynasty was overthrown, and the Manchus established the Ch'ing dynasty which lasted until 1912.

cruel and brutal in the worst way possible. We have done intensive research on the origin of the Manchus; we have found that their progenitor was a white fox which intercrossed with a red dog, thus producing such monstrosities as the Manchus. Throughout the centuries they interbred among themselves, and their number continued to increase. To them proper relationships among men, good customs, and sense of decency were completely alien. They took over China during one of its weakest moments and, like a wild fox or poisonous snake, they will not leave their caves until they are forced to do so. Is it not strange indeed that, instead of plowing under their caves, we let ourselves be beguiled by their clever tricks and be humiliated, insulted, and blackmailed into submission? Sadly enough, many Chinese are evil and avaricious enough to join foxes and dogs and kowtow to them. Even a small boy, ignorant though he is, will become immediately angry if you order him to kowtow to a dog or a pig. Since the Manchu barbarians are no better than dogs and pigs, how can you gentlemen, who have read books and know the ancient ways, be so shameless as to humiliate yourselves before the Manchus? Reading the books, you must be thoroughly familiar with the fact that Wen T'ien-hsiang and Hsieh Fang-te [65] preferred death to submission to the Mongols and that Shih K'o-fa and Ch'ü Shih-ssu [66] fought to the end instead of serving the Manchus. The Manchus have only about 100,000 households, whereas China has more than 50,000,000. Is it not a shameful thing that a people of 50,000,000 households is subject to a small group of 100,000?

Fortunately, the way of Heaven has now changed its course towards the good. That China will be regenerated is as certain as that the barbarians will be eliminated. The days of evil are ending, since the truly great have emerged. As the crimes of the Manchus have reached their utmost limit, the Heavenly God, being so angry with them as He is, has authorized our Prince of Heaven [67] to raise the righteous standard of revolt so as to wipe out the Manchu devils. Wherever you are, you must be inspired by the same patriotic sentiment as we are. Whether you are government officials or ordinary citizens, we believe that your desire to serve a noble cause is as urgent as ours. Our armed forces are enthusiastic in their missions because of the righteousness of their cause, and men and women, full of anger, are volunteering as vanguards on the battlefield. We will not cease marching forward until we kill all banner men, [68] so that once again China can enjoy Heavenly peace.

Through this proclamation we implore you, the talented and the able, to worship God when the first opportunity arrives. Now that we have captured Shou-hsü at Ts'aichou and T'o-huan at Yingch'ang, [69] we are convinced that our long-lost territories will be recovered and that the law of God will be once more established. Any man who can capture the top dog Hsien-feng [70] or kill him and bring his head to us will be recommended for high position in our government. Those who kill the Manchus and surrender their heads to us will be abundantly rewarded. We will not swallow our words! We will definitely keep our promises!

[65] Both were Sung loyalists towards the end of the South Sung dynasty.
[66] Both were Ming loyalists at the beginning of the Ch'ing dynasty.
[67] Hung Hsiu-ch'üan.
[68] The Manchus.
[69] Shou-hsü and T'o-huan were the names of two generals then serving the Manchu regime. Ts'aichou was located in modern Honan province; Yingch'ang in modern Inner Mongolia (Jehol province).
[70] Hsien-feng (r.1851–1861), the reigning Manchu emperor.

Since God, the Supreme Lord, has authorized the Prince of Heaven to rule China, it is a matter of time before these barbarians will be wiped out from the face of the earth.

You gentlemen, as natives of China, are God's children. By obeying the wish of Heaven and joining us to combat the Manchu devils, you will be great heroes in life and receive honor and glory when you arrive in Heaven. If on the other hand you refuse to wake up, continue your evil ways, and insist on fighting against truth, you will be a barbarian in life and an evil spirit after you die. There can be no compromise between good and evil, and the difference between Chinese and barbarians is wide and distinct. Now that you gentlemen have suffered a great deal under the Manchu rule, how can you face God after you die if you do not change your ways and join us in a common effort to eliminate the barbarians? By joining us in this endeavor, not only will you avenge God against those who have lied about Him, you will also help deliver the Chinese people from their sufferings. Only when the barbarians are eliminated can we enjoy the blessing of peace. Those who obey Heaven will be rewarded; those who revolt against it will be punished by death. We are making this proclamation known throughout the world so that all of you will know our intentions.

58 · TSENG KUO-FAN: *A Public Denunciation of Hung Hsiu-ch'üan* [71]

It has been four years since Hung Hsiu-ch'üan and Yang Hsiu-ch'ing launched their rebellion. Millions of people have been adversely affected and more than 5,000 square *li* of land have been ravaged. Wherever the rebels went, they confiscated all ships, large or small, and robbed every man of his last penny, including the very poor. In their search for silver and coins, they stripped off the clothes of those whom they had kidnapped; they killed any man who had more than five taels of silver but refused to surrender the money to them. Each adult male was given one *ko* [72] of rice each day and was then ordered either to fight on the battlefield or build walls and dig trenches. Each woman, after receiving the same amount of rice as a man, was forced to serve as a night watcher on the city wall or transport rice or coal with her bodily strength. These rebels would kill any woman who refused to stop binding her feet, as a warning to those who might choose to disobey orders in this matter. Ship-owners who conspired to escape would be sentenced to death and hung upside down to intimidate those who might have in mind a similar design. These Cantonese bandits [73] treat the people in the middle and lower Yangtze as if they were the lowest animals; meanwhile they themselves enjoy the best the world can offer; wealth, power, glory, and material comfort. Any man who has red blood in his veins cannot but feel bitter and angry once he hears of these wanton brutalities.

Since the days of Yao, Shun, and the Three Dynasties, all of our great sages have striven to maintain orthodox teachings. They emphasize the correctness of human relations: the relative positions of king and ministers, father and son, and

---

[71] *Ch'ing-tai t'ung-shih,* vol. III, p. 132 ff.

[72] One-tenth of a pint.

[73] The Taipings were often referred to by the Ch'ing government as "Cantonese bandits" because most of them came from modern Kwangtung and Kwangsi provinces.

superiors and inferiors are as irreversible as those of hats and shoes. Now the Cantonese bandits, following foreign barbarians, believe in the so-called Christianity. From their kings and ministers to the lowest soldiers and coolie laborers—they call one another brothers. They argue that only Heaven can be addressed as Father, and all men, including one's natural father, should be addressed as brothers. By the same token, all women, including one's natural mother, should be addressed as sisters. Since all land is declared belonging to the Heavenly Father, no farmer can cultivate his own fields to pay his taxes. Since all goods are regarded as the sole property of the Heavenly Father, the merchants cannot buy and sell to make a profit. Scholars are no longer allowed to read Confucian classics which, they say, should be replaced by the teachings of Jesus and the *New Testament*. Thus by one stroke the rebels wish to wipe out our civilization, our morality and ethics, and our sacred books and sound institutions which, as all of you well know, have been flourishing for several thousand years. This proposed change is not only catastrophic to the great Ch'ing dynasty; it is the worst and most damaging event that has happened to our civilization since the beginning of history. It makes Confucius and Mencius weep in the other realm. How can any man, who knows how to read or write, fold his arms without doing something about it?

It has been well known that those who have unusual deeds credited to them will become immortal after they die. The kings rule this world, and the immortals rule the next. All people fear and worship gods and spirits; even rebellious ministers, unfilial sons, and the worst elements of society are not exceptions. When Li Tzu-ch'eng [74] arrived at Ch'üfu,[75] he did not violate the temple of Confucius. When Chang Hsien-chung [76] came to Tzut'ung,[77] he worshipped at the temple of Wench'ang.[78] The Cantonese bandits, on the other hand, burned the Confucian temple at Shenchou [79] and destroyed the wooden tablet that bore the name of Confucius, while those that bore the names of his disciples were scattered about on the floor in both corridors of the sacred temple. Wherever these bandits went, they made the destruction of temples their first business, including the temples to honor loyal ministers and righteous heroes such as Kuan Yü and Yo Fei [80] whose statues they smashed into pieces. Temples were burned wherever and whenever they were found—Buddhist, Taoist, and even those that housed city or local gods. Statues of all religions were smashed; no exceptions whatsoever were made. No wonder that all gods and spirits are angry and will seek revenge against these bandits whenever the first opportunity arrives.

Following an order of the Son of Heaven, I and the twenty thousand men under my command are marching towards the enemy with the avowed purpose of destroying him, so that all the ships that he has stolen will be returned to their original owners and all the people whom he has forcibly detained will be freed.

---

[74] Li Tzu-ch'eng (d. 1645) was a rebel leader towards the end of the Ming dynasty.
[75] Ch'üfu, located in modern Shantung province, was the birthplace of Confucius.
[76] Chang Hsien-chung (d. 1647) was a rebel leader towards the end of the Ming dynasty.
[77] Located in modern Szechuan province.
[78] A Taoist deity.
[79] Located in modern Hunan province.
[80] Kuan Yü (second century A.D.) was a loyal minister and sworn brother of Liu Pei, founder of the kingdom of Shu. Yo Fei (twelfth century A.D.) was a military hero who fought against the Nuchens during the Sung dynasty.

I swear that this purpose will be achieved, whatever the cost. It is only then that our sovereign king can feel easy on earth and that our great sages, Confucius and Mencius, can be comforted in Heaven. Moreover, the one million men and women whom the enemy has murdered will be avenged, and the humiliation which gods and spirits have suffered at his hand will be eradicated.

Through this proclamation I wish to seek the cooperation of all people in this endeavor, wherever they are. I shall consider as my friends all those who, inspired by the sense of righteousness, will organize their own troops in helping me to eliminate these bandits, and in such case I shall be happy to finance their efforts in accordance with their needs. As for those upright gentlemen who have been angered by the spread of Christianity in China and are eager to defend our civilization, I shall invite them to my command where they will be honored as guests and teachers. I welcome all righteous and generous persons to contribute funds for our noble cause; their contribution will be acknowledged with appreciation if it is less than one thousand taels, and the contributor will be recommended to the imperial government for special awards if the contribution is more than one thousand taels. As for those who have been forced to serve in the rebel ranks, I am asking them to kill their superiors and then surrender their cities to us; and in such case, they will be taken under the protective custody of my command and will be then recommended to the imperial government for appointment as government officials. The bandit soldiers who throw their weapons away while engaging in battle and then surrender themselves to my command will be given safe conduct plus traveling expenses, so that they can journey safely home, even though they may have been in the rebel ranks for several years during which their hair has grown several inches in length.[81]

Looking back at our history, we find that the uprisings and rebellions at the end of each dynasty (Han, T'ang, Yüan, or Ming) resulted solely from the presence of a despotic monarch or a corrupt regime. I can assure you that the present Son of Heaven is diligent and compassionate, reverent towards Heaven and full of love towards his subjects. He has not increased taxes; nor has he forcibly conscripted soldiers. Possessing a sense of love as profound as that of the ancient sages, he is waging war against a group of brutal, unprincipled bandits. It does not require great intelligence to know that these bandits will be eliminated, sooner or later. If you, who have been forced to join the rebels, continuously choose to cooperate with them and offer resistance to the imperial government, you cannot expect mercy when the grand army arrives, because at that time it will be impossible to differentiate between the rebels and those who have been forced to join them.

Great virtue and outstanding ability I do not possess; what enables me to command this army is my loyalty and faith. Above in the sky are the sun and the moon, and under the earth are gods and spirits. Before our eyes are the roaring torrents of the Yangtze River, and beyond our sight are the spirits of numerous martyrs who have died for this noble cause. May all of them become my witnesses! I ask all of you to listen to me: the moment this proclamation reaches you, it is as binding as the law. Do not ignore it!

---

[81] Contrary to other Chinese who had shown their loyalty to the Manchu regime, the Taipings did not shave their heads. That is why they were often referred to as "long-haired bandits" (ch'ang-mao tse) by unfriendly contemporaries.

CHAPTER EIGHT

Government in Practice

THOUGH according to Confucian ideology only the virtuous were qualified to rule, most Chinese emperors were the sons of their predecessors. Under normal circumstances the oldest son of a reigning emperor was expected to be designated as the heir apparent. In other cases intrigues or sometimes assassinations played a vital role in the designation of a crown prince. The story of Lü Pu-wei as told by Ssu-ma Ch'ien (Selection 59) reveals not only a circuitous plot of a masterful kingmaker but also an event of great historical significance because the man who emerged as the king later unified China in 221 B.C.

Throughout history Confucian scholars spoke constantly of the great virtues of the founders of the Three Dynasties. Whatever truth their assertion contains, the founders of some of China's later dynasties were anything but exemplary. One of these was Ts'ao Ts'ao (d. A.D. 220) who, either as a man or as a ruler, violated practically every principle which the Confucian scholar had advocated for a virtuous prince (Selection 60). When his son Ts'ao Pi finally forced the reigning emperor to abdicate in his behalf, he was reported to have remarked: "Now I know what the sages meant when they said that Yao and Shun voluntarily abdicated the throne in behalf of the country's most virtuous." Once in power, an emperor was as much interested in personal indulgence as he was in national welfare (Selection 61).

In recruiting governmental personnel, the government was supposed to consider only such factors as academic excellence and personal character. But in practice servility (sometimes mistakenly called "personal loyalty"), influence-peddling, and bribery were equally if not more important factors (Selections 62 and 63). Outside of the emperor's immediate relatives, what people were in a good position to influence or sometimes control him? The eunuchs, of course. The abuse of eunuch power was a major concern to Chinese scholars throughout centuries (Selections 64 and 65). With or without eunuchs, the resort to bribery to sidetrack the normal function of justice was very common in the traditional Chinese society. The story of Fan Li and his three sons (Selection 66) is a case not only involving bribery and influence-peddling; it also reveals an interesting but ironical aspect of human life common to people of all ages.

As far as the people were concerned, on the local level the most important official was the head of a subprefecture or district. He, as the magistrate, was their immediate ruler; he collected taxes, administered justice, and was

137

responsible for the maintenance of peace and order within his jurisdiction. If he were wise and incorruptible, the people benefited; otherwise they would suffer. His importance is well illustrated in a story told by Yüan Mei (Selection 67), a famous man of letters of the eighteenth century. Another example of administrative competence on the local level was provided by Hsi-men Pao whose performance as an able magistrate has been enshrined in Chinese folklore for more than two thousand years. Despite its numerous varieties, the basic account about this man is that told by Ch'u Shao-sun (first century B.C.), a storyteller of unusual talent (Selection 68). To a Westerner who believes in "due process of law," the extraordinary power which a magistrate like Hsi-men Pao possessed (such as his power of putting people to death without a trial) is doubtless disturbing; but to the traditional Chinese the goal of serving justice was infinitely more important than the way whereby justice could be served.

59 · SSU-MA CH'IEN: *Lü Pu-wei the Kingmaker* [1]

Lü Pu-wei was a wealthy merchant in Yangti.[2] A traveling businessman, he bought goods when their price was low and sold them when their price was high. He amassed a large fortune in the process.

In the fortieth year during the reign of King Chao of Ch'in,[3] the crown prince died. Two years later, the king's second son, Prince An-kuo, was designated as the heir apparent. Prince An-kuo had more than twenty sons, but his favorite concubine, Madame Hua-yang, did not bear him any child. She was nevertheless made the principal consort, because the prince loved her most among all of his spouses.

Prince An-kuo's second son was Tzu-ch'u. Tzu-ch'u's mother, concubine Hsia, did not love her son, and consequently Tzu-ch'u was sent to the state of Chao [4] as a hostage to guarantee Ch'in's goodwill towards that state. Since Ch'in had repeatedly attacked Chao, Chao understandably was not particularly enthusiastic about its enemy's hostage. In fact, as the son of a concubine and a hostage in a foreign country, Tzu-ch'u was often short of funds and had a difficult time even to maintain his chariot. When Lü Pu-wei arrived at Hantan on one of his business trips, he heard about Tzu-ch'u and felt sorry for him. "What a priceless merchandise I have found!" he exclaimed. He went to Tzu-ch'u's house and paid him a visit.

"I can enlarge the door of your house," said Lü Pu-wei.

"Never mind enlarging my door; go home and enlarge your own," Tzu-ch'u laughed.

"You do not understand, sir," said Lü. "My door cannot be enlarged unless yours is enlarged first."

Now Tzu-ch'u knew what the visitor had in mind and began to talk with him in a serious and intimate manner.

[1] *Historical Records (Shih chi),* roll 85.
[2] Located in modern Honan province.
[3] 267 B.C.
[4] Hantan was the capital of the state of Chao, located in modern Hopeh province.

"The king of Ch'in is old, and Prince An-kuo is the crown prince," said Lü. "I have heard that the prince is in love with Madame Hua-yang who, despite the fact that she has no child of her own, is nevertheless in a position to decide who the prince's heir apparent will be. You are only one of the more than twenty sons of your father and are not the eldest besides. Moreover, you are presently a hostage in the state of Chao and have not seen your father for a long time. After the present king dies, your father as the crown prince will inherit the throne. As far as your chance of being designated as a crown prince is concerned, how can you possibly compete with his eldest son and many others who are around him every day?"

"What should I do?" asked Tzu-ch'u.

"The fact that you may die in poverty in a foreign country can in no way bring any benefit to your parents. Moreover, poverty prevents you from making friends. Meager in means though I am, I shall be happy to invest one thousand pieces of gold on your behalf and use this money to ingratiate you with Prince An-kuo and Madame Hua-yang, in the hope that eventually you will be designated as the heir apparent."

Upon hearing this, Tzu-ch'u kowtowed to show his gratitude. "If this plan is successfully carried out," he said, "I shall divide the state of Ch'in and give you one half of it."

Lü Pu-wei gave Tzu-ch'u five hundred pieces of gold to be used to win friends. He used the other five hundred pieces to buy curios and playthings to be brought personally to the Ch'in state. Traveling westward, he eventually arrived at his destination and requested an audience with an elder sister of Madame Hua-yang. He told his hostess that the presents he brought with him were his tribute to Madame Hua-yang. Tzu-ch'u was as virtuous as he was wise, he continued, and had among his friends many princes and able men all over China. He worshipped Madame Hua-yang as if she were Heaven, and he cried in sorrow day and night because he had not been given the opportunity to serve her as well as his father the crown prince. After Madame Hua-yang heard about these remarks, she was overjoyed beyond belief.

After winning the confidence of Madame Hua-yang, Lü Pu-wei persuaded her sister to speak to her as follows: "I have heard that a woman who serves a man with her beauty will not be loved when she is old and loses it. You, Madame, have served the crown prince well and are rewarded with affection. Since you do not have a child of your own, it would be wise on your part to choose among the crown prince's offspring a loyal and virtuous man to be adopted as your son and to be designated as the heir apparent. This should be done at the earliest possible moment. While your husband is alive, nobody dares to show you any disrespect. However, after he dies and one of his sons ascends the throne, you will lose all the influence which you now have. To forestall this eventuality and to secure your own position for the future, a word from you with the crown prince will more than suffice at this moment. If you do not choose to safeguard your position today, you will not be able to do it when you are old and no longer beautiful and when the crown prince does not love you so much as he presently does. By then it will be too late. Tzu-ch'u is a virtuous man. However, being the second son of your husband, he knows that he cannot be designated as the heir apparent. Moreover, his mother is not favorably regarded by the crown prince. Now that this young man has expressed his sincere desire to be your protégé, you will never lose your influence in the Ch'in state if you promote him as the heir apparent." Madame Hua-yang agreed.

Catching the crown prince in a listening mood, Madame Hua-yang mentioned Tzu-ch'u in a casual manner. Tzu-ch'u, though serving as a hostage in the state of Chao, was a man of great virtue, she said; and people who knew him praised him highly. "It is my great fortune to serve you, sir," with tears in her eyes she continued; "but unfortunately I do not have a son of my own. Please designate Tzu-ch'u as your heir apparent, sir, so that I will be well protected when you are no longer able to protect me yourself." Prince An-kuo agreed, and jointly they ordered the fashioning of a jade seal unmistakably indicating that Tzu-ch'u had been named as the heir apparent. They sent a large amount of money to Tzu-ch'u and appointed Lü Pu-wei as his adviser. As a result, the name of Tzu-ch'u became widely known among all princes in China.

While serving as Tzu-ch'u's adviser in Hantan, Lü Pu-wei took into his household a beautiful dancer. One day he invited Tzu-ch'u to his house for dinner; Tzu-ch'u, enchanted and fascinated by the young dancer, made the request that she be given to him as a present, though the young woman had already been made pregnant by her present master. Lü Pu-wei was angry with this request; however, considering that he had almost bankrupted himself in advancing the interest of Tzu-ch'u as well as his own, he decided to comply with the request, the refusal of which would doubtless put an end to all of his ambitions. The woman never revealed to Tzu-ch'u that she was pregnant by another man. When the baby was born, he was given the name Cheng.[5] After his birth, Tzu-ch'u elevated the woman to the position of first wife. . . .

King Chao of Ch'in died in the fifty-sixth year of his reign.[6] Crown Prince An-kuo became the king, Madame Hua-yang the queen, and Tzu-ch'u the crown prince. One year later the new king died and was given the posthumous title Hsiao-wen. Tzu-ch'u ascended the throne as King Chuang-hsiang. His foster mother, Madame Hua-yang, became Empress Dowager Hua-yang and his natural mother, Lady Hsia, became Empress Dowager Hsia. In the first year of King Chuang-hsiang's reign,[7] Lü Pu-wei was appointed prime minister and titled Duke Wen-hsin; he was given a fief of ten thousand households in Loyang south of the Yellow River. King Chuang-hsiang died in the third year of his reign, and Cheng, the crown prince, succeeded him as the king.[8] Lü Pu-wei continued as prime minister with the title "Imperial Uncle."

The king was young; time and again the queen mother met secretly with Lü Pu-wei to carry on their illicit sexual relationship. . . . As the king grew older and older, the queen mother's sexual desires became stronger and stronger. Fearing that their illicit relationships might be discovered and that he himself would be condemned, Lü Pu-wei decided to search for a man of unusual sexual capacity to replace him and found such a man in the person of Lao-ai, whom he hired as a servant. He turned Lao-ai loose among the prostitutes and found him highly

---

[5] Cheng, later known as Ch'in Shih Huang-ti, one of the greatest emperors of ancient China, unified the country in 221 B.C. According to hearsay, his mother had been pregnant for twelve months before he was born; that was why, some people contended, his father never found out that he was not his true son.

[6] 251 B.C.

[7] 249 B.C.

[8] This was 246 B.C. when King Cheng was twelve years old.

satisfactory. He ordered that Lao-ai's sexual organ be used as the axle of a small vehicle: the wheel continued to turn without meanwhile bringing any damage to this man's hardy member. Lü Pu-wei then reported his findings to the queen mother who, as expected, wanted Lao-ai for her own pleasure. To make sure that nobody knew the real purpose of Lao-ai's employment with the queen mother, Lü instigated a man to sue Lao-ai for an imaginary crime for which, according to the law, the alleged criminal was to be punished by castration. The man in charge of castration confined his task to the pulling of Lao-ai's beards and eyebrows, having been heavily bribed by the queen mother. Lao-ai was brought to the palace as a eunuch to serve the queen mother who found him sexually satisfactory and loved him dearly. In due course she became pregnant by this supposedly sexless eunuch. . . .

In the ninth year of Shih-huang's reign [9] someone reported to the king that Lao-ai was not really a eunuch; that the queen mother had two sons by him who were carefully hidden; and that one of the two sons would ascend the throne upon the death of the king which, said the informer, was expected to materialize at any moment. The king ordered an immediate investigation, and Lü Pu-wei was implicated in the process. In the ninth lunar month Lao-ai was sentenced to death together with all of his relatives to the third degree.[10] The queen mother's two sons by Lao-ai were also killed. The queen mother was subsequently moved to Yung.[11] As for Lao-ai's followers, their property was confiscated and they were exiled to Shu.[12] At the beginning the king was about to kill the prime minister too. Then, thinking of the great service which Lü had performed for his late father and the pleading for mercy by the prime minister's numerous friends, he decided to spare his life. In the tenth lunar month during the tenth year of Shih-huang's reign,[13] Lü Pu-wei was finally removed from his premiership.

At the suggestion of a man from Ch'i named Mao Chiao, the king invited the queen mother from Yung back to Hsienyang,[14] and Lü Pu-wei was ordered to leave the capital for his fief at Loyang. During the following year when Lü resided in Loyang, all men of influence—dukes and counts, envoys and friends—flocked to Loyang in an almost continuous stream, paying homage and seeking advice. Worried, the king was fearful of a political plot. He sent the ex-premier a letter which read as follows: "What great deeds have you performed for the state of Ch'in which granted you a fief of ten thousand households? How loyal have you been to the state of Ch'in that titled you the 'Imperial Uncle'? You and your family will be moved to Shu." Losing the king's favor, Lü Pu-wei felt that sooner or later he would be executed. He drank poison and died.[15] . . . Seven years later, the queen mother also died. She was given the posthumous title "Imperial Dowager" and was buried with King Chuang-hsiang at Chihyang.

---

[9] 238 B.C. Actually King Cheng did not assume the title of Shih-huang or First Emperor until 221 B.C.

[10] The term *san-tsu* or "relatives to the third degree" has two interpretations. It could mean either "parents, brothers, and wife and children" or "father's relatives, mother's relatives, and wife's relatives." It is not known which one of these two interpretations is applicable here.

[11] Located in modern Shensi province.

[12] Modern Szechuan province.

[13] 237 B.C.

[14] Capital of Ch'in.

[15] This occurred in 235 B.C.

60 · ANONYMOUS: *The Profile of a Tyrant* [16]

As a boy, Ts'ao Ts'ao loved to play with falcons and hounds and was little interested in serious work. His uncle often spoke of his misconduct in front of his father Sung, and consequently Ts'ao was greatly concerned. One day, seeing his uncle on the road, his face suddenly twisted and his mouth contorted. Queried by his uncle as to what had happened, he replied that he had a sudden attack of paralysis. Alarmed, his uncle called his father; by the time his father arrived, however, Ts'ao was as normal as he could possibly be.

"Your uncle says that you have suffered an attack of paralysis. Is it true?" asked his father.

"No, it is not," Ts'ao replied. "Since my uncle does not love me, he has always lied about me."

After this incident, Sung no longer believed his younger brother whenever the latter made some derogatory remarks about his son. Ts'ao, consequently, could do whatever he pleased without fearing punishment.

*   *   *   *   *

As the police chief of the capital,[17] Ts'ao was strict in enforcing the rules that governed the city gates. On each side of a city gate hung a dozen or so five-colored sticks especially made for law enforcement. Whenever a violation occurred, the violator would be beaten to death, however powerful or influential he might be. Several months later, when Chien Shuo's uncle violated the curfew by walking in the streets at night, he was immediately put to death. Since Chien Shuo was a favorite eunuch of Emperor Ling-ti,[18] this incident had a salutary effect upon all officials who from then on did not dare to violate Ts'ao's rules.

Though all the emperor's closest friends and favorite ministers resented Ts'ao bitterly, somehow they could not find a legitimate case to dislodge him. Finally they decided to get rid of him by unanimously recommending his promotion. He left the capital after being promoted to the magistracy of Tunchiu.[19]

*   *   *   *   *

Hearing Hsü Yu's arrival,[20] Ts'ao Ts'ao was so happy that he went out to receive him without bothering to wear his shoes. "Now that you have arrived, I cannot see how I can possibly fail," said Ts'ao. He clapped his hands and laughed loudly.

After being seated in the hall, Yu proceeded to speak: "Please tell me how you

---

[16] The Chinese original of this selection appears as commentaries in "Biography of Wei Wu-ti" *(Wu-ti Ts'ao); History of the Three Kingdoms (San-kuo chih)*, roll 1, by Ch'en Shou who lived in the third century. The author of these commentaries was reported to be a native of Wu (lower Yangtze valley) who otherwise cannot be identified.

[17] The capital of the Later Han, *i.e.,* Loyang.

[18] Emperor Han Ling-ti (r. A.D. 168–188).

[19] Located in modern Hopeh province.

[20] Hsü Yu was then a military adviser to Ts'ao Ts'ao's opponent, a warlord named Yüan Shao. The event of his betrayal described here occurred in A.D. 200.

plan to fight a strong army like General Yüan's. How long can your provisions last?"

"About a year," Ts'ao Ts'ao replied.

"You know that is not the truth. Answer the question again."

"About six months."

"Does Your Excellency not wish to defeat General Yüan? Why do you refuse to tell the truth?"

"I was merely joking with you," Ts'ao replied. "My supplies can last only one month. What should I do?"

"Your army has been isolated and is now defending an area all by itself," said Yu. "It cannot expect any reinforcement, and its food supply is about to be exhausted. I, for one, cannot visualize a more dangerous situation. General Yüan has more than ten thousand vehicles of supplies stored at Wuch'ao which, fortunately, is not well protected. If I were you, I would dispatch a column of lightly armed troops to attack Wuch'ao and burn these supplies. Once they are destroyed, General Yüan will be defeated in three days."

Ts'ao Ts'ao was happy with this suggestion and proceeded to select the best of his troops to carry out this mission. All horses were muffled so that they would not make any noises during the march. The soldiers were carrying inflammable materials such as straw, to be used as kindling to burn General Yüan's supplies. Bearing General Yüan's banners, they marched into the darkness of the night.

On the road some people asked the soldiers where they were going. "His Excellency Yüan was afraid that Ts'ao Ts'ao might attack his rear and consequently dispatched us to strengthen the defense," the soldiers replied. Thinking that the soldiers were telling the truth, the inquirers took the march calmly.

Once arriving at the supply depot, the invaders began to set fire. The garrison troops were caught by surprise and were easily routed. All the stored grain was burned, and Kuei Yüan, the garrison commander, was killed. General Shun-yü Chung-chien's nose was cut off, though he did not die. Altogether more than one thousand enemy soldiers were killed, and all of their noses were cut off and collected. As for the captured cattle and horses, their lips and tongues were also sliced off and collected. Together they were shown to General Yüan's soldiers who, as a result, were greatly frightened.

Chung-chien was captured during the night and was subsequently brought to Ts'ao Ts'ao's headquarters. "How do you end up in this fashion?" Ts'ao Ts'ao asked. "Victory or defeat is determined by Heaven. Why do you have to ask me any questions?" said Chung-chien. Ts'ao Ts'ao was thinking of sparing his life until Hsü Yu interrupted him. "Tomorrow morning when he looks at the mirror," said Hsü Yu, "it is unlikely that he will forget who took his nose away." It was then that Ts'ao Ts'ao changed his mind and ordered Chung-chien's execution.

*　　　*　　　*　　　*　　　*

Acting upon Ts'ao Ts'ao's orders, Hua Hsin, at the head of a squad of soldiers, entered the imperial palace for the purpose of arresting Empress Fu. The empress closed her bedroom door and hid herself inside a wall. Smashing the door and breaking the wall, Hsin pulled the empress out. The emperor [21] was sitting with

[21] Emperor Han Hsien-ti (r.189–220).

the imperial counselor Ch'ih Lü when the empress, barefooted and hair unkempt, was led by. The empress grasped his hand, saying: "Can you save me?" "I do not even know when I shall be put to death myself," the emperor replied. Then, turning to the imperial counselor, he said: "Mr. Ch'ih, have you ever seen a situation like this?"

The empress was subsequently put to death. Her father, Wan, and several hundred of his relatives were also put to death.

*   *   *   *   *

As a person, Ts'ao Ts'ao was frivolous and undignified. He loved music and was often surrounded by entertainers and prostitutes from morning to night. He wore clothes made of light silk and attached to his belt a small bag which contained his handkerchief and other personal effects. Sometimes he put on a conical cap when receiving visitors. During a conversation he was outspoken and joked a great deal; often did he laugh so loudly that he buried his head among the dishes on the table, soiling his headwear. How frivolous he really was!

However, he was strict and harsh in the enforcement of his laws. If he suspected a general to be superior to him in military strategy, he would find some legal excuse to put him to death. He would not hesitate to kill his long-time followers or friends if he found that they had complaints against him. Once he decided to kill a man, no weeping or pleading could make him change his mind. . . .

Once marching his soldiers in a wheat field, he gave the order that under no circumstances would they be allowed to damage the crop and that those who did would be immediately put to death. Observing his order, all of his cavalrymen alighted from their mounts and gently pushed the plants aside so as to thread their way through. Ts'ao Ts'ao's own mount, however, suddenly jumped into the field and caused considerable damage to the crop. Ts'ao ordered the law enforcer to carry out the punishment that was to be inflicted upon himself.

"According to the *Spring and Autumn Annals*," said the law enforcer, "penalty should not be imposed upon the most superior."

"If I am not punished for violating my own law, how can I expect obedience from my subordinates?" said Ts'ao Ts'ao. "However, since I am the commander-in-chief, I cannot very well commit suicide at this moment. Let me punish myself." He unsheathed his sword, cut off his long hair, and threw it to the ground.

*   *   *   *   *

Ts'ao Ts'ao had a favorite concubine whom he often used as a pillow whenever he decided to take a nap during the day. One day, before he went to sleep, he told her to wake him up in a short time. The concubine, seeing him peacefully and soundly asleep, decided not to disturb him, even though she had been instructed to do otherwise. After he woke up by himself, Ts'ao Ts'ao ordered her to be beaten to death.

*   *   *   *   *

During one of his bandit-extermination campaigns, Ts'ao Ts'ao found that his food supply was far from adequate.

"What should I do?" he asked his treasurer.

"We can use small vessels when distributing grain among the soldiers," his treasurer replied.

"That is a good idea!" said Ts'ao Ts'ao.

Later the soldiers complained and accused their commander of cheating.

"I wish to borrow your head to pacify the soldiers," said Ts'ao Ts'ao to his treasurer; "I cannot see how this matter can be otherwise settled."

He cut off the treasurer's head and attached to it a note which read as follows: "This man has been executed in view of the fact that he stole grain from the government and used small vessels to distribute food among the soldiers."

This is a good example showing how cruel and treacherous this man Ts'ao Ts'ao really was.

61 · KO HUNG: *Wang Ch'iang* [22]

Yüan-ti [23] had so many concubines in his palace that he did not have time to meet all of them. He called upon his painters to make a portrait of each of these women so that, by examining the portraits, he could decide with whom he would spend the evening on a particular day. All of his concubines bribed the painters to paint them more beautiful than they really were, paying anywhere between 50,000 and 100,000 standard coins for each portrait. The only exception was Wang Ch'iang who, as a result, was never brought before the emperor's presence.

The king of the Hsiung-nu [24] sent a tribute mission to the Chinese court and requested a beautiful woman as his queen. Yüan-ti checked with his file of portraits and decided that Wang Ch'iang should make the trip. On the day of her departure, he summoned her before his presence. He found that not only was she the most beautiful woman in his palace; she also spoke well and had a refined, elegant manner. Though he regretted the decision which he had made, he nevertheless resolved to send her instead of making a change at the last minute. For the emperor emphasized the importance of keeping a promise to foreign countries, especially in view of the fact that her name had already been put on the record.

After Wang Ch'iang's departure, Yüan-ti ordered a thorough investigation. All painters were subsequently put to death, and their properties confiscated. It was then found that all of them were extremely wealthy.

Among the painters was Mao Yen-shou of Tuling [25] who, specializing in portraits, could paint a person to his exact likeness, regardless of whether he was old or young, handsome or homely. Ch'en Ch'ang of Anling [26] and Liu Hsiang and Kung K'uan of Hsinfeng [27] were expert painters of cattle, horses, and birds in flight. In the field of portrait painting, however, they were inferior to Mao Yen-shou. Both Yang Wang, a native of Hsiatu [28]) and Fan Yü were versatile in the

---

[22] The authorship of *Miscellaneous Notes on the Western Capital (Hsi-ching tsa-chi)*, from which this selection is translated, was traditionally attributed to Ko Hung, a Taoist writer of the third century. This tradition has been contested by modern scholars.

[23] Emperor Han Yüan-ti (r. A.D. 48–33).

[24] As for the Hsiung-nu, see pp. 210–220.

[25] Located in modern Shensi province.

[26] Located in modern Shensi province.

[27] Located in modern Shensi province.

[28] Located in modern Szechuan province.

use of colors. All of these painters were executed on the same day. In fact, famous painters became fewer and fewer after this incident.

62 · ANONYMOUS: *Flattery* [29]

Chou Chi was tall and handsome. One day, standing before a mirror after he had dressed up for the morning audience with the king, he turned around and asked his wife: "Who is more handsome, I or Mr. Hsü of the City North?" "You, sir, are very handsome," replied his wife; "how can Mr. Hsü be compared with you?"

Mr. Hsü of the City North was regarded as one of the most handsome men in the kingdom of Ch'i. Though assured by his wife of his superiority, he was still not certain. "Who is more handsome, I or Mr. Hsü?" he asked his concubine. "You, sir," replied his concubine.

The next day a friend dropped by, and Chou Chi asked him the same question. "You, sir, are much more handsome than Mr. Hsü," said the friend.

When Mr. Hsü came to visit him shortly afterwards, Chou Chi took a good look at him and concluded that the visitor, instead of him, was definitely better looking. Examining himself before a mirror, he was even more convinced. "Why did all of them say that I am more handsome when obviously this is not the case?" he asked himself after he had retired to his bedroom. "My wife flatters me because she wishes to please me. My concubine flatters me because she is afraid of me and dares not tell the truth. My friend flatters me because he wishes to seek favor from me."

The next morning when he had an audience with King Wei, he related to the king his story. "My wife, my concubine, and my friend all say that I am more handsome than Mr. Hsü because of false reasons peculiar to themselves. The kingdom of Ch'i has a breadth of 1,000 *li* and has within it 120 cities. All people in this kingdom, for various reasons, only flatter Your Majesty and dare not to speak the truth. Your concubines only wish to please you; your ministers are afraid of you; and all of your subjects want to curry favor from you. As far as seeking the truth is concerned, you, sir, are more in the dark than I am."

Upon hearing this, the king issued the following order to his subjects: "Those of you who remonstrate with me in person will receive the highest reward. Those who choose to advise me via written memorials will receive the second highest reward. If a person criticizes me in the market and such criticism then finds its way to my ears, he will receive the third highest reward." Soon after the order was issued, thousands of people presented their criticisms. The critics became fewer several months later. After one year they had nothing to criticize; in fact, criticism had completely disappeared.

Other kingdoms such as Yen, Chao, Han, and Wei heard what had happened to Ch'i and decided to send to Ch'i their tribute missions. This is a good example showing how victory against foreign countries can be won by cultivating one's own virtues at home.

[29] The present version of *Documents of the Warring States (Chan-kuo ts'e)*, from which this selection is translated, was edited by the Confucian scholar Liu Hsiang who lived in the first century B.C.

63 · TSUNG CH'EN: *A Letter to a Friend* [30]

Several thousand *li* away I consider myself fortunate to have received a letter from you, a friend whom I have greatly missed. Why did you have to send me any gifts? I do not know how to repay your kindness.

Knowing that you have not forgotten my father, I am sure that my father has missed you greatly. As for your instruction that I should cultivate confidence between superiors and inferiors and that I should improve my ability and virtue to meet the demand of my position, I cannot but feel strongly about it. I know that my ability or virtue is not up to the required standard: I know with even greater certainty that, as far as inspiring confidence is concerned, I am woefully inadequate. Let me elaborate this point.

What kind of man is he who today can inspire confidence? From morning to night he waits with his horse in front of a powerful lord's residence. When the doorman refuses to let him in on some specious excuse, he flatters like a woman and sweetens his request with a piece of gold. The doorman takes his personal card and presents it to the lord of the house, who for his own reasons does not choose to come out to meet him. Meanwhile the caller, standing in the stable, is waiting patiently amidst horses and grooms, both of which emit an odor that is as repugnant as it is disturbing. He is suffering from hunger as well as cold or heat, depending upon the seasons; but he will not leave, intolerable though the situation is. At dusk the doorman finally emerges and says to him: "The lord is tired and will not receive any more visitors today. Please come back tomorrow."

Since the lord has given his order, our caller feels that he must come back the next day. In the middle of the night, he wakes up, throws his clothing on, sits on his bed, and waits for the dawn to break. When the roosters begin to crow, he immediately gets up, washes, and dresses himself. Having arrived on his mount at the lord's residence, he knocks at the door. "Who is it?" the doorman shouts with an angry voice. "It is the same man who came here yesterday," he replies. "Why are you in such a hurry?" the doorman becomes even angrier. "Do you think that the lord will receive visitors at this unholy hour?" "I am helpless; please let me in," he pleads, even though deep in his heart he is as much ashamed of himself as we are ashamed of him. Again he offers money; the doorman gets up and lets him in. Again he is ordered to wait standing in the stable.

The lord agrees to meet him and summons him to his presence while facing the south.[31] Fearful and frightened, our caller prostrates himself below the walking terrace. The lord says "Come in," and he kowtows again. When he finally gets up after deliberately prolonging his prostration, he presents the lord with gold as tribute. The lord pretends that he does not wish to accept it, but our caller insists that he should. This goes on for a considerable time before the lord waves his retainers to take it. The caller kowtows in gratitude and once again prolongs

---

[30] A copy of the Chinese original can be found in *The Most Readable Essays Written in the Ancient Style (Ku-wen kuan-chih)*, roll 12, compiled by Wu Ch'u-ts'ai of the Ch'ing dynasty. A holder of the *chin-shih* degree, the author was a noted writer of the sixteenth century.

[31] The emperor customarily faced the southern direction when meeting with his ministers. In this case, the lord merely shows his contempt for the uninvited visitor.

his prostration deliberately.[32] When he finally gets up, he salutes five or six times before he leaves the lord's presence.

Reaching the front door, he salutes the doorman and says: "Please be nice to me. Do not bar me when I come here next time." The doorman salutes in return. He is happy beyond belief and rushes out quickly from the lord's residence. On his way home whenever he meets someone he knows, he flourishes his whip on the mount and says proudly: "The lord is extremely generous with me." Then he exaggerates the graciousness with which the lord has received him. Whatever doubts they might have, his friends do not wish to take a chance of offending the lord, and they have to take his words for whatever they are worth. Once in a while the lord mentions casually that "Mr. So-and-So is a good man," and his listeners will echo accordingly.

The world regards the man described above as being able to inspire confidence between superiors and inferiors. Do you, sir, wish me to follow his example? As for this powerful lord I have described, I send him two cards each year, one for the summer and the other for the winter; I do not visit him for the rest of the year. Whenever I pass by his residence, I close my eyes and cover my ears, and speed up my horse as if I were chased by an evil spirit. People might say that I am too narrow-minded and thus unable to please my superiors. But I cannot care less. I often shout aloud: "Each man has his own destiny to follow; I shall only do what I regard as right." I do not blame you, sir, if you scold me for my impracticability.

64 · OU-YANG HSIU: *On Eunuchs*[33]

Eunuchs come about because of a monarch's love of sexual indulgence. Yet the harms they cause to a nation are much more serious than those resulting from sexual indulgence. This has been true throughout history.

There are numerous ways in which eunuchs can bring harms to a nation. As they are close to and on familiar terms with a monarch, they have an advantage which no one else possesses. They can afford to be harsh and dictatorial. They do small favors to please and keep their promises in nonessential matters so as to win trust from others. However, once a monarch trusts them and takes them into his confidence, they manipulate or sometimes control him through a simple device: they remind him of the evil consequences that might ensue if he does not listen to their advice. Even though there are loyal scholar-ministers in the court, the monarch will not trust them because, in his judgement, they are too remote and unfamiliar and are not so reliable as those who are around him every day from morning to night.

As the monarch draws closer and closer to the persons surrounding him, his alienation from his scholar-ministers also becomes greater and greater. Meanwhile he becomes more and more isolated from the outside world. The more isolated he is, the more fearful he becomes; the more fearful he becomes, the greater will he be subject to the eunuchs' control. Eventually even his life is at the mercy of his nominal servants who decide whether he should live or die in

---

[32] The caller does this to show his unreserved loyalty or subservience.

[33] Translated from "Biographies of Eunuchs" *(Huan-che chuan); New History of the Five Dynasties (Hsin Wu-tai shih),* roll 38.

accordance with their whims: danger has thus lurked behind every door or curtain in his imperial palace. The persons whom he thought he could trust have now become a source of danger to him.

Once the danger becomes too obvious, the monarch will doubtless try to make an alliance with his hitherto alienated ministers for the purpose of eliminating the very persons who until then have been his closest allies. If for some reason he and his ministers decide to wait for a propitious moment to take such a drastic step, the danger to his life will continue to deepen. If on the other hand they decide to take immediate action, the eunuchs, being close by, can hold the monarch as hostage. In view of this situation, it is extremely difficult for the ministers to initiate an alliance with the monarch against the eunuchs, however capable the ministers happen to be. Even if such an alliance can be formed, it is unlikely that it will be followed by concrete action. Even if action can be taken, it is doubtful that it can really achieve its purpose, because in the end an action of this sort will bring about damage and defeat to the allies as well as the eunuchs. It may cause the monarch to lose his kingdom. Even if the dynasty does manage to survive, the monarch himself may be killed. This in turn will give some strong but unprincipled man the needed excuse to kill all eunuchs so as to allay the anger of all people in the nation. Instances of this description appear time and again in recorded history, and it is clear that the eunuch curse is not confined to a particular generation or period.

No monarch wishes to cultivate danger to himself within his palace ground or to alienate his loyal scholar-ministers deliberately. Nevertheless, the danger comes about because, given the situation described above, it slowly but inevitably feeds itself until it becomes a reality too large to be ignored. In the case of sexual indulgence, a monarch will of course suffer evil consequences if he remains unaware of the danger he is in. However, once he becomes aware of it, he can easily eliminate that danger by dismissing the women who have hitherto surrounded him. The eunuch danger, on the other hand, cannot be easily eliminated even after the danger has been recognized. . . . This is what I mean when I say that the harms caused by eunuchs are much more serious than those resulting from a monarch's sexual indulgence. How can future monarchs afford not to be alert to this danger?

65 · Huang Tsung-hsi: *The Abuse of Power by Eunuchs* [34]

The abuse of power by eunuchs appeared time and again during the Han, T'ang, and Sung dynasties, but at no time did it become so bad as it did during the Ming dynasty. Prior to the Ming period the eunuchs often meddled in policy-making, but rarely were they entrusted with the implementation of policies. In practice as well as in theory only the prime minister and the Six Ministries [35] had the power and the authority to implement policies.

The situation was entirely different during the Ming dynasty. The imperial wish was transmitted orally to the eunuchs before they were forwarded in written form to the government. Tax revenues were transported first to the Inner Treasuries [36]

---

[34] *Ming-yi tai-fang lu,* the 20th essay.
[35] Ministries of Rites, Finance, Personnel, War, Justice, and Public Works.
[36] *Nei-k'u,* in charge of the finance of the imperial household.

before they were allowed to fill the government's warehouses. In the matter of enforcing the law and conducting trials, the East Chamber [37] superseded the regular judicial apparatus. The control by eunuchs of other branches was equally absolute. The prime minister and the heads of the Six Ministries had become the administrative staff who merely carried out the orders issued by the eunuchs in the name of the monarch.

A monarch regards the empire as his household, the government's treasures as his private possessions, and the defense of his person as the national defense. Though his assumption can be challenged on theoretical grounds, it has been the practice in later periods. The Ming monarchs, however, went even beyond this assumption. Since their personal needs, whether they be food, clothing, shelter, transportation, entertainment, or ceremonial equipment, could be obtained within a few miles of the Forbidden City, these monarchs viewed all administrative organs outside of the Inner Court and all the treasures gathered therein as if they were foreign possessions; they demanded more from the government in order to fill up their own private coffers. When a monarch adopted this kind of attitude and acted accordingly, his empire had in fact shrunk to within several miles around the Forbidden City. Who were responsible for this narrow attitude on the part of the emperor? The eunuchs, of course.

During the Han, T'ang, and Sung dynasties the eunuchs could succeed in acquiring power only when the monarch was ignorant, weak, and incapable of administering his government. The situation was different during the Ming dynasty when the entrenchment of eunuchs in power had become a matter of custom and usage, and the emperor could not dislodge them from the position of power even if he wished to do so. Emperor Yi-tsung [38] distrusted eunuchs at the beginning; but, brilliant and wise as he was, he never succeeded in dismissing them from the position of power. Before he died, he did not even have the opportunity of meeting with his own ministers.[39]

The relationship between a monarch and his eunuchs should be the kind of relationship between a master and his slaves. On the other hand, the relationship between a king and his ministers should be the kind of relationship existing among friends, or between a pupil and his teachers, with the ministers playing the teachers' role. The virtue of a slave is obedience, and a good slave serves well his master's whims. The virtue of a teacher, on the other hand, comprises wisdom and knowledge. If a minister acts like a slave, he has lost, by being a flatterer, his usefulness as the monarch's adviser. As a friend and a teacher, a good minister should remonstrate with the king whenever he finds the king in error. The eunuchs, being slaves, commit a serious offense indeed if they attempt to do likewise.

The eunuchs are the king's servants in the Inner Court, whereas scholars and ministers are his servants in the Outer Court. Using the ways of a slave to serve the whims of a king, the eunuchs are at a loss to understand why scholars and ministers are sometimes allowed to defy the king's wishes. "Are they not the king's servants to the same extent we are?" they ask. "Why are they allowed to be so irreverent?" Being used to the slavish way the eunuchs serve him, the king

---

[37] The East Chamber (*tung-ch'ang*), controlled and staffed by eunuchs, tried persons who had allegedly committed treason or other cardinal crimes.

[38] Also known as Ch'ung-chen (r.1628–1644), the last monarch of the Ming dynasty.

[39] The emperor committed suicide in 1644 when the rebels, led by Li Tzu-ch'eng, captured the capital of Peking.

eventually asks the same question. "Is it not true that all of my people are my subjects?" he asks himself. "Why is it that one group is obedient to me and the other group is not?" Then he reaches the conclusion that only the eunuchs love him, while his ministers only love themselves.

When a minister becomes too eager to please and attempts to satisfy every selfish desire of his king, he has in fact abandoned his traditional role as a teacher or friend and adopted the attitude of a flattering slave. As this attitude becomes widespread and is solidified by usage, many superficial scholars begin to rationalize it by saying that the king represents Heaven and should be obeyed at all times regardless of whether he is right or wrong. In their memorials they refrain from criticism even though they know that he is wrong; when on occasion they do venture to criticize, they confine themselves to matters of comparative insignificance. Abandoning the ancient principle of ministership, they merely indulge themselves in expediencies. They are ignorant; yet they honestly believe that this is the proper way of serving their king.

In summary, it may be said that eunuch power not only corrupts sound principles that have degenerated into a rationalization of servitude; it also renders impotent the conscience of man. It surpasses all others as an evil of our political system.

66 · SSU-MA CH'IEN: *Fan Li and His Sons* [40]

Fan Li decided to move to T'ao [41] which, as an important trade center, he hoped would provide him with the opportunity of amassing a fortune. After his arrival, he changed his name to T'ao Chu-kung. He and his sons were simultaneously engaged in farming and the raising of livestock. Besides, he purchased goods and hoarded them when their prices were low, and sold them when their prices were high. Through these efforts he amassed a large fortune in a short period. In fact, he was considered the richest man in China.

Chu-kung had three sons, the youngest of whom was born after the family had moved to T'ao. One day bad news arrived at the Fan household: his second son had committed murder at the state of Ch'u and was now imprisoned. "It is true that the penalty for murder should be death," Chu-kung said to himself; "it is also true that 'a rich man's son should not die in the market'." [42] He loaded an earthen jar containing one thousand *yi* [43] of gold on an ox-drawn wagon and then ordered his youngest son, who by then had reached adulthood, to repair to Ch'u where the money would be used to save his second son's life.

After learning that his youngest brother was sent for this important mission, Chu-kung's eldest son insisted that he should make the trip insead. Chu-kung refused his demand. "The eldest son of a family is called a family supervisor," contended the eldest son. "The fact that you, sir, have chosen your youngest son for this important mission indicates clearly that I have failed as the family supervisor." After saying this, he threatened to commit suicide.

[40] The Chinese original appears in "Biography of Kou Chien, King of Yüeh" *(Yüeh-wang Kou Chien shih-chia); Shih chi*, roll 41.

[41] Located in modern Shantung province.

[42] The market was the place for public execution.

[43] An *yi* was equivalent to twenty taels.

"We may or may not be able to save our second son," said Chu-kung's wife. "But, if we sent our youngest son, we would lose our eldest son even before the attempt is made." Facing this dilemma, Chu-kung had no choice but to reverse his decision. He prepared a letter addressed to a friend of his named Chuang which, together with the gold, was to be delivered personally to the addressee. After the gold was delivered, his eldest son should let Mr. Chuang do whatever he pleased with it. Under no cirsumstances, said Chu-kung, should his son argue with Mr. Chuang about how the money should be disposed.

Besides the one thousand *yi* of gold his father had given him, the eldest son also took with him several hundred taels of his personal gold. He had his own idea as to how his brother's life could be saved.

Mr. Chuang lived in a deserted area underneath the city wall where weeds and wild bamboo grew so profusely that they reached as far as his front door. In fact, he was a very poor man. When the eldest son presented him with the gold, he took it without hesitation. Then he said: "Do not stay in Ch'u even for a moment and hurry home as fast as you can. Your younger brother will be released. Do not ask me, however, how I plan to get him released." Instead of leaving Ch'u as he was instructed, the eldest son stayed without Mr. Chuang's knowledge. Meanwhile he took the several hundred taels he had and presented them to a Ch'u noble who allegedly had a great deal of influence with the king.

Though a poor man, Mr. Chuang was widely known for his incorruptibility. All high officials in Ch'u, from the king down, respected him as greatly as if he were their own teacher. He did not mean to keep the gold that had been presented to him; he merely wished to test Chu-kung's good faith. He would return the gold soon after he had completed the function for which the gold was given. "This is Chu-kung's gold," said he to his wife. "It is like a disease. Do not touch it under any circumstances." Chu-kung's eldest son, however, did not know Mr. Chuang's intentions, and thought that Mr. Chuang was as avaricious and corrupt as most people on earth.

Mr. Chuang went to see the king when the first opportunity presented itself. He told the king that a certain star had moved to a new position and such movement was inauspicious to the welfare of the Ch'u state. Showing his usual confidence in Mr. Chuang, the king asked him what he should do. "Your Majesty should perform a good deed to counteract the evil influence caused by the movement of this star," Mr. Chuang replied. The king agreed with him and gave order that the doors of the treasury be closed.[44]

Surprised by this new development, the Ch'u noble whom Chu-kung's eldest son had bribed rushed to tell the young man that the king would order a general clemency. "How did you know?" "Last night the king ordered the closing of all treasury doors," replied the Ch'u noble; "every time he does this, it means a general clemency."

Knowing that a general clemency was forthcoming and that his younger brother would be released, Chu-kung's eldest son thought that Mr. Chuang was no longer useful to him and that he had simply wasted one thousand *yi* of gold. Again he paid a visit to Mr. Chuang.

[44] According to an ancient custom, the closing of treasury doors preceded the announcement of a general clemency on the theory that robbers and bandits, once released from jail after the clemency was put into effect, might try to steal money from the government's treasury.

"Why are you still here?" Mr. Chuang was surprised because he thought that the young man had gone home a long time before.

"I have not gone home yet," replied Chu-kung's eldest son. "I came here on account of my younger brother. Now that I have heard that he will be released as a result of a general clemency, I come here to bid you farewell."

Mr. Chuang, however, knew the real purpose of this young man's visit. He told him that the gold was in the house and that he could go inside and fetch it himself. The young man did accordingly and was happy with the fact that he had his money back.

Feeling cheated and humiliated, Mr. Chuang went immediately to see the king. "The other day your servant suggested the performance of a good deed to counter-act the evil influence caused by the movement of a certain star," said Mr. Chuang. "This morning while walking in the street, I heard people say that a son of a T'ao millionaire has committed murder in Ch'u and is presently in jail; that this rich man of T'ao has heavily bribed all officials serving Your Majesty; that the real purpose of Your Majesty's proclamation of a general clemency is to save this rich man's son; and that Your Majesty has in mind the welfare of a murderer in-stead of that of the Ch'u state." The king was furious. "Lacking virtue as I do, I will not grant favor to a man simply because his father is rich." He gave the order that Chu-kung's second son be executed immediately. The day after the execution order had been carried out, he announced the general clemency which had been widely expected.

Thus instead of bringing home a live brother, Chu-kung's eldest son brought home a dead body. His mother wept in sorrow; so did all people in the city of T'ao. The only exception was Chu-kung who showed no sadness at all. "I knew that my eldest son would kill his younger brother," said he smilingly. "This is not because he did not love his brother; in fact he did. The reason is that he also loved money and was reluctant to part with it. Both he and I have experienced poverty, and he knew how difficult it was to make money. Consequently, once money was made, he attached great importance to it and was reluctant to give it away. My youngest son, on the other hand, was born to wealth. He rode the best horses and hunted rabbits for recreation; and as far as he was concerned, money came easily and was practically inexhaustible. Since he attached little importance to money and was not unhappy to part with it, my original plan was to dispatch him instead of his eldest brother. Unwilling to give money away, my eldest son killed his own brother. This is the way life is and there is nothing to be sorrowful about. In fact I have been expecting the bad news all the time."

67 · YÜAN MEI: *Lu Liang-chi* [45]

Lu Liang-chi, who at one time served under T'ien Wen-ching, governor of Honan, was a very unusual man. T'ien was harsh and strict, and all officials un-der his jurisdiction, civilian or military, were extremely cautious in the perfor-mance of their duties.

[45] A copy of the Chinese original can be found in *Sample Prose of the Ming-Ch'ing period (Ming-Ch'ing san-wen hsien)* (Nanking, 1937), compiled and edited by Hu Lun-ch'ing, pp. 155–158.

One day the governor ordered Lu to repair to Chungmou [46] to take away the official seal from magistrate Li and succeed him as the new magistrate.[47] Having received the order, Lu purposely changed into ordinary clothes—coarse garments and a straw hat—so that nobody could recognize him as a government official, and proceeded to Chungmou on a donkey. Once in Chungmou, several hundred elders came to comfort him on account of his long journey and inquired about news in the capital. "We have heard that a certain Mr. Lu is about to arrive to replace our magistrate," said they. "Did you heard about this when you were in Kaifeng?" [48]

"Why did you ask this question?" Lu pretended that he did not understand its meaning.

"We have a good magistrate here. We do not wish him to leave us," said the elders.

Several *li* beyond, Lu saw a group of people in scholar's attire, who were discussing something among themselves. "It is a pity that such a good official has to leave us. When Mr. Lu arrives, we shall complain to him," said one. Shaking his head, another man said: "What is the use? Governor T'ien has already given the order. Even if there were ten Mr. Lus, they could not do much about it. Furthermore, Mr. Lu is the very person who is going to replace our magistrate. Do you think that he will sacrifice his own interest to benefit others?" Hearing these remarks, Lu acquired great respect for these people. He did not utter a word, however.

Arriving at the city, Lu met Li and found him to be a gentle, elegant person.

"The seal has been waiting for you for a long time," said Li.

"As I look at you and the clothes you wear, you do not look like an extravagant person," said Lu. "Moreover, your people speak very highly of you as a magistrate. How did you in such a short time become indebted to the treasury?"

"I am a native of southern Yunnan which is ten thousand *li* from this place," Li replied. "I left my mother for the capital and, after ten years, finally received the appointment as magistrate of Chungmou. I borrowed my own salary from the treasury to send for my mother. The moment my mother arrived, I was impeached. What a fate I have!" He burst into tears before he could finish his words.

"I feel very warm. Please prepare some water for my bath," said Lu.

Lu went to another room to take his bath while thinking this matter over. He could not help being moved by Li's remarks. A moment later, he suddenly struck the water with tremendous force and vowed to do something about this. "What kind of man would I be if I did as ordinary people do?" He dressed up in his official garbs and bid Li farewell.

"Where are you going?" Li was astonished.

"Back to the capital," Lu replied.

Li gave him the official seal, but Lu refused to take it. "But I do not want to implicate you," Li insisted.

Taking the seal, Lu threw it to the ground; as it struck, it yielded a tinkling

---

[46] Located in modern Honan province.

[47] A magistrate was the head of a subprefecture, appointed by and responsible to the governor. To take away his official seal was to dismiss him from his office.

[48] The capital of Honan province.

sound.[49] "You do not understand Lu Liang-chi!" he scolded Li in a loud voice. He climbed his mount in anger and then galloped away. All people in the city burned incense to see him off.[50]

Arriving at the capital, he reported the happenings to the responsible officials. "You must have been out of your mind," said they. "No governor will tolerate what you did, let alone His Excellency T'ien."

Early the next morning, when Lu arrived at the governor's official residence, he found that the responsible officials to whom he had spoken were already there. Before he had time to submit his name for an audience, the governor gave the order that he be brought in immediately.

The governor was sitting in his official chair and facing south. His face was as dark as iron;[51] and flanked by a dozen military and civilian officials, he put on an insulting air.

"Why did you not stay in your subprefecture and take care of official business? What did you come here for?" The governor stared at Lu with angry eyes.

"I have something to report," Lu replied.

"Where is the seal?"

"It is still in Chungmou."

"To whom did you give the seal?"

"Magistrate Li."

The governor sneered. Turning to the flanking officials, he said: "Have you ever heard a seal-taker behaving in this manner?"

"No," they replied.

At this moment the responsible officials stood up and offered the governor their apology. "We have failed in our teaching and supervising duties and consequently have a subordinate like this," said they. "He should be impeached as magistrate Li was. Meanwhile give him to us, and we shall try him in the most severe manner. If he is found to have conspired with magistrate Li in this matter, we will punish him as a warning to all other officials."

Lu took off his hat and kowtowed. "Let it be!" he cried aloud. "But I would like to say a few words for myself. As a poor scholar, I came to Honan for the sole purpose of seeking a governmental post. You can imagine how happy I was when I learned of my appointment as magistrate of Chungmou. I was impatient to begin my official duties. However, when I arrived at Chungmou, I found out what kind of person magistrate Li was, how popular he was, and why he owed money to the treasury. If Your Excellency had known all about this man before you sent me to replace him, I would plead guilty for failing to perform my assigned duties and for earning a reputation of selflessness and generosity which I do not deserve. If on the other hand Your Excellency did not know anything about this man before you sent me, I have not committed any offense by reporting to you the situation as I saw it and by waiting for your decision in this matter. I believe that the course I took is more compatible with Your Excellency's desire to patronize all men of talent as well as with His Majesty's wish of elevating filial piety as the most important virtue to govern the nation. If Your Excellency does not believe that magistrate Li deserves pity or sympathy, you can take the seal

---

[49] An official seal was usually made of copper or bronze.

[50] They were showing their gratitude to Lu for helping their magistrate.

[51] Showing anger.

away from him at any time. In fact, there are dozens of officials outside of this office who would be only too happy to obtain that seal for themselves. Who am I who dare to defy Your Excellency's wishes?"

The governor was silent. With their eyes, the responsible officials signaled Lu to leave. Leaving, Lu did not perform the ritual of showing gratitude as dictated by custom. When he was about to leave the hall, the governor's expression suddenly changed. The governor walked down the stairs and shouted: "Come back!" Lu returned and knelt on the floor. The governor took off his coral hat[52] and placed it on Lu's head.

"You are a very unusual man," the governor sighed. "No man deserves this hat better than you do. Without you I have almost dismissed a good official by mistake. But the memorial to dismiss him is already on its way to the imperial government. What can I do?"

"How long has the courier been gone?" Lu asked.

"He has been gone for five days. No horse can catch him, however fast it is."

"With Your Excellency's blessing, I believe that I can," said Lu. "When I was a young man, I used to be able to travel one hundred li per day. If Your Excellency really wishes to withdraw that memorial, please give me your commanding arrow[53] as well as your written order, so that the courier will not raise any questions." The governor agreed, and Lu started his journey.

Five days later, the memorial of dismissal was returned to the governor, and magistrate Li was safe in his post. Because of this incident, Lu became famous throughout the nation.

68 · Ch'u Shao-sun: *The Marriage of the River God*[54]

Hsi-men Pao was appointed as magistrate of Yeh[55] during the reign of Duke Wen of Wei.[56] After arriving at his post, he asked the local elders from what they suffered most. "The marriage of the River God," they replied; "it is the main reason for our being so poor." Asked again how the marriage of the River God could cause poverty, the elders answered him as follows:

Each year before the wedding took place, said the elders, the town chief and the town treasurer imposed heavy taxation upon the people. Of the several million standard coins they collected they spent two or three thousand on the wedding and divided the rest among the sorceresses and themselves. Shortly before the wedding took place, the sorceresses went from house to house and, seeing an attractive maiden, would designate her as the prospective bride. The girl would then be washed clean from head to toe, and new silk clothes would be made for her wedding dress. To wait for the scheduled wedding, she went through a period of fasting and penance in her own house. Meanwhile a structure on a raft, called

---

[52] The official hat of a governor.

[53] A commanding arrow (*ch'i-chien* or *ling-chien*) identified its owner and the authority he exercised. It was usually used on the battlefield by a military commander. Lu requested its use on account of the urgent nature of this matter under discussion.

[54] The Chinese original appears as an appendix to "The Jesters" (*Hua-chi lieh-chuan*), *Shih chi,* roll 126.

[55] Located in modern Honan province.

[56] The story that follows allegedly occurred in c.424 B.C.

penance hall, was built on the bank of the river and richly decorated with yellow and golden silk. Delicious food—meat, wine, and rice—was placed in it. For a period of ten days the girl lived in it; she was powdered and rouged like any other bride. On the day of her wedding to the River God, the raft structure was placed on the river with her in it. It floated downstream for many miles before it submerged into the water.

Because of this custom, continued the elders, many families with daughters had left the city which, consequently, had fewer and fewer people as time went on. Those who were left behind became poorer and poorer on account of the heavy taxes they had to pay, since this annual marriage of the River God had gone on for a long time. People said that if the River God did not receive his bride, he would cause flood and would bring death to all people in this area.

Upon hearing this story, Hsi-men Pao told the elders that at the next wedding of the River God he would like the local officials and the sorceresses to inform him in advance so that he could attend the wedding himself. The elders said that they would be happy to comply with his demand.

On the day of the wedding Hsi-men Pao arrived at the river bank. There were about three thousand people watching the procedure, including the town chief, wealthy and influential citizens of the community, and the elders. Besides, there was the chief sorceress, aged seventy or over, accompanied by ten of her disciples who, dressed in unlined garments made of silk, stood behind her. Hsi-men Pao told the officials in charge that he would like to see the bride himself to make sure that she was attractive enough to be the River God's wife. After the girl was brought before him, he announced to the local officials and the sorceresses that this girl was too plain for the role which she was supposed to play and that he was wondering whether the chief sorceress would be kind enough to inform the River God to wait for a few days until a more attractive girl could be found as his bride. He then ordered the soldiers to throw the chief sorceress into the river.

A moment later Hsi-men Pao said that he could not understand why the chief sorceress had not returned and that a disciple of hers should be sent to hurry her. A young sorceress was then thrown into the river. Neither did she return; so another young sorceress was thrown into the river to hurry the first one. Altogether three young sorceresses were sent down to the bottom of the river.

"You cannot trust women," Hsi-men commented. "They cannot deliver even a simple message. May I bother the town chief for this important mission?" The town chief was then thrown into the river.

The magistrate stood attentively, facing the river and bowing his head in respect. The elders and the officials were as frightened as they were surprised. For a long time the magistrate waited for the messengers' return, but in vain. "What should we do since none of them has returned?" he asked. He suggested that the town treasurer and a member of the local gentry should be sent to the river to fetch them. Upon hearing this both of them prostrated themselves and knocked their heads so hard against the ground that blood gushed out, entailing the change of color on the ground.[57] "Maybe we should wait for a while and see whether our messengers will return by themselves," said the magistrate.

A moment later, Hsi-men Pao spoke again. "Arise, dear treasurer. Since the

[57] This was the way of showing deep repentence and of seeking forgiveness.

River God has obviously decided to retain our messengers as his permanent guests, there is no sense for you to go there now. In fact, I think that all of you should proceed home at this moment." From then on, nobody in Yeh ever dared to speak of the marriage of the River God.

CHAPTER NINE

Recruitment of
Governmental Personnel

Prior to the Ch'in-Han period (221 B.C.–A.D. 220) little distinction was made between the government and the royal household, and all officials were regarded as the king's personal servants. Beginning in 221 B.C. when China was unified, the territory to be administered became a huge empire, and the centralized authority required a large army of civil servants to run governments at various levels. The shortage of qualified bureaucratic personnel was keenly felt by Liu Pang, founder of the Han dynasty, after he had brought the country under his control in the last decade of the third century B.C. (Selection 69). The same shortage was also felt by his great grandson Han Wu-ti (r. 140–87 B.C.) who made the recruitment of "virtuous" men part of an official's normal and required duties (Selections 70 and 71). It was he who introduced the selection system (*hsüan-chü*) which was greatly refined and institutionalized during the Later Han dynasty (A.D. 25–220).

In due course the selection system—the recommendation of "virtuous" men as prospective officials by local governments—deteriorated. When China was again unified late in the sixth century A.D. after a long period of political division and civil war, a new device had to be found for recruiting governmental personnel. This new device was called *k'o-chü*, or examination system. First introduced during the Sui dynasty (590–618), it was followed by all the subsequent dynasties without fail and was not abolished until 1905.

During the early period of the examination system, it was often necessary for a candidate to have an established reputation before he was allowed to pass the examination; and in such a case success in the examination was more a confirmation than a discovery of his talent. Since only high officials or renowned scholars could testify to a man's literary ability, obscure scholars made intense efforts to seek patronage (Selection 72). If the patron happened to be a man of unusual influence, the result of the examination was decided even before the examination took place (Selection 73).

This practice, however, was abolished altogether beginning in the Sung dynasty (960–1279). From then on, the evaluation of a candidate was based solely upon the paper he wrote during the examination. How was it possible to determine a candidate's literary ability in one examination, not to speak of his personal character which would not be revealed? Was it not true that

159

the candidates were primarily motivated by personal gains (power, influence, and wealth) when taking the examination rather than the desire for public service? Was this motive not a reflection on their character which made the examination system itself self-defeating since the purpose of the system was to recruit "virtuous" men? What subjects should be tested in the examination? Should poetry or prose be more emphasized? These questions were raised time and again during the course of Chinese history (Selections 74, 75, 76 and 77). Most scholars, however, regarded the examination system as basically sound, though it needed reform from time to time (Selection 78).

Regardless of the stortcomings of the examination system, success was extremely rewarding to a person who had passed the examination. Overnight he became a celebrity, however humble his origin might be. The rendition of the colorful drama involving the passing of the examination is certainly beyond the capacity of most historians, and we shall do well to leave it in the hands of professional storytellers or novelists. In Wu Ching-tzu (1701–1754), author of the famous novel *An Unofficial History of the Literati* (*Ju-lin wai-shih*), we may have found such a writer (Selection 79). Though written in a fictional form, the story he tells is very typical.

69 · HAN KAO-TSU (LIU PANG): *An Invitation to Virtuous Men to Serve the Government* [1]

I have heard that no monarch is better than King Wen [2] and no prince is superior to Duke Huan of Ch'i. [3] Yet neither of these two would have become famous without the help of able, virtuous men. It is not true that men of wisdom and ability are less numerous today than they were in ancient times. When a monarch does not attempt to communicate with them, they have no way of making their talents available.

Thanks to the blessings of Heaven and the help of my able ministers, I have been able to unify the country: all people in the nation are now members of one family. It is my hope that my descendants will be able continuously to honor their ancestors and worship in the imperial temple until eternity to come. Now that my ministers have helped me pacify the country, it is only fair that they should share with me the blessings of victory.

I can honor and make famous the able and the virtuous who choose to follow me and share with me the burden of the state. Let this wish of mine be publicized throughout the empire so that it will be widely understood. Let it be transmitted from the Grand Counsellor Chou Ch'ang to Prime Minister Hsiao Ho who in turn shall transmit it to all princes throughout the empire. Meanwhile the Deputy Prime Minister should do likewise with regard to provincial governors and their subordinates. If any of the princes or governors discovers a man of talent and virtue under his jurisdiction, he should personally invite him to serve

---

[1] This decree was issued in 196 B.C. Source: "Biography of Han Kao-tsu (*Kao-ti chi); Han shu,* roll 1.

[2] A founder of the Chou dynasty.

[3] Ch'i Huan-kung (686–643 B.C.).

the government. He should see to it that the prospective official be escorted with respect to the Prime Minister's office, and that a description of his age, appearance, and demeanor be forwarded with the recommendation. An official who knows a virtuous man within his jurisdiction and chooses not to report shall lose his position. However, he should not send a man who is either too old or suffering from chronic disease.

70 · HAN WU-TI: *The Recruitment of Talents* [4]

The primary duty of all ministers is to formulate policies, unify the people, universalize our culture, and cultivate good customs. The Five Emperors and the Three Dynasties brought peace and prosperity to the country because they emphasized love and righteousness as the moral foundation of the nation; cultivated virtue and employed the virtuous; and promoted goodness and punished the violent and the wicked. I never cease to hope that I can secure the cooperation of all scholars in the nation to attain this ancient goal.

Consequently I have taken as my task the honoring of the aged, the rewarding of the filial and the respectful, the selection of talented men as government officials, and the promotion of learning and literature. All men of talents can thus participate in the government and transmit to me the wishes and aspirations of the people as a whole. To my officials I have repeatedly emphasized that they should recommend to me the filial and the incorruptible within their respective jurisdictions so as to establish a new tradition of recruiting governmental personnel. Once more we may be able to follow the virtuous path of the ancient sages.

It has been correctly stated that "There is a virtuous man in every ten households" and that "Whenever three men walk together, one of them is good enough to be my teacher." [5] Why is it that sometimes not a single man is recommended to the imperial government for an entire province? To me the reason is very simple: the people have not heard or understood my message, and gentlemen of character, having no means of making themselves known, continue to live in obscurity. You, as governors of the people, can do well in helping me govern the country if you search diligently for the virtuous and the incorruptible, provide inspiration and comfort for my people, and induce them to observe the custom and tradition of each of the communities in which they live.

An ancient law says that those officials who recommend virtuous men should be richly rewarded and those who conceal them should be punished by death. Let the governors, personnel officials, and learned professors deliberate carefully on this matter. Those officials who fail to recommend the filial and the incorruptible will be charged with nonfulfillment of duties and be punished accordingly.

[4] This decree was issued in 128 B.C. Source: "Biography of Han Wu-ti" *(Wu-ti chi); Han shu,* roll 6.
[5] These remarks are attributed to Confucius.

71 · HAN WU-TI: *An Invitation to Join the Government* [6]

I have heard that unusual deeds require unusual men. As a wild, unmanageable horse can sometimes run a thousand *li* a day, an unpopular scholar may likewise perform great deeds. In either case—a trackless horse or an unconventional scholar—its usefulness can only come about if one knows how to harness its energy or utilize its talent. Let all governors and magistrates report to me the unusual talents they can find within their respective jurdisdictions—those who can be ministers or generals or those who can serve as my envoys to distant kingdoms.

72 · LI PO: *A Letter to Han Yü* [7]

When the world's opinion-formers get together, I have heard them say: "I do not care whether I become a duke, but I shall be very happy indeed if I have the opportunity of meeting with Han Ching-chou." [8] How greatly people admire you, sir! Is it not true that you, by following the example of Duke Chou, have become a magnet to all the heroes in the nation who subsequently rush towards your door? Once accepted by you, their reputation will be increased tenfold; that is why they all desire one word of your approval in order to increase their own worth. Since you, sir, do not judge people according to their wealth, it is possible that "Among three thousand guests there is a man named Mao Sui." [9] Will you, sir, make a Mao Sui out of me?

I am a commoner from Lunghsi,[10] and have been wandering through Ch'uhan.[11] I learned swordplay when I was fifteen, and subsequently offended every prince whom I met. As a writer I became proficient when I reached thirty; yet time and again I only succeeded in infuriating the ministers of the state. Though I am no taller than seven *ch'ih*,[12] my ambition is greater than that of thousands of others—

---

[6] This decree was issued in 105 B.C. Source: "Biography of Han Wu-ti *(Wu-ti chi); Han shu*, roll 6.

[7] This letter has a unique place in the history of Chinese literature in view of the fact that it was written by the grestest T'ang poet and was addressed to the greatest T'ang prose writer. At the time of its writing, however, Li Po (701–762) was still a comparatively obscure figure. A copy of the Chinese original can be found in *Ku-wen kuan-chih,* roll 7.

[8] The real name of Han Ching-chou was Han Ch'ao-tsung, governor of Ching-chou (modern Hupeh province) in the 730's. During his tenure of office he was noted for his patronage of talented men of younger generations.

[9] In the fourth century B.C., Hantan, the capital of Chao, was besieged by an invading army from the state of Ch'in. To seek help, the king of Chao ordered Prince P'ingyüan to make a journey to the state of Ch'u. Mao Sui, then one of the least distinguished of the prince's "three thousand guests," volunteered to accompany the prince for the proposed trip. As a result of his "forceful" persuasion ("he grabbed the king of Ch'u with one hand while holding a sword in the other"), the king of Ch'u agreed to send reinforcements to lift the siege. Because of this historical incident, whenever a person volunteers for a task for which others think that he is unqualified, he would say that he is merely "following the example of Mao Sui to recommend himself" (*Mao Sui tzu chien*).

[10] Modern Shensi province.

[11] Modern Hupeh province.

[12] The ancient *ch'ih* (Chinese foot) was much shorter than its modern equivalent (14.1 inches).

men of power and influence have spoken highly of my principle and courage. This is how I feel about myself; how dare I not to share my opinion of myself with you?

You, sir, can be favorably compared with the greatest immortals in the matter of achievement, and your virtuous conduct has moved Heaven and Earth. Your pen has opened the innermost secrets of the universe, and your knowledge has reached the most secluded cloister in the mind of Heaven and man. Will you kindly, sir, open your heart and receive me, even though I do not intend to humiliate myself more than it is necessary when meeting with you?

I shall have no objection, however, if you insist on entertaining me with a lavish dinner and let me speak out what I have in my mind. Should you wish to test my ability in writing, I can assure you that I can complete ten thousand words in a brief moment daily. Now that you are the final authority on the merit of men as well as their literary ability, and now that a scholar will acquire sudden fame once you have passed upon him a favorable judgement, will you, sir, begrudge a small effort of yours to enable me to emerge from obscurity and soar to the clouds?

Formerly, when Wang Tzu-shih was appointed governor of Yü, he invited Hsün Tz'u-ming to join his staff before he journeyed to his post and recruited K'ung wen-chü after he had arrived at his destination.[13] When Shan T'ao was the governor of Yi,[14] he scrutinized men of talent within his jurisdiction and recommended thirty of them, one of whom later rose to become a deputy minister in the imperial government. Both governors were praised highly for their recognition of talent. You, sir, have also recommended Yen Hsieh-lü who subsequently became a secretary in the imperial government. Since then such men as Ts'ui Tsung-chih, Fang Hsi-tsu, Li Hsin, and Hsü Ying [15] have all enjoyed your patronage, either for their talent or their incorruptibility and honorableness. I cannot but feel deeply when I see the loyalty and righteousness with which they carry on their assigned tasks, doubtless inspired by their gratitude to you and their desire to justify your confidence in them. Since I know that you, sir, are honest and sincere with these virtuous men, I have chosen you, instead of any others, to whom I would like to pledge my service. Should you wish to use me in any emergency, you will find me happily and willingly at your disposal.

No man is another Yao and Shun; he cannot possibly be perfect. I cannot brag about any advice or plan which I may be asked to give or design. However, my writings have been accumulated to such a large amount as to be contained in many rolls, and I shall be glad to present them to you for examination, if you do believe that they are not too insignificant for your purpose. Should you feel that they may contain something worthwhile, please provide me with a copiest and some paper and a brush.[16] I shall retreat to my chamber and sweep it clean; and then I shall make copies to be presented to you for inspection. It is my hope that the sword of Ch'ing-p'ing and the jade of Chieh-lu will finally reach Hsüeh Chu and Pien

[13] Wang Tzu-shih lived early in the third century during the Later Han dynasty; Yü was located in modern Honan province. Hsün Tz'u-ming's real name was Hsün Shuang; K'ung Wen-chü's real name was K'ung Yung. Both were famous writers of their times. K'ung Yung was later killed by Ts'ao Ts'ao, founder of the Wei dynasty.

[14] Shan T'ao lived in the middle decades of the third century A.D. during the Tsin dynasty; Yi was located in modern Hopeh province.

[15] All of these people were minor figures in history whose achievement, if any, cannot be easily ascertained. The same thing can be said about Yen Hsieh-lü in the preceding sentence.

[16] A writing brush.

Ho respectively,[17] and that their value will increase because of the recognition of their true worth. I will be most grateful should you choose to extend your benevolence to me and provide me with hope and encouragement. Sir, I am putting myself at your disposal.

73 · Hsüeh Yung-jo: *Wang Wei and the Princess*[18]

Even before he reached the age of twenty, Wang Wei had become widely known for his literary achievement. He was an expert musician besides, specializing in the instrument of *p'i-p'a*.[19] He made his rounds among the notables in the capital [20] and was particularly favored by Prince Ch'i.[21]

Then Chang Chiu-kao [22] was regarded as the most promising young talent in the literary circle; in fact, some of Princess T'ai-p'ing's friends,[23] invoking her name, had already passed his poems on to the examiners in the capital, so that he would be rated "number one" [24] when the examination took place. Wang Wei was about to take the same examination, and when he heard about this arrangement, he reported it to Prince Ch'i and pleaded for help.

"The Princess is a very powerful person, and we cannot openly defy her wishes," said Prince Ch'i. "However, I have a plan. Make a copy of ten of your best poems, and also compose a new song for the *p'i-p'a* which should be both sad and melodious. Come here in five days."

Five days later Wang Wei returned to Prince Ch'i's residence as instructed. "How, as an intellectual, can you hope to see the Princess? Are you willing to follow every instruction I give?" asked the Prince. "Respectfully I am," Wang replied.

Then Prince Ch'i brought out the most luxurious clothes he had and asked Wang to put them on. Carrying his *p'i-p'a*, Wang followed Prince Ch'i to the Princess' residence.

"Knowing that Your Ladyship is at home, I have taken the liberty of bringing you food and music," Prince Ch'i went in and reported. Then he gave the order that a banquet be set up immediately. The musicians, meanwhile, came in one after another in an orderly fashion. In the front row among the musicians stood Wang Wei who was young, handsome, and elegant. The Princess took a look at him and then asked Prince Ch'i who the young man was.

"He is an expert musician," the Prince replied.

The Prince then ordered Wang to play the new song which the latter had

---

17 Here Li Po likens his own writing to the two priceless objects of ancient times.

18 Wang Wei (699–759), the central figure of this story, was not only a great poet and expert musician but also a famous painter. The Chinese original of this story appears in *A Collection of Anecdotes (Chi-yi chi)* by Hsüeh Yung-jo who lived during the first half of the ninth century.

19 A musical instrument similar to the guitar.

20 Ch'angan, capital of the T'ang dynasty.

21 A younger brother of Emperor T'ang Hsüan-tsung (r.713–755).

22 A younger brother of Chang Chiu-ling, then the prime minister.

23 Princess T'ai-p'ing was the daughter of Emperor T'ang Kao-tsung (r.650–683) and Empress Wu (r.684–704), and was later killed by T'ang Hsüan-tsung. Before she died, however, she was the real power behind the throne.

24 *Chiai-yüan.*

recently composed. The song was so sad that all people present were visibly moved.

"What is the name of this song?" the Princess asked Wang directly. The young man stood up and replied: "It is called 'A Revolving Robe'." The Princess was immensely impressed.

"This young man not only knows music," said Prince Ch'i; "he has no peers in the field of poetry."

The Princess was even more surprised. "Have you brought some of your poems with you?" she asked.

Wang Wei took out the poems which he had prepared and presented them to the Princess. Reading them, the Princess was astonished beyond belief. "These are the poems that I have studied and recited regularly," said she. "I always thought that they were the works of the ancient great. Are they your work?" She ordered Wang to change his clothes [25] and be seated on the right side of her guests. At the table Wang was gay, witty, but refined. All the notables at the banquet were impressed.

"Will not the nation be proud to have this young man as the 'number one' in this year's metropolitan examination?" said Prince Ch'i.

"Why do you not ask him to participate in the examination?" asked the Princess.

"He said that he will not take the examination under any circumstances unless he has Your Ladyship's blessings," Prince Ch'i replied. "But it is reported that Your Ladyship has already recommended Chang Chiu-kao as the 'number one'."

"I personally had nothing to do with that recommendation," said the Princess. "I did it at other people's request." Then turning to Wang Wei, she added: "Go ahead and take the examination. I shall do my part to help." Wang stood up and expressed his thanks in a very humble manner.

Later, the Princess summoned the examiners to her residence and ordered her servants to transmit to them her wishes. Wang Wei was then designated as "number one" and passed the metropolitan examination in his first attempt.

74 · HAN YÜ: *Advice to Chang T'ung-tzu* [26]

Each year the total number of candidates who are eligible to take the examination administered by the Ministry of Rites amounts to three thousand in the category of "two classics" alone.[27] The candidates begin their examination career by taking the tests on the subprefectural level, and only those who have succeeded can take the tests on the provincial or prefectural level. Needless to say, the

[25] To change from a musician's clothes to those of a guest.

[26] *Ku-wen tz'u-lei tsuan,* roll 31.

[27] During the T'ang dynasty the government divided Confucian classics into three groups for the purpose of administering examinations in the category of "The Classics" (*ming-ching*). The first group consisted of *Book of Rites* and *Commentaries of Tso;* the second group consisted of *Book of Odes, Chou Institutions,* and *Ceremonies and Rituals (Yi li);* the third group consisted of *Book of Changes, Book of History, Commentaries of Kung-yang,* and *Commentaries of Ku-liang.* A candidate in the "two classics" category could choose one each from the first and the third groups, or both from the second group. See Ma Tuan-lin, "Schools II," *A Study of Cultural Heritage (Wen-hsien t'ung-k'ao).*

three thousand candidates do not include those who have failed on the subprefectural level. The provincial or prefectural governments test them in the same manner as the subprefectural governments have done, and only those who have passed will have their names presented to the emperor, to be tested by the responsible officials in the imperial government. Needless to say, the three thousand previously mentioned do not include those who have failed. The three thousand who have passed come from all parts of China and are called "the country's recommendees" [28] eligible to take the examination on the imperial level. The names of those who succeed in this examination will be presented to the emperor as part of his permanent record, and the candidates themselves will be referred to the Ministry of Personnel for possible appointments in office. Usually they number fewer than two hundred and are called "beginners in life." [29] How difficult it is to become one of these two hundred!

The texts alone of any two classics contain hundreds of thousands of words, not to mention the commentaries and the interpretations which the candidates have to study in order to acquire a general idea. In many cases it will take more than ten years before a candidate is sufficiently prepared to become a member of the three thousand and thus reach the level of the Ministry of Rites.[30] It may take ten additional years before he can become a member of the two hundred and thus reach the level of the Ministry of Personnel.[31] Half of the candidates will have white hair before they ever reach this level, and most of the other half can never make it because of their comparatively low intelligence. Many have tried in vain throughout their lives.

In nine years Chang T'ung-tzu proceeded from the subprefectural level to reach the Ministry of Rites. After one examination he became one of the two hundred. Two years later he was even more proficient in the two classics in which he specialized, a fact which was duly acknowledged by his superiors. As a result he was appointed a captain in the imperial guards. People say that T'ung-tzu is richly endowed with talent and sensitivity; I cannot but express my agreement and say that he stands prominently above others.

Receiving a leave of absence from his superiors, he went home, accompanied by his father, to pay his homage to his mother. He left the capital [32] in the eighth month and did not reach home until the ninth. From the celebrities in the capital to the officials in the cities he passed by—all of them presented him with gifts, and some of them composed poems to praise his accomplishments. T'ung-tzu was glorious indeed.

However, I would like to give him what I consider good advice and say that however earnestly a man wishes to improve himself, he cannot hope to succeed in a short time. The way of judging an elder person is different from that of judging a young man. A young man is valued highly for his difference from others, while an elder person should be evaluated in accordance with his maturity. Since I cannot say that T'ung-tzu is completely self-sufficient in this matter of

[28] *Hsiang-kung.*

[29] *Ch'u-shen.*

[30] The Ministry of Rites was responsible for administering imperial or metropolitan examinations.

[31] The Ministry of Personnel was responsible for assigning governmental posts to the successful candidates.

[32] Ch'angan.

maturity, is it not now the time for him to suspend temporarily the pursuance of that in which he is already proficient and begin to pursue diligently what he has yet to learn?

At one time both T'ung-tzu and I were Mr. Lu's students. Admiring the good relationship between Yen Hui and Tzu-lu [33] who advised and encouraged each other, I write this composition as a gift to my friend T'ung-tzu.

75 · YEH SHIH: *Civil Service Examinations* [34]

Formerly, a successful candidate of the civil service examination was a person who had established a name for himself in the literary circle or had achieved some well-known deeds prior to his participation in the examination. The situation today is entirely different. The candidates who pass the examination are not necessarily those who deserve to pass, and the man who scores the highest often becomes the target of ridicule. Meanwhile even the least talented in the countryside and the most mediocre in a family are busying themselves in books, reciting and memorizing, for the sole purpose of passing the examinations.

A father urges his son to study not because he believes that books are important in themselves but because they are keys whereby his son can open the door to officialdom. While the government attaches great importance to the examination system, the people view it as merely a means to a worldly end. What they like about a successful candidate is not the character of the candidate as a person; rather, it is his writings that they appreciate. In fact, they know nothing about the candidate himself because a man's writings are not necessarily indicative of his person. It is not surprising that our examination system today does not produce men who command esteem, since it has become a vehicle whereby men of dubious motives ride to officialdom. Yet it is the major instrument whereby scholars are transformed into officials from whom ministers of great responsibilities will eventually emerge. Is it not contradictory that a man who is despised on account of his selfish motives when entering the civil service examinations will be relied upon by the nation to shoulder great responsibilities?

A harmful corollary of using the examination to select governmental personnel is to convert all scholars to aspirants of governmental positions. A healthy society cannot come about when people study not for the purpose of gaining wisdom and knowledge but for the purpose of becoming government officials. A person who seeks knowledge will know what "righteousness" means, and a man of righteousness does not need a salary to become rich and a title to become honorable. The outward things that other people envy and seek after will not in any way affect his determination to preserve his own integrity.

Nowadays the situation is different. Beginning with childhood, all of a man's study is centered on one aim alone: to emerge successfully from the three days' examinations, and all he has in his mind is what success can bring to him in terms of power, influence, and prestige. His father and elder brothers push him towards this goal, and so do the best of his friends, because all of them, like him, believe

[33] Both were the students of Confucius. Yen Hui was also known as Yen Yüan.
[34] Yeh Shih (also known as Yeh Shui-hsin), who lived in the twelfth century, was a holder of the *chin-shih* degree and a scholar of considerable originality. This selection is translated from *The Works of Shui-hsin (Shui-hsin chi)*, roll 3.

that this is the only proper path to follow. The old concept of studying for the refinement of one's character and for the acquirement of the sense of righteousness is painfully noteworthy because of its absence. How can one sincerely believe that a system which produces persons of this type as government officials can also generate men of talent eager and able to shoulder great responsibilities? . . .

Formerly, a successful candidate had to wait for a considerable time before he could become a tenured official. This is no longer true under the present system. Once he passes the examination, he is immediately given an official post to hold and can never be dismissed without cause. In some cases the government will regard a man as having passed the examinations and thus deserving an official post if he has tried unsuccessfully for a period of thirty years, on the ground that his perseverance and hard work deserve special consideration. This custom began in the early years of this dynasty when Yi-tsu,[35] feeling compassion for those scholars who were stranded in the capital after failing repeatedly during the Five Dynasties,[36] decided to let them pass as a special favor. Today there are so many scholars in the nation that success in the examination does not carry the same meaning as it once did. The reason for starting this custom is no longer there, and yet the custom persists.

Scholars are the source from which men of talents are drawn and are in fact the very foundation upon which the nation's destiny rests. They cannot live up to their expected usefulness if the government, instead of cultivating them as true scholars, chooses to corrupt and demoralize them. . . .

76 · OU-YANG HSIU: *Proposed Reform for the Imperial Examination* [37]

Let the candidates for an imperial examination be limited to approximately two thousand. The examination period should be longer than it is at present. The first test of the examination should be the writing of a theme answering particular questions. If a candidate commits any of the following seven errors in his papers, he should be automatically eliminated from consideration: vulgarity in language, lack of logic in structure and frequent repetitions, failure to understand the meaning of questions, ignorance of historical precedents which results in the misinterpretation of questions, misquoting of historical precedents, eccentricity in reasoning even though the composition itself is readable, and finally, violation of generally accepted forms that makes the composition itself below standard. By this way anywhere between five and six hundred candidates can be eliminated from consideration.

The second test should consist of writing topical essays. By following the same standards described above, another two or three hundred candidates can be eliminated from consideration. Those who have survived and are thus qualified to take the third or poetry test should not be more than one thousand, from whom it would be easy to select five hundred. If this test is accurate enough to reflect the

[35] Better known as Sung Kao-tsu (or Chao K'uang-yin, r.960–975), founder of the Sung dynasty.
[36] The Five Dynasties (907–960).
[37] A copy of the Chinese original can be found in Ku Yen-wu: *The Daily Accumulated Knowledge (Jih-chih lu)*, roll 16.

candidates' worth, it serves its purpose well. Even if it is not, the result would not be too bad either, because all the opportunitists and the plagiarizers have already been eliminated in the first and second tests. If a candidate is good enough to reach the third or poetry stage, he must have written reasonably well and must have been fairly good in reasoning and knowledgeable in information. It is extremely unlikely that he would be an eccentric person. Even if the poetry test fails its purpose when it is later found that he does not write poetry well, it does little harm that he has passed the examination by mistake.

This reform which I have suggested will bar the young opportunists from successfully exploiting the civil service examination system. Since the government cannot restore the kind of recruitment practiced during the two Han dynasties and has to rely on a candidate's literary work to judge his worth, it is important to see to it that his written composition reflects his integrity as well as his literary ability. In this connection the first thing we have to do is to eliminate the opportunists and the plagiarizers who have infested the examination system. Once we correct the seven errors previously described, the evil-doers will have no chance to succeed, and the number of those who wish to follow their path will also be greatly reduced. The examination system itself will be then rectified.

77 · HUANG TSUNG-HSI: *The Recruitment of Governmental Personnel* [38]

The way of recruiting governmental personnel in ancient times was not only more varied but also more broadly based than it is today. However, the standard whereby a man was actually employed for governmental service was much stricter. If a person was truly virtuous and able, he had no fear that he would not be discovered. As late as the T'ang-Sung period a prospective government employee could choose any of the several categories offered in the examinations to demonstrate his talent. If he failed in one category, he could always try another.

But it was a different matter actually to be employed in the civil service. During the T'ang dynasty, for instance, a man who passed the civil service examination would be tested again by the Ministry of Personnel before he was granted a post to hold. The famous essayist Han Yü failed three times in this test; he was without a govemmental post for ten years after he had passed the civil service examination. Among the successful candidates of the ministerial test only those who had the highest scores would be granted the position of deputy magistrates. The standard whereby a man was chosen as a government official was very strict indeed. No talent would go undiscovered if the policy of recruitment was varied and broadly based, and no man could become a government official on account of his luck if the standard of choosing government officials was high and strict.

Today the situation is entirely different owing largely to the fact that the civil service examination has become the only avenue leading to officialdom. Had our ancestors pursued the same policy, such personalities of heroic stature as Ch'ü Yüan, Ssu-ma Ch'ien, Ssu-ma Hsiang-ju, Tung Chung-shu, and Yang Hsiang would never have had the opportunity of entering governmental service in the first place.

---

[38] *Ming-yi tai-fang lu,* the seventh essay.

This narrow base upon which officials are recruited contrasts sharply with the laxity with which positions are granted to those recruited on this narrow base. Once a person passes the examination, he expects immediate appointment to a governmental post. He may be appointed as the emperor's consultant or adviser if he is fortunate, or as a magistrate on the provincial or subprefectural level if he is not. Those who have failed to receive appointments and are thus forced to return home are nevertheless put on the reserve officials' list, though for all practical purposes they may never again have the opportunity of entering governmental service.

The narrowness of the avenue that leads to governmental service is not conducive to the recruitment of the best available personnel, many of whom remain undiscovered and unknown throughout their lives. On the other hand, the laxity with which governmental posts are granted to those who have successfully threaded their way through this narrow avenue only leads to the appointment of those who are unfit and undesirable. It is true that during the past two hundred years the civil service examination system has produced many prominent men. Based upon this fact, its defenders have contended that it is good and adequate for its purpose and that there is no need for devising other ways of recruiting governmental personnel. These people do not realize that of the hundreds of thousands who have passed the civil service examinations there are bound to be a few unusually talented due to the operation of the law of averages and that the appearance of these few does not in any way reflect the merit of the system itself. In fact, the government could have acquired the same number of unusually talented men by drawing lots among the millions of scholars who have sought governmental positions since the examination system began. In terms of discovering unusually talented persons, it is difficult to say which system is better, drawing lots or examination.

In summary, it can be said that our present way of recruiting governmental personnel through examination is much inferior to the practice followed during the Han and T'ang dynasties, insofar as the discovery of talents is concerned. It merely enables the mediocre and the commonplace to spread their influence throughout the empire. Our problem is not the lack of talented men; it is the lack of sound methods to discover them.

78 · KU YEN-WU: *Miscellaneous Notes on the Civil Service Examination System* [39]

During the T'ang dynasty there were six categories in the civil service examination system. They were "flourishing talent" (*hsiu-ts'ai*), classics, "advanced scholarship" (*chin-shih*), law, calligraphy, and mathematics. Candidates who chose the category of "advanced scholarship" were tested in the composition of poetry; candidates who chose "classics" were tested in their knowledge of Confucian classics. . . . Of the six categories the "classics" had the largest number of successful candidates per examination. The examination emphasized memorization of the commentaries about the classics, rather than the classics themselves. Many critics pointed out that some of the candidates who had passed the "classics" test did not know much about the classics. . . .

The examination administered for the "flourishing talent" was the most

[39] *Jih-chih lu,* roll 16.

difficult, and only about ten candidates were allowed to pass each year. During the Jen-shu period (601–604) three brothers from a certain Tu family passed the examinations of this category; the family, consequently, was highly praised by its contemporaries and enjoyed great prestige. According to *A Record of Successful Candidates During the T'ang Dynasty,*[40] from the Wu-te (618–626) to the Yung-hui (650–655) period, more than twenty candidates in the category of "advanced scholarship" passed each year, while merely one or two passed the "flourishing talent" examination. According to Tu Yu, the author of *A Study of Institutions,*[41] a practice developed during the Chen-kuan period (627–649) whereby a governor was subject to penalties if a candidate he recommended to participate in the "flourishing talent" examination failed to pass. Subsequently this category was abolished.[42] The two categories, "classics" and "advanced scholarship," remained the most popular with candidates. . . .

During the Ming dynasty Wang Wei-chen [43] made the recommendation that the government should follow the example of the Han and T'ang dynasties by introducing other categories besides "advanced scholarship," so that people of unusual talent other than that in literature could be recruited for governmental service; the category of "advanced scholarship," he contended, had been over-emphasized. This overemphasis which had continued for two or three hundred years necessitated a thorough revision of the entire examination system. Without such a revision, he maintained, a person whose talent lay outside the category of "advanced scholarship" could not make his talent available to the government. . . .

Aside from the regular examinations, an emperor during the T'ang dynasty could issue special decrees to invite men of extraordinary ability to serve the government. This was called "imperial invitations" (*chih-chü*). " 'Imperial invitation' was very ancient in origin," says the *T'ang Records* (*T'ang chih*); "it was often referred to as 'invitations by imperial decrees' during the Han dynasty. The emperor made the questions and tested the candidates personally. This tradition of honoring Confucian scholarship was revived during the T'ang dynasty. Individual emperors might vary in wisdom or personal taste; however, their love of goodness and their desire to recruit virtuous men remained constant and unchanged. Governments of all levels selected and then recommended to the emperor what they considered virtuous men from time to time. Sometimes the emperor took the initiative to invite those scholars who were exemplary in conduct, unusual in ability, or versatile in literature. Some of the invitations were extended to the self-effacing and highly principled hermits who, for their own reasons, did not wish to make themselves known. As the emperor's wish might vary, the categories from which talented men were chosen also varied a great deal, including 'military strategy,' 'physical valor,' and 'rare skill.' The regular categories, however, were offered more often and were better known, such as 'virtuous conduct,' 'fearless remonstration,' 'proficiency in classical literature,' 'expertness in teaching,' 'military planning,' 'commandership,' 'administrative skill,' and 'personal management'."

Nowadays the questions used in the civil service examinations are taken from

[40] *T'ang teng-k'o chi.*
[41] Tu Yu, the author of *The Study of Institutions (T'ung tien),* lived in the eighth century.
[42] It was abolished in the second year of Yung-hui, or A.D. 651.
[43] A scholar of the sixteenth century who received the *chin-shih* degree in 1535.

the classics. Though this method is sound in principle, it unfortunately benefits those who are among the least learned. Contrary to this practice, the T'ang and Sung governments used poetry to test a candidate's ability. Though poetry may be characterized as a "literary trifle," a man cannot write poetry well unless he is thoroughly familiar with the mass assemblage of literature dating from ancient times. The use of classics to test candidates began in the Hsi-ning period (1068–1077) of the Sung dynasty when Wang An-shih [44] introduced it for the first time. . . . In the third month of the eighth year of Yüan-yu (1093) the First Secretariat reported that the essays written by candidates were mostly composed in advance prior to the examinations and that it was difficult to tell which one was better or worse. . . .

Chao Ting [45] said that Wang An-shih encouraged candidates to study his sophistical philosophy and destroyed the usefulness of the civil service examination system. Ch'en Kung-fu [46] said that Wang An-shih discouraged students from studying the *Spring and Autumn Annals, Historical Records,* and *History of the Han;* and that the *New Interpretations of the Three Classics,*[47] which he encouraged them to read, was merely a patchwork of useless, empty words. "The so-called contemporary writings [48] are related neither to the classics nor to philosophy or history," he continued. "They are merely a compilation of artificial words not rooted in our literary heritage. Of every ten candidates who have passed the civil service examinations, eight or nine know little about learning. The moment they have passed the provincial examination, they begin to search for connections in order to gain a means of livelihood. They are local bullies when they stay at home and roaming vagrants when they wander about in the empire. If we hope to promote harmony in the world or honesty among the people, we have to retrace the road of our ancient past."

Early in the Ming dynasty the civil service examination consisted of three separate tests, all of which were supposedly of equal importance. However, most of the candidates concentrated their efforts on one classic, paying only scant attention to others. Reading the papers, the examiners exhibited an undisguised prejudice for the first test and were not particularly concerned with the results of the second and the third tests. This situation was completely different from that of the early times when a candidate had to study at least ten years and read a thousand volumes before he could pass all of the three tests. To find a short cut to success, the candidates nowadays devise anywhere from one to two hundred topics from the *Four Books* and the one classic in which they are supposedly specialized, copy other people's essays that correspond to these topics, and memorize them. During the examination they merely copy the essays they have memorized and, if their luck holds, pass the examination with flying colors. This quick but dishonest way to success not only causes the decline of learning but also has a demoralizing effect on the people as a whole. . . .

The worst abuse in the examination system has to do with the making of ques-

---

[44] Wang An-shih (1021–1086) was a famous reformer of the Sung dynasty.

[45] Chao Ting (d.1147) passed the imperial examination and received the *chin-shih* decree in A.D. 1106.

[46] Ch'en Kung-fu (d. c.1140) was a product of Wang An-shih's New University which was designed to replace eventually the civil service examination system.

[47] *San-ching hsin-yi,* written by Wang An-shih.

[48] Writings acceptable in the examinations.

tions. In the first test where the questions are to be drawn from the classics there are four questions. Yet no more than one hundred questions can be normally contrived from these classics. Wealthy and influential families invite famous scholars to take residence in their familial schools, and the duty of these scholars is to write one essay for each of the approximately one hundred questions. They are paid according to the number of essays they write. The prospective examination candidates are ordered by their elders to memorize these essays; sometimes young slaves also join the memorizing work if their masters think that they are intelligent enough. In eight or nine out of ten cases, the questions in the examination are those anticipated in advance, and all the candidates need do is to copy what they have memorized and hand their papers in. Obviously they possess a great advantage over those who have to compose their answers extemporaneously. Besides the classics, they also do the same thing with regard to the *Four Books*.

Once the results of the examination are publicly announced, these people suddenly become the so-called "honorable men." If they are young and handsome, they have a good chance of being appointed as fellows in some of those research institutes in the imperial government. The practice described above has become the fashion of the day, and all scholars are anxious to follow. Having found an easy way to success, they do not even bother to read the classics. . . .

Thus our modern scholars strive to achieve in one year what former scholars failed to achieve in ten years, and to learn in one month what formerly took one year to learn. How do they manage to do so? They plagiarize. If you ask them questions in connection with a Confucian classic, they do not even know to which book you are referring. In my humble opinion, the damage caused by the eight-legged essays [49] is worse than that of burning books,[50] and is more serious than that of burying scholars alive in the suburb of Hsienyang,[51] insofar as the cultivation of talent is concerned. After all, Ch'in Shih Huang-ti buried alive only 460 people. . . .

Yeh Meng-te,[52] in his book *A Swallow's Chatterings from a Stone Forest*,[53] summarizes the situation as follows:

"Prior to the Hsi-ning period the candidates in the civil service examinations were tested in poetry. Scholars would have to study all of the *Five Classics* if they wished to succeed. Even among scholars who did not participate or succeed in the examinations, most of them were able to quote the *Five Classics* with ease. They learned the classics when they were young and did not forget them even after they had become advanced in age.

"Since the change of emphasis from poetry to classics in the examinations, a family usually instructs its children to study only one classic. Even if they do study other classics, they are far from proficient in them. To make the situation worse, their teacher may not be proficient in them either. They often commit errors

---

[49] First developed during the Ming dynasty, the eight-legged style (*pa-ku*) remained the standard form in the examinations throughout the Ch'ing dynasty. An essay written in such a style required parallel phrases or sentences (balanced like a person's legs) and the rigid observance of a well-defined form.

[50] This refers to the book-burning campaign conducted by Ch'in Shih Huang-ti in 221 B.C.

[51] The capital of the Ch'in dynasty, located in modern Shensi province.

[52] Yeh Meng-te, who received his *chin-shih* degree in 1097, was as much known for his ability as a military commander as for his scholarship.

[53] *Shih-lin yen-yü.*

with regard to the texts, let alone the commentaries. Listen to people's conversation today, and you often hear a person refer to another person's field of study as 'your honorable classic' and refer to his own as 'my humble classic.' This is simply ridiculous.

"The problem with the present examination system is that the examination has become too easy. The remedy is to make it more difficult. The more difficult it becomes, the less likely will people wish to take chances with it. By eliminating one chance-taker, we eliminate from society a fortune seeker. This, in my opinion, is the first step towards the rectification of scholars as a group. Moreover, realizing the difficulty of the examinations, the candidates will doubtless study harder. If we can add one diligent scholar to the society, we indirectly substract one member from a group of glib, artificial, and half-learned students whose only goal in life is to pass the civil service examinations. Only in this way can the learning habit of our intellectuals be gradually rectified."

79 · WU CHING-TZU: *A Story of Two Candidates* [54]

After losing his teaching position, Chou Chin faced increasing difficulties in maintaining a livelihood. Chin Yu-yü, his brother-in-law, came to see him one day and gave him some advice.

"If you do not mind me saying so," said his brother-in-law, "I do not think that you should place too much hope on passing the examinations and entering officialdom. Nothing in the world is so important as a steady rice bowl in your hand, and I do not see how you can ever get it with the situation you are in. Some wealthy merchants and I are on our way to the provincial capital to transact some business, and we need an accountant to keep the records. Why do you not go with us? Since you are a bachelor, we can easily put you up in a hotel. We do not pay very much, but at least you will have enough to eat and some warm clothing to wear."

Like a disabled man who has fallen into a deep well, Chou was only too happy that someone had come along to rescue him. He accepted the offer immediately.

Chin and his merchant friends consulted the calendar and chose an auspicious day for their journey. Arriving at the capital, they took temporary residence in a general store.

Without much to do, Chou went out for a stroll. Seeing many workmen in the street, he asked them where they were going. "We are going to do some repair work in the examination yard," they replied. Chou decided to follow them to see what the yard looked like and went as far as its front gate but no further. The gate keeper did not take kindly to the intruder and beat him out with a large strap.

In the evening Chou talked with his brother-in-law, imploring Chin to take him to the examination yard the next day. Chin was reluctant at the beginning, but finally agreed. The next morning all of them, including Chin's merchant friends, went to see the yard, and accompanied by the yard's overseer, they had no difficulty passing through the front gate since the gate keeper, having received a small fee, was only happy to let them in.

[54] *Ju-lin wai-shih*, Chapters II and III.

Reaching the Dragon Portal, the overseer pointed it out to Chou and said: "This is the door through which the candidates come in." Inside the door the visitors saw two lines of cubicles, one on each side. "This is Row One," said the overseer; "why do you not walk along and take a look for yourself, Mr. Chou?"

Entering Row One, Chou saw two number boards neatly arranged on the wall. Suddenly his eyes became sour, and with a long sigh, he smashed his head against one of the boards. He collapsed immediately and became unconscious.

His friends rushed towards him and, without knowing what he had been doing, thought that he must have suffered a sudden attack. "Since this examination yard has not been visited by people for a long time, it must have been taken over by the evil spirits," the overseer explained. "This may be the reason why Mr. Chou has suffered this attack."

"I am holding him," said Chin to the overseer. "Please get some water from the workmen as quickly as you can."

The overseer brought in some water; and, with three or four of his merchant friends holding his brother-in-law, Chin poured water into the latter's mouth. Finally Chou spat out a mouthful of saliva, and all of his friends were relieved. "He is all right!" all of them exclaimed simultaneously. With great efforts, they helped him to stand up. No sooner did he stand up, however, than he saw the number board again. Once more he smashed his head against it, but fortunately he did not knock himself out of consciousness this time. He cried aloud like a baby, and nobody could stop him.

"Are you out of your mind?" Chin scolded. "It is you who wanted to visit this place. Since nobody in your family has recently passed away, why are you crying like an idiot?"

Resting his head upon the number board, Chou continued to cry as if he had not heard his brother-in-law's words. After he had cried long enough on board number one, he moved to board number two and then board number three. Suddenly he slumped and rolled on the floor as if he were in great pain, crying aloud as he rolled. All people around him felt very sad; yet nobody knew how to stop him. Realizing that this scene could not continue forever, Chin asked the overseer to help him to pull Chou up. Chou, however, refused to budge; he cried and cried until his mouth began to spit blood. There was nothing they could do except carry him; with some holding his arms and others holding his legs, they finally succeeded in moving him to a tea house not far from the examination yard. They implored him to drink some tea. While drinking his tea, Chou's nose continued to make noise and his eyes yield tears. How sad he must have felt!

"Mr. Chou must feel deeply about something which we do not know," one merchant commented. "Otherwise he would not have cried in such a manner."

"There is something about my brother-in-law which you gentlemen do not know," said Chin. "He is not really a merchant. He has studied for many years as a scholar, but unfortunately he has not even passed the lowest level of the civil service examination. That is why he felt so sad when he saw this examination yard." These remarks apparently touched Chou's tenderest nerve, and shamelessly he cried again.

"Mr. Chin, I believe that this is your fault," said another merchant. "Since Mr. Chou is a scholar, why did you bring him here as an accountant?"

"You do not understand," Chin replied. "Having recently lost his teaching position and become penniless, he did not have much choice except to take what was offered to him."

"From what I can gather, your brother-in-law is a talented man," said a third merchant: "It is rather unfortunate that his talent has not been appreciated."

"I cannot agree with you more," said Chin. "He just has not received a good break which I believe he deserves."

"A *chien-sheng* is as much qualified to take the provincial examination as a *hsiu-ts'ai* does," [55] said the same merchant. "Since Mr. Chou is a talented scholar, why does he not purchase a permit to take the provincial examination?"

"I feel the same way as you do," said Chin. "But where can we get so much money?"

By then Chou had stopped crying.

"This is not really too difficult a task," said the merchant. "If each of us here contributes forty or fifty taels of silver, Mr. Chou will have enough money to buy a permit. If he succeeds, the money we contribute will not mean very much to him. If he does not, we have to think that as traveling merchants we have lost many times this amount before. Moreover, this is a good deed. How do you gentlemen feel about this matter?"

" 'He who will not help a man in need is not a gentleman indeed'," they all agreed by quoting a well-known proverb. " 'A man cannot be called brave if he, seeing where righteousness is, runs away from it.' Now that we all agree to help, we are wondering whether Mr. Chou will honor us by accepting this offer."

"I am as grateful to you as if you were my own parents," said Chou, "and I will pay this debt even if I have to be reincarnated into a donkey or a horse to do it." He kowtowed to the merchants who saluted him in return. Chin, his brother-in-law, also expressed his gratitude. After a few cups of tea, they left the tea house. Chou did not cry any more; in fact, on his way back to the general store, he chatted and laughed and was in a good mood.

The next day the four merchants handed to Chin Yu-yü two hundred taels of silver as they had promised. Chin, on his part, would provide the extra amount if it were needed. Chou invited his benefactors to a banquet to express once more his gratitude.

Chin took the money to the treasury and obtained a receipt. Fortunately for Chou, the superintendent of examinations had recently arrived at the capital to register new candidates. Chou was the first to register under the *chien-sheng* category.

On the eighth day of the eighth lunar month Chou entered the examination yard to take the first test. Seeing the spot where he had once cried, he was overjoyed. As an ancient proverb says that "A man becomes a genius when enjoying good luck," the seven essays that Chou wrote during the examination were as beautiful as a boquet of flowers. By the time he completed the examination, he found that Chin and his merchant friends had not yet sold all of their merchandise and were still staying in the general store.

On the day when the result of the examination was made public, all of them were overjoyed when they learned that Chou had passed. Together they went

---

[55] A *hsiu-ts'ai* was a person who had passed the lowest or prefectural level of the civil service examination. A *chien-sheng* was a person who had purchased a permit to take the provincial examination even though he had not passed the prefectual examination.

back to Wenshang,[56] their home subprefecture. Arriving home, Chou paid his respect to the magistrate as well as the teacher who once taught him. Meanwhile people swarmed to his door to congratulate him day after day, including the deputy magistrate who called himself Chou's "student." All over the Wenshang subprefecture people came to acknowledge him as either their "relative" or their "friend" even though he had never heard about them before. This continued for about a month. . . .

When time had arrived to take the metropolitan examination, Chin Yu-yü, his brother-in-law, had everything—clothing and traveling expenses—ready for his journey to the nation's capital.[57] He passed it and was awarded the *chin-shih* degree. The palace examination followed,[58] and Chou passed it in the third group.[59] He was assigned a position in one of the ministeries where he worked for three years. Then he was promoted to the position of censor and concurrently the superintendency of examinations in Kwangtung province.

Though he had hired a few scholars to help him out, Chou made up his mind that he was personally to read all examination papers written under his jurisdiction, so that no talent be passed by either through oversight or by mistake. He felt very strongly about this in view of the difficulties he himself had experienced.

The day he arrived at Canton,[60] he worshipped at the Temple of Confucius and thus formally began the examination procedure. After presiding over two tests, he came to the group that consisted of candidates from subprefectures Nanhai [61] and Fanyü.[62] Sitting on an elevated platform, he watched the candidates coming in, some old and some young, some looking respectable and others looking like monkeys just emerging from a cage. Some were well-dressed, while the clothes of some others could only be described as tatters. At the end of the line was a yellow-faced, white-bearded, and extremely skinny man with a worn-out felt hat. Though this was the twelfth lunar month,[63] this man still wore hemp clothes suitable only for summer; he was in fact shivering from cold. Having received the examination papers, he entered the assigned cubicle which was immediately sealed.

When the time arrived for the candidates to hand in their papers, Chou Chin took his seat in the elevated platform. Shortly afterwards the man with hemp tatters ascended with his paper. Taking a look at him, Chou found that a few more pieces had come out from his shabby clothing; they were obviously torn away while he was taking the test in the cubicle. What a contrast there was between this man's shreds and his own silk robe and velvet belt, Chou said to himself.

Checking with the register, Chou found out this man's name. "Are you Fan Chin?" he asked. Fan Chin knelt down and answered "Yes."

"How old are you?"

"The register says that I am thirty, but actually I am fifty-four."

"How many times have you taken this examination?"

[56] Located in modern Shantung province.
[57] Peking.
[58] The palace examination or *tien-shih* was personally supervised by the emperor. The custom began in A.D. 690 during the reign of Empress Wu of the T'ang dynasty.
[59] The third group or *san-chia* was the lowest group that was allowed to pass.
[60] The capital of Kwangtung province.
[61] Incidentally, Nanhai was the birthplace of K'ang Yu-wei, a Confucian scholar and political reformer of the nineteenth century.
[62] The subprefecture where Canton was located.
[63] About January in the Western calendar.

"I began to take it when I was twenty. I must have taken it more than twenty times."

"Why is it that you have always failed?"

"I believe that my writings are simply not good enough to be appreciated by the honorable examiners."

"The examiners are not always right either," said Chou. "You proceed home, and I shall read your paper with great care."

Fan Chin kowtowed and then left.

Since it was still early, none of the other candidates was yet ready to hand in his test. Chou decided to use the time to read Fan's paper in a very careful manner. He was displeased with what he read. "What is this man talking about?" he said to himself; "no wonder that he has always failed." He stopped reading and put Fan's paper aside.

For a long time he waited for people to hand in their tests, but no one else did. "Why do I not read this man's paper once more?" he thought. "If there is something good about it, I shall be generous with him in view of his diligence and perseverance." He read it from the beginning to the end and felt that it did make some sense.

While he was about to read it for the third time, a candidate ascended the platform to hand in his paper. "Please give me an oral test," the candidate knelt down and pleaded.

"All of your literary talent is reflected in this paper," said Chou smilingly. "Why do you need an oral test?"

"Your student knows all about *shih, tz'u, ko,* and *fu.*[64] Please ask me any question about them."

Chou suddenly changed his expression. "The present Son of Heaven emphasizes prose; why should you speak of poetry?" he scolded. "A student should concentrate his efforts on refining his essays; it is a waste of time to study miscellaneous, unrelated subjects. Moreover, I came here to evaluate prose, not poetry. It seems to me that you have been too much occupied with the superficial to know what is really important. This may be the reason that you have made those ridiculous remarks. I cannot stand the sight of a man like you. Guards, throw him out!"

Several guards emerged from both sides, as ferocious as wild beasts. They held the candidate by both arms and, pushing and pulling, carried him out of the front gate.

After the candidate was gone, Chou looked at his paper and learned that his name was Wei Hao-ku and that he wrote fairly well. Chou decided to let him pass with the lowest score and made a mark on his paper so that he would not forget what he had promised himself. Then he took Fan Chin's paper and read it for the third time. "This is a masterpiece," he sighed. "I could not comprehend it even though I had read it twice. Now that I have read it for the third time, every word in it begins to emerge like a pearl. This is one of the best essays I have read in years. Those stupid examiners—how many men of talent have been buried by their stupidity!" Picking up his writing brush, he punctuated the essay with small circles.[65] Then he made three large circles on the face of the examination book

---

[64] Different forms of poetry.

[65] Under no circumstances were the candidates allowed to punctuate their own writings.

and wrote the words "Number One." As for Wei Hao-ku's paper, it was marked "Number Twenty."

On the day that the result was made public, the successful candidates came to Chou to pay their homage and express their gratitude. Fan Chin, being the highest scorer, was received first, and Chou praised highly his work in his presence. Finally it was Wei Hao-ku's turn, and once again the examiner urged him to concentrate his efforts on the examinations and refrain from wasting his energy in such nonessential matters as poetry. The interview was over, and all the successful candidates were escorted out amid music.

The next day Chou left for the capital, and Fan Chin escorted him thirty *li* out of the city. "Success belongs to a man of maturity," said Chou after he had summoned Fan in front of his sedan chair. "Reading your paper, I believe that you have reached that stage. There is no doubt in my mind that you will succeed in the next provincial examination. I shall be waiting for you in the capital." Fan Chin kowtowed to express his gratitude and then stood up. He did not leave the spot where he stood until Chou's sedan chair disappeared behind a hill and was completely out of sight. . . .

Time sped away, and suddenly it was the end of the sixth lunar month before anybody had realized. The successful candidates of the last prefectural examination invited Fan Chin to go with them to take the provincial examination in the capital. Without traveling expenses, Fan went to talk with his father-in-law, Hu the Butcher, to see whether he could help.

Hardly had he made his intention known before Hu the Butcher spat on his face. "You have completely lost control of yourself," he scolded with a vengeance. "Now that you have become a *hsiu-ts'ai*, you are dreaming of transforming yourself into a *chü-jen*.[66] I tell you: it is only a dream! Do you know the reason you passed the last examination? It had nothing to do with your writing which was bad; it was because the examiner felt sorry for you because of your advanced age. You passed because of his charity; do you understand? Those who have passed the provincial examinations are literary stars in the sky, only temporarily reincarnated on earth. Who do you think you are? Have you seen the *chü-jen* in the Chang family? Each of them is a millionaire, and all of them have round faces and large ears. Look at you: you have a pointed mouth and a chin that shapes like a monkey's. If you do not believe me, urinate on the ground and see your own reflection. A frog wishes to eat the meat of a swan, I would say. If I were you, I would forget about taking more examinations. The earlier you forget about it, the better it will be for all of us. Next year I shall find a teaching job for you after I talk with some of my colleagues in the butcher business. You will make a few taels each year to support your old mother who should have died a long time ago but is so stubborn that she refuses to cooperate, and also your own wife. Now you ask me to lend you some money as traveling expenses. I slaughter one pig a day and earn barely enough to support the old and the young in my own family. Do you think that they can survive on a diet of northwestern wind if I allow you to throw my money away in the water?"

The butcher's language was so abusive that it made Fan Chin feel dizzy, so dizzy that he had a difficult time to find the front door. Returning home, he said to himself: "The examiner said that my time to succeed had already arrived. If I do

---

[66] A successful candidate of the provincial examination was called a *chü-jen*.

not take the examination, I will be sorry for the rest of my life. Furthermore, no man has ever passed an examination without taking it." He discussed this matter with some of his fellow candidates and decided to take the examination without his father-in-law's knowledge.

As soon as he completed his examination in the capital, Fan headed straight home. He found that his mother and his wife had had noting to eat for three days. Hu the Butcher gave him a tongue lashing on account of his journey to the capital without his permission.

On the day that the result of the examination was scheduled to be announced, the Fan household did not even have anything for breakfast. "Take my egg-laying chicken to the market and sell it," commanded Fan's mother. "Use the money to buy a few pints of rice and bring them home. I have been starved so long that my eyes are failing." Observing his mother's order, Fan grabbed the chicken, held it with both arms, and walked to the market.

About three or four hours after Fan had left the house, Fan's mother heard a continuous sound from the beating of gongs. Three horses galloped straight towards the village, and finally stopped in front of the Fan house. The riders dismounted and then tied their horses against a thatched canopy at the end of the house. "We request the immediate presence of His Excellency Fan," they yelled at the top of their lungs. "Congratulations!"

Fan's mother was hiding inside the hut and was terrified before she heard the wonderful news. Emerging from her hiding place, she said: "Please sit down, gentlemen. My son has just left the house." "This is the honorable grand madame," they responded. Quickly surrounding her, they requested rewards for having reported the good news. She would be happy to meet their request if she had anything to offer, but she did not have any. While the commotion continued, several other mounters also arrived—they were the second and third groups of messengers dispatched from the capital. There were so many people that the Fan house was soon filled up to its capacity. Meanwhile all the neighbors, having heard the good news, also came to congratulate.

Unable to cope with the situation, Fan's mother asked one of the neighbors to go to the market to fetch her son. The neighbor ran as fast as he could, but nowhere could Fan be found. Finally at the eastern end of the market he saw a man holding a chicken with a straw in one of his hands.[67] The man walked in a halting manner, looking towards the left and then towards the right, in the vain hope that some one would be interested in his merchandise.

"Mr. Fan," yelled the neighbor. "Please come home immediately. You have passed the examination, and your house is packed with people from the capital."

"This man is poking fun at me," Fan said to himself and continued to walk as if he had not heard his neighbor's words. Failing to receive any response, the neighbor ran towards him and tried to snatch his chicken away from him.

"Why are you trying to take my chicken away? You are not going to buy it, are you?"

"Listen! You have passed the examination. Your mother wants you to come home to cope with the messengers."

"My dear neighbor," said Fan. "You know that we have not had anything to eat for a long time, and I need to sell this chicken in order to get some money to keep

[67] The straw indicated that the chicken was for sale.

us alive. Why are you poking fun at me? Go home yourself. I have to sell this chicken."

Unable to convince him, the neighbor snatched the chicken from his hands and threw it to the ground. He then pulled Fan all the way toward home.

"The new honorable has finally come home!" cried the messengers in jubilation.

Pushing his way through the crowd, Fan quickly stepped into the house. Right in the middle of the house hung a long banner with words that read as follows:

"Good Tidings to the Honorable Fan Household: His Excellency Fan Chin has passed with high honor the provincial examination in the Province of Kwangtung; rank: number seven. The aforesaid fact has been reported to the Imperial Government."

Fan Chin read it once and then twice. He clapped his hands and laughed. "Ha! Ha! I have passed!" Hardly had he finished his words before he collapsed on the floor and became unconscious. Frightened, his mother poured water into his mouth. Gradually he regained his consciousness; then he clapped his hands and laughed again. "Ha! Ha! I passed!" he kept on repeating. Suddenly he took off, running as fast as he could towards the outside. Not far from the house, he ran right into a water pond. Drenched, with his hair spread all over his face and his hands covered with mud, he struggled out of the pond. Several people tried to hold him, but did not succeed. Still laughing and clapping his hands, he walked straight towards the market.

"The new honorable is so happy that he is now crazy," the neighbors commented.

"Why should I have a fate like this?" Fan's mother cried. "Who knows when he will recover!"

"This morning when he went out, he was absolutely normal," said Fan's wife. "What can I do, now that he is suddenly ill?"

The neighbors did their very best to comfort the two women. "Please do not worry," said one. "We will send two men to follow him, wherever he goes. Meanwhile we shall take the responsibility of feeding these messengers." Before long some neighbors brought chickens and eggs and others brought rice and wine. The two women, with tears in their eyes, went to the kitchen to prepare food.

Fan Chin's sudden illness was naturally the topic of conversation among the messengers who were then enjoying their dinner. "I have a suggestion to make with regard to the new honorable's illness," said one of the messengers.

"What is it?" others asked.

"We need a man whom His Excellency is most afraid of. You see, his illness came about because he was too happy. If a man whom he fears slaps his face and tells him that all the good news which he has heard is really a lie, he will be shocked to normalcy."

They all agreed that this was a good idea.

"The man whom His Excellency is most afraid of is his father-in-law, Hu the Butcher. He is now selling meat in the market," said one of the neighbors.

"He went to work at dawn and is about to come home soon," said another.

One man volunteered to fetch Hu the Butcher, only to meet him on the road. Hu by then had already heard of Fan's success in the examination; now, accompanied by an assistant, he was bringing eight pounds of meat and five thousand standard coins to his son-in-law's house to congratulate him. Entering the door, he saw Fan's mother and found her crying. He learned about Fan's illness and was surprised at this sudden turn of events. Then he heard that the people outside wanted to speak to him. After handing the meat and the money to his daughter, he stepped outside.

The people outside told Hu the Butcher what they wanted him to do, but Hu refused to cooperate. "Though he is my son-in-law," Hu explained, "he is also a *chü-jen*. A *chü-jen* is a star in the sky; who, tell me, dares to slap a star? I have heard the priests say that a man who slaps a star will receive one hundred blows by an iron bar after he dies and will be condemned to the eighteenth hell from which he can never hope to emerge. I will not do it."

"Mr. Hu," said one neighbor who was known for having a sharp tongue. "Since you slaughter hogs everyday, you must have accumulated thousands of blows in your name without realizing this fact yourself. What difference does it make that you receive one hundred more? Even if the king of Hades broke all of his iron bars, still he would not be able to keep straight with your record. On the other hand, if somehow you can help your son-in-law to recover from his illness, the king of Hades might have mercy on you and lift you up from the eighteenth to the seventeenth hell."

"He is merely joking with you, Mr. Hu," said one of the messengers. "This is an emergency. You have to cooperate."

With all people urging him to cooperate, Hu the Butcher finally agreed to try. He swallowed two cups of wine so as to give him the necessary courage. Rolling up his oily sleeves, he put on his normal air of ferociousness. He walked straight towards the market, followed by five or six of the neighbors.

"Just scare him a little! Do not hit him too hard!" Fan's mother cried aloud.

"Do not worry," the neighbors replied.

In the market the neighbors found Fan Chin sitting on the door steps of a Buddhist temple. His hair was unkempt; his face was covered with mud; and one of his shoes had been lost. "I passed! I passed!" He yelled loudly while continuing to clap his hands.

Hu the Butcher walked towards him like a devil reincarnated. "You beast! What did you pass?" With all of his energy, he slapped Fan's face. Seeing his performance, the neighbors had a difficult time to stifle their laughter.

Though Hu did manage to muster enough courage to strike his son-in-law, he was nevertheless fearful at heart. He felt pain in his right hand which had become too shaky for a second effort. Meanwhile Fan had already fainted and collapsed on the ground. The neighbors rushed towards him, some gently beating his back and others massaging his chest. Gradually he began to breathe; his eyes were shining; and more important, he was no longer crazy. The neighbors pulled him up and seated him on a bench in front of the temple.

Standing away from the crowd, Hu the Butcher felt that his striking hand had become more and more painful as time went on. It remained open and refused to bend. "I knew that a man should never strike a literary star in the sky," he murmured to himself with deep regret. "Now the gods are punishing me!" The more he thought of what he had done, the more painful his hand became. He asked a nearby doctor to put a plaster on his palm.

"How did I get here?" Fan looked around and was puzzled. "I must have had a nightmare."

"Congratulations!" said the neighbors. "You passed the examination with high honor."

"That is right. I recall that my rank was seven."

Fan tied up his hair and asked for water to wash his face. Meanwhile somebody had found his lost shoe.

Seeing his father-in-law, Fan was afraid that the butcher might use abusive language to scold him again. "My honorable, virtuous son-in-law," Hu stepped forward and addressed Fan in the most endearing manner. "I did not mean to do what I just did. It was your mother who implored me to do it."

"Mr. Hu, the slapping which you delivered was solid and crisp," said one of the neighbors. "When the new honorable washes his face, his washing basin will doubtless be half filled with grease."

"From now on," said another neighbor, "you cannot slaughter pigs any more."

"With such a virtuous son-in-law," said Hu the ex-Butcher, "why do I need to slaughter more pigs? As far as I can see, my livelihood has been assured for the rest of my life. I often say that my son-in-law is not only scholarly and wise but also unusually handsome. How can those *chü-jen* in the Chang and Chou families be compared with him who is infinitely better looking? Though my eyes are small, they are uncanny in recognizing great men when they see one. I recall that my daughter, before she was married at the age of thirty, had many suitors, all of whom were extremely wealthy. I said that she was a girl born with good luck and that I would not marry her to any man except a *chü-jen* with admirable quality." He laughed heartily after he had finished his remarks. The neighbors laughed too. Then they escorted the new honorable back home. Fan walked in the front, and all others, including his father-in-law, followed a few paces behind.

CHAPTER TEN

Law Enforcement

THE apparent contradiction between the humanistic tradition of Confucianism and the draconic nature of the Chinese penal code has been a puzzle to many Western observers. All Confucians emphasized the importance of morality to prevent wrong-doings rather than the importance of law to punish the wrongdoers. However, once they became government officials, they either condoned or actually participated in some of the most inhumane practices in the enforcement of the law. The use of torture to exact confessions was a normal court procedure and some of the penalties inflicted upon the convicted (such as face branding and castration) could only be described as diabolic. Whenever an emperor was compassionate enough to reduce the harshness of the penal code, the historians duly recorded the event with great jubilation (Selections 81, 82, and 83).

Was severe punishment really necessary? Some answered the question negatively (Selection 84), while others believed that it was essential to the maintenance of an orderly society. The arguments advanced by Mei Tsengliang, a scholar of the nineteenth century, summarized the official attitude: that the purpose of severe punishment was not vengeance against a particular individual for a particular crime; rather, it was to deter others from following his example and thus indirectly help them from going legally astray and perhaps even save their lives (Selection 85). Presumably, the more severe the punishment was, the stronger the deterrent would be.

One of the best examples of the arbitrary nature of the Chinese law enforcement was provided by the sad episode involving two of the most prominent figures in Chinese history, Li Ling and Ssu-ma Ch'ien, both of the second century B.C. In any other culture Li Ling would have been regarded as a great hero; but he was viewed as a villain in the eyes of the Chinese law and was dealt with accordingly (Selection 86). Ssu-ma Ch'ien, whose only "crime" was to have testified to Li Ling's good character, was punished by castration which, next to the death sentence, was regarded as the worst punishment imaginable (Selection 87).

On the local level the magistrate was the judge as well as the administrative head of the subprefecture under his jurisdiction. If he were intelligent, wise, and most important of all, compassionate, the accused would of course have a fair trial. If he were not, the chance for a miscarriage of justice would be great, especially in view of the fact that he was free to use torture to exact confessions. The story that appears as Selection 88 illustrates this point well. Though written in fictional form, it could have occurred anywhere in China prior to the twentieth century.

80 · SSU-MA CH'IEN: *On Punishment* [1]

Confucius says: "To guide the people by political means and rectify their conduct by the use of punishment can only succeed in making them shameless and opportunistic. On the other hand, they will acquire a sense of shamefulness and can easily be induced to goodness if they are guided by moral precepts which impose propriety upon their conduct." Lao-tzu says: "A truly virtuous man does not speak of virtues and consequently becomes more virtuous. A man who shows off his virtues has little virtue in him. The more the laws are, the more numerous the thieves will be."

"How right these remarks are," comments the Grand Historian.[2] "Laws are only the means of governing; they cannot eliminate the causes that prompt people to commit crimes. During the Ch'in dynasty the laws were broad and minute enough, but crimes multiplied and knew no end. All people, high or low, conspired to violate the law, and the government was weakened as a result. During this period the officials governed the people as if they were fighting fire with hot water; they had to be militant, relentless, and unusually cruel in order to meet the demand of their assigned role. Those who spoke of virtues were regarded as having failed in the performance of their duties. 'When presiding over a trial,' says Confucius, 'I, like all other judges, hope that there will never be another trial again.' 'An ignorant man laughs loudly when he hears of true virtues,' says Lao-tzu.

"After the establishment of the Han dynasty, the government abolished all cruel laws, eliminating those that were superficial but maintaining those that were basic and essential. The law was so lenient that it could be compared to a fishing net with huge holes through which the largest fish could easily escape. Yet the government functioned better and better each day, and there were no dishonest dealings among government officials. Meanwhile people enjoyed peace and security. It seems clear that the best way to govern lies in the cultivation of virtues rather than the imposition of harsh punishment."

81 · HAN WEN-TI: *A Decree to Abolish Punishment by Mutilation* [3]

I have heard that during the time of Yu-yü Shih [4] the most severe penalty for any crime was to make the offender dress differently from others; there was no

---

[1] "Biographies of Harsh Officials" *(K'u-li lieh-chuan); Shih chi,* roll 122.
[2] There is a debate among historians as to whom the author referred when he used the title "Grand Historian" *(T'ai-shih kung)*: his father Ssu-ma T'an or himself.
[3] This decree was issued in 167 B.C. Source: "A Treatise on the Penal Code, III" *(Hsing-fa chih ti-san); Han shu,* roll 23.
[4] A legendary emperor of the remote past.

such thing as capital punishment. Yet few people committed crimes. How perfect the governing was!

The present law provides three kinds of punishment by mutilation,[5] and yet the violation of the law continues to occur. Where is the blame to be placed? Is it true that I am not virtuous enough to set a good example to my subjects, or that I have failed to teach them as well as I should have? People commit crimes because they are ignorant. They are ignorant because they have not been properly taught. I feel deeply ashamed. Says the *Book of Odes:*

> Gentle and loving are our rulers
> Whom we admire and emulate
> As if they were our parents.

It is wrong to punish a man who has not been properly informed. Once the punishment is inflicted, it will be too late for him to change his conduct. I feel sorry for him indeed.

The suffering from punishment will be permanent and can never be relieved when punishment means the maiming of the body or the impairment of the flesh and the skin. Severe and inhuman as this punishment is, how can those who impose it be still referred to as "fathers and mothers of the people?"

Let the punishment by mutilation be eradicated from the Penal Code and be replaced by punishment in other forms.

82 · HAN HSÜAN-TI: *On Punishment* [6]

The imposition of punishment adversely affects the life of the punished. Its purpose should not be more than the prevention of violence and the forestalling of wrong-doings: to punish one person so that all others can live in peace and security. An official is considered just and equitable if the punishment he chooses to impose does not cause the living to complain and the spirit of the dead to resent.

Many of our officials today, however, act in violation of this basic concept. Relying on their own cleverness, they interpret the law differently at different times and impose different penalties over the same crime. They add inflammatory words to the proceedings and exaggerate the wrong-doings of the offender, so as to make sure that the accused will receive what they consider just punishment. When they present the case and the sentence they suggest to the imperial government for confirmation, how can the latter, far away from the scene, know that they have presented the complete truth? Ignorant as I am and incompetent as my officials are, on whom can the people depend for the rendering of justice?

Let all governors examine closely their subordinates to make sure that they do not have in their employment this kind of official. An official should apply the law fairly and in an equitable manner. He is not allowed to impose corvée duties without compelling reasons or to entertain lavishly a passing envoy or dignitary for the sole purpose of publicizing himself. He should know that overstepping the

---

[5] Face branding, maiming of the nose, and amputation of toes.
[6] This decree was issued by Emperor Han Hsüan-ti (r.73–49 B.C.) in 72 B.C. Source: "Biography of Han Hsüan-ti" *(Hsüan-ti chi); Han shu,* roll 8.

official boundary in violation of the law is like walking on thin ice waiting for daylight: he is in danger of being punished.

I feel deeply sorrowful that our empire has recently suffered a pestilence. Let those provinces that have been severely affected by it be exempted from taxation for this year.

83 · HAN HSÜAN-TI: *On Criminal Implications Between Close Relatives* [7]

The affection between father and son and between husband and wife is natural with man. It is not altogether unexpected that after one of the parties has committed a crime, the other tries to conceal it at the risk of his own life. It merely shows how deep this affection is. How can a law be considered wise when it operates in opposition to this natural affection?

Let it be known that from now on a son does not commit a crime if he attempts to conceal the crime of either of his parents; a wife does not commit a crime if she attempts to conceal the crime of her husband; and a grandson does not commit a crime if he attempts to conceal the crime of any of his grandparents. On the other hand, parents are not allowed to conceal a crime committed by their children; a husband is not allowed to conceal a crime committed by his wife; and grandparents are not allowed to conceal a crime committed by their grandchildren. The penalty is death in each case, and the proceedings should be reported to the Governor of Punishments.

84 · LU WEN-SHU: *On the Severity of Punishments* [8]

It is said that the Ch'in regime committed ten errors during its existence.[9] Since then all of these errors have been eliminated with the exception of one, *i.e.,* cruel punishment of the violators of the law.

The Ch'in regime looked down upon cultural pursuits while glorifying valiancy in warfare. It considered men of virtue insignificant while attaching great importance to officials who enforced the law with harshness and cruelty. A man who spoke on behalf of justice was characterized as a slanderer, and any criticism of the government was denounced as the advocacy of heresy. Consequently, upright scholars could not be found in the employment of the government, and good advice and sound admonitions were conspicuously absent. Flattery filled up the air, and nothing but arrogance existed in the mind of the monarch. Disasters, whenever they occurred, were carefully concealed as a matter of routine; they were never reported to the emperor. It is no wonder that the Ch'in regime fell in the end.

[7] This decree was issued in 66 B.C. Source: "Biography of Han Hsüan-ti" *(Hsüan-ti chi); Han shu,* roll 8.
[8] This was a memorial submitted to Emperor Han Hsüan-ti in 73 B.C. Source: "Biographies of Chia, Chou, Mei, and Lu" *(Chia Chou Mei Lu chuan); Han shu,* roll 51.
[9] The ten errors were abolition of feudalism, construction of the Great Wall, melting weapons and casting them into huge statues, construction of the Afang Palace, burning books, burying scholars alive, construction of a mausoleum to house Shih Huang-ti's body, search for immortal drugs, dispatching the crown prince to supervise an army in the northern frontier, and finally, cruel punishment of law offenders.

Blessed by Your Majesty's effort, the country is now peaceful and prosperous. Father and son; husband and wife—all work diligently for a secure home. Yet the peace we enjoy is still marred by one imperfection: the complete chaos in meting out punishment. The imposition of penalties concerns the life of man and is second to nothing in importance. For a man, once dead, cannot live again; and a limb, once separated from the body, cannot be rejoined. "It is preferable to let the guilty escape than to kill the innocent," says the *Book of History*. The criminal judges today act in direct opposition to this ancient precept. All of them, high or low, attempt to outdo each other in harshness which to them is an indication of impartiality. The harsher they are, the more likely they will be characterized as objective and just, while those who believe in a fair trial may suffer evil consequences. As a result, all judges want their charges to die, not because they hate people as such, but because these deaths will assure their own security. Time and again the market is spattered with blood,[10] and condemned criminals are so numerous that they stand shoulder to shoulder. Each year the condemned and the executed are numbered in thousands—these killings make all men of goodwill sorrowful and sad. This is the reason, I believe, why we have not reached an era of unspoiled peace.

People love life as long as they are bodily secure; they prefer death if the punishment inflicted upon them has become too painful to bear. By the means of torture, a judge can obtain whatever confession he wishes to have, because the accused, unable to stand the pain, will confess a crime which he may have never committed. All judges understand this easy method of obtaining confession and use it to good effect; then they can invoke the law and impose a sentence which supposedly reflects the seriousness of the crime. Fearful that the severe penalty may not stand the scrutiny of their superiors, they distort the case in their petition to the imperial government,[11] in such a way that even a Chiu-yu [12] examining the case would have to conclude that the death sentence is only too light for the accused. Not only do they edit the accused's confession to suit their purpose; they also trace in detail his motives, so as to make sure that he cannot escape capital punishment. Obsessed with the idea of being strict and severe, they are cruel and brutal to the greatest extreme. Following the principle of expediency and indifferent to the welfare of the nation, these criminal judges are the true criminals of the nation.

An old proverb says: "Do not enter a circle even if it is chalked on the ground; [13] do not speak to a judge even if he is carved from a piece of wood." How pathetic this remark is! How much the people hate the judges! Of all the problems we face today, none is more serious than this inhumanness in meting out punishment. Of all the people who abuse the law and violate its intentions, none is worse than our criminal judges. Not only do they separate people who love each other; they have also made a mockery of true justice.

This is what I mean when I say that of the ten errors made during the Ch'in regime one is still very much in existence.

---

10 In ancient times the market was often used as an execution ground.

11 Capital punishment had to be sanctioned by the imperial government before it could be carried out.

12 A brilliant jurist who served under the legendary emperor Shun.

13 The circle symbolizes confinement or imprisonment.

85 · Mei Tseng-liang: *On Capital Punishment* [14]

There is no law which can be long enforced without generating abuse. The simpler the law is, the less likely it will be abused. The more complicated it is, the more likely it will be subject to misinterpretation. A law, however good it is when it is enacted, will bring harm to all concerned if its enforcers continue to interpret it literally. Once abuses begin to accumulate, it will be extremely difficult to go back to the law as it was originally intended.

Killing a man without justifiable cause is called murder. According to the law of Kao-t'ao,[15] the penalty for misconduct was branding and the penalty for murder was death. As late as the Han dynasty, the law said that "The penalty for murder is death; assault and robbery will be punished in accordance with the seriousness of the offense." In both cases, the law was simple, clear, and easily understood.

This does not mean that people of ancient times did not understand that there were different degrees of murder and that the circumstances under which murder was committed could vary. But they knew that no law, however thorough and specific, could possibly cover all circumstances under which murder could be committed. They preferred a simple, uniform law which was easy to understand, but the violation of which would entail the most severe penalties. The execution of one man would serve as a warning to thousands of others who, knowing the severity of punishment, would not commit crimes and thus save their own lives.

People of later ages maintained that this simple but harsh law was incomplete and devised new laws to replace it. The same murder was divided into several kinds: murder with intent to kill, murder with causes, combat murder, murder through mistaken identity, murder by accident, murder disguised as unintended error, murder caused by repeated strikes by one's own hands, etc. A variety of circumstances was introduced to underline the same physical act: murder. Since the varied circumstances had to be ascertained before the death sentence could be carried out, the judge had to decide whether the execution should or should not be postponed. In many cases the execution was postponed time and again until the death sentence itself was commuted to long imprisonment. Meanwhile the amount of paper work involving the whole procedure—prosecution, inquiry, rebuttal, and finally, confirmation—could be piled up one foot in depth. Even after the death sentence was confirmed, the subprefecture or district that handled this case would have to petition the Ministry of Justice in the capital before the sentence could be carried out. Even then there was a good chance that the sentence would be commuted. The law was so complicated that it was difficult to know where it stood.

Today people say that this law is a good law and that we invite harsh criticism from posterity if we attempt to change it. Even those who believe that it is wrong tend to compromise and simply follow the majority. They do not realize that to follow the majority when the majority is wrong entails a loss for all concerned. Our law makers say that as long as there are people who live by mistake, there

[14] *Ku-chin wen-tsung,* vol. I.
[15] Kao-t'ao was said to be the minister of justice under the legendary emperor Shun.

must be people who die by mistake, thus underlying the theory that it is more important to save the living than to avenge the dead. Our law enforcers say that as the dead cannot be restored to life, we should be more concerned with the life of the living; that we should have no more right to kill the murderer than the murderer has the right to kill the murdered; and that our overwhelming desire to save life will be understood and appreciated by all members of our society.

This line of thinking, when put into practice, will not only fail to save the life of the living, but will actually encourage them to proceed to the road of the dead. It will not only cause more people to be murdered; it will also cause more murderers to be sentenced to death. Whenever a person is murdered, the news spreads fast. All people know the difference between life and death, but few people know the subtle differences between combat murder, murder through mistaken identity, murder by accident, and murder disguised as unintended error. It is extremely confusing to them that a murderer sometimes does and sometimes does not have to pay with his own life. They may feel sorry for a murderer who has to die, but they will be very angry indeed if he is not punished for the beastly crime he has committed.

If a man dies immediately after he has eaten a piece of poisonous meat, no one else will eat the same meat and no one else will die. If, on the other hand, three men eat the same meat and only one of them dies, more people will eat the same meat and more will die. By the same token, a law, not strictly enforced, will cause more people to lose their lives. Why is it that we should be concerned with the life of one murderer at the expense of the lives of thousands of others who will be tempted to follow his example if he were not punished so severely as he should be? People say that by sparing his life, the official-in-charge will not run the risk of killing him by mistake. This argument, seemingly reasonable, is disastrous in reality. Do they realize that the official-in-charge, by sparing a murderer's life, may have encouraged many others to indulge in killing as long as they have "legitimate reasons" to do so? If the law is to be interpreted this way, I am afraid that it will kill more people than it can save.

86 · LI LING: *A Letter to Su Wu* [16]

Let me congratulate you for exemplifying the best of all virtues [17] and establishing a great name for yourself in time of peace. I, on the other hand, live far away in a foreign country, a fact grieved by all people since ancient times. Thinking of you, my old friend, can I not feel sadness at heart? Not considering me unworthy, you have honored me with your letter in which you provide me with advice as well as comfort, a favor that is more generous than what one brother can give to another. Ignorant though I am, how can I not feel a strong sense of gratitude?

Since the time of my surrender, I have lived in poverty and misery, accompanied each day by my own sorrows. From morning to night I see no one except those who are strange and alien. My clothes are made of animal skins, and my home is a felt tent that protects me from the elements. I eat lamb (which smells)

[16] *Ku-wen kuan-chih,* roll 6.
[17] This referred to Su Wu's refusal to surrender despite the Hsiung-nu's demand and the honor accorded to him after his return to China in the summer of 81 B.C.

to appease my hunger and drink milk to quench my thirst. With whom can I share a word or a smile? In these northern territories the ice is black and the earth cracks under the impact of the bitter cold. A deadly quiet shrouds the entire land, only to be broken by the bleak, chilly sound of the wind. As early as the ninth month, the air becomes cool, and the grass withers over the landscape. At night I cannot sleep; I incline my ears and listen to the sounds from the distance. The reed whistles [18] echo one another, and the neighing of grazing horses moves sadly through the air. The horses moan in groups: strange sounds come from every corner of this remote land. Early in the morning I sit on my bed and listen: I cannot hold back my tears. Oh, Tzu-ch'ing,[19] I am not a man without sensitivity; how can I not but feel sad?

Since your departure, I feel more lonely than ever. I think of my mother who, as old as she was, had to suffer capital punishment. My wife and children were completely blameless; yet, they were also punished by death. Where can a man seek pity after he has been accused of betraying his own country and of repaying favors with ingratitude? Now that you have returned home and enjoyed honor, how sorrowful my own fate is that I have to remain here to be continuously humiliated! How sad it is that I, born to a high civilization, end my days in the nation of the ignorant; abandoned by my own sovereign and parents, I am now living in the land of the barbarians! I grieve over the fact that an inheritor of the ancient culture has become a member of the barbarians.

It has not been clearly understood that my accomplishments were great compared to the offense I committed. The nation has not been grateful for what I intended to achieve. Whenever I thought of this ingratitude, I did not believe that I should die by my own hands. It is not difficult to commit suicide if, by doing so, my true motive could be better understood. In view of what the nation has done to me,[20] what use is it for me to end my own life? I merely humiliate myself. I continue to live not because I value life above everything else but because the alternative seems to be much worse. Knowing my conditions, my retainers try to comfort me, using words which indicate their own misunderstanding of my feelings. Whatever pleasure one might have in this alien land only makes one all the more sorrowful.

Oh, Tzu-ch'ing, to understand a man is to understand how he feels. In my previous letter, I did not express myself fully since I wrote it in haste. Let me retrace what I would like to say. The late emperor [21] granted me a command of five thousand infantrymen and ordered me to march towards the remote areas of the distant north. Five other generals failed to arrive in accordance with a plan that had been previously arranged, and I alone met the enemy. Let me remind you of the conditions under which we fought. We had carried our food supplies for ten thousand li, and our fighting forces consisted entirely of infantry. We were far away from China and were deep in the heartland of a powerful enemy. Five thousand men were pitched against one hundred thousand of the enemy's soldiers, and our infantry, tired and exhausted, was face to face with his fresh cavalry. Yet, we fought: we routed his men, captured his banners; we chased

[18] Whistles made of reed leaves.
[19] Su Wu's courtesy name.
[20] This referred to the capital punishment imposed by the Han authorities upon his mother, wife, and children.
[21] Han Wu-ti.

him throughout the north until he disappeared; and in the process we killed his most brilliant commanders. All of our soldiers fought so bravely that they marched towards death as if they were about to return home—how proud I was to be their commander and how fortunate I was to be in charge of this great responsibility! At that time I thought that my contribution to the nation was incomparably great.

After this defeat, the Hsiung-nu [22] mobilized the entire nation, regrouped their best troops, and sent one hundred thousand men to face us. The khan took personal command of his troops that subsequently encircled us. The odds against us were overwhelming, not only in numbers but also in the fact that infantry was pitched against cavalry. Yet our weary soldiers stood up and fought again; each of them was counted to fight as if he were one thousand. Neglecting his wounds and bearing his pain, he rushed forward to exchange his life for that of his enemy. The dead and the wounded lay helplessly throughout the battlefield, and the remaining numbered less than one hundred, all of whom could not fight because of their illness. Yet, when I raised up my arm and shouted, the wounded and the sick stood up, raised their swords, and pointed them at their enemy; the enemy turned his horse around and fled. Then only a few of us were still alive, the supply of arrows was exhausted, and not a single person had a weapon in his hand. Shouting loudly, each of us rushed towards the enemy with his bare hands. At this moment I felt that Heaven and Earth were angry in expressing their sympathy for me and that every soldier of mine was shedding blood and tears on my behalf. Being convinced that I could not be captured, the khan proposed to leave the battlefield and lift the siege. However, listening to the advice of a traitor,[23] he ordered the renewal of the fighting, and consequently I could not escape the fate that was destined for me.[24]

Formerly Emperor Kao,[25] commanding three hundred thousand troops, was besieged by the Hsiung-nu at the city of P'ingch'eng.[26] He had under his command many great generals and brilliant strategists; yet he had to suffer starvation for seven days before he could escape.[27] How could people expect me to do better under more limited circumstances? They condemned me on the ground that I did not commit suicide after I had been captured, a great crime to which I readily admit. You know me well, Tzu-ch'ing; do you believe that my failure to commit suicide was due to cowardice: that my love of life was so great that I was willing to sacrifice high principles in order to preserve it? Am I such a person who would betray his king and his parents and abandon his wife and children so that he alone could live? The reason I refused to die was that I had a more constructive purpose in mind. As I indicated to you in my previous letter, I wished to preserve my life so that in some future time I could repay the favor which the nation and the king had previously bestowed upon me. It was my belief then as it is my

[22] For a description of the Hsiung-nu and China's relation with them, see pp. 210–220.
[23] His name was Kuan Kan, a Chinese general who had previously surrendered to the Hsiung-nu.
[24] He was captured.
[25] Also known as Emperor Kao-tsu, founder of the Han dynasty. His real name was Liu Pang.
[26] Located in the northern section of modern Shensi province.
[27] This incident occurred in 199 B.C. Two years later, a peace treaty was concluded between the two countries whereby Liu Pang agreed to marry one of his princesses to the Hsiung-nu king, send him silk, wine, and rice as gifts, and call him "brother."

belief now that to live for a useful purpose is much wiser than to die for a vain glory. . . .[28]

In your letter you said that the Han dynasty had always been generous towards those who had accomplished great deeds for the nation. Being a minister of the Han, how could you say anything different. . . .[29] My grandfather was regarded as one of the bravest generals the Han dynasty had ever produced and his military deeds against the Hsiung-nu were considered incomparably great. Yet, because he had offended a favorite minister of the king, he was forced to commit suicide in the remote area of an alien land.[30] This incident has made many courageous men sigh in grief. How can you say that the Han government is not ungrateful to its meritorious ministers and courageous generals?

You, sir, once served as Han's envoy to the Hsiung-nu; you traveled to the heart of a powerful enemy with only a few retainers. Once it was clear that you could not successfully complete your mission due to circumstances beyond your control, you did not hesitate to attempt to end your own life.[31] Constantly moved about and enduring immense sufferings, you almost died in the wilderness of the remote north.[32] You were a young man when you went to the north as an envoy; by the time you returned, your hair was already white. Your mother had died then, and your wife had been remarried. What you had done for the Han dynasty was unprecedented in history. Even the barbarians, let alone the emperor of China, know that a man of such high principles deserves honor and esteem. I thought that after your return you would be invested with a feudal domain and be awarded thousands of chariots. Yet, your cash reward was only two million,[33] and your position was that of a department head in charge of barbarian affairs.[34] There was no investiture for your efforts. On the other hand, those ministers who specialized in slandering their betters were awarded titles of dukes; flatterers and the emperor's relatives were installed as high-ranking officials. Since the Han government treated you in this manner, how could I hope for anything better?

[28] This was followed by the mention of two historical figures who refused to die even though humiliated by defeat and who eventually won victories against their enemies.
[29] This was followed by the listing of nine persons who had accomplished great deeds for the Han dynasty but to whom the royal house had been extremely ungrateful.
[30] There was no exaggeration on the part of Li Ling whose grandfather, Li Kuang, is regarded by historians as one of the greatest generals during the Han dynasty. In 127 B.C. Wei Ch'ing, here referred to as "favorite minister," was appointed as commander-in-chief of an expeditionary force to fight against the Hsiung-nu, and Li Kuang was to serve as his deputy to command a separate detachment on his eastern flank. Li Kuang and his troops lost their way and were late when meeting with the main force in a previously agreed rendezvous. Asked by Wei Ch'ing why he had lost his way, Li unsheathed his sword and committed suicide because to him this question amounted to open reproach, a humiliation which a gentleman could not bear.
[31] In 100 B.C. Su Wu was sent by Han Wu-ti as his personal envoy to the Hsiung-nu court, accompanied by approximately one hundred retainers and personal guards. When the khan tried to persuade him to renounce his allegiance to the Han authority, Su unsheathed his sword and fell on it, with the intended purpose of committing suicide. He was only seriously wounded, however. After his recovery, he was detained for eighteen years before he was allowed to return to China.
[32] In order to prevent the Han authority from knowing his whereabouts, Su Wu was moved about from place to place. For the most of the eighteeen years during which he was detained, he served as a shepherd near the Arctic Ocean.
[33] Two million standard coins.
[34] In this position Su Wu received two thousand piculs of grain as his annual salary, equivalent to that of a governor.

It punished me so severely for the simple fact that I failed to commit suicide; yet, it did not reward you, a man of the highest principle, in a way that you truly deserved. Following a policy like this, how can it expect its subjects in the remote areas to be completely loyal and obedient? I may have been ungrateful to my government, but my government was equally ungrateful to me.

An old proverb says that to be unfearful of death does not require unusual courage. Even if I did die, do you really think that His Majesty would have any sympathy for me? Even though I cannot establish a great name for myself, I still prefer to die and be buried in a barbarian land, instead of returning to my own country where I will be subject to humiliation at the hands of the clerks whose only ability, as you well know, consists of playing with words. Please, sir, do not expect me to return. What else can I say, Tzu-ch'ing? We are ten thousand *li* apart; our roads are different. I stay in a different world while I live and will become a ghost in an alien land when I die. Farewell, Tzu-ch'ing. Please give my best regards to my friends at home, and work diligently for His Majesty the Emperor. Your young son is well; please do not worry about him.[35] Do take care of yourself, however. Facing the northern wind, I am looking forward to a word from you. Your friend, Li Ling.

87 · SSU-MA CH'IEN: *A Letter to Jen An*[36]

Though I regarded myself as unusually talented during my younger days, I did not enjoy a great reputation when I reached adulthood. The emperor, however, granted me a position in the court on account of my deceased ancestor so that I could contribute whatever talent I might have.[37] Being limited in outlook, I cut off my relations with my friends and purposely foundered in my duties towards my family, so that I could devote all of my time and energy to the position I held. I was anxious to ingratiate myself to the emperor, but the result proved to be otherwise.

Though both Li Ling and I served as officials-in-attendance at one time, we were merely acquaintances. Each of us went his own separate ways; we never drank wine together, nor had we entertained each other. Yet, from what I could observe, he was a gentleman of the highest principle. He was dutiful towards his parents and never broke a promise with his friends. He was incorruptible with regard to money; he gave and took in accordance with the highest principles. He would graciously withdraw whenever in conflict with others; he was respectful and modest towards all the people whom he knew. Often did he express the wish to sacrifice his own life whenever a national emergency called upon him to do so. With a selfless ambition like this, he, in my opinion, was a true patriot.

A man who was unconcerned with his own life in order to serve the nation in a time of crisis was to me very unusual indeed. Yet, once he made a mistake, all those ministers, whose only desire was to save their own lives and those of their

---

[35] During his detention Su Wu married a Hsiung-nu woman who bore him a son named T'ung-kuo.

[36] This is a translation of the last two-thirds of the Chinese original. Source: "Biography of Ssu-ma Ch'ien" (*Ssu-ma Ch'ien chuan); Han shu,* roll 62.

[37] Ssu-ma Ch'ien succeeded his father, Ssu-ma T'an, as the royal historian.

families, began to criticize him and inflate his shortcomings. Personally, I strongly deplored this outcome of events.

Li Ling commanded an infantry regiment of less than five thousand, penetrated deep into cavalry territory,[38] and went as far as the nerve center of the Hsiung-nu. Like a bait in front of a tiger's mouth, he challenged the power of the barbarians who numbered hundreds of thousands. For more than ten days he and his men killed their enemies; so many did they kill that the enemy hardly had time to recover the dead and attend the wounded. The Hsiung-nu chieftains were terrified; they called upon their Left and Right Princes [39] to send all the archers of their nation to encircle the expeditionary force. Li Ling fought from place to place for a distance of one thousand *li* even though he and his compatriots were completely surrounded at all times. The end finally approached when the supply of arrows was exhausted and the relief forces failed to arrive. Meanwhile the dead and the wounded piled up upon one another. Yet, when Li Ling called for more efforts, all the wounded stood up; with tears in their eyes and blood on their clothes, they drew their empty bows, braced the enemy's sharp knives, and rushed northward to kill or to be killed.

Before Li Ling's defeat, a messenger arrived and reported on his military feat. All princes and ministers toasted the emperor and celebrated. Several days later, the news of the defeat reached the capital.[40] The emperor was so worried that he could not eat well; he showed his unhappiness when he met with his ministers. His ministers were sorrowful and afraid, but did not know what to do. It was then that I, forgetting my inferior position and concerned only with the emperor's unhappiness, wished to express my humble but sincere opinion in this matter. I felt that since Li Ling was extremely generous in his relation with others, he could always count on other people's help and support; he, in my opinion, could be favorably compared with the greatest generals of the past. It seemed to me that even though he was defeated, he merely waited for another opportunity to serve the Han government better. He had done his best prior to his defeat—his deeds were good enough to be made known throughout the empire. While I was looking for an opportunity to express these private thoughts of my own, the emperor inquired. In response I praised Li Ling's achievements, in the hope that the emperor would feel better after lending his ears to my presentation and that other people's slandering of Li Ling could therefore be stopped. The emperor misinterpreted my intention which apparently I had failed to make clear, thinking that I was merely propagandizing on Li Ling's behalf and that I was disparaging the efforts of General Erh-shih.[41] He ordered that I be imprisoned at once; to the very end I was not given the opportunity to present my case in front of the emperor towards whom I had always been unswervingly loyal. Since I was charged with calumination against the sovereign, the judge went along with the charge.

My family was poor, and I did not have the money to buy my redemption. All of my friends did not utter one word or lend one hand to help. Alas! I was not made of wood or stone and thus devoid of sensitivities. Yet, I was shut behind

[38] This referred to modern Outer Mongolia, the home of the Hsiung-nu.
[39] They were the Hsiung-nu's highest officials, second only to the Great Khan.
[40] Ch'angan.
[41] Also known as Li Kuang-li, one of the greatest generals of the Han dynasty, who was then fighting in the north.

the prison door, keeping company with the jailers. To whom could I complain or present my case? You, sir, have personally seen all of this. Did I ever do anything that could justify this misfortune of mine? The reputation of Li Ling's family was completely ruined after his surrender, and I myself was punished by castration and thus became a laughing stock throughout the world. How can I explain to an ordinary person this tragic turn of events?

My late father did not accomplish political or military deeds of great importance. His position as a historian, astronomer, and calendar maker was similar, like mine, to that of a magician or diviner, to be kept like an entertainer or prostitute, and was looked down upon by all the people. Had I suffered capital punishment, my death would be like that of an ant, an insignificant event as far as the world was concerned. People would not compare me with those who died on a matter of high principle and would say that, coming to the end of my wits, I deserved the punishment I had received.

Every man must die. His death can be either highly honorable or totally insignificant, depending upon the situation in which he dies. The best is a situation in which he does not bring humiliation to his ancestors; next best is a situation in which he does not bring humiliation to himself. The situation becomes worse and the humiliation greater in the following order: die after being insulted with an angry countenance, die after being insulted with angry words, die after pleading for mercy, die after being changed into brown clothes,[42] die after being tortured in jail, die after his hair has been shaved and his neck fettered with iron rings, die after being maimed and mutilated, and the worst of all, die after being castrated.

The ancient saying that "corporal punishment should never be inflicted upon scholars" is designed to strengthen the self-respect of all intellectuals. A tiger in deep mountains is feared by all the beasts. Once it is caged, however, it wags its tail to beg for food. Why? Slowly and gradually it has lost confidence in itself and its own self-respect. "Do not enter into a circle even if it is chalked on the ground; do not speak to a judge even if he is carved from a piece of wood." A man should plan ahead and commit suicide before he can be tortured. Once his hands and feet are tied up to receive torture; his body is exposed to receive beatings; and he himself is confined within four walls—he does not mind kowtowing to the warden whenever he sees him, and he trembles with fear whenever a prison guard passes by. Why? Slowly and gradually he has lost confidence in himself and his own self-respect. . . .

It is the nature of man to love life and abhor death. He is concerned with his parents, and he wishes to protect his wife and children. When he chooses to die for a matter of principle, this is because he has not been given a better choice. It is my misfortune that my parents died early and that I do not have any brothers. Of course, you know how I feel about my wife and children. A man who chooses to die on a matter of principle is not necessarily brave; nor is a man cowardly who chooses to live in order to attain a noble goal. Cowardly though I might seem, I did not choose to live for the mere sake of living. When I allow myself to be humiliated as a prisoner by refusing to die, I must have a good reason for such a behavior. Even a slave or concubine has the courage to commit suicide; how could I possibly not have it in view of the circumstances?

---

[42] Customarily worn by prisoners.

The reason that I chose to live with humiliation and under the worst circumstances [43] was that my private wishes had not been fulfilled at the time of my misfortune. I was fearful that my literary work would not be known to posterity. . . .

Untalented though I am, I have been devoting myself to literary pursuit. I collected all known works about the past, examined each historical event, and traced its beginning and end. I studied and commented on the success or failure, rise or fall, of each person or regime. The book begins with Hsien-yüan [44] and ends with the present. It consists of ten charts, twelve royal biographies, eight treatises, thirty biographies for the aristocrats, and seventy ordinary biographies, totalling one hundred thirty rolls. The purpose is to find the laws that govern Heaven and Earth and the reasons that underlie the changes of ancient and modern times. I wish to be the originator of a new school of writing totally different from any others. [45]

The misfortune fell upon me before the book was completed. Knowing what I had to accomplish, I went through the worst punishments without anger or fear. I felt that I could more than redeem myself for the humiliations I had suffered if my book were completed. It would be then kept in a famous mountain, waiting for those who, understanding its value, would distribute it in all of the large cities. I should have no regret then even if my body were slashed into thousands of pieces. This private wish of mine can only be communicated to a wise man; how can I expect an ordinary person to understand it? . . .

88 · LIU OH: *A Case of Murder* [46]

"In the northeastern section of the Ch'iho subprefecture [47] and forty-five *li* from the city is a village named Ch'itung," said Huang Jen-shui. "The village, which has three or four thousand households, has one main avenue and several side streets. On the third side street south of the main avenue lived a man named Chia Chih, popularly known as Old Chia. Old Chia, aged fifty or a little above, had two sons and one daughter. At the age of twenty, the elder son married the daughter of a Wei family which, like the Chia family, depended upon farming for its livelihood and owned forty or fifty *ch'ing* [48] of land. Wei Ch'ien, head of the Wei family, adopted a nephew as his son whose duty was to help him to manage household affairs. The adopted son, however, proved to be less than reliable, and Old Wei, as Wei Ch'ien was popularly called, showered all of his affection on his son-in-law instead. In the seventh month of last year, his son-in-law incurred a seasonal disease and died one month later. After a mourning period which lasted one hundred days, Old Wei, to comfort his daughter, often invited

[43] This refers to his castration.
[44] Hsien-yüan is also known as Huang-ti or Yellow Emperor, a legendary ruler of the remote past.
[45] From hindsight this was hardly an exaggeration. For the next two thousand years all dynastic historians followed the format of *Shih chi* with only minor modifications.
[46] This is a condensed, abridged version of the Chinese original that appears in *Lao-ts'an yu-chi*, Chapters 15–18.
[47] Located in modern Shantung province.
[48] Sixty or seventy-five acres.

her to his home where she stayed anywhere between ten and fifteen days each time.

"Old Chia's second son, aged twenty-four, looked decent and wrote fairly well since he had been studying at home. After the death of his elder son, Old Chia did not want him to study any more because he was afraid that overwork might be harmful to his son's health. The old man also had a daughter, aged nineteen, who was not only beautiful but also able and intelligent; she made decisions on all matters relating to the family, large or small. Because of her beauty and talent, the villagers gave her a nickname: Early Spring. Her brother, on the other hand, was docile and spoke little; the villagers gave him a nickname too and called him Chia the Stupid. Chia the Stupid was married to a daughter from a scholarly family in the same village, but Chia the Early Spring remained a maiden at the mature age of nineteen.

"Why is it that she was not married at this late age? The reason was very simple. Since she was unusually beautiful and talented, there was not a single man in the village with whom she could be properly matched. There was one man in the village, however, who seemed to be able to fill the bill. His name was Wu Erh, nicknamed Wu the Prodigal, a handsome, eloquent, and wealthy young man who loved to ride horses and practice archery. He was remotely related to the Chia family and came to visit often. Time and again he sent go-betweens to ask for Early Spring's hand. At the beginning Old Chia was favorably disposed; then, learning what kind of man Wu Erh really was, he changed his mind. He heard that the young man had already stolen several women in the village, that he loved to gamble, and that he often went to the capital for a spending spree which lasted one or sometimes two months. He concluded that with a son like this the Wu family would eventually become bankrupt, even though it was the wealthiest family in the village. After Wu Erh had been ruled out as a prospective son-in-law, Old Chia continued to search for a promising candidate, but in vain. Meanwhile Early Spring became older and older without a husband.

"The first anniversary of the death of Chia's elder son fell on the thirteenth day of the eighth month this year. The family invited monks to perform a Buddhist ritual which lasted three days, the twelfth, the thirteenth, and the fourteenth. After the ritual was over, Old Wei invited his daughter home to celebrate the moon festival together.[49] In the afternoon of the festival day, he heard that all the members of the Chia family, with the exception of Early Spring, had suddenly died. He and his daughter rushed towards the Chia household and found that altogether thirteen persons had become the victims of an unknown hand. Three bodies were found in the gate house: one doorman and two hired hands. Another body, that of a boy servant, lay on the floor of the main hall. In the antechamber behind the main hall Old Chia was dead in his bed. The bodies of young Chia and his wife were found in their own room in the living quarter of the house, next to the body of an amah. On the bed was their baby, aged three. In the kitchen two more bodies were found: an amah and a young female slave. Another amah's body was found in a side room. The family accountant, the last to be counted, died in his quarters located near the front hall.

"Because of the mysterious nature of these sudden deaths, the village immedi-

---

[49] The moon festival, which is still celebrated by the Chinese today, falls on the fifteenth day of the eighth lunar month, about mid-September.

ately reported their occurrence to the magistracy of the subprefecture in the city. Early the next morning the magistrate, accompanied by the subprefectural coroner, arrived and conducted an autopsy. He found that none of the dead persons had suffered from wounds prior to their deaths, that their joints were not rigid, and that there were no blue or purple marks on the skin whose color seemed to be absolutely normal. In other words, there was no indication that the victims had been either beaten or poisoned. 'Their deaths are a mystery,' the magistrate concluded and ordered the Chia family to go ahead with the funeral.

"Returning to the city, the magistrate, whose name was Wang Tzu-chin, proceeded to make a report to the provincial government. Hardly had he completed the draft of his report when he received a petition from the Chia family, saying that evidence of murder had been found in connection with this case."

"What was the evidence?" Huang Jen-shui continued. "Both Chia Kan (a young man who had been installed as Old Chia's legitimate heir shortly after the multiple deaths) and Early Spring claimed that a half piece of poisoned moon cake [50] had been found on Old Chia's table and that all the victims seemed to have eaten the same moon cakes prior to their deaths. These cakes had been sent by the Wei family as a present two days before the moon festival, and the mass murder was prompted by the fact that Widow Chia, the sister-in-law of Early Spring, had a paramour with whom she had carried on an illicit relationship. So the plaintiffs claimed.

"The magistrate summoned Chia Kan for questioning, but the latter could not name the so-called paramour. Widow Chia maintained that the moon cakes were delivered on the twelfth when she was still at home and that some members of the family did eat them then without suffering any evil effects. Her father Old Wei testified that the moon cakes were ordered from the Ssu-mei Bakery and that if they did contain poison, he, Old Wei, was not responsible. The manager of the Ssu-mei Bakery admitted that these cakes were his shop's products, but the cakes stuffing, he added, was provided by the Wei family. Since the stuffing in the half piece found on Old Chia's table did contain a small amount of arsenic, Old Wei and Widow Chia were taken into custody. They were thrown into an empty room in the city jail, but so far no torture had been applied to exact confessions.

"The magistrate did not know what to make out of this case. He had personally examined the bodies that gave no indication that the victims had been poisoned. If arsenic was the cause of their deaths, they should not have died simultaneously since they had not eaten the cakes at the same time. Moreover, how could one explain the fact that the net result of the poisoning was the same death, in view of the fact that some had obviously eaten only a small amount of the cakes and could conceivably have survived while others had eaten more? Because the plaintiffs had pressed hard on their charges, the magistrate had no choice except to make a detailed report to the governor and request an able official from the provincial government to conduct the trial."

"Several days ago," Huang Jen-shui continued, "a presiding judge was dispatched from the provincial capital. His name was Kang P'i, a disciple of Lü Chien-t'ang. Like his teacher, he was harsh, strict, and incorruptible. No sooner did he arrive than he used torture to exact confessions. Both defendants, Old

---

[50] The consumption of moon cakes (a Chinese delicacy) during the moon festival is a custom still followed by most Chinese today.

Wei and Widow Chia, died several times over on account of the excessive pain, but none made any confessions."

"What happened next?" Lao-ts'an was anxious to know.

"Well, the situation became worse as far as the defendants were concerned," Huang replied. "The manager of the Wei household, a naive but good-hearted old man, was fully convinced of his master's innocence and decided to do something about it on his own. Putting some money in his pocket, he came to the city and appealed to a man named Hu for help. Hu was a member of the local gentry and a holder of the *chü-jen* degree.[51] Seeing him, the old man kowtowed, saying that the gods would reward Hu abundantly if the latter could somehow save his master's life. 'Never mind the gods,' Hu replied. 'Only money can do the trick. I know the presiding judge very well; in fact, we had at one time dined together in the capital. Give me one thousand taels of silver, and I will take care of your problems. Mind you, this amount does not include my fee.' The old man took two checks from his pocket, each bearing a face value of five hundred, and handed them over to his host. 'I only want this case to be amicably settled,' he added; 'I do not care how much it will cost.' Hu nodded his head in agreement. After finishing his lunch, Hu dressed up properly and went to see Kang P'i."

"The defendants were really in trouble now," Lao-ts'an cried aloud.

"After some conventional talk, Hu presented the two checks to Kang P'i with both hands. 'This is the humble tribute presented to Your Excellency by the Wei family in connection with the murder case,' said Hu. 'Please have mercy on them.' "

"I am sure that Kang P'i was extremely angry," said Lao-ts'an.

"The situation would not have been so bad if he were angry," said Huang Jen-shui.

"What happened?"

"Well, Kang P'i took both checks with a smiling face. He examined them carefully and then said that he was not sure whether they were genuine and redeemable. 'These are certified checks issued by the T'ungyü Bank, the largest bank in our subprefecture,' Hu replied; 'there is no question about their authenticity.'

" 'How can you expect me to settle a murder case of such monstrosity with only one thousand taels of silver?' Kang asked.

" 'The Wei family says that it is willing to pay more if the case can be dismissed at the earliest possible moment.'

" 'The murder involves the death of thirteen persons,' said Kang; 'and I would like to charge one thousand taels for each person, totalling thirteen thousand taels. However, since you are an old friend of mine, I will do you a favor by reducing my fee by one-half. Are sixty-five hundred taels all right with you?'

" 'Yes, yes,' Hu agreed promptly.

" 'Since you are only the go-between, I would like you to speak with the Wei family so as to secure its approval of this deal. They do not have to write checks to that amount at the moment. All I need is a promissory note indicating that it will pay the agreed total. Once I receive the note, I will dismiss the case the very next day.'

"Hu was happy beyond belief and went to talk with the manager of the Wei household. Hearing that the case would be dismissed promptly, the old man, being so naive as he was, decided to make a decision on his own. He thought that his

[51] As for the *chü-jen* degree, see p. 179, Footnote 66.

master would not mind this deal when he was told of it after his release from the prison, especially in view of the fact that he, as the household manager, had been a faithful employee for so many years. Moreover, all he had to do was to write a promissory note rather than to pay the demanded amount in cash. He wrote the note accordingly and handed it over to Mr. Hu. Besides he wrote a check of five hundred taels as the latter's fee. Hu took the promissory note, together with a letter of request which he himself had written, to Kang P'i, the presiding judge. After accepting the note, Kang gave out a receipt.

"The next day the trial took place as scheduled. Magistrate Wang Tzu-chin, who knew nothing about this deal, was to sit as an assessor. Once the judges were seated, the guards brought in the two defendants: Old Wei and his daughter Widow Chia. The defendants, kneeling on the floor, looked half alive and half dead. Kang took from his pocket three evidences of attempted bribery: two checks of one thousand, a promissory note of sixty-five hundred, and Hu's letter of request, and showed them to magistrate Wang. Wang knew that the defendants were in serious trouble, but did not say a thing.

" 'Do you know how to read?' Kang asked Old Wei. Old Wei replied that he did.

" 'Do you know how to read, Mrs. Chia?'

" 'I had a few years of schooling when I was a child,' Widow Chia replied, 'but I do not recognize too many characters.'

"Kang then ordered the guards to show the defendants the checks and the promissory note. He asked the defendants whether they understood the meaning of these documents.

" 'We do not,' the defendants replied.

" 'All right, you do not understand,' retorted the judge. 'Look carefully at the handwriting and also the name of the person who wrote this promissory note.'

" 'The promissory note was written by your servant's manager,' said Old Wei. 'But I have no idea why he wrote it.'

" 'You have no idea, eh?' the judge laughed loudly. 'I will tell you why he wrote it.' Then he related to the defendants how their manager had attempted to bribe him during the previous day. 'I want you to understand that I do not have any grudge against you; all I am interested in is serving justice. I am an official of the court, specially sent by His Excellency the Governor to help magistrate Wang to try this case. If you were not guilty, why was your manager willing to spend several thousand taels of silver for the purpose of bribing me? This is evidence number one. Since he has spent sixty-five hundred taels to bribe me, I am not surprised that he has spent even more to bribe others. But for the time being, I shall not go into that. If you had nothing to hide, your manager would have responded differently when I demanded bribes. He would say, for instance, that you, the defendants, were really innocent; that you were glad to spend seven or eight thousand taels if your names were cleared; and that it was improper to pay sixty-five hundred taels while the trial was still pending. Instead he promptly agreed to my demand of paying five hundred taels for each of your victims. If you were innocent, why did he agree to this kind of demand which could not be interpreted in any other way except as an admission of guilt? This is evidence number two. If I were you, I would confess my guilt right at this moment so that you do not have to suffer from any pain resulting from the use of torture, a process that would become necessary if you refuse to cooperate.'

"Both father and daughter kowtowed, repeating successively that they were innocent. Suddenly Kang P'i pounded the table. 'I can see that you do not appreciate my persuasion,' said he in a loud voice. 'Guards, bring me the instruments of torture.'

"The guards answered with a loud 'Cha,' and threw the squeezers, which landed with a thunderous noise, to the floor.

"The judge asked the guards to step forward before they were about to apply the instruments to the defendants. 'I am familiar with you people's techniques,' said he. 'If a crime is not serious, after you have taken money from the defendant, you will not squeeze very hard. If on the other hand you know that he is guilty and that there is no way that he can prove himself innocent, after you have accepted his or his relatives' bribes, you will make one harsh squeeze so as to kill him on the spot. In this way you will do him or his relatives a favor by preserving his body in total; the judge, meanwhile, will receive the blame and perhaps be punished for causing death during a trial. Do not try to fool me; I know all of your tricks. Today I want you to apply your instruments to Mrs. Chia first. Do not kill her! Once you see that she is about to die, loosen the squeezer and let her revive. Then squeeze her again. This we shall continue for ten days. No matter how stubborn she is, I have the feeling that she will confess.'

"The torture of Widow Chia did not last for ten days because on the second day with tears in her eyes, she was ready to confess. She was unable to endure the pain any longer; and moreover she did not want her old father to be tortured in the same manner as she was.

" 'I am alone responsible for this mass murder,' she testified; 'my father did not and does not know anything about my crime.'

" 'Why did you murder the whole family?' the judge asked.

" 'I merely intended to kill my sister-in-law Early Spring with whom I had not gotten along very well.'

" 'If what you say is true, why did you not just kill her instead of the whole family?'

" 'My intention was to kill her and her alone. I put the poison in the cake stuffing because I knew that she, more than anybody else, loved the moon cakes and would eat them first. After she ate them, I thought, she would die, and others, seeing her death, would not eat them and consequently would not die. However, the plan was miscarried, and its miscarriage caused the deaths of so many people.'

" 'What kind of poison was it that you put in the cake stuffing?'

" 'Arsenic.'

" 'Where did you get it?'

" 'It was purchased in a drugstore.'

" 'What drugstore was it?'

" 'I do not know. I did not buy it myself.'

" 'Who bought it for you?'

" 'I sent the hired hand Wang Erh to buy it. Wang Erh was one of those thirteen who was killed by mistake.'

' 'How is it possible that Wang Erh, who bought the poison, also ate the moon cakes that resulted in his own death?'

" 'He did not know that I intended to use the arsenic to poison people. I told him that I needed it to kill mice in the house.'

" 'You said that your father had no knowledge of your planned murder. How is it possible that you did not discuss with him a matter of such importance?'

" 'I bought the arsenic when I was at my own house and planned to place it in the food of my sister-in-law. But before I had the opportunity to carry out my plan, my father invited me home for a visit. The servants were preparing cake stuffing, and I asked them what it was for. They told me that it was to be used in the moon cakes to be sent to my own house as a gift. I took the opportunity and placed the arsenic in it.'

" 'That is all. I congratulate you for being so frank. I have heard that your father-in-law did not treat you well.'

" 'That is not true. My father-in-law treated me as well as any man treats his own daughter. He could not treat me better.'

" 'He is already dead. Why do you wish to protect him?'

"Upon hearing this Widow Chia raised her head and became suddenly angry. 'All that Your Excellency wants from me is my confession, and I have cooperated to the fullest extent and to your heart's true desire. I know that by making this confession I will be punished by slicing. It seems to me that you should be satisfied with that, but you are not. You want me to confess a premeditated murder against my own father-in-law. This is too much. Do you not have any children of your own? I hope that you will think carefully about this matter before you ask me any more questions.'

"Kang P'i smiled. 'As a government official and the presiding judge, I consider it my duty to know as much as I can about this case. Since you have confessed your guilt, I would like you to sign your own confession.' "

After Huang Jen-shui had described in detail the murder case, he mentioned the fact that Widow Chia's confession occurred only two days before and that Kang P'i was very unhappy about the eventuality that Old Wei, because of his daughter's confession, might get out from the trial unscathed. "I had lunch with magistrate Wang yesterday," he added; "he was as angry as he could possibly be. But he did not dare to utter one word. If he did, Kang P'i would make him sound as if he had taken bribe from the Wei family. I do not know what we can do about this case. If there is one man who might be able to do something about this, that man would have to be Pai Tzu-shu. Pai is as incorruptible as, if not more than, this devil-reincarnated Kang. Moreover, he is intelligent, scholarly, and upright, and commands great respect among his colleagues. Even devil Kang does not dare to slight him. The defendants will have a better chance if Pai is sent from the capital to conduct a retrial. In a day or two the case will be reported to the governor. If that happens, all hopes of proving the defendants' innocence will be gone. You know how happy I was when I met you unexpectedly yesterday. I thought that you might be able to do something about this."

"I do not have any plan at the moment," said Lao-ts'an. "Since this is an emergency, I shall write a letter to the governor immediately, reporting the details of this case.[52] I shall request him to send His Excellency Pai Tzu-shu here to conduct a retrial. If this does not work, there is nothing more I can do. Each year there are many innocent people sentenced to death. Since we happen to know this case, we shall do the very best we can."

"Hear, hear!" Huang Jen-shui applauded. "We have the stationeries ready. Please write this letter at this very moment." He then ordered a servant to bring in candles and tea. . . .

---

[52] Lao-ts'an, though a commoner, was a personal friend of the governor.

About 2 P.M. in the following day the governor's reply arrived. There were two letters, in fact. The one in the governor's own handwriting was very brief. The other, written by the governor's secretary, said that a man had been sent to replace Pai Tzu-shu for the time being, that Pai would arrive at the city of Ch'iho in six or seven days, and that the governor would like Lao-ts'an to stay in Ch'iho for a few days so that when Pai arrived they could discuss this case together. . . .

After receiving the governor's letter, Lao-ts'an decided to go to the court house to take a look himself. Entering the front gate, he saw many people going in and out, indicating that a trial was being conducted at the moment. He went straight to the courtroom, a huge hall lined by guards on both sides. Standing behind the guards, he could not see the procedure very well.

"I want you to understand, Mrs. Chia, that there is no way that you can escape the death sentence," he heard the judge shouting aloud. "Your assertion that your father knew nothing about this crime is obviously motivated by your desire to save his life. You want to be a good daughter, and you shall have my sympathy and cooperation on this score. However, I will not guarantee your father's life if you refuse to name your paramour. This paramour of yours has made you suffer so much and is in fact the primary cause of this sad state of affairs you are in. I do not understand why you still wish to protect him. You are in jail on account of him, and yet he does not even care to pay you a visit. What love does he really have for you? Our sage once said: 'A woman can have any man in the world as her husband, but she has only one father.' When a woman is faced with the choice between her husband's life and her father's, she is obligated by law and custom to choose the latter. This paramour of yours is not even your husband; why do you wish to protect his life at your father's expense? I want you to tell me who he is. Do you hear me?"

Lao-ts'an heard a woman's weeping from the floor.

"You still refuse to confess," the judge shouted. "Now you are forcing me to torture you again."

The woman muttered a few words, but her voice was so feeble that the words were inaudible.

"What did she say?" the judge asked the clerk of the court.

"Mrs. Chia said that since her life is her own, she is willing to sacrifice it so as to cooperate fully with Your Excellency," the clerk replied. "She will confess whatever you want her to confess as long as it involves only her own life. She is not willing, however, to invent a paramour and thus cause the death of an innocent person."

The judge pounded the table in anger. "You adulteress, you think that you can outsmart me! Guards, bring in the instruments!"

The guards responded with a simultaneous "Cha," and some of them quickly went out and then came back with the squeezers. They threw the instruments to the floor with such violence that all men present were visibly shaken.

Inasmuch as he tried to control his anger, Lao-ts'an could not do it any longer. In violation of the sanctity of the court, he pushed the guards aside and said loudly: "Let me pass!" The guards yielded, and Lao-ts'an went to the center of the court. One guard had already pulled up Widow Chia's head by her hair, and two others were applying the squeezers to her hands. He pushed them aside, yelling, "Stop!" The guards, completely taken by surprise, stopped. Then in a leisurely manner he walked towards the elevated platform where the judges were seated. He recognized the judge who sat on the lower side as magistrate Wang; the one who sat in the center was obviously Kang P'i, the presiding judge. Seeing the presiding judge, he bowed in respect.

Magistrate Wang stood up immediately as soon as he recognized that the intruder was Lao-ts'an. Kang P'i, not knowing who the intruder was, remained seated. "Who are you who dare to violate the sanctity of this court?" Kang shouted. "Guards, grab him!"

The guards responded with a loud "Cha," but chose not to move one inch. They had seen magistrate Wang stand up when faced with this stranger, and they rightly concluded that this man must be of some importance, even though he was dressed in ordinary civilian clothes.

Seeing Kang P'i's angry face and his self-centered importance, Lao-ts'an decided to play with him for a while. "Never mind my name which is not important," he said to the presiding judge in a soft voice. "I would like to have a few words with you first. If you do not agree with me, you can torture me in the same manner you have tortured this woman. I am not speaking with you about the merit of this case which is none of my business. I only wish to ask one question: is it proper and correct to handcuff the hands and enchain the feet of these two defendants, one a dying old man and the other a helpless woman? Are you afraid that they might break the jail? The handcuffs and the chains are only proper for bandits, and now you are using them against ordinary civilians. Where, tell me, is your conscience?"

Magistrate Wang did not know that the governor's reply had arrived; he, consequently, did not wish to see a showdown occur at this moment. "Honorable Pu," [53] said he to Lao-ts'an, "it is inconvenient to discuss this matter here. Let us all go to the inner chamber." Hearing the magistrate call Lao-ts'an "Honorable," Kang P'i knew that the stranger must be more than ordinary; angry though he was, he chose not to say a word. Not wishing to embarrass the magistrate, Lao-ts'an decided not to play the game any longer. He walked towards the magistrate and saluted, and the magistrate saluted in return. "Let us all go to the inner chamber," the magistrate repeated. "Just a moment," Lao-ts'an replied. Then he took from his sleeve the letter in the governor's own handwriting and handed it over to Wang Tzu-chin. The first thing that caught the magistrate's eyes was the governor's huge seal; Wang was happy beyond belief. Opening the letter, he read it loudly so that everyone present could hear it:

"Your letter received. Pai Tzu-shu will arrive shortly. Please transmit the order to the two judges: Kang and Wang. Under no circumstances are they allowed to use torture to exact confessions. The two Wei defendants are to be released on bonds, pending a retrial to be conducted by Pai Tzu-shu. Your friend, etc."

Having read the letter, the magistrate handed it over to Kang P'i for examination. "By the order of His Excellency the Governor," he shouted to the whole court, "the two defendants are to be immediately released on bonds, pending a new trial to be conducted by His Excellency Pai Tzu-shu." Meanwhile the guards were busy taking off the defendants' handcuffs, foot chains, and neck rings. This being done, the captain of the guards ordered the two hapless creatures to step forward and kowtow to the judges. "Our thanks to His Excellency the Governor,

---

[53] Pu was Lao-ts'an's courtesy name.

His Excellency Kang, and His Excellency Wang," the captain shouted aloud on behalf of the defendants, a ritual which he was required to perform under the rule of the court. When the presiding judge heard the words "Our thanks to His Excellency Kang," they sounded like a sword that pierced right through his heart. He became restless; he quietly left the courtroom without a word. . . .

On the day of the new trial, the clerks had everything ready as early as ten o'clock in the morning, even though the trial was not supposed to take place until the afternoon. "Since both the plaintiffs and the defendants are here," announced Pai Tzu-shu, the presiding judge, "why do we not start the hearings now? I would like to have three seats placed on the judge's platform."

Upon hearing this both Kang and Wang stepped forward and saluted. "Your humble servants wish to be absent during the trial," they pleaded. "Our presence may be an inconvenience to the proceedings."

"Not at all," Pai replied. "I may overlook things, and I need you gentlemen's help." Shortly afterwards, the chief clerk came in and announced that everything was ready. Pai and his two assessors changed into official robes and went promptly to the courtroom.

Once seated, Pai Tzu-shu picked up his vermillion brush and checked the name of Chia Kan, one of the two plaintiffs. As soon as he was brought in, Chia Kan quickly knelt on the floor.

"Is your name Chia Kan?" Pai asked.

"Yes."

"How old are you?"

"Seventeen."

"Are you the natural or adopted son of the deceased Chia Chih?"

"I am actually his nephew; I was adopted as his son."

"When were you adopted as his son?"

"I was adopted shortly after my father—I mean my foster father—had been murdered. He was scheduled to be put into the coffin the very next day, and he did not have a male heir to serve as the chief mourner. The clan elders decided to designate me as his son and chief mourner so that the mourning ritual could take place in a proper manner."

"Were you there when the magistrate came to examine your father's body?"

"Yes, I was."

"Were you there when the body was put into the coffin?"

"Yes, I was."

"What did his face look like? I mean: what was its color?"

"White and pale; just like any other dead person."

"Did it have blue or purple marks?"

"I did not see any."

"Were his joints rigid?"

"No."

"Did you feel his chest to see whether it was still warm?"

"I did not. But some one who did feel it said that it was not warm."

"When was it discovered that the moon cakes contained arsenic?"

"The second day after my father had been put into the coffin."

"Who discovered it?"

"My sister." [54]

[54] Early Spring.

"How did your sister know that the moon cakes contained arsenic?"

"She did not know at first, but somehow she became suspicious. She took a close look at the stuffing and found pink dots in it. She asked people what these dots were, and they said that they were arsenic. She invited a druggist to examine them, and the druggist said the same thing. It was then that she concluded that the deceased had been poisoned."

"That is all. You can go," said the presiding judge.

Using his vermillion brush, Pai checked the next testifier. It was the Ssu-mei Bakery. The guards brought a man before the judges.

"What is your name? How are you related to the Ssu-mei Bakery?"

"My name is Wang Fu-t'ing. I am the manager of the Ssu-mei Bakery."

"How many moon cakes did the Wei family order from your shop?"

"It ordered twenty catties." [55]

"Was the cake stuffing provided by the Wei family?"

"Yes, it was."

"How many moon cakes did you make for an order of twenty catties?"

"Eighty-three."

"Was the stuffing the same for all these cakes?"

"Yes, it was."

"What kind of stuffing was it?"

"It was a mixture of rock sugar, sesame seeds, and almonds."

"How many kinds of cake stuffing does your bakery sell?"

"Several kinds."

"Among the several kinds you have in your bakery, is there one similar to the mixture which you have decribed?"

"Yes, there is."

"How does yours compare with the one provided by the Wei family?"

"Theirs is better."

"In what way is theirs better?"

"I do not know exactly. But I have heard our chef say that they used better materials and that their cake stuffing was sweeter and more fragrant than ours."

"Are you telling me that your chef tasted the stuffing provided by the Wei family while he was using it to make the moon cakes?"

"Yes, I was."

"Did the chef feel that the stuffing had poison it it?"

"No, not at all."

"That is all. You are dismissed."

Pai Tzu-shu then ordered Old Chia to be brought in. Once in, the defendant knelt down and ceaselessly knocked his head against the floor. "I am innocent; I am innocent," he kept on repeating.

"I am not asking you whether you are innocent," said the presiding judge. "You should confine your answers to my questions. You are not allowed to say anything unrelated to my inquiry." Upon hearing this, the guards on both sides responded with a thunderous "Cha."

Dear reader, you may wish to know why the guards repeatedly yelled "Cha" during the court procedings. This loud "Cha" is popularly referred to as "voice of awe;" its purpose is to intimidate a defendant so that he will confess whatever the

[55] A little over twenty-seven pounds.

judge wants him to confess. We do not know during which dynasty this custom was originated, but it has been followed in all of the eighteen provinces.[56]

Now let us go back to the hearings.

"How many moon cakes did you order from the bakery shop?" Pai asked the defendant.

"Twenty catties."

"How many catties did you send to the Chia family?"

"Eight catties."

"Did you send the moon cakes to anybody else?"

"Yes. I sent four catties to the father-in-law of my son."

"What happened to the remaining eight catties?"

"We ate them ourselves."

"Are there any persons in this courthouse who have eaten them?"

"All members of our family have eaten them, including those who are here in this courthouse."

Pai Tzu-shu turned to the guards and ordered them to bring in all members of the Wei household who were presently in the courthouse. Shortly afterwards three men appeared, one quite old and the other two middle-aged. The three men knelt down before the judges.

"The older man is the manager of the Wei household," the guards reported; "the other two are its hired hands."

"Did you all eat the moon cakes?"

"Yes, we did."

"How many did each of you eat?"

"I received four as my share," said the manager. "I have eaten two; there are still two left."

"Each of us received two," said the two hired hands. "We have eaten them already."

"Do I understand correctly that you still have two moon cakes left?" the presiding judge asked the manager.

"Yes," the manager replied. "When I heard that the cakes contained poison, I did not dare to eat them again."

"Have you brought these two cakes with you?"

"Yes, I have."

"That is fine," said the presiding judge. "Guards, escort this man outside and bring in the two cakes of which he has just spoken." Turning to the chief clerk, he asked where the half piece of poisoned cake was. The clerk replied that it was in the court's storage. Pai ordered him to bring it to the courtroom.

Moments later, the two uneaten cakes, together with the half piece of poisoned cake, were brought to the judge's platform. The presiding judge gave the order that Wang Fu-t'ing, the manager of the Ssu-mei Bakery, be again called in to testify.

Meanwhile the presiding judge was showing the cakes to his assessors. "I feel that the crust of the three cakes look exactly the same," he remarked. "Do you gentlemen agree?" Kang and Wang bowed slightly and answered "yes." By then Wang Fu-t'ing was already brought in; he testified that these cakes were indeed his shop's products. After signing his testimony, he was then dismissed.

[56] This story was set against a nineteenth century-background.

Once more the presiding judge examined the half piece of poisoned cake. "Look carefully, Mr. Kang," he said. "The stuffing of this cake is a mixture of rock sugar, sesame seeds, and almonds, all of which are oily materials. If the arsenic were mixed with them at the time the stuffing was made, it would have been mingled with them completely. But this is not the case as far as this cake is concerned. It is obvious that the arsenic was added to the stuffing after the cake had already been made. Moreover, since all of the cakes are of the same manufacture, it does not seem right that some who ate them would die of poison while others would not. In my humble opinion, the arsenic was added to the stuffing of this particular cake after the victims had already died. It is obvious to me that the deaths of the thirteen persons had nothing to do with the moon cakes. What do you two gentlemen think?" Wang quickly expressed his agreement. Kang did likewise, though he was very much depressed and embarrassed. "Since it has been clearly established that the moon cakes which the victims ate did not contain poison," Pai continued, "the defendants who were accused of having used the moon cakes to poison the victims are in fact innocent. They should be cleared of all charges, and the case is closed as far as they are concerned."

The presiding judge then gave the order that Old Wei be again brought in. "I have reached the conclusion that the moon cakes which you sent to the Chia family did not contain any poison," said the judge. "You and your daughter are therefore innocent. You can proceed home." Old Wei kowtowed and then left.

Now it was Chia Kan who had to face the judge. Being a boy of low intelligence, he had neither the capacity nor the intention of implicating any person in a crime. It was his sister Early Spring who had prompted him to become an involuntary plaintiff. Seeing that the defendants had been released, he was extremely worried and regretted deeply the role he himself had played. So far, the people behind him had coached him well; now, with this sudden, unexpected turn of events, they did not know what words they should put into his mouth. For the first time during the trial he was on his own.

"Chia Kan," he heard the judge call him, "as the adopted son of the deceased, you should have carefully examined the case before you made this groundless charge. If you were not able to do so because of your youthfulness, you should have consulted others before you took this drastic step. Did you add arsenic to the cake stuffing so as to implicate the defendants? If not, who asked you to start this lawsuit? Do you realize how severe the punishment is for those who have made false accusations?"

Chia Kan kowtowed ceaselessly like a woodpecker. He was so frightened that his body was shaking. "I knew nothing about this case," he cried. "I only did what my sister told me. It was she who claimed that she had discovered arsenic in the cake stuffing. Honestly, I know nothing except what I am now telling you."

"I am extremely reluctant to call a woman to the court to face a judge," said Pai Tzu-shu. "Now that you have implicated your sister, I guess I do not have much choice. . . ."[57]

[57] The real murderer turned out to be Wu Erh, the unsuccessful suitor of Early Spring. The story is too long to be translated in its entirety.

CHAPTER ELEVEN

Foreign Relations

PRIOR to the modern period the history of China's external relations was largely a history of peace and war with her nomadic neighbors. For more than three thousand years all Chinese governments were occupied with one important concern: how to defend the comparatively abundant agricultural south against the less productive and more warlike nomadic north. The Great Wall, completed in the third century B.C., is the most eloquent testimony of such an effort.

The study of China's relations with the Hsiung-nu, a Turkish-speaking group who dominated the northern grassland for almost a millennium after the fourth century B.C., will throw much light on the basic difficulties between China and her nomadic neighbors. Dynasties rose and fell in the south and nomadic kingdoms came and went in the north, but the basic social structure of both sides and their respective economic needs remained the same. The conflict between the Han dynasty and the Hsiung-nu was essentially the same conflict that existed between China and other nomadic tribes during the later periods. It was a conflict involving the basic differences between an agricultural and a pastoral society.

One of the earlist records describing the Hsiung-nu appears in *Han shu* by Pan Ku (Selection 89). Though primarily known as a historian, Pan Ku served ably in an expeditionary force against the Hsiung-nu headed by General Tou Hsien in A.D. 89. By then the enemy had plagued the Han dynasty for almost three hundred years. During this period the Han statesmen continually advocated the adoption of a more effective policy, and their memorials to the emperor reveal some of the basic difficulties which the Chinese government had to face in dealing with a nomadic tribe (Selection 90). Such difficulties prompted people like Ch'ao Ts'o, a statesman of the second century B.C., to propose strengthening the frontier through the establishment of military settlements in the border areas (Selection 91), while others like Chu-fu Yen, also of the second century B.C., were openly dubious about the feasibility of an agricultural society like China bringing a nomadic horde under her control (Selection 92). Facing this unpleasant reality, most Chinese emperors such as Han Wen-ti were happy to buy off the enemy whenever they were allowed to do so (Selections 93 and 94).

Though there were times when a Chinese emperor (such as Han Wu-ti of the second century B.C. and T'ang T'ai-tsung of the seventh century A.D.) felt strong enough to send troops to the northern grasslands and seek out the enemy so as to destroy him, the balance of power in the long run seems to have been in favor of the nomads. From the fourth to the thirteenth centuries they established a number of Sinicized or semi-Sinicized kingdoms in North China, and during the next seven hundred years they twice conquered all of China, once in the thirteenth and again in the seventeenth century.

A major exception to this nomadic-agricultural relationship was China's relationship with Japan. This exception becomes "major" only from hindsight and largely because of Japan's importance in the modern world; traditional China and traditional Chinese historians gave only scant attention to the Japanese. For instance, the spread of Chinese culture to Japan during the T'ang dynasty was unquestionably a most important event from the Japanese point of view; yet both dynastic histories dealing with this period (*T'ang shu* and *Hsin T'ang shu*) allocate only a few terse, dull, and uninspiring passages to it. One of the reasons for this negligence was that Japan, located far out in the sea, was not so politically important to China as, say, Korea or Annam.

Two of the most important Chinese documents describing early Japan appear in the *History of the Three Kingdoms* (*San-kuo chih*) by Ch'en Shou (third century) and the *History of the Sui* (*Sui shu*) by Wei Cheng (seventh century). They are translated here and appear as Selections 95 and 96 respectively. China's relationship with Japan was mainly a peaceful one; throughout the long history there were only four major military encounters. The first two (in the seventh and again in the sixteenth century) had to do with the contention over Korea; the third was Japan's piratical raids against China's southeast coast during the Ming dynasty; and the last and perhaps the most dramatic was the attempted conquest of Japan by the Mongols in the thirteenth century. This latter event, as recorded in the *History of the Yüan* (*Yüan shih,* by Sung Lien of the fourteenth century), throws much light on the Chinese concept of foreign relations as well as the operation of the tributary system (Selection 97).

On Japan's part there was no serious attempt to conquer all of China until the modern period. The Japanese expansionist moves began in the 1870's and did not come to an end until the conclusion of World War II.

89 · Pan Ku: *The Hsiung-nu* [1]

The Hsiung-nu live in the north and are a nomadic people. They raise a variety of animals, most of which are horses, cattle, and sheep. Other animals such as camels and donkeys are comparatively small in number. They move constantly to seek water and grass; they have no cities, houses, or crop fields. Land, however, is divided among different tribal groups.

The Hsiung-nu do not have any written language; consequently all agreements or promises are made in oral form. Small children are taught to ride sheep and

---

[1] "The Hsiung-nu" (*Hsiung-nu chuan*); *Han shu,* roll 94a.

shoot birds and squirrels. When they grow older, they begin to shoot foxes and rabbits. Meat, instead of grain, is their staple food. All able-bodied men are expert archers and are members of the cavalry in their respective tribes.

Under normal circumstances when life is comparatively easy, the Hsiung-nu earn their livelihood by tending their herds and augment it by hunting. When life becomes difficult, all men are taught the art of warfare, preparing ardently for the launching of attacks. This, you might say, is the nature of the Hsiung-nu. They rely on bows and arrows if the enemy is at a distance and switch to knives and spears in close combat. They attack when they are certain of victory, but are not ashamed to run away from the battlefield if they think that the odds are heavily against them. They go wherever there are profits to be realized; they do not know of such things as righteousness and propriety.

From the king down, all the Hsiung-nu people eat animals' meat, wear their skins, and convert their furs into garments. The young and the strong have priority to the best food; the elderly have to be satisfied with the leftovers. They highly value youth and strength, and look down upon the old and the weak. After the death of his father, a man will marry his step-mother. Likewise he takes his brother's wife as his own when and if his brother dies. . . .

In the first month of each year the khan holds court with all people in his tribe. In the fifth month he gathers all tribal members at Lung [2] where he offers sacrifices to Heaven, Earth, gods, and spirits. Again in the fall when horses are strong and alert, he calls into session another assembly in a forest region, offering sacrifices to gods and spirits and counting the numbers of men and animals.

According to the Hsiung-nu law, he who kills another man will be punished by death. A robber will be condemned to slavery together with all members of his family. Small offenders will be lashed with a stick; serious offenders, on the other hand, will be thrown into jail where they usually die within a period of ten days. Thus throughout the Hsiung-nu empire there are fewer than ten people in jail at any time.

The khan worships the rising sun early in the morning and the moon in the evening. In seating arrangement the person who sits on the left and faces the north is the most honored among the group. The dead are buried in coffins, accompanied with gold, silver, and clothing. But the graves are not marked with trees,[3] nor do the mourners wear mourning clothes. Upon the death of a khan approximately one hundred of his favorite ministers and concubines will be put to death so that their spirits will be able to follow his.

During a military campaign the Hsiung-nu watch closely the size of the moon. They attack when the moon is large and bright and withdraw when it becomes small and dim. A Hsiung-nu soldier who kills an enemy will be awarded one goblet of wine plus whatever material goods he has taken from his victim. If he captures a man or woman alive, the latter becomes his slave. Thus on the battlefield all Hsiung-nu soldiers fight valiantly for their own material ends, upon which they converge like hungry vultures. Upon a setback, however, they disintegrate quickly and disperse like flying clouds. Their favorite strategy is to entice

[2] Located in modern Outer Mongolia.
[3] According to an ancient Chinese custom, a tree was planted near the grave as soon as the dead man was buried.

their enemy to a pre-arranged place and then encircle him. After a battle, the warrior who brings home the body of a dead comrade will inherit all of the latter's worldly possessions.

90 · CH'AO TS'O: *On the Military Strength of the Hsiung-nu* [4]

Since the establishment of the Han dynasty, the northern barbarians have time and again invaded our border areas. Each time they succeed in what they set out to achieve. During the time of Empress Kao,[5] they attacked Lunghsi,[6] captured many cities, and looted, carrying away with them animals and other properties. Subsequently they launched an even larger invasion in the same area: they killed soldiers and officials and practiced banditry on a large scale.

I have heard that popular morale rises with each succeeding victory and that an army, once defeated, can never win a victory again. Lunghsi was thrice raided by the Hsiung-nu; the morale of its people was so low that they were despondent of any victory. Yet, blessed by our national gods and wisely guided by Your Majesty's instructions, recently the officials in Lunghsi have been able to rally the soldiers and instill in them a fighting spirit. Leading a group of people who had been hopelessly demoralized shortly before, against great odds they defeated the hitherto victorious enemy. They killed one Hsiung-nu chieftain, dispersed the rest, and won a great victory.

The people in Lunghsi are the same people. It is the leadership of the officials and the military commanders that makes them either cowardly or extremely brave. "There is no such thing as an invincible people," says an ancient book on military strategy, "but there is such a thing as an invincible general." Therefore, to secure the frontier and accomplish great deeds, the government has to consider the selection of good generals one of its first priorities. . . .

The difference between large and small countries is not only a difference in military strength but also a difference in policies and in the strategy of defense. The normal course for a small country to follow is to admit its inferiority and be subservient to a country of great strength. If it wishes to attack a larger and stronger country, it will have to make alliances with other small countries. However, as far as China is concerned, her basic policy is to use barbarians to fight barbarians.

Not only is the Hsiung-nu terrain different from that of China; there is also a vast difference in the military skills of these two groups of people. The Hsiung-nu horses are superior to those of China if the terrain is rugged, bisected by steep mountains and deep streams. Their riders can easily outdo their Chinese counterparts when maneuvering on dangerous roads and narrow passes, and compared with the Chinese, can shoot better while galloping at full speed. Moreover, the Hsiung-nu soldiers can stand the elements better, become tired less easily, and can

[4] "Biographies of Yüan Ang and Ch'ao Ts'o" (*Yüan Ang Ch'ao Ts'o chuan*); *Han shu,* roll 49.
[5] Empress Kao, also known as Empress Lü, was the wife of Liu Pang, founder of the Han dynasty. She ruled China from 187 to 180 B.C.
[6] The western section of modern Shensi province.

fight for a much longer time without water or food. These are the Hsiung-nu's advantages.

In combatting the Hsiung-nu, China has her advantages too. If the terrain is level and easy to traverse, the Chinese light-chariots and cavalry elite can easily rout a Hsiung-nu force even though it is larger in number. The Chinese bow is stronger, can cover a longer distance, and is far superior to that used by the enemy. In group combat, the Chinese can take full advantage of their strong armour, sharp knife, effective bow and arrows, and strict discipline among the rank and file; as a group, the Hsiung-nu soldiers are inferior. Once they reach their targets, the Chinese arrows, coming from a strong bow, can easily penetrate the leather armour or wooden plate [7] of a Hsiung-nu soldier. Fighting on foot in close combat, a Chinese soldier uses his sword and spear much more skillfully than his Hsiung-nu opponent and can move with a dexterity which his enemy cannot match.

In short, the Chinese have five advantages as compared to the Hsiung-nu who have only three.

Now that Your Majesty has mobilized hundreds of thousands of fighting men against an enemy who can muster only tens of thousands, it seems that, with a ratio of ten to one, the victory is almost assured. Yet war is by definition a dangerous undertaking; in as short as a moment's time the strong can become the weak and the great can become the small. When a nation has staked so much on victory, the effect of demoralization will be all the greater and the regret more profound if it is defeated. When victory or defeat is involved, there is no such thing as over-cautiousness.

The barbarians who have surrendered to us number several thousands. Their habits and their skills are the same as those of the Hsiung-nu. It is hereby suggested that they should be given strong armour, tough clothing, powerful bows and sharp arrows, to be mounted on the best horses available in the border provinces. To be commanded by Your Majesty's generals, they should be used on rugged terrain and dangerous passes. Meanwhile, in battles to be fought on level plain and open space, the Chinese cavalrymen and light chariots can be used to good effect. Our strategy will reach a flawless stage if, in addition to our numerical superiority, we command the advantages of both China   and her nomadic opponents.

91 · CH'AO TS'O: *The Defense of Our Northern Frontier* [8]

Despite the fact that their territories are barren and unproductive, the northern barbarians have no difficulty in mustering enough strength to invade our border areas repeatedly. Why?

The northern barbarians eat meat, drink milk, and wear animal furs and skins. They have no fields, houses, or cities. Like birds and beasts, they move from place to place and stop only when they find water and good grass. When water or grass is exhausted, they move again until they find the same in some other place. There is no way of telling from where they have come or to which place they will go; nor do we know when they will come or go. This constant migration is the way they

---

[7] Strapped on the chest, a wooden plate was used to protect a soldier's vital organs against piercing arrows.

[8] *Han shu*, roll 49.

make their livelihood, to the same extent as we derive our livelihood from tilling the fields.

During their constant migration they often venture as far as our border provinces. Sometimes they set foot on Yen and Tai,[9] and other times they penetrate as deep as Shangchün.[10] Consequently garrisons have to be maintained throughout the northern frontier and also in the Lunghsi area.

The defense of the frontier by garrison soldiers poses a number of problems. If their number is small, the imperial government will have two choices when encountering a barbarian invasion. It can abstain from sending reinforcements, and in such case the people in the border areas, losing all hope of defending their territories, may decide to surrender themselves to the enemy. Suppose, say, that the imperial government makes the other choice and decides to send reinforcements. If the reinforcements are small, they may not be able to cope with the situation. If they are large, they will have to be dispatched from places far from the border areas; by the time they reach the frontier, the invaders may have already fled. Moreover, once a large force has been gathered on the frontier, the government will have a difficult time to decide what to do with it. If it is not sent back to the districts from where it came, the cost of maintaining it will be exhorbitant. If it is, the barbarians will certainly invade again. While this kind of situation continues, not only will China become poorer and poorer, her people will also become less and less secure.

Having in mind the security of our northern frontier, Your Majesty has sent troops to defend the people in the border areas. The problem is, the soldiers who are sent there from faraway places have a tour of duty of only one year, which is too short a period for them to appreciate the capacity of their opponents. It is the humble opinion of your servant that instead of rotating the soldiers, permanent settlements, with houses and fields, should be maintained on the frontier for the purpose of defense. On each strategic point or thoroughfare a settlement of no less than one thousand households should be established, to be surrounded by high walls and deep moats which in turn are protected by bamboo stockades further beyond. About 150 paces inside the outer wall an inner wall should also be built within each settlement. The construction of houses should be completed and all farm equipment provided before the residents move in.

As for the prospective residents, they should be first recruited from convicted criminals or those who, presently on parole under an act of clemency, have not yet served their full term. If this source is inadequate, additional source may be found among male and female slaves who have committed crimes, or those slaves voluntarily surrendered by their owners in order to win titles of honor from the government. In the former case the slaves in question, once recruited, will be regarded as having redeemed in full whatever crimes they have committed. If ordinary law-abiding citizens wish to volunteer for frontier service, they will be granted titles of high honor and will be exempted from all taxations and corvée duties.

The immigrants are to be provided with food and clothing until they are self-supporting. Part of the money used for this temporary support may come from the selling of titles of honor to those who wish to buy them; the titles can go as high

[9] Yen was located in modern Hopeh province, and Tai in modern Shansi province.
[10] Located in the northern section of modern Shensi province, around the Yenan area.

as that of deputy ministers in order to enhance the income. Since men without families cannot be expected to stay permanently in the frontier, the government should instruct all district magistrates to buy widows who have lost means of support and marry them to bachelor immigrants. Material rewards have to be great if we expect people to be settled permanently in those dangerous areas of the frontier.

Whenever the barbarians attempt a raid and are then stopped, the local magistrates should see to it that those responsible for stopping the raid be rewarded with half of the property that would have been lost to the barbarians had the raid not been stopped. When people are brave enough to help each other at the risk of their own lives, they do not mean to ingratiate themselves with the emperor or the imperial government; rather, they are motivated by their desire to protect themselves and their families and to win material rewards. Facing a barbarian attack, these permanent residents would act differently from the garrison soldiers from the East who do not know the geography of the frontier and are generally fearful of the barbarians. Their substitution for the garrison soldiers will bring a result many times more rewarding. If Your Majesty chooses to accept the proposal outlined above, not only will the people in China no longer have to perform garrison duties in the remote frontier, the people in the frontier will have great incentive to protect each other and thus free themselves from barbarian raids or incursions. The benefits you bestow upon them will pass from generation to generation, and your wisdom will be remembered with gratitude until eternity to come.

92 · CHU-FU YEN: *On the Proposed Expedition Against the Hsiung-nu* [11]

I have heard that an enlightened monarch welcomes outspoken admonitions in order to broaden his perspective, and that an upright minister does not hesitate to remonstrate frankly with his king even though by doing so he may risk capital punishment. If a king and his ministers cooperate fully in this matter, there will be no problems which cannot find solutions, and their accomplishments will be remembered for thousands of years to come. Mindful of my duty to you as a loyal minister and not wishing to escape death by remaining silent, I wish to contribute a few humble ideas of my own. I hope that Your Majesty will forgive me for my impudence and lend your ears to one of your humblest servants.

"A nation which loves war will be eventually and inevitably destroyed, however large and strong it might be," says *Ssu-ma's Military Strategy*.[12] "On the other hand, a nation is in danger indeed if, enjoying peace, it is unprepared for the eventuality of war." Even after the country has been pacified and long after the singing of victory songs has become a matter of the past, an ancient custom dictates that the Son of Heaven hunts in the fall and again in the spring; his vassals, meanwhile, continue to drill their troops and conduct military maneuvers

[11] This memorial was presented to Emperor Han Wu-ti in *c*.134 B.C. Source: *Han shu*, roll 64a.

[12] The authorship of *Ssu-ma's Military Strategy* (*Ssu-ma fa*) was attributed to a man named Ssu-ma Jang-chü who lived in the state of Ch'i in the seventh century B.C.

in the countryside. Why? This is because even in time of peace the nation should not forget the possibility of war.

Anger is the antithesis of virtue; warfare is an inauspicious and often dangerous way of carrying out policies, and feuds and strifes, whenever they occur, are the least indicative of the righteousness of the parties involved. Whenever a monarch is angry, blood runs like rivers and corpses spread far and wide. That is why the sage kings of the past thought twice before they resorted to war as a means of resolving differences. Those monarchs who loved military virtues and were constantly engaged in warfare were without an exception regretful in the end.

Formerly Ch'in Shih-huang used his victorious forces to conquer one territory after another until the six rival kingdoms [13] were annexed and all of China was brought under the jurisdiction of a unified government. His achievement was as great as that of the previous Three Dynasties. Yet he was unsatisfied with this achievement and wished to attack the Hsiung-nu to score even greater victories. Li Ssu,[14] his minister, protested: "The Hsiung-nu have no walled cities where people reside; nor do they have grain storages and warehouses which they must protect. They move about like birds; and, even if they were conquered, it would be extremely difficult to govern them. Nor is it easy to conquer them. If our troops are lightly equipped while marching deep into the enemy's territory, the supply of food will be soon and inevitably exhausted. If on the other hand they have to carry all the food they need, they will lose their speed and maneuverability and will not be able to achieve the purpose for which the campaign is conducted. We reap no economic gains by conquering the Hsiung-nu territory, and we cannot move the Hsiung-nu people and thus protect them when and if we have brought them under our control. In fact, we have to abandon them almost as soon as we have won victories on the battlefield. How can the father of the people [15] exhaust China's manpower and economic resources with no other purpose to be achieved except to satisfy an emotional grudge? In my humble opinion, this is not the best policy to follow."

Ch'in Shih-huang ignored this protest and ordered General Meng T'ien to attack the Hsiung-nu. General Meng conquered a thousand square *li* and pushed the Chinese border to the bank of the Yellow River.[16] The border areas, however, were unproductive in the growing of crops: their land was compact and dry, and their lakes were salty and sterile. Soldiers drafted from all parts of China were sent northward to defend the river areas; and, isolated and exposed for more than ten years, an uncountable number of them perished. Throughout the Ch'in dynasty the government was unable to extend its control north of the Yellow River. Did this failure result from the inadequacy of manpower or the insufficiency of military equipment? The answer was "No." The real reason was that all objective conditions were against China in this particular case.

Moreover, all of the military supplies, from food for the soldiers to feed for the horses, had to be shipped by boats and vehicles from such coastal areas as Huang, Ch'ui, and Langya [17] to the northern river by a tortuous route. The distance

---

[13] The six rival kingdoms were Ch'i, Ch'u, Chao, Han, Wei, and Yen.
[14] See pp. 29–30.
[15] The emperor of China.
[16] This refers to that part of the Yellow River located in the Ordos Desert.
[17] All of the three places were located in modern Shantung province.

was so great that it took 1.92 piculs of grain consumed on the road to deliver 1 picul of grain to the frontier. Taxation was so heavy that farmers could not produce enough to meet the military demand even though they had worked hard in the field; dilegently as a woman spun and wove, she had little cloth left to make her own curtains. The economy continued to deteriorate until the people could no longer support the orphaned, the widowed, the aged, and the weak, many of whom had to perish in the streets. This was the time when the people began to stage a revolt.

After Emperor Kao-tsu [18] had unified China, he led his troops in seizing territories along the frontier. Having heard that the Hsiung-nu forces were gathering beyond the Tai Valley,[19] he proposed to attack them. Ch'eng, an imperial counselor, protested. "This cannot be done," said the imperial counselor. "The Hsiung-nu gather like beasts and disperse like birds. To chase and attack them is like chasing and attacking one's own shadow. Great as the virtue of Your Majesty is, I feel that the proposed attack is as unwise as it is inauspicious." Emperor Kao-tsu ignored this advice and marched his troops to the Tai Valley. The result was the siege of P'ingch'eng.[20] Regretful afterwards, the emperor sent Liu Ching as his envoy to the Hsiung-nu court to establish a peaceful relationship through the bond of marriage. Peace was established shortly afterwards.

An ancient military book says: "The mobilization of ten thousand men entails a cost of one thousand gold pieces per day." The Ch'in regime regularly maintained a garrison force of several hundred thousand along the frontier. While this force did score occasional victories and held the enemy at bay, it also created and then deepened the Hsiung-nu's hatred for China. The victories it was able to score could in no way compensate for the financial losses which China had to suffer.

Robbery and pillage are part of the Hsiung-nu's occupation; nature had made them this way. The ancient dynasties—Yü, Hsia, Yin, and Chou—did not attempt to rectify their character; they tolerated them in the same manner as they had to tolerate wild beasts. The Hsiung-nu were not regarded as human beings and were thus not subject to human standards. I shall be greatly worried if for any reason we fail to follow the traditional policy of the past dynasties or choose to ignore the lessons we have learned in modern times. If we did so, the sufferings of our people would be very great indeed.

Moreover, the longer a war lasts, the more it is subject to unexpected eventualities. The tougher the goings become, the more men are inclined to waver. Meanwhile the people in the border areas will suffer from mental agonies as well as economic distress, and we shall not be surprised should they harbor disloyal thoughts. Generals and officials become suspicious of one another, and many of them will not hesitate to fraternize with the enemy. This happened during the Ch'in dynasty when Wei T'o and Chang Han [21] succeeded in carrying out their own private designs at the expense of the government. The government could no longer implement its policies as its power had been undermined by these two persons. This is the lesson to be remembered.

[18] Liu Pang, founder of the Han dynasty.
[19] Located in modern Shansi province.
[20] See p. 192, Footnote 27.
[21] The real name of Wei T'o was Chao T'o who, sent by Ch'in Shih-huang to defend China's southwest, later declared himself independent. Chang Han was a famous Ch'in general who later surrendered to the rebel leader Hsiang Yü. As for Hsiang Yü, see pp. 261–263.

The *History of the Chou* [22] says: "The prospect of safety or danger depends upon the kind of order to be issued; a nation's survival or destruction lies with the efforts, or the lack of them, of its own people." It is my hope that Your Majesty will think carefully about this matter.

93 · HAN WEN-TI: *A Letter to the Great Khan* [23]

The emperor respectfully inquires about the health of the Great Khan and wishes him well. The gift of two horses has been gratefully received.

Our ancestors built the Great Wall in order to separate the nomadic north from the agricultural south. Following their example, I have endeavored to promote peaceful pursuits in the territories within my jurisdiction so that each man is able to earn a livelihood by whatever means he chooses: tilling, weaving, or hunting. We emphasize peaceful pursuits in the hope that children do not have to be separated from their parents and that all people in the empire, from the emperor to the lowest subjects, can enjoy the fruits of their respective endeavors. We have never committed an act of violence.

Recently there have been people so evil and avaricious that they violated the principle of righteousness as well as the agreement of friendship between our two countries.[24] They were unconcerned with the thousands of lives that might be lost as a result of their activities; they were scornful of the good relations that had existed between us. In view of what has happened in the recent past, I am pleased to read your letter in which you stated that since an agreement of friendship has been concluded between our two countries and since the two sovereigns have sworn in brotherhood, all hostilities between us should hereafter cease, so that people of both sides can enjoy peace and prosperity for generations to come. To a wise man each day is always fresher and brighter than the day before, and it is never too late to start something better anew. With peace secured, not only can the elderly enjoy their old age, the young will also be able to grow to maturity—all of them will be hereby assured a natural span of life. As peace will please Heaven as well as comfort man, let it be passed from one generation to another until eternity to come. Let all men rejoice in it!

Han and Hsiung-nu are two neighboring countries facing each other across a common boundary. Since your country is located in the north where winter is long and cold, we have agreed to present to you a sizable amount of grain, gold, silk, and many other items each year as gifts. Now that peace has prevailed throughout the world, how wonderful it is to see people rejoice in it. You and I are fathers of our respective peoples and are responsible for their welfare. When I think of the unpleasant incidents in the past, I only blame my own ministers for their ill advice; these incidents, I hope, will not harm the brotherly relationship between you and me.

I have heard that Heaven, being impartial, bestows its blessings upon all men without discrimination. It is my earnest hope that the unpleasant incidents of the past be eradicated from our memory and that all of us march on the broad road of

---

[22] The authorship of the *History of the Chou (Chou shu)* is unknown.

[23] This letter, written in 162 B.C., can be found in "The Hsiung-nu" *(Hsiung-nu chuan)*; *Han shu,* roll 94a.

[24] This refers to invasions by the Hsiung-nu of the Chinese border areas.

peace and goodwill. Let us abandon the hostility of the past and face hopefully towards the future. Let the people of both of our countries cherish each other as if they belong to one family. All animals—birds that fly in the sky, fish that swim in the water, and insects that crawl on the ground—love peace and security; note how they run away from a place of danger to an area of security. This is the law of nature, the way of Heaven!

Not wishing to indulge myself in the unpleasant past, I hereby declare that I shall not concern myself with those Chinese who have been either captured or kidnapped by your side. It is my hope that you in turn will not mention people like Ch'ang-ni.[25] Emperors of ancient times never broke a promise, and I shall not rescind my vow of friendship for you either. If you are equally concerned, peace will prevail throughout the world from now on. I am looking forward to your favorable response.

94 · HAN WEN-TI: *A Letter to the Great Khan*[26]

Benighted as I am, I have not been able to exercise a good influence abroad. Foreign countries are not enjoying peace, and our foreign bretherns are insecure in their pursuits. Meanwhile in my own country people work diligently without peace in mind and security in body. Who is to blame for these occurrences both here and abroad? It is I who am not virtuous enough and fail to make my good intentions known abroad.

During the past few years the Hsiung-nu have repeatedly invaded our border areas and killed our people and officials. My officials and soldiers have failed to convey my intention for peace to the invaders, and their failure has increased my sense of guilt. Continuous warfare between our two countries has brought harm to both sides; when shall all of us enjoy peace again? I am fearful and often sleepless at night when I think of the sufferings of thousands of persons occasioned by the war.

I am therefore sending to you my ambassador, trusting that he will convey to you my sincere desire for peace. It is my hope that you will return to the way of old, so that once again peace between our two countries will prevail and citizens of both sides be secure in their lives. Let both you and me forget about the past, and march together on the broad avenue of brotherhood. All the good people in the world will be thus protected.

Let peace begin from this very year!

95 · CH'EN SHOU: *The Japanese*[27]

The Japanese live in mountainous islands located in that part of the ocean southeast of the province of Taifang.[28] They were grouped into more than one hundred countries at one time, and some of these countries sent tribute missions

---

[25] A Hsiung-nu leader who had surrendered to the Han authority.

[26] This letter, written in the sixth lunar month of 162 B.C., can be found in "Biography of Han Wen-ti" (*Wen-ti chi*); *Han shu,* roll 4.

[27] "The Japanese" (*Wo-jen*), *History of the Wei* (*Wei chih*), roll 30; *San-kuo chih.*

[28] Located in the northern section of modern Korea.

to China during the Han dynasty. Now only about thirty countries on the islands maintain relations with China. . . .

Regardless of age, all male Japanese brand their faces and tattoo their bodies. Since ancient times all Japanese envoys have claimed their country's close relationship with China. The founder of their nation, said they, was a son of Shao-k'ang [29] of the Hsia dynasty who received an investiture from his father to govern K'uaichi.[30] They further stated that the ancient Japanese cut their hair short and tattooed their bodies because they believed that by doing so they would not be harmed by flood-dragons [31] that infested the area where they lived. Today the Japanese still tattoo their bodies partly because they wish to camouflage and thus protect themselves from such dangerous carnivores as the shark whenever they dive into the ocean to catch fish, oysters, and clams. For most Japanese, however, tattoos are merely decorations. The way they are tattooed is altogether different from one Japanese country to another. Sometimes the tattoos are on the left side of the body and sometimes on the right side. The size of the colored marks also varies, depending upon the rank and position of the tattooed in the society where he lives.

Judging from the known distance between China and Japan, the Japanese islands must be located east of K'uaichi.[32] The Japanese are a moral people and they have good customs. All men bind their hair into a bundle without covering it with a hat; they wear head bands made of cotton instead. Their attires are made of strips of cloth sewed together horizontally, and they are so well sewed that one can hardly notice the seams between them. The hair of a Japanese woman spreads dishevelled at its lower end but is thereafter coiled into a tail that hangs on her back. Her clothes are like a bed sheet with a hole in the center from which the head emerges.

The Japanese raise such crops as paddy rice and hemp. Their sericulture is so advanced that they know how to make the finest silk. On their islands there are no oxen, horses, tigers, leopards, or magpies.

As for weaponry, they use spears, shields, and bows and arrows. Their bows, made of wood, are longer on the upper end and lower at the bottom. They use bamboo to make arrows to which are fastened barbs made of iron or animal bones. . . .

The Japanese islands have a warm climate, and the Japanese eat their vegetables raw regardless of winter or summer. They go bare-footed in their daily routine, but they do live inside houses. Inside a house, parents and children live in separate quarters. All Japanese cover their bodies with red paint, a custom similar to that in China where people love to rub their skin with white powder. Their eating and drinking utensils are made of bamboo, and they eat with their own hands.

A dead man is laid inside a coffin without being protected by an outer vault, and the coffin is buried underneath a mound made of dirt or earth. The dead body is kept within the house for more than ten days before it is taken out for burial. During these days the chief mourner will abstain from eating meat and cry

[29] Shao-k'ang was an able, enlightened king who, according to tradition, ruled China for twenty-two years in the twenty-first century B.C.

[30] Modern Chekiang province.

[31] A flood-dragon or *chiao-lung* was a mythological animal that supposedly caused flood or earthquake.

[32] Actually, they were located northeast of K'uaichi.

constantly, while other mourners will sing, dance, and drink wine. After the burial, all members of the family bathe themselves in water, a ritual which the Japanese call "baptism." [33]

Whenever the Japanese decide to communicate with China, they send only one person each time. Before his journey, the designated envoy is not allowed to comb his hair, clean his body from lice, change his clothes which should remain dirty, or have sexual intercourse with women. In fact, he acts as if he were undergoing a period of mourning. If nothing inauspicious occurs during this period of fasting, all people in the village will take good care of his family, livestock, and whatever valuables he might have during his absence. If on the other hand he incurs sickness or disease or suffers from violent attacks by others, they will kill him on the ground that he has not been sincere and strict with himself.

The Japanese islands produce high-quality pearls and blue jade. In their mountains can be found mercury. Among the trees are cedar, scrub oak, camphor, papaya, oak, and many others. There is also a variety of bamboos. There are other plants such as ginger, orange, pepper, and wild ginger which could be used as condiments, but the Japanese do not know how to use them. Wild animals include monkey and black pheasant.

Before a Japanese travels or undertakes any important task, he consults oracles by burning animal bones. The words of the oracle sound like an order from a superior to an inferior, and the inquirer must be explicit in his inquiry before the ritual takes place. The oracle will indicate whether the proposed undertaking is an auspicious one. The other way of conjuring oracles is by burning tortoise shells, and the diviner examines the crackings of the shell to ascertain the omens.

There are no discernible differences between father and son or men and women as far as outward conduct is concerned. All Japanese love to drink wine. Whenever a person salutes a man of noble birth, he strikes his own hands instead of kneeling and kowtowing. Some Japanese live to be one hundred years old; others live to eighty or ninety years of age.

According to the Japanese custom, a man of noble birth can have four or five wives; even a man of meagre means sometimes has two or three wives. Japanese women are not licentious by nature; they do not know such things as jealousy. The good custom of Japan is also manifested by the fact that her people do not rob or steal and that they rarely resort to lawsuits to resolve their differences. If a man commits a minor crime, his wife will be confiscated by the government, but he and all of his relatives will be put to death if his crime is that of a serious nature. There is a clear line of demarcation between the superiors and the inferiors, and each person acts and behaves in accordance with his social status. An inferior is obedient to the person socially above him. . . .

In the sixth month of the second year of Ching-ch'u (A.D. 238) the Queen of Japan sent her minister Nan-sheng-mi and others to the province of Taifang where they requested the honor of paying homage to the Son of Heaven so as to present their tribute. Liu Hsia, the governor of Taifang, dispatched officials to escort personally the Japanese envoys to the capital.[34]

In the twelfth month of the same year (A.D. 238) the Chinese emperor [35] issued an edict to the Queen of Japan which read as follows:

[33] *Lien-mu.*
[34] Loyang.
[35] Emperor Wei Ming-ti (r. A.D. 227–239).

"By this edict I hereby confer upon you, Pei-mi-hu, the title 'Ruler of Japan: Friend of Wei.'[36] Liu Hsia, the governor of Taifang, ordered officials personally to escort your minister-envoys, Nan-sheng-mi and Niu-li, to the capital, and I wish you to know that they have safely arrived and that I have received the tribute which they presented to me on your behalf: four men, six women, and cloth of different colors totalling two bolts and two *chang* in length. The fact that you sent me tribute despite the great distance between our two countries shows clearly your loyalty and fealty as a vassal state. I cannot but feel compassionate towards you and have thus decided to confer upon you the title 'Ruler of Japan: Friend of Wei.' In a separate case you will find a golden seal with purple ribbon attached to it. This seal, to be forwarded to you by the governor of Taifang, indicates your newly acquired investiture. It is my hope that you will rule your people in a proper manner and continue your loyalty towards me without fail.

"In view of the fact that your two envoys, Nan-sheng-mi and Niu-li, have traveled a long distance to pay me tribute on your behalf, I have decided to confer on the former the title 'General of the Imperial Guards with the Propensity Towards Goodness' and the latter, 'Colonel of the Imperial Guards with the Propensity Towards Goodness.' Silver seals with blue ribbons attached to them will be awarded to these two envoys to indicate their respective positions. They will be given a farewell audience before they are sent home.

"To reward you for the tribute you sent me, I am giving you the following items: 5 bolts of crimson silk with embroidered dragons, 10 sheets of crepe woolens in red color, 50 bolts of bright crepe, 50 bolts of violet silk, 3 bolts of violet silk with embroidered scenery, 5 sheets of woolens with polka dots of various colors, 50 bolts of white silk, eight taels of gold, two knives of five feet in length, 100 bronze mirrors, fifty catties of high-quality pearls, and fifty catties of mercury. All these will be packed in cases, to be brought to you by your two envoys. Upon their arrival you shall examine these gifts to see for yourself that they are in good order. It is my hope that you will show these gifts to your countrymen so that all of them will know that being compassionate towards you, I have given you so many of my treasures."

In the first year of Cheng-shih (A.D. 240) Governor Kung Tsun sent a delegation to Japan headed by Colonel T'i Chün. The delegation brought with it the edict issued by the Chinese emperor and the official seal whereby the Japanese king would be formally proclaimed "Ruler of Japan." To the Japanese king it also brought many gifts from the Chinese emperor: gold, silk, embroideries, knives, swords, mirrors, and other valuables. Upon receiving the items described above, the Japanese king sent to the Chinese emperor a memorial to express his gratitude. . . .

96 · WEI CHENG: *Japan* [37]

Japan is located southeast of Pai-chi and Hsin-lo,[38] 3,000 *li* away from China via land and sea. It consists of mountainous islands in the midst of the Great Sea.

---

[36] Wei was then the dynastic title of China's royal household.
[37] "Japan" (*Wo-kuo*); *Sui shu*, roll 81.
[38] Both countries were located in modern Korea.

During the Wei dynasty [39] more than thirty of its kingdoms communicated with China, and each of their rulers called himself "king." Since the Japanese have not yet invented the lineal measure, they measure distance in terms of the time needed to travel such a distance. Thus they say that their country is five-month long from west to east and three-month long from north to south. It is surrounded by water on all sides. Its elevation is high on the east but slopes down westward. Its capital is Hsieh-mi-tui, called Hsieh-ma-t'ai in the *History of the Wei*.[40] "Japan is located 12,000 *li* from the provinces of Lo-lang and Taifang [41] and is east of K'uaichi," says an ancient record; "it is very close to Tan-erh." [42]

During the reign of Han Kuang-wu (r. A.D. 25–57) the ruler of Japan, calling himself a "minister," sent an envoy to China to pay his tribute. Another tribute mission was sent to China during the reign of Han An-ti (r. A.D. 107–125); the country from which the mission came was referred to as the "Kingdom of the Dwarfs." [43] During the Huan-Ling period (147–188) the Japanese nation was plunged into chaos; different groups fought among themselves; and no common sovereign existed for a long time. Finally there was a woman named Pei-mi-fa who, as a soothsayer, knew how to confuse people with her magic and was consequently proclaimed by her countrymen as the new ruler. After her accession, her younger brother helped her rule the country. She reportedly had more than one thousand female slaves waiting on her in the palace, though few had ever seen them. What people did see, however, was the repeated presence of two men who not only waited on her during meal time but also served as liaison officers between her and the outside world. Among her palace buildings were observation towers, all of which were protected by palisades. Entrance into and exit from the palace were strictly regulated.

From the Wei (220–265) to the Liang (502–556) dynasty all Chinese regimes had communicated with Japan.

In the twentieth year of K'ai-huang (A.D. 600) the reigning ruler of Japan was a man with the surname of A-mei. He had two personal names: To-li-ssu-pei-hu and A-pei-chi-mi. It was he who sent an envoy to China. Upon the envoy's arrival, the reigning Chinese emperor [44] ordered responsible officials to learn as much as possible about Japanese customs. "The king of Japan regards Heaven as his elder brother and the sun as his younger brother," said the Japanese. "He grants audiences and determines policies each morning before the sun rises, while sitting cross-legged on his throne. He stops immediately after the sun rises, saying: 'It is my younger brother's turn to take care of the rest.'" The Chinese emperor considered the Japanese king impudent and issued an order saying that the latter should strive to improve his manners.

The Japanese king had a wife named Chi-mi; he also had six or seven hundred girls in his palaces. His crown prince was Li-ko-mi-to-fu-li. He did not have any walled cities, however.

There were twelve ranks of Japanese officials. They were, in the order of importance: "Greater Virtue," "Lesser Virtue," "Greater Love," "Lesser Love,"

[39] 220–265.
[40] *Wei chih.*
[41] Both provinces were located in modern Korea.
[42] Its modern equivalent cannot be easily located.
[43] *Wo-nu kuo.*
[44] Sui Wen-ti (r.589–604).

"Greater Righteousness," "Lesser Righteousness," "Greater Propriety," "Lesser Propriety," "Greater Wisdom," "Lesser Wisdom," "Greater Faith," and finally, "Lesser Faith." The number of officials for each rank was unspecific and indefinite. Besides, there were 120 district rulers comparable to the magistrates in China. Every eighty households were headed by an official called *yi-mi-yi* whose functions were similar to those of a Chinese village chief. Ten of these village units made one district.

As for clothing, all Japanese men wore jackets and skirts. The sleeves of their jackets were unusually short. Their so-called shoes were really sandals varnished with lacquer, and they were tied to the feet with strings. Most Japanese did not wear socks. Their custom prohibited the use of gold and silver to decorate their clothes which, consisting of strips of cloth sewed together horizontally, did not have any vertical seams.

Formerly the Japanese did not wear hats, and they let their hair hang loosely over their ears. It was not until the Sui dynasty [45] that the king of Japan first designed a headwear. This headwear was made of embroidered silk and was decorated with artificial flowers fashioned from gold or silver. A woman tied her hair into a bundle which hung on her back. Her clothes, like those of men, consisted of jackets and skirts, all of which were embellished with fringes. Combs were fashioned from bamboo, and mats were made of straw. Some of the mats were covered with leather and were fringed with the finest animal skin.

The Japanese weapons included bows, spears, knives, lances, cross-bows, hand hatchets, and many others. Lacquered sheets of animal skin were used as materials to make shields. Points of arrows or spears were fashioned from animal bones. Though soldiers were a common sight, rarely did war take place. Early in the morning the king met his ministers amidst the displaying of the royal insignia and the playing of the national anthem. The total number of the Japanese households was about 100,000.

According to Japanese customary law, murder, robbery, and adultery were punishable by death. Thievery was compounded into a fine; the larger the value of the stolen goods, the heavier the fine would be. A person who could not pay the imposed fine would be condemned to slavery. Lesser crimes were punishable by flogging or banishment from the local community. During a trial, torture was often used to exact confessions. The various ways of applying torture included the placing of heavy logs upon the knees of the accused and the sawing of the accused's neck by the chord of a strong bow. Sometimes a trial by ordeal was ordered. In this case the contestants in a lawsuit were instructed to search for a small stone with their hands in a jar filled with boiling water, and the person whose hand was badly burned was declared the guilty party. Sometimes a snake was placed in the jar; a person whose hand was stung by the snake was considered guilty.

Generally speaking, the Japanese were a quiet, peaceful people. Rarely did they resort to law for the settlement of their differences. Banditry and robbery were infrequent occurrences.

Japanese musical instruments included a variety of flutes and a lyre which had five strings. All Japanese, both male and female, branded their shoulders, marked their faces, and tattooed their bodies. They dived into water to catch fish. They

45 This refers to the Chinese Sui dynasty (590–618).

did not have any written language in the early years; they knotted chords or carved marks in the wood for the purpose of reckoning or recording. Only after they imported Buddhist scriptures from Pai-chi did they have a written language.

The Japanese climate was warm and temperate; trees and grass were green even in winter time. The land was fertile and productive, though there were more areas covered by water than by land. To fish, the Japanese attached a small ring around the neck of a cormorant and then threw the bird into the water.[46] A fisherman could make a daily catch of more than a hundred fish this way. The Japanese did not use dishes or plates when eating; they used tree leaves instead. Food was helped to the mouth by hand.

The Japanese were an honest, straightforward people, and they had good customs. There were more women than men in the country. People with the same surname could not marry each other. They married only those with whom they were in love. When the bride came to the man's house on the wedding day, she had to pass through the ritual of riding a dog before she was brought face to face with her husband. Generally speaking, Japanese women were not licentious by nature.

After a Japanese died, his body would be put inside a coffin, and his friends and relatives performed the funeral ritual by singing and dancing around it. The wife, children, and brothers of the deceased wore white clothes during the period of mourning. If the deceased was a man of noble birth, his coffin would be stationed in the fields for three years before it was buried. A dead commoner, however, would be buried as soon as a propitious day could be found. During the day of the burial the dead body was transported to the site of the grave on a wooden sleigh or, in some cases, in a small carriage.

In Japan there was a mountain called A-su which for unknown reasons burst into fire from time to time. The flame was so high that it seemed to have reached the sky. The Japanese considered this phenomenon so mysterious that they worshipped and prayed before it.

Japan also produced the valuable ju-yi [47] pearls which were as large as eggs and had a sky-blue color. They reflected light even in complete darkness. Both Hsin-lo and Pai-chi regarded Japan as a great country with many valuables and held her in high esteem. They frequently exchanged envoys with this island kingdom.

In the third year of Ta-yeh (A.D. 607) To-li-ssu-pei-hu, the king of Japan, sent an envoy to China to pay his tribute. The envoy said: "The king of Japan, having heard that the Buddhist emperor of China is promoting Buddhism on the Chinese soil, is sending me, together with other monks, to learn about Buddhist teachings in China." The letter from the king of Japan read in part: "The Son of Heaven in the place where the sun rises is hereby addressing the Son of Heaven in the place where the sun sets. It is my earnest hope that you are healthy, etc. etc." The emperor [48] was very much displeased with this letter; he gave the order that from then on the minister in charge of barbarian affairs should not present him with any letter from a barbarian chief that showed disrespect.

---

[46] The ring prevented fish from being swallowed by the bird, and the fish would then be retrieved by the fisherman. This kind of fishing is still widely practiced in both China and Japan.

[47] Ju-yi, literally, means "as you like it."

[48] Sui Yang-ti (r.605–616).

In the following year (A.D. 608) the emperor sent an official named Fei Ch'ing as his envoy to Japan. The envoy passed across Pai-chi and landed on the island of Chu, north of the kingdom of Jan-lo. Passing through the kingdom of Tu-ssu-ma[49] which was located in the midst of the ocean, he traveled eastward to the kingdom of Yi-chih and then the kingdom of Chu-ssu. Further eastward, he arrived at the kingdom of Ch'in-wang where people acted and behaved like the Chinese, but for unknown reasons they were still regarded as barbarians. After passing through ten more countries the envoy finally reached the coast of Japan. All the kingdoms east of Chu-ssu were in fact Japan's vassals.

The Japanese king sent A-pei-t'ai, who bore the rank of "Lesser Virtue," to head a delegation of several hundred to receive the Chinese envoy in the suburb. The Japanese displayed the royal insignia, beat drums, and blew horns to welcome the visitor. Ten days later, the king sent "Greater Propriety" Ko-to-pi, accompanied by a retinue of more than 200 horse riders, to visit and comfort the Chinese. Subsequently Fei Ch'ing entered the Japanese capital and was introduced to the king. The king was overjoyed and remarked as follows:

"I have heard that west of the Sea there is a country called Great Sui, the land of righteousness and propriety. I, therefore, once sent envoys to pay my tribute. I, a barbarian, live in a remote corner of the Sea and, consequently, have not learned the proper manner in which a great envoy is to be received. That is why I have hesitated for a long time before I receive you today. Now that I have swept the roads and decorated my guest house for the purpose of meeting with you, I wish you to tell me with your own words how the great country of yours has regenerated its civilization."[50]

Fei Ch'ing replied to the king as follows:

"The virtue of my sovereign is as great as that of the sun and the moon and is spreading towards the four corners of the earth. Knowing your desire to be influenced by a superior culture, he has sent me here to express his appreciation."

The king then led him to the guest house.

Shortly afterwards, Fei Ch'ing sent a messenger to report to the king that since he had already completed his mission of transmitting his master's message, he wished to leave Japan for home. Upon hearing this, the king gave a banquet to bid the Chinese farewell and ordered an envoy to go with Fei to China where he would present Japanese products to the Chinese emperor as tribute.

After this no more communication between China and Japan took place throughout the Sui dynasty.

97 · SUNG LIEN: *Yüan's Relations with Japan*[51]

In the first year of Chih-yüan (A.D. 1264) during the reign of Yüan Shih-tsu[52] a Korean named Chao Yi petitioned the government, saying that it was possible to establish contact with Japan and that envoys should be selected for this pur-

[49] Tu-ssu-ma seems to be Tsushima. The other places mentioned in this paragraph cannot be easily identified.
[50] There had been a long period of civil war before China was unified under the Sui regime in 590.
[51] "Japan" *(Jih-pen); Yüan shih,* roll 208.
[52] Better known in the English language as Kublai Khan.

pose. In the eighth month of the third year (1266) the government appointed Hai-ti, the vice president of the Ministry of War as envoy to Japan and granted him the Tiger Seal for this particular purpose. Yin Hung, the vice president of the Ministry of Rites, was appointed as his deputy bearing the Golden Seal. They were to carry with them the message from the Mongol emperor to the king of Japan. The message read as follows:

"The Emperor of the Great Mongols addresses the King of Japan as follows: I have heard that since ancient times even a small nation emphasizes the importance of mutual trust and reciprocal friendship in its relationship with neighboring states. How can we be any more different? Our ancestors received the mandate of Heaven to establish a great empire and brought a large number of peoples under their jurisdiction. Even peoples in the remotest areas feared our military might and longed for the benevolent influence we might be able to extend to them. I can assure you that their number was very large indeed.

"When I ascended the throne as the emperor, I immediately ordered the cessation of hostilities and the restoration to Korea the territories we had conquered, feeling compassionate for the innocent Korean people who had suffered so much during the previous war. Grateful for the favor we had shown to them, the Korean king and his ministers bore tribute to China, and the relationship between China and Korea, though legally a relationship between lord and vassal, has been as cordial as a relationship between a father and his son. Of this fact I am sure that you are fully aware.

"Korea is our buffer state in the east and Japan, being close to Korea, has had contact with China since time immemorial. Yet there has not been any exchange of envoys to express mutual friendship in the recent past. Fearing that you might not know my intention in this matter, I am sending to you my envoys bearing my personal message. It is my hope that the communication between our two countries be opened and maintained and that our mutual friendship be established. A sage regards the whole world as one family; how can different countries be considered one family if there is no friendly communication between them? Is force really necessary to establish friendly relations? I hope that you will give this matter your most careful attention."

Following the order of the Mongol emperor, Wang Chih, the king of Korea, sent Sung Chün-fei, the vice premier and Chin Tsan, the vice president of the Ministry of Rites, to accompany Hai-ti to Japan. The Japanese did not respond, and the envoys came home.

In the sixth month of the fourth year of Chih-yüan (1267) the emperor, disappointed with the fact that the envoys had failed in their mission to establish communications with Japan, again sent Hai-ti to Korea and gave Wang Chih the order that the mission to Japan must be successfully completed. Wang Chih, being fearful that the envoy from the Celestial Empire might encounter danger on the treacherous sea route to Japan, decided to send his own envoy instead. Consequently, in the ninth month of the same year, he sent to Japan P'an Fu, an official in the royal household, with the necessary credentials. P'an Fu stayed in Japan for six months, but nothing consequential came from this trip.

In the ninth month of the fifth year of Chih-yüan (1268) Hai-ti was ordered to bring the emperor's message to the Island of Tui-ma. The Japanese refused to receive him. Hai-ti captured two Japanese, T'a Erh-lang and Mi Erh-lang, and brought them home.

In the sixth month of the sixth year of Chih-yüan (1269) the emperor ordered Chin Yu-ch'eng of Korea to return the two Japanese to Japan and to bring to the Japanese government a state message from Korea. The Japanese government, however, did not choose to reply. Chin Yu-ch'eng stayed in Japan for a considerable time before he returned home.

In the twelfth month of the same year (1269) the emperor sent Chao Liang-p'i, the secretary-general of the Secretariat, as his envoy to Japan. The message the envoy carried to the king of Japan read as follows:

"I have heard that a king, to be truly great, does not discriminate against foreigners on behalf of his own subjects. Since Korea has become a member of our family, Japan is in fact our neighbor. I once sent envoys to your country to establish friendly relations, but unfortunately they failed in their missions, due to obstructions by your border officials. The two Japanese they arrested and detained were subsequently released by my order; they were comforted before they were sent home with my credentials. Since then I have not heard anything from you in this matter. Was your failure to send envoys to China caused by the disturbances that accompanied the rebellion led by the powerful minister Lin Yen in Korea? Or, is it true that your envoys, having been sent by you, were delayed by unpredictable eventualities on their way to China? I do not know the answer to either of these two questions.

"It is difficult for me to understand why Japan, which has long been known as a cultured and civilized country, will do things without thinking carefully about them. Now that I have reestablished peace in Korea by eliminating Lin Yen and restored the legitimate Korean king to the throne, I am sending you Chao Liang-p'i, secretary-general of the imperial government, as my envoy bearing with him my personal message. It will be a joy to all parties concerned if you could see your way to send your envoys to accompany him when he returns to China, so that the good relations between our two countries will be established from now on. It saddens me whenever I think that I may have to use force to achieve this purpose if for any reason you hesitate to respond to my call for the establishment of friendly relations. I hope that you will give this matter your most careful attention."

Before Chao Liang-p'i began his journey, he requested to know the proper rites to be performed when meeting with the Japanese king. The consensus of the court was that since the relative order between the two countries had not been established, there should not be any special rule with regard to the rites to be performed. The emperor agreed.

In the twelfth month of the seventh year of Chih-yüan (1270) the emperor ordered Wang Chih to provide escort for envoy Chao Liang-p'i on his way to Japan. The emperor stressed the importance of this mission and said that it must succeed. Generals Hu-lin-shih, Wang Kuo-ch'ang, and Hung Ch'a-ch'iu led their troops to escort the envoy as far as the coast. The troops were to be stationed in Chinchow [53] and its neighboring areas until the envoy safely returned.

In the sixth month of the eighth year of Chih-yüan (1271) Ts'ao Chieh-sheng, an expert on Japan, sent a memorial to the emperor which read as follows: "The route to Japan via Korea whereon our envoys have thus far traveled is long and circuitous. There is a shorter route outside Korea which will enable us to reach

[53] Located in modern Liaoning province in Manchuria.

Japan in one-half day if the wind direction is right. I shall not wish to go to Japan alone. If on the other hand the government has decided to send an expeditionary force for the subjugation of Japan, I shall be happy to serve as a guide." The emperor said that he would have to think more carefully before making a decision.

In the ninth month of the same year (1271) Wang Chih, the king of Korea, ordered Hsü Ch'eng, an expert on Japan, personally to escort the envoy Chao Liang-p'i to Japan. Japan responded for the first time and sent Mi Ssu-lang to pay homage to the Mongol emperor on his behalf. The emperor gave a banquet in honor of the visiting Japanese and then sent him home. . . .

In the second month of the ninth year of Chih-yüan (1272) the Korean king Wang Chih wrote a letter to the king of Japan. In the fifth month he wrote another letter emphasizing the fact that Japan must send an envoy to the Great Court [54] to establish friendly relations. The Japanese did not respond.

In the sixth month of the tenth year of Chih-yüan (1273) Chao Liang-p'i again journeyed to Japan as the Mongol envoy and returned shortly afterwards.

In the third month of the eleventh year of Chih-yüan (1274) the emperor ordered Hsin-tu, the garrison commander of the Fengchou District,[55] and Hung Ch'a-ch'iu, the viceroy of Korea, to prepare nine hundred ships and 15,000 men for the conquest of Japan. The preparation was to be completed by the seventh month.

In the tenth month of the same year (1273) the expeditionary force arrived in Japan and defeated the Japanese. But due to the lack of morale on the part of the soldiers and the exhaustion of arrows, the expeditionary force returned to China after pillaging the Japanese countryside.

In the second month of the twelfth year of Chih-yüan (1275) the emperor sent Tu Shih-tsung, vice president of the Ministry of Rites, Ho Wen-chu, vice president of the Ministry of Defense, and Sa-tu Lu-ting, imperial counselor, as his envoys to Japan. The Japanese, however, did not respond to the emperor's message.

In the fourteenth year of Chih-yüan (1277) Japan sent her merchants to China to exchange gold for Chinese copper coins. The government granted them permission to make such an exchange.

In the second month of the seventeenth year of Chih-yüan (1280) the Japanese killed the Mongol envoys, including Tu Shih-tsung. Marshals Hsin-tu and Hung Ch'a-ch'iu requested the permission to lead their army personally for the conquest of Japan. A conference was held among the imperial ministers and it was decided to postpone the decision for the time being.

In the fifth month of the same year (1280) Fan Wen-hu was summoned to the imperial court to discuss possible military action against Japan.

In the eighth month of the same year (1280) an imperial decree ordered the recruitment of soldiers for the conquest of Japan.

In the first month of the eighteenth year of Chih-yüan (1281) the emperor ordered A-la-han and Fan Wen-hu, the vice president and deputy chief of the Administration of Japanese Affairs respectively, together with Marshals Hsin-tu and Hung Ch'a-ch'iu, to lead an army of 100,000 for the conquest of Japan.

[54] The Mongol Court of China.
[55] Located in modern Liaoning province.

In the second month of the same year (1281) the generals went to the imperial palace to bid the emperor farewell. The emperor instructed them as follows: "We sent envoys to Japan in response to her ambassadorial mission to China. Yet the Japanese chose to detain our envoys and refused to give them permission to return home.[56] That is the reason you gentlemen must make this trip. I have heard the Chinese say that the primary purpose of conquering another country is to acquire its land and people, and we defeat our own purpose if we indulge in killings. What use does land have if there are no people on it? There is another thing that worries me greatly—I am afraid that differences and feuds might develop among you generals. If the Japanese choose to negotiate with you, you should consult among yourselves and then speak with one voice."

In the fifth month of the same year (1281) Fei Kuo-tso, a counselor-adviser in the Administration of Japanese Affairs, submitted a report to the emperor which read as follows: "Previously this Administration decided that the naval forces would head for the Chinchow District of Korea where they would meet the army led by Marshals Hsin-tu and Hung Ch'a-ch'iu before the expeditionary forces moved eastward for the conquest of Japan. Later this plan was found impractical due to transportation problems caused by the wind. The officials of this Administration met again, and it was decided that the army and the navy should rendezvous at the Island of Yi-ch'i instead. In the third month of this year a Japanese ship was wrecked by storm and floated to our shore, and we asked the shipwrecked sailors to draw maps of the Japanese islands. We found an island called P'ing-hu west of the Japanese capital which was surrounded by water on all sides and could be conveniently used to anchor our battleships. Moreover, this island was and perhaps is still undefended. Our present plan calls for the occupation of this island. After this island is occupied, a boat will be sent to the Island of Yi-ch'i calling the army led by Marshals Hsin-tu and Hung Ch'a-ch'iu to join forces. We believe that the strategy we have outlined will yield good results." The emperor replied that Peking was far away from the areas of battle and that the planning of military operation should be left in the hands of A-la-han, the field commander.

In the sixth month of the same year (1281) A-la-han became sick and could not make the trip. A-t'a-hai was appointed as commander-in-chief of the expeditionary force to replace him.

In the eighth month the generals lost their whole army even before they made contact with the enemy. The Administration of Japanese Affairs reported the situation as follows: "After the expeditionary forces had arrived in Japan, a heavy storm destroyed most ships before attempts could be made to attack the Japanese capital. Despite this disaster, the high command still decided on the course of war, only to abandon it when it was found that commanders like Li Te-piao, Wang Kuo-tso, and Liu Wen-cheng had refused to obey orders, deserted the ranks, and fled. Under these circumstances this Administration had no choice except to ship the remaining army to Ho-p'u where it was dissolved, and all the soldiers were ordered to go home by themselves."

Shortly after the above report was made, Yü Ch'ang, a soldier who had managed to come home alive despite his army's defeat reported the situation as follows: "In the sixth month the expeditionary forces left for the sea and arrived

[56] They were actually killed by the Japanese.

at the Island of P'ing-hu in the following month. Subsequently they moved to the Wu-lung [57] Mountains. On the first day of the eighth month a heavy storm destroyed most of the ships. Four days later Fan Wen-hu, together with many other generals, boarded the strongest ships they could find and left, leaving behind them more than 100,000 soldiers who were then stationed at the base of the mountains. Having been deserted by their generals, the soldiers elected Lieutenant Chang as their commander-in-chief and pledged allegiance to him. While they were cutting trees to build ships for the purpose of sailing home, the Japanese arrived and the battle began. Most of the soldiers were slaughtered in combat, and the rest, numbering 20,000 to 30,000, were taken by the Japanese as prisoners. On the ninth day the Japanese attacked the Island of Pa-chüeh [58] and killed all Mongolian, Korean, and Northern Chinese soldiers. They spared the lives of Southern Chinese soldiers and condemned them to slavery instead, on the ground that South China had been only recently conquered by the Mongols. I was one of those whose lives were spared and who were condemned to slavery. The real reason for this defeat is that the commanders could not agree among themselves and chose to desert their own soldiers."

A long time elapsed before two more soldiers, named Mo Ch'ing and Wu Wan-wu, also managed to come home. Thus out of 100,000 soldiers who left China for this military campaign, only three returned.

In the twentieth year of Chih-yüan (1283) A-t'a-hai was appointed the president of the Administration of Japanese Affairs, and Ch'e-li T'ieh-mu-erh and Liu-erh Pa-tu-erh were appointed as his first and second deputy chiefs respectively. They were ordered to recruit troops and build ships for another military campaign against Japan. In a memorial to the emperor, Ang-chi-erh, the inspector-general of Huaihsi,[59] said that the nation's resources had been depleted by the recent campaign and that the proposed military action should not take place. . . .

In the twenty-third year of Chih-yüan (1286) the emperor said that since Japan had never invaded China the proposed campaign against that country should be cancelled for the time being, especially in view of the fact that the people in Chiao-chih [60] were invading the border provinces.

In the second year of Ta-te (1298) during the reign of Yüan Ch'eng-tsung,[61] Yeh-su-ta-erh, the governor-general of Kiang-Che [62] made the suggestion that military forces should be used for the purpose of subjugating Japan. The emperor replied that this was not the proper time to take this action, though he would think carefully about it.

In the third year of Ta-te (1299) a monk named Ning-yi-shan was granted the title "Master of Infinite Mercy" before he was appointed as an envoy to Japan. The monk went to Japan via a commercial ship, but the Japanese failed to respond by sending their envoys to China.

[57] Literally, "Five Dragons."
[58] Literally, "Eight Angles."
[59] Located in modern Anhwei province.
[60] Modern Indochina.
[61] Emperor Yüan Ch'eng-tsung (r. 1295–1307).
[62] Modern Kiangsu and Chekiang provinces.

Part III

Economics

CHAPTER TWELVE

Land, Population, Famine, and War

LOOKING at the available land-population figures of historical China, one may reach some tentative conclusions. First, with each rising dynastic cycle both population and the amount of cultivated field increased steadily, though the former increased at a greater rate than the latter. Population continued to increase long after the area of cultivation had been stabilized. Second, when the population reached its highest level within each dynastic cycle (while the amount of arable land remained substantially the same), a major social upheaval was in the offing, accompanied by famine, civil war, and sometimes foreign invasions. Third, during a dynastic interregnum (period between two dynastic cycles) both population and the amount of cultivated land dropped sharply as a result of war, famine, and disease. The interregnum could last from scores to sometimes hundreds of years (such as the interregnum between the dissolution of the Later Han dynasty and the founding of the Sui-T'ang Empire). Lastly, all population and land figures were inaccurate and too low to reflect the actual situation. Generally speaking, population figures were more distorted than land figures. This inaccuracy, however, does not invalidate the conclusions reached above, which are based upon the numerical differences between figures rather than the absolute accuracy of individual figures. These differences are so large that the above conclusions remain correct even though an individual figure may not be so accurate as it should be.

The inaccuracy of population and land figures stems from the fact that taxes were assessed on the basis of either population or amount of land under cultivation, and often both; to evade taxes by reporting small figures was too great a temptation to resist. Such falsification was in fact a common practice. "Sometimes from thirty to fifty households were reported as one household" (Selection 99); other times an average household was said to have only 1.5 to 2.0 members (Selection 100), a ridiculous figure even if we do not take into consideration the fact that the Chinese, until modern times, had glorified large families.

Taxes were heavier during the later periods (Selection 104), and the requirement that part of the taxes be paid in cash (instead of produce) made the situation even worse (Selections 105 and 106). Beginning in the T'ang dynasty, most of the government's tax revenue came from areas south of the Yangtze River. Though these areas were more productive than any other region in China, heavy taxation plus large rent reduced a large number of tenant farmers to a level of recurrent starvation (Selection 107). How heavy taxation adversely affected the life of the people is well illustrated by an apocryphal story told by the T'ang essayist Liu Tsung-yüan (Selection 108).

After food and population had reached a delicate balance and when most peasants were living on a starvation level, a drought or flood would tip the balance and send thousands of peasants to their deaths. Facing death, people acted like wild animals (Selection 109), and those who did not wish to die gathered as bandits and rose in revolt. A civil war would follow, fought with bitterness. The bitterness would become greater if a foreign power tried to take advantage of the situation so as to conquer all of China (Selection 110).

Of all the heroes who have fought in a Chinese civil war, none is perhaps more colorful than Hsiang Yü (third century B.C.). His defeat and subsequent suicide are a household story known to practically everyone who has attended a Chinese theatre or opera (Selection 111).

98 · MA TUAN-LIN: *The Population of China* [1]

When Yü (*c.*2205–*c.*2198 B.C.) of the Hsia dynasty introduced a provincial system after he had successfully brought the Great Flood under control, the total population of China was 3,553,923. . . . When Duke Chou administered China as the prime minister under King Ch'eng (*c.*1115–*c.*1079 B.C.) the total population of China was 13,704,923. This was the time when the economy of the Chou dynasty reached its most prosperous stage. . . .

About thirty years after King P'ing (r.770–720 B.C.) had moved his capital to Loyang,[2] the total population of China was 11,941,923. . . .

During the Han dynasty, from the reign of Kao-tsu (r.206–195 B.C.) to the reign of Hsiao-p'ing (r. A.D. 1–5) the total number of households in China was 12,-233,062, and the total population was 59,594,978.[3] This was the time when the economy of the Han dynasty reached its most prosperous stage.

In the second year of Chung-yüan (A.D. 57) during the reign of Han Kuang-wu (r.25–57) the total number of households in China was 4,279,634, and the total population was 21,007,820.

In the eighteenth year of Yung-p'ing (A.D. 75) during the reign of Han Ming-ti (r.58–75) the total number of households in China was 5,860,173, and the total population was 34,125,021.

In the second year of Chang-ho (A.D. 88) during the reign of Han Chang-ti (r.76–88) the total number of households in China was 7,456,784, and the total population was 43,356,376.

In the first year of Yung-hsing (A.D. 105) during the reign of Han Ho-ti (r.89–105) the total number of households in China was 9,237,112, and the total population was 53,256,229.

In the fourth year of Yen-kuang (A.D. 125) during the reign of Han An-ti

---

[1] The author was a famous historian of the thirteenth century. This selection is taken from his monumental work, *A Study of Cultural Heritage (Wen-hsien t'ung-k'ao)*, roll 11.

[2] This occurred in 770 B.C.

[3] Both figures were actually those of A.D. 2, the highest ever recorded during the Former Han dynasty.

(r.107–125) the total number of households in China was 9,946,919, and the total population was 48,690,789.

In the first year of Chien-k'ang (A.D. 144) during the reign of Han Shun-ti (r.126–144) the total number of households in China was 9,946,919, and the total population was 49,730,550.

In the first year of Yung-chia (A.D. 145) during the reign of Han Ch'ung-ti (r.145) the total number of households in China was 9,937,680, and the total population was 49,524,183.

In the first year of Pen-ch'u (A.D. 146) during the reign of Han Chih-ti (r.146) the total number of households in China was 9,348,227, and the total population was 47,566,772.

In the second year of Yung-shou (A.D. 156) during the reign of Han Huan-ti (r.147–167) the total number of households in China was 16,070,906, and the total population was 50,066,856. . . .

During the period of the Three Kingdoms (220–265) Ts'ao Ts'ao of Wei occupied the Central Plain,[4] Liu Pei of Shu controlled the Pa-shu area,[5] and Sun Ch'üan of Wu had within his jurisdiction all the territories in the Lower Yangtze. These three kingdoms fought against one another constantly. The kingdom of Wei (220–265) had a total of 663,423 households and a population of 4,432,-881. . . . At the time when the kingdom of Shu (221–264) was conquered, it had 280,000 households and 940,000 people approximately. The number of people under arms was about 102,000, and the number of officials was about 40,000. In the third year of Ch'ih-wu (240) the kingdom of Wu (222–280) had 520,000 households and 2,300,000 people approximately. At the time when it was conquered, it had about 530,000 households, 32,000 officials, and 230,000 soldiers. Its population was 2,300,000 approximately. The total number of people in the royal household was more than 5,000. . . .

In the first year of T'ai-k'ang (A.D. 280) during the reign of Tsin Wu-ti (r.265–290), the year when Wu was conquered and when all of the nine provinces were brought under the control of a unified government, the total number of registered households was 2,459,804, and the total population was 16,163,863. This was the time when the economy of the Tsin dynasty reached its most prosperous stage. . . .

In the eighth year of Ta-ming (A.D. 464) during the reign of Sung Hsiao-wu-ti (r.454–464) the kingdom of Liu Sung (420–479) had 906,870 households and 4,685,501 people. . . .

In the second year of Ch'ung-hua (A.D. 577) when it was conquered by North Chou (557–581), the kingdom of North Ch'i (550–577) had 3,032,528 households. . . .

In the first year of Ta-hsiang (A.D. 580) the kingdom of Later (North) Chou (557–581) had 3,590,000 households and 9,009,604 people. . . .

Emperor Wen-ti (r.589–604) of the Sui dynasty was modest and thrifty; he did not impose taxation on the increased population. In the second year of Ta-yeh (606) during the reign of Sui Yang-ti (r.605–616) the total number of households in China was 8,907,536, and the total population was 46,019,956. This was the time when the economy of the Sui dynasty reached its most prosperous stage.

[4] North China.
[5] Modern Szechuan province.

During the Chen-kuan period (627–649) of the T'ang dynasty it was reported that the total number of households in China did not exceed 3,000,000. . . . In the first year of Yung-hui (650) the Ministry of Personnel reported an increase of 150,000 households during the previous year and that the total number of households in China was approximately 3,800,000. . . .

In the first year of Shen-lung (705) during the reign of Empress Wu (r. 684–705) the total number of households in China was 6,356,141.

In the fourteenth year of K'ai-yüan (726) during the reign of T'ang Hsüan-tsung (r. 713–755) the total number of households in China was 7,069,565.

In the thirteenth year of T'ien-pao (754) during the reign of T'ang Hsüan-tsung (r. 713–755) the total number of households in China was 9,619,254.

According to T'ung tien,[6] in the fourteenth year of T'ien-pao (755) the total number of households in the nation was 8,919,309, of which 3,565,500 were non-taxpaying households and 5,349,208 were taxpaying households. The total population was 52,919,309, of which 44,700,988 were non-taxpaying subjects. This was the time when the economy of the T'ang dynasty reached its most prosperous stage.

In the second year of Chih-te (757) during the reign of T'ang Su-tsung (r. 756–762) the total number of households was 8,018,701. . . .

In the third year of Ch'ien-yüan (760) the total number of households was 1,933,125.

According to T'ung tien, the population in the third year of Ch'ien-yüan was as follows: For the 169 districts that had reported, the total number of households was 1,933,134. Among them 1,174,592 were non-taxpaying households and 758,582 were taxpaying households. The total population was 16,990,386, of which 14,619,587 were non-taxpaying subjects and 2,370,799 were taxpaying subjects. From the fourteenth year of T'ien-pao (755) to the third year of Ch'ien-yüan (760) the total loss of households amounted to 5,982,584 units and the total loss of population amounted to 35,928,723 people.[7]

In the second year of Kuang-te (764) during the reign of T'ang Tai-tsung (r. 763–779) the total number of households in China was 2,933,125.

In the first year of Chien-chung (780) during the reign of T'ang Te-chung (r. 780–804) the total number of taxpaying households in China was 3,805,076.

In the Yüan-ho period (806–820) during the reign of T'ang Hsien-tsung (r. 806–820) the total number of households in China was 2,473,963.

In the Ch'ang-ch'ing period (821–824) during the reign of T'ang Mu-tsung (r. 821–824) the total number of households in China was 3,944,595.

In the Pao-li period (825–826) during the reign of T'ang Wen-tsung (r. 827–846) the total number of households in China was 4,955,151. . . .

In the first year of Chien-lung (960) during the reign of Sung T'ai-tsu (r. 960–975) the total number of households was 976,353. In the first year of Ch'ien-te (963) when the territory of Chingnan [8] was conquered, the emperor brought under his jurisdiction 142,300 households. Another 97,388 households were added when the territory of Hunan [9] was conquered in the same year. In the

---

6 T'ung tien (or The Study of Institutions) was written by Tu Yu, a famous historian of the eighth century.

7 This loss of population was caused by An Lu-shan's revolt which began in A.D. 755.

8 Modern Hupeh province.

9 Modern Hunan province.

third year of Ch'ien-te (965) Shu [10] was conquered, and 534,029 households were brought under the jurisdiction of the central government. In the third year of K'ai-pao (970) the territory of Kuangnan [11] was annexed, and another 170,263 households were added to the empire. In the eighth year of K'ai-pao (975) when the territory of Kiangnan [12] was conquered, 655,065 households were brought under central administration. In the ninth year of K'ai-pao (976) the total number of households in China was 4,132,576.

In the fifth year of T'ien-hsi (1021) during the reign of Sung Chen-tsung (r. 998–1022) the total number of households in China was 10,162,689, and the total population was 21,830,064.

In the eighth year of Chia-yu (1063) during the reign of Sung Jen-tsung (r. 1023–1063) the total number of households in China was 12,462,317, and the total number of population was 26,421,651.

In the third year of Chih-p'ing (1066) during the reign of Sung Ying-tsung (r. 1064–1067) the total number of households in China was 12,917,221, and the total population was 29,092,185.

In the eighth year of Hsi-ning during the reign of Sung Shen-tsung (r. 1068–1085) the total number of households in China was 15,684,529, and the total population was 23,807,165.

In the sixth year of Yüan-feng (1083) the total number of households in China was 17,211,713, and the total number of population was 24,969,300. . . .

In the sixth year of Yüan-yu (1091) during the reign of Sung Che-tsung (r. 1086–1100) the total number of households in China was 18,655,093, and the total population was 41,492,311.

In the second year of Yüan-fu (1099) the total number of households in China was 19,715,555, and the total population was 43,411,606. . . .

In the thirteenth year of Shao-hsing (1160) during the reign of Sung Kao-tsung (r. 1127–1162) the total number of households in China was 11,375,733, and the total population was 19,229,008.

In the second year of Ch'ien-tao (1166) during the reign of Sung Hsiao-tsung (r. 1163–1189) the total number of households in all of the provinces was 12,335,450, and the total population was 25,378,684.

In the fourth year of Shao-hsi (1193) during the reign of Sung Kuang-tsung (r. 1190–1194) the total number of households in all of the provinces was 12,302,873, and the total population was 27,845,085.

In the sixteenth year of Chia-ting (1223) during the reign of Sung Ning-tsung (r. 1195–1224) the total number of households in all of the provinces was 12,670,801, and the total population was 28,320,085.

99 • MA TUAN-LIN: *The Unreliability of Population Figures as They Appear in Tax Registers* [13]

We shall not indulge ourselves in the discussion of the population figures of the Three Dynasties. As for the Former Han dynasty, the largest population was

---

[10] Modern Szechuan province.
[11] Modern Kwangtung and Kwangsi provinces.
[12] Lower Yangtze.
[13] *Wen-hsien t'ung-k'ao*, roll 3.

reached in the second year of Yüan-shih (A.D. 2) during the reign of Han P'ing-ti when the total number of households was reported to be 11,233,000. The largest number of households during the Later Han dynasty occurred in the third year of Yung-shou (A.D. 157) when it reached 10,677,960.[14] During the period of the Three Kingdoms (220–265) the total number of households in the three kingdoms was less than 1,200,000, a figure no larger than that of the two districts, Nanyang and Junan,[15] during the best years of the Han. This small figure should not surprise us, in view of the fact that wars were incessant during this period and that among every ten households scarcely one had survived this devastation. The surprising thing is that as late as the T'ai-k'ang period (280–289) of the Tsin dynasty, long after the country had been unified and peace restored, the total number of households was only 2,459,800. Shortly afterwards, China was divided into the Southern and Northern Dynasties; each of these dynasties was short in duration and their population figures were too scanty to be reliable. Even during their best years the total number of households was far from impressive. For instance, during the reign of Sung Wen-ti (r. 424–453) and shortly after the Yüan-chia period (420–423) the total number of households in the Liu Sung kingdom (420–479) was only a little more than 906,800. The number of households in North China was not impressive either; it was about 5,000,000 during this period immediately following the movement of the capital by Wei Hsiao-wen-ti (r. 471–499) from P'ingch'eng to Loyang.[16] Thus, even during the most prosperous years of the Southern and Northern Dynasties the total number of households in both North and South China was only about 6,000,000. After the Sui dynasty had unified China, the total number of households was only a little more than 8,907,000 as late as the second year of Ta-lieh (A.D. 606).

The question is often raised why the Sui and the T'ang, which had a territory no smaller that that of the Former and the Later Han, had a population only two-thirds as large. The answer is that the household and population figures of the Former and the Later Han dynasties are more accurate; because poll and household taxes were low, the figures reported by provinces and districts were closer to reality than those of a later period. After the Wei and the Tsin dynasties, poll and household taxes became increasingly heavy, and it is inevitable that there should be concealment in reporting the population and household figures so as to evade taxes. During the period when China was divided into the Southern and Northern Dynasties population registers became even more unreliable. Some called themselves "sojourning families," [17] and others claimed familial relationship to powerful clans—all of them refused to register so as to evade the payment

---

[14] This is the same figure as that recorded in *T'ung tien*. However, according to the *History of the East (Later) Han (Tung-Han shu)*, the largest number of households ever recorded during the Later Han dynasty was 16,070,906, considerably larger than the largest figure recorded during the Former Han dynasty. One might also note that in both the Former and the Later Han cases the country was plunged into civil war shortly after the largest population figure was recorded.

[15] Both were located in modern Honan province.

[16] P'ingch'eng and Loyang were located in modern Shansi and Honan provinces respectively.

[17] These families moved to the Yangtze Valley from North China early in the fourth century during the period of barbarian invasions. They shared a gentry background, and most of them were wealthy.

of taxes and the performance of corvée duties. Sometimes from thirty to fifty households were reported as one household. That is why the number of households appearing in population registers continued to decrease, even though the actual situation might be the reverse.

After China had been unified under the Sui and the T'ang regimes, it was inevitable that population should increase. During the Sui-T'ang era (590–906) the periods of great prosperity were those of K'ai-huang (581–600) and Chen-kuan (627–649). As far as population census was concerned, those taken during the T'ien-pao period (742–755) were the most thorough and presumably most accurate. Yet the total number of households was reported to be only 8,914,909, of which 3,565,500 were classified as "non-taxpaying." The non-taxpaying households were those of the nobility and high-ranking government officials, as well as the households maintained by the widowed, the disabled, the incurably ill, and male or female slaves. How is it possible that these households were so numerous as to constitute more than one-third of the total? The answer is only too obvious. By using households and individual persons as the basis to levy taxes, the government not only accentuated the difference between the rich and the poor, but also inadvertently fostered cheating and falsehood on the part of the taxpayers.

During the Yüan-shih period (A.D. 1–5) of the Han dynasty the total amount of cultivated land was reported to be 8,275,036 ch'ing, averaging 67 mou and 146 square paces per household, approximately.[18] During the K'ai-huang period (581–600) the total amount of cultivated land was reported to be 19,404,267 ch'ing, averaging two ch'ing per household. The territory of China remained substantially the same from the Han to the T'ang dynasty; why is it that arable land had increased while the numbers of registered households and population had decreased? The answer is not difficult to find. Land was immovable, and the total amount of cultivated land would remain the same once the war was over and peace restored, because all the land that had been laid in waste during the course of the war was once more put under cultivation. Population or number of households, on the other hand, could increase or decrease. In the wake of a long period of civil strife when most of the properties had been destroyed, people conspired to make false reports on population or household figures so as to evade taxes; tax registers existed only in name and certainly could not be relied on as the basis for an equitable tax system.

In his book T'ung tien, the T'ang historian Tu Yu says that during the 138 years from the beginning of the Wu-te period (618–626) to the end of the T'ien-pao period (742–755) the economic prosperity of the T'ang dynasty was comparable to that of the Han, and yet in population as well as in the number of households the figures for the T'ang period were much smaller. He attributed this discrepancy to the fact that the T'ang officials, short-sighted and irresponsible, were negligent in their duties to enforce the law, and consequently a large number of households and people never appeared in the tax registers. Though there is no question about the correctness of Tu Yu's statements, he fails to mention the fact that as taxes continued to increase, the number of people or households that

---

[18] One ch'ing (100 mou) is equal to 15.13 acres; 240 square paces make one mou or one-hundredth of one ch'ing.

appeared in tax registers was bound to become smaller and smaller. This was not only true during the T'ang dynasty but also true during all of the dynasties beginning with the Wei and the Tsin. . . .

100 · LI HSIN-CH'UAN: *The Unreliability of Population Figures* [19]

During the most prosperous years of the Former Han dynasty, each household reportedly had 4.8 members in average; the average increased to 5.2 during the Later Han dynasty. In either case the size of an average household was similar to that of a small peasant household during the Chou dynasty.

When population increase reached its apex during the T'ang dynasty, each household was said to have an average membership of 5.8. This average was similar to that of middle-sized peasant households during the Chou dynasty.

From the Yüan-feng (1078–1085) to the Shao-hsing (1131–1162) period of the present dynasty [20] the average membership of each household was said to be only 2.1. To say that an average household had only two members is obviously absurd. Why is it that there was such a large discrepancy between actual and reported figures? The reason is clear: a large number of people was never reported.

It is officially recorded that the average membership of each household in Chekiang is now 1.5 while that in Shu [21] is 2.0. Since it cannot be said that the people in Shu are more generative than the people in the Southeast,[22] the difference seems to have stemmed from the fact that Shu does not have a poll tax and consequently has a large average of membership per household.

101 · MA TUAN-LIN: *The Amount of Cultivated Land Throughout Chinese History* [23]

During the reign of Emperor Yao [24] the Great Flood isolated different parts of China, and communication and transportation between various regions became virtually impossible. The emperor ordered Yü to devise ways to stop the flood, and after the flood was brought under control, all the territory in China was divided into nine administrative provinces. . . . The total amount of cultivated land in the nine provinces was 9,108,020 *ch'ing*. . . .

During the prime years of the Former Han dynasty the total amount of arable land was 145,136,405 *ch'ing*. But of this amount, 100,090,947 *ch'ing* were marginal land. The land under profitable cultivation was 8,270,536 *ch'ing*. In the

[19] Li Hsin-ch'uan (d.1243), a famous historian of the Sung dynasty, was the author of *Annals of Sung Kao-tsung (Kao-tsung hsi-nien lu)* and *Miscellaneous Notes In and Outside of the Court (Ch'ao-yeh tsa-chi)*, two primary sources in the study of the Sung history. This selection was quoted by Ma Tuan-lin in *Wen-hsien t'ung-k'ao*, roll 11.

[20] Sung dynasty.

[21] Modern Szechuan province.

[22] Chekiang is located in the Southeast.

[23] *Wen-hsien t'ung-k'ao*, roll 1.

[24] A legendary emperor of ancient times.

second year of Yüan-shih (A.D. 2) the total number of households in China was 12,233,000. This means that if the cultivated fields were divided equally among all of the households, each household would receive 67 *mou* and 146 square paces approximately. . . .

In the first year of Yung-yüan (A.D. 89) during the reign of Han Ho-ti (r. 89–105) the total amount of cultivated land was 7,320,170 *ch'ing, 80 mou,* and 140 square paces.

In the fourth year of Yen-kuang (A.D. 125) during the reign of Han An-ti (r. 107–125) the total amount of cultivated land was 6,942,892 *ch'ing,* 33 *mou,* and 85 square paces. . . .

In the first year of Chien-k'ang (A.D. 144) during the reign of Han Shun-ti (r. 126–144) the total amount of cultivated land was 6,896,271 *ch'ing,* 56 *mou,* and 194 square paces. The total number of households in the same year was 9,946,990. This means that if the cultivated fields were divided equally among all of the households, each household would receive 70 *mou* approximately.

In the first year of Yung-chia (A.D. 145) during the reign of Han Ch'ung-ti (r. 145) the total amount of cultivated land was 6,957,676 *ch'ing,* 20 *mou,* and 108 square paces.

In the first year of Pen-ch'u (A.D. 146) during the reign of Han Chih-ti (r. 146) the total amount of cultivated land was 6,930,123 *ch'ing,* and 38 *mou.* . . .

In the ninth year of K'ai-huang (A.D. 589) the total amount of cultivated land was 19,404,267 *ch'ing.* During the K'ai-huang period (581–600) the total number of households was 8,907,536. This means that if the cultivated fields were divided equally among all of the households, each household would receive more than two *ch'ing.* . . .

During the Ta-yeh period (605–616) the total amount of cultivated land was reported to be 55,854,040 *ch'ing.* (This figure, quoted from the official history, seems to be too large to be accurate. If it were, cultivated acreage per household would be as large as 5 *ch'ing* plus, since the total number of households was approximately 8,907,536 during this period.)

During the middle years of T'ien-pao (742–755) the total amount of cultivated land was 14,303,862 *ch'ing* and 13 *mou.* In the fourteenth year of T'ien-pao (755) the total number of households was more than 8,900,000. This means a cultivated acreage of approximately 160 *mou* per household.

Towards the end of the T'ien-pao period the total amount of cultivated land was 3,125,251 *ch'ing* and 25 *mou.*

In the fifth year of T'ien-hsi (1021) the total amount of cultivated land was 5,247,584 *ch'ing* and 32 *mou.* . . .

During the Huang-yu period (1049–1053) the total amount of cultivated land was 2,280,000 *ch'ing* approximately.

During the Chih-p'ing period (1064–1067) the total amount of cultivated land was 4,400,000 *ch'ing* approximately. . . .

In the eight year of Yüan-feng (1085) the emperor,[25] learning about the disturbances that land survey had caused among the people, ordered the cessation of such a survey. The cultivated fields which had been surveyed and duly recorded amounted to 2,484,349 *ch'ing.*

[25] Sung Shen-tsung (r.1064–1085).

During the Yüan-feng period (1078–1085) the Sung empire had four capitals and eighteen provinces. The total amount of cultivated land was 4,616,556 *ch'ing*. Of this amount, 4,553,163 *ch'ing* and 61 *mou* were private possessions and 63,393 *ch'ing* were public land which belonged to the government. . . .

During the Yüan-shih period (A.D. 1–5) the Han government had within its jurisdiction more than 8,275,000 *ch'ing* of cultivated fields. The amount was 19,404,000 *ch'ing* for the Sui government during the K'ai-huang period (581–600) and 14,308,000 *ch'ing* for the T'ang government during the T'ien-pao period (742–755). In other words, the cultivated land of each of the three dynasties were two, three, or even four times larger than that of the Sung dynasty.[26] The fact that the Sung territory was smaller than any of the above-mentioned dynasties due to the loss of the Yu and Chi provinces[27] may account to some extent for this difference, but the difference is too large to be explained away by this fact alone. According to the *Chih-p'ing Records,* the computation of cultivated fields during the Sung dynasty was based upon the amount of land taxes collected within each administrative area, and the owners of 70 percent of all cultivated fields never filed tax returns. When this factor is taken into consideration, it would seem that the total amount of cultivated land within the Sung empire exceeded 30,000,000 *ch'ing*. Greatly concerned with the harm which a strict enforcement of the tax laws could have caused to the people, the Sung emperors chose to be lenient in this matter. Consequently we have no way of knowing how much land was under cultivation during the Sung dynasty. . . .

102 · CHANG T'ING-YÜ *et al.*: *Land and Population During the Ming Dynasty* [28]

The population of the Ming dynasty, insofar as it can be ascertained, has been recorded as follows:

In the twenty-sixth year of Hung-wu (1393) the total number of households in China was 16,052,860, and the total population was 60,545,812.

In the fourth year of Hung-chih (1491) the total number of households in China was 9,113,446, and the total population was 53,281,158.

In the sixth year of Wan-li (1578) the total number of households in China was 10,621,436, and the total population was 60,692,856.

It is not surprising that the population of China should reach a high peak after T'ai-tsu[29] had pacified the country;[30] it is strange, however, that the population should decrease from that peak after China had enjoyed a long period of peace.[31] During the civil war period[32] the areas north of the Huai River[33]

[26] North Sung dynasty (960–1126).

[27] Both were located in modern Hopeh province.

[28] The authors were famous scholar-officials of the seventeenth and eighteenth centuries. This selection is taken from "Economics I" *(shih-huo yi); History of the Ming (Ming shih),* roll 77.

[29] Ming T'ai-tsu or Chu Yüan-chang (1328–1398), founder of the Ming dynasty.

[30] This refers to the population of 1393.

[31] This refers to the population of 1491.

[32] This refers to the war between Ming Hui-ti (r.1399–1402) and his uncle Chu Ti. The latter won and ascended the throne in 1403 as Ming Ch'eng-tsu or Yung-lo (r.1403–1424).

[33] Located in modern Anhwei province.

were so devastated that nothing was left except a sea of tall grass. Yet the population of China increased during this period. Moreover, it began to decline from then on until it reached a very low point in the T'ien-shun period (1457–1464). It rose again during the Ch'eng-te period (1506–1521).

What were the factors that caused the population to decline? According to Chou Ch'en,[34] a major cause of the increase or decrease of population was the strict enforcement, or the lack of it, of the population registration law; it had little to do with the actual increase or decrease of the population in question. When the law was not strictly enforced, people simply failed to register. Many of them had either secured the protection of powerful, influential families or, disguising themselves as artisans, had taken residence in either of the two capitals.[35] Some were traders who traveled all over China; others lived in boats with their families. In any of these cases they were extremely difficult to trace.

There was, however, an even more important factor. Emperor Ming Hsüan-tsung (r. 1426–1435) once remarked to his ministers that throughout the long history of China, population increased when there was peace and declined when there was war. This is the truest statement insofar as the increase or decrease of population is concerned. . . .

A land survey was conducted in the twenty-sixth year of Hung-wu (1393), and the total amount of cultivated fields in China was reported to be 8,507,623 *ch'ing*. This amount was so large that it seemed that all arable land had been put under cultivation. . . .

In the fifteenth year of Hung-chih (1503) the total amount of cultivated land in China was 4,228,518 *ch'ing*. The ratio between privately owned and government-owned land was seven to one.

In the sixth year of Wan-li (1578) the emperor,[36] acting upon the recommendation of Grand Chancellor Chang Chü-cheng (d.1582), ordered the survey of all cultivated fields in the empire. . . . The total amount of cultivated fields was 7,013,976 *ch'ing*, about 3,000,000 *ch'ing* larger than that of the Hung-chih period (1488–1505). . . .

103 · MA TUAN-LIN: *The Advantages and Disadvantages of Different Tax Systems* [37]

The Ch'in dynasty abolished the well-field system,[38] together with the traditional tax which amounted to 10 percent of the land's yield. Farmers were allowed to own or till as much land as they could afford; and persons, instead of land, became the basis upon which taxes were levied. The amount of taxes actually paid by each individual was thirty times more than the prevailing amount prior to the abolition of the well-field system.

It was not until Han Kao-tsu (r.206–195 B.C.) acceded to the throne that taxation on land was rectified. The new tax amounted to one-fifteenth of a farmer's

[34] Chou Ch'en (*chin-shih,* 1404), serving in the Ministry of Public Works in the 1420's, was an able administrator of finance.
[35] Peking and Nanking.
[36] Ming Shen-tsung (r.1573–1619).
[37] *Wen-hsien t'ung-k'ao,* roll 3.
[38] See pp. 264–287.

produce; it was further reduced to one-thirtieth in a later period. But the Han government levied taxes on persons as well as on land. The poll tax of the Han dynasty was first introduced in the fourth year of Han Kao-tsu's reign (203 B.C.) and amounted to a yearly payment of 120 standard coins for each of all individuals between the age of fifteen and sixty-five, and 20 standard coins between the age of seven and fifteen. At the time of Han Wen-ti (r.179–157), however, it was reduced to 40 standard coins for each adult male, a reduction by two-thirds of the original amount. Moreover, it was levied only once every three years, amounting to approximately 13 standard coins per year. This was a very small amount indeed. After the reigns of Han Chao-ti (r.86–74 B.C.) and Han Hsüan-ti (r.73–49 B.C.) even this small amount was sometimes reduced and occasionally abolished altogether.

One reason for this low rate of poll tax was that the Han government did not rely on this source for most of its revenue. There was no such thing as land distribution, nor was there a limitation on land holdings. The rich and the powerful amassed large tracts of land, while the very poor did not have a spot of earth of their own. The larger the holdings an owner had, the larger the amount of land tax he would have to pay. Poll tax, on the other hand, did not take into consideration the difference between the rich and the poor. It is encouraging to note that the poll tax of the Han dynasty was only a little more than 13 standard coins per year.

The poll tax increased considerably during the early years of Wei Wu-ti (A.D. 210's).[39] Then a governor named Yüan Shao ordered the payment of four pints [40] of grain for each *mou* of cultivated field and two bolts of silk and two catties of floss for each household. The household tax was further increased to three bolts of silk and three catties of floss during the reign of Tsin Wu-ti (r.265–289). But this increase was more apparent than real. According to the Tsin statutes, each adult male was granted seventy *mou* of land for cultivation; women and minors also received land from the government in various amounts. Thus people who paid the household tax were all landowners; it is not surprising that it was larger than that during the Han dynasty. However, once a precedent was established, it was followed without question. Household tax tended to become larger and larger with the passage of time.

The system of land distribution reached its most glorious age during the time of the Later Wei (386–535) and was followed with modifications by the North Ch'i (550–577), the North Chou (557–581), the Sui (590–618), and the T'ang regimes. The tax systems of these regimes seem to differ from one another only slightly; extant materials are too scanty to reconstruct a picture in detail. Generally speaking, there are more royal decrees in these materials concerning taxation on households than those on land. Since each household received land from the government, taxation on households and taxation on land were really the same thing; there was no need to separate these two. In other words, land taxes were included in household taxes.

The T'ang dynasty, however, changed this situation. It divided a citizen's obligations to the government into three categories: the payment of rice or other kinds of grain as land tax, the payment of silk, floss, and cloth as household tax,

39 Wei Wu-ti was the posthumous title of Ts'ao Ts'ao.
40 A measure equivalent to 31.6 cubic inches.

and finally, the performance of corvée duties on the part of all adult males. One thing, however, remained the same. Each adult male received one hundred *mou* of land from the government for cultivation; some of these would be returned to the government for redistribution upon the death or retirement of the grantee and others could be inherited by his children. A person's tax and service obligations were based upon the fact that he had received from the government one hundred *mou* of land for the maintenance of his livelihood.

After the middle period of the T'ang dynasty this system began to deteriorate. The government could no longer prohibit the buying and selling of distributed land once the land was in the hands of a grantee. Eventually the land distribution system had to be abandoned. As a result most of those who paid taxes in produce and performed corvée duties were actually landless. Is it fair that these people should pay the same amount of taxes as the rich and the powerful who had acquired for themselves large tracts of land? Moreover, during and after the An-Shih revolt[41] people were forced by circumstances to move from one area to another. The old population registers became useless; how could they still be used as the basis for collecting taxes? After a social upheaval of enormous proportions in which millions of people had either perished or been routed from their homes, how was it possible to continue a tax system which could only thrive in peace?

During the time of war and civil disturbances the only thing that could not be moved or lost was land. For this reason the semi-annual tax system,[42] introduced in the fourteenth year of Ta-lieh (779), was clearly a laudable remedy because it was based upon the total amount of land actually under cultivation. It did, however, have some shortcomings, one of which was the requirement that tax payments be made in cash rather than local produce such as silk. As the prices of produce continued to drop, the amount of taxes in terms of produce would continue to rise. A point was eventually reached when the amount of taxes a farmer had to pay was twice as much as the amount levied at the time when the semi-annual tax system was introduced, and taxpayers suffered greatly from this increasing taxation in terms of their produce. It should be remembered, however, that most of the complaints voiced by the taxpayers were centered on the harshness of the tax collectors who wished to collect as much as possible; they bore no relation to the basic nature of this system which, I believe, was fundamentally sound.

While the arguments raised by Lu Hsüan-kung and Ch'i K'ang no doubt have great merits,[43] it is still true that a primary prerequisite to the payment of taxes in produce was the reestablishment of the land distribution system so that all farmers in China would have an equal amount of land for cultivation. As long

[41] This refers to the rebellion led by An Lu-shan and Shih Shih-ming. The rebellion began in 755, a year that marked the end of a glorious period and the beginning of the T'ang dynasty's decline.

[42] The semi-annual tax system (*liang-shui fa*) was introduced by Yang Yen, the prime minister, during the reign of T'ang Te-tsung (r.780–804). It was a graduated tax system, based upon the ability to pay, and all payments were to be made in cash, instead of produce as had been hitherto the case. It was called the semi-annual tax system because the payments were made twice a year, one on the sixth and the other on the eleventh month of the year.

[43] The real name of Lu Hsüan-kung was Lu Chih (d.805), a famous scholar-official of the eighth century, who opposed the introduction of the semi-annual tax system. Ch'i K'ang (d.804), his contemporary, took a similar stand.

as the equalization of land ownership remained an impossibility, there was no better alternative to the semi-annual tax system.

For many dynasties in the past the sole criterion in differentiating the amount of poll tax was the difference in age. It did not take into consideration the difference in wealth, a difference which had existed for a long time. Was it not absurd to impose the same amount of tax on a destitute man and a youngster who had recently inherited a large fortune? The semi-annual tax system corrected this inequity by making income, instead of age difference, the basis to determine the amount of taxes each individual had to pay. Lu Hsüan-kung maintained that the government's assessment of each individual's cash payment was often partial and unfair and that it cultivated falsehood and generated cheating on the part of the taxpayer. Since money was light in weight compared with produce, he continued, a wealthy person could easily carry his money with him, leave his home community, and move to another area where he did not have to pay taxes and perform corvée duties. Those who were left behind would have to work doubly hard so as to shoulder the burden which he, a dishonest person, had successfully evaded. Thus the semi-annual tax system, concluded Lu Hsüan-kung, only succeeded in encouraging the evasion of corvée duties as well as cheatings in tax payments.

Though there is plenty of justification in this criticism of the semi-annual tax system, it should be pointed out that the abuse of this system stemmed from the lack of honesty and impartiality on the part of government officials and had nothing to do with the system itself which was basically sound. To become wealthy, a person could either pursue the essential profession by working diligently on his farms or follow such non-essential profession as trade. It is true that rich merchants could easily evade their tax obligations on account of their mobility and that farmers, attached to land, had no way of escaping from whatever taxes were imposed upon them. But, under the semi-annual tax system, the farmers who were obligated to pay taxes were those who were able to pay. Is it not true that this system was still better than the inflexible system of paying taxes in produce in which all people, regardless of whether they were rich or poor, had to pay the same amount simply because their names happened to appear in the tax register?

That the amount of taxes to be paid to the government should be in proportion to the amount of land held by the taxpayer is a principle sound and valid at all times. There was a different tax system for each of the Three Dynasties, but all of them used land holdings as the basis for taxation. There were no such things as poll or household taxes.

The tax system throughout Chinese history may be summarized as follows: During the Three Dynasties there were no taxes on households even though each household was granted land for cultivation by the government. During the Former and Later Han dynasties the land-granting system was abolished, but the household taxes, upon which the government depended for most of its revenues, were generally light. The worst tax system was that practiced between the Wei and the middle period of the T'ang dynasty. The government imposed heavy taxes on households under the pretense that it had granted land to the taxpayers. The truth is that while the taxpayers could not depend upon the government for land-granting on a regular basis, they had to pay taxes nevertheless; and once taxes were raised, rarely were they reduced. All of these abuses were eliminated under the semi-annual tax system. Can we belittle it simply because it was introduced by Yang Yen? [44]

104 · HUANG TSUNG-HSI: *Land Taxation* [45]

Emperor Yü conducted a land survey to determine the amount of taxes to be levied. When the Chou dynasty was established, it did likewise. Since this process was repeated, the Chou government apparently felt that it could not rely on the findings obtained during the Hsia dynasty. Then each feudal state was responsible for its own well-being; the fertility of cultivated fields, the size of population, and whatever changes occurred in either of them were the concerns of an individual state, not those of the central government.

The situation changed with the abolition of the well-field system. Early in the Han dynasty land taxes were one-fifteenth of a farmer's produce, and they were reduced to one-thirtieth during the Wen-Ching period.[46] During the reign of Han Kuang-wu (r.25–57) the tax rate was one-tenth at the beginning but was reduced to one-thirtieth shortly afterwards. In each case the tax rate was low. The imposition of a light taxation stemmed from the consideration that since the empire was large, the government could not grade all lands in accordance with their productivity so as to determine different tax rates, and that, by levying taxes at a low rate, it was hoped that even people on the poorest land, after paying their taxes, would have a tolerable livelihood. If the peasants on the poorest land did not complain about their taxes, went the argument, nobody else would either, and consequently all people in the empire would feel economically secure. Meanwhile the work and expenses involving the survey of land and the differentiation of land productivity would be avoided.

A rate of one-thirtieth in produce was the lowest tax rate ever recorded. It corresponded to the lowest rate of the nine-rate system [47] prevalent during the best years of the Three Dynasties. Why is it that the Han dynasty could afford a low tax rate which the Three Dynasties were not even able to match? Is it true that the Han dynasty was more enlightened than the Three Dynasties?

The Three Dynasties practiced the well-field system; the peasants tilled the land which was owned exclusively by the government. Private ownership of land began in the Ch'in dynasty after the well-field system had been abolished, and the government began to levy taxes on land which it no longer owned. Though the rate of one-thirtieth in produce seemed small, it was actually higher than the rates prevalent during the Three Dynasties. People of later ages did not understand this and contended that since the rate of one-tenth was the ancient practice and since the rate of one-thirtieth was only a temporary measure of the Han dynasty, the tax rate should be increased to one-tenth in order to conform to the law of ancient times. They did not realize that since the government did not own the land, a tax rate of one-tenth would be equivalent to the highest rate of the nine-

[44] Yang Yen was regarded as a bad minister by most Confucian scholars.
[45] *Ming-yi tai-fang lu,* Essay No. 11.
[46] The reigns of Han Wen-ti (r.179–157 B.C.) and Han Ching-ti (r.156–141 B.C.).
[47] The nine rates were high-high, high-middle, high-low, middle-high, middle-middle, middle-low, low-high, low-middle, and low-low.

rate system practiced during the Three Dynasties. How could the people not become economically distressed when such a high tax rate was imposed? During the time of Han Wu-ti, time and again the government felt that it needed a larger revenue to meet its expenses. It raised money by selling titles, floating loans, increasing commercial tax, monopolizing the manufacturing of iron and salt, and many other measures. But it never increased taxation on land. Had the increase of land taxes been a sound course to resort to, it seems unlikely that his finance ministers would not have thought of it.

Though often labelled as an ancient practice, the one-tenth rate was anything but such a practice. Moreover, even this rate was not constantly adhered to whenever a government needed additional revenue as a result of recurrent warfare. In other words, land taxation was no longer based upon what the land could produce, but what the government needed in meeting its expenses. The increased taxation, introduced as a temporary measure to meet a contemporary need, remained in the law book long after such a need had disappeared. It was further increased when another contemporary need occurred. In short, once taxes were increased, they were rarely reduced. That is why taxes become increasingly heavier with the passage of time and people of later ages were more financially distressed than people of an earlier period. "After the abolition of the well-field system," said a Confucian scholar of the Han dynasty, "the policy of love [48] was no longer observed, and consequently people have become poorer and poorer."

What the Han scholars could not foresee was that because of the increasingly heavy taxation, the people of the Wei-Tsin period (220–420) were poorer than the people of the Han period (202 B.C.–A.D. 220) and that the people of the T'ang-Sung period (618–1279) were poorer than the people of the Wei-Tsin period. Since the well-field system was not practiced during any of the above-mentioned periods, we cannot say that the increasing poverty of the people resulted primarily from the government's failure to restore such a system.

Today most of the government's revenues are collected in areas south of the Yangtze River. As far as land taxes were concerned, they did not become unbearably heavy in these areas until the time of Ch'ien Shu.[49] The Sung dynasty continued this heavy taxation throughout its existence. This heavy taxation became even heavier during the time of Chang Shih-ch'eng,[50] and throughout the Ming dynasty no attempt was made to reduce the increased rate. Thus taxes on cultivated fields, beginning at the rate of 3 pecks per *mou,* were eventually increased to 7 pecks per *mou.* Besides there were charges on "official depreciation," [51] plus non-official collections. Since a *mou* of cultivated fields could not yield more than 1 picul (10 pecks) of grain, such heavy taxation meant that even if a peasant turned in all of his harvests as taxes, he would still be in debt to the government. This heavy taxation, begun as an expedient measure in a turbulent age, has become a major curse of our own time.

[48] *Jen cheng.*
[49] Ch'ien Shu was an independent ruler of the Lower Yangtze (Wu-Yüeh) in the middle decades of the tenth century. He later surrendered his principality to the Sung regime soon after the latter's establishment.
[50] A warlord who controlled the Lower Yangtze in the 1350's.
[51] On the assumption that a sizable portion of grain, after being collected and stored in the government's warehouses, would become rotten and thus useless, the government collected a larger amount than that allowed by the statutory rate.

I feel that if a truly great monarch ever comes to rule China, he would rectify the entire tax structure and make the lowest tax rate of ancient times the norm for all areas in the empire. Some people might say that the government cannot meet its expenses if the tax rate is reduced to one-thirtieth of the produce. To these critics I would say that the central government in ancient times derived its income from a small area of only 10 *li* in radius around the capital, plus 10 percent of each feudal state's revenue shipped to the central government as tribute. Nowadays the provinces and districts keep only 10 percent of the collected revenue for their administrative expenses and ship 90 percent of the tax income to the central government. If a 10 percent collection was adequate for the maintenance of an ancient government, how is it possible that a 90 percent collection is inadequate today?

105 · Po Chü-yi: *The Harmful Effects of Using Money to Pay Taxes* [52]

A good tax system is one in which all forms of taxation, including land and household taxes, are paid in what the people produce. Since grain and silk are the items which the people produce, to require people to pay taxes in cash in addition to what they have already paid in produce is a violation of this principle. Where can the people obtain copper coins for the fulfillment of their tax obligations when their mulberry groves do not yield copper and when they themselves are not allowed to mint copper coins? When the tax collector presses them for the fulfillment of such obligations, they have no choice except to trade their produce for copper coins. In a bumper year when grain is cheap in terms of money, they will have to sell it at half of its normal price in order to meet the tax payment; even then it is doubtful whether their produce can yield enough cash for the tax purpose. In a bad year the situation will be considerably worse. They will have to borrow money to meet their tax obligations by paying an interest of 100 percent per year; and once a debt is incurred, it is doubtful that they can ever get out of it. Thus the farmers have no hope for a better future even in good years.

The big landlords and the wealthy merchants, taking advantage of this situation, have become more and more wealthy and have bought large tracts of land. Meanwhile those who work diligently in the fields all year round have become poorer and poorer. Our social ills have become increasingly serious as the gap between the rich and the poor continues to widen.

Under these circumstances, how can we blame a farmer if he wishes to abandon farming and take up trading, or if his wife desires to stop weaving and occupy herself with a more profitable engagement such as embroidery? If a large number of farmers decide to follow his example, the fields will lie fallow and the people will become poorer. While land resources remain to be exploited, manpower continues to be wasted. The four seasons evolve in vain when they are not utilized for the raising of crops. The more carefully this problem is scrutinized, the more

---

[52] The original appears in *The Ch'ang-ch'ing Collection of Mr. Po (Po-shih ch'ang-ch'ing chi)*, by Po Chü-yi (772–846), a famous poet of the T'ang dynasty. A copy can also be found in *Jih-chih lu,* roll 11.

convincing is the conclusion that the high price of money in terms of produce is one of the most serious weaknesses of our economy.

While it is true that a high price of grain will be harmful to the consumers, it is also true that a low price will be injurious to the farmers. High price of grain will entail budgetary difficulties for those families that do not produce it; low price of grain, on the other hand, will lessen the farmers' interest in farming. An enlightened monarch, therefore, should see to it that the price of grain is neither too high nor too low, that goods circulate freely, and that all of the four classes [53] in our society will benefit from the operation of a dynamic economy. When this goal is achieved, not only can the government collect enough revenue to meet its administrative expenses, the people will also become economically secure.

The total number of coins now in circulation has become smaller and smaller. Some of them are stored in the government's treasury while others are held by individuals. The number in circulation will be drastically reduced if the government continues to demand the payment of taxes in cash. Meanwhile, as money becomes more scarce, grain and silk will be worth less and less in terms of money. Such a development will be very harmful to farming and sericulture. If this trend continues, it is not difficult to visualize how disastrous the situation will be ten years from today.

A good tax system has two important features: first, all taxes are paid in produce and second, the amount to be paid varies with the size of the crop or the size of mulberry groves. Under this system not only will the land resources be fully developed, the harmful effects that result from the selling of produce for cash will be also eliminated. The farmers will feel economically secure in continuing farming, while those who have left farming for trade may return to their original occupation. Even the mercenaries and the professional wanderers may decide to take up farming. The first step to all of these healthy developments is an order from the government that from now on money will no longer be required for tax payments.

106 · KU YEN-WU: *The Disadvantages of Using Money to Pay Taxes* [54]

A nation's wealth is determined by the amount of grain it produces; money is necessary only in the sense that it facilitates exchange or trade.

From the Three Dynasties to the T'ang period, land taxes were paid in produce such as grain and silk. It was not until the introduction of the semi-annual tax system by Yang Yen that land taxes began to be paid in copper coins. Even then silver was not used for tax payments.

According to *Han shu*, the Ch'in regime had two kinds of money in circulation, none of which was made of tin or silver. These metals were only used for making utensils or for decoration purposes. It was not until the Liang dynasty (502–557) that gold and silver were reported to have been used as mediums of exchange in Chiao-Kuang.[55] In the second year of Ching-yu (1035) during the reign of

---

[53] The four classes were scholars, farmers, artisans, and merchants.
[54] *Jih-chih lu,* roll 11.
[55] Modern Kwangtung Kwangsi, and Vietnam.

Sung Jen-tsung (r.1023–1063) the government for the first time ordered that silver be used for tax payments in Fukien, Kwangtung, and Kwangsi; it would, on the other hand, accept silk in Chiangtung,[56] and copper coins in all other provinces. There were two reasons why silver was required for tax payments for the three provinces mentioned above; namely, the large number of silver mines in this area, and the sea trade conducted by the coastal people. However, it was not until the time of Chin Chang-tsung (r.1190–1208) that silver was minted to make coins. The coins, formally named "Treasures of Peace," [57] were legal tender for all business transactions, public or private. Despite the existence of silver coins, we know that people continued to use unminted silver as medium of exchange as early as the Cheng-ta period (1224–1231).

Silver has been so customarily used as money that we tend to forget how this custom began. As late as the Yüan dynasty the amount of taxes paid in silver constituted only a small portion of the total tax revenue. In other words, the important role which silver played in tax collection has a history of only two or three hundred years. . . . Had silver been designated as the only acceptable item for paying taxes, where would the additional silver come from if, say, taxes were suddenly doubled?

Some people have convincingly argued that since farmers cannot produce money in the field, to require them to pay taxes in money is to encourage them to abandon such an essential occupation as farming so as to take up such a non-essential occupation as trade. They suggest that all taxes should be paid in produce. Few people have cash in hand, let alone cash in the form of silver. It seems to me that the interests of both the government and the people will be better served if a large degree of flexibility is introduced insofar as tax payment is concerned. Taxes should be paid in produce in areas where trade does not play an important role in people's economic life; even if money is considered necessary as part of the tax payments, it should not constitute more than 30 percent of the total assessment. . . .

107 · KU YEN-WU: *Heavy Taxation in the Lower Yangtze Valley* [58]

Ch'iu Chün,[59] in his book *Supplementary Notes to an Elaboration of the Great Learning,*[60] remarked as follows:

"Han Yü (768–824) once said that of the total amount of taxes collected in the empire, 90 percent came from the areas south of the Yangtze River. Today, of the total amount of taxes collected in the areas south of the Yangtze, 90 percent comes from the Lower Yangtze Valley. Of the total amount collected in the Lower Yangtze Valley, 90 percent comes from five prefectures. These five prefectures are Soochow, Sungkiang, Changchow, Chiahsing, and Huchow.[61]

---

[56] Lower Yangtze.
[57] *Ch'eng-an t'ung-pao.*
[58] *Jih-chih lu,* roll 10.
[59] Ch'u Chün (d.1495) was a famous scholar and economist.
[60] *Ta-hsüeh yen-yi pu.*
[61] The first three were located in modern Kiangsu province, and the last two were located in modern Chekiang province.

"During the Hung-wu period (1368–1398) the total amount of land taxes averaged 29,430,000 piculs of grain per year. To this amount the Chekiang province contributed 2,752,000 piculs; Soochow prefecture, 2,809,000 piculs; Sungkiang prefecture, 1,209,000 piculs; and Changchow, 552,000 piculs. It is easy to see how heavy the tax burden was for people in these areas.

"Now that the national capital has moved to Peking,[62] the amount of land taxes transported to Peking from areas south of the Yangtze River is more than 4,000,-000 piculs of rice per year. The amount collected in the five prefectures mentioned above is about half of the total amount collected in Kiangsi, Hukuang, and South Chihli provinces. Take Soochow as an example. It has seven subprefectures under its jurisdiction and has a total of 96,506 ch'ing of cultivated fields, as compared to a grand total of 8,496,000 ch'ing for the nation as a whole. Yet it pays as much tax as 2,809,000 piculs of grain per year, as compared to 29,400,000 piculs of grain for the entire nation. Taxes being so heavy in the Lower Yangtze Valley, it is no wonder that people in this region have been financially exhausted. . . ."

In the seventh (leap) month of the first year of Hung-hsi (1425) Chou Kan, the lieutenant governor of Kwangsi, made the following report after his return from an inspection tour in the Soochow, Changchow, Chiahsing, and Huchow prefectures.

"In the areas I have visited, I found that a large number of people had deserted their homesteads and fled to other places. The reason for this disheartening phenomenon, according to the village elders, was the unbearably heavy taxation imposed upon the villagers.

"Formerly land tax amounted to 5 pints (0.05 piculs) of grain per *mou* in the Wukiang-Kunshan area,[63] and a tenant farmer usually paid 1 picul of grain as rent to his landlord for every *mou* of land he tilled. Whenever a landlord's land was confiscated by the government, the rent was reduced by 20 percent, and the tenant would pay 8 pecks (0.8 piculs) per *mou* to the government as rent. In the case of land formerly owned by the members of the royal household, the situation was different. There was no reduction of rent whenever the land was returned to the government; in other words, the tenant continued to pay a rent of 1 picul per *mou*. If a rent of 0.8 piculs per *mou* was too burdensome to a peasant, a rent of 1 picul per *mou* was doubtless worse. Suffering from cold and hunger, he had no choice except to flee from his homestead.

"It is hereby suggested that the rent for all government-owned land in this region—the land confiscated from landlords and the land formerly owned by the members of the royal household—should be made the same as the rent for government-owned land in other areas of the empire, namely, 6 pecks per *mou*. Then the abandonment of land to waste by deserting peasants will be discontinued, and those who remain will have a tolerable livelihood."

Upon reading this report, the emperor issued an order saying that this matter should be discussed thoroughly among the responsible officials.

In the second month of the fifth year of Hsüan-te (1430) the emperor [64] issued a decree which read as follows:

"It has been made known to me that the rent for government-owned land varies from place to place and that, the rent being so high, the farmers have encountered

---

[62] The capital of the Ming dynasty was Nanking from 1368 to 1402. It was Peking beginning in 1403.
[63] Located in modern Kiangsu province.
[64] Ming Hsüan-tsung (1426–1435).

difficulties in fulfilling their obligations towards the government. Let it be known that from this year on the rent that has been 1 to 4 pecks per *mou* be reduced by 20 percent and that the reduction be 30 percent if the rent has been hitherto 4.1 pecks to 1 picul per *mou*. Let it be also known that this reduction is meant to be permanent. . . ."

In the Lower Yangtze the farmers who till their own land constitute only 10 percent of the total number of farmers. The overwhelming majority of the farmers, or 90 percent of them, are tenant farmers. The fields they till are small in size. In assessing land for tax purposes, the government considers all ditches and roads that run through the farm as taxable areas. A tenant farmer reaps one harvest each year in the fall and collects anywhere between 1 and 3 piculs of unpolished grain for each *mou* of land. From this amount he pays his landlord anywhere from 8 pecks (0.8 piculs) to 1.3 piculs as rent. He works hard all year round, and a considerable time is devoted to the collection of human and animal waste to be used as fertilizers. His cash expenses for each *mou* of cultivated land are about one string of cash. Thus after the expenses are deducted, his harvest amounts to less than 1 picul per *mou*. It is not unusual that after his rent is paid today, he has to beg for food tomorrow.

108 · LIU TSUNG-YÜAN: *The Snake Catcher* [65]

The wilderness outside Yungchow [66] produces strange snakes whose black bodies are spangled with white dots and stripes. They are so poisonous that whatever trees, shrubs, or grass they touch will soon wither and die. No man can survive long when suffering from their bite. However, their meat, when dried and salted, can be used as a wonder drug to cure a variety of diseases such as apoplexy, rheumatism, and ulcer. It kills germs and produces new flesh.

Because of the medicinal qualities these snakes possess, the imperial physicians recommended that the government collect them, and the government followed the recommendation by imposing on Yungchow an annual quota of two snakes as part of the tax load. The local government then called upon people to catch these snakes, and those who handed their catches to the government would be exempt from taxation. Responding to the government's call, a large number of the Yungchow people were anxious to catch these snakes. However, only the Chiang family has survived this undertaking; in fact, it has monopolized snake-catching consecutively for three generations.

I had the opportunity of meeting with Mr. Chiang, and I asked him how he liked his job of catching snakes. "My grandfather died of it; so did my father," he replied. "I have been in it for twelve years since the death of my father, and I myself almost died on several occasions." He looked very sad, and I felt sorry for him. "Are the snakes really so poisonous?" I asked. "I shall report your grievance to the proper authority, and I am sure that some arrangement can be made whereby you will not have to catch any more snakes. Of course, you will have to pay taxes and perform corvée duties as other people do. Do you wish me to do this for you?"

Upon hearing this Mr. Chiang became even sadder, and tears began to stream

---

[65] *Ku-wen kuan-chih,* roll 9.
[66] Located in modern Hunan province to which the author was then exiled.

from his eyes. "You, sir, no doubt feel sorry for the kind of life I am leading," he replied. "Do you realize that unpleasant though my present duty is, it is still better than the duty of paying taxes? If I did not have my present duty, my life would be much worse. My family has lived in this area for three generations, totalling sixty years. During these years the people became poorer and poorer, and all my neighbors had a difficult time to maintain a tolerable livelihood. They could not meet their tax payments, even though they had contributed all that their land produced and everything that their houses contained. In desperation many left their homes, moved to other places, and never returned, while others who chose not to leave continued to suffer from hunger. These people worked diligently under all kinds of climatic conditions: rain, wind, heat, and cold. Breathing the poisonous air that was prevalent in this part of China, they died in droves.

"Of every ten households that lived in this township during my grandfather's lifetime, less than one has remained. Of every ten households that lived in this township during my father's time, less than two or three have remained. Since I became a snake catcher twelve years ago, more than 50 percent of the original households have become empty. Some perished, and others have moved to other places. Because I am a snake catcher, I have survived.

"Whenever the tax collector came to our township, he caused so much disturbance and fear that even chickens and dogs could not enjoy their tranquility. I woke up from my sleep and, seeing my snake in the jar, I went back to my bed with peace of mind. I fed my snake dutifully, and when the time arrived, I delivered it to the government as my taxes.

"Thus only twice a year I risk my life when I attempt to catch the snakes. For the rest of the year I enjoy what the land produces, and I have a pleasant time. Who among my neighbors has the sense of peace and serenity that I have? Should I die while catching snakes, I shall still have lived longer than most of my neighbors who have died a long time ago. How can I complain that the snakes are poisonous?"

After hearing Mr. Chiang's talk, I felt very sad indeed. Until then I had been doubtful about Confucius' assertion that "Bad government is worse than tigers." Now I am convinced of its accuracy. How many people really know that heavy taxation is worse than poisonous snakes? I write this story in the hope that those who are interested in people's welfare will give adequate attention to the problem of taxation.

109 · MA MAO-TS'AI: *An Eyewitness' Report on Famine Conditions* [67]

Your humble servant was born in Anse subprefecture, Shensi province. I have read many memorials submitted by Your Majesty's officials in connection with the present state of affairs. They say that famine has caused fathers to desert their

[67] This memorial was addressed to emperor Ming Ch'ung-chen (r.1628–1644) in 1629. The famine situations described in it prompted a revolt which blossomed to a nationwide rebellion shortly afterwards. The rebellion eventually toppled the Ming regime in 1644. The original of this memorial appears in the *Shensi Gazette (Shan-hsi t'ung-chih)*, roll 86. A copy can also be found in Li Wen-chih, *The Popular Uprisings towards the End of the Ming Dynasty (Wan-Ming min-pien)* [Shanghai: The Chung-hua Book Company, 1948], pp. 15–16.

children and husbands to sell their wives. They also say that many people are so starved that they eat grass roots and white stones. But the real situation is worse than what they have described. Yenan,[68] the prefecture from which your humble servant comes, has not had any rain for more than a year. Trees and grass are all dried up. During the eighth and ninth months of last year people went to the mountains to collect raspberries which were called grain but actually were no better than chaff. They tasted bitter and could only postpone death for the time being. By the tenth month all the raspberries were gone, and people peeled off tree bark as food. Among tree bark the best was that of the elm. This was so precious that in order to conserve it, people mixed it with the bark of other trees to feed themselves. Somehow they were able to prolong their lives. Towards the end of the year the supply of tree bark was exhausted, and they had to go to the mountains to dig up stones for food. Stones were cold and tasted musty. A little taken in would fill up the stomach. Those who took stones found their stomachs swollen and they dropped and died in a few days. Others who had no wish to eat stones gathered as bandits. They robbed the few who had some savings, and when they robbed, they took everything and left nothing behind. Their idea was that since they had to die either one way or another it was preferable to die as a bandit than to die from hunger and that to die as a bandit would enable them to enter the next world with a full stomach. . . .

There were situations even more pathetic than those described above. For instance, there was a dumping ground to the west of Anse, to which two or three infants were abandoned by their parents each morning. Some of these infants cried aloud; others merely whimpered because they had lost all strength to cry. Some yelled for their parents; others, being so hungry as they were, ate their own excrements.

What seemed strange at the beginning was the sudden disappearance of children or single persons once they wandered outside of the city gates. Later it was discovered that some people in the suburb had been eating human flesh and using human bones as fuel for cooking. By then people knew that those who had disappeared were actually killed and eaten. Meanwhile the cannibals themselves became sick as a result of eating other people. Their eyes and faces became red and swollen in a few days; their body temperature kept on rising until they died.

Wherever a person went, he saw dead bodies. Their odor was so odious that it was simply unbearable. Outside of the city wall people dug several pits, and the pits were so large that each of them could contain several hundred dead bodies. When your humble servant passed through the city, three of these pits had been filled up. Two or three miles further away from the city the number of dead bodies that was not buried was even more numerous. If the number of people who perished in a small city like Anse is so large, just imagine the number of those who died in a large city! One only needs to visit one place to know the situation in all other places. . . .

At the beginning of the Ming dynasty, every ten households were organized as a *chia* and every ten *chia* were organized as a *li*. Most of these households have become empty, and each *chia* or *li* no longer has the number of households it used to have. . . . If a household has now only one or two members, these one

---

[68] This is the same Yenan that served as the capital for the Chinese Communists during World War II.

or two members are still obligated to pay taxes for the entire household. If a *chia* has now only one or two households, these one or two households are still obligated to pay taxes for the entire *chia*. The same is true all the way from the *li* to the subprefectural level. Unable to shoulder the tax burden of the entire organizational unit, the people that have not left or died are forced to flee from their home, reluctant and unhappy as they are. With their roots cut off from the land which once they tilled, they wander from place to place until eventually they lose all the money they originally carried with them. By then they can only dream about their home, while facing the reality of death. Under circumstances like these, it is no wonder that they should choose to become bandits.

110 · SHAO CH'ANG-HENG: *The Siege of Kiangyin* [69]

Two years after the present dynasty [70] was established, Duke Yü [71] led his grand army across the Yangtze River. Nanking surrendered, and King Hung-kuang,[72] accompanied by his ministers, fled, only to be captured shortly afterwards. Fresh from victory, Duke Yü dispatched many Manchu princes and generals to annex all territories in southeast China. The defending officials either surrendered or fled; those who chose to defend their cities only defended them long enough to see them captured—the defense lasted anywhere from a few hours to at most ten days. South of Chinkiang [73] a hundred famous cities fell in less than a month. Yet Kiangyin, a small, insignificant city, managed to hold its ground for more than eighty days before it was finally captured. The man responsible for this heroic effort was the police-master Yen Ying-yüan.

Previously, when the head-shaving order [74] was issued, a Confucian student named Hsü Yung-te chose the first day of the sixth (leap) month to hang an image of Ming T'ai-tsu [75] in the main hall of the local Confucian temple and led people in worshipping and crying before it. Suddenly a crowd of about ten thousand gathered around the temple. The crowd wanted to elect the police chief Ch'en Ming-yü as their leader to defend the city. "I am not so able and brave as Mr. Yen," Ch'en replied. "We cannot undertake this tremendous task without his help." A messenger galloped in the middle of the night to invite Ying-yüan who, without hesitation, arrived at the city with forty of his men in the same evening.

Then the total number of soldiers in the city was less than one thousand, and the total number of households was about ten thousand. Nobody even knew where the food would come from. Soon after Ying-yüan's arrival, he recruited soldiers

---

[69] Shao Ch'ang-heng (1637–1704) was a native of Changchow (Kiangsu province), not far from Kiangyin where the event described in this selection took place. A copy of the Chinese original can be found in *Ming Ch'ing san-wen hsien*, pp. 139–143.

[70] The Ch'ing or Manchu dynasty that was established in 1644.

[71] Better known as Dorgon.

[72] Also known as Prince Fu.

[73] East of Nanking, on the southern bank of the Yangtze River.

[74] In 1645 the Manchu government issued an order that all Chinese should shave part of their heads as an indication of their loyalty to the new government. The penalty for disobeying this order was death.

[75] Chu Yüan-chang, founder of the Ming dynasty.

and repaired defense towers. He ordered each household to contribute one able-bodied man to mind the defense of the city wall while the rest of the adult males would prepare food and transport military provisions. In the defense towers he stored guns and ammunitions that had been manufactured under the direction of the circuit commander Tseng Hua-lung, and he requested rich families to contribute whatever they had for defense: "grain, cloth, silk, and useful items, but not necessarily money." However, a college student named Ch'eng Pi took the leadership of contributing 25,000 taels of silver, and his example was followed by others. Because of these contributions, the city was well equipped with materials of defense when the siege began, including 300 jars of gunpowder, 1,000 piculs of lead and iron balls, 100 cannons, 1,000 rifles, hundreds of thousands of taels of silver, 10,000 piculs of rice, wheat, and beans, and large quantities of wine and spirits, salt, iron, animal feed, and straw.

The defense of the city was assigned to four leaders. Huang Lioh, a man who had passed the civil service examination in military affairs, was responsible for the Eastern Gate; a certain captain, whose name I can no longer remember, defended the Southern Gate. Ch'en Ming-yü was in charge of the Western Gate, while Ying-yüan himself defended the Northern Gate. Hardly had the defense plan been put into effect before the siege began.

The attacking force that gathered outside of the city wall numbered approximately 100,000, encamped in about 100 barracks. It surrounded the city tens of layers in depth. Its soldiers shot upward with bows and arrows and wounded many of the defenders. The defenders, taking advantage of their high position on the wall, fought back with catapults and cannon, and killed a large number of the attackers. Then the attackers moved in some of their largest cannon and tore a huge hole in the city wall. Ying-yüan filled up the hole with chained doors encased in iron plates and strengthened the bulwark by piling earth-filled coffins behind it. Once again the enemy attacked the northern wall, and again there was a huge hole. An order was issued that every man should bring a huge rock towards the hole, and overnight a strong fortification was built inside the city wall and behind the breached point.

The city was then short of arrows. In the darkness of the night Ying-yüan placed straw men between parapets on the wall and hung a lamp besides each of these straw men. The soldiers, hiding behind the wall, beat drums and shouted loudly as if they were about to come down over the wall to raid the enemy's camps. Surprised, the attacking forces rained the straw men (who, they thought, were real soldiers) with arrows. When dawn arrived, Ying-yüan collected a large amount of arrows for his own use. At other nights, however, he did let down soldiers over the wall. These soldiers, taking advantage of favorable winds, set fire to enemy camps, and during the ensuing chaos several thousand enemy troops trampled each other to death.

The headquarters of the attacking force was encamped three *li* outside of the city. One day, its commander, Liu Liang-tso, appeared with his banners below the city wall. "I know Mr. Yen," he cried aloud, "and I would like to speak to him." Ying-yüan agreed to his request. Formerly, Liu was one of King Hung-kuang's four garrison generals, titled Earl of Kuang-pai, who since then had surrendered to the present regime.[76] "Huang-kuang has already fled and there is no

[76] The Ch'ing or Manchu regime.

ruler south of the Yangtze River," Liu spoke from the distance. "If you surrender early, you can keep your position and wealth."

"Though I am only a police-master of the Ming government, I know what the word 'principle' means," Ying-yüan replied. "You, sir, were a general of the Ming regime that rewarded you with a fief and a title and charged you with the responsibility of the Kiang-Huai area.[77] Yet, not only did you fail to defend the territory to which you had been assigned, you have become a vanguard for the enemy. How can you face the righteous people in our city?" Liu was ashamed of himself and left without a word.

Ying-yüan was strong in build, dark in complexion, and wore a small mustache. Stern and strict, he saw to it that his orders were always obeyed. Those who violated them were whipped without mercy. However, he was generous with money and rewarded abundantly those who were deserving. He personally dressed the wounded; and, when a soldier died, he gave him a good funeral, performed the libation, and cried. He never called a soldier by his name but addressed him as "good brother." Ch'en Ming-yü, his lieutenant, was also generous, sincere, and kind. Whenever he toured the wall and inspected its defense, he was often in tears as he comforted the soldiers and complimented them for their industry. The two men were dearly loved by their subordinates who were happy to die for them.

Previously, a Manchu prince had been in charge of annexing territories in the Soochow-Sungkiang area.[78] Now that all of the large cities had been captured, the prince moved his command to strengthen the attacking force that had surrounded Kiangyin. He tied up two Ming generals who had previously surrendered and sent them to an area below the city wall where they knelt and tearfully pleaded for Ying-yüan's surrender. "As defeated commanders, why did you not quickly commit suicide once you were captured?" Ying-yüan scolded them. "What right do you have to come to speak here?" The prince sent a messenger to the city, saying that the siege would be lifted if Ying-yüan would kill one official responsible for the defense of each of the four city gates. Ying-yüan cried aloud in anger: "I prefer to chop off my own head than to kill any of my own people." He scolded the messenger and sent him away.

When the moon festival [79] arrived, Ying-yüan distributed monies among soldiers and civilians as gifts. The soldiers took turns drinking on top of the city wall. For this occasion Hsü Yung-te composed a song called "Ten Hours at Night" and asked a good musician to sing it. The singing mingled with the beating of cooking-pots [80] and the blowing of reed pipes. The celebration continued for three consecutive evenings.

Knowing that the city had no intention of surrendering, the prince intensified his attack. The suicide attackers, wearing heavy armor made of iron, climbed the wall by ladders. The defenders cut them with their knives and axes; hearing a tinkling sound, they noticed that the edges of their weapons had been badly dented. Day and night the cannon roared, and the shaking of the earth was felt as far as one hundred *li* away. Inside the city the dead and the wounded kept

---

[77] The area between the Huai River and the Yangtze.

[78] Both cities were located in modern Kiangsu province, south of the Yangtze River.

[79] Celebrated on the fifteenth day (full moon) of the eighth lunar month.

[80] The beating of cooking-pots signaled alarms, such as a new attack.

on piling up, and weeping and crying could be heard in every lane or street. Standing on top of the city wall, Ying-yüan was even more determined.

One day at dawn the sky broke, and it rained heavily throughout the morning. At noon a red flash rose from a wooden bridge outside of the city wall and sped towards the western section of the city. The wall collapsed, and the attackers, amid rain, fog, and smoke, climbed the wall through the broken point in massive numbers. Leading his suicide squad, Ying-yüan fought from street to street, totalling eight engagements and killing about a thousand. He rushed towards one of the city gates, but the gate had already been closed. Realizing that he could not escape, he jumped into the Front Lake; but, because the lake was too shallow, he failed in his attempt to commit suicide. Liu Liang-tso gave the order that Ying-yüan be captured alive, and he was.

Liu was sitting cross-legged in the main hall of the Ch'ien-ming Temple when Ying-yüan was brought in. Seeing the prisoner, he jumped to his feet, held his captive, and cried. "What are you crying about?" said Ying-yüan. "Now that I have failed, I am waiting for death." Later, when he was brought before the prince, he stood erect and refused to kneel. A soldier nearby hit one of his legs with a spear. The spear pierced through and broke his shinbone; and he collapsed. When the evening drew near, the soldiers took him to the Hsi-hsia monastery. Throughout that night the monks heard him shouting continuously: Kill me quickly; kill me quickly!" Suddenly there was silence, and Ying-yüan was dead.

The siege of Kiangyin lasted eighty-one days. The besieging army consisted of 240,000 men, of whom 67,000 died outside of the city and 7,000 died in street fighting. Its total loss was more than 75,000. Those who died in defense of the city numbered somewhere between 50,000 and 60,000. Every lane or street was full of unburied bodies. Not a single person had chosen to surrender.

After the city had fallen to the enemy, Ch'en Ming-yü dismounted and fought on foot. He was killed in front of the garrison headquarters after suffering severe wounds in several parts of his body. Holding a sword, he stood erect against a wall long after his life had departed from the face of the earth. Other people say that he closed all doors inside a house and then burned himself to death.

111 · Ssu-ma Ch'ien: *The End of a Hero* [81]

Hsiang Yü's troops built a walled camp at Kaisha,[82] but their number was few and their provisions exhausted. They were soon surrounded by several layers of the Han army and its allies. In the night Hsiang Yü heard the songs of Ch'u [83] from the Han soldiers all around him, and he was astonished beyond belief. "Has the Han army already conquered Ch'u?" he exclaimed; "why are there so many Ch'u people in the Han army?" He rose from his bed and began to drink in his tent. With him were a beautfiul woman named Yü who, as his favorite, followed him wherever he went, and a fine steed named Chui, his cherished mount. Full of emotions, he began to sing the sad song which he himself had composed:

[81] Source: "Biography of Hsiang Yü" *(Hsiang Yü pen-chi); Shih chi,* roll 7.
[82] Located in modern Anhwei province.
[83] Hsiang Yü's home state.

> My strength can pluck up a mountain;
> My energy overshadows the earth.
> But in a wrong time I have lived!
> My Chui will cease to run—what can I do?
> Oh, Yü, dear Yü,
> What can you do?

For several times he sang this song, and his favorite Yü joined him in response. Tears streamed from his eyes, and all of his retainers wept with bowed heads. Then he mounted his horse and was followed by more than eight hundred brave horsemen under his command. Under the darkness of the night they broke through the encirclement to the south and galloped as fast as they could.

The Han army did not discover Hsiang Yü's escape until the next morning. When it did, it ordered the cavalry commander Kuan Ying to head a cavalry force of five thousand in hot pursuit. Hsiang Yü crossed the Huai River; [84] by then only about one hundred horsemen were able to follow him. At Yinling [85] he lost his way, and he asked a farmer for directions. The farmer deliberately lied to him by saying "Left"; riding toward the left, he was trapped in a huge swamp. Thus the pursuing Han army was able to overtake him.

Once more he decided to lead his soldiers eastward. By the time he reached Tungch'eng, [86] he had with him only twenty-eight horsemen, while the Han army, which was pursuing him, numbered several thousand. He knew then that he could not possibly escape. "It has been eight years since I led my troops in war," he said to his followers. "I fought and won more than seventy battles before I became the leader of all of China. Here I am—in such a desperate situation! It is Heaven who wishes to destroy me: I myself have never committed any error on the battlefield. Today I have resolved to die, gentlemen; but I shall win three victories for you before that comes to pass. I shall break through the encirclement, kill the enemy commanders, and cut their banners into pieces, so that you gentlemen will know that it is Heaven who wishes to destroy me and that I myself am not short of generalship on the battlefield."

Upon saying this Hsiang Yü divided his horsemen into four bands to face four different directions. Meanwhile the Han army was closing in several layers in depth. "I will get one of their generals for you," he said to his horsemen. He ordered his men to gallop down on four directions, to meet later on in three groups east of the hill. He shouted aloud and down the hill he went. Before him the Han soldiers scattered, and he had no difficulty in cutting down one of the Han generals. Duke Ch'ih-ch'üan, [87] the Han cavalry commander, took pursuit. Staring at him ferociously, Hsiang Yü scolded with a loud voice, so loud that the duke's men and animals panicked and did not stop running until several *li* later. Hsiang rejoined his horsemen who were then divided into three groups.

The Han army did not know which group Hsiang Yü was in and consequently decided to divide its soldiers into three groups likewise, so as to encircle each and

---

[84] Originated from the Honan province, the Huai River passes through the Anhwei province and pours into Lake Hungtze, between Anhwei and Kiangsu provinces.

[85] Located in the northern section of modern Anhwei province.

[86] Located in modern Anhwei province.

[87] His real name was Yang Hsi. He did not receive the title of duke until Hsiang Yü was killed.

all of the enemy's units. Hsiang galloped about among the Han soldiers, killing one capitain and four or five scores of men. Then he gathered his horsemen and found that he had lost only two of them. "Have I not kept my promise?" he asked his followers. "Your words never fail, sir," they all bowed in respect.

Hsiang Yü then thought of crossing the river [88] at Wuchiang [89] and going east-ward. Arriving at Wuchiang, he found that the village chief already had a boat waiting for him in the river. "Even though the area east of the river is compara-tively small," said the village chief, "it still measures one thousand *li* in breath and has a population of several hundred thousand. It does not degrade anyone to become its ruler. I beg you, sir, to cross the river immediately. Since I am the only person who has a boat, the Han army will not be able to get across the river when it arrives." "Why should I cross the river when Heaven has already decided to destroy me?" Hsiang Yü laughed. "When I crossed the river westward, I had with me eight thousand native sons from the area east of the river. Now none of them is returning with me! The elders might have pity on me and choose me as their king, but I cannot bear to face them. How can I face my own conscience even though they might not speak anything about it?" "I know that you are a respectable, honorable man," Hsiang Yü continued. "This is my horse which I have ridden for five years. It has never met its equal and can often run as much as one thousand *li* per day. I cannot bear to kill it, and I would like to present it to you as a gift."

Then Hsiang Yü ordered his horsemen to dismount and to fight on foot with knives and swords in close combat. Though he single-handedly killed several hundred Han soldiers, he himself suffered more than ten wounds. Looking around, he saw Lü Ma-tung, a Han cavalry marshal. "You are an old friend of mine; are you not?" said Hsiang Yü. Lü took a glance at him and then pointed him out to Wang Yi: "This is King Hsiang!" "I have heard that the Han authorities have offered a reward of one thousand catties of gold and a fief of ten thousand households for my head," said King Hsiang; "let me do you a favor." Upon finishing these words, he committed suicide by slitting his own throat.[90] Wang Yi rushed forward to seize his head, while the rest of the horsemen trampled over each other in a struggle to get their shares of his body,[91] killing a few dozen in the process. . . .

With the death of Hsiang Yü, all of the Ch'u territories surrendered. Only Lu [92] refused to follow suit. The King of Han [93] led his troops towards Lu with the avowed purpose of putting to the sword all of its inhabitants. Then, thinking that Lu was a state of cultural and moral refinement and that it merely wished to die for its lord [94] as a matter of principle, he decided not to carry out his original plan. He showed Hsiang Yü's head to the elders of Lu who subsequently sur-rendered their state. . . .

[88] The Yangtze River.
[89] Located on the western bank of the Yangtze, Anhwei province. The river moves along a general north-south direction in this area.
[90] Hsiang Yü died in the twelfth lunar month, 202 B.C., when he was thirty-one years old.
[91] For the purpose of getting rewards.
[92] The home state of Confucius.
[93] Liu Pang, founder of the Han dynasty.
[94] Hsiang Yü.

CHAPTER THIRTEEN

Landownership

B Y THE second century B.C. practically all territories within what we today call China had been brought under the Chinese jurisdiction, and the frontier of agriculture had virtually disappeared. As population continued to increase while the total arable acreage remained substantially the same, a point would eventually be reached when the limited amount of land could no longer support the ever-increasing population. Population pressure and land shortage were the major causes of the dynastic cycle, as we have noticed in an earlier chapter.

Unable to enlarge total land acreage, many Chinese believed that the next best thing was to make the limited amount of land available to all who needed it, so that everyone in the nation would have a tolerable livelihood. This was the principle behind the well-field system, so called because each tract of land, for distribution purposes, was divided into nine equal sections that were shaped like the Chinese character for "well" or 井. This system was said to have been put into practice during the Chou dynasty, though details about its operation are not known. As early as the fourth century B.C. when Mencius was asked to elaborate on it, his answer, as one can find in Selection 112, was far from satisfactory. Land concentration had gone on for a long time by then, and it did not seem that the well-field system could ever be restored. When the Ch'in state, acting upon the recommendation of its chief minister Shang Yang (d. 338 B.C.), formally abolished feudal land tenure and permitted the buying and selling of landownership, it only legally confirmed an existing practice.

The abolition of feudal land tenure sped up the process of land concentration. While the wealthy accumulated hundreds or thousands of *mou* of land, said the Han scholar Tung Chung-shu, the very poor did not have a spot of earth which they could call their own. Ch'ao Ts'o, a statesman of the second century B.C., suggested the selling of titles to the wealthy so as to reduce the tax burden of the poor (Selection 113); one hundred fifty years later, K'ung Kuang, then the prime minister, recommended the limitation of land-ownership to 30 *ch'ing* (or 3,000 *mou*) per household (Selection 114). K'ung's recommendation was brushed aside, and it was not until the assumption of power by Wang Mang (d. A.D. 23) that a drastic measure was taken to nationalize all land and to divide it equally among the farming households (Selection 115). The reform was short-lived, however; and with the establish-

264

ment of the Later Han dynasty, the landed interests once again took over the control of the government.

There were no more attempts at land reform until late in the fifth century when the Later Wei regime, acting upon the recommendation of a scholar-official named Li An-shih (d. 495), introduced and carried out a land distribution system (Selections 116 and 117). Historians regard this land reform as the most successful after the abolition of the well-field system largely because a long period of foreign and domestic wars had reduced population to a very low level and once more there was land available for distribution. In other words, the government did not have to take land away from the wealthy (as in the case of Wang Mang's land reform) so as to give it to the poor (Selection 118).

Following the Later Wei's example, the Tsin, the North Ch'i, the North Chou, and the Sui regimes carried out the land distribution system in various degrees, but details are not known. However, we know a great deal more about the land distribution system implemented during the early period of the T'ang dynasty (Selection 119), though the T'ang effort, like those preceding it, lasted only a short period. Beginning in the Sung dynasty no attempt was ever made to equalize landownership until the Taipings tried a similar measure in the nineteenth century.

From the eighth to the nineteenth centuries and over a period of more than one thousand years, statesmen and scholars argued among themselves as to whether the land distribution system of ancient times could be restored. Some answered the question negatively (Selections 120 and 121), while others were more optimistic (Selection 122). The Taipings failed in their attempt since their regime lasted only a brief period; future historians will doubtless make their own judgement as to how successful the Chinese Communists are in trying to solve one of China's most difficult problems.

112 · MENCIUS: *The Well-Field System* [1]

Duke Wen of T'eng asked Mencius about the best way to govern a country; Mencius answered him as follows: [2]

"The tax system of the Hsia dyansty was called *kung* in which each farmer was required to pay as taxes the produce of five of the fifty *mou* granted to him by the government. The tax system of the Yin dynasty [3] was called *tsu*. According to this system, a tract of land was divided into nine sections, each section consisting of seventy *mou*. The eight surrounding sections were tilled separately by eight different households, while all of them tilled the central section in common. The produce of the central section would go to the government as taxes. The tax sys-

---

[1] "T'eng Wen-kung" *(T'eng Wen-kung p'ien); Book of Mencius,* roll 3.
[2] Part of the answer unrelated to the well-field system is not included in this translation.
[3] Shang dynasty.

tem during the Chou dynasty was called *ch'e*. This system was the same as *tsu*, except that each household tilled one hundred instead of seventy *mou* of land. In all cases the taxes paid to the government amounted to approximately 10 percent of the produce.

"Lungtzu [4] once said: 'As for land taxation, the best system is *tsu,* and the worst system is *kung.*' In the latter system the average yield of several years is used as the basis of taxation, and taxes remain the same in each and every year. As a result, in good years the amount of taxes is proportionally small in terms of the bumper crops, while in lean years people have to pay the same amount even though they may not even have the resources to fertilize their own fields. How can a ruler be still considered father and mother of the people when his subjects look at him with hatred because they work hard all year round and yet do not have enough means to support their parents? How can he call himself father and mother of the people when his subjects have to borrow money to make both ends meet, while the aged and the young are suffering from starvation in the gutter?

"As for the system of hereditary salary for the scholars, Your Highness has already put it into practice. Says the *Book of Odes:*

> Oh, rain!
> Come down to the lord's common first
> Before descending on my own section.

"Only when the *tsu* system is practiced can there be such an institution as the lord's common. From the above quotation we know that the *tsu* system was put into practice during the Chou dynasty." . . .

Duke Wen of T'eng sent his minister Pi Chan to obtain more information from Mencius about the well-field system. Mencius replied as follows:

"Your lord has chosen you to carry out the 'policy of love,' and it is my sincere hope that you should do your very best. The first step to the implementation of the 'policy of love' is to make clear and distinct the boundary lines between fields, otherwise the amount of land for each section would not be the same and, consequently, the harvest collected from it as officials' salaries would be different. This is the reason why a tyrannical ruler or corrupt official should wish to confuse boundary lines. Once the boundary lines are made clear and distinct, the division of land and the amount of salary each official receives will become fair and equitable.

"Your country, T'eng, is located in a remote area and its territory is small. Nevertheless, it has scholar-officials as well as common people. These two groups of people are interdependent on each other. Without scholar-officials the common people would not have anyone to govern them; without common people the scholar-officials would not have anyone to give them a means of livelihood. I propose that in the border areas the *tsu* system should be adopted and farmers should pay one-ninth of their produce as taxes. In the central areas of the country, however, farmers should pay only one-tenth of their produce. All public officials with ranks below that of a minister [5] should receive fifty *mou* of land for their own support. Upon reaching the age of sixteen, a boy will be considered an associate

[4] An ancient sage about whom we know little.
[5] *Ch'ing.*

member [6] of his family and should receive from the government twenty-five *mou* of land.[7]

"All people should live and die in the areas where they are born, and they should not be allowed to leave their own communities. The farmers who till land under the well-field system will be brotherly towards one another, whether at home or in the field. They will cooperate in preventing thievery and banditry, and they will help and support the unfortunately ill. A sense of love and harmony will prevail upon the people in the countryside.

"I propose that every square *li* (or 900 *mou*) of land should be divided into nine sections of 100 *mou* each. The central section is the common, and the eight surrounding sections are owned by eight different households. All the eight households should jointly till the common before they can work on their individual sections. This is the way of differentiating common people from scholar-officials.

"What I have said is merely an outline. It is up to you and your lord to make whatever additions or subtractions deemed necessary."

113 · CH'AO TS'O: *On the Value of Grain* [8]

To prevent cold and hunger from inflicting his people, an enlightened monarch does not grow food to feed them or weave to clothe them; he only opens for them the existing natural resources. During the reigns of Yao and Shun there was a flood that lasted nine years; and when T'ang [9] was the emperor, a drought continued for seven years. In each case, not a single person died of starvation. Why? This was because these monarchs had stored enough food in preparation for natural disasters. Now that the country has been unified and that its land and population are no smaller than those during the period of Shun and T'ang, why is it that the stored grain is less than adequate, in view of the fact that we have neither natural disasters nor flood and drought that last for several years? The reason is that land resources and manpower have not been fully utilized. Not all arable land has been put under cultivation; forest and water resources have not been duly utilized; and the unemployed have not been put to work as farmers.

Only when people are poor do they go morally astray. Poverty results from the inadequacy in material supplies which in turn is caused by the lack of efforts in agricultural activities. Those who are not engaged in agriculture are not attached to the land where they live; and like birds and beasts, they leave their home casually without regret. As a means to deter people from moving away from their homesteads, harsh laws and severe punishments are no more effective than high walls and deep moats which cannot stop them. When a man suffers from cold, he is not particular about the clothing he is going to wear; when he is hungry, he eats whatever is available. After cold and hunger have arrived, he cares little about honesty and shamefulness. It is a common knowledge that we would suffer from hunger if we were denied two meals a day and that we would be at the mercy of the weather if we did not add new clothes each year. When a man is

[6] *Yü-fu.*
[7] According to Chu Hsi's interpretations, the boy's allotment would be increased to one hundred *mou* once he reached adulthood and was married.
[8] "Economics, Part I" *(Shih-huo chih shang); Han shu,* roll 24a.
[9] Founder of the Shang dynasty.

hungry and cannot find food, or when he is cold and cannot find clothing, even his loving mother cannot keep him as her son. How, in such a case, can a monarch keep him as his subject?

Knowing this truism, an enlightened monarch promotes agriculture and seri-culture, reduces taxes and requisitions, and encourages savings so as to fill up the grain storages—these storages would be open for the needy during a period of drought or flood. Only by adopting these measures can he keep all the people as his subjects. His functions are like those of a shepherd who guides his flocks along a proper path. Without such a guidance people will seek profit as water seeks the lowest ground regardless of directions.

Pearl, jade, gold, and silver can neither quench hunger nor clothe one's body; yet all people value them highly. Why? It is because the monarch uses them. They are light in weight and small in volume and can be easily stored. Carrying them in his hand, a man can travel the world without worrying about cold or hunger. Their light weight and high value enable a minister irresponsibly to desert his king, a man easily to leave his home, and a bandit or thief effortlessly to get away from the law. Grain and cloth, on the other hand, are raised from the ground, grow slowly with the passage of time, and require collective efforts be-fore they can be utilized. Since an average person cannot carry a weight of several piculs, grain and cloth cannot be as easily hidden or carried away as precious stones or metals are. Yet, without them for a single day, a man will suffer from cold and hunger. This is why an enlightened monarch values highly the five grains [10] and regards lightly precious stones or metals.

Now, in a household of five, at least two of them have to work in the field. The amount of land they can cultivate cannot be more than 100 *mou* which yield approximately 100 piculs of grain. They plow in the spring, weed in the summer, harvest in the fall, and store their harvest in the winter. They cut wood and grass for fuel; they support the government with taxes as well as labor services. They expose themselves to wind and dust in the spring, heat in the summer, dampness and rain in the fall, and freezing cold in the winter. All year round they do not have a single day when they can rest themselves. Besides, there are guests to be entertained, bereavements to be condoled, and sick people to be comforted. Orphans have to be supported, and the young have to be raised. Working dili-gently like this, these small farmers still cannot escape from the harsh treatment at the hands of unsympathetic officials or cruel laws. Taxes and requisitions are imposed often and repeatedly; a law is proclaimed in the morning, only to be changed in the afternoon. Those who have things to sell are forced by circum-stances to sell them at half of their true worth; those who have nothing to sell have to borrow money by paying an interest of 100 percent. As their debt continues to increase, sooner or later they may have to sell their land, houses, or even children.

The situation is entirely different with the merchants. The big merchants store and hoard their merchandise; and when they sell, they sell things at a price twice their cost. The small merchants sit beside their goods which are displayed to attract customers. All of them hold in their hands the rare and the profitable and

[10] There are several versions of "the five grains." According to one version, the five grains are rice, wheat, barley, beans, and sesame seeds.

travel daily in large cities. Taking advantage of an urgent need, they sell goods to the government at such a price as to bring a hundred percent return on their investment. Because profits are so large, their males need not plow or weed, and their females do not have to weave or raise silkworms. Yet they wear the best kind of clothes and eat the choicest meat. They do not have the hardships experienced by farmers, but they enjoy a material comfort equivalent to that of a great landlord. As they are rich, they are able to communicate with those in power, and the influence they can exercise is greater than that of government officials. They befriend one another as they possess a common denominator, wealth; and they travel thousands of *li* to seek pleasures. Their carriages line the road for a long distance, and they ride on the best of horses. Their shoes are made of silk; so are their robes. It is no wonder that the merchants have successfully exploited the farmers who are forced to desert their homesteads.

Our law degrades the merchants, but the merchants have become increasingly wealthy nevertheless. It honors farmers, but farmers have become poorer and poorer. Those the people honor are exactly those the monarch despises; those the law elevates are those for whom the officials show contempt. As the government and the people march towards the opposite directions, how is it possible that the law will be respected and the nation be enriched?

To promote agricultural production is our most urgent task today. To do so, we shall place a high priority on the value of grain. Grain, in fact, should be used as a means of reward and punishment. Let the order be issued that those who contribute grain to the treasury be granted official titles, or given clemency should they be found to have committed crimes. By using this device we achieve three purposes simultaneously: the rich will acquire the coveted titles, the poor will become financially better off, and the government will have grain at its disposal. Taking the surplus from the rich to meet governmental expenses, we do not need to tax heavily the poor; the surplus will go wherever it is needed. Once such an order is issued, it will benefit all people concerned. Specifically, it will enable the government to acquire enough funds to meet its expenses, to reduce tax load, and to promote agricultural production.

According to the present law, a household which makes available to the government a chariot-horse whenever it is needed is entitled to exemption from military services for three of its members. Shen-nung [11] once said: "Even though the stone wall is as high as eighty feet, the moat is as wide as one hundred paces, and the military force is as large as one million men, a city cannot be defended if it lacks food." Such being the case, the promotion of grain production should be a monarch's first concern and a basic item in the government's policy. Yet, according to the present law, a person who contributes grain to the government's treasury is entitled to only one military exemption for his household and is awarded a title no higher than that of the fifth rank. This is a far cry from the honor awarded to those who contribute horses. The granting of titles is a monopoly of the monarch who, in fact, can grant as many titles as he desires. Grain, on the other hand, is raised by the people; and, since it grows only from the ground, its supply is clearly limited. All men desire high titles and all criminals want to receive clemency. I hereby propose that those who contribute grain to the border

[11] A legendary culture-hero.

regions should be given official titles and that, if they happen to be convicted criminals, their guilt should be considered nullified. If the proposed measure is adopted, there will be plenty of grain in the northern border regions.

114 · PAN KU: *The Limitation of Landownership* [12]

After Ai-ti (r.6–1 B.C.) ascended the throne as the emperor, Shih Tan, who served as the regent, reported to him as follows:

"After a long period of war which followed the dissolution of the Chou-Ch'in regimes, the country was woefully inadequate in the supply of natural and man-power resources. Emperor Hsiao-wen,[13] upon ascending the throne, promoted farming and sericulture and personally led the nation in cultivating the virtue of thrift. There was no land aggrandizement then, and consequently there was no need to limit the ownership of either land or slaves.

"Now that the nation has enjoyed peace for several generations, a situation has meanwhile developed whereby the extremely wealthy, including many government officials, have succeeded in amassing large fortunes, while the very poor have become poorer still. While it is understandable that a gentleman should wish to follow established policies rather than to initiate innovations, innovations are necessary if the situation has deteriorated to such an extent that it presents an urgent need for reform. Though I have no detailed plans at the moment, I do feel that there should be some limitation on landownership."

The emperor ordered that discussions be held among responsible officials in connection with this proposal.

In response to the emperor's request, K'ung Kuang, the prime minister and Ho Wu, the Grand Counselor, made the following proposal:

"It is suggested that the limitation of landownership be applied to all principalities, all princes who presently reside in the capital of Ch'angan, all princesses who have landholdings in provinces and districts, all the princes with the Kuan-nei title,[14] and all government officials and common citizens. Let the maximum amount of land a person can own be limited to 30 *ch'ing*. As for the number of slaves a person can own, let it be limited to 200 for princes with the rank of 'king,'[15] 100 for all princesses or princes with the rank of 'duke,'[16] and 30 for the Kuan-nei princes, government officials, or common citizens. The excessive amount of land or slaves will be confiscated by the government should they not be disposed of by individual owners in a period of three years."

The prices of both land and slaves dropped as a result of this proposal.

The proposal was never carried out, however, largely on account of the opposition expressed by the powerful Ting-Fu families [17] and also the emperor's favorite, Tung Hsien.[18] The emperor issued a decree saying that the implementation of this proposal be postponed for the time being, but the postponment turned out to be more than temporary.

[12] "Economics, Part I" *(Shih-huo chih shang); Han shu,* roll 24a.
[13] Han Wen-ti (r.179–157 B.C.).
[14] Princes who did not have fiefs of their own and resided in the capital area *(Kuan-nei).* They were of a lower rank (19th) among the princes.
[15] *Wang.*
[16] *Lieh-hou.*
[17] The emperor's relatives.
[18] A handsome man with whom the emperor was reported to have had homosexual relationship.

115 · WANG MANG: *The Reestablishment of the Well-Field System* [19]

In ancient times when the well-field system was in operation, every eight households shared one well-field, and each household, consisting of a husband and a wife, tilled one hundred *mou* of land. Since taxes were only one-tenth of the produce, not only was the nation sufficient, the people were also well-to-do. Being happy and contented, they sang praises to their rulers. This was the situation in the times of Yao and Shun and during the Three Dynasties.

The wicked Ch'in rulers, however, changed this state of affairs. They increased taxes for the enhancement of their personal comfort and imposed heavy corvée duties to satisfy their selfish desires. They destroyed a sound institution devised by our ancient sages by abolishing the well-field system. As a result, people annexed the land of one another and became avaricious and greedy. The strong acquired land amounting to thousands of *mou,* while the weak did not have even a small lot where they could build their own house. Slave markets were established, and slaves were housed in the same places as cattle and horses. In the eyes of the government the lives of the slaves were of no consequence. Moreover, cruel and unscrupulous men, taking advantage of their connections with high officials, went to such extremes as to kidnap people's wives and children and offer them for sale in the slave market. Their activities violated the principle of Heaven as well as that of sound relationship among men. It was in direct contrast to the nature of Heaven and Earth and the dignity of individuals. The *Book of History* says: "Enslave you I shall." By this it meant that only those who refuse to obey the law will suffer this severe punishment.

When the Han dynasty was established, taxes on land were considerably reduced, to something like one-thirtieth of the produce. But often were there additional levies, from which even the aged and the sick were not exempted. Moreover, the wealthy and the powerful frequently encroached upon the rights of the poor, forcing the latter to share their harvests with them without in the meantime sharing the tax burden. As a result, while in name the tax rate was one-thirtieth of the produce, the actual amount was something like 50 per cent. No matter how hard a family worked all year round, it rarely received enough to keep its members above the starvation level. While the wealthy had surplus grain to feed dogs and horses, the poor did not even have chaff to fill up their empty stomachs. Proud and arrogant, the wealthy were inclined to be villainous; destitute and helpless, the poor were tempted to engage in lawless activities. Both groups became victims of their own environment and had to be punished in accordance with the law. The cases of such punishment are too numerous to enumerate.

Formerly, when I was at Talu [20] I issued my first order in connection with the nationalization of land and the reestablishment of the well-field system. At that time the omen was good and we had bumper crops. Unfortunately, due to the opposition of certain rebellious elements, this order had be revoked. Now let me reiterate the order that from now on all land belongs to the nation, all slaves are private possessions, and neither land nor slaves are subject to trade. A household which has a male membership of less than eight but a landholding of more

---

[19] "Biography of Wang Mang, Part II" *(Wang Mang chuan chung); Han shu,* roll 99b.
[20] This place cannot be easily identified.

than one *ch'ing* should distribute the excessive amount among its relatives, neighbors, or fellow villagers. The landless will receive land from the government in
accordance with the law. Those who dare to criticize this well-field system, a
system devised by our ancient sages, will be exiled to the frontier where they will
serve as defenders against the monstrous barbarians.

116 · LI AN-SHIH: *On the Restoration of the Land Distribution System* [21]

I have heard that to divide land among the people is an important policy of all
times and that to coordinate the needs between urban and rural areas is a prerequisite to good government. To achieve this dual purpose, the ancient governments practiced the well-field system in which the total amount of land a person
could own was subject to a legal limit. By this device it was hoped that no land
would lie in waste and every unit of manpower would be effectively utilized. As
long as the well-field system was enforced, no families were powerful enough to
monopolize all land in the countryside and to enjoy the yields of nature to the
exclusion of others, while an unattached individual, however insignificant he was,
could have his share of land from which he derived a tolerable livelihood.

For several generations in the past there have been people who either sold or
abandoned their fields in bad years, wandered aimlessly in different parts of the
country, and did not return home until the three-elder system [22] was established.
Upon their return they found that their deserted homesteads had been buried in
wilderness, and the trees around their houses had long since disappeared. Owing
to the fact that a long time had elapsed since they or their ancestors had left their
native villages, it could not be established for certain that they were in fact the
rightful owners. In the minds of others, they might be imposters. Meanwhile, the
powerful and the wealthy, invoking evidences which might date as early as the Wei
(220–265) or Tsin (265–317) dynasties or calling witnesses that were often their
friends or relatives, laid claims to large tracts of land which, justifiably or
unjustifiably, they called their own. As they continued to press their claims for
years, even the respectable elders in the village became confused. In a lawsuit
involving land titles, the judges were at a loss to differentiate truth from falsehood, as both sides supported their claims with written documents as well as oral
statements from their friends or relatives. As the lawsuits dragged on for many
years without the prospect that they could ever be resolved, even the best land
was allowed to continue to lie fallow and mulberry leaves grew and then withered
without being utilized.[23] Under such circumstances, how was it possible that
people had enough means to support themselves?

---

[21] "Biography of Li An-shih" (*Li An-Shih chuan*); *Wei shu,* roll 53.
[22] The three-elder system or *san-chang chih* was introduced during the early years of
Wei Hsiao-wen-ti's reign (r.471–499). Under this system village chiefs or elders were
chosen from experienced farmers among the villagers. Besides giving advice on better
farming methods, a village chief administered justice, collected taxes, and saw to it that
the destitute in the village—the incurably ill, the disabled, the orphaned, and the
widowed—were financially taken care of by the entire village. He did not receive any
salary; his remuneration consisted of tax exemptions and exemption from labor and
military services.
[23] Silkworms are fed on mulberry leaves.

Though it would be difficult to restore the well-field system of ancient times in its entirety, attempts should be made to put into effect that part of the sysem which is both proper and applicable under our present conditions. Each person should be granted land in accordance with his occupation and ability, so that not only would the most insignificant individual be able to acquire the means of a livelihood, the land of the wealthy would also be fully utilized to yield maximum results. Mountains, rivers, lakes, and ponds—all of these should be declared public property, and their yields should be enjoyed equally by all. As for lawsuits involving land title, they should be resolved in a specified time; if evidences are not clear or adequate enough to render a decision, the side that is at present in physical control of the land in question should be declared the legal owner. In this way the dishonest will be stopped in their efforts to win land from others, while the honest will be able to keep the land which is legally their own.

117 · WEI SHOU: *Land Distribution During the Later (North) Wei Dynasty* [24]

In the ninth year of T'ai-ho (485 A.D.) the emperor [25] issued a decree ordering land distribution. The decree reads as follows:

"A male subject, upon reaching the age of fifteen, is to be granted 40 *mou* of open fields. [26] A woman is to be granted 20 *mou* of open fields. Slaves will be granted the same amount of land as common people.

"After a male subject has attained full adulthood, he is to receive from the government one ox and 30 additional *mou* of land. The maximum of oxen a household can own is limited to four.

"If the granted land is of such low quality that one half of it has to lie idle each year, the amount of granted land will be doubled. If two-thirds of the land have to lie idle each year, the amount of granted land will be trebled. All land granted under this category is for the tillers only; the amount can be increased or decreased. It is returnable to the government for redistribution.

"A person is granted land upon reaching the taxable age. The granted land will be returned to the government upon the retirement or death of the grantee.

"Slaves and oxen are granted by or returned to the government in accordance with their presence or absence in the households of the grantees.

"In addition to the open fields described above, there are mulberry fields [27] that are not required to be returned to the government for redistribution. . . . Each adult male is to receive 20 *mou* of mulberry fields upon which he should plant 50 mulberry trees, 5 dates, and 3 elms. He will further receive one additional *mou* of land for the sole purpose of growing dates and elms, but not mulberry trees. Slaves will be granted the same amount of land as common people.

"The trees described above should be planted within three years after land is granted. The government will forcibly take away that part of the land from the grantee who has not planted trees on it. The grantee will be allowed to plant mulberry trees or elms in excess of the minimum amount or to plant fruit trees in areas designated for mulberry trees or elms.

---

24 "Economics" *(Shih-huo chih); Wei shu,* roll 110.
25 Wei Hsiao-wen-ti (r.471–499).
26 *Lu-t'ien,* fields that had no trees planted on them.
27 *Sang-t'ien,* fields that were planted with trees, especially mulberry trees.

"Fields that are returnable to the government for redistribution [28] should not be planted with trees—mulberry trees, elms, or fruit trees. Those who violate this rule are punishable in accordance with the law.

"All mulberry fields are hereditary property and are not required to be returned to the government upon the death of the grantee. The amount of mulberry fields a household can own depends upon the size of its membership. Those households who own more than the legal minimum will not receive land from the government; nor will the government take away from them the excessive amount. On the other hand, those households who own less than the legal minimum will receive the difference from the government. A person who owns more than the legal minimum can sell the surplus to others if he chooses to do so; a person who owns less than the legal minimum can buy the difference from others if he is able to do so. But under no circumstances should a person sell below, or buy above, the legal minimum.

"In addition to the open and mulberry fields described above, each adult male is to receive 10 *mou* of hemp fields from the government. It is five *mou* for an adult female. Slaves will be granted the same amount of land as common people. All hemp fields are returnable to the government for redistribution.

"A household that consists of disabled or crippled persons and does not have among its members able-bodied men or women who receive lands as those described above will receive one half of the amount generally granted to adult males for each of its members over the age of eleven. Land thus granted is not required to be returned to the government if the disabled or crippled person is presently seventy years old or above.

"A widow who chooses not to remarry will receive the same amount of land as that granted to other women. Moreover, her land is exempt from taxation.

"All land transactions—the granting of land to the cultivators or the returning of land to the government for redistribution—should be conducted in the first month of each year. All events that occur during the intervening period, such as the death of the grantee and the buying or selling of oxen and slaves, will not be taken into consideration until the first month of the following year when the granting or returning of land, oxen, and slaves is scheduled to take place.

"In areas where land is abundant and population is small, local officials should do their utmost to borrow laborers from other areas to cultivate the hitherto uncultivated land. If any of these borrowed laborers choose to settle down in the areas permanently, he should be granted land in accordance with the law.

"In areas where the population density is large and the amount of arable land is small, a person's mulberry fields will be subject to redistribution if he refuses to migrate to the less populated areas when requested to do so. The rule of doubling grant in the case of inferior land will be suspended if, after mulberry fields in an area have been made redistributable, there is still not enough land to go around. If land shortage is still encountered despite the measures described above, the amount of land granted to each of the members in a household will be proportionally reduced in accordance with the seriousness of the shortage. The above rules are applicable to all areas where there is no distribution of mulberry fields.

"In densely populated areas where there is a land shortage, people are allowed

---

[28] Open fields.

to emigrate to any other district or province where there are virgin or abandoned fields to be opened up. However, under no circumstances should this rule be interpreted to mean that the government is encouraging people to avoid a life of hardship so as to pursue a life of ease. In areas where there is no land shortage, people are not allowed to emigrate to other areas.

"The grantees who establish their homesteads for the first time should be given one *mou* of land for every three persons for the purpose of building houses. The allotment for slaves is one *mou* for every five persons. . . .

"The land of those who have been exiled or banished upon criminal convictions and those who have no heirs upon their death will be declared public land and is subject to redistribution among the needy. The same rule is applicable to abandoned houses and mulberry trees and elms that have not been attended to. . . .

"The amount of public land government officials are entitled to receive varies with their positions and ranks. A governor-general is to receive 15 *ch'ing* of land; a governor, 10 *ch'ing*; a governor's deputy or assistant, 8 *ch'ing*; and a district magistrate, 6 *ch'ing*. Land thus granted is attached to the office, not to the person. After an official leaves his office, the aforesaid land is to be taken over by his successor. Those who sell it during their tenure of office are punishable in accordance with the law."

118 · CHENG CH'IAO: *The Success of Wei Hsiao-wen-ti's Land Distribution System* [29]

After the abolition of the well-field system, seven hundred years elapsed before Hsiao-wen-ti of the Later Wei dynasty, acting upon the recommendation of Li An-shih, successfully carried out the land distribution system. This example of land distribution was followed by the Tsin dynasty which, during the reign of Tsin Wu-ti (265–289), granted seventy *mou* of land to each adult male and thirty *mou* to each adult female. Fifty *mou* of the land granted to each adult male were taxable; it was twenty *mou* in the case of adult females. All minors, male or female, were exempt from taxation. Since extant records are far from detailed, we do not know in what ways land was actually distributed; nor do we know the process in which land was returned to the government for redistribution upon the death or retirement of the grantee.

The question is often raised: how could the Later Wei regime practice land distribution long after the well-field system had been abolished? Would confusion not be created and complaints raised when the government, in its attempt to equalize landownership, took land away from the rich to give it to the poor?

If we examine the land distribution law of the Later Wei carefully, we will see that the land which was subject to redistribution was confined to open fields only and that mulberry fields were not subject to redistribution. The open fields did not have trees planted on them, while the mulberry fields, which could be inherited by the owners' heirs, were planted with mulberry trees and elms. It seems that the fields which had been appropriated by the government for distribution

[29] Cheng Ch'iao, a historian who lived early in the twelfth century, was the author of *General Record (T'ung chih)* in which this selection appears. A copy of the Chinese original can also be found in *Wen-hsien t'ung-k'ao*, roll 2.

purposes were abandoned and ownerless land; the former owners could either have been exiled to faraway places as a result of criminal conviction or have died without leaving legitimate heirs. The abandoned fields, plus the homesteads and the trees on them, were all public properties and could therefore be used for distribution among the landless. It is not true that the land which was given to the poor had been taken away from the rich.

Again, according to the law, those who had landholdings larger than the amount distributed among the landless did not have to hand over to the government the excessive amount, even though they were not entitled to receive land from the government. On the other hand, a farmer whose landholdings were smaller than the amount distributed among the landless would receive the difference from the government. Besides, those whose landholdings exceeded the legal amount could sell the excess if they chose to do so; those with small acreage could of course purchase land from others until the total holdings were on a par with the legal limit. But no man was allowed to sell if his landholdings were below those of the legal limit, and no man was permitted to buy beyond the legally allowed amount. Thus the trading in land was even encouraged in order to achieve the purpose of equalization of landownership. It is obvious that the government did not forcibly take land away from the rich so as to give it to the poor.

In short, Wei Hsiao-wen-ti's land reform was vastly different from that of Wang Mang. Such difference may have been the reason why the land reform of the Later Wei was devoid of abuses and lasted much longer.

119 · LIU HSÜ: *Land Distribution During the T'ang Dynasty* [30]

In the seventh year of Wu-te (A.D. 624) the law governing the measurement and distribution of land was promulgated for the first time. The law read as follows:

"Five feet are to be considered one pace. Two hundred forty square paces are equal to one *mou*. One *ch'ing* consists of one hundred *mou*.

"Each adult male [31] is to be given one *ch'ing* of land. A person who is incurably ill or disabled will receive forty *mou* of land. Widowed wife or concubine will receive thirty *mou*. The head of a household will receive twenty *mou* in addition to his regular allotment. Of the amount of land each person receives, 20 percent is hereditary and the rest is redistributable.[32] Upon the death of the grantee, the hereditary portion can be inherited by the head of the household next in line, while the redistributable portion is to be returned to the government for redistribution among other people.

"As for the grantee's obligations towards the government, each adult male is to pay two piculs of grain each year as rent.[33] Besides, there are requisitions [34] that vary in accordance with the products of his native district. He is to deliver

[30] "Economics, Part I" *(Shih-huo chih shang); T'ang shu,* roll 48, by Liu Hsü (d. c.940), a scholar-official during the early period of the Five Dynasties.
[31] The term "adult male" includes both *chung-nan* or "middle adult" (from eighteen to twenty-one years old) and *ting-nan* or "full adult" (twenty-one years old and older).
[32] The Sung historian Ma Tuan-lin maintained that this particular regulation was applicable to adult males only.
[33] *Tsu.*
[34] *T'iao.*

to the government each year two *chang* [35] of damask silk. If he chooses to pay in cloth instead of silk, the assessment will be increased by 20 percent. For a person who selects to pay in silk, he should add three ounces [36] of floss to his payment. If he pays in cloth, he should add three catties of hemp. In addition to the payments in produce, he is required to work twenty days each year for the government.[37] He can, if he wishes to, translate his corvée obligations into payment in kind, at the rate of three feet of silk for each day of corvée service. He will be exempt from silk or cloth payment if, when the necessity arises, he is called upon to work twenty-five instead of twenty days. He is to be exempt from both grain and silk or cloth payment if he is called upon to render labor services for a period of thirty days. Under no circumstances should the corvée duties last a period longer than fifty days.

"Rent is to be paid in rice in the Lingnan provinces.[38] For tax purposes all households in these provinces are to be divided into three categories: high income, medium income, and low income. Each year they are to pay 1.2, 0.8, and 0.6 piculs of rice respectively. These amounts are to be reduced by 50 percent if the taxpayers belong to the Yi or Liao minorities.[39]

"As to the northern barbarians who have been Sinicized and live under Chinese jurisdiction, cash instead of produce will be accepted for tax payment. The payment is ten standard coins for a member of the high income household and five standard coins for a member of the medium income household; the members of a low income household are exempt from poll tax. However, if these barbarians have lived under Chinese jurisdiction for a period of two years or more, each of their male adults is required to deliver to the government two heads of sheep each year for high income households and one head of sheep for medium income households. The tax rate for low income households is one head of sheep for every three male adults.

"Taxes will be reduced in proportion to the seriousness of natural disasters, such as flood, drought, plague of locusts, and frost. If more than 40 percent of the planted crop is destroyed during a natural disaster, the affected taxpayer does not have to pay any rent. Both rent and silk or cloth obligations are cancelled if more than 60 percent of the planted crop is destroyed. All obligations towards the government, including corvée duties, cease automatically if more than 70 percent of the planted crop has been destroyed.

"All households in the nation are to be divided into nine categories in accordance with the amount of properties they possess. Under the supervision of its magistrate, the grading of households in each district should be done once every three years. Such grading should be then examined, checked, and made official by the provincial authorities.

"One hundred households form a hamlet, and five hamlets form a township. A neighborhood consists of four households, and a *pao* is composed of five households. Those who live in cities are organized into wards, and those in the countryside are grouped into villages. All people in each of the organizational units—

---

[35] One *chang* is equivalent to ten Chinese feet.
[36] *Liang,* a Chinese ounce.
[37] According to Ma Tuan-lin, it was twenty-two days in leap years.
[38] Modern Kwangtung and Kwangsi provinces.
[39] These minorities can still be found in modern Kwangsi, Kweichow, and Yunnan provinces.

village, ward, neighborhood, or hamlet—are urged to emulate one another in good behavior.

"The four classes of people—scholars, farmers, artisans, and merchants— earn their livelihood by engaging in their respective professions; they should not compete with people socially below them for the purpose of making profits. Artisans, merchants, and people of miscellaneous occupation are not allowed to associate themselves with scholars.

"After a person is born, he or she is classified as an infant. When he reaches the age of four, he is called a child. A child becomes a junior adult when he is sixteen. He attains full adulthood when he reaches the age of twenty-one. Beginning in his sixtieth year, he is classified as a senior citizen.

"Each year responsible officials should record people of different age groups in accordance with the above classifications. The registration of all households should be made once every three years. Five copies of the registration should be deposited with district and provincial authorities, and three copies should be filed with the executive branch [40] of the central government."

120 · YEH SHIH: *The Impossibility of Restoring the Well-Field System* [41]

Those who say that they love the people can be classified into two categories: worldly officials who are concerned with a present need; and scholars who indulge themselves in the discussion of idealistic but impractical solutions. Thus, insofar as our land problems are concerned, the more conservative of the reformers wish to design a program whereby the process of land concentration can be stopped and the more radical of them openly advocate the restoration of the well-field system. All of them are doubtless motivated by their desire to bring benefit to the people.

The various measures designed to prevent land concentration in the hands of a few have been carried out in districts and provinces where government officials happen to be alert, steadfast, and upright. As for the restoration of the well-field system, scholars for the last hundred years have been mapping and designing various means to achieve this purpose and exchanging information and ideas among themselves. However, knowing the impracticability of their programs, they have not ventured to present these programs to the imperial government for possible adoption. Even if they did, it is unlikely that their programs would be given much attention.

Their programs may be praiseworthy from a logical or theoretical point of view, but it is doubtful that these programs, even if they could be carried out, would be beneficial to our society. In my opinion, the restoration of the well-field system is not one of the best policies to follow. The prerequisite to its restoration is the nationalization of all land in China. Even if this prerequisite could be met, it is still doubtful that the system itself could be restored. King Wen, King Wu, and Duke Chou would not be in favor of its restoration if they were living today.[42]

[40] *Shang-shu sheng.*
[41] *Wen-hsien t'ung-k'ao,* roll 1. As for the author, see p. 167, Footnote 34.
[42] They were the founders of the Chou dynasty and were regarded as China's model rulers by traditional historians.

Why is it that the well-field system cannot be revived? One reason is that this system requires detailed planning and minute regulation which are no longer possible today. From the time of the Yellow Emperor [43] to the time of the Chou dynasty the territory under the king's direct jurisdiction was very small; and such being the case, it was not difficult to survey and record every small lot of land within this jurisdiction. Moreover, government officials had no important functions other than the supervision of a smooth operation of the well-field system throughout the year. Their duties included the recruitment of workers, the rectification of boundary lines between fields, and the maintenance of irrigation ditches and canals. Outside the king's domain each feudal lord managed his country in a similar manner. And all this work was made comparatively easy by the fact that governmental posts were hereditary. All things considered, it is not surprising that the well-field system was successful in ancient times. Even then the areas south of the Yangtze and the Han and east of the Wei and the Tzu did not implement this system.[44]

After China was unified, officials at all levels were under the direct jurisdiction of the central government. They were replaced every two or three years as a matter of routine; local officials with high ranks were usually replaced in a period of less than a year. How could an official introduce and then carry out a program in less than a year when ten or twenty years are required to put it on a firm basis? What would the farmers do in the meantime? What would become of the nation when farmers ceased to cultivate their fields while waiting for the implementation of the well-field system?

The disestablishment of the well-field system by Shang Yang was followed by the abolition of feudalism. Since the well-field system was closely related to feudalism, it is inconceivable that the former could exist after the latter had been abolished.

To run a successful farm in accordance with the well-field system requires the most efficient utilization of all labor forces. The digging and the maintenance of surrounding and separating ditches, for instance, are both laborious and time-consuming. These ditches look pleasant to the eyes, but the farm they serve do not yield more crops than a modern farm of the same size. Today farmers dig canals to lead water from its mountain origin to the low land, and by the use of brooks and ditches, successfully irrigate their fields. They break a confining dam whenever water is needed, and with a minimal effort they manage to achieve a maximum result. In this respect they are not inferior to the farmers of the Three Dynasties who practiced the well-field system. Despite the change of time, the goal of agriculture remains the same, namely, to produce an amount of food large enough to meet the need of the entire nation.

The fact that farmers of the later periods were not so well off as farmers of the Three Dynasties has nothing to do with the failure to implement the well-field system; it has a great deal to do with the fact that in ancient times there were no poor farmers. What is gone cannot be retraced; what has been abolished cannot be restored. The dykes and the embankments, the streams and the ponds—some of them were in existence one hundred years ago but have since then disappeared. If these landmarks can be obliterated and become untraceable in a short

[43] Huang-ti, a legendary emperor of the remote past.
[44] The Han River originates from modern Shensi province, flows southeastward, and pours into the Yangtze near Hankow in modern Hupeh province. The Wei River and the Tzu River are located in modern Shantung province.

period of one hundred years, how can we trace the original designs of the well-field system which existed more than two thousand years ago? Over the many million acres of land, villages formed and then moved, established and then lost—how is it possible to trace the well-field system before Shang Yang abolished it?

Confucius and Mencius lived in a period when the Chou dynasty had already declined. Though the well-field system was then no longer in force, its general principles were well known. The two sages sighed with regret that this good institution of the ancient kings had been destroyed by tyrranical despots and corrupt officials and admonished their contemporaries to pay great attention to the rectification of boundary lines between fields. Later scholars, who have never seen or heard how the well-field system was actually operated, echo the two sages with the same sorrow and regret, saying that the well-field system should be restored. The question is this: can it be restored?

Nowadays there are unthinking officials who wish to bankrupt the wealthy in order to support the poor. Their suggestion is at best a temporary, remedial measure and should not be relied on as a permanent policy. Why should these officials wish to make this suggestion? One of the reasons is that these officials, especially those on the provincial and district levels, have to busy themselves all year round with the lawsuits started by the wealthy; these officials become impatient and angry with the wealthy, and would like to eliminate them if they could. But is this the fault of the wealthy? It is unfortunate that district officials could not provide a means of livelihood for the people under their jurisdiction and their duties in this respect have been taken over by the local wealthy. This transfer does not come about overnight; it becomes finalized only after a long period of evolution.

The poor who have no land of their own become the rich men's tenants. Those who are extremely poor sell either their service as servants or their bodies as slaves. The artisans, the entertainers, and the loafers—all of them depend upon the wealthy for making a living. In each community there are numerous requisitions in addition to the regular taxes. Local officials, pressed by higher authority to collect these requisitions, appeal to the wealthy and receive what they need. It is no exaggeration to say that the wealthy are the pillars in any district or province and are relied on by both the government and the people for rendering essential services. They support the poor as well as provide the government with what it needs. It is true that they continue to enrich themselves by buying more land, but in view of the amount of work they have to do and the services they have to render, it does not seem that the profits they realize are too excessive. To be sure, there are those who are harsh and oppressive and acquire land as if they could never stop. In such a case, local officials should warn them against their selfishness, and if they do not take heed, punish them in accordance with their offense. The purpose is to make these rich people aware of their mistakes and to correct and reform them whenever the necessity arises. It is wrong for a local official to go beyond this limit, harbor hatred at heart, and punish them in a severe manner in order to show off his own authority or earn a reputation.

It is very sad indeed that government officials should regard the destruction of the wealthy as one of their primary objectives, while the government itself cannot and does not provide a livelihood for the poor. This objective will set the poor against the rich and vice versa, and no man will be happy in the end. I believe that a better purpose can be served if the scholars cease to talk about the possibility of restoring the well-field system and the unthinking officials tone down their ideas about curbing the rich's acquisitive activities. A wise policy is one well-adjusted to its time, and a good law is a law that has taken into consideration the changing circumstances. It is my belief that if sound institutions are established above, the wide gap between the affluence of the very wealthy and the poverty of the extremely poor will be greatly narrowed in ten years and the acquisitive activities of the wealthy will stop by themselves. And all people, including the very poor, will enjoy a more satisfactory livelihood. This is the objective that the king and his ministers should constantly and diligently strive for. People render a great disservice to the nation by indulging in idle talks and artificially creating divisions between the government and the people, while knowing only too well that the well-field system of ancient times cannot be restored and that our urgent need is a new system for the present. How can a good government come about when unthinking officials continue to regard illusions as reality and scholars continue to seek a reputation for themselves by pretending to be lofty and idealistic?

121 · MA TUAN-LIN: *On the Restoration of the Well-Field System* [45]

Since the abolition of the well-field system by the Ch'in regime, scholars and gentlemen have sighed with regret that their rulers are either unwilling or unable to restore this system of the Three Dynasties to benefit the people and that they are closing their eyes to the fact that the powerful and the wealthy have continued to enlarge their landholdings to enrich themselves. While there is much justification in their complaint, their arguments are nevertheless misleading. In this regard Su Hsün [46] and Yeh Shih [47] are two standouts because, in discussing the well-field system, they alone take into consideration the changing circumstances from ancient to modern times and evaluate objectively the merits and demerits of the system in question. I shall elaborate further the arguments advanced by Yeh Shih.

It is difficult to talk about the well-field system since we know little about its operation. According to the Chou law, each household was granted one hundred *mou* of land for cultivation if the land was so fertile that it could be cultivated consecutively year after year. The granted land would be increased to two hundred *mou* if one half of the land had to be fallowed every year. If the land was so poor that two-thirds of it had be fallowed each year, the amount of granted land would be increased to three hundred *mou*. It is clear that before the well-field system was put into practice, the ancient government must have known the various degrees of fertility of each tract of land. Again, according to the Chou law, a household of seven persons would receive the best kind of land; it would receive land of medium productivity if its membership was six and poor land if its membership was five. Thus the government must have known in advance the size

---

[45] *Wen-hsien t'ung-k'ao*, roll 1.
[46] Su Hsün, though overshadowed by his more illustrious son Su Shih (1036–1101), was nevertheless a great scholar in his own right.
[47] The author of the preceding selection.

of each household within its jurisdiction. Under the well-field system it was estimated that an efficient farmer could support a family of nine, and the number of persons a farmer could support would be reduced to eight or even seven if he was less efficient. Thus the ancient government must have known the diligence, or the lack of it, of each of the farmers to whom land was granted. Again, according to the Chou law, each of the male members of a household would receive twenty-five *mou* of land once he reached the age of sixteen, in addition to the one hundred *mou* of land granted to the head of the household. People who were engaged in professions other than farming—scholars, artisans, and merchants— would receive twenty *mou* of land per household; *i.e.,* five non-farming households were equivalent to one farming household insofar as land granting was concerned. Thus the ancient government must have had a thorough knowledge of not only the age difference of all of its people but their professions as well. In other words, it must have known in minute detail every street or village in the nation before it could foresee and consequently prevent the pitfalls inherent in the process of land granting and its subsequent returning to the government for redistribution. The well-field system could not be put into practice without such detailed knowledge.

How is it possible that the ancient kingdoms possessed such knowledge? At that time, outside the king's personal domain the country was divided into feudal fiefs, each of which was ruled by a duke, marquis, earl, viscount, or baron.[48] Within the king's personal domain the land was further divided among the king's ministers and deputy ministers. Each member of the nobility, whether outside or inside the king's personal domain, ruled a territory no larger than one hundred square *li*. The territory was hereditary, and the ruler knew his subjects as well as if they were his own children. Such being the case, the ruler did not encounter any difficulties when he divided his subjects' fields in the well-field fashion, rectified the boundary lines whenever necessary, and made them responsible for each other's welfare. Meanwhile government officials also received a fair share of the harvested crops. There were no greedy, aggressive bullies who encroached upon other people's rights in violation of the law; nor were there corrupt officials who tampered with the books so as to benefit themselves.

During the Spring and Autumn period (722–481 B.C.) the feudal lords fought among themselves and annexed each other's territories. As the total number of principalities was reduced to less than one hundred, the size of each principality increased. However, with the passage of time each of the principalities was broken into small entities by powerful ministers who, nominally serving the prince, were hereditary rulers within their respective domains. The Fei domain of Chi and the Ch'eng domain of Meng in the state of Lu; the Ch'üwo domain of Luan and the Tsinyang domain of Chao in the state of Tsin—these were the outstanding examples of hereditary domains ruled by powerful ministers.[49] Even such small principalities as Chu, Chü, T'eng, and Hsieh [50] lasted several hundred years. Each of these hereditary domains or principalities had a territory of fifty to seventy square *li*; being so small in size as well as in population, it did not encounter any difficulties whenever it decided to introduce new laws or institutions.

It is my opinion that the rulers of those days, who granted one hundred *mou*

48 *Kung, hou, pai, tzu,* and *nan.*
49 Lu and Tsin were located in modern Shantung and Shansi provinces respectively.
50 All of the four principalities were located in modern Shantung province.

of land to each of their subjects upon his attainment of adulthood and took the land away from him upon his retirement, acted no differently from the great landlords of our own times who inherited landholdings from their ancestors and rented them out to their tenants. In both cases the tillers of the land are either given or deprived of the land they till in accordance with the degree of their industriousness or the lack of it. The amount of rent a landlord collects varies with the amount of crops that have been harvested. Growing up in the countryside, he knows the strong and weak points of each of the fields he owns; he does not need thorough study or investigation to locate responsibility whenever things do not go so smoothly as they should have. Consequently, cheating and duplicity do not arise.

The situation changed during the period of Warring States (403–221 B.C.). After a long period of incessant warfare, only seven major states remained, and the small states, which had somehow managed to survive, were few in number. Each state became larger and larger in size, and its population became more and more numerous. Its ruler was primarily concerned with military conquests, paying little attention to the welfare of its people. Though the well-field system was not completely abolished, it was rampant with abuse. It was then that Mencius remarked: "Nowadays people, working diligently as they do, cannot support either their parents or their wives and children," and he accused tyrannical rulers and corrupt officials of treating with contempt the boundary lines between people's fields. It is clear that land-granting was still practiced then and that the causes of abuse lay in the difficulties of enforcing the rules that governed the well-field system, difficulties that resulted from the large size of the states and their numerous populations. Cheating and duplicity became more and more serious as the well-field system continued to deteriorate.

The Ch'in dynasty abolished the well-field system altogether, and each person was allowed to own or till as much land as he was able to. Taxes were levied in accordance with the amount of land a person owned. According to Ts'ai Tse,[51] Shang Yang's purpose of abolishing the well-field system and the boundary lines between the fields was to "purify the people and strengthen their will." It is obvious that by the time of the Ch'in regime the land-granting system of the Chou dynasty had become so chaotic that it was no longer a fair, equitable system.

The Han dynasty was unable to restore the well-field system of the Three Dynasties after it had succeeded the Ch'in. Why? Local officials were transferred from one post to another on short order, while the distribution of land and its returning to the government for redistribution were so complicated that the procedure, if attempted, was bound to be abused. Even the most enlightened and the shrewdest officials could not make this system work. Since a local official could not stay in his post for a reasonable length of time, how was it possible for him to know all about the land and the people within his jurisdiction, a knowledge necessary to the operation of the land-granting system as practiced during the Chou dynasty? In the absence of officials with long tenure, the responsibility of distributing land would have to be vested in the hands of local clerks. How could these clerks be able to carry on this stupendous task without causing ill effects

---

[51] A native of the state of Yen, Ts'ai Tse served as Ch'in's chief minister during the middle decades of the third century B.C.

that would be felt for many generations to come? There would be lawsuits involving land titles which could not be resolved for many, many years. Fairness and impartiality had to be observed at all times if the operation of the well-field system were to be successful. In what ways could the government achieve this noble goal? . . .

Beginning in the Ch'in-Han period there were two basic difficulties in carrying out the land distribution system. First, the empire was large; so was the population. Second, after the abolition of feudalism and the establishment of central administration, land was no longer the ruler's private possession, nor were administrative posts hereditary. During the T'ai-k'ang period (280–289) of the Tsin dynasty each adult male was reported to have received seventy *mou* of land in accordance with the law, but unfortunately, due to the inadequacy of documentary evidence, we know little about the operation of this system. Shortly afterwards the barbarians invaded and then occupied North China, and we know even less about their land system. It was not until the time of Wei Hsiao-wen-ti that the system of land distribution was revived. Unlike the system carried out during the Three Dynasties, the system of Later Wei merely called for the redistribution of land that had long been under private ownership. Hardly had this system been enforced for one generation than it began to deteriorate. The North Ch'i (550–577), North Chou (557–581), and Sui (590–618) regimes operated the land distribution system in the same manner as the Later Wei and met with similar results. According to the land distribution system introduced by T'ang T'ai-tsung (r.627–649), some of the distributed land could be inherited by the grantee's heirs, while the rest was to be returned to the government for redistribution upon the death or retirement of the grantee. Within certain limitations the law allowed the grantee to buy or sell land whenever necessity arose. Even this system did not last indefinitely. After the Yung-hui period (650–655) the process of land concentration was revived, and the land distribution system was abolished *de facto,* if not *de jure.* Thus from the Han dynasty to the present, a period of more than 1,400 years, the land distribution system was practiced for only 200 years approximately, *i.e.,* from the reign of Hsiao-wen-ti of the Later Wei to the early period of the T'ang dynasty.

Why is it that the well-field system of the Three Dynasties could last more than 1,000 years while a similar system of later periods could not? This is because feudalism existed in ancient times side by side with the well-field system and provided the basis upon which the latter thrived. Then land in China did not belong to the emperor as his private possession but was divided among the feudal lords. After the Ch'in dynasty had abolished feudalism, for the first time in history all land in China became the emperor's private source of income. Moreover, with the abolition of feudalism came the institution of private ownership, an institution which did not exist during the Three Dynasties. Once the institution of private landownership was established, it was extremely difficult to reverse the trend so as to revive the ancient system. To advocate the reestablishment of feudalism today is to advocate the division of the empire and, in fact, to advocate confusion and anarchy. Under the present circumstances, the restoration of the well-field system cannot mean anything except the confiscation of private property which would be resented by the people as a whole. The pedantic view of many of today's scholars simply could not be put into practice, however attractive it might look on the surface.

122 · HUANG TSUNG-HSI: *The Feasibility of Restoring the Well-Field System* [52]

Long after the well-field system had been abolished, the Han scholar Tung Chung-shu proposed the limitation of landownership. Similar proposals were also made by Shih Tan and K'ung Kuang.[53] According to K'ung's proposal, the maximum amount of land a person could own should be limited to thirty *ch'ing*, and any excess over that amount would be confiscated by the government, were it not disposed of by its owner within a period of three years. Though no one could doubt the good motive behind this proposal, there were nevertheless misgivings. In ancient times the government granted land and thus supported the people; the implementation of K'ung's proposal, on the other hand, would mean that the government was to take away land from the people by a legal device. It was bad enough not to grant land to the people; it was doubtless worse to take their land away from them. A government should under no circumstances be engaged in wrongdoing, however minor it seems to be.

Contending that to seize land from the wealthy to give it to the poor would create social disturbances, many who believe in the soundness of the well-field system suggest its restoration at the end of a long period of civil war when land is plentiful and population is small. They regret that Han Kao-tsu [54] did not restore it after his elimination of the Ch'in regime and that Han Kuang-wu,[55] when in a similar position, let a golden opportunity pass by without doing something about it. They do not realize that the ancient sage kings, when implementing the well-field system, had as their goal not only the maintenance of the people's livelihood but also the multiplication of their offspring. How can people today possibly relish the slaughtering of millions of people to provide an opportunity to carry out their cherished well-field system? Would they consider it unfortunate that, after the system has been put into practice, population continues to increase and such an increase entails great difficulties in continuing this system?

Among the latter scholars the two men who argued most convincingly about the feasibility and infeasibility of restoring the well-field system were Hu Han and Su Hsün respectively.[56] Su Hsün's argument, conceded by Fang Hsiao-ju,[57] was that it would take several hundred years to make the preparatory work involving irrigation ditches and canals, drainage, road construction, and delimitation of boundaries between different fields before the well-field system could be successfully carried out. My point is, if the government has made the cardinal decision to implement the land distribution system, other considerations such as the construction of roads and irrigation works will be taken care of in due course, and the delimitation of boundaries between different fields will not pose an

---

[52] *Ming-yi tai-fang lu,* Essay No. 11.
[53] Both were high-ranking officials towards the end of the first century B.C.
[54] Founder of the Former Han dynasty.
[55] Founder of the Later Han dynasty.
[56] Hu Han, a native of Chinhua (Chekiang province), was a scholar of the fourteenth century. As for Su Hsün, see p. 281, Footnote 46.
[57] Fang Hsiao-ju was a well-known scholar who served under Ming Hui-ti (r.1399–1402) in the early period of the Ming dynasty and was later killed by Ming Ch'eng-tsu (or Yung-lo) upon the latter's ascension to the throne in 1403.

insurmountable problem. What Su Hsün worried about is not really the center of the issue. Both Hu Han and Fan Hsiao-ju maintained that the well-field system could be restored; yet nowhere in their writings did they indicate by what means it could be restored.

I have observed the operation of the military-field system [58] in the frontier, and it is my conclusion that the operation of the well-field system cannot be too different. The scholars who contend that we can successfully operate one but cannot successfully restore the other are really contradicting themselves.

In the operation of the military-field system, each soldier is granted 50 *mou* of cultivated fields which corresponds to the 100 *mou* of cultivated fields granted to each adult male during the Chou dynasty. Regular taxes for the 50 *mou* of land amount to 12 piculs of grain that go to the treasury of the garrison headquarters, while an additional levy of 12 piculs is kept within each garrison unit for paying officials' salaries and other administrative expenses. Thus the regular taxes amount to 0.24 piculs per *mou,* a rate similar to that in the *kung* system [59] practiced during the Chou dynasty. Today the area of military fields is 644,243 *ch'ing,* while the total amount of land under cultivation for the nation as a whole was reported to be 7,013,976 *ch'ing* and 28 *mou* in the sixth year of Wan-li (1578). In other words, military fields constitute approximately one-tenth of the total amount of land under cultivation. If the land distribution system can be successfully carried out in 10 percent of the total cultivated acreage, there is no reason why it cannot be implemented with equal success in the remaining 90 percent of the acreage. Moreover, approximately 30 percent of the total cultivated fields is presently owned by the government.

If the total area of cultivated fields is divided equally among the 10,621,436 households in China, each household will receive 50 *mou,* plus an undivided amount of 170,325,828 *mou* for the nation as a whole. This undivided amount is large enough to be bought and sold among the wealthy; the necessity of limiting landownership will be avoided, and the wealthy will not feel that they are unnecessarily deprived of their rightful ownership. The fact that the military-field system can be successfully carried out convinces me that the well-field system can be restored.

If the military-field system is a good example to follow, some might say, why is it that it has not brought prosperity to its participants as it should have? There are several reasons for this lack of prosperity, none of which will be found in the well-field system if it were restored. First, the participants in the military-field system are not natives to the areas where they are; even though they have been granted land to till, they are always homesick for the areas from which they originally came. Second, under the military-field system, the young and the strong are engaged in military activities, while the farming is done by the old and the weak. This situation not only reduces the output of the field; it also mitigates the incentive of the tillers who cannot see why those who do not till should have the same share of produce as the tillers. Third, since each *mou* cannot produce more than 1 picul of grain per year, a levy of 2.4 pecks per *mou* means a heavy taxation of 25 percent of the produce. This is considerably higher than the

[58] Under the military-field system or *t'un-t'ien chih,* the government granted land to garrison soldiers (usually in the frontier) who tilled it for their own support.
[59] See pp. 265–266.

one-tenth rate practiced in ancient times. Fourth, tax collectors in the military-field system are not civilian officials; they are military men who tend to be harsher and more ruthless than their civilian counterparts. Because of the reasons stated above, the participants in the military-field system have not been as prosperous as they should be.

CHAPTER FOURTEEN

The Search for Economic Security

TOTAL dependence on agriculture and the unreliability of weather conditions created one of the most difficult problems for the Chinese, namely, how to provide enough food for all members in the society in case of flood or drought and consequently famine. The problem became particularly acute if the flood or drought lasted, say, a period of two or three years. Most Westerners are familiar with the seriousness of this problem today; many, however, do not realize that it has existed in China for more than two thousand years.

To reduce the problem to manageable proportions, the Chinese developed a remarkable institution several centuries before the Christian era, and with modifications here and there and interruptions now and then, it lasted until the twentieth century. The ever-ready system was first introduced by Li Hui, the chief minister of the state of Wei early in the fourth century B.C. (Selection 123). Subsequent regimes developed it further, and a variety of granary systems was introduced from time to time. Although names differed, three major institutions stood most prominently under the ever-ready granary system; sometimes they existed simultaneously and other times they did not. They were the ever-normal granary (*ch'ang-p'ing ts'ang*), the relief granary (*yi ts'ang*), and the communal granary (*she ts'ang*). The primary purpose of the ever-normal granary was to stabilize grain prices: to purchase grain immediately after the harvest when the supply was abundant and prices were low and to sell it in the spring or summer when the demand was strong and prices were high. It was hoped that this practice would keep the small, independent farmers from being exploited by the merchants and the money lenders who operated in the same fashion, but unlike the ever-normal granary, had as their sole purpose the realization of the largest profit. During a period of famine when the price of grain was exorbitant, the ever-normal granary would either sell its stored grain at below-the-market prices or lend it to poor peasants on easy terms. The primary purpose of relief or communal granary, on the other hand, was to provide food for the extremely poor who, in a period of prolonged famine, would have perished had there been no relief measures.

The operation of the ever-ready granary system met with varying degrees of success during the course of Chinese history (Selections 124, 125, and 126). Whatever defects it might have, all Chinese governments attached great importance to it. When, during the Sung dynasty, Wang An-shih (1021–1086) suggested using the assets of the ever-normal granary as the capital to

288

finance his green sprouts program (*ch'ing miao fa*), he encountered a chorus of vigorous protest (Selection 127). To people like Ssu-ma Kuang (1018–1086) the ever-normal granary was too important and useful an institution to be tampered with (Selection 128). Successfully utilized, it could become a very effective weapon in fighting a local famine (Selection 129).

The uncertainty of economic life in the countryside necessitated other forms of cooperation besides the every-ready granary system, cooperation not only in the sharing of what the land produced but also in the efforts that were made to produce it. Sometimes this cooperation was institutionalized under a directive from the central government (Selection 130). If a local official was so inclined, he could extend this cooperation to non-economic fields as well and make the farmers responsible for not only each other's economic welfare but also moral behavior or conduct (Selection 131).

123 · Li Hui: *The Storage of Grain for Relief* [1]

High price of grain brings harm to the consumers; low price of grain, on the other hand, will affect the producers adversely. When farmers cannot make a tolerable living as a result of depressed prices, they will leave their home to seek a new livelihood somewhere else. How can a country remain prosperous if the fortune of its farmers goes from bad to worse? Whether the price of grain is too high or too low, the country will suffer just the same. An enlightened ruler should see to it that agriculture is continually promoted and that none of his subjects suffer from inflated or depressed prices.

Now a farmer with four dependants cultivates 100 *mou* of land. Each *mou* yields 1.5 piculs of grain per year, and his total yearly income is 150 piculs. After he pays his taxes which amount to 10 percent of his income or 15 piculs, he has 135 piculs at his disposal. Each person consumes 1.5 piculs of grain per month, and the yearly consumption for a family of five is 90 piculs. This leaves him 45 piculs. Each picul of grain commands a price of 30 standard coins; when the farmer sells his 45 piculs, he receives a cash income of 1,350 standard coins. After he has made his contributions to his family temple and other communal activities which average 300 standard coins per year, he has 1,050 standard coins at his disposal. The cost for clothes for each person is about 300 standard coins per year, and the total cost for the entire family is 1,500 standard coins. Thus in a normal year he winds up with 450 standard coins in deficit. If there are sicknesses and deaths in the family or if the government decides to increase the tax load, the deficit would be even larger. That is why farmers are often beset with financial difficulties and are not so industrious as they should be in pursuing their agricultural activities.

An enlightened ruler bases his tax collections upon the amount of harvests his subjects have reaped and varies them accordingly. In terms of the amount of harvests collected, a bumper year can be classified as excellent, good, or fair. In an excellent year, a farmer reaps 600 piculs of grain in the 100 *mou* of land he tills, and after all of the daily necessities are paid for, he should have 400 piculs

---

[1] "Economics, Part I" (*Shih-huo chih shang); Han shu*, roll 24a.

of grain at his disposal. The government, in this case, should impose upon him a tax load of 300 piculs. In a good year, he reaps 450 piculs of grain, and after his daily necessities are paid for, he should have 300 piculs at his disposal. The government should then impose upon him a tax load of 200 piculs. In a not so bumper but fairly good year, he should have 100 piculs left after all of his living expenses have been met, and the government should, in this case, collect from him 50 piculs of grain as taxes.

In the same fashion, all lean years can be classified as poor, very poor, and exceedingly poor. A poor year is a year when the farmer reaps 100 piculs of grain for the 100 *mou* of land he tills. In a very poor year and an exceedingly poor year he reaps 70 and 30 piculs of grain respectively.

In short, in an excellent year the government collects as taxes 75 percent of a farmer's disposable produce, and reduces its take to 66.6 and 50 percent for a good and a fairly good year respectively. The purpose of collecting taxes according to a graduated scale is twofold: it guarantees a satisfactory livelihood for all taxpayers, and it prevents the fluctuation of grain prices.

In lean years when there is a shortage of grain, the government will sell in the open market the stored grain which has been collected as taxes during the bumper years. The amount it allocates for sale varies with the urgency of the consumers' need. In a poor year the amount released for sale will be the same as that collected as taxes during a fairly good year. The amount for a very poor year and an exceedingly poor year will be the same as that collected as taxes in a good year and an excellent year, respectively. By this device the price of grain will not rise, and farmers will not leave their home to seek food even after a severe famine has occurred as a result of a drought or flood. The underlying principle of this device is to take away the surplus during the bumper years so that the surplus will be available to meet people's need during the lean years.

124 · CH'ANG-SUN WU-CHI: *The Ever-Ready Granary of the Sui Dynasty* [2]

In the fifth month of the eighth year of K'ai-huang (A.D. 588) Ch'ang-sun P'ing, minister of Public Works and duke of Hsiangyang Hsien, presented the emperor [3] with a memorial which read as follows:

"In ancient times by farming consecutively for three years, a farmer would be able to accumulate a grain surplus which would last one year, and a grain reserve equivalent to an accumulated harvest of a three-year period could be attained when there was a succession of nine good years. Since there were grain reserves to meet any emergency, no man suffered from food shortage even when natural disasters such as flood and drought occasionally occurred. The ancient governments were farsighted and enlightened enough to persuade people to store away grain surplus in good years to meet whatever emergencies might arise in bad years.

"Last year there was a drought in Kuannei [4] which ruined most of the crops.

---

[2] "Economics" *(Shih-huo); History of the Sui (Sui shu),* roll 24. The author had been a scholar and high-ranking official before he was forced to commit suicide in A.D. c.660.
[3] Sui Wen-ti (r.589–604).
[4] Modern Shensi province where the capital of the Sui dynasty, Ch'angan, was then located.

Full of compassion for the people whom you loved more than your own children, Your Majesty ordered that the surplus grain in Shantung be shipped to Kuannei, that the grain in the government's storages be made available to the people, and that the posts of grain officials be created to coordinate all relief measures. Those who had little to eat were then given sufficient food. The generosity of Your Majesty was unprecedented in history! Moreover, wealthy families that had surplus grain of their own emulated Your Majesty's good deed by competing among themselves in making their private wealth available to the poor. 'The grass bends towards the direction in which the wind blows,' [5] and people will follow the good example set by their rulers.

"It is the hope of your humble servant that the policy of storing surplus grain for relief purposes be made permanent and institutionalized."

Upon receiving this memorial the emperor ordered all of his subjects, military as well as civilian, to combine their efforts in the establishment of relief granaries. During the days of harvest each farmer was to contribute a portion of his crops, whether wheat or other kinds of grain, to the local granary, and the contributions would be stored in structures that were to be constructed. Grain officials were not only to record the amount of grain that had been received, but also to make periodical inspection of the storages to make sure that the stored grain did not become rotten and thus useless. In a bad year when people had little to eat, the stored grain would be made available for relief purposes.

From then on communities of all provinces began to build relief granaries to store grain surplus.

Shortly afterwards, Kuanchung [6] suffered from drought for several consecutive years, while other districts such as Ch'ing and Yen [7] were plagued with a devastating flood. Crops failed, and people had nothing to eat. Emperor Kao-tsu [8] ordered Su Wei to open imperial granaries for relief and instructed Wang Tan to make available to the people at Kuanchung the three million piculs of grain that had been stored in the Kuangt'ung Granary. The aged grain previously stored during the defunct Chou dynasty [9] was sold to the needy at below-the-market prices. Moreover, the imperial government purchased more than six thousand head of oxen and donkeys and distributed them among the exceedingly poor who were then ordered to proceed to Kuanchung where food was provided for them. The areas devastated either by drought or by flood were exempted from land taxation.

In the fourteenth year of K'ai-huang (594) Kuanchung suffered a serious drought and people had nothing to eat. The emperor arrived at Loyang and ordered people to seek food from local officials. Each person was given food when he physically presented himself to the official-in-charge, regardless of the fact that he might not have a rank or position with the government.

In the following year the emperor traveled eastward in his inspection tour and offered sacrifices to the T'ai Mountain.[10] He found that the relief granaries in

---

[5] This quotation comes from the *Analects of Confucius* which compares rulers to wind and people to grass, and says people will follow the example set by their rulers.

[6] Located in the southern section of modern Shensi province.

[7] Both districts were located in modern Shantung province.

[8] Sui Wen-ti.

[9] North Chou dynasty (557–581) which Sui replaced.

[10] T'ai Mountain or Tai Shan is located in modern Shantung province.

local areas had been greatly depleted because of the lack of replenishment. Consequently, in the second month of the same year, he issued the following decree:

"The purpose of establishing relief granaries was to provide an effective remedy in times of drought or flood. Now many people are shortsighted enough to take grain from these granaries on the slightest excuses. Where will the grain come from when there is a real need for it?

"Agriculturally, the districts in the northern frontier such as Yün and Hsia [11] were different from other areas. It is hereby decreed that the relief granaries in these disticts should accept grains of a miscellaneous variety [12] as well as regular crops such as wheat. Whenever a granary in any of these districts is open for relief purposes, the official-in-charge should see to it that grains of a miscellaneous variety and grains that have been stored for many years be distributed first."

In the first month of the sixteenth year of K'ai-huang (596) the emperor decreed that in assessing contributions to the relief granaries all households in the empire be divided into three categories: high income, middle income, and low income. The maximum assessment for a high-income household was 1 picul of grain per year; it was 0.7 piculs for a middle-income household and 0.4 piculs for a low-income household.

Shortly afterwards, there were continuous rains in Shantung year after year. All the areas, from Ch'i and Sung to as faraway as the sea,[13] suffered from a devastating flood. Many people perished in the water. In the eighteenth year of K'ai-huang (598) the emperor sent his river engineers to the head of each of the flooding rivers with the intended purpose of examining the river topography so as to recommend corrective measures. Subsequently male adults in the nearby areas were mobilized to work on river projects: to lead the torrential water along the natural paths of the flooding rivers. The stored grain in the relief granaries was distributed among the needy, and the total amount thus distributed was more than five hundred piculs. All forms of taxation, with the exception of corvée duties, were cancelled in the flooded areas.

From then on there were succeeding years of good harvests.

125 · T'o-T'o: *The Ever-Ready Granary of the Sung Dynasty* [14]

The ever-normal granary and the relief granary were the two institutions of the Han and the Sui dynasties that had been successfully operated to the great benefit of the people. In the Hsien-te period (954–960) of the Later Chou dynasty (951–960) an order was issued to establish the people's benevolent granaries [15] to

[11] Yün was located in the northern section of modern Shansi province, and Hsia in the northern section of modern Shensi province. Both districts were semi-arid.

[12] "Grains of a miscellaneous variety" or *tsa liang* include such crops as kaoliang which is drought-resistant, does not require a long growing season, and can therefore grow well in the northernmost part of China proper. They are not so highly priced as regular crops like wheat.

[13] Both Ch'i and Sung were located in modern Honan province, and the sea was the Yellow Sea.

[14] "The Ever-normal and Relief Granaries" in "Economics, Part I, Section 4" *(Shih-huo shang ssu); History of the Sung (Sung shih),* roll 176, by T'o-t'o, a historian who lived in the fourteenth century.

[15] *Hui-min ts'ang.*

which the government assigned those grain collections which, as miscellaneous taxes,[16] had been hitherto paid in cash. The stored grain would be sold at below-the-market prices whenever there was a food shortage. After the Sung dynasty was established, it inherited this institution and kept it in operation.

As wars were frequent during the Five Dynasties, the communal granaries gradually disappeared from the national scene. Early in the Ch'ien-te period (963–967) T'ai-tsu[17] ordered all provinces to establish relief granaries in the sub-prefectures within their respective jurisdiction. Each year when the semi-annual taxes were collected, a taxpayer was to contribute one peck of grain to the relief granary for every picul of grain they paid to the government. Whenever a person was short of food, he could apply to his subprefectural magistrate for a loan, and the magistrate would in turn submit his request, together with those of others, to the provincial government for authorization. Only after the loan had been granted was it necessary to report the transaction to the imperial government. Later, this system was abolished, largely on account of the inconvenience caused by the shipping of grain to and from the provincial capital.

In the third year of Ch'un-hua (992) the areas around the capital[18] had an unusually bumper harvest. The government sent its officials to each of the four city gates to purchase grain at above-the-market prices. The purchased grain was then stored in the nearby warehouses, to be sold at below-the-market prices in some future time when there was a shortage of food on account of bad harvest. These storages were named ever-normal granaries.

During the Hsien-p'ing period (998–1003) Ch'eng Su, an official in the treasury department, suggested the establishment of people's benevolent granaries in Fukien province. Subsequently a decree was issued ordering their establishment in all the provinces.

In the third year of Ching-te (1006) a suggestion was made to establish ever-normal granaries in Chingtung, Chinghsi, Hopeh, Hotung, Shensi, Kiangnan, Huainan, and Liangche provinces. Each of these provinces was to retain a certain amount of its tax revenue as capital for the said granaries, the amount varying with the total number of population within its jurisdiction, ranging from two to twenty thousand strings of standard coins. Each granary was to be headed by an able and incorruptible official appointed by the Transport Administration.[19] The entire system was to be put under the direct jurisdiction of the Department of Agriculture, and under no circumstances was the Finance Commission[20] allowed to transfer its capital or asset for other purposes. The official-in-charge would buy grain at above-the-market prices during summer or fall when supply was abundant, and would sell at below-the-market prices whenever there was a food shortage. But the price at which he would sell should not be lower than the

---

[16] Payments in addition to the regular taxes.

[17] Sung T'ai-tsu or Chao K'uang-yin (r.960–975).

[18] Kaifeng.

[19] The Transport Administration or *Chuan-yün ssu* was created at the beginning of the Sung dynasty. It was in charge of collecting tax revenues throughout the empire and the transportation of such revenues directly to the imperial government and independently of provincial authorities.

[20] Created during the Later T'ang dynasty, the Finance Commission or *San ssu* supervised the work of the Salt and Iron Administration, the Ministry of Finance, and the Board of Expenditure. The Sung dynasty inherited this institution, but abolished it sometime during the Yüan-feng period (1078–1085).

price at which he bought. The ever-normal granary system was not to be established in the border provinces, however.[21] The emperor [22] ordered that discussions be held among the officials in the Finance Commission with regard to this proposal. These officials, after deliberation, recommended its adoption.

In the fourth year of T'ien-hsi (1020) the ever-normal granary system was extended to Hupeh, Hunan, Szechuan, Shensi, and Kwangnan provinces.

It was reported that during the fifth year of T'ien-hsi (1021) the ever-normal granaries in all the provinces bought 183,000 piculs of grain and sold 243,000 piculs.

During the Ching-yu period (1034–1037) Wu Tseng, the deputy envoy of transport in Huainan, reported that the total reserve in the ever-normal granaries in his province amounted to only 400,000 piculs of grain which were inadequate to meet emergencies in case of famine. He requested permission to increase the reserve to 2,000,000 piculs on his own initiative, if the imperial government would agree that it would not transfer the increased amount to be used for purposes other than relief. The imperial government granted his request. Subsequently it issued the order that under no circumstances would the Finance Commission or the Transport Administration be allowed to appropriate the reserve in the ever-normal granaries for its own uses.

During a period of several years the grain reserve in the ever-normal granaries continued to increase while the supply of food for the nation's military forces remained inadequate. To meet military expenses, the imperial government ordered the Department of Agriculture to transfer part of its holdings in the ever-normal granaries to the Finance Commission, totalling one million *min* [23] in cash value. Once the precedent was established, the transfer continued until eventually there was little left in the ever-normal granaries.

From the beginning of the Ching-yu period it was the policy of the imperial government to open its ever-normal granaries to the poor whenever famine occurred in the capital area. Some of these granaries bought grain at above-the-market prices during the famine period so that it would have more grain available for relief purposes, thus ingratiating themselves with the poor. In the third year of Huang-yu (1051) the imperial government ordered the immediate cessation of this practice.

Ch'en Sheng-tzu, the comfort envoy [24] in charge of Huainan and Lianche provinces, reported that the ever-normal granaries in the devastated areas sold their grain at a price ten or fifteen standard coins above the cost and that such a practice was incompatible with the government's policy of showing compassion for the poor. The imperial government responded by ordering local officials to desist from such a practice; they were told to sell their grain at the price at which it was bought.

In the fifth year of Huang-yu (1053) the emperor [25] issued a decree which read as follows: "Lately the harvest in Hupeh has been bad, and it is only proper

---

[21] The storage of grain in these provinces might attempt foreign enemies to invade the border regions.

[22] Sung chen-tsung (r.998–1022).

[23] One *min* equals to 1,000 standard coins.

[24] *An-fu shih,* usually sent by the imperial government during a period of famine or after the pacification of a local disturbance or uprising.

[25] Sung Jen-tsung (r.1023–1063).

that the ever-normal granaries should be open for relief purposes. However, the Department of Agriculture reported that some of these granaries are still collecting grain to enhance their reserves. Is this the proper way to show the government's concern for the welfare of the people? These collecting activities should be stopped at once."

In the second year of Ming-t'ao (1033) responsible officials were ordered by the emperor to discuss the feasibility of restoring the relief granary system. Nothing consequential came from their deliberations.

During the Ching-yu period (1034–1037) Wang Ch'i, a scholar in the Chi-hsien Institute,[26] proposed the reestablishment of the relief granaries and presented the emperor with the following memorial: "It is hereby suggested that all households above the fifth rank be required to contribute one pint of grain to the relief granary for every two pecks of grain paid as regular taxes. Such a requirement will be dropped in case of a flood or drought, however. Local officials should be made responsible for locating convenient places to construct storages, and the relief granaries, once established, should be operated under the direction of the Transport Administration. In a medium-sized district where the regular taxes amount to 100,000 piculs of grain per year, the collection for the relief granaries will be as much as 5,000 piculs. The total collection for the nation as a whole will be very large indeed. During a famine in the Ming-t'ao period (1032–1033), the government was unable to lend all of its grain reserves to the poor because, if it did so, it would not have enough left to feed the nation's armed forces. Many people, facing starvation, were forced to leave their home to seek food. In order to raise funds, the government then appointed as an official anyone who had contributed several thousand piculs of grain for relief. This is not because it wished to degrade governmental posts; full of compassion for those who were then suffering, it did not feel that it had any choice. If the relief granaries were established, each household would contribute grain in accordance with its income, and the poor would not have to wait for a drought or flood in order to enjoy the generosity of the rich." The emperor ordered that this proposal be discussed among the responsible officials. Since there were disagreements among these officials, no action was taken with regard to its implementation.

In the first year of Ch'ing-li (1041) Wang Ch'i again proposed the establishment of the relief granaries. Emperor Jen-tsung accepted his proposal and ordered their establishment throughout the empire. By an imperial decree every household above the third rank was required to contribute grain to the local relief granary. The decree was not carried out, and the matter was soon dropped.

Later a man named Chia An [27] also advocated the reestablishment of the relief granaries. He submitted to the emperor a memorial which read as follows:

"In recent years we have been enjoying peace and bumper crops. People are happy and secure, and few families are broken up because of the lack of food. However, once there is a drought or flood, the situation will immediately change. Many will be forced by hunger to leave their homes, and thousands will perish on the roadside. When a tragedy of this magnitude occurs, the government will find that the reserve in the granaries is inadequate to meet the need and that to increase

[26] The Chi-hsien ("Collection of Talents") Institute was a research institute supported by the central government.
[27] A brilliant scholar-official who served during the reign of Sung Jen-tsung and died in c.1065.

taxes so as to obtain additional grain from the rich is a poor substitute. To move grain from the surplus areas to the region of famine involves a transportation over a thousand *li,* and by the time the grain finally arrives, many may have already perished. To move the famine-stricken to the areas of food surplus is hardly more convenient; it creates difficulties for the refugees as well as the people in the surplus areas. All officials, high or low, are at a loss in knowing what to do. Meanwhile the destitute and the starved are dying in droves.

"Having in mind the great tragedy that may occur again, I wish to suggest the reestablishment of the relief granaries, to be operated in the same fashion as those during the Sui dynasty. Local governments should be ordered to impose grain collections in good years, to be made available to the needy whenever there is a natural disaster. This measure, if adopted, will be in full accord with the ancient saying that 'To collect more in good years when there is a large surplus is anything but tyrannical.' [28] I should not think that it is tyrannical in view of the fact that the sole purpose of this collection is to benefit the people."

After receiving this memorial, the emperor requested the opinion of all provinces with regard to the feasibility of restoring the relief granary system. Only four provinces responded positively, and all others were opposed to its reestablishment. They opposed its establishment on a variety of grounds, such as the great increase in taxation as a result of imposing additional levies, the temptation these granaries would provide for bandits and thieves, and the disturbances the construction of storages would create among the people. Some provinces maintained that they had already had the ever-normal granaries within their jurisdiction and that these granaries could be used effectively to combat famine whenever it occurred.

Not to be discouraged, Chia An submitted another memorial which read as follows:

"Your humble servant has had the occasion to look into the files of the Ministry of Justice and has noticed that the total number of criminals sentenced to death amounts to more than four thousand per year. Anywhere between 60 and 70 percent of the capital cases involves banditry. Why? Many of the poor, facing hunger and cold during a period of drought or flood, were forced by necessity to commit capital offenses which they would not have done under normal circumstances. This is the reason why I have repeatedly urged the reestablishment of relief or communal granaries as a precautionary measure against the evil consequences that follow in the wake of failing crops.

"It is my humble opinion that the provinces opposing the reestablishment of the relief granary system are wrong in their arguments. They say that the additional levy necessary to the financing of the new project amounts to double taxation. They do not realize that this additional levy is really forced savings in preparation for a drought or flood and that it is not another form of taxation which will be appropriated by the government. I feel that once the relief granaries are established, they will win increasing support with the passage of time, and in the end people will be more than willing to contribute for its continual success.

"As to the argument that the relief granaries will tempt bandits and thieves, the critics forget that these evildoers are only interested in precious metals or stones,

---

[28] This remark was made by Mencius.

instead of such bulky materials as wheat and rice. Today some of our wealthy people store tens of thousands of piculs of grain in the countryside, and rarely are they worried about the possibility that their stored grain will be robbed or stolen. Moreover, the cause of banditry or thievery is poverty. If my proposal to reestablish relief granaries is accepted, people will have enough to eat during the period of a drought or flood, and there will be no reason for them to wish to forgo their self-respect by violating the law. In fact, the implementation of my proposal will eradicate the very cause of banditry or thievery.

"The argument that the ever-normal granaries are sufficiently supplied to meet emergencies is equally erroneous. The purpose of the ever-normal granaries is to stabilize prices. Such a purpose is lost when their reserves are used for relief during the time of famine. Moreover, these reserves legally belong to the government which often finds them too small even to meet its own expenses. The nation has operated the ever-normal granaries for many years. Yet, whenever there is a drought or flood, people suffer from starvation and are forced by hunger to leave their homes. This is a clear indication that the ever-normal granaries are not well equipped to serve the goal of providing relief.

"As to the last argument that the people will be unnecessarily disturbed when such materials as wood have to be requisitioned in order to build storages, I would say that the people are no more disturbed by the construction of relief granaries than they are by the construction and repairing of postal stations which the local governments force them to do each and every year. Why should they be unduly disturbed by one project while not disturbed at all by the other?

"The nature of man is such that he is more interested in good results than the hard work necessary to bringing them about. It is my sincere hope that Your Majesty will forcibly implement the relief granary system regardless of the opposition that might arise."

The government, facing strong opposition from the public, decided not to reestablish the relief granary system. . . .

126 · CHANG T'ING-YÜ et al.: The Ever-Ready Granary of the Ming Dynasty [29]

The relief granary system of the Ming dynasty began during the reign of Ming T'ai-tsu (r.1368–1398) who invited a group of elders to contribute cash or grain for relief purposes. Later, all provinces and districts in China were ordered by the imperial government to carry out a similar program. The program worked so well that local governments had a large amount of grain reserves to meet emergencies whenever they arose. Unfortunately this remarkable system was allowed to deteriorate as time went on.

When Yü Ch'ien [30] was the governor-general of Honan and Shansi, he revived the relief granary system within his jurisdiction. When Chou Ch'en [31] was a governor in the south, he likewise restored a system known as "granaries for farmers'

[29] *Ming shih,* roll 79.
[30] One of the greatest statesmen of the Ming dynasty; was put to death by emperor Ming Yin-chung in 1458 on a charge of alleged treason.
[31] See p. 245, Footnote 34.

relief." [32] Successful as his program was, other governors were unable to duplicate it.

During the Cheng-t'ung period (1436–1449) a new law was enacted to punish more severely those who had committed robbery. People who had been convicted of this crime would be exiled to the frontier, and their wives, if any, would be confiscated by the government. Meanwhile, a man would be officially classified as a "righteous citizen" [33] if he chose to make a contribution of 1,500 piculs of grain to the government; as a "righteous citizen," his household would be exempt from miscellaneous corvée duties. The poor who received one picul of polished rice in a year of famine were required to pay to the lender, namely, the government, 2.5 piculs of unpolished rice in some future time when there was a bumper crop.

In the third year of Hung-chih (1490) an imperial decree stipulated the minimum amount of grain reserve for each community as follows: 15,000 piculs for a community of 100 square li, 20,000 piculs for a community of 400 square li, 15,000 piculs for a military unit of one "thousand," and 300 piculs for a military unit of one "hundred." [34] The grain reserve of each community was to be inspected from time to time, and the official-in-charge was to be rewarded or punished in accordance with the fulfillment or non-fulfillment of the grain quota within his jurisdiction. If the grain reserve was more than 30 percent below the assigned quota, his salary as an official would be proportionally reduced. If it was more than 60 percent, he would be demoted and transferred.

In the eighth year of Hung-chih (1505) a law was enacted to allow criminals to redeem their crimes by paying fines in grain which would be then stored for relief purposes. Officials who had been convicted of corruption and bribery were allowed to do likewise.

A decree issued during the Cheng-te period (1506–1521) stated that a prisoner upon whom the court had imposed a fine could pay to the government's granary an amount of grain equivalent to 80 percent of the imposed fine. Military officials who had committed crimes were allowed to do likewise. Meanwhile they were put under probation until they performed new deeds to redeem themselves. Prior to this time each granary had been headed by a specially designated official who was solely responsible for its operation. This post was then abolished, and the prefectural and district magistrates, together with the regular granary officials, were placed in charge of the granaries within their territorial jurisdiction.

In the first year of Chia-ching (1522) Ku Ting-ch'en [35] presented the emperor [36] with a memorial which read as follows: "During the Ch'eng-hung period (1465–1505) the yearly grain surplus of each community was transferred to the relief granary to meet whatever emergency might arise. Now that the autumn harvests of each community are barely large enough to meet the grain require-

---

[32] *Chi-nung ts'ang.*

[33] *Yi min.*

[34] Under the imperial garrison system (called *wei-so*) of the Ming dynasty, garrisons of various strength were stationed throughout the empire. A garrison unit of one "hundred" had actually 112 men; that of one "thousand" had actually 1,200 men. The largest unit was *wei* ("guard") which had 5,600 men.

[35] Ku Ting-ch'en, a native of Kunshan (modern Kiangsu province), received the highest honor in the *chin-shih* examination of 1505; he died in 1540 after serving the Ming government in a variety of capacities.

[36] Ming Shih-tsung (r.1522–1566).

ment of the government, there is not a single kernel that goes to the relief granary. Whenever a natural disaster occurs, local officials, as a matter of routine, will petition the imperial government to allow them to retain part of the grain for relief, the grain that has been assigned for other uses. Meanwhile, they try to borrow from the wealty for the same purpose. I beg Your Majesty to quickly restore the ever-ready granary system in order to benefit all people in the empire."

Upon receiving this memorial the emperor ordered responsible officials to store and accumulate paddy rice and other types of grain by whatever means at their command so that the ever-normal granary system of ancient times could be successfully revived. Poor people were entitled to borrow from the ever-normal granary in the spring, on the condition that they would pay their debt in the fall after harvests had been collected. No interest would be charged on these transactions. The law stated that for lending purposes each prefecture was required to maintain a grain reserve of 10,000 piculs; each district from 4,000 to 5,000 piculs; and each subprefecture from 2,000 to 3,000 piculs. As the size of each jurisdictional area increased, the amount of grain reserves should also be increased, from 15,000 piculs for an area of 100 square li to 190,000 piculs for a region of 640,-000 square li.

The grain reserves, though successfully accumulated, were reduced year after year, as poor people continued to buy grain from the government at bargain prices. By the Lung-ch'ing period (1567–1572) a large prefecture had no more than 6,000 piculs in reserve, while a small city had only 1,000 piculs. While grain reserves continued to decrease, the penalty for violating the granary law was also reduced. During the middle years of the Wan-li period (1573–1619) a large prefecture had a grain reserve of no more than 3,000 piculs, while a small city had as little as 100 piculs. The officials-in-charge regarded the law as something to be conveniently ignored; when the imperial government reprimanded them for their inactivity, they merely fabricated figures to hide their own failures.

During the Hung-chih period (1488–1505) Lin Ching, governor of Kiangsi, petitioned the imperial government for the reestablishment of ever-normal and communal granaries. However, it was not until the eighth year of Chia-ching (1529) that the government finally decided to establish communal granaries in all the provinces. According to the royal decree, every twenty to thirty households were to form a commune, and each commune was to be headed by a commune chief, chosen from those who were wealthy and upright. He was to be assisted by a deputy chief, chosen from those who were known for their fairness and impartiality, and by a secretary-treasurer who knew his calligraphy and arithmetic. They were to meet on the first and the fifteenth days of each month to discuss matters concerning the communal granary. All households in the commune were to be divided into three groups: the high income, the middle income, and the low income; and each was to contribute an amount of grain to the communal granary. The amount ranged from one to four pecks per year, depending upon the group to which the household belonged. A 5 percent levy was added to each peck of contributions to allow in advance for its forthcoming depreciation. Only people from the high-income households were eligible for assuming the duty of collecting contributions.

In a year of famine, the decree continued, people of the high-income households could borrow from the communal granary if their harvests were inadequate to meet their expenses, but they would have to return the amount they borrowed once there was a good year. People of middle- or low-income households, on the other hand, could draw from the communal granary an amount in proportion to their needs without assuming any obligation to return it in a future date. Local officials were required to keep account of each of these transactions, and the books they kept were to be filed with the provincial governor. Moreover, the grain reserves in a communal granary were to be verified by on-the-spot inspections each year. Should it be found empty, the commune chief would be fined by an amount equivalent to one year of his harvests.

This system was unquestionably sound, but unfortunately few of the communities had the necessary resources to make it last in a later period.

127 · T'o-T'o: *The Controversy over the Green Sprouts Program* [37]

After Wang An-shih was appointed prime minister, he spoke to Emperor Shen-tsung (r.1068–1085) about his economic programs. Impressed with his presentation, the emperor authorized the creation of the Rules Commission [38] to implement Wang's programs. Lü Hui-ch'ing, an editor in the Chi-hsien Institute,[39] was made a secretary of the commission. From then on Wang concentrated all of his efforts on the implementation of his new economic policy, the first of which was the green sprouts program.

Su Shih, then stationed at Tamin,[40] sent a memorial to the emperor expressing his opinion. He was called to the capital and, like Lü Hui-ch'ing, was made a secretary in the Rules Commission. One day Wang An-shih showed him a draft of the green sprouts program, and the latter immediately voiced his opposition. "Though the government's purpose is not to realize profit when, under the green sprouts program, it lends money to the people at an interest of 20 percent," said Su Shih, "the people will nevertheless suffer because no law, however detailed it is, can prevent officials-in-charge from engaging in irregular activities during each of the monetary transactions. Moreover, once money is made so readily available, even the most prudent will wish to spend it; when the payment is due, few, even among the wealthy, can meet the deadline. If the green sprouts program is put into practice as you have suggested, I am afraid that there will be numerous beatings of those who have defaulted, and disturbances will be created among the people when there should be none."

"When Liu Yen [41] was in charge of the nation's finance during the T'ang dynasty, many people criticized him for not extending credit to those who needed it," Su Shih continued. "He replied that it is not good for the nation if its people think that money is easy to obtain. The result will be very harmful indeed if the law has to be invoked to force payments. 'Though I do not extend credit,' he continued, 'I know the economic conditions—the success or failure of crops and the fluctuation of grain prices—in every corner of the empire. I buy grain for the government when the price is low and sell it when the price is high. There

---

[37] *Sung shih,* roll 176.
[38] *T'iao-li ssu.*
[39] See p. 295, Footnote 26.
[40] Located in modern Hopeh province.
[41] Minister of Finance during the reign of T'ang Tai-tsung (763–779).

is no need to extend any credit.' What Liu Yen described was the operation of the ever-normal granary system. If you, sir, follow his example in administering the nation's finance, I am sure that your achievement will be as great as his."

After hearing these remarks, Wang An-shih did not mention the green sprouts program for more than a month.

Meanwhile Wang Kuang-lien, the transport envoy in charge of Hopeh province, was called to the capital for consultation. Previously when Wang was the transport envoy in Shensi, he sold several thousand permits to those who wished to become Buddhist monks,[42] and used the money thus collected as capital to finance his own green sprouts program. Now, arriving at the capital, he requested that the same program be carried out in the Hopeh province. It was then that Wang An-shih decided to carry out this program for the entire nation. Once such a decision was made, the ever-normal granary system was suddenly transformed into the green sprouts program. Because of his opposition to this program, Su Shih was dismissed from his post as a secretary in the Rules Commission.

To ingratiate themselves with the prime minister, the officials-in-charge in each of the provinces attempted to lend as much as possible in order to show their "achievement." Since only the poor wished to borrow while the wealthy were understandably reluctant, they imposed a quota on each of the households within their jurisdiction: the richer a household was, the more it had to borrow. To make sure that the poor would pay their debts, every ten households, the rich as well as the poor, formed a group to guarantee each other's payment. In Hopeh where Wang Kuang-lien was in charge, each household of the first rank had to borrow 15,000 standard coins; even a household of the fifth rank had to borrow 1,000 standard coins.[43] People protested in noisy clamor, but Wang Kuang-lien, in a memorial to the emperor, said that the people rejoiced at the great benefit that the government had chosen to bestow upon them. Despite Wang's optimism, others in the capital continued their criticisms. . . .

In the third year of Hsi-ning (1070) Han Ch'i, then magistrate of the Tamin prefecture, submitted to the emperor the following memorial:

"The purpose of the green sprouts program, insofar as I can discern in the royal decree, is to benefit the poor. It enables them to escape from the usurious interest charged by the wealthy whenever they need extra cash to meet emergencies. Its purpose is definitely not the enrichment of the government. The actual situation, however, is in direct contrast to the stated ideal. In the countryside every household from the first rank down is required to borrow money in direct proportion to its wealth, and any household above the third rank can contract additional loans above its required norm. In the cities a family that has properties to its name is required to borrow in the same fashion as its counterpart in the countryside. In short, the borrowers, whether in the city or in the countryside, are mostly those who do not need to borrow. Since for each 1,000 standard coins borrowed they have to pay 300 standard coins in interest, the government is in fact a money lender, enriching itself to the same extent that the wealthy used to do. This practice, I believe, violates the very intention of the green sprouts program.

---

[42] A man could not become a monk unless he had bought a permit (called *tu-t'ieh*) from the government.

[43] These households were graded in accordance with income.

"Though the law says that there should not be any compulsion in the implementation of this program, a less well-to-do person cannot borrow any without his payment being guaranteed by the well-to-do. Most people in the world are not so wise as they should be; they can only see what is immediately beneficial and do not wish to bother themselves with the distant future. They only know that it is easy to borrow, and borrow accordingly; rarely do they stop to think that they have to repay with interest what they have borrowed. Since the promulgation of the green sprouts program, both the officials and the people are at a loss to know what to do. If no compulsion is used, the wealthy would naturally not wish to borrow, while the poor and the unemployed, who are willing to borrow, may pose great problems when payment is due. Unable to pay, a defaulter will suffer punishment at the hands of government officials, and those who have guaranteed his payment wind up paying his debt.

"Last year the areas north of the Yellow River had bumper crops, and polished rice was sold as low as seventy to eighty standard coins per peck. The government should have bought grain then so that it would have enough to sell should prices become high. In such a case, it would have conformed to the ancient practice of stabilizing prices by taking away the surplus that glutted the market, thus bringing benefit to all people concerned. This year when the ever-normal granaries were about to sell their grain to the public, they were stopped by their superiors in the capital. Their superiors wished to show off their 'achievement' by using the stored grain as capital to make a profit of 30 percent under the green sprouts program; they were not concerned with either the welfare of the poor or the future of the nation as a whole. . . ."

The emperor took the memorial from his sleeve and showed it to Wang An-shih. "Han Ch'i is truly a loyal minister of mine," he commented. "I thought that the green sprouts program was beneficial to the people; I had no idea that it could be so harmful. How could there be green sprouts in the streets? Yet our officials are forcing the city people to borrow money to grow them."

Wang An-shih suddenly changed his countenance and retorted: "I do not see how the city people can be harmed if we let them do whatever they wish to do." To refute Han Ch'i's arguments, he continued: "To collect interest from one's investment is as much the teaching of Duke Chou [44] as the ever-normal granary system. Formerly Sang Hung-yang [45] monopolized all the wealth in the nation to satisfy the private needs of one man, the emperor; and he was correctly criticized as a profit-minded minister. Now we are trying to help the poor by clamping down the money-lending activities of the greedy rich, and our purpose is not to manage finance in such a way as to help satisfy the private desire of any one person. How can we be characterized as profit-minded ministers?"

Both Tseng Kung-liang and Ch'en Sheng-tzu argued strongly against the extension of the green sprouts program to the cities. They debated with Wang An-shih for a long time before finally giving up. Because of Han Ch'i's arguments, the emperor himself was also doubtful of the wisdom of the whole program.

Pretending that he was ill, Wang An-shih did not show up in his office. The emperor was debating with himself as to whether the green sprouts program should be cancelled altogether. Tseng Kung-liang and Ch'en Sheng-tzu suggested

[44] A saintly ruler early in the Chou dynasty.
[45] A finance minister during the reign of Han Wu-ti (r.140–87 B.C.).

that a decree to cancel it be issued right away, but Chao Pien alone insisted that Wang An-shih should be consulted and be given the responsibility to cancel it himself. For several days the debate went on, and no conclusion was reached. Meanwhile the emperor was even more doubtful about the wisdom of the green sprouts program.

Finally the emperor ordered Lü Hui-ch'ing to draft a decree to reinstate Wang An-shih. Being reinstated, Wang went to the palace to express his gratitude. Thinking that he had received a new mandate, he became even more ruthless. He scolded Tseng Kung-liang and others who had opposed him, and was more determined than ever to carry out his new programs. . . .

128 · SSU-MA KUANG: *The Ever-Normal Granary System and the Green Sprouts Program* [46]

Most of those who criticize the green sprouts program only know that the officials-in-charge, being young, inexperienced, and of lower ranks, abuse the authority entrusted to them, and annoy and oppress people wherever these officials happen to be located. The critics are unquestionably right, but unfortunately the harm which they have pointed out is merely a contemporary one. I, your humble servant, am more concerned with a harm of permanent nature, the harm that will come about ten years from today.

The reason that there is a difference between the rich and the poor is because there is a difference between natural endowments: some are wise and able and others are not. The people who become rich are those who possess more knowledge and think far ahead; they prefer to work hard and live thriftily instead of borrowing money from others. As a result, they always have some extra money in their purse and consequently will not suffer financial embarrassment. The people who become poor, on the other hand, are those who prefer a day to day existence and do not wish to bother themselves with what the future holds. When they have money, they spend it on liquor; since they have no savings, they have to borrow from others whenever an emergency arises. When the debts continue to accumulate, eventually they may be forced to sell their wives and children to meet the payments, while they themselves wind up in the gutter where hunger and cold become their constant companions. Even then they are not regretful for the miserable state of affairs they have brought to themselves.

It is true that a wide difference exists in the standard of living between the rich and the poor, but their interests are really complementary. The rich need to lend money to the poor to enrich themselves, and the poor need to borrow money from the rich to preserve their very existence.

The green sprouts program has changed this mutual dependence drastically. Under this system the district official lends money to the people twice a year, once in the spring and again in the fall, and charges interest on the money borrowed. As one would expect, the wealthy do not wish to borrow, and the people who do borrow are those among the poor. The officials-in-charge, being anxious to impress their superiors with their lending activities, impose a quota system among all households within their jurisdiction and force people to borrow from the gov-

46 *Wen-hsien t'ung-k'ao,* roll 21.

ernment, regardless of whether the prospective borrowers are rich or poor, or whether they need the money or not. The amount of loan imposed on each household varies with the financial capacity of the reluctant borrower; the richer he is, the more he has to borrow. It ranges from one to as much as fifteen *min* of cash. The local officials-in-charge, fearing that the poor may not be able to pay the debt when the payment is due and that in such a case they will incur the wrath of their own superiors, force the local wealthy to countersign the loan agreements concluded with the poor and make them responsible for all the payments. By this device the local wealthy are made liable for any delinquency in debt payment in their respective communities.

As one would expect, the poor squander the money away as soon as it is in their hands. If the harvest is only a little below expectation, they cannot even pay the regular semiannual taxes, let alone the interests that have accumulated on the loan which they contracted with the government. When the officials press for payment, they evade and then, as a last resort, flee from their homes and may never return. The rich, on the other hand, cannot and will not leave their own community; consequently one rich family is often forced to pay the debts of several poor families that have defaulted. If a rich man is found unable to pay after he has exhausted his financial resources, the officials may decide to grant him a moratorium. Meanwhile his debt to the government continues to increase; hardly has the spring deadline passed before the autumn deadline arrives. This may continue for a number of years. In a year of famine, he, like the poor, may be forced to leave his own village and wander from place to place until eventually he dies. If fortunately the harvest is good, the officials will press him to pay all the debts that have accumulated for years and will leave little or nothing for himself. Thus, whether the year is good or bad, he will not have a moment of peace. The net result is that while the poor have either died or disappeared, all of the wealthy have also become poor. I am afraid that ten years from now there will be few who can be considered rich.

Once the wealthy class is eliminated, upon whom can the government rely for the provision of military supplies such as grain and silk, if unfortunately our enemy decides to invade our frontier and the government is forced to mobilize its troops? I do not know how many *min* have been so far lent out under the green sprouts program—the amount must be immensely large. It should be expected that whenever there are such natural disasters as flood or drought, local officials who have a sense of compassion for the people will petition the imperial government to forgo the collection of the accumulated debts or the cancellation of these debts altogether, after it has been established that the borrowers' financial resources are totally exhausted. I am afraid that the government will have no choice except to grant the petitioners' request. In such a case, the large amount of money then in arrears will never be returned to the lender, namely, the government, and the people will be in as much financial distress as before. Meanwhile the village chiefs and the street elders, who are charged with the duty of collecting debts from the people, continue to demand fees for their services. Is this really a good policy?

The ever-normal granary system was introduced by the sage kings during the Three Dynasties; it was not invented by such people as Li Hui and Keng Shou-ch'ang [47] as has been generally assumed. Its basic purpose is the stability of grain

---

[47] Keng Shou-ch'ang was a minister of agriculture during the Former Han dynasty.

price so that farmers will not suffer from depressed prices when supply is abundant; nor will the consumers be harmed when there is a scarcity of grain in the open market. The people rely on the ever-normal granaries for a steady supply of food; meanwhile the government makes a handsome profit in each of the grain transactions. Unquestionably the ever-normal granary system is sound and beneficial to all concerned.

Why is it that lately this system has begun to deteriorate? The fault does not lie with the system itself; it has a great deal to do with the kind of people who operate it.

Now the Rules Commission is using the cash reserve of the ever-normal granaries as capital to finance the green sprouts program. Besides, it has transferred all grain reserves in the ever-normal granaries to the Transport Administration. To me this means the *de facto* destruction of the ever-normal granary system and its replacement by the green sprouts program. In a year of bad harvest, the government has a difficult time to meet its military expenses and consequently does not have any surplus for famine relief. It has consistently depended upon the cash and grain reserves in the ever-normal granaries for this purpose. When all these reserves are lent out under the green sprouts program, where can the government find the necessary cash to buy the surplus grain that gluts the market during bumper years, and where can it find the necessary grain for famine relief during the years of failing crops?

The late emperor [48] was generous enough to appropriate one million *min* of cash from the treasury so that the ever-normal granaries could use the appropriation as capital to purchase surplus grain in the market. Only recently I have heard that the total holdings of all the ever-normal granaries in the empire amount to more than ten million *min,* in grain as well as in cash. If these holdings are dispersed as they will be under the green sprouts program, when and how can they be reaccumulated if, in some future time, we decide to reintroduce the ever-normal granary system? This is why I believe that the harm incurred during the implementation of the green sprouts program is small compared with the irreparable damage that results from the destruction of the ever-normal granary system.

129 · TSENG KUNG: *How His Excellency Chao Combats Famine* [49]

In the summer of the eighth year of Hsi-ning (1075) there was a serious drought in the Wu and Yüeh provinces.[50] In the ninth month His Excellency Chao, the Grand Secretary of the Tzu-cheng Palace and concurrently the Vice President of the Board of Censors, was appointed as the governor of Yüeh. After arriving at his post, he sent the following inquiries to all subprefectures under his jurisdiction: "How many townships have been affected by the famine? How many people can support themselves? How many people need the government's

[48] Sung Ying-tsung (r. 1064–1067).

[49] A copy of the Chinese original can be found in *A Collection of Essays (Ching-shih wen-tsung)* [Chungking: Huang-chung Press: 1943], pp. 184–185, by Su Yüan-lei. Tseng Kung (*chin-shih,* 1057), a contemporary of such men as Ou-yang Hsiu and Su Shih, was regarded as one of the greatest essayists of the Sung dynasty.

[50] Modern Kiangsu and Chekiang provinces respectively.

support? How many people can be mobilized to construct ditches and canals? How much money is in the treasury and how much grain is in the granary that can be used for relief? How many households can contribute grain for relief? How much surplus grain do the Buddhist and Taoist monks have that can also be used for this purpose?" When the reports were in, the total number of the needy, including the orphaned, the aged, and the chronically ill, was more than 21,900.

According to a Yüeh custom, the total amount of grain allocated for relief purposes should not exceed 3,000 piculs per year. In that year, however, His Excellency raised more than 48,000 piculs from wealthy citizens and Buddhist and Taoist monks to be added to the official allocation. Beginning on the first day of the tenth month each adult was given one pint of grain per day and each minor one-half as much. Fearful that the crowd might trample and thus injure each other when it came to receive food, His Excellency ordered that men and women come on alternative days to collect a two-day supply. To prevent the needy from leaving their home town, fifty-seven distribution centers were installed outside the cities and in the suburbs, and the receivers were warned that the granting of relief grain would be discontinued as far as they were concerned if they left for the city. Former officials who resided in the areas of famine were invited to help the regular staff to carry on the relief duties. They were given food to eat; they were not paid any salaries. By these devices those who could not support themselves were thus saved from starvation.

His Excellency informed all wealthy citizens within his jurisdiction that they should continue to sell grain to the needy if they had any to sell. Besides, he made available more than 52,000 piculs of government-owned grain, to be sold in the open market at below-the-market prices. Eighteen stores were established for this purpose. As an additional relief, 38,000 men were recruited to build irrigation canals totalling 4,000 *chang*. Money lenders were urged to grant moratorium to the borrowers who would not have to pay their debts until harvests were collected; and, if the creditors agreed to such an arrangement, the government would guarantee payments. Pending adoption, abandoned children were supported by public funds.

In the spring of the following year, an epidemic struck the province. His Excellency ordered the establishment of a temporary hospital to house those who were ill but homeless. Two Buddhist monks were employed to attend the patients, to see to it that they receive adequate food and medical care. Those who died would be properly buried.

According to the law, the relief for the poor should end by the third month each year. In that year, however, it did not end until the fifth month. In cases where the letter of the law was violated, His Excellency took the full responsibility, thus freeing his subordinates from whatever legal consequences might arise. He granted any request that was considered beneficial and reasonable. He worked tirelessly day and night, and often he used his own money to buy food and medicine for those who were ill. It is due to his efforts that the unfortunate were saved from death during the drought and the epidemic and that those who died were properly buried.

130 · K'o Shao-min: *The Agrarian Commune of the Yüan Dynasty* [51]

Of the agricultural policies introduced and carried out during the Yüan dynasty, none was more beneficial than the establishment of agrarian communes. Previously, in a memorial presented to the emperor,[52] Chang Wen-ch'ien, then the minister in charge of agrarian affairs, drafted fifteen articles as a guideline for the proposed communes. In the twenty-third year of Chih-yüan (1286) the emperor issued a decree ordering the establishment of communes in all the provinces of China in accordance with the aforesaid fifteen articles. The important points of these articles were as follows:

1. Every fifty farming households were to be organized as a commune in each and every district. Each commune was to be headed by a commune chief chosen from the village elders who were well experienced in farming. Once the number of households within a commune multiplied to one hundred, a separate commune, headed by a different chief, should be established. If a village had fewer than fifty households, it should form a commune jointly with a neighboring village. In remote and sparsely populated areas where this kind of arrangement was infeasible, each village was allowed to form its own commune even though its total number of households was fewer than fifty. The primary function of a commune chief was to teach and promote farming and sericulture, and local officials were not allowed to assign to him duties that were not related to this primary function.

2. In promoting farming and sericulture, the commune chief should consider it his duty to reward the diligent and punish the laggard. He should see to it that the farmers under his jurisdiction complete their work in each of the seasons when it was due. To achieve this purpose, he should erect a post on the embankment of each of the commune fields and write on it the name of the person in charge of this particular field. Such identification would help him to locate responsibilities during his periodic inspection tours.

3. Each adult male was required to plant twenty mulberry and date trees each year. He could, if he so chose, plant twenty mulberry trees around his house. If the soil was not condusive to the growth of either mulberry or date trees, he could plant elms and willows instead. But the total number of trees planted should not be fewer than twenty. If he chose to plant fruit trees, he should not plant more than ten. On the other hand, he should be encouraged to plant as much clover as possible as a famine prevention measure.

4. As for irrigation works, they were the responsibility of local officials who, with the assistance of irrigation experts, should see to it that they were in good order at all times. Barring unusual circumstances, villagers were allowed to dig irrigation canals to lead water from higher to lower ground. If water wheels were needed to move water from lower to higher ground, the government should

---

[51] K'o Shao-min (d.1933), a Hanlin scholar towards the end of the Ch'ing dynasty, became the president of the Institute of Ch'ing Studies (*Ch'ing-shih kuan*) after the establishment of the republic. His monumental work, *A New History of the Yüan (Hsin Yüan shih),* was formally listed as a dynastic history by an order of the President of the Chinese Republic in 1919. This selection appears in "Economics, Part II" *(Shih-huo chih erh); Hsin Yüan shih,* roll 69.

[52] Yüan Shih-tsu or Kublai Khan, r.1264–1294.

see to it that the villagers made them with their own resources. It would provide free materials, however, if the villagers were found to be too poor to undertake this task alone.

5. To provide an additional supply of sustenance, villages that were close to water sources should dig ponds for the purpose of raising such animals as ducks, geese, and fish, and such plants as lotus, water-chestnut, and reeds.

6. All people in a commune were obligated to help a fellow member who, because of illness or death in the family, could not attend to his fields.

7. Whenever an unusually large number of people in a commune suffered from illness and consequently could not work, two of the neighboring communes would be obligated to help them during the crisis. Such mutual help should also be arranged with regard to the raising of silkworms. Whenever a person's ox died, all of his fellow members should contribute money to purchase or rent a new one.

8. With the exception of those abandoned fields that had been assigned to the military services or designated as public land, all others that were illegally occupied by unauthorized personnel should be taken over by the government, after such an illegal act had been clearly established by responsible officials. These fields would be first distributed among poor villagers and, should there be a surplus, distributed among the rest of the villagers.

9. Each commune should establish a relief granary to be supervised by the commune chief. In a good year each household was required to contribute one peck of grain for each of its members. Those who did not have grain to contribute should deliver to the relief granary materials of comparable value. The stored grain or materials were to be distributed among the needy in a year of famine.

10. The commune chief should take notice of any person who was lazy in his work or disobedient to his parents or elder brothers. He should report the man's misconduct to the inspection official whenever the latter arrived. Upon verification of his guilt, the commune chief should write down his name, together with his misdeeds, on a white wall in the village. If he still refused to mend his ways, he would be forced to serve as a coolie laborer for the entire commune as a punishment.

12. A school should be established in each and every commune. The teacher should be versed in the classics.[53] All parents were urged to send their children to school during the period of comparative leisure when the children's help was no longer needed in the field. A pupil who did exceptionally well should be reported to responsible officials for verification and then commendation.

13. In the tenth month of each year the district headquarters would send an official to each of the communes for inspection purposes. If the eggs of locusts were found within a commune's jurisdiction, no efforts should be spared to exterminate them.

It can be seen from the above articles that the regulations governing the agrarian commune were thorough and detailed. Prior to the Yüan dynasty nothing like this had occurred for a long time.

---

[53] Confucian classics.

131 · Wang Shou-jen: *A Rural Compact* [54]

An old proverb says that a reed stands erect without support if it grows among the hemp and a white sand becomes black if it is buried in the mud. Is it not true that a good or bad man is really the product of his environment? Formerly there were those among us who deserted their homes and committed crimes. Is it really true that they were bad by nature and deserved all the blame placed upon them? I believe that we, as officials, were equally at fault because we had failed to teach them proper conduct and to set good examples for them to follow.

Neither are you elders completely blameless. You have failed to teach and discipline your children at an early age, and without your guidance, they are influenced instead by the evil elements in our society. You have failed to encourage them to walk along a righteous path; and you do not know how to make them affectionate members of your household to which they should feel that they belong. Moreover, you have aggravated their grievance by your impulsive anger and constant complaint; and by being dishonest with them, you have brought damage to yourself. As a result, their conduct becomes worse and worse each day, and they become even more unmanageable. All of us—we as officials and you as parents—are equally responsible.

However, there is no use grieving about the past; there is much we can do about the future. I therefore draft and proclaim this rural compact whereby you can live harmoniously together. All those who endorse this compact pledge themselves to be dutiful towards their parents, show respect for their elder brothers, teach and discipline their children, and be friendly towards their neighbors. They will help and provide comfort for one another during the time of distress, adversity, or death; they will encourage one another towards goodness and warn each other against evil. They will refrain from engaging in feuds and lawsuits, and they will instead be harmonious and faithful. All pledge themselves to be good citizens and to do their very best to cultivate fine customs.

Even the most ignorant man can find fault with others; the most intelligent man becomes suddenly ignorant when the fault lies with himself. Do not hold a grudge against those who you believe have wronged you. Nor should you think that you are so good that you cannot be made better. To be good or evil is decided in a fraction of a second, and such a decision can only be made by you and you alone. I hope that you will keep in mind these words.

1. A compact leader and three deputy leaders shall be chosen by all members of this compact. These leaders should be elderly and virtuous and enjoy the respect and confidence of the constituting members. . . . Three books should be kept. The first book is to record the names of all participating members and their daily behavior. The second and third books are to record their good deeds to be recommended and their errors to be corrected, respectively.

2. A member of this compact contributes 3 percent of a tael for each meeting, to be collected by the compact treasurer. The fee thus collected is used

---

[54] This rural compact was written by Wang Shou-jen (1472–1529), a famous philosopher of the Ming dynasty, sometime after 1516 when he was made a governor of South Kiangsi (Nan Kan). Source: *Ching-shih wen-tsung*, pp. 188–191.

to disburse all expenses connected with the meeting, such as food and beverage. Its amount should be kept small.

3. The compact meeting should be held once a month, on the day of the full moon. Those who cannot attend the meeting due to illness or other legitimate reasons should notify the treasurer in advance. A member who fails to attend without legitimate reasons will receive a demerit and will be fined one tael of silver. The money will go to the common treasury.

4. Whenever a dispute occurs between two contending members, a general meeting of all members will be called in a spacious Buddhist or Taoist temple to resolve the differences.

5. To be more on the generous side, all commendations should be clear and decisive and all reproofs should be subtle and perspicuous. If a man has shown disrespect for his elder brothers, instead of recording the misconduct as it has happened, the record should read something like this: "We have heard that so-and-so has not done his best in honoring his elders. We personally do not believe that this is true. Before we have time to ascertain the truth, we record on a tentative basis what we have heard." All reproofs recorded for the purpose of reforming the offending person should be written in this manner.

In the case of an unrepentent offender who will not change his ways despite repeated remonstrations, he should nevertheless not be reprimanded in public. If he were, he would have no place to retreat, and it is more likely that he would be aggravated to go further on his evil path. Instead, the compact leader should approach him in private and persuade him to report his error of his own accord. Other members shall reason with him and help him to see the light through his own efforts. For the time being, his wrongdoings shall not be recorded, but will be recorded if they are continued. If he insists on following his evil ways after they have been recorded in the compact book, his misconduct will be reported to the government. If this report fails to impress him, his fellow members are obligated to arrest him and hand him over to the government, to be punished in accordance with his offense. If he resists arrest, they will request government troops to exterminate him.

5. Disputes among members should be settled by arbitration, and the compact leader should serve as the arbitrator. The decision should be reasonable, just, and equitable to both sides. Under no circumstances should a member be allowed to shift responsibility, defame others, or unjustifiably accuse the commune leader and other officials of wrongdoings.

6. People from other areas often return home whenever tax payments and corvée duties are due, leaving the evaded burden to be shouldered by those in their immediate neighborhood. The compact leader should inform them that they should fulfill their obligations towards the government within the stipulated time limit, and that if they continue to evade them, their misdeeds will be reported to responsible officials who will punish them in accordance with their offense. Moreover, they will no longer be allowed to reside among us.

7. Local landlords and traveling merchants are allowed to lend money at an interest not to exceed the customary rate. If the debtor cannot pay when payment is due, he should be given additional time to fulfill his obligations. There are among the money lenders heartless and ruthless elements who seize the first opportunity of default to grab the debtor's land; the debtor, losing his means of support, is forced by hunger to commit crimes. From now on a debtor who cannot meet his payments

should report this to the compact leader who in turn will make an arrangement with the creditor to pay as much as the debtor can, with the balance to be either reduced or paid in the future, or both. If the debtor has overpaid, the overpayment shall be returned. If the creditor refuses to refund the overpaid amount, the compact leader and his fellow members will take the case to the government for redress.

8. There are people who join the bandits in order to seek revenge against their relatives or neighbors on account of some differences or disputes which they have not been able to resolve by peaceful means. By resorting to violent methods, they bring damage to not only their intended victims but also innocent bystanders. From now on all disputes should be reported to the compact leader who will then serve as the arbitrator to resolve the differences. The compact leader can, if he chooses, volunteer his good offices whenever a dispute arises. In short, no person is allowed to commit banditry in order to seek revenge. If an act of banditry is committed, the compact leader, together with his fellow members, should report it to the government which shall then send armed forces to exterminate the offenders.

9. There are those in the military as well as in the civilian ranks who, looking respectable, are actually engaged in illegal activities. They serve as informers for bandits, or trade cattle and horses in a clandestine manner. They enrich themselves at the expense of thousands of others. The compact leader and his fellow members should warn a person of this kind against his evil ways and encourage him to reform. If he does not, his wrongdoings shall be reported to the government, to be punished in a manner he deserves.

10. In the process of performing their official duties, all village officials, civilian or military, are not allowed to seek compensation from villagers. If they actively seek compensation, the compact leader should report their misconduct to the government, to be punished in a manner they deserve.

11. Men and women should be married when they reach the marriageable age. Wedding is often delayed when the family of the prospective bride complains of the insufficient amount of betrothal money that has been paid, or when the family of the prospective groom regards the amount of dowry as inadequate. In each case, the compact leader should inform the parties concerned that the amount of betrothal money or dowry should vary with the ability to pay and that weddings should not be delayed on financial grounds.

12. After the death of one's parents, funeral services should be conducted in such a way as to demonstrate adequately the sense of loss which he feels. The amount of expenses should not exceed his ability to pay. What good does it do to the deceased that their survivors risk financial bankruptcy in order to perform the most elaborate Buddhist rituals or to give the most ostentatious banquets? Let the compact leader inform all of his members that funeral services only need to be proper and that the compact book will record a man as an unfilial son if he insists on lavishness in the performance of funeral services.

13. The day before the monthly meeting the officials of this compact should repair to the meeting hall to prepare for the forthcoming meeting. After sweeping and washing the place clean, they shall place the admonition tablets,[55] together with the incense burners, at the northern end of the hall. Upon the arrival of the

---

[55] Tablets on which were carved or written words of admonition such as "loyalty," "filial piety," "love," "righteousness," "propriety," and "shamefulness."

members on the day of the meeting, they will be brought before the incense burners when the signal drum is beaten for the third time. They will kneel down with their faces facing northward, to listen attentively to a recitation of the compact beliefs. After this is done, the compact leader will speak loudly to them as follows:

All of us who have submitted ourselves to the observation of the compact beliefs will strive for goodness to the best of our ability. If anyone of us deviates from this goal or works for it in appearance but sabotages it in reality, let gods and spirits punish him by death!

The members will then respond as follows:

If anyone of us deviates from this goal or works for it in appearance but sabotages it in reality, let gods and spirits punish him by death!

This being done, the members will prostrate themselves on the ground, stand up, and leave the hall in single file. Outside of the hall and on the temple ground they will be divided into two groups. One group will line up on the eastern end of the ground and the other on the western end of the ground; and they will face each other. It is then that the secretary will begin the reading of the rural compact. After finishing his reading, he shall shout loudly: "Do all of us wish to observe this compact?" The members will yell in unison: "Yes." Then they will salute each other by prostration, stand up, and take their respective seats. . . .

CHAPTER FIFTEEN

Money and Trade

THE great emphasis placed upon agriculture, from which the over-whelming majority of the Chinese people derived their livelihood, over-shadowed the importance of other economic activities such as industry and commerce. This situation was not helped by the traditional anticommercialism which began during the Former Han dynasty and continued until the modern period. Such a prejudice did not exist prior to the Han dynasty, however. As late as the second century B.C. the contribution of the merchant class was sometimes recognized (Selection 132), and Pan Ku (and earlier Ssu-ma Ch'ien) thought it suitable to include the biographies (brief though they were) of some of the leading entrepreneurs in his monumental work (Selection 133). A merchant or industrialist could occasionally rise above the general prejudice and acquire power and influence in the process (Selection 134).

Popular and influential though it was, the anticommercial attitude could not in any way outweigh the basic need of earning a livelihood. A Chinese of talent would avoid the pursuance of an industrial or commercial career if he had a choice, but many Chinese did not have such a choice. The southeast coast of China was hilly and agriculturally unproductive, and the southeastern Chinese had depended upon trade for their livelihood since time immemorial. This trade acquired a new dimension beginning in the Sui-T'ang period when the merchants of the Middle East—Persians, Jews, and Arabs—came to China in large numbers. Some of them did exceptionally well (Selection 135), while others did not (Selection 136). One of the most successful was an Arab with a Sinicized name of P'u Shou-keng who, coming to China during his boyhood, rose to become a high-ranking official with the Sung government and one of the most wealthy and influential men in all of China. His switch of loyalty to the Mongols in the 1270's exterminated whatever hope the Sung loyalists might have had of preserving the southeast for the Chinese govern-ment (Selection 137). To reward him, the Mongols made him the governor of a Chinese province.

Trade needed medium of exchange or money to facilitate it. Though a variety of currencies developed from as early as the Shang dynasty, it was the standard coins made of copper (called *ch'ien* in Chinese) that became the most popular money throughout the course of Chinese history. But the term "standard coins" conveyed different meanings in different periods (Selection 138), and a person's wealth or income was often measured in terms of the land he owned or the amount of grain he received each year. For in-

313

stance, a government official's annual salary was expressed more frequently in the number of piculs of grain he received than the amount of cash he obtained. A picul of grain denoted a value fairly constant and easily understood, while the value of a standard coin varied from time to time, depending upon not only its copper content, but more importantly, the abundance or scarcity of money vis-à-vis the amount of goods in the market. Coinage was a government monopoly, though there were occasional exceptions (Selection 139).

The use of money to facilitate trade took another forward step when paper currency was introduced. Though its origin could be traced to the "flying cash" of the T'ang dynasty, paper currency was not in wide use until the Sung dynasty. First developed by private sources, it became a government monopoly shortly afterwards. The issuance of paper currency was institutionalized, and the temptation to print more of it was too strong for any government to resist (Selection 140). As more and more new issues were rushed into the market, prices of commodities rose and the face value of a paper note bore no relation whatsoever to its counterpart in silver or copper coins. Eventually people objected to accepting the paper money at all (Selection 141).

132 · SSU-MA CH'IEN: *An Introduction to Economics* [1]

"When the world reaches the stage of perfection," said Lao-tzu, "political units are so small that people in one state can hear the crowing of a cock or the bark of a dog in its neighboring states. Citizens of each state love their own food, admire their own clothes, feel satisfied with their own customs, and rejoice in their own occupations. They do not visit people in the other states for the entire duration of their lives." If we use Lao-tzu's standards to measure man and his activities, we might say that the authorities in modern times are totally shameless and that they have succeeded in covering people's eyes and ears.

I do not know what the situation was before the Shen-nung [2] period, says the Grand Historian.[3] From the information provided in the *Book of Odes* and *Book of History,* we know that since the beginning of the Yü-hsia period [4] people have always wanted to see the most beautiful, listen to the most musical, and eat the most delicious. They love comfort and ease, and they brag about their power and influence which to them means glory. This popular attitude has been deeply embedded for a long time; no philosophical persuasion could change it even if it were conducted from door to door. Under the circumstances the best thing to do is to leave the people the way they are, and the next best is to channel their materialistic desires through reason. Less desirable is to educate them so that they will reduce or lose such desires, and worse still, to use coercion to achieve the same purpose. Of all the possible courses to take, the worst the government can do is to join the people and compete with them for material gains.

[1] "Biographies of Merchants and Industrialists" *(Huo-chih lieh-chuan); Shih chi,* roll 129.
[2] A legendary ruler of the remote past.
[3] The author refers to himself.
[4] Twenty-third century B.C. approximately.

Shensi produces lumber, bamboo, grain, hemp and flax, ox tails, and jade. Shantung produces fish, salt, lacquer, silk, and musical instruments. Kiangnan [5] produces cedar, *tz'u*,[6] ginger, cassia, gold, tin, lead, mercury, sandstone, rhinoceros, tortoise-shell, pearls, and animal teeth and skin. The areas north of the Lungmen and Chiehshih Mountains [7] breed a large number of horses, sheep, and oxen, besides producing such items as felt, fur, meat, and horn. Over the mountains that stretch thousands of *li* can be found copper and iron mines that dot the landscape like pawns on a chessboard. This is a brief account of the products in China.

All these products the Chinese love dearly. They are the materials for their food and clothing; they are used to send off the dead as well as prolong the life of the living. The farmers raise crops; the miners bring forth minerals; the artisans fashion into articles what others have produced; and the merchants move raw materials as well as finished products to the market. These activities have gone on and will continue to go on with or without a government, and each person will do his very best to obtain what he desires. That the price of a product is low is a good indication that it will go up; likewise, the price of a product that is too high is bound to come down soon. Each man works diligently on his occupation and rejoices in it; he seeks profits as water seeks the lowest ground, ceaselessly and tirelessly, unobservant of day and night. Wherever profit is, he does not wait for an invitation, and he produces even though nobody has asked him to do so. Does this situation not conform well with the principle of Tao? Is it not a vindication of the soundness of the "naturalist" theory?

"If the farmers do not raise crops," says the *Book of Chou*,[8] "the people will have nothing to eat. If the artisans do not manufacture goods, the people will have nothing to use. If the merchants do not pursue their trade, where can the people obtain the three treasures? [9] If the miners do not bring forth minerals, there will be a shortage of money. When money is in short supply, it will be impossible to exploit the natural resources that exist in mountains and rivers." Upon these four groups of producers—farmers, artisans, merchants, and miners—do the people depend for their supply of food and clothing, and the size of this supply will determine the degree of material welfare which they enjoy. If the supply is large, it will enrich the nation as well as the households that constitute it. The underlying principle of affluence versus poverty is as simple as it is immutable: the masterful will have a surplus, and the awkward will have to be satisfied with an inadequate livelihood.

When Grand Duke Wang [10] was granted a fief at Yingch'iu,[11] he found that his new domain was salty and unproductive and that the population was sparse. He promoted spinning and weaving and improved upon the manufacturing of handicraft products; he also strengthened and invigorated the salt and fishing industries. Being economically successful, his fief Ch'i became a center of attrac-

[5] The Yangtze valley.
[6] *Catalpa kaempferi.*
[7] The Lungmen Mountains were located in modern Shensi and Shansi provinces. The exact location of the Chiehshih Mountains has been debated for centuries; it remains unknown.
[8] *Chou shu,* an ancient classic.
[9] Pearl, jade, and gold.
[10] His real name was Chiang Tzu-ya who reportedly lived in the twelfth century B.C.
[11] Located in modern Shantung province and close to the sea. The fief was later known as Ch'i.

tion to which people, old or young, migrated in large numbers. Its products—hats, belts, clothes, and shoes—could be found all over the nation. People throughout the Shantung coast went to Ch'i to pay their tribute.

Subsequently the state of Ch'i declined. It was revived, however, under the premiership of Kuan-tzu.[12] Kuan-tzu strengthened the state's financial position through the establishment of a treasury department to supervise the implementation of his economic policies and enabled Duke Huan [13] to become the leader of the Chinese states. Duke Huan called nine interstate conferences and exercised influence in all parts of China. Because of this success, Kuan-tzu was awarded the House of San-kuei and the position of "tributary minister"; [14] his wealth rivalled that of many princes in other states. The wealth and strength which Ch'i enjoyed continued until the period of King Wei and King Hsüan.[15]

Kuan-tzu once said: "Only when the granaries are full of grain can people know the meaning of propriety and righteousness; only when people are adequately supplied with food and clothing can they understand the difference between honor and shamefulness." The sense of propriety thrives in plenty and dies in poverty. When a gentleman becomes wealthy, he uses his wealth to promote good deeds. When a small man becomes wealthy, he uses his wealth to satisfy his selfish desires. A deep river breeds fish; a high mountain invites beasts. It is easy for a wealthy man to be loving and righteous. If he has power and influence to go with his wealth, he is simply irresistible. However, once he loses his power and influence, the people who have lived on him as guests will leave his door and disappear. If he is unhappy about his losses, he can be more barbarious than the barbarians. The saying that a millionaire's son does not die in the market [16] contains a great deal of truth.

For what do people cooperate and live harmoniously together? Profit. For what do they compete and fiight against one another? Profit. Even a king or a duke is worried about poverty; how can an ordinary citizen be possibly an exception?

133 · PAN KU: *The Merchants* [17]

After Kou Chien, the King of Yüeh, had been defeated at K'uaichi,[18] he employed Chi Yüan and Fan Li as his advisers. "To know the inevitability of warfare is to learn to prepare for it," said Chi Yüan. "To use materials timely and effectively is to understand truly the meaning of natural resources. Keeping constantly in mind this truism, a king will be able to create wealth and strength for his kingdom. When there is a drought, he should make boats so as to be

---

[12] Kuan Chung who lived in the seventh century B.C.

[13] Duke Huan of Chi (686–643 B.C.).

[14] *P'ei-ch'en* which was equivalent to a minister on the imperial level.

[15] Ch'i Wei-wang and Ch'i Hsüan-wang, both of whom lived in the fourth century B.C.

[16] The market was traditionally used as a place for public execution.

[17] "Biographies of Merchants and Industrialists" (*Huo-chih chuan*); *Han shu,* roll 91. Some of the merchants that appear in this selection are described in virtually identical language in *Shih chi,* roll 129.

[18] He was defeated by Fu Ch'ai, King of Wu, in about 483 B.C. K'uaichi was located in Yüeh (modern Chekiang province).

prepared for a flood. When there is a flood, he should manufacture vehicles so as to be prepared for a drought. To anticipate what the future holds and act accordingly is the soundest principle underlying all rules." The king followed his advice in all matters concerning the state, and in ten years the kingdom was economically prosperous and militarily strong. He paid his soldiers generously and defeated the powerful state of Wu in a single battle. The humiliation which he once suffered at K'uaichi was finally avenged.

"Chi Yüan's advice, even when it was partially followed, has brought excellent results," said Fan Li. "I shall follow his advice in managing my household." He left Yüeh in a small boat and wandered in many parts of China. He changed his name too; he called himself Ch'ih-yi Tzu-p'i when he was in Ch'i and Mr. Chu when he finally settled down at T'ao.[19] He chose T'ao as his home because T'ao was an important trade center where goods of all states gathered and changed hands. He bought, hoarded, or sold, depending upon the time and the circumstances. He relied on his own judgement and would not blame others whatever the result. Moreover, as a businessman of unusual ability, he knew whom he should entrust with responsibility and at what time he should buy or sell.

In a period of nineteen years, Mr. Chu made one thousand gold pieces three times. Each time after the money had been made, he distributed it among his poor friends and younger brothers. Later, having reached the old age, he handed over his business to his children and grandchildren. The business continued to grow until eventually it was valued at tens of thousands in assets. From then on, whenever people discussed rich men, the first name that came to their minds was Mr. Chu of T'ao.

After finishing his studies with Confucius, Tzu-kung was employed as an official at the state of Wei.[20] Later, he became a merchant, buying and selling in all of the places between Ts'ao and Lu.[21] Of the seventy disciples of Confucius, he was defintely the most wealthy. While Yen Yüan [22] lived a gutter existence with little to eat, Tzu-kung was at the head of scores of chariots, visiting dukes and counts to whom he brought money and silk as gifts. Wherever he went, the head of the state received him as warmly as if he were an equal. Yet Confucius praised highly Yen Yüan and spoke condescendingly of Tzu-kung. "Is Hui [23] not close to being a sage even though he had little to eat?" said Confucius. "As for Tz'u,[24] he has not followed what I taught. Whether he buys or sells, he always manages to realize the largest profit."

Pai Kuei was a native of Chou. At the time when Li K'e was assisting Duke Wen of Wei [25] to develop land resources, Pai Kuei was focusing his eyes on the fluctuation of commodity prices. He bought when others sold and sold when others bought. Moreover, he was frugal in the use of food and clothing and had few material desires. He lived no better than his employees or even his servants. Whenever there were profits to be realized, however, he dashed towards his

---

[19] Tingt'ao, modern Shantung province.
[20] Located in modern Honan province.
[21] Both were located in modern Shantung province.
[22] A disciple of Confucius.
[23] Yen Yüan.
[24] Tzu-kung.
[25] Early in the fourth century B.C.

targets as audaciously as a hungry vulture sweeps down on its prey. "I manage my business," said he, "in the same way as Yi Yin and Lü Shang [26] administered a government, Sun Pin and Wu Ch'i [27] planned a battle, and Shang Yang [28] implemented a provision of the law.[29] If a man is not intelligent enough to change with the circumstances, brave enough to make sudden and drastic decisions, benevolent enough to give whenever it is wise to give, or persevering enough to hold to what he believes to be sound and correct, he should not go into my field, the field of business." From then on, all businessmen, to be successful, followed Pai Kuei's advice.

Ch'i Tun became wealthy by manufacturing salt, and Kuo Tsung, a native of Hantan,[30] amassed a large fortune by the mining and smelting of iron. Their wealth was so great that it rivalled that of the kings.

Wu-chih Ying was in the livestock industry. He sold his animals whenever they became large and numerous. With the money he thus acquired, he bought high-quality silk and presented it to the king of Jung [31] as tribute. The king paid him a price ten times his cost, and gave him cattle and horses so numerous that they were measured in "valleys" instead of "heads." Ch'in Shih-huang [32] granted him the title of prince and the privilege of meeting with him in the same manner as his ministers.

The ancestors of Widow Ch'ing of Pa discovered a mine containing mercury deposits, and the family monopolized its profits for several generations. Needless to say, the family was extremely wealthy. Widow Ch'ing inherited this business and ran it successfully. She hired guards to protect her person, and consequently nobody dared to approach her in an improper manner. Ch'in Shih-huang invited her to be his guest and called her a lady of chastity. He even built a palace in honor of her.

The ancestors of the Cho family of Shu [33] came originally from the state of Chao where they amassed a large fortune by engaging in the iron mining and iron smelting business. After the conquest of Chao by the state of Ch'in, the Cho family, together with many others, were forced to move to Shu. Having lost everything they had, the heads of the Cho family—husband and wife—had to push wheelbarrows with their own hands on their way towards the territory of Shu.

Those among the evictees who had some money of their own requested the officials-in-charge to settle them in a place not too far from their original home. The officials agreed and settled them at Chiamen.[34] The Cho family, however, wished to proceed further. "This place is mountainous and unproductive," the

---

[26] Yi Yin was the prime minister under T'ang, founder of the Shang dynasty. Lü Shang, also known as Chiang Tzu-ya, served King Wen of Chou during the twelfth century B.C.

[27] Famous military strategists of ancient China.

[28] The chief minister of the Ch'in state during the fourth century B.C.

[29] This remark should not be taken literally because Pai Kuei, who lived late in the fifth and early in the fourth century B.C., could not have possibly heard of Shang Yang who did not become Ch'in's chief minister until the latter part of the fourth century B.C.

[30] Capital of the state of Chao.

[31] A non-Chinese, nomadic tribe located in modern Kansu and Chinghai provinces.

[32] Founder of the Ch'in dynasty.

[33] Modern Szechuan province.

[34] Located in modern Szechuan province.

Chos commented. "We have heard that the valleys below the Ming Mountains [35] are wide and fertile. Taros of unusual size grow in this part of the world, and no person has ever died because of the lack of food. Moreover, the people are industrious; they make cloth and love to trade." They requested to be moved to Linch'iung.[36]

Arriving at their destination, the Chos were extremely pleased with their new home. They began to smelt iron which they found in the nearby mountains and sold their products in all the areas between Shu and T'ien.[37] Soon they became wealthy enough to own eight hundred slaves. They fished and hunted for recreation and lived like kings.

Ch'eng Cheng, an evictee from Shangtung, was also engaged in the iron smelting industry. He traded among the barbarians with whom he was in good terms. His wealth matched that of the Cho family.

After the fortune of the Cho and Ch'eng families had declined, another millionaire named Lo P'ou emerged in Chengtu during the Ch'eng-Ai period (32–1 B.C.). Previously, as a merchant in the capital,[38] he had already amassed a large fortune. Then he became a financial agent for the Shih family of P'ingling whose fortune was even greater than his own. The Shih family gave him a large sum of money as capital and ordered him to operate between the capital and Pashu.[39] In a period of several years, his profits multiplied to tens of millions. He gave half of his profits to Duke Tingling of Ch'üyang on whose political power he relied to facilitate his money-lending activities. Because of the duke's support, no debtor of his dared to default on his payments. Lo P'ou also monopolized the salt-producing wells in Szechuan and reaped a return of 100 percent on his investment each and every year. He succeeded in what he had set out to achieve.

The ancestors of Mr. K'ung of Yüan came from Liang [40] where they were engaged in the iron smelting industry. After the conquest of Wei by the Ch'in state, the K'ung family was moved to Nanyang.[41] Mr. K'ung followed the family tradition and reestablished the iron business on an even larger scale. He invested his money in crop fields besides, and traveled among the princes whose support he sought for his commercial activities. Called a "gentleman of leisure and refinement," he was not so ruthless as other merchants; yet the amount he earned was more than enough to maintain a life of ease and comfort. He eventually amassed a fortune of several thousand gold pieces. His example of a leisurely life was followed by other Nanyang merchants.

The people of Lu were known for their frugality, and the Ping family was even more frugal than most. It built its fortune on the iron smelting business and was extremely wealthy. Yet all members of this family made a pledge among themselves that they would not let a single profit-making opportunity pass by, however insignificant it might be. They traded all over the empire. Because of the example they set, many people in Lu abandoned the pursuit of literature and took up trade instead.

[35] Located in the western section of modern Szechuan province.
[36] Located in Szechuan, southwest of Chengtu.
[37] Modern Yunnan province.
[38] Ch'angan.
[39] Modern Szechuan province.
[40] Wei, modern Shansi province.
[41] Located in modern Honan province.

The people in Ch'i had an unusually low opinion of slaves, but Tiao Chien was an exception. He, in fact, placed a high value on them. He collected slaves of high intelligence whom other owners wished to get rid of, and sent them to seek after profits in the fishing and salt industry as well as in trade. His slaves rode in carriages and made friends with government officials, but he trusted them as usual. His confidence in them paid him handsomely, and he amassed a fortune valued at tens of millions. As a popular saying went, it was preferable to be Tiao Chien's slave than to be a citizen with a high-ranking title. An able and intelligent slave, successfully utilized, could bring wealth to his owner. After the Tiao family's fortune had declined, there was a Wei family in Lintzu [42] who accumulated wealth valued at fifty millions during the Ch'eng-Ai period (32–1 B.C.).

The people of Chou [43] were shrewd, and Shih Shih was the shrewdest. Shih moved goods from one place to another and would go wherever there were profits to be realized. Loyang, the capital of Chou, was to China as the main street to a city: it was the distribution center for all goods that came from Ch'i, Ch'in, Ch'u, and Chao. [44] The rich people in Loyang strove to impress one another with their wealth, and some of them were so busy making money that they stayed in other cities for a prolonged period, and when they did occasionally return to Loyang, could not find time even to visit their own home. Shih Shih employed men of such aggressiveness that he eventually amassed a fortune of hundreds of millions.

After the Shih family's fortune had declined, Chang Ch'ang-shu and Hsüeh Tzu-chung, both of Loyang, also amassed a fortune of hundreds of millions during the period of Ch'eng-ti, Ai-ti, and Wang Mang. [45] Wang Mang, following the example of Han Wu-ti, hired them as his advisers, but he was unable to obtain much benefit from this association.

The ancestors of Mr. Jen of Hsüanch'ü were granary officials. When the Ch'in regime was about to collapse, he purchased large quantities of grain, while other rich people competed with one another to hoard gold and jade. Shortly afterwards the Ch'u and the Han armies faced each other at Yingyang, [46] and farmers could no longer till their fields. The price of polished rice rose to ten thousand standard coins per picul. By selling the hoarded grain, Mr. Jen acquired all the gold and jade that had been hitherto in other people's hands. He, consequently, became very wealthy. While other wealthy men loved luxuries, Mr. Jen continued to be frugal and worked diligently in the fields and in attending his livestock. Other merchants bought things because they were cheap; he bought them because they were good, however expensive they were. His good example as a rich man was followed by his descendants for several generations. His father made him promise that he would not eat or wear anything that did not come about as a result of his own labor and that he would never eat meat or drink liquor prior to the successful completion of a day's work. He was a good example to his neighbors and was highly respected by the emperor despite his wealth.

After the Han government had opened up the frontier, Ch'iao T'ao acquired a

[42] Located in modern Shantung province.
[43] Located in modern Honan province.
[44] Modern Shantung, Shensi, the middle Yangtze valley, and Shansi respectively.
[45] From 32 B.C. to A.D. 24.
[46] The Ch'u and the Han armies were led by Hsiang Yü and Liu Pang respectively. Yingyang was located in modern Honan province.

fortune that consisted of one thousand horses, two thousand cattle, ten thousand sheep, and ten thousand *chung* [47] of grain.

When Wu and Ch'u revolted,[48] all nobles in Ch'angan [49] were required to join the armed forces. To furnish themselves with food and equipment, they went to the money-lenders to borrow. Owing to their uncertainty about the outcome of the forthcoming warfare, the money-lenders did not wish to lend because they were not sure that the prospective borrowers could honor their debt obligations. The Wu-yen family alone decided to risk one thousand gold pieces and charged the borrowers an interest of 1,000 percent. In three months the rebellion was suppressed, and the Wu-yen family multiplied its investment by ten times in a single year. . . .

Outside the capital and in the countryside there were numerous people rich and shrewd enough to engage in industry and trade and to enter into monopolistic enterprises. All of them won esteem from local populace because of their wealth. There were, for instance, Ch'in Yang whose landholding was the largest in his province, Weng Pai who peddled animal fats, the Chang family who sold pickles and sauces, the Chih family who sharpened swords and knives, the Cho family who specialized in the making of spices, and Chang Li who was an expert on horse diseases. . . . There were others whose occupations were outright immoral, such as digging out dead bodies to steal the buried treasure, or running gambling houses in violation of the law. Yet people like Ch'ü Shu, Chi Fa, and Yung Lo-ch'eng who were engaged in these lawless activities resided side by side with ordinary citizens and were regarded as respectable. There was nothing more disastrous to a nation than the destruction of good customs.

134 · PAN KU: *Pu Shih* [50]

Pu Shih, a native of Honan, was a rancher as well as a farmer. He had a younger brother. When his younger brother reached adulthood, he gave him the house, the fields, and all the valuables in the household. He left the house with one hundred sheep and headed for the mountains. He shepherded in the mountains for a period of ten years, at the end of which his sheep had multiplied to more than one thousand. He bought houses and land and divided what he bought with his younger brother because by then the latter had already bankrupted himself. As his younger brother repeatedly bankrupted himself, Pu Shih had to come to his rescue again and again.

Later, when the emperor [51] was about to launch a military campaign against the Hsiung-nu,[52] Pu Shih sent him a petition in which he expressed his desire to contribute half of his wealth to the war funds. Having read the petition, the emperor dispatched an envoy to speak with him.

"Do you wish to become a government official?" asked the envoy.

---

[47] One *chung* equals 0.4 piculs.
[48] This refers to the Seven States Rebellion. See p. 126, Footnote 44.
[49] Then the national capital.
[50] "Biography of Pu Shih" *(Pu Shih chuan); Han shu,* roll 58.
[51] Han Wu-ti.
[52] See pp. 210–220.

"I have been a shepherd since I was a child," Pu Shih replied. "I have never learned to be a government official; nor do I wish to become one."

"Do you have any complaints to which you want the government to listen?"

"No," Pu Shih replied. "I have never feuded with anyone in my life. I lend money to the poor who need my help, and I teach those who seek my advice. All people in my area listen to me; against whom should I have any complaints?"

"What do you really want then?"

"Now that the emperor has decided to launch a military campaign to conquer the Hsiung-nu, I believe that the virtuous should volunteer to die and the wealthy should contribute funds," Pu Shih replied. "Only by cooperative efforts can the Hsiung-nu be conquered."

The envoy reported the conversation to the emperor who in turn asked the opinion of Kung-sun Hung, the prime minister. "This man speaks and acts against common sense and, in my opinion, cannot be trusted," said the prime minister. "I hope that Your Majesty will not grant his request." Accepting the prime minister's advice, the emperor did not answer Pu Shih's petition. Several years later when his request was formally rejected, Pu Shih returned home to attend to his livestock and crop fields.

One year after his returning home, a Hsiung-nu tribe called Hun-yeh surrendered to the Han authorities. The treasury was empty, and there were no financial resources to meet these increased expenses. Meanwhile a large number of poor people were forced by hunger to leave their homes, and they too depended upon local governments to feed them. Having sensed the difficulties faced by local officials, Pu Shih presented the governor of Honan with 200,000 standard coins to be used to help the refugees.

Looking at a list of the wealthy people of Honan who had contributed to the relief of the poor, the emperor spotted the name of Pu Shih. "This is the same man who had at one time expressed his desire to contribute half of his wealth to the government's defense fund," he said to himself. He ordered that Pu Shih be given 120,000 standard coins as a reward. Accepting the honor, Pu Shih nevertheless returned the money to the government. At a time when the rich wanted to hoard their wealth, he alone wished to contribute. Having been convinced that Pu Shih was an elder of great integrity, the emperor decided to make him an official with the tenth rank and award him ten ch'ing of land. Moreover, by an imperial decree his name was made known throughout the empire, and he was hailed as a good example for all people to follow.

But Pu Shih did not want to become a government official. "I have some sheep in the imperial forest," said the emperor; "I would like you to tend them for me." Thus, after he had been formally made an official, Pu Shih was tending a herd of sheep, dressed in coarse clothes and wearing straw sandals like any other shepherd. One year later, the emperor paid him a visit and was pleased to see that the sheep had grown well and had multiplied. "The principle of tending sheep is the same as that of governing men," said Pu Shih. "It is important to eliminate the bad elements whenever they are found. If left alone, they will contaminate the whole group." The emperor thought that this advice was very wise and decided to try him as a shepherd of the people. He was given a minor post first at which he did well, and was then promoted to the magistrate of Ch'engkao [53] where he supervised

[53] Located in modern Honan province.

the transport of tax revenue to the imperial government. Fully convinced of his honesty as a man and his loyalty as a minister, the emperor made him an imperial counsellor to King Ch'i and then promoted him as the latter's chief minister.

Later when Lü Chia [54] revolted, Pu Shih presented the emperor with the following memorial: "I have heard that when a king suffers humiliation, his ministers should die to avenge it. As for the rest, they should contribute funds to finance the military efforts. Only in this way can the nation become strong and inviolable. Therefore I and my children will proceed to Lintzu [55] to learn archery and Poch'ang [56] to study seamanship so that we, as loyal subjects, can also die for the nation."

Impressed with Pu Shih's sentiments, the emperor issued the following decree: "I have heard that a man should 'return kindness for kindness and honesty for injury.' [57] Though the nation is now in difficulty, few have volunteered their efforts and valiancy so as to serve it. The chief minister of Ch'i [58] was exemplary in conduct and worked diligently in tilling the fields. Each time his livestock had multiplied, he divided it with his younger brother with his usual generosity. Commanding great wealth, he was never corrupted by it. Formerly when there was an alert in the northern frontier, he petitioned the government to allow him to help. Later when there was a bad harvest in Hsiho,[59] he led the people of Ch'i to contribute grain for relief. Now he is volunteering again. Though he has not yet entered the battlefield, I cannot but admire the sense of righteousness that inspires his effort. He shall be from now on titled Duke of Kuannei and be awarded forty catties of gold and ten ch'ing of land. Let this fact be known throughout the empire."

During the Yüan-ting period (116–111 B.C.) Pu Shih replaced Shih Ch'ing as the Grand Censor. He did not like the government's monopoly of the salt and iron industry and its taxation on boating, and suggested abolishing both. The emperor was not pleased with his suggestion. In the following year the emperor was scheduled to perform the grand ritual to honor Heaven, and Pu Shih, without literary training, could not write anything appropriate for the occasion. He was demoted and was made an adviser to the crown prince, and his post as the Grand Censor was taken over by Erh K'uan. He died of old age.

135 • Yo K'o: *The Arabs in Canton* [60]

The "sea barbarians" [61] lived side by side with the Chinese in Canton and the most powerful of them was a man named P'u.[62] Mr. P'u, a white barbarian, came

[54] A ruler in Nanyüeh (modern Kwangtung province).

[55] Located in modern Shantung province.

[56] Located in modern Shantung province.

[57] A remark attributed to Confucius.

[58] Pu Shih.

[59] The section of the Yellow River that serves as the dividing line between modern Shensi and Shansi provinces.

[60] The author (b. c.1183), who lived early in the thirteenth century, was a grandson of Yo Fei, the famous general of the Sung dynasty. The Chinese original appears in his work, *History of the Ch'eng (Ch'eng shih)*, roll 11.

[61] *Hai-liao.*

[62] Believed to be the transliteration of the Arabic word Abu.

from Chan-ch'eng [63] where he was reported to be a man of great importance. On his way to China, he encountered a heavy storm; and fearful of the sea, he requested his employer to let him stay in China as a commercial agent so that he did not have to risk his life on the stormy sea again. His employer agreed to his request. . . .

Having been in the city for a long time, the P'u family lived a life of luxury far exceeding the level permitted under the law. However, since the local government was interested in encouraging more traders to come and since the family involved was not Chinese, it did not wish to concern itself with the violation. Thus, the P'u house became bigger and more luxurious as its wealth continued to grow at a fast rate.

In the Jen-tzu year of Shao-hsi (1192) when I was ten, I followed my father to Canton and had the opportunity of visiting the P'u house. The house was several stories high and covered a large area, though I can no longer remember all the details. I recall that there was a tall building several hundred ch'ih [64] in height, towering over a running stream. Whenever a visitor entered the building, he saw a golden plate underneath which an ingenious machine was hidden. Pressing the plate, he heard a musical, metallic sound. Going up, he noticed beautiful carvings all around him, painted gold or blue, and sometimes both. Besides the building was a garden which contained a pond and a pavilion. The pond was several *chang* on each side, and in its center was a golden fountain. The fountain was covered with decorations shaped like the scales of a fish; I was told that thousands of gold pieces had been spent in building it. The main hall of the building was supported by four pillars made of garu-wood which reached as high as the main beam. The side halls and anterooms were equally elegant.

The barbarians worshipped spirits and loved cleanliness; it seemed that they had nothing to do all day long except to worship and pray for better fortunes. The deity they worshipped sounded like Buddha but there was no image of him in the place where he was worshipped. Frankly, nobody knows what kind of deity he really was. In the place of worship there was a stone stele several *chang* high on which were carved strange, cursive words, and all worshippers prostrated themselves before it instead. . . .

Behind the place of worship was a high, slender pagoda protruding skyward towards the clouds. It did not really look like a pagoda, and viewed from a distance, it looked more like a silver brush. It was made of earthen tiles and was painted with white powder. At the ground level was a door which led to a flight of circular stairs, and a person ascended the stairway to reach the top. The stairway, however, was invisible from the outside. Before ships arrived from the sea in the fourth or fifth lunar month, the barbarians went up and down the pagoda, making strange, unintelligible noises and praying for southern winds to come. Often the winds responded. At the pinnacle of the pagoda was a golden rooster which turned around with the change of wind. As I understand, one leg of the rooster has been missing. . . .

One day my father invited the head of the P'u family for dinner and entertained him in the most luxurious manner. All members of our family watched the stranger from behind a curtain, including me who was then a child. I saw him throw money

---

[63] Modern Vietnam.
[64] A Chinese foot.

away as if it were made of dirt; all of our servants—sedan-chair carriers and errand boys—were tipped generously. He displayed on the table the treasures he had brought with him, including pearls and perfumes, in order to show how wealthy he was. "He always loves to show off," commented one of our servants.

136 · Li Fang: *An Old Man from Persia* [65]

Early in the K'ai-yüan period (713–741) Li Mien served as a military commander at Chünyi.[66] At the end of his tenure of office, he decided to take a boat voyage along the Pien River[67] eventually to reach Yangchow where he intended to amuse himself.[68] At Suiyang [69] he met an old Persian who, being very ill, supported himself with a crutch. "I am stranded in a foreign land and also dangerously ill," said the old Persian. "I wish to return to Yangchow. Knowing that you are a man of compassion, I hope that you will protect me and be kind enough to let me ride in your boat." Li felt sorry for the old man and asked him to come aboard. Having been fed with rice and meat, the old man felt better and spoke again: "I was a man of noble birth and came to this country as a merchant more than twenty years ago. I have three sons at home, and I am sure that one of them will come here to look for me."

When the boat reached Ssushang,[70] the old man's illness took a sudden turn for the worse, and he knew that he was going to die soon. He informed Li Mien that he wished to talk with him alone. "Many years ago our country lost its national treasure in the form of a precious stone, and nobody was able to find it. Knowing what it would mean to me if I could locate it, I left my country twenty years ago to search for it. Eventually I found it, and had planned until now to bring it home. With it I should be very wealthy indeed since this stone is worth at least a million. Fearful that it might be lost or stolen while I traveled such a long distance, I cut part of my body and buried it inside my flesh. Unfortunately I have become ill and am now going to die. You have been very kind and generous to me, and I shall give it to you as a present." Upon finishing these words, the old Persian unsheathed his sword and cut open his buttock. The stone slipped out, and the old man died.

Li Mien washed and dressed him and buried him on the bank of the river. Before he pushed the dirt back to the grave, however, he put the stone inside the dead man's mouth.

Arriving at Yangchow, Li Mien stayed in a hotel. One day he met a group of foreigners and began to speak with them. Standing beside the group was a young boy who looked very much like the old Persian who had recently died. He paid a visit to this boy, inquired about his background, and was satisfied that the boy was indeed the old Persian's son. He told the boy about his father's death, and the

---

[65] "Li Mien" *(Li Mien); T'ai-p'ing Records (T'ai-p'ing kuang-chi),* roll 402, by Li Fang who lived in the tenth century.

[66] Located in modern Honan province, near Kaifeng.

[67] Modern Honan province.

[68] Yangchow, located in modern Kiangsu province, was one of the gayest cities of the T'ang-Sung period.

[69] Located in modern Honan province, south of Shangch'iu.

[70] Located in the northern section of modern Anhwei province.

latter was overwhelmed with grief. Then he mentioned about the precious stone and the place where the old Persian was buried. The young man went to his father's grave, opened it, and took the stone away.

137 · K'O SHAO-MIN: *P'u Shou-keng* [71]

P'u Shou-keng, a native of the "Western Regions," came to Ch'üanchou [72] with his elder brother Shou-ch'eng as traders. Towards the end of the Hsien-shun period (1265–1274) he ably served the Sung government by suppressing piracy on the coast. Later, after the new government [73] had appointed him as Minister of Pacification of Fukien and Kwangtung Provinces, he surrendered all of his military forces to the Mongols. When the young prince of Sung [74] arrived at Ch'üanchou, the people in the city wished to welcome him; but Shou-keng closed the city gates and would not let him in. General Chang Shih-chi [75] attacked the city, and the members of Sung's royal household planned to stage an uprising inside the city so as to bring him in. Learning about their plans, Shou-keng invited them to discuss the city's defense. In the midst of drinking, he killed all of them. For three months General Chang attacked the city in vain; finally he lifted the siege and left.

Greatly pleased with Shou-keng's achievements, Emperor Shih-tsu [76] promoted him to the rank of a grand marshal. In the fourteenth year of Chih-yüan (1277) he was appointed as governor of Kiangsi. All of his children and grandchildren also distinguished themselves in governmental service.

138 · YEH SHIH: *The Development of Currency* [77]

Opinion differs when people discuss the advantages and disadvantages of coined money.

In the ancient times money played only an auxiliary role to goods, whereas in the later periods the situation was exactly the reverse. The invention of money resulted from the necessity of conducting trade; its circulation enabled the merchants to make purchases in faraway places as well as those at home. It was difficult to transport goods, but it was easy to ship money.

Money was only infrequently used during the Three Dynasties. It was not until the Ch'in-Han period (221 B.C.–A.D. 220) that it attained wide usage. Nowadays no business can be conducted without it.

The question arises as to why money was rarely used during the Three Dynasties. In those ancient times each person had a steady occupation and was content with it. He was self-sufficient in the sense that he himself produced

[71] Despite his importance, information about P'u Shou-keng is scattered and scarce. This brief account appears in "Biography of P'u Shou-keng" *(P'u Shou-keng chuan); Hsin Yüan shih,* roll 74.
[72] Located in modern Fukien province.
[73] The Mongol or Yüan government.
[74] Prince Shih. This event occurred in 1276.
[75] A Sung loyalist.
[76] Kublai Khan.
[77] A copy of the Chinese original can be found in *Wen-hsien t'ung-k'ao,* roll 9.

practically all the things he and his family needed, from grain and cloth to vegetables, fish, and meat; there were few things he needed to buy from others. As far as money was concerned, only merchants needed it as a medium of exchange, and only the government depended on it as a common standard to measure and compare the values of all things in the empire. In a later period when Li Hui introduced his grain purchase program, it was reported that a typical household spent only a little more than one thousand standard coins per year.[78] They were considered a large sum then. It was certainly larger than the amount that a typical household during the Three Dynasties had either the opportunity or the need to use.

The fact is that during the Three Dynasties the things that a person needed, such as grain, silk, and cloth, grew from the ground,[79] and he raised all of those things himself. Since he was content with the occupation he was pursuing, he did not need money to buy things from others. Rarely had he the opportunity of using money and, as far as he was concerned, money might as well be non-existent. Even when money was used, it was used by the government as a common standard of measuring so as to compute and compare yearly expenditures. It was an expedient, though a necessary one.

The situation changed during the later periods. All goods were expressed in monetary terms. As *chang* and *ch'ih* [80] were used to measure the length of silk and cloth, money became the standard of measurement for all of our daily necessities. It was a gauge whereby the value of all things was determined. The government's revenues and expenditures were computed in terms of money; so were the taxes and tributes that the people paid to the government. The material reserves of local governments were expressed in monetary terms, and needless to say, all merchants used money as a means to facilitate trade. The question may be asked: why did the people of later ages need so much money in circulation as compared to so little during the Three Dynasties?

During the Three Dynasties China was divided into many feudal, autonomous states. Each of these states was economically self-sufficient, and it produced what it needed. People lived such a simple life that unless an item was essential to the maintenance of their livelihood, an item which they did not produce,[81] they would not exhaust their efforts and energy in order to obtain it. Moreover, the government made it clear that it would not allow people to procure goods in faraway places, goods which they did not really need. The *Book of History* says:

> Only goods yielded on the home soil
> Shalt thou love and cherish.

Lao-tzu once said: "When the world reaches the stage of perfection, political units are so small that people in one state can hear the crowing of a cock or the bark of a dog in its neighboring states. Citizens of each state love their own food, admire their own clothes, feel satisfied with their own customs, and rejoice in their own occupations. They do not visit people in the other states for the entire dura-

---

[78] See pp. 289–290.
[79] Silkworms were fed on the leaves of mulberry trees that grew from the ground.
[80] One *ch'ih* is equal to 14.1 inches, and one *chang* is equal to ten *ch'ih*.
[81] The author perhaps had in mind such things as salt.

tion of their lives." It is not surprising that people who lived in such a society needed little or no money at all.

This situation changed after China had been unified. Though the country was divided into districts and provinces, there was no bar against communication and transportation across administrative boundaries, because all administrative units were under the direct control of a centralized government. Geographical mobility increased, and the merchants, to practice their trade, traversed across the length and breadth of the empire. It was then that the use of money greatly increased.

In the ancient times people used jade to decorate their clothes, accumulated tortoise shells as if they were great treasures, and converted gold and silver into mediums of exchange. Gold and silver were merely two of the items considered unusually valuable. As the government began to expand, so did its expenditure; and we know that whenever a king decided to reward his ministers, he rewarded them with gold. However, since jade, heavy though it was, was used to decorate clothes, it seems that its value was regarded as higher than that of gold or pearls.

The Han dynasty continued to use gold and silver as currency. It was not until the reigns of Han Hsüan-ti (73–49 B.C.) and Han Yüan-ti (48–33 B.C.) that gold as a currency began to disappear from the market. After his accession as emperor, Wang Mang tried to restore the currency of ancient times and classified all currencies into three grades. But his monetary reform did not survive his regime. With the establishment of the Later Han dynasty gold became even more scarce. Much of the gold which had been in circulation was now used to decorate Buddhist and Taoist temples after Buddhism and Taoism had become more and more the popular faiths of the masses. Gold and silver were no longer used as money; instead, it was used to decorate vessels, clothes, and articles that were designed to amuse. Jade also became more and more scarce, and to embellish their clothes, people used gold and silver instead. It was then that coined money, made of copper, became the sole medium of exchange. Its circulation continued to increase during the subsequent centuries.

Despite the continuous increase of coined money, no uniform system ever existed to govern coinage. The weight and size of minted coins varied from time to time, and it was not until the introduction of the K'ai-yüan coin [82] during the T'ang dynasty that an optimum weight of the standard coins was finally achieved. The coins of ancient times were extremely light in weight. The coins circulated during the Three Dynasties can no longer be found, but *Wu-chu* and *Pan-liang,* the two kinds of money coined during the Han dynasty which can still be found in the market, are too light to be of universal usage. The reason those ancient coins were so light was because they were designed as the lowest of the currency then in use, and above them were such currencies as gold and silver. In the later ages coins became the most valuable currency in the market after gold and silver ceased to be mediums of exchange; it was obvious that coins of light weight such as *Wu-chu* and *Pan-liang* were no longer suitable as currencies. Since the K'ai-yüan coins were neither too heavy nor too light, they became extremely popular immediately after their introduction; they had a wide circulation throughout the empire. Even today they can still be found in the market. Despite their popularity, the T'ang government continued to feel the shortage of coins.

[82] It was so-called because it was introduced during the K'ai-yüan period (713–741) during the reign of T'ang Hsüan-tsung (713–755).

During the Sung dynasty time and again the government's mint was called upon to issue new coins to meet the coin shortage. Generally speaking, the mint followed the K'ai-yüan example; there were, however, some exceptions. For instance, the coins produced during the T'ai-p'ing (976–983) and T'ien-hsi (1017–1021) periods were actually heavier than the K'ai-yüan coins. The T'ai-p'ing coins were the best of the Sung coins prior to the reign of Sung Jen-tsung (r.1023–1063); the quality of Sung coins deteriorated after the Hsi-ning period (1068–1077). During the early period of the Sung dynasty the government was concerned with the quality of the coins it produced rather than the cost necessary to produce them, and consequently the coins produced in this period were good. Later, its sole concern in manufacturing coins was the amount of profits it could realize; it reduced cost at the expense of the quality of the coins it produced. The coins produced during the Shao-hsing (1131–1162) and Ch'ien-tao (1165–1173) periods were even worse than those produced during the Hsi-ning and Yüan-feng (1078–1085) periods. In short, the quality of coins continued to worsen throughout the Sung dynasty.

The reason why such a large number of debased coins existed during the T'ang dynasty was because the government allowed private individuals to coin money in competition with the government. Coinage was by its very nature a government monopoly. The profits from its operation rightly belonged to the government; it was certainly unwise to share these profits with private individuals. During the Han dynasty Emperor Wen-ti (r.179–157 B.C.), wishing to set an example of thrift for his subjects to follow, announced that he did not need to spend much money and that he was relinquishing the government's monopoly of coinage. What happened then? The coins that were produced by the private houses of Wu and Teng [83] circulated throughout the empire, and the King of Wu, using this money, was able to start a rebellion in the Southeast.[84] During the T'ang dynasty there was a prolonged war after the K'ai-yüan and T'ien-pao period (713–755). To raise revenue to meet its mounting expenditure, the government increased taxes so as to take away money from private sources. New taxes were imposed on such items as tea, wine, and salt. Thus, beginning with Emperors T'ang Su-tsung (r.756–762) and T'ang Tai-tsung (r.763–779), not only was the government unable to create new money to meet new demands; it also tried, through a variety of unorthodox taxes, to seek money from the people. As the government and the people competed to obtain more money, no household in the empire could maintain its daily livelihood without it. Meanwhile goods had slowly disappeared from the market.

The change in world events and the prices of marketable goods—these are the things which defy predictions. But money, one of those magic things created by man, is useful to its creator only when it is in constant circulation; it loses its meaning of existence when it is taken away from the market and locked up in an iron chest. Now the wealthy are doing their utmost to collect and hoard as much money as possible, and the government, on its part, is trying to tax money away from the people so that it can hoard all the money in the empire in its vaults. Money, once entering its vaults, is not allowed to emerge. To meet the demand for a medium of exchange, the government issues paper currency instead.

---

[83] The house of Teng was the house of Teng T'ung. See pp. 330–331.
[84] This refers to the Seven States Rebellion. See p. 126, Footnote 44.

Most people do not realize that circulation is the very function of currency and that once circulation is denied, money loses its usefulness as money. In such a case, it would not have been different from other objects. Now people say that since there is a shortage of coined money, we should print more paper currency. Do they realize that as paper currency increases, it will not only chase goods from the market but coined money as well? The disadvantages resulting from the printing of paper currency are not new; they have existed ever since there was paper currency.

Any situation, once reaching its furthermost point, cannot develop further and has to reverse itself. A new way must be found if our monetary system is to remain sound. These are the questions: what are the steps that we should take to improve our monetary system? What kind of system is it that it is so good as to be unchangeable? The first step, in my opinion, is to abolish paper currency. Only then will coined money reappear in the market. The wealth of a nation lies with the abundance of goods. Only when goods become abundant will their prices fall and will the value of money increase. Only when the value of money remains constant can money be used as a gauge to measure the value of other things and can serve effectively as a medium of exchange.

Due to the scarcity of goods in the market, the value of money has greatly declined in recent years. It will take the efforts of a great statesman to reverse the trend and to find a new way for the future.

139 · SSU-MA CH'IEN: *Teng T'ung* [85]

Teng T'ung was a native of Nanan, Shu province.[86] He became a yellow-capped official on account of his expertness in boating.

One night emperor Hsiao-wen [87] had a strange dream in which he was trying in vain to climb to Heaven and finally succeeded when some one gave him a push from behind. Turning his head and looking backward, he saw a yellow-capped official who wore his cloth belt in reverse. Waking up, he went to the Chien Palace and secretly looked for the yellow-capped official whom he had seen in his dream. He was greatly pleased when he found Teng T'ung who, like the man in his dream, wore his cloth belt in reverse. From then on the emperor showered on him one favor after another. As a cautious, modest man, Teng T'ung did not like to socialize with other officials; in fact, he refused to go out to meet with them even after the emperor had granted him a special bath.[88] Time and again the emperor showered him with money—thousands of standard coins each time and altogether ten times. He was promoted to the rank of a senior minister.[89]

Frequently the emperor went to Teng T'ung's house to amuse himself. Being a prudent man of modest ability, Teng never suggested any man the emperor could

---

[85] "Biographies of Favorites" *(Ning-hsing lieh-chuan); Shih chi,* roll 125. An almost identical account also appears in *Han shu,* roll 93.

[86] Modern Szechuan province.

[87] Han Wen-ti (r.179–157 B.C.).

[88] *Tz'u-yü* or "granting of a bath" was one of the ways in which an emperor indicated his approval of the person involved.

[89] *Shang ta-fu.*

use. All he knew was to conduct himself properly and to please the emperor to the best of his ability.

One day a fortune teller remarked that Teng T'ung was destined to die of starvation. "Nonsense!" the emperor retorted. "The man who can make Teng T'ung rich is I, and I shall do my very best." He gave the order that the Copper Mountains [90] be handed over to Teng T'ung who from then on could mint his own copper coins. Soon T'eng's coins circulated throughout the empire.

The emperor suffered from a boil which Teng T'ung frequently sucked in order to reduce the pain. One day he felt very depressed, and asked Teng T'ung who in the world loved him most. "The crown prince," Teng replied. The crown prince came in to inquire about his father's health, and the emperor asked him to suck his boil. Very reluctantly the crown prince did as he was told. Later, when he heard that Teng T'ung had regularly sucked his father's boil, he began to hold resentment against him.

Emperor Wen-ti died and the crown prince succeeded him as emperor Ching-ti.[91] The new emperor ordered Teng T'ung to be dismissed from his official post and to return home as a private citizen. Shortly afterwards some one reported that Teng T'ung had conspired with bandits to ship coins to the border regions in violation of the law. The emperor ordered an investigation, and Teng T'ung was found guilty as charged. As a punishment, all of his properties were confiscated; even then it was reported that he was still in debt to the government for tens of thousands. The First Princess [92] wanted to give him some money for his support, but it was confiscated by the government before it could reach him. She ordered a kind man to take him in so he would be provided with food and clothing, since by then he did not have a single penny to his name. He died in another man's house and without a home.

140 · SUNG LIEN: *The Paper Currency of the Yüan Dynasty* [93]

Paper currency began with the "flying cash" of the T'ang dynasty. It was called "medium of exchange" [94] during the Sung dynasty and "notes of exchange" [95] during the Chin dynasty (1115–1234). The basic principle underlying all paper currencies was the representation of goods in terms of paper notes, in the hope that the circulation of both goods and notes would bring about the greatest material benefit possible. The principle corresponded well with the principle of complements that was expressed in the *Chou Institutions*.[96]

Soon after the Yüan dynasty was established, it followed the example of its predecessors, T'ang, Sung, and Chin, in issuing paper currency. Unfortunately no

[90] Located in northwestern section of modern Szechuan province.
[91] Han Ching-ti (r.156–141 B.C.).
[92] Ching-ti's elder sister and Wen-ti's daughter.
[93] "Economics, Part I" *(Hhih-huo yi); History of the Yüan (Yüan shih)*, roll 93, by Sung Lien who lived in the fourteenth century.
[94] *Chiao-hui.*
[95] *Chiao-ch'ao.*
[96] The authorship of *Chou Institutions* or *Chou kuan* was traditionally attributed to Chou Kung or Duke Chou who lived in the twelfth century B.C. It was most likely the creation of a later period.

written documents exist today which enable us to know how this system of paper currency actually functioned prior to the Yüan period.

In the first year of Chung-t'ung (1260) during the reign of Yüan Shih-tsu [97] the government issued the first notes of exchange after it had entered China proper. The bulk of each note was actually made of silk. Each silk note bearing a face value of 1,000 taels was declared to be worth 50 taels in silver. The prices of all goods were to be expressed in silk notes, not silver.

In the tenth month of the same year the Chung-t'ung paper currency was for the first time issued. There were three series altogether, the tens, the hundreds, and the thousands. There were four denominations among the tens: ten, twenty, thirty, and fifty standard coins; three denominations among the hundreds: one hundred, two hundred, and five hundred standard coins; and, finally, two denominations among the thousands: one thousand and two thousand standard coins. A paper note bearing the denomination of 1,000 standard coins was equivalent to a silk note bearing the denomination of one tael; two of these paper notes were equivalent to one tael of silver. Besides, there were the Chung-t'ung silver certificates made of embroidered silk. Five denominations were planned, each bearing a face value of one, two, three, five, or ten taels of silver; each tael on silk was to be worth one tael in silver. Despite the planning, the government failed to authorize their circulation.

In the fifth year of Chung-t'ung (1264) the imperial government ordered the establishment of the Office of Price Stabilization in each of the districts in the empire. The function of this office was to make certain that price fluctuation of any commodity would fall within a prescribed range so as to prevent the sudden drop of commodity prices. The government authorized 12,000 *ting* [98] in paper currency to be used as capital for each of the offices to be established.[99]

In the twelfth year of Chih-yüan (1275) paper currency in "minute" denominations was added to those issued before. Each of the new issues bore a face value of two, three, or five standard coins.

At the beginning wooden plates were used to print paper or silk currencies. In the thirteenth year of Chih-yüan (1276) copper plates replaced wooden blocks for this purpose.

In the fifteenth year of Chih-yüan (1278) a decree was issued to stop the printing of the "minute" notes, since they had been proven to be inconvenient to the people.

As the government printed more and more paper and silk currencies, prices of goods continued to rise. In the twenty-fourth year of Chih-yüan (1287) the government issued a new series of paper currency called Chih-yüan, and the Chih-yüan currency was to be used side by side with the Chung-t'ung currency. The new series had eleven denominations, from five standard coins to as much as two *kuan* or 2,000 standard coins. One *kuan* of the new currency was to be worth five *kuan* of the Chung-t'ung currency. Following the precedent established during the early years of Chung-t'ung, the government was to operate banks in all districts of China to trade in gold and silver, in the hope that the purchasing power of its paper currency would be stabilized. At each of these banks a tael of

[97] Kublai Khan.

[98] One *ting* is equal to ten taels.

[99] This money was to be used to buy a certain good in the open market if its price had fallen to a point below the prescribed range.

silver could be exchanged for two *kuan* of Chih-yüan currency, but the bank would demand an additional 5 percent of the amount in exchange if the bearer presented the bank with a note of two *kuan* to exchange for one tael of silver. Likewise one tael of gold could be exchanged for twenty *kuan* of Chih-yüan currency, but the bank would demand twenty *kuan* plus five hundred standard coins for one tael of gold. A counterfeiter of paper currency was punishable by death. Those who provided information which led to the arrest and then the conviction of a counterfeiter were to be rewarded with five *ting* of paper currency made available from the confiscated property of the convicted. The law seemed to be equitable and just.

In the second year of Chih-ta (1309) Emperor Wu-tsung, greatly concerned with the continuous rise of commodity prices in terms of paper currencies, ordered the printing of the Chih-ta silver certificates. The new issues had thirteen denominations, from two *li* [100] to two taels. A silver certificate bearing a face value of one tael was to be worth five *kuan* of the Chih-yüan paper currency, one tael in silver, or one-tenth of a tael in gold. These silver certificates issued during the Chih-ta period (1308–1311) might be described as the third generation of Yüan's paper currency.[101]

Generally speaking, the Chung-t'ung currency was converted to the Chih-yüan currency at the ratio of five to one, and the Chih-yüan currency was likewise converted to the Chih-ta currency at the same ratio. In less than a year after the Chih-ta silver certificates were issued, Emperor Jen-tsung (r.1312–1320) ascended the throne, and he quickly withdrew these certificates from the market on the ground that they had been over-priced in terms of other currencies. However, the Chung-t'ung and Chih-yüan currencies continued to circulate throughout the Yüan dynasty.

In the second year of Chih-yüan (1265) the law governing the exchange of worn-out notes for new certificates was enacted. According to this law, a worn-out currency note, plus thirty standard coins for cost, could be presented to any of the government banks for a new issue. In the following year (1266) the charge for cost was reduced to twenty standard coins. Nineteen years later (1285) it was restored to the old amount. The law also stated that as long as the face value on a note was clear and legible, the note should continue in circulation even though it had been slightly damaged; those who refused to accept it were punishable by law.

As for the worn-out notes that had been exchanged for new issues, each district should see to it that they were transported to the provincial capital to be burned and that the head of its tax bureau personally supervised the transportation. The worn-out notes in such banks as those under the direct jurisdiction of the provincial government need not be transported and could be burned within the banks concerned.

In the second year of Ta-te (1298) the Ministry of Finance divided all worn-out notes into twenty-five categories, and any of them could be exchanged for new notes. In the fourth year of T'ai-ting (1327) the Ministry made public the places where worn-out notes could be legally burned. When these notes were to be burned, the Ministry would dispatch an official from the Office of Investigation [102]

[100] One-thousandth of a tael.
[101] The other two were Chung-t'ung and Chih-yüan.
[102] *Lien-feng ssu.*

to supervise the burning. If the banks whose worn-out notes were to be burned belonged to the provincial government, a specifically designated provincial official and an official from the Office of Investigation would jointly supervise the burning.

141 · HUANG TSUNG-HSI: *Paper Currency* [103]

Paper currency began with the "flying cash" of the T'ang dynasty which served the same function as the promissory notes of today. It was not until the Sung dynasty, however, that the issuance of paper currency was institutionalized as a governmental policy. This policy was successful for two reasons. First, for each issue of paper notes to be put into circulation, the government provided a cash backing that amounted to 360,000 *min,* in addition to the revenues it derived from the selling of salt and liquor. Second, paper notes and standard coins were interchangeable, and a citizen could obtain from the government coins for his paper notes or paper notes for his coins. Moreover, he could buy salt or liquor with his paper notes from the government-owned stores. In short, paper notes were as good as coined money.

The value of paper currency was further strengthened by the fact that the total amount of each issue was limited to the total amount of cash backing then available. This limitation enabled the government to know how much of a given issue was currently in circulation and how much of it had been returned to the treasury for destruction. It also enabled the government easily to discover counterfeiting whenever it occurred. Because of the reasons stated above, it is not surprising that the paper currency of the Sung dynasty was successful.

During the Yüan dynasty the government operated banks in each of the provinces where a citizen could exchange his paper notes for gold or silver, and vice versa. Such being the case, the government did not encounter too many difficulties in circulating its paper currency.

The situation was different during the Ming dynasty. Then the bureau of paper currency only allowed people to exchange old issues for new ones; there was no mention as to how the paper notes could be exchanged for hard money or goods. It is no wonder that the paper currency of the Ming dynasty remained a failure throughout its existence.

During the reign of Ming Yi-tsung (r.1628–1644) many profit-minded ministers, seeing the easy advantage of transforming a piece of paper into gold or silver and knowing little about the principles that governed a sound monetary system, suggested the reestablishment of the paper currency. They spoke a great deal about the advantage of manufacturing paper notes but little about how to make them work. How could they expect people to trust a piece of paper that had no cash backing behind it?

If the government had in its treasury enough hard money to back up its paper currency, issued the currency only once every five years, provided free exchange of old for new issues, burned the old issues that had been returned to the treasury, and accepted all issues as legal tender for paying taxes on commercial transactions and for buying goods manufactured by the government such as salt, there was

[103] Translated from "Finance, Part II" *(Ts'ai-chi); Ming-yi tai-fang lu,* Essay No. 17.

no reason why its paper currency would not have worked. If meanwhile it abolished gold and silver as mediums of exchange, the people—officials and scholars
as well as merchants—would have been only too happy to use paper notes for
business transactions since they were small in size, light in weight, and easy to
carry, as contrary to grain, silk, and copper coins which were difficult to transport. . . .

Part IV

Family and Society

CHAPTER SIXTEEN

The Gentry and Its Ideals

THE word "gentry" *(ssu-shen* or *shen-ssu)* is an ambiguous term, and it is subject to different interpretations. There were, however, three attributes which the members of the gentry had in common: education, independent income, and a favorable public image. Since there were numerous degrees within each of the three factors, there were numerous degrees of "gentility." From this group most of traditional China's leaders were drawn, from the prime minister in the imperial government to a village chief in the countryside. As officials or in private life, they were supposed to set a moral example for the rest of the population to follow, and they took their self-assigned role very seriously (Selection 142).

While the general moral precepts were those recorded in the ancient classics, each member of the gentry might give special emphasis to a particular virtue. To a man like Ku Yen-wu no virtue was more important than the sense of "shamefulness" (Selection 143), while others, influenced by the Taoist philosophy, tended to look at morality in a broader context (Selections 144 and 145). To all of them a sense of meekness or humility was not only morally compelling but also a physical necessity if one wished to survive in this cruel and uncertain world (Selections 146 and 147).

Since the overwhelming majority of the gentry came from the landowning class, it is not surprising that they should feel a strong attachment to the land and emphasize the importance of agriculture (Selection 148). This affinity for the land, plus the great uncertainty in agrarian life due to drought, flood, famine, etc., generated certain values generally associated with rural life, such as mutual help and thrift. In extending financial help, one should follow the Confucian doctrine of "graded love" by helping one's clan members first (Selection 149).

Practically all Chinese scholars emphasized thrift as a model way of life and indoctrinated their children on its importance (Selection 150). To the seventeenth-century scholar Huang Tsung-hsi the avoidance of wastefulness should be one of the most important factors in shaping a nation's policy as well as in regulating a man's personal life. Any custom that was wasteful in nature, including religious rites and rituals, should be eliminated (Selection 151).

An old Chinese proverb says, "No family can be rich or poor consecutively for three generations." Knowing the uncertainty of his family fortune, a man of the gentry would naturally want to make sure that when the truism of this proverb began to materialize, he and his family would have something to go back to (Selection 152). At the time of affluence, one should always think of and be prepared for the time of scarcity.

142 · LÜ K'UN: *A Gentleman's Code* [1]

A gentleman does not have any of the ten attributes commonly shared by others. These ten attributes are those of a soldier, a woman, a juvenile, a vulgar man, a prodigal son, a country bumpkin, a defendant in front of a judge, a female slave, an informer, and finally, a merchant.

He should hide a large portion of whatever goodness he might have and thus cultivate his "ethical profoundness." Likewise he should conceal to a great extent the shortcomings of others and thus enlarge his "magnanimity." Patience is essential to planning, and a peaceful mind is a prerequisite to the management of affairs. Modesty is the most important item in the preservation of one's life, and tolerance and forgiveness should be the basic attitude towards others. To cultivate his mind, a gentleman should not be unduly concerned with such things as affluence or poverty, life or death, constancy or change.

Every event has its reality, every word its abode of beautitude, and every object the reason that sustains its existence. Likewise there are ways that make man a man; the purpose of education is to learn these ways. A gentleman learns them whenever and wherever he is, constantly and tirelessly. He will not cease to learn until he knows them all and knows them well.

Scholars of today are different. They bury themselves in mountains of books and concern themselves with miscellaneous details. They spend much of their time in articulating beautiful but artificial ornate words, and concentrate their efforts on improving skills that merely enable them to confuse truth with falsehood and replace good customs with pomp and superficiality. They rival one another in the performance of exact, detailed, but meaningless rituals. What a pity! Neurotic and senseless, they live in a world of nightmare. Besides tasteful food and good clothing, there is nothing else with which they are truly concerned. How pathetic! A good scholar not only loves learning, but more important, knows what he is learning.

Not concerned with learning when there is plenty of time to learn, a person is completely at a loss when an emergency suddenly occurs. He meets the situation in a hazardous and confused manner and does not care whether he will succeed or not, or whether he will be regretful in the future. When the whole thing is over, he goes back to his original ways, unchanging and seemingly unchangeable. "Only when you plan ahead can you succeed"—few statements are wiser than this one.

When ordinary people are engaged in wrongdoings, we can understand, though we do not condone them. But scholars should never be engaged in wrongdoings! If they are, who will teach and set the example for the rest of the population? When ordinary people commit crimes, we can understand, though we do not condone them. But government officials should never commit crimes! If they do, who will be there to prevent crimes?

---

[1] Lü K'un (d.1621) served as a governor of Kiangsi province during the Ming dynasty. This selection appears in his book entitled *Groanings (Shen-yin yü)*.

In ancient times people of equal fame or station were brotherly towards one another. Today they do not even hide their envy or jealousy.

A man's ability, or the lack of it, is made clear for all to see when he is assigned to perform an important but difficult task. How he acts and behaves in adverse vis-à-vis prosperous circumstances is the true measurement of his intelligence. His capacity of self-control is shown clearly at the moment of joy or anger. Does he have foresight? Observe him when he is a member of a crowd.

To love a child by feeding him with sweets is to harm his body; to let him do whatever he pleases is to ruin his sense of values. This is not love; it is indicative of a womanly weakness.

143 · KU YEN-WU: *On Shamefulness* [2]

"Propriety, righteousness, incorruptibility, and shamefulness are the four cardinal virtues of a nation," said Kuan-tzu.[3] "When these four virtues are not fully developed, the nation will die by itself." How correct Kuan-tzu was!

Propriety and righteousness are the basic rules that govern a man's conduct; incorruptibility and shamefulness are the two qualities that make him stand erect as a man. A corrupt person will take whatever can be taken; a shameless person will do whatever his selfishness dictates to him. When an individual is corrupt and shameless, he will bring damage or even death to himself. When a nation's high-ranking officials take whatever can be taken and do whatever their selfishness dictates to them, they will bring about chaos and anarchy and may even cause the nation to disappear from the face of the earth.

Of the four cardinal virtues the most important is shamefulness as far as a scholar is concerned. "A scholar should conduct himself in accordance with the principle of shamefulness," said Confucius. "A man cannot live without a sense of shamefulness," said Mencius. In fact, the most shameful thing in the world is the failure to recognize the value of shamefulness. "Of all the things that concern man none is more important than shamefulness," said Mencius on another occasion. A man who is clever and opportunistic has no use for shamefulness. When he becomes corrupt or violates the principle of propriety or righteousness, it is because the sense of shamefulness has already left him. A nation is in shame if its intelligentsia have lost their sense of shamefulness.

Since the end of the Three Dynasties the moral fiber of the nation has become weaker and weaker. The lessening influence of the four cardinal virtues upon the people has not come about overnight. Yet the leaves of a pine do not fall even in winter, and the cocks continue to crow even in the most stormy weather. When most people are soundly asleep, there are a few who remain constantly awake. Recently I read the *Family Instructions for the Yen Clan* [4] in which the author speaks of a scholar-official in the Ch'i regime who had a seventeen-year-old son who was proficient in calligraphy and literature. "I intend to teach him the Hsien-pei language and the *p'i-p'a*," [5] the author quotes the official. "When he is fairly

---

2 *Jih-chih lu,* roll 13.

3 Kuan Chung of the seventh century B.C. See also pp. 369–370.

4 See p. 342, Footnote 7.

5 Hsien-pei was a nomadic, non-Chinese tribe; *p'i-p'a* was a musical instrument.

good at both of them, he will be able to serve the ministers well and win affection from them. I believe that this is a very important part of his education." The author says that he lowered his head and did not make any comment after he had heard these remarks. "If this is the way of becoming a minister," he continues, "I hope that none of you, my children, will ever succeed in becoming one." [6]

Unfortunately Yen Chih-t'ui had to live in an age of degeneration and serve a corrupt regime.[7] Yet he could make remarks that echoed the sentiments of the poets in the *Book of Odes*. Compared with him, will today's flatterers not be ashamed of themselves?

144 · YEN TSENG: *The Mottoes on My Desk* [8]

A man cannot escape from his shadow however fast he runs. He will hear his own whisper however feeble he tries to make it. However, once he steps into a shade, the shadow disappears; once he closes his mouth, no whisper emerges. Likewise, if a man wishes to avoid misfortunes or disaster, he should always remain weak, humble, and meek.

Of all things in the world, the tongue is the major cause of trouble and the most effective way of inviting disaster. The power of speech, endowed by Heaven, is incorporated in man. Yet, one improper remark, once emerging from the mouth, may bring disaster or even death to the utterer. Therefore a sage speaks nothing if he has a choice and speaks with great caution if he does not have one. Whenever he does speak, he approaches his task with as much fear as if he were to be burned in a fire, drowned in a river, or pushed towards a precipice. In short, he will not speak unless he absolutely must.

A gentleman regards tasteful food as destructive to his stomach and wealth as an invitation to danger. He has no use for jealousy, envy, slandering, or flattery. He believes that cruelty will boomerang against its practitioner, and betrayal will eventually entrap the betrayer. To him sexual indulgence is the road to a family's destruction, and a habitual drinker will surely wind up in the gutter.

A gentleman, on the other hand, will embrace the virtues of loyalty and filial piety as a means to acquire personal wealth, and rely on temperance and thrift as the most reliable source of financial adequacy. He criticizes himself three times everyday and instructs his descendants to do likewise until eternity to come.

[6] The same story is told in the author's own words in Selection 156, pp. 365–367.

[7] Yen Chih-t'ui, the author of *Family Instructions*, lived in the sixth century when China was divided.

[8] The author was a Taoist philosopher who lived in the first century B.C. Source: *Sample Prose of the Han Period (Liang-Han san-wen hsien)*, edited by Hu Lun-ch'ing, pp. 124–125.

145 · FANG HSIAO-JU: *Mosquitoes* [9]

Suffering from summer heat, Mr. T'ien-t'ai [10] slept inside a mosquito net at night. His servant, a young boy, was fanning him to keep him cool. He felt comfortable and was soon soundly asleep. Shortly afterwards the boy went to sleep too; throwing away his fan, he was crouching against the bed. His snores sounded like thunder.

Suddenly Mr. T'ien-t'ai woke up: he thought that a thunder storm was coming. He sat up and held his knees. In a second he heard the sound of flying. How could one describe this sound? It sounded like singing; no, it was more like complaining. It sounded like hums of desire; no, it was more like murmurs of resentment. The fliers brushed against his forearms and then stabbed his skin. They struck his knees, and they bit his face. All his hair, on his body as well as on his head, rose up and stood; his body shook so violently that its flesh seemed to be falling off. He clasped his perspiring hands and caught something in the middle. He smelt it and found it frowsy and bloody. Startled and alarmed, he did not know what to do. He kicked the servant boy and cried aloud: "Something is bothering me. Bring a candle quickly and see what it is."

Once the candle was brought in, Mr. T'ien-t'ai saw that the mosquito net had been wide open and that thousands of mosquitoes were gathering on the net. Under the candlelight, these mosquitoes, like dragonflies, flew in confusion. Their mouths were sharp, and their stomachs were bunchy. In fact, they had eaten so much that they were red and round.

"Are these not the same creatures that have drunk my blood?" Mr. T'ien-t'ai scolded the servant boy. "It is all your fault! You carelessly opened the net and thus they managed to get in. Since mosquitoes are not so intelligent as human beings, they would not have been able to harm me had you taken preventive measures."

The servant boy plucked some straw and tied it into a bundle. He lit one end of the bundle, and shortly there was a huge smoke. The mosquitoes turned to the left and then to the right, and circled the bed several times before they left. "Now that they are gone, you can go back to sleep," said the servant boy.

Mr. T'ien-t'ai rearranged his bed and was ready to go back to sleep. Then he cried for Heaven and sighed. "Why does Heaven have to create these creatures to bother me?" he asked.

Hearing this, the servant boy burst into laughter. "Why do you attach so much importance to yourself and blame Heaven?" he retorted. "Between Heaven and Earth are *yin* and *yang,* the two generative elements. When provided with form and substance, they transform themselves into all things in the universe. They transform themselves into large things such as elephants, strange things such as flood-dragons, violent things such as tigers and leopards, tame things such as deer and sheep, feathered things such as birds and fowls, and finally, naked things such as human beings and insects. Each of these animals has its own source of

[9] A copy of the Chinese original can be found in *Sample Prose of the Ming-Ch'ing Period (Ming Ch'ing san-wen hsien),* edited by Hu Lun-ch'ing, pp. 30–32. As for the author, see p. 285, Footnote 57.
[10] T'ien-t'ai was the name of a mountain in T'aichou, Chekiang province, where the author was born. Thus the author referred to himself as Mr. T'ien-t'ai.

food supply; and regardless of their sizes and lengths, the essence that lies inside the form is all the same. From man's point of view, man is superior to other animals. From the point of view of Heaven and Earth, however, no animal is superior to others.

"Now man considers himself superior and calls himself 'the dominator.' All other animals, on land and in water, are captured to serve his ends. Even frogs cannot run away for their lives, and wild geese cannot hide their traces. The number of animals man eats is certainly very large indeed. Why may not other animals eat man for a change? Tonight, as soon as you have been bitten by mosquitoes, you are crying for Heaven and complaining to Him about it. If all animals that have been eaten by man complain to Heaven the way as you do, what do you think the penalty upon man will be?

"It may be argued that it is all right for man to eat animals and animals to eat man, since they belong to different species. As for the mosquito, it is a cautious and fearful animal. It does not dare to make its appearance under daylight, and attacks people only in darkness when they are weary and tired.

"Here on earth there is one species of animals who eat the same food, drink the same water, marry and raise their children in the same manner, wear the same clothes and hats, and even have the same kind of mannerisms. Yet they attack each other in broad daylight, sucking each other's brain and drinking each other's blood. While they are fighting, others are stumbling in the wilderness, lost and hungry. Their cryings for Heaven can be heard miles away, and yet nobody shows the slightest sympathy.

"As soon as you are bitten by mosquitoes, you, sir, become restless and cannot sleep at night. Yet you do not seem to be the least concerned when one group of human beings bites another. Does this attitude of yours not violate the principle of a gentleman who places the welfare of others above that of his own?"

Having heard the servant boy's argument, Mr. T'ien-t'ai threw his pillow to the ground, reflected, and sighed. He put on his clothes, walked out of the room, and sat outside throughout the night.

146 · LIU HSIANG: *A Letter to My Son Hsin*[11]

This is to tell you, Hsin, not to be careless. You have not accomplished anything special, and yet you have been bestowed with such a great favor.[12] You should ask yourself how you are going to repay this conferred honor.

Mr. Tung[13] once said: "When a condoler arrives at the front door, a congratulator is already somewhere in the village." This means that worry and grief will make a person careful and diligent, that diligent work will bring about good deeds, and that in the end good fortune will result. He also said: "When a congratulator arrives at the front door, a condoler is already somewhere in the village." This means that good fortune gives birth to arrogance and extravagance

11 Liu Hsiang, who lived in the first century B.C., was the author of several books, including one on Dualism (*Hung-fan wu-hsing chuan*). Source of this letter: *Liang-Han san-wen hsien,* pp. 124–125.

12 This referred to the fact that Hsin had been appointed as a member of the imperial guards.

13 Tung Chung-shu, second century B.C.

which in turn will bring about disasters. In the wake of disasters come the condolers.

At the beginning of his reign, Duke Ch'ing of Ch'i,[14] taking advantage of the great power which the Ch'i state then possessed, insulted and invaded other states. He did not have a cautious and modest attitude and consequently suffered the disaster at An from which he fled in the most unbecoming manner.[15] This is what Mr. Tung meant when he said that "when a congratulator arrives at the front door, a condoler is already somewhere in the village." After this defeat, people came to Duke Ch'ing and expressed their sympathy. Becoming more fearful and consequently more cautious, he changed his ways and reformed himself. His subjects loved him, and other states decided to return to him the territories which they had previously conquered. This is what Mr. Tung meant when he said that "when a condoler arrives at the front door, a congratulator is already somewhere in the village."

You are so young and yet you have been appointed to such an honorable and important position as a member of the imperial guards. You should express your thanks to all of those who have made this possible and kowtow to all of the nobles. You should face your task with diligence and humility and, in doing so, you might be able to avoid disasters.

147 • MA YÜAN: *A Letter to My Nephew*[16]

I hope that when you hear about other people's faults, you will feel as if you had heard the mention of your parents' names: *i.e.,* once you have heard it, you should never mention it to others.[17] I detest people who criticize others behind their backs and speak of rights and wrongs in the most casual and arbitrary manner. I prefer to die rather than to see my children commit this serious error. You know how strongly I feel about this matter; the reason I reiterate it is to make sure that you will not forget it.

Lung Pai-kao is sincere, honest, considerate, and careful. He does not satirize or criticize. He is modest, thrifty, incorruptible, just, and dignified. I love and respect him; I would like you to look up to him as a model and an example. Tu Chi-liang, on the other hand, is courageous and loves to perform righteous deeds. He shares other people's happiness or sorrows. He has among his friends all kinds of people, evildoers as well as honest, law-abiding citizens. After his father died, he invited guests from several provinces to attend the funeral. I love him and respect him, but I do not want you to follow his example. If you cannot live up to Pai-kao's standard, you will be still a respectable gentleman. This is like saying that if you attempt to sculpture a snow-goose but are unsuccessful, the sculpture will still look like a duck.[18] If on the other hand you cannot live up to Chi-liang's

---

[14] Lived in the first half of the sixth century B.C.

[15] In 589 B.C. the Battle of An (modern Shantung province) was fought, and the Ch'i forces were soundly defeated by an army from the state of Tsin.

[16] Ma Yüan, who lived in the first century A.D., was a famous general of the Later Han dynasty. Source: *Ku-wen kuan-chih,* roll 6.

[17] In order to show his deep reverence, a son was not supposed to mention his parents' names in front of others.

[18] This is equivalent to saying that if you aim high, you will wind up in the middle which is still respectable.

standard, you will wind up as a flippant buffoon. This is like saying that if you attempt but are unsuccessful to draw a tiger, your picture will look like that of a dog.[19]

I do not know what Chi-liang's future will be. But the generals of the province have been resentful whenever they speak of him. Since he has become a conversational topic in a wide area, my blood runs cold whenever I think of his future. That is why I do not want my own children to imitate him.

148 · CHENG HSIEH: *A Letter to My Younger Brother* [20]

I have always believed that of the four classes [21] in our society the farmers should be ranked as the highest and the scholars the lowest. Today a well-to-do farmer cultivates 100 *mou* of land and a less well-to-do 50 or 60 *mou* of land. Working diligently all year round, the farmer sows, plows, and harvests so as to support all the people in the society. Without him all of us would have starved to death. If we intellectuals do what we are supposed to do—practice filial piety at home and brotherly love in our relationships with others, preserve and transmit a great heritage, work for the welfare of the people when given an official post to hold, and set a moral example to others while in retirement, I would say that we are superior to the farmers.

But today's intellectuals are different. With a book in his hand, the only thing an intellectual can think of is to pass the civil service examinations, first on the local and then on the imperial level, so that he can become an official, amass a large fortune, build mansions, and buy more and more land. Since his motive is wrong, he goes from bad to worse, with no ending whatsoever. If he fails to pass the civil service examinations, he winds up as a local ruffian, swinging his weight around and bullying others.

To be sure, not all intellectuals are bad. There are those among us who, following the great examples of the past, are selfless and wish to do whatever they can to advance the welfare of all of mankind. In the eyes of the public, however, these few are also suspect because the majority of the intellectuals are bad. Nowadays I am afraid even to open my mouth. If I did, people would laugh and say: "You intellectuals know how to talk about beautiful things. Once you become a government official, you will not talk about the same things any more." While they are scolding and laughing at me, I choose not to say a word to defend myself. The artisans make equipment for us to use, and the merchants ship goods from one place to another. All of them bring benefit to society in some tangible manner. Only we intellectuals cause inconveniences to others and should be in fact ranked the lowest among the four classes. Even the lowest rank seems to be too high for us.

It is the farmers for whom I have had the greatest respect. We should treat our new tenants with consideration and courtesy. They call us "hosts" and we call them "guests." "Hosts" and "guests" are people of equal footing; they are not superiors and inferiors. We should always be sympathetic towards their needs:

---

[19] This is equivalent to saying that if your goal is so high as to be beyond your capacity to reach, you will end up being ridiculous.

[20] Cheng Hsieh (1693–1765), also known as Cheng Pan-chiao, was a calligrapher, painter, as well as an essayist. Source: *Ming Ch'ing san-wen hsien,* pp. 149–150.

[21] Scholars, farmers, artisans, and merchants.

lend them money when they need it and be generous with them when they cannot pay it.

I often laughed when I read the *Song of the Seventh Night* in which the T'ang author [22] describes the Herd-boy and the Spinning Damsel speaking in sorrowful terms when they meet and then must say good-bye to each other.[23] The author does not understand the true meaning for naming these two stars "Herd-boy" and "Spinning Damsel." "Herd-boy" symbolizes the source of food, while "Spinning Damsel" denotes the origin of clothing. Since these two are the most important stars in Heaven, how can man not attach great importance to the things which they symbolize? The shining of these two stars keeps reminding us of their importance.

The women in our community can neither spin nor weave. Yet they know how to cook and sew, and they cannot be said to be too lazy in this sense. Lately I have heard that some of them begin to attend theaters and play cards. How much our good customs have deteriorated! Against these bad habits our women should be warned.

Though our family has 300 *mou* of land, it is mortgaged property and cannot be counted upon for long. Sometime in the future we shall buy 200 *mou* of land, divided equally between you and me. This is in conformity with the ancient principle that an adult male should have 100 *mou* of land. If we sought more than this amount, we could succeed only by taking away what rightly belongs to others, a cardinal sin we shall not commit. There are many people in the world who have no property of their own. If I become so greedy, what would happen to the poor who have no means of support? Some would say that there are people whose fields spread over a large area, measuring several hundred *ch'ing*. In response I would say that other people have their way of doing things while I have my own, and that, while it is good to follow other people's examples in an era of sainthood, it is definitely wrong to try to "keep up with the Changs" in a time when good customs have already deteriorated. I wish you to know that this is an important principle in our family code.

149 · CH'IEN KUNG-FU: *A Model Member of the Gentry* [24]

Fan Chung-yen, a native of Soochow,[25] was a very generous philanthropist. He chose his beneficiaries from two groups of people: clan members of meager means and men of good character who might or might not be related to him. When he

---

[22] An author of the T'ang dynasty.

[23] This is one of the best known folktales in China. Herd-boy and Spinning Damsel were two stars across the Milky Way (which the Chinese called "Heavenly River") that were banished to earth because of their "improper" behavior in Heaven. On earth they fell in love as they did in Heaven. Finally moved by their devotion towards each other, the Heavenly God decided that they could see each other, but only once a year: on the seventh evening of the seventh lunar month. On that day all birds on earth would fly to Heaven to build a bridge across the Heavenly River, so that these two eternal lovers could meet on schedule. Meanwhile on earth an unmarried maiden, if she wished to marry as romantic a husband as Herd-boy, could offer flowers and fruits as sacrifices and pray for the blessings of the eternal twosome who were then meeting in Heaven.

[24] The author, a native of Changchow (modern Kiangsu province), lived in the eleventh century. Source: *Ku-wen kuan-chih,* roll 9.

[25] Fan Chung-yen (990–1053) was a famous statesman of the Sung dynasty. Soochow is located in Kiangsu province.

was a high official and wealthy, he bought 1,000 *mou* of good land just outside the city wall and called it "righteous fields." The yield of this land was to be used to support all of his clan members so that they would not suffer from cold and hunger, and such expenses as those during the time of wedding or funeral would be also provided for. A clan elder of high integrity was chosen to administer this program.

According to this program, a clan member was entitled to receive one pint of rice each day and one bolt of silk each year. He would receive 50,000 standard coins as wedding expenses for his eldest daughter's marriage and 30,000 standard coins for each of his younger daughters. The cash subsidy for his eldest son's wedding was 30,000 standard coins and 15,000 standard coins for each of his younger sons. The funeral expenses for an adult and a minor were 15,000 and 10,000 standard coins respectively. A total of ninety clan members received benefits in this manner, and the total expenditure amounted to 8,000 pecks of grain per year. However, the expenditure was small in view of a much larger income. Only those who lived at home were entitled to these benefits. They were not entitled to them once they found employment with the government outside of their own home district.

For twenty years Fan Chung-yen had this project in mind but was unable to carry it out. He finally succeeded when he became the governor of Shensi, participated in the high council of the imperial government, and received a large salary. After he died, his descendants continued this project as a memorial to him. Though his position was high and his salary large, he was personally poor throughout his life. When he died, he did not leave his children enough money for his funeral expenses. What he did leave his descendants was something much richer: the principle of helping the needy, especially among one's own clan members.

150 • TSENG KUO-FAN: *Letters to My Sons* [26]

To Chi-hung, the 29th day of the 9th month, 1856
For a family of scholar-officials it is easy to change the habit from thrift to extravagance; but once the habit of extravagance is formed, it is very difficult to go back to that of thrift. You are very young: under no circumstances should you acquire a fondness for extravagance or the habit of being lazy. People of any profession—scholars, farmers, artisans, or merchants—can prosper if they are industrious and thrifty. On the other hand, they will eventually bankrupt themselves if they are complacent, extravagant, and lazy.

Reading books and practicing calligraphy should be a daily routine and should never be interrupted. Get up early each morning so that you will not violate the family tradition established by your forebears. You know very well that both my father and my uncle get up as soon as the day breaks.

The achievement of fame and wealth is half determined by fate and half by one's own efforts. However, if one wishes to become a good man, his success or

[26] Source: "Letters to My Sons" in *The Complete Works of Tseng Kuo-fan (Tseng Wen-cheng kung ch'üan-chi)*, Vol. VII. The author (Tseng Kuo-fan, 1811–1872) was a scholar and statesman of the nineteenth century most noted for his suppression of the Taiping Rebellion.

failure depends solely upon his own efforts; it has nothing to do with fate.

I have always wanted to follow the examples of the great sages of the past. When I was young, I did not succeed well in cultivating the habit of reverence or serenity. Even today I can still have an occasional slip when I joke with words or actions. You should be serious in manner and should never say a word which you do not mean. Minding this advice is the first step towards the road of virtue.

To Chi-tseh, the 3rd day of the 3rd month, 1859

I have received your reproduction of Ho Tan-lu's [27] epitaph. Each character is gracefully and beautifully done; the spaces between the main strokes are broad and loose. I am very pleased with your work. However, I have noticed that the intervals between strokes are sometimes too wide. You should work more diligently to correct this error.

In practicing calligraphy there are two important considerations. One is the movement of strokes and the other is the structure of strokes within each character. To learn about the former, you should study more diligently the calligraphy of the great masters of the past. As for the latter, the common way to achieve your goal is to place a transparent paper on an ancient masterpiece and trace it. These two rules are the most basic in attaining good calligraphy. Children begin their calligraphic work with tracing. If they work hard, they should be able to produce copies similar to the original.

By the time I was thirty, I already knew the meaning of stroke movement as evidenced in the works of the ancient greats. But I did not do well in stroke structure. One of my hopes in life was to be able to combine the style of Liu Ch'eng-hsüan with that of Chao Tzu-liang.[28] However, due to the lack of sufficient work in stroke structure, I have not been able to achieve the goal which once I set out to achieve. It is my hope that from now on you will work specially hard on structure. Each day you should use transparent paper to trace the great masterworks of the past, anywhere from one hundred to two hundred characters a day. In a period of several months you will find that your style will come close to that of the great masters insofar as stroke structure is concerned. I shall be greatly pleased if you can succeed in what I have failed to achieve: to combine the Liu and the Chao styles in your own calligraphy. If you feel that you cannot achieve this purpose and you have decided to follow a particular school, it is still all right with me. The important thing is not to switch lightly when you see something different and new.

To Chi-tseh, the 21st day of the 4th month, 1859

Outside of the *Four Books* and the *Five Classics,* the books I like most are the *Historical Records, History of the Han, Chuang-tzu,* and *Han Yü.* My love for them has lasted for more than ten years, but unfortunately I have not had time to study them as thoroughly as I should. Besides, I also like *History As a Mirror,*[29]

[27] A famous calligrapher.

[28] Ch'eng-hsüan was the courtesy name of Liu Kung-ch'üan who lived in the ninth century and was noted for his strong and "bony" strokes. Tzu-liang was the courtesy name of Chao Meng-t'iao who lived in the thirteenth century and was famous for his graceful lines. They were two of the best known calligraphers in Chinese history. Their calligraphic styles are still being imitated today.

[29] *Tzu-chih t'ung-chien,* by Ssu-ma Kuang (1018–1086).

Selected Works by Prince Chao-ming,[30] *Selected Works in the Ancient Style* by Yao Pao-hsi,[31] and finally, *Selected Poems from Eighteen Schools,*[32] also by Yao Pao-hsi. During my younger days when I diligently pursued my studies, I was hoping not only to master these dozen or so books, but also to follow the example of Ku T'ing-lin and Wang Huai-tsu to write commentaries on them.[33] I am now getting old, and being occupied by worldly affairs of the most difficult nature, have not been able to accomplish what I once wanted very much to do. Whenever I think of my failure, I am deeply ashamed. My son, if, besides the *Four Books* and the *Five Classics,* you read carefully and think deeply about the eight books which your father loves so much, and then write notes to indicate what you have gained from reading them or what you do not understand, I shall be so happy that I will sleep well every night. This will be the best gift you can give to me.

To Chi-tseh, the 14th day of the 10th month, 1859

I received your letters of the 19th and the 29th and learned that the wedding had taken place. It is the fortune of our family that your newly married wife has learned to endear herself to your mother.

For more than two hundred years the emperors of our dynasty have had the habit of getting up at the *yin* hour.[34] The forebears of our family established a similar tradition. Both the honorable Ching-hsi and the honorable Hsing-kang had the habit of getting up before daybreak. In wintertime they got up and sat for about two hours before daylight appeared. My father, the honorable Chu-t'ing, got up every morning as soon as there was daylight. He would not wait for daybreak if there was something important that had to be taken care of. You must have observed this yourself.

Recently I have also formed the habit of getting up as soon as the day breaks, in the hope that I shall be able to continue the tradition of our forebears. Now that you have attained adulthood and have been married, the first thing you should remember and devote yourself to is getting up early each morning. You should set an example to your newly married wife and urge her to do likewise.

Throughout my life my main shortcoming has been the lack of perseverance, and consequently I have not been able to achieve anything worthwhile. I have not succeeded in the establishment of virtues nor the accomplishment of good deeds; I am deeply ashamed.[35] Since I began to manage military affairs, I have not had the time to devote myself to other subjects. I frequently change my mind about what I really want to do; this is a good indication of my lack of persever-

---

[30] *Chao-ming wen-hsien,* by Hsiao T'ung (better known as Prince Chao-ming) who lived in the sixth century A.D.

[31] Pao-hsi was the courtesy name of Yao Nai (eighteenth century) who edited and compiled *Ku-wen tz'u-lei-tsuan.*

[32] *Shih-pa chia shih-ch'ao.*

[33] The author apparently had in mind *Daily Accumulated Knowledge (Jih-chih lu)* by Ku Yen-wu (courtesy name: T'ing-lin; seventeenth century) and *Random Notes from Book Reading (Tu-shu tsa-chi)* by Wang Nien-sun (courtesy name: Huai-tsu; eighteenth century).

[34] From 4 to 6 A.M.

[35] This remark came from a man who, more than anyone else, was responsible for the suppression of the Taiping Rebellion and thus saved the Ch'ing dynasty for another fifty years.

ance, for which I feel a strong sense of shame within myself. If you wish to accomplish something in your life, you should begin with the word "perseverance."

From my observation of the honorable Hsing-kang, I have concluded that his extraordinary mannerism can be summarized in one word: dignity. I have followed his example, and I believe that my mannerism, whether in sitting or in walking, is also a dignified one. One of your main shortcomings is that you are too flippant in your manners. From now on you should watch yourself at all times with regard to this matter. You should be serious and dignified, whether you are sitting or walking.

In summary, these three requirements—early rising, perseverance, and dignity—are most important to you at the moment. Early rising is our family tradition; the lack of perseverance is one of my worst shortcomings of which I am greatly ashamed; and the lack of dignity is a shortcoming of yours. I cannot possibly overemphasize these words.

To Chi-tseh, the 4th day of the 3rd (leap) month, 1860

Your letter of the 16th was received on the first day of the month.

Since Uncle Ch'eng has moved to the new residence, you are now the lord of our old homestead, the Golden House. My grandfather, the honorable Hsing-kang, attached great importance to the successful management of the household. First, he insisted that every member of our family should get up early in the morning. Second, the house should be washed and swept regularly to keep it clean. Third, the offering of sacrifices to the deceased ancestors should be performed in the most sincere manner. Fourth, all of our neighbors, relatives, and clan members should be well treated. Whenever they came to our house, they were always received with great respect. We gave them financial help if they were in need. We offered them our good offices if they were involved in lawsuits; congratulated them on wedding and other festival occasions; provided comfort when they were sick; and sent them condolences after the death of any of their family members.

Besides the four items described above, the honorable Hsing-kang paid constant attention to the study of books and the raising of vegetables. Recently when I wrote letters home, I often reminded you of the importance of "books, vegetables, fish, and hogs." I want you to know that whenever I did this, I merely followed the tradition established by my grandfather.

Now that you are busy pursuing your studies, you may feel that you are not able personally to supervise all of the eight activities described above. But in any case you should understand the meaning behind these activities. Ask Mr. Chussu [36] to be particularly careful in this matter because all of these activities are extremely important. As for the sacrificial ceremonies, tell your mother that she should have them in mind constantly. Only the best food and vessels can be used for the purpose of offering sacrifices. A family's fortune cannot last long if the family is not particular when offering sacrifices, no matter how prosperous it is at the moment. Remember this!

To Chi-tseh, the 24th day of the 12th month, 1860

You are weak in body, and I am greatly concerned with your coughing. However, it is still better not to take any medicine. Medicine can save people, but it

[36] A family steward.

can also kill people. A good doctor saves seven out of every ten patients, but he kills the other three. A mediocre doctor, on the other hand, kills seven of every ten patients, and saves the lives of only three. The doctors I have seen in the countryside are all mediocre; and fearful of the harm they can do, I have not taken any medicine prescribed by doctors for the past three years. I am now ordering you not to do it either. The reason is simple and clear, and I cannot overemphasize this point. I want you respectfully to obey this order without fail.[37]

Walking several thousand paces after every meal is the best way of preserving one's health. After each meal you should walk to the village of T'angchiap'u or Uncle Ch'eng's house; this round trip amounts to approximately three thousand paces. I am sure that keeping this habit will enable you to feel much better after a period of three months.

After the *History of the Han,* you should read *History As a Mirror.* Use the copy which I previously sent to you from the capital. Follow my instruction: punctuate the entire text with a writing brush.

Do you walk with more dignity nowadays? Have you been able to hide your cleverness when you speak? Emphatically you should mind these words!

To Chi-tseh, the 14th day of the 1st month, 1861

Your strokes are weak;[38] it is advisable that from now on you should follow the style of Liu Kung-ch'üan.[39] . . . Trace one hundred characters each day so as to imitate his stroke structure and acquire the feel of the original. Each time you write me, enclose a few sheets of your calligraphy for me to examine.

After you finish reading the commentaries on the *Commentaries of Tso,* you should immediately begin reading *History As a Mirror. . . .*

I am glad to hear that teacher Teng speaks well of your brother Hung. Since Hung is reading *History As a Mirror* at the moment, you, being the elder brother, should also teach him from time to time.

Your reading ability is good, and you are also doing well in calligraphy. But your ability to compose, in prose as well as in poetry, is comparatively low. Had you been well instructed in this matter when you were fifteen or sixteen, this shortcoming could have been easily avoided. But you are now twenty-three. The future depends upon your own efforts; your father, brothers, or teachers cannot give you much help. Knowing that composition is your weakest point, you should apply yourself more intensively in this field. Since reading and calligraphy are your strong points, you should still strive to improve them.

Walk with dignity and speak with clumsiness. Can you always remember this instruction? I am well; tell your mother that she should not be worried about me.

To Chi-tseh and Chi-hung, the 13th day of the 3rd month, 1862

As I acquire more experience in life, I feel strongly how difficult it is to play the role of a teacher. You two should concentrate your efforts on your studies; you should not think of pursuing either a military or a bureaucratic career at this moment.

---

[37] The reader might be interested in knowing that Tseng Chi-tseh shortly recovered from this illness. After entering governmental service, he later became China's ambassador to England, France, and finally Russia.

[38] The author was speaking of calligraphy.

[39] See above, Footnote 28.

My teachings to the family's younger members can be summarized in what I call "eight essentials and three inducements." The study of commentaries is essential to the understanding of ancient classics; the study of phonetics is essential to the composition of poetry and prose; the pleasing of parents is essential to the performance of filial duties; the suppression of anger is essential to a healthy life; the abstention from uttering untruthful remarks is essential to the cultivation of personal ethics; early rising is essential to the successful management of a household; incorruptibility is essential to the pursuance of an official life; and finally, friendship and harmony with the people are essential to the successful commanding of an army. The three inducements are inducements of good fortunes by observing filial piety, industriousness, and forgiveness.

My father, the honorable Chu-t'ing, emphasized one thing in his teaching: filial piety. He was respectful towards his parents when he was young, and was loving towards them when he became older. His love and respect, coming from the bottom of his heart, were genuine and sincere. When I wrote his epitaph, I emphasized one thing: filial piety. . . . There were three kinds of people whom my grandfather, the honorable Hsing-kang, did not trust. They were Buddhist monks, Taoist priests, and medical doctors.

During the present time of chaos and war, the smaller the amount of money one has, the less likely he will encounter disaster. The more economical he is, the more likely he is to receive good fortunes. As for you two brothers, I can see no other way whereby you can serve your mother and yourselves well except through industriousness and thrift. The military situation is extremely serious at the moment; [40] I have only two words as my instruction: industry and thrift. Report this wish of mine to your mother and your uncles. They should not forget it either.

To Chi-tseh, the 4th day of the 4th month, 1862

I have received your two letters, dated the 14th and the 22nd of last month, which you sent from the provincial capital.[41] I am pleased to learn that our second daughter lives happily after joining the Ch'en family where she is amply supplied with food and clothing.

Though you have been busy with social activities for the last few months, I am glad that you have not neglected your studies which will be further improved if you keep your present pace. The first virtue in life is constancy. During my early years I was poor in calligraphy, and I was unable to improve it despite my worries over my inadequacy and my determination and efforts to improve it. Recently I have been copying and tracing every morning without interruption, and my calligraphy has been slowly improving.[42] As far as learning is concerned, age makes little difference; nor is there such a thing as inherently easier or more difficult. All important is the word "perseverance." A tree or an animal grows each and every minute; however, since we see it everyday, we do not even notice its growth.

You have three shortcomings. Your speech is too clever and lacks clumsiness; [43] you cannot interpret the books you read in a very profound manner; and your

---

[40] This refers to the author's campaign against the Taipings.

[41] Changsha, Hunan province.

[42] The author was then fifty-two years old.

[43] According to traditional Chinese thinking, a man clever in speech created the impression of being untrustworthy.

compositions lack ruggedness and are too prosaic. If you work hard on these three points, steadily as well as intensively, I believe that you will make great improvement in one or two years without realizing it yourself. Clumsiness in speech and dignity in manner will pave the way for virtue. Ruggedness and fluidity in composition will help you in your scholarship.

You have made some progress in poetry. Have you written much poetry lately? The seven-character poems of Li Po, Tu Fu, Han Yü, and Su Shih are extraordinarily heroic.[44] Have you read any of them?

To Chi-tseh, the 24th day of the 1st month, 1863

I am concerned with my son-in-law Lo's temperament, but there is not much we can do about it. Instruct your third sister [45] to be pliable, obedient, and respectful, and under no circumstances should she openly defy her husband's wishes. There are three cardinal bonds in human relationships, all of which are between superiors and inferiors. The king is superior to his ministers; the father is superior to his sons; and the husband is superior to his wife. This is the basic principle that governs Heaven and Earth. "The king is Heaven; the father is Heaven; and the husband is Heaven," says one of our ancient records. "The king is supreme; the father is supreme; and the husband is supreme," says *Cermonies and Rituals*.[46] "Even though the king is not benevolent, his ministers have to be loyal. Even though the father is not loving, his sons have to be filially dutiful. Even though the husband is not virtuous, his wife has to be obedient." We are a family of scholars and officials and have obeyed the instructions in the *Cermonies and Rituals* for many generations. You should instruct your first and third sisters to be patient and obedient, no matter how unpleasant their environment is.

To Chi-shui (nephew), the 14th day of the 12th month, 1863

For generations the motto of our family has been "filial piety, brotherly love, industry, and thrift." I did not see personally how this motto was observed prior to the honorable Fu-ch'en's generation since this was before my time. However, I did see that the honorable Ching-hsi and Hsing-kang got up before daybreak every morning and that they worked hard all day long without a moment's rest. When the honorable Ching-hsi was a young man, he studied at the Ch'en family's temple. When he went to school in the first lunar month, his father, the honorable Fu-ch'en, gave him one hundred standard coins as pocket money. By the time he returned home in the fifth lunar month, he spent only two standard coins and returned the rest to his father. How thrifty he was! Even after his grandson had acquired a position in the Hanlin Academy,[47] he was still thrifty enough to grow his own vegetables and collect animal waste as fertilizer. People of your generation have seen for yourselves how industrious and thrifty my father, the honorable Chu-t'ing, was. Even though our family has become well-to-do, you and your brothers should not forget how much your ancestors have gone through. One should never over-enjoy his good fortune; nor should he over-use his power and influence.

[44] Heroic in style, not necessarily in content.
[45] Younger sister.
[46] *Yi li.*
[47] The nation's highest academic institution, to which only the most successful of the imperial examination candidates were assigned.

There are two important things underlying the word "industry": early rising and perseverance. As for the word "thrift," it means at least two things. First, do not own or wear expensive clothes. Second, do not hire too many servants. Ministers and generals do not necessarily come from what we might call the best families; nor are sages and heroes born as such. They are made through a determination of will and constant efforts. Now you are living under the most enviable circumstances and enjoying the best time of your life. Moreover, you will have one of the most virtuous men as your teacher next year. At this moment you should make an iron resolution with regard to your own future. If you do so, I do not see why you should fail in whatever tasks you might choose to undertake and why you cannot become the man you admire. I hope that being so young as you are, you will think hard about my advice.

To Chi-tseh, the 1st day of the 9th month, 1865

I heard that you fell ill on the 11th and that by the 16th you still felt tired and dizzy. Have you recovered from your illness yet?

My philosophy in life can be summarized in one statement: "I will do my very best; let Heaven decide the outcome." The same philosophy is also applicable to the preservation of one's health. As a rich man will become richer if he avoids luxuries, a healthy man will become healthier if he does not abuse his own body. By the same token, as a poor man will not become bankrupt if he is thrifty enough, a physically weak person will be able to preserve his health if he exercises enough self-control. By self-control is meant not only that related to food and sex, but also that in the pursuance of studies. You should never overwork yourself even in the matter of acquiring knowledge.

In my essay on the "eight essentials," I said that the abstention from anger is essential to the preservation of health. I have also taught you not to let worry occupy your mind, that you should take an optimistic attitude towards life and the world in general. To cultivate a cheerful outlook is one way of eliminating anger. If you know how to abstain from anger and how to exercise self-control, you have already mastered the way of preserving health.

The length of a man's life span, like that of his illness, is determined by Heaven. Since it has been determined, any attempt intended to prolong it is merely wishful thinking. The same thing can be said about the occurrence or length of an illness. Taking medicine and praying to the gods are worse than useless. I remember what the honorable Hsing-kang said about medicine and prayers; I have elaborated on his teachings so as to transmit them to you people of the younger generations. From time to time you should convey my thinking in this matter to other members of our family.

151 · HUANG TSUNG-HSI: *On Wastefulness* [48]

Even after taxes have been reduced, the people will still have financial difficulties as long as they maintain their irrational customs, superstitions, and luxurious habits. What are the irrational customs? They are the rites and rituals in marriage and funeral that bear no resemblance to their long-lost counterparts of ancient times. In the matter of marriage, there are such customs as "filling up the

[48] *Ming-yi tai-fang lu,* Essay No. 18.

baskets," "equipment for the journey," and the giving of banquets.[49] In the matter of funeral, there are such customs as the dressing of the dead, the offering of sacrifices, the performance of Buddhist rituals, the giving of banquets, and the invocation of the spirits. The rich compete with one another in displaying lavishness in the observance of these rituals, and the poor struggle to emulate them.

What are the popular superstitions that are also wasteful in nature? The Buddhists build their costly temples, and all the things they need, including food, clothing, equipment, and services come from the people. The wizards and the witches are an equal drain on the people's financial resources. Their paper money,[50] candles, incense, sacrifices, music, dances, fasting, and prayers are as extravagant as they are useless.

What are the luxurious habits prevalent in our society? They can be seen in such institutions as brothels, taverns and restaurants, and embroidery plants. A customer in a brothel can spend as much in one night as the total assets of a middle-income person. An extravagant meal in an expensive restaurant can cost as much as an average person's expenditure on food for a whole year. One suit that emerges from these embroidery plants may involve an expense that can keep ten people warm for an indefinite period.

If the nation is to be governed well, we should eliminate all the Buddhist and other mystical practices and return to the simple rites of ancient times in relation to funeral and marriage. We should rely on schools as the institution for educating the people. All brothels should be closed down, and no man should be allowed to drink liquor. As for clothing, it should be made of ordinary cloth or silk.

Today nine out of every ten stores in our large cities are catering to the needs of the Buddhists, the wizards and the witches, the prostitutes, the curious, and the leisurely. All of these stores should be closed down immediately and for good. This is not the final solution to this problem, but at least it is a step towards the right direction.

When the sage kings of ancient times spoke of suppressing the non-essential occupations so as to elevate the essential ones, they had in mind the kind of occupations described above. Later scholars did not understand the sages' true intentions and mistakenly classified commerce and craftsmanship as non-essential, saying they wanted to suppress these occupations. Both merchants and artisans perform great services and are in fact essential to the welfare of our society. It is wrong to say that the sage kings of ancient times wished to suppress them.

[49] "Filling up the baskets" or k'uang-fei denoted the presents which the family of the prospective groom gave to the family of the prospective bride. "Equipment for the journey" or chuang-tzu denoted dowry. The banquets were given during the time of the wedding.

[50] During a Buddhist or Taoist service, paper money was burned so that the deceased could receive it. It was not the paper currency issued by the government; it was more like play money.

152 • TS'AO HSÜEH-CH'IN: *No Feast Can Last Forever* [51]

At midnight when Feng-chieh was about to close her eyes, she saw Mrs. Ch'in walking from the outside towards her bed.[52] "You are soundly asleep, dear aunt," said Mrs. Ch'in. "Now that I am returning home,[53] you do not even wish to escort me for a short distance. We have been good friends; so I come here to bid you farewell. I know that I will miss you. Before I leave, I want to tell you a wish of mine which only you can help to fulfill."

"What is your wish?" Feng-chieh heard herself ask this question. "I shall do my very best."

"Dear aunt, you are a natural hero among the powdered and the perfumed; [54] even many scholar-officials cannot surpass you in native ability. Have you forgot the old sayings that 'the moon will wax after the fifteenth' [55] and that 'when a tank is over-filled, the water will spill?' There is also the saying that 'the higher you climb, the heavier you will fall.' Now that our family has been influential and prosperous for almost one hundred years, we should be prepared for the day when 'sorrow comes in the wake of happiness.' How can it maintain its reputation as an old, scholarly family should it become in some future time a victim to an old saying that 'when the tree falls, all monkeys inhabiting it will disperse and be gone?' "

Feng-chieh was not pleased when she heard these words. But they were too serious to be brushed aside. "You are right, but what would you suggest to keep this family permanently secure?" she asked.

"How foolish you are!" Mrs. Ch'in chided. "Have you not heard the proverb that 'a fortune comes in the wake of a misfortune?' Happiness and sorrow—and honor and shame—take turns in governing the world and the life of a man. There is nothing we, as human beings, can do about this irony. If, during the days of glory, we take steps to prepare ourselves for the days of sadness and decline, we might be able to keep the family permanently secure. Now we have taken steps in all respects except two. If we can do equally well in these two respects, the family will be safe indeed."

"What are these two respects?" asked Feng-chieh.

"First, there is no estate specially assigned for the maintenance of the ancestrial cemetery and its seasonal worship. Second, though the family school has been established, there are no funds available for permanent support. Though we have no difficulty in maintaining both of them now, being so prosperous as we are, where will the money come from if in some future time the family fortune declines? In my humble opinion, we should buy more land and houses near the ancestrial cemetery, and the income from these sources will provide steady support for all expenses in connection with the worship of our ancestors. The family school might be located there too and be supported by the same financial resources. Meanwhile a rule should be formulated whereby each section of the

[51] *The Dream of the Red Chamber (Hung-lou meng),* roll 13. As for the author, see p. 49.
[52] Mrs. Ch'in had died only a few minutes earlier.
[53] According to Buddhist ideology, to die is to return home.
[54] The fair sex.
[55] The full moon.

family will take turns administering the land estate, performing the ritual of worship, and managing the family school. Since this responsibility is rotated among the different sections of the family for only a one-year period, rivalry or quarrel among different family members will not come about, and there is little likelihood that part or all of the estate will be sold or mortgaged."

"If in some future time the government condemns the family and confiscates its properties," Mrs. Ch'in continued, "it will not take over the estate which I have described, since it has been particularly assigned for sacrificial purposes. In such a case our descendants can go back to the estate and will have something to lean on: managing their farms and continuing their scholarly pursuits. Moreover, they will not have to interrupt the sacred duty of worshipping their ancestors. It is unwise to think that our prosperity will last forever; it is important to plan ahead. Before long another happy event will occur and will make our family even more glorious. But you should remember that this glory, like all others, is only transient and temporary. Let nothing blind you to the eternal truth, namely, 'No feast can last forever.' If you do not plan ahead, you will regret, and regret does not serve any useful purpose."

"What will be the happy event you spoke of?" asked Feng-chieh.[56]

"This is a heavenly secret which I cannot reveal to you at this moment," said Mrs. Ch'in. "Dear aunt, we have been good friends. Before I bid you farewell, let me give you this advice:

>All flowers disappear after the spring;
>Each of us seeks his own door, silently!"

Feng-chieh wished to ask more questions, but she was suddenly awakened by the beating of signal boards outside. The boards were beaten four times which signified that a member of the family had died. "Mrs. Ch'in, the honorable mistress of the Eastern Residence, has passed away!" a man shouted aloud outside the window. Feng-chieh was so startled that her whole body was covered with cold perspiration. . . .

[56] The happy event, which Mrs. Ch'in, as a departing spirit, could predict, was the forthcoming visit of a female member of the family who was then a high-ranking concubine of the reigning emperor. Ts'ao Hsüeh-ch'in described this visit in great detail later in his book.

CHAPTER SEVENTEEN

Human Relationships

THE Chinese believed that philosophies were ways of life to live by rather than ideologies to be discussed in abstract terms. Theoretically, how a person conducted his life spoke more eloquently of his philosophy than anything he might have said or written. Since no man except a hermit could conduct his life in a social vacuum, to learn the proper behavior or conduct was in fact to learn the accepted rules that governed human relationships. No other people in the world gave so much attention to the maintenance of harmonious relationships among men as the traditional Chinese.

The Confucians spoke of *wu-lun* or five cardinal relationships: relationships between king and subjects, father and son, husband and wife, elder and younger brothers, and finally, between friend and friend. The first two relationships were considered the most important, though there was considerable debate as to which one of these two was more important (Selection 54). The relationship between a king and his subjects has been elaborated upon in some detail in Chapter Seven, and Chapter Eighteen will be devoted to women and their relationships with others, including their husbands. Here we shall concern ourselves with the other three relationships.

Though Confucius said that a father should be loving *(tz'u)* if he expected his son to be pious *(hsiao)*, the father-son relationship was often one-sided in practice. In other words, the son should remain "pious" regardless of whether the father is "loving." Under normal circumstances, a child of traditional China enjoyed the same love and care that a child does in any other culture (Selection 153). However, once a father had stopped loving his son for some reason of his own, he put his son in an untenable position, and there could be tragic consequences (Selection 154). The virtue of filial piety was strongly emphasized throughout Chinese history, and from such emphasis developed many customs peculiarly Chinese. While some of these customs (such as the mourning for a three-year period after the death of either parent) were understandable if not approvable from a Westerner's point of view, others were bizarre or even brutal. The story that appears in Selection 155 is a verification of the truism that a virtue, when carried to great extremes, will become a vice instead.

To cultivate in a child's mind a strong sense of respect for his elders, his parents should see to it that he be indoctrinated with the socially approved values; if necessary, they should not hesitate to resort to corporal punishment to achieve that purpose (Selections 156 and 194). One of the most celebrated examples of brotherly love was the story of Pai-yi and Shu-ch'i (Selection 158) told by Ssu-ma Ch'ien, though modern scholars may have strong reservations about its authenticity as a historical episode.

Whenever a Chinese wished to emphasize the close relationship between two friends, if he were familiar with ancient literature, he would say that their friendship was as great as that between Kuan Chung and Pao Shu-ya *(ch'ing t'ung Kuan Pao)*. If, on the other hand, he wished to stress mutual understanding, he would cite the example of Lü Pai-ya and Chung Tzu-ch'i (Selection 159). While friendship was supposed to be as "pure" as the two examples cited above, ulterior motives were not altogether absent in some other cases (Selection 160). Sometimes the pledge of mutual help marked the very beginning of friendship, and frequently such a pledge was formalized in a friendship pact known as "sworn brotherhood" (Selection 161). The principle of "sworn brotherhood" formed the ideological foundation of China's numerous secret societies which, under able leadership, were often diverted to political activities. The Yellow Turbans of the third century A.D. and the White Lotus Society of a later period were among the most noted examples.

Outside the five cardinal relationships described above there were such relationships as those between teachers and students and among neighbors. After a student had passed the civil service examinations, the person before whom he must perform the kowtow was his teacher. If he committed a crime and could not be located, sometimes his teacher was punished as a substitute (Selection 154). By teacher-student relationship was meant more than the relationship in the Western sense; it also included the relationship between the man who supervised a civil service examination and the candidate who passed it under his direction. In the latter case it was more like a relationship between a patron and a protégé, a relationship which was sometimes closer than the usual teacher-student relationship (Selection 162).

At the bottom of the social scale were the slaves whose relationship with their masters was so one-sided that few scholars of traditional China bothered to elaborate on it. In practice the treatment of slaves varied a great deal. It ranged from the thoroughly brutal (Selection 154) to the fairly lenient (Selection 164). From time to time the government took the initiative to regulate the master-slave relationship in the hope that some of the worst abuses in the treatment of slaves could be eliminated (Selection 165), though we have no idea to what extent its directives were carried out. Slaves were generally employed in domestic work; the nature of their work may have accounted for the fact that unenviable though their position was, slaves in China were perhaps treated more humanely than those in some other countries.

153 · OU-YANG HSIU: *My Father* [1]

It was my misfortune that my father died when I was only four. Though the family was poor, my mother decided not to remarry so that she could devote herself to raising me to adulthood. "Your father was an honest official," said she; "he loved to entertain and was very generous with others. He saved little with the small salary he received and was proud of the fact that he did not have any savings. 'I will never let money corrupt me,' he used to say. When he died, he did not leave a single roof to cover our heads and not even one acre of land to grow our food. How difficult it was when I had to raise you alone! But I knew your father well. His whole hope was placed upon you, then only a small child.

"I came too late to serve my mother-in-law who had already died when I married your father. But I knew that your father had been a dutiful son before I arrived. When your father died and left behind him a helpless child, I did not know whether alone I could raise you to adulthood. But somehow I felt that the family line would be maintained.

"I married your father one year after the ending of a mourning period which he had observed for his own mother. Each year on the day of her demise, he would offer sacrifices to her departed spirit and sob audibly: 'How much I would prefer to serve her with simple food rather than honor her with rich sacrifices!' Whenever he was enjoying his food, he would say: 'Why was I not well-to-do when my mother was still alive?' And tears would stream down from his eyes. At the beginning I attributed this strong emotion to the fact that his mother had only recently passed away; I was hoping that it would fade away with the passage of time. However, when he maintained it for a long period and in fact throughout his whole life, I knew with certainty that he had been a truly dutiful son to his mother, even though I myself had never had the honor to serve her personally.

"As a government official, your father often worked late at night in examining criminal cases. Sometimes he pushed his paper aside and began to sigh. 'Why are you so unhappy?' I asked him. 'This is a case of capital punishment, but I have no way of saving this man,' he would reply. 'Can you not do your very best?' 'If I have done my best to save him and yet cannot reach my goal, both he and I will have no regret. If, on the other hand, I do reach my goal and succeed in saving his life, the person who has died at his hands will not forgive me. The whole world wants him to die. He will probably die, however hard I try to save him.'

"Turning around, he saw the nurse standing on the side and holding you in her arms. Pointing at you, he sighed: 'The diviner says that I shall die soon. If he is correct, I would not be able to raise this child myself. After I die, please instruct him in the same way as I would have done myself.' In fact, he made similar remarks with regard to the education of all members of the younger generation. Since these remarks were repeated often, I could not forget them even if I tried to.

"I cannot make any comment on the way your father conducted his official business, since I know little about it. But I do know that he was an honest, unpretentious man at home. Judging from what I observed at home, I know that he

---

[1] *Ku-wen kuan-chih*, roll 10. As for the author, see pp. 458–459.

was a man who would not do anything against his convictions. Since his heart was full of love for others, I was convinced that he would have an heir. Oh, my son, kindly remember the words which your father once told me: 'It is more important to serve one's parents with love than with material goods. Not every man is able enough to work for the benefit of all of mankind; it is important, however, that whatever he does, he should be motivated by love.' I cannot teach you better than to repeat your father's words."

How can I possibly forget these words?

My grandfather died when my father was still a small child. He studied diligently and passed the imperial examination in the third year of Hsien-p'ing.[2] He became a prefectural judge first in Taochow and then in Ssuchow and Mienchou.[3] He was finally transferred to T'aichou.[4] He died on his fifty-ninth year and was buried at Mount Lung in the district of Shahsi.[5]

154 · SSU-MA CH'IEN: *The Death of Prince Shen-sheng* [6]

In the fifth year of Duke Hsien's reign (672 B.C.), the Duke attacked Li-jung [7] and acquired Madame Li. Both Madame Li and her younger sister became the Duke's favorites. . . .

In the twelfth year (665 B.C.) Madame Li gave birth to a son named Hsi-ch'i. The Duke began to think seriously about the possibility of replacing Shen-sheng by Hsi-ch'i as the crown prince. . . .

In the seventeenth year (660 B.C.) the Duke ordered crown prince Shen-sheng to head an army to attack Tung-shan. . . .[8]

"I have several sons," said the Duke to Li K'e; [9] "I do not know which one of them should be designated as my heir apparent." Li K'e did not reply. Later he went to see the crown prince.

"Is it true that I am going to be replaced as the crown prince?" Shen-sheng asked.

"You should do your best while you are commanding the army," said Li K'e. "As long as you believe that you are respectful towards your father, why should you be afraid of being replaced? Moreover, a man should be more concerned with his performance as a loyal son than with the possibility, or the lack of it, of being designated as the heir apparent. You will be very safe indeed if you diligently cultivate your virtue and never place any blame on others."

One day in the nineteenth year (658 B.C.) the Duke told Madame Li privately that he intended to replace Shen-sheng by Hsi-ch'i as the crown prince. "No, you should not," Madame Li protested in tears. "The fact that Shen-sheng is the crown prince is known to all the states throughout the country. Moreover, he is at the head of an army and is very popular with the people. You must not replace

---

[2] A.D. 995.

[3] Taochou was located in modern Hunan province, and Ssuchou and Mienchou were located in modern Anhwei and Szechuan provinces respectively.

[4] Located in modern Kiangsu province.

[5] Located in modern Kiangsi province.

[6] "The State of Tsin" (*Tsin shih-chia*); *Shih chi*, roll 39.

[7] A non-Chinese tribe.

[8] A non-Chinese tribe.

[9] A minister.

the eldest son of a legal wife by the young son of a concubine on my behalf. If you insist on carrying out your plan, I will commit suicide."

Despite what she said in front of the Duke, Madame Li secretly sent her agents to spread rumors for the purpose of slandering the crown prince, though outwardly she kept on praising him. She, of course, wanted her own son to be installed as the crown prince.

One day on the twenty-first year (656 B.C.) Madame Li told the crown prince that she had dreamed about Madame Chiang, the crown prince's deceased mother, and that he, the crown prince, should proceed to Ch'üfu [10] to offer sacrifices to comfort his deceased mother. After the ritual of offering sacrifices had been completed, the crown prince brought back the sacrificial meat to his father as tribute. The Duke was then in a hunting trip outside the capital, and Madame Li ordered her servants secretly to place poison in the meat.

Two days later the Duke returned from his hunting trip, and the royal chef presented the sacrificial meat. The Duke was about to eat it when he was stopped by Madame Li. "Since the meat comes from a place faraway, it should be tested before you eat it," she said. The Duke threw the meat to the ground, the ground began to bulge.[11] Fed with it, a dog died immediately. Tested it on a slave, the slave also dropped dead. "How cruel the crown prince is!" Madame Li said in tears. "He wants to kill his own father whom he is anxious to replace. How can he possibly have mercy on others? You, sir, are very advanced in age, and yet he cannot wait. The reason he wants to kill his father is because he cannot stand me and my son Hsi-ch'i. Under the circumstances I and my son can either flee to another country before it is too late, or commit suicide before the crown prince slaughters us with his own hands. Formerly when you wanted to replace him as the crown prince, I was strongly opposed to it. Now I know how wrong I was."

As soon as he learned that he had been implicated by Madame Li in the alleged attempt to murder his father, the crown prince fled to Hsinch'eng.[12] Unable to locate the crown prince, the Duke was furious enough to kill the prince's tutor Tu Yüan-k'uan as a substitute.

Some one told the crown prince that the poison was placed by Madame Li and that he should inform his father about his innocence. "My father is very old," said the crown prince. "He needs Madame Li for his old age. Without her he could not eat or sleep well. If I tell him the truth, he will be very angry with her. I cannot bear to see that his only comfort is taken away from him during his old age." Some one suggested that he should flee to another state. "With a bad reputation such as I have,[13] which state in the country will take me in as its guest?" said the crown prince. "The only course open to me is to commit suicide."

On the *wu-shen* day of the twelfth month, crown prince Shen-sheng committed suicide at Hsinch'eng.

[10] The former capital of Tsin, located in modern Shansi province.

[11] According to Chinese hearsay, an object unusually poisonous, once thrown to the ground, could make the ground rise slightly.

[12] Located in modern Shansi province.

[13] This refers to the alleged attempt of murdering his own father.

155 · HOU FANG-YÜ: *Wan the Dutiful Son* [14]

Wan the Dutiful Son cut a piece of flesh from his thigh to feed his mother and was consequently able to cure her illness. People say that this honorable occurrence should be reported to higher authorities so that his virtuous conduct could be exemplified in testimonials, to be remembered by posterity for years to come. Others say that this cannot be done because it is explicitly prohibited under the present law.

A dutiful son, pure in heart and sincere in conduct, appears only once in a long time. It is a pity that, due to the legal restriction, he cannot be honored in the way he should be. If he could be, the example of filial love and obedience which he set would have exercised a benevolent influence over an increasingly large number of people. I shall elaborate on this point.

Many years ago there was in Ch'üanchou a dutiful son named T'ang Yen who cut a piece of flesh from his right arm to feed his father. His motive was the same as that of Wan. Commenting on this incident, the historian Yao Lai [15] maintained that to mutilate one's own body, for whatever purpose, is incompatible with the concept of righteous conduct and should not be regarded as a good example to follow. Since then people have considered this statement the final word on this subject.

That we should not mutilate our own body, including its hair and skin, has been an ancient adage handed down by our sages. If this adage is to be interpreted literally, the loss of one hair by artificial means would be considered improper and should therefore be avoided. I, for one, do not believe in this literal interpretation. On the contrary, when vital principles are involved, principles that have to do with our loyalty towards our sovereign or parents, we should not mind the pulverizing of our brain and the slicing of our bodies, let alone the loss of one limb, if we are to be sincere in the belief of our principles. Han Yü maintained that self-inflicted death can be justified only under extraordinary circumstances, and that this principle is equally applicable in cases wherein a person's loyalty towards his sovereign or parents is involved. Only then, he continued, should the dead man be exemplified as a model to follow.

What does Han Yü mean by "extraordinary circumstances"? He means a situation in which the prevention of disaster or the seeking of revenge has become a compelling necessity. What situation be more compelling than the suffering of unbearable pain by one's parents as a result of injury or illness? If a person decides to mutilate his own body so that his parents can live, I cannot see any reason why he should not be allowed to do so. Furthermore, a man who mutilates himself will be on the verge of death; unless he is absolutely sincere, he would not have taken such a step in the first place. It is wrong to compare him with those hypocrites who take drastic actions for the sole purpose of earning an undeserved reputation. His example will inspire others to show the same boundless love for their parents. Those who do not understand this point and denounced him for mutilat-

---

[14] *Ku-ching wen-tsung,* vol. III, pp. 30–31. The author was a scholar-official who lived in the seventeenth century.
[15] A Ming historian who lived in the first half of the sixteenth century.

ing his own body commit the same error of extremism that Han Fei once did.[16]

When King Wu was seriously ill, Duke Chou prayed to Heaven to substitute his own life for that of his brother.[17] He went further than merely mutilating his body; he was willing to die for the person to whom he had pledged his loyalty. Can we blame him for attempting to exterminate himself? The answer is obviously "no." By the same token, we cannot say that Mr. T'ang committed an extremist act when he mutilated himself in order to save his father. He should in fact be praised.

Filial piety was one of the cardinal virtues of ancient times. During a period of moral decline such as we experience today, our leaders no longer encourage or promote the cultivation of good customs. Our scholars, who neglect their duties towards their parents in normal times, are indifferent during the time of crisis. They ignore the sufferings of their parents as if they were the sufferings of strangers, while quoting ancient classics to cover up their cowardliness. In fact, they defend their lack of action as the normal course to follow, a course which they claim is becoming to a virtuous person. They regard a man as impulsive or hypocritical and criticize him severely if he chooses to sacrifice his own life for the benefit of his king or parents. If this line of thinking goes unchallenged, how can our customs be improved and our people be led to a righteous path?

Suppose that there is a man who is impulsive or hypocritical by nature. Today he performs one good deed because of his impulsive or hypocritical nature. Tomorrow he will perform another good deed for the same reason. Day after tomorrow he will do it again. He does it day after day and year after year with no intention of discontinuing it whatsoever. While his good deeds are accumulating, should we still accuse him of being impulsive or hypocritical? If we characterize a man as impulsive or hypocritical simply because he is willing to sacrific his life for his king or is doing his best for his parents, what is the use of the so-called virtues that have been praised so highly by today's intellectuals?

It is because of this reason that I think highly of Wan the Dutiful Son. . . . I believe that his virtuous conduct should be reported to higher authorities so that it will be made widely known for all of us to follow.

156 · YEN CHIH-T'UI: *On the Teaching of Children* [18]

It is unnecessary to teach the naturally superior; it is useless to teach the inherently stupid. As for most people, they need to be taught.

The sage kings of ancient times believed in prenatal education and introduced a system whereby a child was taught before he was actually born. Three months after the conception, the expectant mother left her husband's chamber to reside in a separate suite of her own. From then on, she was not to see anything vulgar

---

[16] Han Fei (d.233 B.C.), a Legalist philosopher, did not believe that genuine, selfless motive could exist behind an action. All actions, however cleverly disguised, were meant to bring benefits to the person who performed them.

[17] Duke Chou was the younger brother of King Wu (twelfth century B.C.). According to the legend, Heaven was so moved by the Duke's selflessness that He spared the king's life.

[18] "On the Teaching of Children" *(Chiao tzu)* in *Family Instructions for the Yen Clan (Yen-shih chia-hsün),* Chapter II, by Yen Chih-t'ui who lived in the sixth century.

and not to hear anything improper. She should be nourished with good food and imbued with wholesome music. Never should she be subject to any form of excess. This was the law of ancient times, written on a jade plate and safeguarded in a golden vault. . . .

The parents who do not discipline their children are not necessarily those who wish their children ill. The trouble with them is that, thinking that they love their children, they do not want to scold or be angry with them, let alone beat them. When a person is ill, he has to take medicine and to undergo such operations as acupuncture and cauterization if he is to stay alive, even though none of these operations is a pleasant one. No parent wants to punish his child more than it is necessary; when he does, it is because he believes that in the long run the punishment will bring his child more good. Being a good parent as he thinks he is, he does not believe that he has a better choice.

Madame Wei was the mother of General Wang. She continued to be strict with her son long after the latter had passed forty and was a commander of 3,000 troops at P'ench'eng.[19] She whipped him whenever she thought that he had acted or behaved in an improper manner. Because of her discipline, General Wang was able to achieve great deeds.

During the reign of Yüan-ti (r.552–554) of the Liang dynasty there was a gentleman unusually talented and bright. Needless to say, he was his father's favorite. Because of his partiality, the father neglected to teach his son in a proper manner. Whenever his son did something well, he praised him all year round. Whenever his son did something wrong, he concealed or rationalized it in the hope that the latter would reform by himself; he did not punish his son as a good father should have. Later, the son was married and then appointed as a government official. However, because of the lack of good teachings on the part of his father, he became less respectful and more arrogant towards others. One day he made some intemperate remarks in front of Chou T'i, and the latter was infuriated and slaughtered him in the most brutal manner.

A father's dignity is too great to suffer from an intimate relationship with his son. His love, on the other hand, is too strong to make such a relationship casual and distant. If the relationship is too distant, the father will not be able to express his love adequately, nor can his son remain pious and obedient. If the relationship is too intimate, there will be negligence of parental duties on the part of the father and disrespect on the part of the son. . . .

Duke Lang-ya was the son of Emperor Wu-ch'eng of Ch'i and the brother of the crown prince. Since he was born with high intelligence, the emperor and the empress were particularly partial towards him. For instance, he was given the same rights and privileges in the matter of food and clothing as the crown prince. "This is an unusually intelligent child who will achieve a great deal when he grows up"; the emperor made this remark time and again in front of his favorite son.

After the crown prince ascended the throne as the emperor, Duke Lang-ya was moved to a side palace. Yet he enjoyed a leniency and a tolerance from the new emperor far exceeding those shared by other princes. The empress dowager, however, still felt that he had not received enough privilege and often spoke to the emperor on his behalf. Thus, at the tender age of his teens, he became arrogant,

---

[19] Kiukiang, modern Kiangsi province.

reckless, and intemperate. He demanded the same kind of clothing, utensils, and playthings as the emperor had. Visiting the main palace one day, he saw officials present to the emperor fresh ice and "early dates"; [20] he demanded the same but was refused. "Why can I not have the same thing as the emperor has?" he protested. This is only one of the examples showing how misguided he was.

Duke Lang-ya had grievances against the prime minister and decided to falsify a royal decree so as to kill him. Being fearful that others might come to the rescue of his intended victim, he ordered the soldiers under his command to prevent anyone from entering the palace. Since his action was not interpreted as part of a larger design to overthrow the emperor, he was not punished so severely as he should have been. However, he was imprisoned eventually and died in prison.

Though a parent loves his children, rarely can he maintain absolute impartiality between all of them. Since the beginning of mankind, the showing of partiality has been one of the worst parental abuses. A parent should know that though it is easy to love a child who is intelligent and good-looking, he has even a greater obligation towards a child who is clumsy or retarded. To show partiality for a child whom one believes one loves defeats the very purpose one tries to achieve; it will spoil and eventually ruin him. . . .

A scholar-official of the Ch'i dynasty once told me that he had a seventeen-years-old son who was proficient in calligraphy and literature. "I intend to teach him the Hsien-pei language and the p'i-p'a," [21] he continued. "When he is fairly good at both of them, he will be able to serve the ministers well and win affection from them. I believe that this is a very important part of his education." I lowered my head and did not make any comment. How strange this man's way of educating his son was! If this is the way of becoming a minister, I hope that none of you, my children, will ever succeed in becoming one.

157 · YEN CHIH-T'UI: *On the Relationship Between Brothers* [22]

The relationship between husband and wife began as early as the emergence of mankind. The relationship between father and son came about after the relationship between husband and wife had been established. The relationship between brothers came naturally when the parents had more than one child. From ancient to modern times these three relationships are the cornerstones of a family. All familial relationships to as far as the ninth degree are only ramifications of these basic relationships. As basic relationships, they should be as genuine and true as they are natural, and their importance cannot be overemphasized.

Brothers come from the same origin and are consequently of the same spirit, even though they are separate in form. While they are little, they tag along with the same parents, eat at the same table, and wear each other's clothes. They study the same subjects when they are in school, and travel in the same areas when they are old enough to be out of their home. Even if one of them acts improperly, the others will love him just the same. The situation begins to change, however, when they reach adulthood and are married. Each of them has his own wife and

[20] Tradition dictated that the first dates plucked from the tree should be presented to the emperor as tribute.
[21] See p. 341, Footnote 5.
[22] *Yen-shih chia-hsün,* Chapter III.

children, and the brotherly love, however great it has been, will suffer some degree of deterioration. The relationship between sisters-in-law can never be so close as that between brothers, and it is absolutely wrong to allow one's wife to interfere with the natural love which one has for his brothers. In reality, however, only when brotherly affection is unshakably strong can it stand interference from outsiders. You, my children, should keep this constantly in mind.

After the death of the parents, the brothers should love and care for each other more than ever before. They should be as close as a shadow to an object and as an echo to a sound. Loving their parents as they did and thinking that they are the branches of the same tree, how can they possibly feel otherwise? Their relationship is totally different from their relationships with others: whenever a misunderstanding develops, it should be quickly eliminated before it can bring about permanent harm. Like a man living in a house, he should quickly repair the damage whenever a hole develops on the floor or in the wall, otherwise rats and birds will come in, and so will wind and storm. If he does not, the hole will become larger and larger, and the whole house will eventually collapse. In the destruction of brotherly love, one may compare servants and concubines to birds and rats and one's wife and children to wind and storm. The only difference is that servants, concubines, and so on can be more destructive to brotherly love than birds, rats, and so on can be destructive to a house.

If brothers are not friendly towards each other, it is unrealistic to expect that their children will love one another as cousins. When cousins do not love one another, all members of the clan will feel remote and distant. When that occurs, even a man's servants can become his enemies. He is in danger wherever he goes, and there is no one who will lend him a helping hand. I have seen people who can win the friendship of hundreds of scholars in the nation but none from his elder brothers. Why is it that they can be so successful with many and yet so unsuccessful with a few? I have seen others who can command thousands of troops that are willing to die for them but who cannot command a semblance of respect from their own younger brothers. Why is it that they are so able in winning loyalty from strangers while remaining helpless in trying to gain respect from people to whom they are close? . . .

158 • SSU-MA CH'IEN: *Two Brothers* [23]

Pai-yi and Shu-ch'i were the eldest and youngest sons of Prince Ku-chu respectively. It was the prince's wish that after he died, his youngest son Shu-ch'i would succeed him as the prince. After the prince died, Shu-ch'i insisted that his eldest brother Pai-yi should inherit the throne. "We cannot disobey the wish of our father," said Pai-yi who then fled from the principality. Shu-ch'i did not want to become the prince either, and he fled from the principality too. After they left, the people in the principality installed a brother of theirs as the new ruler.

Having heard that Hsi-pai treated well the country's elders, Pai-yi and Shu-ch'i went westward with the intended purpose of becoming his subjects. By the time they arrived, however, Hsi-pai had already died. His son King Wu placed the tablet of his father (whom he called King Wen) on a carriage and was proceeding

---

[23] "Biography of Pai-yi" *(Pai-yi lieh-chuan); Shih chi,* roll 61.

eastward to conquer Cheo.[24] The two brothers knelt before King Wu's horse and protested: "Now that you have started a military campaign shortly after your father's death, can you still regard yourself as a dutiful son? Can you say that it is a benevolent act for a vassal to kill his king?" [25] The king's guards wanted to kill the two brothers, but they were stopped by T'ai-kung.[26] "These two are men of principles," said T'ai-kung; "let them be escorted away in peace."

King Wu conquered the Yin regime,[27] and all people in China pledged allegiance to him. Determined that they would not eat any grain raised in the Chou territory,[28] the two brothers went to Shouyang Mountains [29] and collected thorn-ferns as food. When they were about to die of starvation, they composed a song which read as follows:

> Climbing the Western Mountains,
> We collect ferns.
> One form of violence replacing another—
> Is it really justice?
> Shen-nung, Shun, and Yü [30]—they are all gone;
> Where will our home be?
> We are withering away, alas!
> Die we shall and must.

They died of starvation in the Shouyang Mountains.

159 · SSU-MA CH'IEN et al.: Ideal Friendship

Two Friends [31]

Kuan Chung, a native of Yingshang,[32] befriended Pao Shu-ya during his boyhood. He often cheated his friend in financial matters, but his friend, knowing his poor financial condition and taking into consideration his basic goodness, never complained. Throughout these long years, Pao Shu-ya continued to befriend him and treat him well.

Later, Kuan Chung became an adviser to Prince Chiu, and Pao Chu-ya, on the other hand, served Prince Hsiao-pai.[33] Subsequently Prince Chiu died, and Prince Hsiao-pai was consequently installed on the throne as Duke Huan of Ch'i. Kuan Chung was thrown into prison because he had previously served the Duke's rival.

[24] The last ruler of the Shang dynasty, sometimes romanized as "Chou."
[25] Then King Wu was still a nominal vassal of King Cheo.
[26] Chiang Tzu-ya, the prime minister under King Wu.
[27] The Shang dynasty.
[28] King Wu was the founder of the Chou dynasty.
[29] Located in the northern section of modern Shensi province.
[30] The sage emperors of the ancient past.
[31] "Biographies of Kuan Chung and Yen P'ing-chung" *(Kuan Yen lieh-chuan); Shih chi,* roll 62.
[32] Located in modern Anhwei province.
[33] Princes Hsiac-pai and Chiu were two brothers who competed for the same throne. By agreement each of the two friends volunteered to serve one of the two rival princes so that, whichever prince won, one of them would gain power and influence and was thus in a position to help the other.

However, at the suggestion of Pao Shu-ya, not only was Kuan Chung released; he was also made the chief minister of Ch'i. He soon proved his worth by making Ch'i the most powerful state in North China and Duke Huan the most influential person in all of China. Without his efforts Duke Huan's success would not have been possible.

"When I was poor," said Kuan Chung, "Pao Shu-ya and I formed a business partnership. When profits were divided, I always took the larger share. Pao did not think that I was greedy because he knew that I was poor and needed the money. The business decisions I made were often wrong and sometimes disastrous, but Pao did not regard me as stupid; he knew that there were circumstances which I could not control. Three times I was employed by a prince and three times I lost my position through dismissal. Yet Pao did not think that I was incompetent; he attributed my misfortunes to bad luck. I fought as a soldier three times and three times I ran away from the battlefield. Pao, however, did not consider me a coward; he knew that I had an old mother whom I had to support. After Prince Chiu had been defeated, I chose imprisonment instead of following the example of the prince's other lieutenants by committing suicide. Pao did not think that I was a man without any principle; he understood that I was more ashamed of my inability to accomplish great deeds and make my name known throughout the world than of my failure to follow a principle that was insignificant and commonplace. My parents gave me my life, but it was Mr. Pao who really understood me."

After Pao Shu-ya had recommended Kuan Chung as Ch'i's chief minister, he became his recommendee's subordinate. Following his footsteps, his descendants served as Ch'i's ministers for more than ten generations. As far as other people were concerned, they valued more highly Pao Shu-ya's ability to discover and to understand a great man than the greatness which Kuan Chung had obviously displayed.

Chi Cha and His Sword [34]

In his role as a roving ambassador, Chi Cha [35] passed through the principality of Hsü. Prince Hsü liked the ceremonial sword which Chi Cha had carried with him, but was too modest to make a suggestion. Knowing what the prince had in mind, Chi Cha would have been happy to present it to him as a gift had he not needed it in his official capacity as a roving ambassador.

Passing through the principality of Hsü again on his return trip, Chi Cha found that Prince Hsü had already died. He went to the latter's cemetery and hung the sword over a tree beside his grave.

"What is this for since the prince is already dead?" asked one of his servants.

"I promised this sword to him in my heart even though he did not know it," said Chi Cha. "How can I break my promise simply because he is dead?"

Lü Pai-ya and His Harp [36]

Lü Pai-ya, one of the greatest harpists of ancient China, once played for his friend Chung Tzu-ch'i.

[34] "Biography of Wu T'ai-pai" (Wu T'ai-pai shih-chia); Shih chi, roll 31.
[35] A prince from the state of Wu.
[36] Lü's Annals (Lü-shih ch'un-ch'iu), roll 14, written under the direction of Lü Pu-wei. As for Lü Pu-wei, see pp. 138–142.

"You are thinking of the mighty T'ai Mountains,[37] the noblest of all," said Chung.

When another piece was played, Chung again remarked: "How serene the river is, running thousands of miles without losing its majesty!"

A few years later, Chung Tzu-ch'i died. Lü Pai-ya broke his harp and never played again.

160 · SSU-MA CH'IEN: *Chang Yi*[38]

Chang Yi was a native of Wei and had at one time studied statecraft with Su Ch'in under Mr. Kuei-ku. He believed that Su Ch'in was superior to him in both intelligence and ability.

After he had completed his studies with Mr. Kuei-ku, Chang Yi traveled in different parts of the country, hoping to secure a position with one of the states that then divided China. In one instance, he was accused of having stolen a piece of jade by the retainers of the chief minister of Ch'u who had invited him to dinner, on the ground that he was "poor and unprincipled" and consequently must have stolen the jade. The retainers seized him by force and flogged him with a stick for several hundred times. Gaining no confession from him, they finally let him go.

Returning home, he faced a sarcastic wife. "Ha, ha!" she sneered; "if you were not a roaming scholar, you would not have received this kind of insult!" "Look at my tongue," said Chang Yi; "is it still there?" "It is there," his wife laughed. "As long as it is there," he said, "I will be all right."

Meanwhile his friend Su Ch'in, as a roaming scholar, had successfully convinced the king of Chao of the necessity of forming a grand alliance against the state of Ch'in. Though the alliance was formed, he was afraid that it would collapse once Ch'in attacked any of the allied states. Consequently he needed a man to be in power in Ch'in to prevent it from attacking the allied states, and he believed that no man could serve that purpose better than his friend Chang Yi. With this purpose in mind, he sent an agent to talk with Chang Yi in the most casual manner; Chang Yi, of course, had no idea that this man was sent by Su Ch'in. "You, sir, were once a good friend of Su Ch'in," said the agent. "He is in power now; why do you not pay him a visit since he might help you to secure a position which you desire?"

Accepting this man's advice, Chang Yi traveled to Chao where he requested an audience with Su Ch'in. Time and again Su Ch'in refused to receive him; in fact, he ordered his retainers not even to report to him Chang Yi's presence. Several days passed before he finally agreed to a meeting. The visitor, however, was seated in the lower hall to eat with the servants; and to add insult to injury, Su Ch'in scolded him repeatedly for his lack of ambition: "How is it possible that a man of your ability can continue to stand such poverty and humiliation? There is no way I can help you to secure power and wealth which, frankly, I do not believe you deserve. If I were you, I would leave here at this very moment."

When Chang Yi came to Chao, he thought that Su Ch'in, being an old friend,

---

[37] Located in modern Shantung province.
[38] "Biography of Chang Yi" *(Chang Yi lieh-chuan); Shih chi,* roll 70.

could somehow help him to secure what he wished. Not only did Su Ch'in refuse to help; he also insulted him. In an angry and vengeful mood, Chang Yi decided to visit the state of Ch'in because, of all the states in China, only Ch'in had the power to put Chao in its "proper" place. Su Ch'in, meanwhile, knew exactly what his friend intended to do. "Chang Yi is one of the ablest men in this country and his ability is far superior to mine," he remarked to one of his retainers. "I am fortunate to have secured a high position first, and it is my judgement that the man who can successfully guide the Ch'in state is he. Now he is poor and desperate and has requested my help. I was afraid that if I did help him, he would be satisfied with a small position and would not have the opportunity to develop his ability fully. That is why I brought him here and then deliberately insulted him, in the hope that feeling a strong sense of humiliation, he would be vengeful enough to revive his own ambition. You should follow him to Ch'in in secret and make sure that he receives everything he needs."

Su Ch'in asked the king of Chao to provide chariots and money for Chang Yi's travel. Without identifying himself, the agent followed Chang Yi wherever he went and stayed in the same hotels as if by accident. Slowly and gradually they became friends, and the agent was able to persuade Chang Yi to take the chariots and the money made available to him by Su Ch'in. It was through this help that Chang Yi finally reached the Ch'in state where he had an audience with King Hui. King Hui appointed him as his guest minister and planned with him the grand strategy of attacking the allied states. His mission completed, Su Ch'in's agent requested the permission to leave.

"It is due to your help that finally I have a day like this," said Chang Yi. "I intend to show you my gratitude. Why do you wish to leave?"

"I am not your friend, sir," replied the agent; "your real friend is Mr. Su. Mr. Su was afraid that the Ch'in state might attack Chao and destroy the alliance, and he thought that you were the only person who could acquire a decision-making position in Ch'in and prevent this from occurring. Therefore he deliberately insulted you to make you angry, while dispatching me in secret to provide you with the money you needed. All I did was part of Mr. Su's planning. Now that you, sir, have acquired the power you aspired to, my mission is completed, and I shall return home to report to Mr. Su the successful completion of my mission."

"How strange this is!" Chang Yi sighed. "All the time I was part of Mr. Su's planning; yet I did not realize it. Since Mr. Su is much more intelligent than I am, how dare I plot an attack against the Chao state? Please convey my thanks to Mr. Su and tell him that as long as he is in power in Chao,[39] I will not even think of such a thing as an attack on that state. Even if I did, how could I possibly hope to succeed?"

[39] Su Ch'in was then the chief minister of Chao.

161 · LO KUAN-CHUNG: *Sworn Brotherhood in a Peach Orchard* [40]

Liu Pei [41] was twenty-eight when Liu Yen, governor of Yu,[42] issued a public proclamation to invite volunteers to join his army to combat the Yellow Turbans.[43] Looking at the proclamation one day, he could not help uttering a long sigh in view of the anarchy the country had been plunged into. "What is the use of sighing if, as a patriot which I presume you are, you do not intend to do something about this miserable state of affairs?" he heard some one shouting behind him. Turning around, he saw a man about eight *ch'ih* in height, with a head looking like that of a leopard and a neck that was shaped like that of a swallow. He had a pair of big round eyes and a wide spread of whiskers, so long and bushy that they looked like those worn by a tiger. When he spoke, he sounded like a thunderbolt.

Greatly impressed with this man's appearance, Liu Pei asked him who he was. "My full name is Chang Fei and my courtesy name is Yi-te," the man replied. "My family has lived in the prefecture of Cho [44] for many generations and owns a sizable amount of land. As for myself, I peddle wine and I slaughter pigs. My hobby is to make friends with all the heroes I can find. I noticed you reading the proclamation and heard you sighing. I was interested in knowing why you were sighing."

"My name is Liu Pei, a descendant of the imperial household. Having learned that the Yellow Turbans have revolted, I wish that I had the power to crush them and bring about peace among the people. But I do not have that power; that is why I sighed."

"I have some money to my name," said Chang Fei; "maybe we can recruit volunteers of our own. Do you wish to join me for this important undertaking?" Liu Pei quickly agreed.

While drinking wine in a village tavern, the two friends saw a big man pushing a huge wheelbarrow towards the store. In front of the store the man parked his vehicle. He then went inside and ordered the bartender to give him some wine. "Bring the wine jug quickly because I am in a hurry," he yelled. "I have to go to the city to join the army."

Liu Pei took a good look at this man who must have been nine *ch'ih* in height. His face was as dark as a ripened date, and his lips were flashing red. His eyes were long and narrow, and his eyebrows looked like two crouching silkworms. He grew a long beard which certainly must have been two *ch'ih* in length. How impressive he was!

Liu Pei invited the stranger to his table and asked his name. "My full name is Kuan Yü, and my courtesy name is Yün-ch'ang. I came from Chiehliang, Hotung

[40] *The Romance of the Three Kingdoms (San kuo yen-yi)*, roll 1, by Lo Kuan-chung who lived in the fourteenth century.
[41] Founder of the Kingdom of Shu during the period of the Three Kingdoms (220–280).
[42] Modern Hopeh province.
[43] The Yellow Turbans began as a Taoist secret society, raised the standard of revolt in 184, and were crushed in A.D. 190.
[44] Located in modern Hopeh province, near Peking.

province, where I killed a local bully and was wanted for murder. For more than five years I have been wandering all over the country. Having heard that this place needed volunteers to crush the rebellion, I came here to enlist."

Liu Pei told Kuan Yü of his own plan, and the latter was more than pleased.

The three friends went to Chang Fei's villa and planned the next step. "In the back of my villa is a peach orchard where the flowers are in full blossom at the moment," said Chang Fei. "Tomorrow we shall go to the orchard to offer sacrifices to Heaven and Earth and report to them what we intend to do. Before their presence we three should be sworn in as blood brothers—one for all and all for one. Only in this way can we succeed in our undertaking." Both Liu Pei and Kuan Yü quickly agreed.

The next day in the orchard all sacrifices were carefully prepared, including a black ox and a white horse. After burning the incense, the three friends knelt down and recited the following oath: "We—Liu Pei, Kuan Yü, and Chang Fei—hereby make the pledge that from now on we are blood brothers, even though our surnames are different. We will help one another in rescuing the poor and supporting the weak; we want to bring about peace among the people and to show our gratitude towards our country. Even though we were not born in the same time, we ardently hope that we shall die in the same day, the same month, and the same year. Let Heaven and Earth witness this pledge. If we violate the principle of righteousness and betray one another, let Heaven or man put us to death!"

After the oath was taken, Liu Pei was designated as the eldest brother, Kuan Yü the younger brother, and Chang Fei the youngest brother. The sacrifices were then offered to Heaven and Earth.

The completion of the ritual was followed by a banquet in the peach orchard, attended by three hundred able-bodied men recruited from the countryside. There was plenty of wine and meat, and all of them, including the three brothers, ate and drank to their hearts' desire.

162 · FANG PAO: *An Episode That Lasts a Lifetime* [45]

The following story was related to me by my late father:

Tso Kuang-tou, an elder from our subprefecture,[46] once served as a superintendent in the capital area.[47] During a snow storm on a bitter winter day, he and a few companions of his, dressed in civilian clothes, rode in the countryside. Entering an old temple, he found a young man on the veranda; his head crouching on a table, the young man was soundly asleep. There was a piece of composition on the table, apparently just completed. After reading it, Tso Kuang-tou took off his sable robe and used it to cover the young man's body. Then he left and closed the door gently behind him. Asked who the young man was, the monks replied that his name was Shih K'o-fa.

In the civil service examination that followed, Tso Kuang-tou was the chief

---

[45] *Ming Ch'ing san-wen hsien*, pp. 171–173. The author (Fang Pao, 1668–1749), a famous essayist, once served as the Vice President of the Ministry of Rites.

[46] Both Fang Pao and Tso Kuang-tou were born in T'ungch'eng, modern Anhwei province.

[47] The area around Peking.

examiner and Shih K'o-fa one of the candidates. When the latter's name was called, Tso stared at the candidate with close attention. After the examination was over and when Shih presented him with the paper, he marked "Number One" on the paper right in front of the candidate. Subsequently he summoned the young man to his home so that the latter could pay respect to his wife in person. "All my own sons are ordinary," said Tso to his wife. "The only person who can follow my footsteps is this young man."

After Tso Kuang-tou was thrown into jail,[48] Shih K'o-fa was outside the prison door everyday from sunrise to sundown, waiting for a chance to see his patron. But the eunuchs had taken strict preventive measures; even Tso's personal servants were not allowed to enter the prison. Later, Shih heard that Tso had been tortured by fire and that he would die at any moment. He presented fifty taels of silver to the jailer and tearfully pleaded for the latter's help. The jailer was moved and agreed to do whatever he could.

One day the jailer told Shih to change into the costume of a jail cleaner—a shabby jacket and a pair of straw shoes—and equipped him with a bamboo basket and a shovel with a long handle. He led Shih to Tso's cell and pointed to him where the prisoner was. Tso was sitting on the floor against a wall: his face was burned beyond recognition and all the bones and flesh below his left knee had completely disappeared. Shih knelt down, held Tso's knees, and wept.

Tso recognized Shih only by his voice since he could no longer open his eyes. With great efforts, he raised up one of his arms and plucked one of his eyes open with his fingers. The eye was staring in anger, as radiant as a torch. "You idiot," he roared. "Where do you think this place is? Why do you come here during a time when the nation is in serious difficulties? Now that I, as an old man,[49] have already been finished, you neglect great principles and risk your life by coming to this place. If anything happens to you, who will be there to shoulder the burden of national affairs? Get out of here quickly before those evil men [50] have a chance to implicate you. If you do not hurry, I will kill you." He groped on the ground and found an instrument of torture. He picked it up and proceeded to throw it at the visitor. Without uttering a word, Shih quickly left the cell. Later, when he tearfully related this incident to others, he said: "The heart of my teacher was cast from iron."

During the latter part of the Ch'ung-chen period,[51] the bandit Chang Hsien-chung and his followers ravaged the areas of Ch'i, Huang, Ch'ien, and T'ung,[52] and Shih K'o-fa was appointed by the imperial government as an intendant to defend the Feng-Lü area.[53] Whenever he was engaged in a military campaign, Shih would not sleep in a comfortable bed for as long as several months. He asked his generals and soldiers to take turns sleeping, while he himself would sit outside his tent throughout the night. He selected ten strong soldiers and divided them into five groups; each group of two would squat on the ground, and Shih would

---

[48] Tso Kuang-tou was thrown into jail by the eunuch Wei Chung-hsien whom he had denounced in a memorial to the reigning emperor. He was jailed in the latter part of 1624 and died in the summer of 1625 while still in prison.

[49] He was then fifty-one years old.

[50] The eunuchs.

[51] 1628–1644.

[52] Ch'i and Huang were located in modern Hupeh province, and Ch'ien and T'ung in modern Anhwei province.

[53] Fengyang and Lükiang, modern Anhwei province.

lean against them to rest until they were replaced by another group in two hours. In winter nights when he sometimes stood up to shake his clothes, the sheet of ice that had formed on his armour was suddenly broken up and made a tinkling sound. Some one advised him to take a rest, but he refused, saying: "I do not wish to fail my government; nor do I want my teacher [54] to be ashamed of me."

While commanding the army, Shih often passed through T'ungch'eng. During each sojourn he would repair to the Tso household, paying his respect to Tso's parents and wife.

T'u-shan, an elder in our clan, was Tso Kuang-tou's nephew by marriage and my late father's good friend. The incident that occurred in the prison cell was related to him by Shih K'o-fa himself.

163 · SHENG JU-TZU: *A Debt of Gratitude* [55]

Before he passed the civil service examinations, His Excellency Chao Ch'ing-hsien served as a tutor to a boy of the Ch'en family who resided in the same village. To show her appreciation, the boy's mother made new shoes each year to be presented to the teacher as gifts. When Chao left the village to participate in the civil service examinations, the Ch'en family showered him with farewell presents. Meanwhile it provided generous aid whenever the Chao family, which was poor, was short of funds. It even sent a house servant all the way to Peking to bring to Chao all of his personal belongings.

Chao passed the examinations in his first attempt and subsequently became more and more important in the bureaucracy.

Later, the Ch'en boy, whom Chao had once tutored, committed a capital offense and was thrown into jail. Somebody said to the boy's father that Chao, being such an influential official as he was, might be able to lend a helping hand to save the boy's life. The boy's father talked with his wife about this matter, and she agreed. "You should make this trip yourself," said she. "I shall make a pair of shoes as his present."

Arriving at Pien,[56] Ch'en went to Chao's residence, but the doorman refused to announce his presence. He continued to wait outside, however, until Chao came back from his office. He saluted the latter in front of his mount and was ordered to come in. Once in, he presented the shoes which his wife had made. Chao held the shoes for a long time and then went inside. He washed his feet,[57] put the new shoes on, and came out. He asked Ch'en the purpose of his trip, and the latter told him what it was. "Make yourself comfortable in my study room [58] and stay here for a while," said Chao.

For a ten-day period, Chao did not give Ch'en a chance to mention the plight of his son. When the latter insisted, he merely replied "yes, yes." One month

---

[54] Tso, his teacher, had died by then.

[55] The original appears in *Conversations of an Old Scholar (Lao-hsüeh ts'ung-t'an)* by Sheng Ju-tzu who lived in the fourteenth century. A copy can also be found in *Random Notes by Famous Writers of the Past (Li-tai min-chia pi-chi lei-hsien)*, edited by Hu Lun-ch'ing, p. 34.

[56] Modern Kaifeng, Honan province.

[57] To show his respect for the person who made the shoes.

[58] In most houses of the gentry, a study room doubled as a guest room.

passed by, and Ch'en mentioned his intention to leave for home. "Do not worry; stay for a while," said Chao.

One more month later, Chao showed Ch'en a letter which came from the latter's family. The boy's life had been spared!

As soon as His Excellency had learned about the boy's plight, he sent a personal servant to Ch'üchou [59] where the boy was imprisoned. Each day this servant carried food to the jail so as to feed the prisoner. After the judge learned whose servant this man was, he ordered the sentence to be reduced from capital punishment to imprisonment.

Even today people in Ch'üchou are still talking about this incident.

164 · Ts'ao Hsüeh-ch'in: *Hsi-jen* [60]

Finally all the other people were gone, leaving Precious Jade and his female slave, Hsi-jen, alone in the room.

"Who is that girl who wears the red jacket?" asked Precious Jade with a smile.

"She is my cousin," Hsi-jen replied. Precious Jade sighed.

"What are you sighing about?" she asked. "I know what you are thinking. You are thinking that people like her are not good enough to wear red-colored clothes."

"No, that is not what I meant at all," Precious Jade smiled. "If she is not good enough to wear red-colored clothes, who is? She seems to be a very nice girl. I am just thinking how wonderful it would be if she could join our family."

"Now, listen," Hsi-jen sneered. "I was destined to become a slave, but that does not mean that all my relatives are destined to become slaves too. It seems that you will never be satisfied until all nice girls in the world become your family's slaves."

"You are too sensitive. I said how wonderful it would be if she could join our family. I did not say that I wanted her to become our slave. She could become a relative of ours, for instance."

"You know that you did not really mean that," she retorted.

Precious Jade did not reply. He picked up more chestnuts and continued to crack them.

"Why do you all of a sudden become so quiet?" she asked. "Did I offend you? All right, spend a few taels of silver and buy her tomorrow."

"What can I say if you continue to talk in this manner?" he finally resumed his smiling. "I was praising her and was thinking that only people like her were really good enough to live in a huge, beautiful mansion like this. But instead of her, this mansion has no better inhabitants than vulgar people like us. I thought that this was unfair."

"Well, I do not think that she will ever have a good luck as the one which you have described. Though she was born poor, she is nevertheless the apple of her parents' eye. She is seventeen now and she will be married next year."

Precious Jade was taken aback when he heard that the girl was to be married. He made some unintelligible sound and became restless.

[59] Located in modern Chekiang province where the author of this selection was born.
[60] *The Dream of the Red Chamber (Hung-lou meng),* Chapter 19.

"I have not had many opportunities to visit my cousins," Hsi-jen sighed. "Now that I am about to return home, they are leaving."

Precious Jade immediately sensed that something was going on which he did not know. As if suddenly struck by a thunderbolt, he threw away the nuts which he was cracking and asked: "What are you talking about? Do you want to leave here?"

"When I was home, my family asked me to be patient for a while, and they would have enough money next year to ransom me and take me home."

Precious Jade became more alarmed. "What on earth do they want to ransom you for?" he asked.

"What a silly question this is! Your home is not my home which is somewhere else. How can you expect my mother to leave me permanently at your house?"

"But I will not let you go."

"Now, look, how can you become so unreasonable? Even the imperial household follows the ancient tradition of buying slaves in certain years and freeing them in certain other years. There is no rule that entitles a household to keep a slave permanently. Do you think that your household can be an exception?"

Thinking the matter over, Precious Jade concluded that Hsi-jen was right. "What would you do if the Dowager Mother [61] refuses to let you go?"

"Why should she wish to keep me? If I were of unusual kind or had served particularly well the Dowager Mother and the Honorable Lady,[62] I could understand that they would wish to keep me, and in that case they could easily achieve their purpose by paying my family a few additional taels of silver. But you know that I am only ordinary and that there are many female slaves in this household who are more capable than I am. I came here when I was little. First I served Lady Shih;[63] since then I have been serving you for several years. When my family comes here to ransom me, I see no reason why the Dowager Mother and the Honorable Lady will not let me go. They may be even generous enough to forego the ransom payments. As for the fact that I have served you well, I do not think that it should be an important factor in their thinking, because to serve you well is part of my duty. After I am gone, there will be some one better than I am to take over my place. I am not indispensable, you know."

Precious Jade did not know what to say. There seemed to be a hundred reasons why she should leave. Yet he was determined that she should stay. "Despite what you have said," said he in an anxious manner, "I simply will not let you go. I will talk with the Dowager Mother and ask her to give your mother more money. In such a case, I think your mother will be polite enough to let you stay."

"If the Dowager Mother insists, my mother will of course have no choice except to let me stay. Even if you do not give her any money, she will still have no choice as long as you insist on keeping me in your family. But your family has never used its power and influence to force other people to do things which they do not want to do. After all, people are not like merchandise which can be easily obtained as long as you are willing to pay a high price. To keep me permanently here will split my family and in the meantime will not benefit you in any material way. Do you think that the Dowager Mother and the Honorable Lady will do a thing like that?"

[61] Precious Jade's grandmother.
[62] Precious Jade's mother.
[63] Precious Jade's cousin.

Precious Jade was silent. After a long while, he said: "Judging from what you have said, you will definitely be going."

"Yes, I will definitely be going," she replied.

"I never realized that she is so heartless," Precious Jade said to himself. "If people here all have to go, why should Heaven send me here in the first place?" he sighed. "After all of you are gone, I will be nothing but a lonely ghost." He was so depressed that he went to bed immediately.

What Precious Jade did not know was that Hsi-jen engaged in this conversation merely to find out how he felt towards her; she had long made up her mind that she was not going to leave the Chia household. When during a recent visit home her mother and elder brother mentioned their desire to ransom her, she immediately protested: "I will never return home even if you threaten to kill me. Formerly you were so poor and starved that you had nothing to sell except me, and sold me you did for a few taels of silver. Then I did not protest because no daughter in her right mind could bear to see her parents die in starvation without doing something about it. Fortunately I was sold to a good household. Now I eat and wear the same thing as my master, and nobody in his household has ever beaten me. Since my father died, you have been doing well financially, and the family has been restored to its former solvency. If you were in financial difficulties, I could understand that you may wish me to come home to help you out. But right now you do not really need me. What is the sense of ransoming me anyway? From now on, think of me as if I were dead." After finishing these remarks, she burst into tears.

Having sensed her feelings, both her mother and her brother decided not to insist. Moreover, the contract whereby Hsi-jen was sold was an unredeemable contract: the seller could not ransom the sold person as long as the buyer did not agree. Her mother and brother were in fact counting on the generosity of the Chia household to relinquish its rights voluntarily and to let them ransom her if they merely pleaded for kindness. Being so generous as it was, it might even decide to forego the ransom payments. All members of the Chia household treated their slaves well, and there was no such thing as cruelty or brutality. The young female slaves who had been assigned to work as personal servants were treated even better. They received more consideration and esteem than a girl of an average family received in her own household. All things taken into consideration, Hsi-jen's mother and brother decided not to raise again the question of ransoming her.

165 · MA TUAN-LIN: *Slavery* [64]

By the order of emperor Han Kao-tsu (r.206–180 B.C.) people were allowed to sell their children as slaves.

In the fifth year during the reign of Han Kao-tsu (202 B.C.) it was decreed that those who had sold themselves during the time of famine were then legally free.

Emperor Han Wen-ti (r.179–157 B.C.) promoted agriculture and set the example as a man of thrift. His good influence was felt by the people as a whole,

[64] *Wen-hsien t'ung-k'ao,* roll 11.

and there was little evidence of land grabbing. It was considered unnecessary to impose a limitation on either the amount of land or the number of slaves that a person could own.

In the fourth year during the reign of Han Wen-ti (175 B.C.) the emperor issued a decree to free all of the government-owned slaves.

In the first year of Chien-yüan (140 B.C.) during the reign of Han Wu-ti, the emperor issued a decree of clemency whereby the women and children of the rebel leaders who had been condemned to slavery during the Seven States' Rebellion [65] were declared free.

Later, when the government was short of funds, it declared that any man who made a contribution of slaves to the government could be appointed as an official for life and could be promoted if he was already an official.

To prosecute people for tax evasion, Yang K'o [66] sent inspectors to all parts of China to bring the evaders to justice. The properties confiscated from the convicted tax dodgers were worth millions of standard coins in cash, and the confiscated slaves numbered tens of thousands.

During the reign of Han Yüan-ti (r.48–33 B.C.) Kung Yü [67] reported to the imperial government that government-owned slaves numbered anywhere between 100,000 and 200,000 and that there was no useful work for them to do. He said that it was wrong to tax law-abiding citizens to support these slaves and that these slaves should be set free.

In the fourth year of Yung-shih (13 B.C.) during the reign of Han Ch'eng-ti (r.32–7 B.C.) the government issued the following decree: "It is known that many high officials and feudal lords, together with their relatives and subordinates, have each in their possession a large number of male and female slaves. It is also known that these slaves are so pampered that they are allowed to wear silk clothes. The responsible officials should see to it that this situation should not be allowed to continue; it should in fact be gradually reversed."

After the accession of Han Ai-ti (6–1 B.C.) as the emperor, he issued a decree which read as follows: "The dukes, counts, imperial princesses, and high government officials, in addition to wealthy commoners—each of them has in his possession not only large tracts of land and numerous houses and villas but also a large number of slaves. A limitation should be imposed on their holdings. In accordance with the suggestion made by responsible officials, the limitation of slave ownership should be as follows: For kings and dukes the maximum number of male and female slaves each of them is allowed to own is 200; for counts and and imperial princesses, 100; and for counts who reside in the capital and its environs and for all officials and commoners, 30. Slaves over the age of sixty or below that of ten are not included in this limitation. The slaves above and beyond the legal maximums should be surrendered without compensation to the district magistrates. Government-owned slaves, male or female, should be set free if their age is fifty or above."

Wang Mang (d.A.D. 23) decreed that all slaves were private properties and were not subject to buying and selling.

In the fifth month of the year of Chien-wu (A.D. 26) emperor Han Kuang-wu

---

[65] See p. 126, Footnote 44.
[66] A high-ranking official under emperor Han Wu-ti.
[67] A government official.

(r.25–57) issued the following decree: "People who wish to sell their children should be allowed to do so. Officials who dare to arrest them are punishable by law."

In the eleventh month of the sixth year of Chien-wu (A.D. 30) the emperor decreed that officials and commoners who, during the time of Wang Mang, had been convicted of violating the old statutes and condemned to slavery were thereafter free citizens.

In the seventh year of Chien-wu (A.D. 31) the emperor decreed that any person who had sold himself or herself as a slave during the time of famine or who had been kidnapped by the Ch'ing-Hsü bandits [68] and was forced to serve as a slave or a concubine, should be allowed to leave his or her owner if he or she chose to do so. The slave owner who forcibly detained a person against his or her will would be prosecuted in accordance with the Slave Trade Act.

In the eleventh year of Chien-wu (A.D. 35) the government issued the following decree: "Among all things created by Heaven and Earth, man is by far the most valuable. Those who have been convicted of the murder of their slaves should not have their sentences reduced."

In the eighth month of the same year (A.D. 35) the government issued another decree which read as follows: "Those who dare to punish their slaves by boiling or burning are punishable in accordance with the law. Those slaves who have suffered injuries as a result of such punishment should be set free."

In the eleventh month of the same year a royal decree invalidated the law that stipulated death sentence for male or female slaves who shot and wounded people by bow and arrows.

In the third month of the twelfth year of Chien-wu (A.D. 36) it was decreed that those people in Lung and Shu [69] who had been kidnapped and later enslaved should be set free whenever they started legal proceedings for their freedom against their owners. They were legally entitled to their freedom even if they chose not to start the aforesaid legal proceedings, said the royal decree.

In the twelfth month of the thirteenth year of Chien-wu (A.D. 37) it was decreed that those people in the province of Yi [70] who had been kidnapped and enslaved after the eighth year of Chien-wu (A.D. 32) should be set free. Women who became concubines as a means of seeking protection during the time of famine or turmoil should be allowed to leave their spouse-owners if they chose to do so. Those who forcibly detained these women were prosecuted in accordance with the Kidnapping Act which was then operative in the provinces of Ch'ing and Hsü. [71]

In the twelfth month of the fourteenth year of Chien-wu (A.D. 38) it was decreed that the male and female slaves in the provinces of Yi and Liang who had started legal proceedings to obtain their freedom after the eighth year of Chien-wu (A.D. 32) should be set free. A person who had sold himself into slavery was not required to return the money with which he was purchased.

In the first year of Yen-p'ing (A.D. 106) during the reign of Han Shang-ti it was decreed that the names of public slaves, together with private slaves who

[68] Ch'ing and Hsü were located in modern Shantung and Kiangsu provinces respectively.
[69] Modern Shensi and Szechuan provinces.
[70] Modern Szechuan province.
[71] See above, Footnote 68.

were owned by princes and government officials, should be reported to government authorities if their surname was Liu [72] or they were sick and old. The decree emphasized the importance of accuracy and thoroughness in making the aforesaid report.

In the fourth year of Yung-ch'u (110) during the reign of Han An-ti (r.107–125) it was decreed that male and female slaves who had been confiscated by the government should be set free.

After Tsin Wu-ti (r.265–289) had conquered the Kingdom of Wu it was decreed that princes and government officials were entitled to the possession of protectees. These protectees could be classified as either retainers [73] or subordinates. [74] The maximum number of subordinate households for each of the officials was stipulated as follows: officials of the first or second rank, 50; officials of the third rank, 10; officials of the fourth rank, 7; officials of the fifth rank, 5; officials of the sixth rank, 3; officials of the seventh rank, 2; and officials of the eighth or ninth rank, 1.

In the fourth year of T'ai-hsing (321) during the reign of Tsin Yüan-ti (r.317–322) the emperor issued the following decree: "Formerly the two emperors of the Han dynasty [75] and Emperor Wu [76] of the Wei dynasty—all of them exempted people of good families from being enslaved. After a rebellion had been crushed in the province of Liang [77] during the reign of Tsin Wu-ti (r.265–289), all slaves, male or female, were restored to their freemen status. Thus the exemption of members of good families [78] from being enslaved has been the established custom for successive dynasties. Let it be known that people of North China [79] who have lost their freedom and are now slaves in such provinces as Yang [80] should be set free, provided that they had come from good families before they lost their freedom. Their emancipation is a prerequisite to their enlistment in the army."

In the first year of T'ien-hu (566) during the reign of Chou Wu-ti (r.561–577) the emperor issued the following decree: "Formerly it was decreed that all public slaves in Kiangling [81] who were more than sixty-five years old should be set free. Now let it be known that all slaves of more than seventy years old, whether they be owned by the government or private individuals, should be allowed to purchase their own freedom."

In the first year of Chien-te (572) it was again decreed that the prisoners-of-war captured at Kiangling who have been hitherto reduced to the status of public slaves should be given their freedom.

According to the statutes of the T'ang dynasty, the male or female relatives of those who had been convicted of treason were condemned to serve as public

[72] The surname of the royal household.
[73] *Yi-shih k'e.*
[74] *T'ien k'e.*
[75] Believed to be Han Wen-ti and Han Ching-ti, two of the most enlightened rulers of the Han dynasty.
[76] Wei Wu-ti or Ts'ao Ts'ao.
[77] Modern Kansu province.
[78] *Liang chia.*
[79] *Chung chou.*
[80] Modern Kiangsu province.
[81] Modern Hupeh province.

slaves. However, when and if a general clemency was proclaimed, the households maintained by these slaves would be reclassified as "probationary households." [82] If a general clemency was proclaimed for the second time, these households would be elevated to those of the miscellaneous category.[83] When and if the third clemency occurred, the former slaves would be restored to full citizenship.

In the first year of Yung-ch'ang (684) when King Cheng of Yüeh was executed on account of treason, it was found that he had in his household more than one thousand domestic slaves. It was then decreed that all nobles, beginning with the kings and the dukes, should not have more than a specified number of male and female slaves.

In the first year of Wan-sui T'ung-t'ien (696) it was decreed that domestic slaves and servants who were versed in military skills would be drafted into the army for the forthcoming war against the Khitan Tartars, and that their owners would be compensated by the government in accordance with the market value of the slaves or servants involved.

In the first year of Ta-tsu (701) it was decreed that people of northern frontiers were not allowed to own male or female slaves whose origin was in T'u-chüeh.[84]

In the fourteenth year of Ta-lieh (779) it was decreed that the prefecture of Yung [85] which had hitherto sent male and female slaves each year to the central government as tribute should no longer be allowed to do so. To separate these people from their homes where they might have lived for generations and to take them forcibly from their beloved ones were not compatible with the principle of love, continued the royal decree.

In the fourth year of Yüan-ho (809) the imperial government issued the following decree: "Many people in Lingnan,[86] Ch'ien,[87] and Fukien have been kidnapped by government officials as well as private citizens and then sold in the open market as slaves. The responsible officials in the aforesaid provinces are hereby instructed to round up these slaves and closely examine their origins. Only those who are not of good family background are allowed to remain slaves. Those who have kidnapped freemen [88] and condemned them to slavery should be punished in accordance with the law."

In the first year of Ch'ang-ch'ing (821) a royal decree warned against the laissez-faire attitude which local officials of Teng, Lai, and other coastal areas [89] had taken with regard to the kidnapping and then the selling of Hsin-lo people [90] as slaves. Such an attitude, said the royal decree, was strictly forbidden.

In the fourth year of Ch'ang-ch'ing (824) the imperial government decreed that all central and local officials should see to it that those public slaves, male or female, who were suffering from incurable diseases or disabilities or were seventy or older, should be freed from their bondages and be given full citizenship.

[82] *Shen fu.*
[83] *Tsa fu.*
[84] T'u-chüeh was a Turkish tribe that then posed a potential threat to T'ang China's northern frontier.
[85] Located in modern Kwangsi province
[86] Modern Kwangtung province.
[87] Modern Kweichow province.
[88] *Liang jen* or people of good standing.
[89] Both Teng and Lai were located in modern Shantung province.
[90] Hsin-lo was a Korean kingdom.

In the fifth year of Hui-ch'ang (845) the First and Second Secretariats [91] submitted a joint petition to the emperor which read as follows: "Among the Buddhist temples those in Kiang-Huai [92] have the largest number of male and female slaves. Some of these temples have been deteriorating due to the lack of care, and none of them have any monks or nuns in them. The deserted temple slaves, male or female, are forced to find a means of livelihood for themselves, having been deprived of their source of supply of food and clothing. . . . We hereby suggest that all of them should be relieved from their slave status."

In the first year of T'ai-chung (847) the imperial government ordered the abolition of slave trade in Lingnan. . . .[93]

In the second year of T'ung-kuang (924) during the Later T'ang dynasty [94] the imperial government declared that women who had been captured during the time of war and later sold as slaves or concubines should be given their freedom. Once their identities were established, they should be returned to their relatives.

In the second year of K'ai-pao (969) during the reign of Sung T'ai-tsu (r.960–975) it was decreed that upon the death of a slave the responsible official should immediately investigate and determine the cause of his death before his owner was allowed to bury him if for any reason the cause of his death was suspect. No investigation would be conducted if the slave died of illness.

In the fourth year of K'ai-pao (971) the imperial government decreed that the custom—prevalent in the Kwangnan districts [95]—of purchasing boys and girls as slaves and then hiring them out as servants and manual workers for the purpose of making a profit should be abolished. Those who dared to violate this order, said the imperial decree, would be punished by flogging, followed by banishment from local communities.

In the second year of Shun-hua (991) the imperial government issued a decree which read as follows: "During the recent famine the poor and starving people in Shensi and other frontier provinces were forced by circumstances to sell their children to the Jung people [96] as slaves. It is hereby decreed that provincial officials on the frontier, in cooperation with the transport envoy in each province,[97] should ransom these children and return them to their respective parents with funds drawn from the public treasury."

In the second year of Chih-tao (996) a decree issued by the imperial government read as follows: "It is found that the poor people in Kiangnan, Liangche, and Fukien, who have incurred debts and are unable to pay interest or principal to their creditors, are often forced to sell their children to the latter as slaves. Upon the day when this order arrives, these children, after being carefully identified, should be returned to their respective parents. Those who dare to conceal the origin and identity of these children are punishable in accordance with the law."

In the first year of Hsien-p'ing (998) during the reign of Sung Chen-tsung (r.998–1022) it was decreed that people in Szechuan and Shensi who had incurred

[91] *Chung-shu sheng* and *Men-hsia sheng.*
[92] The areas drained by the Yangtze and the Huai River.
[93] See above, Footnote 86.
[94] 923–936.
[95] Modern Kwangtung and Kwangsi provinces.
[96] A non-Chinese, nomadic tribe in China's northwest.
[97] See p. 293, Footnote 19.

debt to the government should not be forced to pay their debt with the male or female slaves they owned.

In the sixth year of Hsien-p'ing (1003) it was decreed that scholars and common people alike were not allowed to brand the faces of their servants, no matter what offenses these servants had committed against their employers.

In the third year of T'ien-hsi (1019) the imperial government issued the following decree: "From now on those who kidnap or buy people and then transport them to the territories of the Khitan [98] are punishable in accordance with the law. Their leaders are subject to capital punishment; so are their accomplices. If the intention of transporting people to the Khitan territories has been established but the physical act has not yet taken place, the offenders will not suffer the death penalty. Instead, they will be flogged, branded, and exiled to the frontier."

[98] A Mongolian tribe beyond China's northern frontier.

CHAPTER EIGHTEEN

Women in Chinese Society

A TRADITIONAL Chinese family was organized on two well-defined, unwritten rules: the superiority of the elder over the younger generation and the superiority of males over females. In case of conflict, the first rule prevailed over the second. These rules made the role of the females, especially those of the younger generation, the least enviable. She was expected to be obedient to her parents before she was married; and once married, she was supposed to place the welfare of her husband and her parents-in-law above that of her own (Selection 166). A good wife should strive to please her husband in every way, including sometimes finding for him an attractive concubine (Selection 167). Most of her usefulness to her family was considered gone if unfortunately her husband died while she was still young and if by then her parents-in-law were already deceased. Legally she was allowed to remarry, but the fact that her children would be taken away from her in such a case served as a strong deterrent against remarriage. Very likely she would devote the rest of her life to the raising of her children. If she had no children to raise, was too old to find a suitable husband, or had a strong moral aversion to remarriage, her future was as uncertain as it was gloomy. In such a case, she might choose to follow the example of the woman described in Selection 168 by committing suicide, and the traditional Chinese society, instead of seeing anything terribly wrong with her act, would praise her instead (Selection 169). Throughout history few societies have harbored so much injustice to their women as did the traditional Chinese society.

All marriages were arranged, and a "good" girl was supposed to be completely innocent about sex and related matters until the wedding night. She was to marry whomever her parents had selected as her groom, and needless to say, she was not supposed to meet her future husband until the wedding ceremony was over. Had she been "exposed to strangers" even in the most innocent manner during her maidenhood, her moral character was suspect, and no man with "self-respect" would wish to marry her (Selection 170). Once her reputation was ruined, it would be extremely difficult for her family to find for her a suitable husband to whom she might have been otherwise entitled.

Arranged marriages are not necessarily synonymous with bad marriages. In fact we find in ancient Chinese literature many celebrated examples of arranged but nevertheless happy marriages. Once in a while these happy marriags came to tragic endings, and in the case of *The Peacock Flies Southeast*

(K'ung-ch'üeh tung-nan fei) the man was forced to divorce his beloved wife since she, in the eyes of his mother, had failed as a satisfactory daughter-in-law (Selection 171). According to the Confucian teachings, a man's loyalty towards his parents should always have a higher priority than his love for his wife.

The matter of marriage and family was usually regulated by custom and tradition; rarely would the government interfere with it. When the government did enact laws to regulate it, it wished not only to universalize what custom had long accepted but also to reduce or eliminate some of the worst abuses of the existing customs (Selection 172). The law would not go beyond what custom would accept, however, though by making the punishment for a crime clear and definite, it may have helped to reduce excessiveness and humanize the punishment (Selection 173).

166 · CHU CH'EN-YING: *A Testimonial in Memory of My Wife* [1]

My wife Chin, who came from the Hsü family, was born on the third day of the fifth month in the second year of Yung-cheng [2] and was married to me in the tenth year of Chien-lung.[3] She died on the twenty-sixth day of the ninth month in the year of Hsin-ssu,[4] seventeen years after our marriage.[5] She was then thirty-eight years old.[6]

My wife was born with high intelligence and learned to sew at an early age. Whenever she had time in the evening, she read extensively the great works of the past. Being versed in the classics, she understood large issues better than most people do.

Shortly after she joined our family, my younger sister was to be married. My late mother was worried about her inability to provide enough furniture for the forthcoming wedding because of the lack of funds.[7] Believing that my mother should not burden herself with this worry on account of her advanced age, my wife voluntarily contributed all of her own furniture for this purpose. My mother was pleased and began to eat heartily for the first time in a long period.

The year after my sister was married, I lost my teaching position and had to eat at home. Shortly afterwards my mother left us and went to Heaven. I tried to borrow money from every source I could find, but I did not succeed. Having sensed my helplessness, my wife sold all of her jewels to meet the funeral expenses. During the period of mourning I slept next to my late mother's tablet,[8]

[1] *Ku-chin wen-tsung,* vol. 26, pp. 33–34.
[2] 1724.
[3] 1745.
[4] 1761.
[5] Sixteen years according to the Western custom.
[6] Thirty-seven years old according to the Western custom.
[7] According to the Chinese custom, the bride's family was to provide the furniture for the bride's bedroom such as dresser and chest.
[8] Usually made of wood, the tablet bore the name of the deceased and was placed on the most sacred spot in the household. The tablet was where the dead person's spirit was supposed to be whenever it returned home.

while my wife took care of our infant son in the regular bed. The bed was not equipped with a mosquito net, and the time being summer, the baby cried all night and every night because it could not stand the mosquito bites. My wife chased the mosquitoes with a broken fan until she was so exhausted that she fell asleep herself.

When in the winter I again obtained a teaching position, I took with me the only quilt that we had in our house. My wife was left with a worn-out blanket made of cotton which she held tightly to keep herself warm while sleeping on a bare plank which was our bed. Each evening after the children had gone to sleep, she lit the lamp and began to work. By midnight the little fire in the jug had disappeared, and she was shivering from cold. She walked around the room to keep herself warm, and when she felt warm enough, she started to work again. When finally she did go to bed, she found that the children were as cold as frozen ice. They vomited when they were fed with milk. Consequently none of our children has been able to grow to adulthood. Meanwhile my wife, worried and exhausted, became increasingly ill and never did recover normal health.

My wife wrote poetry well. Reaching middle age, she was particularly fond of the *Book of Changes*. At the end of a copy of this book she wrote the following comment: "Fortune and misfortune, like growth and decay, are complementary to each other in the world where we live. . . . A gentleman should be content with whatever fate has assigned to him." On the wall of our bedroom she penned the following words: "If a man cannot enjoy poverty, he should at least be able to make peace with it. If he cannot make peace with it, he should at least be able to endure it. Once he learns how to endure it, he will be able to appreciate the truism that the acquirement of wealth is as much beyond our control as the occurrence of life or death."

During the early spring of this year her health deteriorated even further. Time and again she kept on reciting an old poem until a dark cloud passed over her face and then she stopped. The poem read:

> Die will the silkworm
> When the last bit of its silk is emitted;
> The candle's tears will become dry
> When it is burned to its end.

Early in the fall our young son fell into a river and was drowned before rescue could arrive. My wife was overwhelmed with grief, and attacked from within as well as without, her much weakened body could not endure any longer. Her mind, however, remained clear to the very end, and she talked about our family affairs without the slightest confusion. She said to herself: "Heaven gives me life so I can labor; now He is giving me death so that I can enjoy leisure and peace. I have toiled for seventeen years. Now it is the end." And then she sighed. With tears in my eyes, I asked her whether she had any more to say, "You, sir, have been proud of your writings. Please write something about me after I die. Describe me as I am; please do not exaggerate." After saying these words, she closed her eyes.

My wife did not die of illness; she really died of poverty. No, she did not die of poverty; she died of weariness. Useful as words are, they are inadequate to express what she had suffered and endured.

167 · T'ANG SHUN-CHIH: *A Eulogy for Wang, My Sister-in-Law* [9]

Wang married my younger brother when she was eighteen. Though coming from a wealthy family, seeing the emphasis we as a scholarly family attached to thrift, she adjusted herself accordingly. She sold her gold hairpins and earrings and exchanged her expensive clothing for simple attire. She personally supervised servants in the preparation of food as well as other domestic work such as sewing and embroidery. She used as capital the money she acquired from selling ornaments to invest in trade; however, she herself was as thrifty as she was industrious and acted as if she had always lived in meager means.

She was intelligent, alert, energetic, and generous. She understood the proper way of dealing with people and handling affairs without ever learning about them, and she got along well with all members of our household, high or low. Her father-in-law praised her highly and once said: "My second daughter-in-law knows exactly what I want when she prepares tea or cooks food." Whenever there were guests for tea or dinner, it was Wang who took the primary responsibility for preparing it, while other women in the household only helped. Hearing about her good work in our household, her mother Hsü once said: "Knowing how she once served me, I have no doubt that she will serve her father-in-law equally well." My wife Chuang also praised her, saying that it was Wang who understood her best. Whenever she had misgivings which she could not very well discuss with her husband, she sought advice from Wang. Hearing this, Wang's sisters remarked: "She was the same way with us when she was at home. We knew even then that she would get along well with her future sisters-in-law."

In the first three years after her marriage, Wang had two miscarriages. From then on she was greatly concerned with the fact that my brother might not have an heir. One day, returning home from a trip that he had made with me to Yihsing,[10] my brother saw a strange girl in his room. Surprised, he asked his wife who the girl was; he was told that this was the concubine that she had bought for him. Protesting that he, barely over twenty, was too young to have a concubine, he sent the girl home without being intimate with her. Five or six years later when there was still no male child, she again bought a concubine for her husband. She personally dressed up the girl, being fearful that the latter might not be attractive enough for her husband. The arrival of the concubine did not in any way affect the relationship between Wang and her husband which remained affectionate. In fact, she encouraged her husband to stay with his concubine for as many evenings as he wished.

Among her mother's five daughters, Wang was the favorite. Previously, when her father died, her mother, observing the wish of the dead man, gave Wang two hundred taels of silver. She refused to accept the gift on the ground that her mother, being so young as she was, needed the money herself. Later, when her mother distributed her jewels as a farewell gift before she died, Wang received

---

[9] *Ming Ch'ing san-wen hsien,* pp. 46–49. T'ang Shun-chih (1507–1560), a famous essayist, was also known for his efforts to suppress the Japanese pirates along China's southeast coast in the 1550's.

[10] Located in modern Kiangsu province.

twice as many as any of her sisters. Hoping not to offend her sisters, she refused to take even her own share. . . .

Not only did my brother and his wife love each other dearly; they also admonished each other so as to refine each other's character. At one time only we two brothers stayed at the old house when our father was away as a government official. Whenever my brother became over-active, Wang would show her displeasure and say to him: "If you are not concerned with your own health, how can you face your elder brother who is concerned with yours?" Whenever my brother did something wrong, she would conceal it, being fearful that it might offend me and thus sow the seeds of dissension between us brothers. Whenever my brother did something well, she would be greatly pleased and say: "Do not believe for a moment that you did well because of your own ability. The credit should go to your elder brother who has had such a good influence upon you." Remarks like these moved my brother deeply who, consequently, wished to move even closer to me in brotherhood. The credit should go to this woman Wang who not only encouraged my brother along the road of goodness but also helped the good relationship between us brothers.

It seems that with her ability and virtue she should have enjoyed a long life and been rewarded with many sons. Yet she died young without a child and, more ironically, died of childbirth. These are the things we mortals simply cannot understand. After two miscarriages early in her married life, she did not expect any more pregnancy; instead, she was praying for the pregnancy of the concubine after the latter had been brought in to our household. When later Wang did become pregnant, people said that possibly Heaven had decided to reward her for her lack of jealousy. Yet she died because of this pregnancy. Why? Why?

She died on the fifth day of the sixth month, in the year of Ting-yi [11] of the Chia-ching period, at the age of twenty-nine. . . .

168 · KUEI YU-KUANG: *Mrs. T'ao, a Chaste Woman* [12]

Mrs. T'ao, a chaste woman, came from the Fang family. She was the wife of T'ao Tzu-k'o, a native of K'unshan.[13]

One year after she was married, her husband died. Overcome with grief, she wished to commit suicide. Some one reminded her that she had a responsibility to live as long as her mother-in-law lived. She thought about this for some time, agreed, and did not speak of death any more. Meanwhile she served her mother-in-law with even greater diligence. Since the latter was also a widow, the two women shared one room during the day and one bed in the evening. They loved and comforted each other. However, the idea of dying for her late husband did not leave the young woman's mind even for a single moment.

In choosing a burying ground for her late husband, she decided on the Bay of Pure Water. A magician, however, raised objection to this choice on the ground that it was inauspicious. "How can this place be inauspicious when it has such a beautiful name as 'Pure Water'?" she replied. Her husband's younger brother

[11] 1547.
[12] *Ku-wen tz'u-lei tsuan,* roll 38. Kuei Yu-kuang (1506–1571) was a famous essayist of the Ming dynasty.
[13] Located in modern Kiangsu province.

went to the West Mountain to buy stones, and he had in his mind the idea of building a grave for his brother alone. Mrs. T'ao, however, bought bricks with her own money and built her grave next to that of her dead husband.

Several years later, her mother-in-law fell ill with diarrhea. For more than sixty days she waited on her, day and night. This was late summer, and the odor was simply unbearable. She often removed the sick woman's underwear and washed it herself. The servants vomited whenever they saw these garments by accident. "Do they really smell so bad?" she said. "I am with them everyday, but I do not smell anything." She congratulated herself when she heard that a sick person was likely to get well if her waste had an unusually bad odor.

When her mother-in-law's illness went from bad to worse, Mrs. T'ao realized that the chance of her recovery was practically nil. For five days she cried in grief and did not eat anything. When the elder woman finally died, she supervised the funeral.

Tzu-k'o, her late husband, had two younger brothers. Tzu-fang, one of the two, had also died by this time, so only the youngest son survived his mother. Of the three T'ao women who attended the funeral, only one had a husband. "Now that our mother-in-law is dead," said the widow of Tzu-fang, "what are we going to do?" "You and I can easily dispose of ourselves," said Mrs. T'ao. "I feel sorry for my brother-in-law and his wife who from now on have to maintain the T'ao household and face an uncertain future." The two women looked at each other and cried.

Shortly afterwards, Mrs. T'ao went to her own room. She mixed gold dust with water and drank it, but she failed to die. She then decided to plunge herself into a well, but the opening of the well was too narrow for her body to go down. About nine o'clock in the evening, she asked a slave girl of hers to accompany her on a walk on the west side of the house. In the middle of the way, she ordered the slave girl to return home, and she herself quickly plunged into the river. The river was shallow, and the woman's body alternately sank into the water and then emerged from the surface. The moon was then bright, and the slave girl saw this through tall grass from a distance.

After the members of the T'ao family had located the body, they found that her face, having been buried in the water, was as radiant as if she were still alive. Her hands held tightly the roots of some of the river reeds, and it was extremely difficult to separate them.

Mrs. T'ao married Tzu-k'o when she was eighteen and lost her husband the year after. She served her mother-in-law for nine years before they died on the same day. She was buried at the Bay of Pure Water, in the area of Ch'ientunp'u which is located in the southern section of the subprefecture.

169 · CHOU CHI: On Widowhood [14]

In ancient times marriage came about as a result of mutual affection between the parties involved, and there was no pressure exercised by outsiders. Once the matrimonial relationship was established, rarely would the parties wish to dissolve

---

[14] *Ku-chin wen-tsung,* vol. 3, pp. 32–33. The author was a scholar of the Ch'ing dynasty.

it. While the service of go-betweens was considered essential to bring marriageable men and women together, there was no law prohibiting elopement. Nor was divorce forbidden. Permissiveness of this nature was meant to meet situations other than normal. Without it marriage would become a burden rather than a joy, and adultery would become a commonplace.

Emotions are part of our human nature, and desires are merely their extensions. A superior man knows how to preserve his natural self, while an average person succeeds only in making good use of his emotions. As far as an inferior man is concerned, he merely indulges himself in the satisfaction of his desires. When a man is successful in eliminating his desires, he will be able to use his emotions in a proper manner; eventually he may be even able to return to his natural self. However, not every man wishes to eliminate his desires.

For most people not only do desires exist, they also change. As desires change, so do emotions. When emotions change, a man becomes distant to the person to whom he was once close, and his loving gestures, once genuine and true, are now perfunctory or even hypocritical. While still living together, they are remote within and hypocritical without. Yet, with the reputation of both sides at stake, they believe that they cannot end the situation by simply separating one from the other. They endure each other's presence and complain bitterly inside. As this situation continues, the danger to each other's physical and emotional security is hiding in the corner and is waiting to emerge at any moment. When a marital status depends upon outward correctness rather than inner affection for its continuance, it has a shaky foundation which will eventually collapse. . . .

I believe that a new custom should be cultivated whereby divorce will be no longer viewed as a social disgrace. This new custom, instituted to meet abnormalities, will enable people to follow their own emotions as they arise and prevent many unhappy eventualities.

The reason for honoring widowhood is the difficulty with which it can be maintained. Knowing the difficulty for a woman to maintain her widowhood, do we have any right to condemn or punish a woman who chooses not to maintain it?

A concubine is not legally tied with the man with whom she lives because their union does not come about through proper rituals. Yet she is legally entitled to her son born of this union. On the other hand, a widow who chooses to remarry is forced to cut off all ties with her children. The law places her in an inferior position, lower than that of a concubine. Not wishing to leave her children, a widow has no choice except to comply with what the society approves or demands, namely, continuous widowhood. The widowhood which we honor and glorify may have been achieved under false pretense, a hypocrisy imposed by society upon a woman against her true wishes. Knowing the difficulty of maintaining widowhood, many women choose to commit suicide after the death of their husbands, leaving behind not only their parents and parents-in-law to whom they owe gratitude but also their children who need their love and care.

I believe that a widow who chooses to remarry should be treated in the same manner as a concubine. She is to cut off all ties with her former husband's family according to the custom, but she should be allowed to maintain relationship with her children. This new rule, if adopted, will be beneficial to all concerned for two reasons. First, her parents and parents-in-law cannot force her to continue her widowhood by denying her the access to her children; and, second, her continuous widowhood, if she chooses that status, will be voluntary and therefore genuine.

Under present circumstances, a young woman has only two alternatives open to her after the death of her husband. She could either follow her husband by committing suicide or enter a long period of widowhood with all hardships and privations implied in that term. If she chooses the latter course, she would have to serve her parents-in-law loyally and faithfully as well as raising her own children. People say that she should be honored as an example to follow if she chooses widowhood instead of committing suicide, on the laudable ground that life is valuable. Many loyal ministers commit suicide during the period of dynastic change, and philosophers and kings of later ages honor them so as to cultivate good customs, even though their self-inflicted death does not help the dynasty which they have hoped to preserve. Is it not contradictory that we glorify the ministers and scholars who die for their dynasties while condemning severely a helpless woman who simply wishes to follow her dead husband? I believe that a widow who commits suicide during or shortly after the mourning period should be exemplified as an inspiration to others.

The teachings of our ancient sages are broad enough for us to live by comfortably without the necessity of violating any of them. Narrow-minded and pedantic scholars intensely search out the errors in our conduct and condemn them accordingly. Even Shen Pu-hai and Han Fei [15] cannot match them in harshness. Their harshness drives people to hypocritical acts which can in no way help the cultivation of good customs. If this situation continues, nobody knows what the result will be. All of us should be rightfully concerned.

170 · Ts'ao Hsüeh-ch'in: *The Death of Yu San-chieh* [16]

"As far as my sister is concerned, she has already made up her mind whom she wants to marry," said Yu Erh-chieh. "She is not the kind of person who changes her mind easily. The best course we can take is to help her to find that man."

"Who is he?" Chia Lien asked.

"This is a long story," Erh-chieh smiled. "Five years ago there was a birthday party in honor of the Grand Madame, and my mother and we two sisters all went there to participate in the celebration. Our hostess invited a troupe of actors to entertain, and mind you, all of these actors came from good families. Among the actors was a man named Liu Hsiang-lien who played the romantic lead. He is the man my sister has had in mind for these five years. Last year I heard that this man had fled from the city and disappeared; allegedly he had committed some kind of crimes. I have no idea where he can be located."

"Should I be surprised!" said Chia Lien. "Let me congratulate your sister for her good taste. But I should remind you, however, that handsome and dashing as he is, this man is really cold-blooded. He does not have many friends and does not care to have any. The only person he seems to be able to get along with is Precious Jade, and we should ask Precious Jade's servants whether he has returned to the capital or where he is. But keep in mind that he is a wanderer, and nobody knows when he will return or whether he will ever return. How can we expect your sister to wait, say, five or ten years?"

[15] Both Shen Pu-hai (fourth century B.C.) and Han Fei (d.233 B.C.) were Legalist philosophers.
[16] *The Dream of the Red Chamber,* Chapter 66.

"I know my sister," said Erh-chieh. "If she says she is going to wait, she is going to wait, no matter how long the waiting period is. It is useless to try to change her mind."

At this moment Yu San-chieh walked in, and apparently she had overheard the conversation. "Brother-in-law," said she to Chia Lien, "you do not understand what kind of people we are. When we say something, we mean it. The moment this man named Liu comes home, I will marry him. He is the only man for me, and I do not want anybody else. From now on I shall fast and recite Buddhist scriptures and shall devote all my time to the service of my mother. I will wait until he returns. If he does not return in a period of one hundred years, I shall cut off my hair and go to a nunnery." Upon finishing these remarks, she took a jade hairpin from her head and broke it into two pieces. "If I violate my own promise, let me look like this hairpin!" Then she went inside. . . .

In a business trip several days later, Chia Lien accidentally ran into Liu Hsiang-lien. Only a short time before Liu had saved the life and the merchandise of Hsüeh Fan, a relative of Chia Lien. Hsüeh Fan was so grateful that he insisted that from then on he and Liu Hsiang-lien should become sworn brothers.[17] The ritual of sworn brotherhood was duly performed; now they were on their way back to the capital.[18]

"After I have had the opportunity of taking care of my business at home," said Hsüeh Fan, "I shall find a house for my sworn brother. Maybe we can find a nice girl for him too."

"That is splendid!" Chia Lien exclaimed. "I have a girl in mind who is just right for Mr. Liu." Then he told the two friends that he had taken Yu Erh-chieh as his concubine and that he was looking for a good man for his concubine's sister. He did not mention, however, that Yu San-chieh had selected Liu Hsiang-lien herself.

"That is wonderful," said Hsüeh Fan. "I do not see how you can possibly refuse."

"Well, a long time ago I made a promise to myself that I would not marry until I met a woman of unusual beauty. Since you two are so enthusiastic about this matter, I guess I will have to violate my own promise. I will do whatever you two want me to do."

Chia Lien laughed. "Words are not enough," said he. "We want something tangible from you as a pledge. As far as my sister-in-law is concerned, I can give you my word that she is as virtuous in personal character as she is beautiful in appearance."

Hsiang-lien was pleased to hear what a great beauty San-chieh was. "I shall be in the capital in about a month. Shall we discuss it then?"

"I hope that you will not misunderstand me," said Chia Lien. "I do trust your word. But, having been living like a floating duckweed [19] all your life, who knows when you will be back in the capital? How long has my sister-in-law to wait? I shall be happy if you will give me the engagement presents for me to take home."

17 As for the definition of "sworn brothers," see p. 360.

18 This paragraph is an abridged and paraphrased version of the original. Materials that have no bearing on the main topic of this selection are deleted.

19 A floating duckweed moves according to the constant change of wind directions and leaves no traces.

"A gentleman never violates his promises," Liu Hsiang-lien replied. "I came from a poor family. Where can I have so much money for engagement presents at this time when I am away from home?"

"That can be easily taken care of," said Hsüeh Fan. "I have some money here, more than enough to buy some engagement presents."

"I do not mean gold, silver, pearls, or precious stones," said Chia Lien. "I mean some personal belongings of yours which I can take home as a pledge. They do not have to be very expensive."

"I have nothing valuable in my baggage except a sword called Mandarin Duck. This sword has been in our family for many generations and is so valuable that I carry it wherever I go, even though I never use it. I will give it to you as my pledge. I may be a floating duckweed, but I certainly will come back for this sword."

After a few more drinks, all of the three went their separate ways. . . .

Returning home, Chia Lien told the two sisters how he had accidentally met Liu Hsiang-lien and the subsequent engagement. He took the sword from his baggage and presented it to Yu San-chieh. San-chieh unsheathed it and found that there were actually two swords. The handle of each sword was carved with a dragon playing with a fire ball and was inlaid with pearls and precious stones. On the reverse side one handle was carved with the character "Yüan," [20] and the other the character "Yang." [21] As for the swords themselves, they were shining and bright, like two streams of water in an autumn night. San-chieh was happy beyond belief. She put the swords back to the sheath and hung them on her bedpost. She looked at them every day, confident that she had found a man on whom she could rely for the rest of her life. . . .

It was not until the eighth month that Liu Hsiang-lien returned to the capital. He went to the Hsüeh family to pay his respect to Hsüeh Fan's mother and found that his sworn brother had been sick in bed. Hsüeh's mother thanked him for having saved her son's life and informed him that everything had been prepared for the wedding and that all he needed to do was to pick up a propitious date. Liu Hsiang-lien thanked her copiously for the trouble she had gone through.

On the second day after his arrival at the capital, Liu Hsiang-lien paid a visit to Precious Jade. The two friends were very happy to see each other. Hsiang-lien inquired about Chia Lien's secret marriage to Yu Erh-chieh without his wife's knowledge, and Precious Jade replied that though he had heard about this from his servants, he did not think that he should interfere with a matter of this sort. "I have heard that he wants to talk with you. Is that true?" he asked. Liu Hsiang-lien then told him about the circumstances that led to his engagement to Yu San-chieh.

"Congratulations! Rarely can you find a great beauty as she is. A great match!"

"If she is so wonderful as all of you said she is, why should Chia Lien pick me? I have never been friendly with him, and there is no reason why he should be so concerned with my welfare. He pressed for my immediate consent to this marriage, and I was stupid enough to agree to it. Is it not odd that the family of a prospective bride should seek after the family of a prospective groom? The more

[20] The drake of the mandarin duck.
[21] The female of the mandarin duck.

I think about it, the more puzzled I become. I regret very much that I gave my sword as the pledge. Later I thought of you; I thought that you might be able to help me to solve this puzzle."

"Being a cautious man as I believe you are, why did you not ask these questions before the engagement?" said Precious Jade. "You have always wanted a great beauty, and here she is. If I were you, I would not ask any more questions."

"How do you know that she is a great beauty since you obviously do not know her background?"

"Why, these two girls are related to cousin Chen of the Eastern Residence. I have been having gay times with them for about a month.[22] Both girls are exceptionally beautiful."

Liu Hsiang-lien stamped his feet on the ground with great anxiety. "My Heavens!" he exclaimed. "What a fool I have been! In all of the Eastern Residence the only clean pair is the two stone lions that guard its front entrance." Upon hearing this Precious Jade suddenly changed his expression; his face was now flashing red. Liu Hsiang-lien knew that he had been too impulsive and had said something which should not have been said. He saluted and he apologized. "My big mouth—I will never forgive my own big mouth! However, please tell me what kind of person she really is—I mean her moral character."

"Since you already seem to know so much about her, why should you ask me? I may not be very clean myself," Precious Jade replied.

"I am sorry for my intemperate remarks. Please forgive me."

"There is nothing to be forgiven. If you insist that I should forgive you, the whole thing may sound more serious than it really is," Precious Jade smiled.

After leaving Precious Jade, the first thing Liu Hsiang-lien thought of was to pay a visit to Hsüeh Fan. He changed his mind when he recalled that Hsüeh Fan was sick in bed and had a bad temper besides. Then he decided to go straight to Chia Lien to demand the return of his sword.

Hearing that Liu Hsiang-lien was in the front door, Chia Lien rejoiced and immediately went out to escort him to the inner room to meet Madame Yu. Liu saluted instead of performing the kowtow. He called Madame Yu "elder aunt" instead of "honorable mother-in-law." He called himself "your humble student" instead of "your humble son-in-law." Chia Lien was puzzled about his behavior.

Only after the tea was served did Liu Hsiang-lien mention the purpose of his visit. "I learned only recently that my aunt has engaged me to marry a girl of her choice," said he. "I did not know this until I returned home in my last trip. Inasmuch as I would like to obey your order, Mr. Chia, it does not seem right to disobey my own aunt. If the engagement present were something money could buy, I certainly would not request its return. But this sword was given to me by my grandfather. I hope that you will not mind returning it to me."

Chia Lien became restless and did not know what to say. "A promise, once made, should never be broken," he protested. "It was exactly for this reason that I asked you to give me a pledge. Marriage is one of the most important things in a man's life. How can a person make a firm promise about it and then break the promise? To me this simply cannot be done."

Hsiang-lien smiled. "I will take whatever punishment you choose to impose on

---

[22] Precious Jade was known for his "talented" ways with women. However, as far as Yu San-chieh was concerned, he was never successful.

me. But as far as this matter is concerned, I am afraid that I simply cannot go through with it."

Chia Lien continued to argue, in the hope that somehow he could persuade Liu Hsiang-lien to change his mind. "Let us go outside to talk; shall we?" Hsiang-lien suggested.

Yu San-chieh heard every word of the conversation in her own room. She had been waiting for him for such a long time; now, when he finally arrived, he wanted to cancel the engagement! Obviously he had heard some derogatory remarks about her in the Chia household and mistook her as a cheap woman unfit to become his wife. What would people think of her if Chia Lien continued to argue with this man for the sole purpose of pushing her to his arms? Having heard that the two were about to go outside to continue their conversation, she took the sword down and carried it in such a way as to place its sharp point behind her elbow. She rushed out and said: "You two do not have to speak about this matter any more. Here is your sword!" Her tears streamed down like raindrops. Then she proceeded to hand the sword to Liu Hsiang-lien with her left hand. When Liu was about to take it, she unsheathed the sword with her right hand and quickly slit her own throat. When the people in the house rushed towards her, it was already too late.

Madame Yu cried and cried and cursed Liu Hsiang-lien with all the bad words she could find. Chia Lien grabbed his shoulder and ordered the servants to take him to the officials. "What is the use?" said Yu Erh-chieh, while wiping her tears. "He did not force her to commit suicide; she did it herself. Once you report him to the officials, all people will know about this, and what they know will not help our family's reputation. Let him go!" Chia Lien then ordered Liu Hsiang-lien to get out.

Instead of getting out, Liu Hsiang-lien stood motionless. He took out his handkerchief and began to wipe his tears. "I did not realize what a resolute person she was. I wish I had! I owe her my esteem and respect. It is my misfortune that I cannot have her as my wife." He cried and cried and finally left when he could not cry any more.

171 · ANONYMOUS: *The Peacock Flies Southeast* [23]

(In this prose translation of a famous Chinese poem, an attempt has been made to retain insofar as possible the tempo and, hopefully, the feeling of the original poetry.)

The peacock flies southeast, circling about every five *li*.

"I began to weave silk at thirteen; at fourteen I learned to make clothes. I was playing the lute at fifteen; at sixteen I recited the *History* and the *Odes*.[24] At

[23] According to the author, the story described in this selection occurred during the Chien-an period (196–219) of the Han dynasty. The author, who can no longer be identified, lived in the third century A.D. when divorce and remarriage were more socially acceptable than they were in a later period. A copy of the Chinese original can be found in most collections dealing with ancient Chinese poetry.

[24] *Book of History* and *Book of Odes*.

seventeen I became your wife. But alas! My heart has been filled with sadness. You, my lord, are a government official; I, as your faithful wife, cannot complain of your frequent departures. Many nights I am left alone in the empty chamber; rarely have we seen one another!

"At dawn when the cock crowed, I was already at the loom. Night after night I worked without rest; in three days I wove five *chang* of cloth. But the Honorable One [25] said I merely dawdled. I dawdled not, my lord; it is too difficult to be a wife in your household. This misery is unbearable. I should quickly end it. Kindly request the Honorable Ones [26] to return me to my home as soon as possible."

The official sought out his mother upon hearing these words.

"Fortunate indeed is your son," he said, "to have this woman as his wife, unlikely though he is to obtain fame or wealth. We married each other at a tender age; we wish to be man and wife throughout our lives. After we die, we wish still to be friends. She has been with us but two or three years. Never has she done anything wrong. How can she possibly displease?"

"You have been deceived, my son; your woman has no manners. She does what she pleases, never asking how your mother feels. Against her I have many grievances. I have made up my mind—I am afraid you have no choice. Our neighbor to the east has a daughter truly virtuous. She calls herself Ch'in Lo-fu; a delicate, beautiful girl she is. I shall ask her hand for you; hesitate not to send away your wife."

The official went down on his knees.

"If you send away my wife, I will never marry again," said he.

The Honorable One was angry when she heard these unfilial words. She pounded her sitting stool, denouncing the official in harsh terms.

"How dare you, scoundrel, side with your wife! No more love can you expect from me; I will not agree with you in this matter."

Once again he prostrated himself before the Honorable One and left quietly without a word. Into his own chamber he went, bringing the sad tidings to his beloved. He sobbed much, and could barely make himself understood.

"I do not desire your departure," said he, "but my mother has given me no choice. Please go home for the time being. I, meanwhile, shall sojourn to the capital. I shall return soon and reunited we will then be. Bear with me in your grievance; do not disobey my words."

"Why is it necessary," she inquired, "to make this elaborate arrangement? In the early spring of a bygone year, I left my own home for your honorable household. Serving the Honorable Ones I have been diligent; disobedient to them I have never been. Day and night I worked alone. Who was there to share my misgivings? Doing nothing wrong and waiting on her daily, I should deserve some consideration. Now I am asked to leave. How can you ask me to return?

"I have embroidered coats with golden trimmings. I have a pink bed-net [27] made of silk, with perfume bags hanging on its four corners. Many, many more

---

[25] Her mother-in-law.

[26] Her parents-in-law.

[27] A bed-net, usually shaped like a box, hangs over the bed. It prevents mosquitoes as well as provides privacy.

things I have—including boxes and cases tied with many-colored silk strings. Each has its individuality; all of them their owner cherishes. As a person becomes less worthy, so do the things which she owns. They are not good enough for the coming one.[28] Please give them away to whomever you please. Farewell, my lord. Take care of yourself, always! As long as we live, let us not forget each other, please!"

The cock crowed; the dawn was near. The official's wife rose to dress up for the departure. She put on her silk shirt, and changed and changed again her clothes, unable to decide what was proper to wear. She put on her silk shoes and a hat embedded with tortoise shells. Around her waist hung a silk belt glossy and white. To and fro her earrings swung, tinkling like a bell. Her fingers were like white scallions newly cut; her lips were as red as rubies. Here she came—how daintily she moved! How beautiful she was!

She went to say farewell to the Honorable One. The Honorable One was angry still.

"I came from a humble background," she said; "as a daughter at home I had not been well taught. I have been truly shameful, dear mother; I have not served you and my husband well. Now I have to leave because I have not been a satisfactory daughter-in-law. Today I am going home, but forget you I shall not."

She bid farewell to her husband's sister who was little and sweet. Tears streamed down her cheeks, since they had been great friends.

"When I came to this household, you, dear sister, were a baby learning to walk. Now that you are almost as tall as I am, you should be diligent in serving your mother since I can no longer do so myself. Whatever you do—play or work—remember your poor, lost sister-in-law."

Tears rushed down like hundreds of streams when she mounted upon her carriage. The official escorted his wife to the main road, and on the main road he dismounted. Into the carriage he went; into her ears he softly whispered.

"I will never let you go, no matter what the Honorable One says. I am now leaving for the capital but I shall return home. May Heaven be my witness, betray you I will not."

"I shall be waiting for you," she replied, "feeling as deeply as you do. You, my husband, are like a rock; I, your humble wife, can be compared to a rush. A rush is soft, yet flexible and strong; a rock is immovable and solid. But I should tell you, dear husband, I have parents whose wishes I cannot predict. There may be circumstances, my lord, when I cannot do what I have promised."

Raising their hands, they said good-bye. How sad and forlorn they must have felt.

Into the main hall she went to see her mother, uncertain though she was because she knew not what to expect. Her mother clasped her hands in surprise.

"Is this my daughter?" She could not believe her eyes. "I taught you to weave at thirteen; at fourteen you tailored like an expert. At fifteen you played the lute; at sixteen you knew all about proper manners. At seventeen you were married.

[28] The woman whom her husband might marry in the future.

Have I not done everything proper and right? Now you are home unexpectedly. Have you misbehaved?"

"A disgrace to you I truly am, dear mother, but I have not misbehaved."

Her mother was greatly grieved.

After ten days at home, a go-between arrived with words from the magistrate.

"The magistrate's third son," said the messenger, "is eighteen and unmarried. He is handsome, eloquent, and talented."

"Talk with the go-between," commanded her mother; "I cannot explain to him myself."

With tears in her eyes she sadly explained.

"On my way home," she said, "My former husband and I made a pledge: we will not desert each other, and we will be reunited. Would it not be strange if I should violate the pledge? Be gone, my friend; violate my own pledge I will not."

"The daughter of your humble servant," said the mother, "has come home only recently. If she served poorly as a clerk's wife, how can she serve well the son of a magistrate?"

Several days passed. Another go-between, the district secretary, came to the household.

"The Lan family," said he, "has produced many officials in the past. The fifth son, handsome and unmarried, requests the hand of a daughter from your honorable household. The Prefect, his father, instructs me to serve as the go-between, the message being transmitted to me through the keeper of the records. I was instructed to say that the Prefect has a son whose sincere intention is to engage in holy matrimony. To your honorable household I have come, madame, to bring to you his respect."

Her mother thanked the go-between, but declined the honor he had bestowed.

"My daughter has taken an oath not to remarry; what else is there to be said?"

Upon hearing this her elder brother was disturbed, not knowing why she did not wish to be remarried.

"Why do you decline an offer," he asked, "with so many advantages in it? Formerly you were married to a government clerk; now the Prefect's son is requesting your hand. What a difference! To marry this young man will bring you great honors. If you do not wish to do so, I am truly at a loss to understand you."

She raised her head and answered him as follows:

"You are right, dear brother; your words are always wise. I left home to serve my husband, only to return home at this early date. I will do whatever you think best. How dare I act according to my own wishes? Though a pledge has been made to my former husband, I realize it can no longer be fulfilled. Now that I have given my consent, the wedding may soon take place."

The go-between left the house, muttering "Yes, yes, yes." Happily he went to see the Prefect to report the good news.

"Your humble servant has not disappointed you, honorable sir; my speech was made of lucky words."

The Prefect was overjoyed upon hearing these words. He opened the calendar; he consulted the books.

"The stars and the planets are in the right positions; this is the month most propitious. Today is the twenty-seventh; the luckiest day is the thirtieth. On that day, my dear son, the wedding will take place."

Words came down to prepare the bride's clothes. They were so many and beautiful that they looked like a stream of floating clouds. The wedding boat was painted with orioles and snow-geese. On its corners stood four flags embroidered with flying dragons—gracefull they turned around with the breeze. The chariot was painted gold with jade-colored axles. The horses, grey and white, strutted slowly; the golden saddles were lined with silk trimmings. Three hundred bolts of silk and three million coins tied with purple strings—these were the bride's presents. Food and drink—how delicious they were! They were collected from many distant places. Five hundred servants were running hither and thither— joyously they served for this grand occasion.

The mother remarked to her daughter that a message from the Prefect had arrived.
"He is coming to take you tomorrow; you should prepare your clothes."
Her daughter gave no answer; with a handkerchief she covered her sobbings. Down her cheeks the tears streamed.
She moved her glass table beside the window. Her left hand held a pair of scissors and a ruler; her right hand was busy with velvet and silk. Skirts she made in the morning; in the evening she finished her blouses. As it became darker and darker, she carried her sadness outside the front door.

Her former husband then heard of the sudden change of events. He took leave from his duty and rode home as quickly as he could. Two or three *li* from her house his mount neighed loudly as if to share his sorrows. The woman heard the neighings of the horse, rushing forward to meet her beloved. From the distant horizon came the man she had awaited. As her heart was torn into pieces, she placed her hand on the saddle and sighed.
"Since you left," she said, "the unexpected has occurred. I can no longer keep my word. Oh, how much I hope you can understand! My family has betrothed me to another man. Forget and forgive me, my dearest one; we shall never see each other again."
"Congratulations!" he said; "you have climbed high indeed. The rock is hard and strong, lasting thousands of years. What has happened to the rush? It is strong one day, only to be changed overnight. Being wealthy, you will enjoy life; I will walk alone in the other world."
"How can you say this, my husband, since we are forced to do what we loath? I will join you in the other world; we shall keep our word."
They clasped hands and said good-bye, each going to his own house. How sad it is, dear reader, when two lovers make a pledge to die together! They swore to relinquish this world, which would be imperfect as long as they were not united.

The official went to his own house. He knelt before the Honorable One.
"Bitter winds sweep across the land," he said, "killing trees and causing heavy frost. My life will come to an end soon, dear mother; I regret leaving you alone. I am doing this of my own accord; do not blame the ghosts or spirits. Soon my

body will be like a rock in the Southern Mountains—hard, unyielding, and solid."

Tears streamed from his mother's eyes, when she heard these words of doom.

"You were born to a great family; you are now a government official. Why do you wish to die for a woman unworthy of your affection and love? Our neighbor to the east has a virtuous daughter whose beauty the entire city admires. I shall ask her hand for you. In a day or two I will bring you the good news."

Once more the official prostrated and to his own room he then returned. The room was empty—how things had changed! Looking at the Honorable One's chamber, how much he grieved!

Horses and cattle were neighing outside the wedding tent into which the official's former wife went. It was dark. It was quiet.

"I am going to die today; I shall have no regret leaving this world."

She lifted up her skirt; she cast off her silk shoes. Quietly, she walked towards the river that was crystal and clear.

The official eventually heard the sad news. Now the end had finally arrived. Walking round and round a tall tree, he hanged himself on its southeastern branch, in his own front yard.

172 · SUNG LIEN: *The Yüan Code: Marriage and Family* [29]

6. Boys and girls who have been sold by their parents in order to raise money to pay taxes should be freed from their bondage and be returned to their parents. A government official who is so harsh in exacting tax payments as to cause taxpayers to sell their children is punishable by law. The money which the parents have collected when selling their children is not returnable to its original owner.

7. The parents who kill their girl infant immediately after her birth are to be penalized by a fine assessed at one-half of their total assets. If the informer of an infanticide happens to be a male or female slave, he or she will immediately regain his or her freedom. A government official who knows that infanticide has taken place and chooses not to prosecute the offender is punishable by law.

8. Widows, widowers, and orphans, together with the aged, the weak, the crippled, the incurably ill, the extremely poor, and all those who have no relatives or friends to support them, should be admitted to the houses of relief. The responsible official should see to it that those who are qualified for relief have been admitted and those who are not qualified are discharged. Any violation of this regulation on his part is punishable by law. His superior should conduct periodical investigation so as to make certain that this regulation is constantly observed.

14. After a bandit has surrendered himself to the government, the government official who accepts his surrender shall under no circumstances accept as gifts the men and women whom the bandit has kidnapped or detained. He should instead set these men and women free immediately. If these people do not have any relatives and have consequently no place to go, the official should match them as hus-

---

[29] *History of the Yüan (Yüan shih),* roll 103.

bands and wives so that they can establish their own households. All people who have been detained by bandits are to be set free.

15. After a woman has been freed from captivity in the hands of a bandit and if for any reason she has lost her memory about where she comes from and has consequently no relatives to go to, the official who has taken her into custody should see to it that she is properly married and that the betrothal money he has received from her future husband is spent on her trousseau.

20. Only in those households where there are more able-bodied men than the number necessary to meet the government's requirement of labor services can some of their members be allowed to leave home to join the monastic ranks. Besides, these prospective monks or priests must have brothers who during their absence can continue to support their parents. If these conditions are satisfactorily met, the families concerned can then petition local authorities who, having made their own investigations and being satisfied with the result, will recommend to the provincial authorities the granting of permissions. Only the provincial authorities can issue a certificate that enables a person to become a monk or a priest. Those who become monks or priests without obtaining such certificates in advance are punishable by law and will be ordered to return to civilian life.

21. Those monks in Hohsi [30] who have been legally married are subject to such legal obligations as paying taxes and providing shelters for government troops, obligations that are shared by all civilians. The unmarried monks, however, are exempt from these obligations.

22. If a man neglects his duty as a son by not providing financial support for his parents who are in need, he shall be severely punished in accordance with the law, even though his parents have a household of their own and the family property has long been divided. The same penalty will also be imposed upon a person who refuses to take into his home a member of his clan who has been widowed, orphaned, aged, crippled, or ill, cannot support himself, and consequently has to be admitted to a house of relief at the public's expense. However, if it has been clearly established that he is as poor as his relatives or clan members who need help, he is not obligated to support them. In such a case, the houses of relief will take over the duties that are normally his.

28. It is legally forbidden to mortgage one's own daughters; it is equally forbidden to accept as mortgage the sons and daughters of another person. However, the government will not start legal proceedings against the mortgagee if he has taken steps to officially marry the mortgaged girl as either a wife or a concubine.

29. It is legally forbidden to mortgage one's wife or concubine. It is permissible, however, to accept as mortgage a married couple who, in this case, will live together after they have been mortgaged.

30. It is legally forbidden to sell one's wife, concubine, or younger foster brothers or sisters.

31. It is permissible to petition for the custody of homeless children; it is not permissible, however, to sell these children as slaves after their custody has been granted. It is illegal to adopt slaves as foster children.

32. The government official who forces people within his jurisdiction to become his own slaves will receive a corporal punishment of seventy-seven blows by

[30] Modern Kansu province.

a wooden stick. He will be suspended from his office for one year and will be demoted by two ranks when he is reinstated.

33. Any person who mistakes a man of good family as a slave and then brutalizes him will receive a corporal punishment of eighty-seven blows by a wooden stick. If he is a government official, he will be dismissed from his office.

34. If a slave has given evidence that he comes from a family of good standing, he should be given a paper to certify the same and should be allowed to live in peace, until such time as his relatives come to take him home. If he has no home to go to, he should be allowed to make his own choice with regard to the future of his life.

35. A runaway slave will receive a corporal punishment of seventy-seven blows by a wooden stick when and if he is captured.

36. It is legally forbidden to betroth one's sons or daughters who are not yet born.

37. The wedding ceremony should be conducted in such a way that it will not entail unnecessary expenses. It should not be used as an occasion for extravagance for the sole purpose of impressing one's friends and relatives. It is forbidden to stage an all-night celebration.

38. If a go-between is accused of having demanded and received more betrothal money for the prospective bride's family or more commission for himself than what has been customary in either case, a public inquiry will be conducted to ascertain the truth. If he is found guilty, from then on, he can never serve as a go-between in marriage proposals.

39. The family of a betrothed girl is allowed to cancel the engagement and to betroth her to a third party if the family of her fiancé has been accused and then convicted of treason, and as a consequence, all members of the said family have been condemned and confiscated by the government. The engagement is likewise cancelled and the girl in question can be betrothed to a third party if her fiancé has been convicted of banditry or robbery and is destined to be exiled to a remote area. However, if the girl is currently married and has borne her husband a son or sons, she is not allowed to marry another person even though her husband has been convicted of bandity or robbery and is being punished accordingly.

40. If a betrothed girl has illicit relations with another man, the family of her fiancé can, if it chooses, break off the engagement, and in such a case, is entitled to the reimbursement of the money which it paid at the time of the betrothal. If on the other hand it chooses to honor the engagement despite the knowledge that the girl in question has had illicit relations with another man, it is entitled to the reimbursement of only one-half of the betrothal money. If a family deliberately creates rumors that throw doubts on a maiden's character and thus creates a situation in which she will not receive a proposal for marriage from any family except the one which has created these rumors but is fully aware of her innocence, the head of this family will receive fifty-seven blows by a wooden stick, and the girl in question, if she has already been married into this family, is free to leave.

41. A man will receive eighty-seven blows by a wooden stick and his marriage is declared invalid if he marries during a period when he is supposedly mourning the death of one of his parents.[31] If he is a government official, he shall be dismissed from his office. His wife is not held responsible and is free to leave his

[31] The mourning period usually lasted three years.

house. The money which he paid to his wife's family at the time of the betrothal will be confiscated by the government.

42. Those who betroth their children during the period of mourning are punishable by law, but the punishment will be two degrees less than that imposed upon those who marry their children during the said period. The engagement is invalid, and the betrothal money will be confiscated by the government.

43. If a man has agreed to marry his daughter to the son of another man, orally or by written agreement, or he has accepted the betrothal money and has thus implied his consent to the proposed marriage, he is not allowed to break his own promise. If he does, he will receive thirty-seven blows by a wooden stick. The penalty will be increased to forty-seven blows if in the meantime he has betrothed his daughter to a third party. The punishment will be further increased to fifty-seven blows if in the meantime he has married his daughter to a third party. If the third party knows that she has been engaged to another person and yet marries her, he will be punished too, not to the extent, however, that her father is punished. In any event, the marriage is invalid and the girl will be returned to her parents. The family of her fiancé, to whom she was originally engaged, is not held responsible for the illegal conduct of her father and can cancel the engagement if it chooses to do so. If it chooses to cancel the engagement, it is not entitled to the reimbursement of the money it paid to her family at the time of the betrothal. If it does not choose to cancel the engagement and yet, without giving valid reasons, continues to refuse to honor the marriage contract for as long as a period of five years, the responsible official will issue her family a certificate which enables it to marry her to some one else.

44. If a person accepts a man into his own house as his son-in-law and then chases him out so that his daughter can and later does marry another man, he and his second son-in-law will each receive sixty-seven blows by a wooden stick. The woman will return to her first husband as his legally married wife. The betrothal money that was paid by his second son-in-law will be confiscated by the government.

45. A government official who marries a prostitute will receive fifty-seven blows by a wooden stick. He will be dismissed from his office, and the marriage is invalid.

46. A man who takes in more concubines despite the fact that he has already had a wife and a concubine will receive forty-seven blows by a wooden stick. The said concubines shall leave his house, and he is not entitled to the reimbursement of the money with which they were purchased. If he is a government official, he will be dismissed from his post.

47. If a man has been convicted of having illicit sexual relations with a woman and if subsequently he marries this same woman as a wife or concubine, such marriage is invalid despite the fact that she may have borne him children.

48. A woman who lives and has been brought up in her fiancé's house cannot be married to anybody else. Anyone who is responsible for marrying her to a man other than her fiancé will receive sixty-seven blows by a wooden stick. The woman will be returned to her parents, and the betrothal money paid prior to the illegal marriage will be confiscated by the government.

49. A man who gives his wife in marriage to another man after receiving money from the same will receive sixty-seven blows by a wooden stick, and the money will be returned to its original owner. The man who marries another man's wife

is not punishable if he does not know that she is a married woman. The woman will be returned to her parents.

50. A man who takes a woman as his concubine by approved ceremony and subsequently gives her in marriage to another man after receiving money from the same will receive fifty-seven blows by a wooden stick. The money in question will be confiscated by the government. The woman will be returned to her parents. If he is a governmental official, he will be dismissed from his post.

51. A Buddhist or Taoist priest who marries in violation of the law of his faith will receive sixty-seven blows by a wooden stick. He will be ordered to return to civilian life, and his marriage is invalid. The money he paid at the time of the betrothal will be confiscated by the government.

52. It is legally forbidden to mortgage one's tenants. Only a tenant's parents, not his landlord, can arrange his marriage.

53. A man who marries his younger brother's wife will receive one hundred seven blows by a wooden stick. The woman will receive ninety-seven blows by the same instrument. The marriage is invalid. The man who presides at the marriage ceremony will receive fifty-seven blows by a wooden stick, and the go-between who arranges this marriage will receive thirty-seven blows by the same instrument.

54. A man who takes his step-mother in marriage after the death of his parents will receive one hundred seven blows by a wooden stick. The marriage is invalid. If he is a government official, his name will be deleted from the official roster and he can never hold an official post again.

55. It is legally forbidden for a Northern or Southern Chinese [32] to marry his step-mother after the death of his father or marry his sister-in-law after the death of his elder brother.

56. It is legally forbidden to take into marriage the wife of his deceased cousin.[33] If he does, he will be regarded as having had illicit sexual relations with the woman in question and will be punished accordingly.

57. A slave who marries his mistress after the death of his master is regarded as having committed adultery and will be punished accordingly. A slave who forces the daughter of his deceased master to marry him is punishable by death.

58. If a man gives the concubine of his deceased father to another man who then keeps her as a mistress, he will receive seventy-seven blows by a wooden stick. The man who keeps her as a mistress will receive fifty-seven blows by the same instrument.

59. A man who is the custodian of another man's wife and then, having received money from a third party, gives her in marriage against her will and in violation of the trust that has been placed in him will be regarded as having deliberately and purposely violated the law and will receive seventy-seven blows by a wooden stick. The money he has received will be confiscated by the government, and the woman in question will be returned to her former husband.

60. A woman of good family who willingly marries a slave will be considered a slave. A woman who comes from a good family and is then sold by her husband as a slave is not a slave. The buyer and the seller are equally guilty and will be

---

[32] During the Yüan dynasty the government divided all people in China into four groups: Mongols, people of Western regions (most of whom were Muslims), Northern Chinese, and finally, Southern Chinese.

[33] The word "cousin" here means a son of one's father's sister.

punished accordingly. The money with which she was purchased will be confiscated by the government.

61. If a man marries his son's fiancée (who has lived and been brought up in his own household) [34] to one of his own slaves, he will receive fifty-seven blows by a wooden stick. The woman will be returned to her parents who, in this case, are not required to return the money paid to them at the time of the betrothal.

62. The marriage between the daughter of a runaway slave and the son of a good family is legally valid if children have been born to this union. However, the original owner of this runaway slave is entitled to collect betrothal money from the man to whom his slave's daughter has been married.

63. A woman who has been deserted by her husband may return to her parents and be remarried. Her first husband has lost all rights in relation to her by his act of desertion.

64. A woman who has been deserted by her husband can take in marriage a second husband. The husband who once deserted her cannot remarry her even after her second husband has died. Such a marriage is illegal.

65. It is not permissible for a man to sell his wife even though he and his wife detest each other; nor is it permissible to buy another man's wife. Both the buyer and the seller will be punished in accordance with the law. It is permissible, however, for a man to marry a woman who has been divorced from her husband by mutual agreement.

66. A divorce between a man and his wife or concubine is legal only when it is explicitly expressed in a written document. Possessing such a document, the woman in question can remarry. Any evidence other than a written document is not valid in divorce cases.

67. A woman who deserts her husband and parents-in-law to become a nun will receive sixty-seven blows by a wooden stick. She will be returned to her husband.

68. A man who sells or buys a woman of good family with the intended purpose of making her a prostitute will be punished in accordance with the law, and the woman will be returned to her family. One-half of the purchasing price will be confiscated by the government, while the other half will be awarded to the informer who reports to the government this illegal transaction. All of the purchasing price will be confiscated by the government if the woman informs the government herself or if the illegal transaction is discovered without the help of an informer. Despite her good family background, a woman can be bought or sold as a prostitute if she has committed adultery thereby causing her husband to abandon her. The relative of a prostitute or entertainer can become a prostitute without violating the law.

69. A man who forces abortion upon a pregnant prostitute will be punished in accordance with the law, and the prostitute in question, from then on, is free from her bondage as a prostitute.

70. A man who forces his wife or concubine to become a prostitute will receive eighty-seven blows by a wooden stick. He will receive seventy-seven blows by the same instrument if he makes a woman of good family appear as a singer or dancer

[34] In old China it was permissible to take a female child or sometimes infant into one's own house with the intended purpose of marrying her to one's own son once she reached the marriageable age. The female child usually came from a poor family, or in some cases, had been abandoned by her own parents.

in a party or banquet, or if he forces her to become a prostitute. He will receive forty-seven blows by a wooden stick if he forces a female slave to become a prostitute. The slave in question will be then freed from her bondage as a slave.

71. A man who makes his wife or concubine a prostitute with her consent and collects money from her customer or customers will receive eighty-seven blows by a wooden stick. The woman in question and the customer or customers will receive the same punishment. The woman will not be punished, however, if she takes the initiative to report her prostitution to the government. She will be still subject to punishment if she has waited days or months before she makes such a report.

173 · SUNG LIEN: *The Yüan Code: Illicit Sexual Relations*[35]

1. A woman who has illicit sexual relations with a man will receive seventy-seven blows by a wooden stick; eighty-seven blows if she is married. The penalty will be heavier by one degree if the man, having had illicit sexual relations with her, succeeds in persuading her to elope with him. In such a case both the man and the woman are equally guilty and are to be punished by flogging. When a woman is punished by flogging, her clothes are to be stripped off before the blows are delivered. If a woman attempts illicit sexual relations but has not succeeded in her attempt, her penalty will be reduced by four degrees.

The penalty for raping a married woman is death. The penalty is one hundred seven blows by a wooden stick if the woman is unmarried; the penalty is reduced by one degree in cases of attempted but unsuccessful rape. In each or any of the above cases the woman is not held responsible.

An illicit sexual relationship arranged by a go-between and attained via mutual agreement is still considered a violation of the law, but the penalty will be reduced by three degrees from that normally imposed for committing such a crime. The penalty will be reduced by four degrees if the families of the parties involved are informed in advance of and are in agreement with the illicit sexual relationship.

2. A person who informs the government of the illicit sexual relations of others is not punishable for providing such information.

3. An unmarried woman who becomes pregnant is punishable by law. The man whom she accuses as the father of her unborn child is not punishable on the sole basis of her accusation.

4. A soldier of the palace guards who has illicit sexual relations with a palace slave will receive a dishonorable discharge from the guards.

5. A man who forces illicit sexual relations upon his daughter-in-law will receive the death sentence; he will receive one hundred seven blows by a wooden stick if he attempts such relationship but fails to achieve his purpose. In either case she will be returned to her parents. If the woman voluntarily and without compulsion agrees to her father-in-law's advances, both she and her father-in-law will receive the death sentence. If a woman accuses her father-in-law of having raped her and if her accusation proves false, she will receive the death sentence. If she accuses her father-in-law of having attempted to rape her and if her accusation proves false, she will receive one hundred seven blows by a wooden stick

[35] *Yüan shih,* roll 104.

and will be then returned to her husband who, in this case, can either marry her off or sell her as a slave. In cases involving illicit sexual relations between a man and his daughter-in-law, the penalty will remain the same regardless of whether the man or the woman reports such relations to the government. If a woman accuses her father-in-law of having raped her whereas in fact he has only attempted but failed to rape her, she will receive thirty-seven blows by a wooden stick and will be then returned to her parents.

6. A man who forces sexual relations upon the wife of his adopted son will receive one hundred seven blows by a wooden stick. If he attempts to rape her but does not succeed, the penalty will be eighty-seven blows by a wooden stick. The woman is not held responsible and will not be punished. . . .

7. A woman who, in conspiracy with her paramour, falsely accuses her father-in-law of having raped her for the purpose of obtaining a divorce from her husband so as to marry her paramour will receive one hundred seven blows by a wooden stick. The paramour will receive a penalty one degree below that of hers, and the money which he has paid to her husband for the purpose of obtaining the divorce will be confiscated by the government. The woman will be returned to her husband who can either marry her off or sell her as a slave.

8. A man who has illicit sexual relations with his younger brother's wife will receive one hundred seven blows by a wooden stick and will be exiled to the frontier. The adulteress will be at the disposal of her husband who can do whatever he wishes with her.

9. A man who rapes the widow of his elder brother will receive ninety-seven blows by a wooden stick.

10. A man who has illicit sexual relations with the wife of his nephew [36] will receive one hundred seven blows by a wooden stick. The same penalty will be also imposed on the woman. If he is a government official, his name will be deleted from the official roster and he can never hold a governmental post again.

11. A man who attempts to rape the wife of his nephew but does not succeed will receive one hundred seven blows by a wooden stick.

12. A man who has illicit sexual relations with the daughter of his brother will receive the death sentence; so will his brother's daughter. If she is the daughter of his first cousin,[37] the penalty will be reduced by one degree. If she is the daughter of a distant cousin, the penalty will be reduced by two degrees.

13. A man who forces illicit sexual relations upon his father's concubine while mourning the death of his parents will receive ninety-seven blows by a wooden stick. The woman will be returned to her parents.

14. If, having been convicted of illicit sexual relations, a man commits the same offense again, the penalty to be imposed on him will be doubly severe. The woman in question will be returned to her husband who can either marry her off or sell her as a slave.

15. A man or woman who steals from his or her own household, a larceny related to, or part of, his or her illicit sexual relationship with another person, will be punished for the illicit sexual act only; he or she will not be punished for the larceny.

16. It is permissible to take another man's wife as concubine under a contract

[36] A son of his brother.
[37] A son of his father's brother.

of hostage mutually agreed, but the woman should be returned to her husband after a period of time specified in the contract. If the former hostage holder continues to have sexual relations with the woman after she has been returned to her husband, such relations are considered illicit and are punishable by law. If he conspires with the woman to kill her husband and succeeds, both he and the woman will receive the death sentence.

17. A man is held responsible if his son has illicit sexual relations with a woman. The responsibility remains the same even if he has taken the initiative to report these relations to the government. He is not held responsible, however, if he has warned his son against, and has done his best to prevent, such relations before they take place.

18. A boy born of illicit sexual relations belongs to his natural father; a girl born of illicit sexual relations belongs to her natural mother.

19. A Buddhist (or Taoist) monk or nun who has illicit sexual relations with another person will be forced to return to civilian life after he or she has been duly punished for his or her crime.

20. A man who rapes a girl child will receive the death sentence. He is still regarded as having raped her even if she agrees to his advances. In both cases the girl child is not held responsible. By a girl child is meant a girl under the age of ten throughout these statutes.

21. An old man who rapes a girl child will receive one hundred seven blows by a wooden stick. This penalty cannot be compounded into a fine.

22. A boy under the age of fifteen who has sexual relations with a girl under the age of ten is regarded as having raped her even though she agrees to his advances. The boy will not be punished by death, but will receive one hundred seven blows by a wooden stick. The girl is not held responsible.

23. A man who rapes a woman above the age of ten will receive one hundred seven blows by a wooden stick.

24. A man who rapes the daughter-in-law of his wife's former husband or the daughter of his wife's former husband will receive one hundred seven blows by a wooden stick. His wife is free to leave him.

25. When three men conspire to rape one woman and succeed in their attempt, each and all of them will receive the death sentence. The woman is not held responsible and will not be punished.

26. An official who has illicit sexual relations with a woman will be punished in the same manner as any other citizen. Besides, his name will be deleted from the official roster and he can never hold a governmental post again. An official who is salaried but does not hold any specific post will be punished to the same extent as any other official if he commits the crime described above.

27. An official who attempts illicit sexual relations with a woman but does not succeed will receive fifty-seven blows by a wooden stick. He will be dismissed from his present office and will be demoted to a rank of the miscellaneous order.

28. An official who flirts with a man's wife and thus causes the man to desert his wife will receive sixty-seven blows by a wooden stick. He will be dismissed from his present post and will be demoted by two ranks when and if he is reinstated. . . .

29. A government official who attempts to rape a married woman but does not succeed in his attempt will receive one hundred seven blows by a wooden stick.

His name will be deleted from the official roster and he can never hold a governmental post again.

30. A government official who has illicit sexual relations with another man's concubine and subsequently purchases her as his own concubine will be punished for the second crime only: *i.e.,* he has violated the law by purchasing the concubine of a man who resides within his territorial jurisdiction, provided that his illicit sexual relations are not known to the government prior to his purchase of this woman as a concubine. He will receive thirty-seven blows by a wooden stick and be transferred to another post.

31. A jailer who has illicit sexual relations with the wife of one his prisoners will receive ninety-seven blows by a wooden stick, and his name will be deleted from the official roster.

32. A government official who has illicit sexual relations with a prostitute or the wife of an entertainer and subsequently takes her as a concubine will receive seventy-seven blows by a wooden stick and will be dismissed from his office.

33. A jailer who allows anyone to have illicit sexual relations with a widow prisoner under his custody will receive eighty-seven blows by a wooden stick, and his name will be deleted from the official roster.

34. A government official in charge of barbarian affairs who willfully marries a confiscated woman under his custody will receive eighty-seven blows by a wooden stick and be dismissed from his office. The woman in question will receive forty-seven blows by the same instrument.

35. No penalty is provided for a man who has illicit sexual relations with his slave's wife.

36. The daughter of a slave who has been betrothed to a man of good family is considered a woman of good family. If her master [38] forces illicit sexual relations on her, he will receive one hundred seven blows by a wooden stick. If these illicit relations are made possible by the permissiveness of his wife, his wife will receive fifty-seven blows by a wooden stick. If the fiancé of this slave's daughter still wishes to marry her after the aforesaid illicit sexual relations have taken place, he is entitled to the reimbursement of one half of the money which he has paid to the slave owner. If he does not wish to marry her, he is entitled to the reimbursement of the total amount. In the latter case she will be placed in the custody of her father as a woman of good family, to be married to someone else.

37. A slave who has illicit sexual relations with his master's daughter will receive the death sentence.

38. A servant who has illicit sexual relations with his employer's wife will receive the death sentence. A woman who elopes with her husband's servant will receive the death sentence.

39. A slave who rapes his master's wife will receive the death sentence.

40. A slave who has illicit sexual relations with his master's concubine will receive ninety-seven blows by a wooden stick. The concubine will receive the same penalty.

41. The son born from an illicit sexual relationship between a man of good family and a woman slave belongs to his natural mother who in turn belongs to her master. The son born from an illicit sexual relationship between a male slave

[38] The owner of her father.

and a woman of good family belongs to his natural mother and will be regarded as a man of good family.

42. When an illicit sexual relationship between a male and a female slave occurs, each of the two parties will receive forty-seven blows by a wooden stick.

43. A man who collects money from the prostitution of his wife will receive eighty-seven blows by a wooden stick. His wife and her customer or customers will receive the same punishment. The bond of marriage is hereon dissolved. If a man forces his wife or concubine to engage in prostitution for pecuniary reasons, the woman will be punished only to such an extent as the situation warrants.

44. A man who has illicit sexual relations with a married woman and then conspires with her to buy a divorce agreement from her husband so as to marry her will receive ninety-seven blows by a wooden stick. The woman will receive the same penalty. She will be returned to her legally married husband.

45. A man who cannot get along with his wife and then forces her to have illicit sexual relations with another man will receive seventy-seven blows by a wooden stick. She is not held responsible and is free to leave him.

46. A man who falsely accuses his father-in-law of having illicit sexual relations with his wife will receive ninety-seven blows by a wooden stick. His wife is free to leave him.

47. Suppose that a man accuses his wife of having illicit sexual relations with another man and then deserts her. Subsequently she is married to the man with whom she has been accused of having such relations. Both marriages are invalid; she cannot be married to either.

48. A man who has illicit sexual relations with a married woman and succeeds in a joint conspiracy to kill her husband will receive the death sentence. The woman will be punished in the same manner. The family of her paramour is responsible for the funeral and burial expenses of her deceased husband.

49. If a woman is not a party to the murdering of her husband by her paramour, her penalty will be that short of the death sentence.

50. If a woman conspires with her paramour to poison her husband but does not succeed in killing him, the penalty will be the same as that had she succeeded in killing him.

51. A woman who takes the initiative in conspiring with her paramour to kill her husband and then kills him with her own hands will receive a sentence of slow death by slicing.[39] Her paramour who has participated in this conspiracy will receive penalties provided elsewhere in these statutes.

52. A man who kills his wife is not guilty if his wife resists arrest when he catches her in the midst of having an affair with another man.

53. A man who kills his wife in order to marry a widow with whom he has illicit sexual relations will receive the death sentence.

54. A man who conspires with his mistress to poison his wife and succeeds will receive the death sentence. His mistress will be also put to death.

55. A man who kills his wife (or concubine) and her paramour is not guilty if he catches and kills them at the place where the illicit sexual relations take place. Nor is a woman guilty who kills the man who rapes or attempts to rape her. If a man who catches his wife (or concubine) having an affair with another man kills the man on the spot but decides to spare the life of his wife (or concu-

[39] A death by the slow process of slicing limbs, etc. before beheading.

bine), his wife (or concubine) will nevertheless receive the death sentence. If on the other hand he kills his wife (or concubine) but decides to spare the life of her paramour, her paramour will receive one hundred seven blows by a wooden stick.

56. A man who kills the woman with whom he has illicit sexual relations will receive the same penalty as if he had killed any other person.

57. If a man kills a woman who resists his advances, he will be punished in the same manner as a common bandit who kills a man with a wooden stick.

58. Suppose that a woman has two paramours and she, for her own reasons, has a date with both in the same evening. The paramour who arrives first fights and then kills the paramour who arrives later. The killer will be punished in the same manner as if he has killed with premeditation.

CHAPTER NINETEEN

The Pursuit of Pleasure

THE Chinese have been universally known for their industry, and they deserve their good reputation. Yet no person can work all his waking hours, however industrious he is. It can be strongly argued that the existence of leisure is essential to the development of a civilization, and no country can advance far in cultural achievements if all of its people are occupied with the daily necessity of making a living. Scholarship, literature, and fine arts are the products of leisure, and their flourishing requires the continuous support of a devoted audience. In traditional China this support was provided by the gentry and to a lesser extent the well-to-do commercial class. The wide gap between the rich and the poor, while deplorable from a social or economic point of view, was nevertheless beneficial in some respects. Had there been equal landownership throughout Chinese history as many Chinese economists have advocated, there would not have been a leisure class willing and able to promote or participate in cultural activities. The population was so large and arable acreage so small that the leveled income would have been too low to allow anyone to live above the peasant level. In such a case no Chinese would have had either the inclination or the time to engage in such "nonessential" activities as editing an ancient text or writing a piece of sophisticated poetry.

Of all the talents the Chinese emphasized, none was more important than the literary talent. Such emphasis was evidenced by the fact that prior to the modern period the Chinese produced more books than the rest of the world combined. As for fine arts, the art form which the Chinese cherished most was calligraphy, and the works of such great masters as Wang Hsi-chih (321–379), Liu Kung-ch'üan (d. A.D. 865), and Chao Meng-t'iao (d. A.D. 1322) were imitated throughout history (Selection 174). Perhaps second to calligraphy in importance was painting which, unlike calligraphy that could be made presentable through studious effort and constant practice, required a special talent of its own which could not be easily acquired (Selection 175). A cultured gentleman of traditional China was supposed to be versed in the four arts: the lute, chess, calligraphy, and painting; of the four, playing the lute was perhaps the least widespread.

Since not every Chinese could become a cultured gentleman, the pursuit of pleasure could not be always high-brow. In China as well as in many other parts of the world, the enjoyments most popular with a large section of the leisured class consisted of "wine, woman, and song" (Selections 176, 177, 178, 179, and 180). Prostitution was legal throughout Chinese history; in fact, it was not abolished until the Communists took over the country in 1949. Popular though it was, sexual indulgence was an expensive habit, and most Chinese, for economic if not other reasons, preferred more prosaic entertainments such as attending a theater or watching an animal show (Selections 181, 182, and 183). If expenses were an important consideration when seeking entertainment, a Chinese could not do better than to visit a tea house where for a penny or two not only could he have a fresh pot of tea but would also be entertained by a professional storyteller. Among the tales spun by the storyteller, few were more popular than those in *The Romance of the Three Kingdoms*. One of the tales he told might be a variation or elaboration of a general theme that appears here as Selection 184.

The audience of a storyteller in a tea house was mostly illiterate, and rarely could one find among the listeners a scholar-official, because he tended to regard such form of entertainment as below his dignity as a member of the gentry. For one thing, the stories told by the professional storytellers were conveyed in oral or colloquial form, and the scholars of traditional China looked down upon everything written in the spoken style. Generally speaking, they preferred short narratives, whether they be parables, fables, anecdotes, or short stories (such as the *ch'uan-ch'i* of the T'ang dynasty), all of which, of course, had to be written in the classical or literary style. From hindsight this facet of the Chinese literary heritage is perhaps the most interesting if not the most significant, though it is little known in the Western world. Selection 185 is a collection of parables, and the reader can make his own judgment as to their merit.

174 · T'ANG T'AI-TSUNG *et al.: Famous Calligraphers*

Wang Hsi-chih [1]

Wang Hsi-chih loved geese and would go a great distance to see one that was considered unusual. An old widow in K'uaichi [2] had a goose which crowed well, but which she refused to sell. Unable to obtain it, Wang and his friends decided to make a special trip to her house so as to see it themselves. Having heard that the famous calligrapher loved her goose and flattered by his forthcoming visit, the old widow killed the goose and prepared it in the most delicious manner. By the time he arrived, Wang found a tasteful but dead goose on the table instead of a live, talented goose which he had come to see.

A Taoist priest in Shanyin [3] loved to raise geese; and Wang Hsi-chih, after taking a look at the flock, was very pleased and wanted to buy some for himself. "I will give you all of my geese if you will handwrite for me the *Book of Taoist Virtue*," said the priest. Wang agreed and brought the geese home in a cage after he had completed the penmanship.

[1] Though the *History of the Tsin (Tsin shu)* was written by a committee headed by Fang Hsüan-ling, the "Biography of Wang Hsi-chih" (*Tsin shu*, roll 80), from which this selection is made, was believed to have been penned by the T'ang emperor T'ai-tsung (r.627–649) who was among Wang's most ardent admirers.
[2] Located in modern Chekiang province.
[3] Located in modern Chekiang province.

Paying a visit to a student of his one day, he was disappointed that his host was not home. He saw a bright, shining table in the house and decided to write a message on it. The student's father, not knowing the value of Wang's calligraphy, erased the message shortly after the visitor's departure. Returning home, the student learned what had happened and was sorrowful and depressed for several days.

One day at Chishan,[4] Wang Hsi-chih saw an old woman selling fans made of bamboo. To her surprise and chagrin, Wang wrote five characters on each of her fans. When the woman was about to voice her anger, he said to her: "Tell your customers that this calligraphy belongs to Wang Hsi-chih. You should charge no less than one hundred standard coins for each of your fans." The woman did according to what she had been told; to her happy surprise, people competed among themselves to buy her fans. Several days later, she came back for more calligraphy; Wang laughed and refused to honor her request.

Liu Kung-ch'üan [5]

Liu Kung-ch'üan, whose courtesy name was Ch'eng-hsüan, had loved learning since childhood and was able to write poetry well at the tender age of twelve. He passed the metropolitan examination and received the *chin-shih* degree in the first year of Yüan-ho (A.D. 806).

After Mu-tsung (r.821–824) ascended the throne as the emperor, he summoned Liu Kung-ch'üan for an interview. "I saw your penmanship in the Buddhist temples I have visited, and I have been looking forward to meeting you for a long time," said the emperor. He immediately appointed Liu as an adviser to the imperial government and an academician in the Hanlin Academy.

Mu-tsung was not considered an able, enlightened ruler. One day he asked Liu Kung-ch'üan about the proper methods whereby a person could become a good calligrapher. "The movement of the brush is directed by the mind," Liu replied. "The brush will move properly if the mind is rectified." The emperor changed his expression immediately since he knew that Liu's remarks had a double meaning. They were a remonstration, though indirect and implied.

At the beginning Liu Kung-ch'üan followed the style of Wang Hsi-chih and later diligently studied the contemporary great. Eventually he became the founder of a school of his own. His work was characteried by energy and strength as well as a sensual attractiveness. It was so popular that if a minister had failed to obtain his penmanship for his family's gravestones, he would be regarded as less than filial to the deceased. Whenever the barbarians bore tribute to China, they set aside a large sum of money marked: "For the purchase of Liu Kung-ch'üan's calligraphy only."

His mind being totally absorbed in his work, Liu Kung-ch'üan paid little attention to his own financial wellbeing. Meanwhile the mighty and the powerful were so anxious to obtain his calligraphy for their ancestors' gravestones that they paid him tens of thousands of standard coins each year for his service. He put the money in any utensil that happened to be nearby—a wine jug, a flower vase, or a water bowl. When his servants reported to him that the money had disappeared, he would smile and say: "Well, the money must have gone to Heaven." He would not mention the theft any more as if it had never occurred.

[4] Located in modern Chekiang province.
[5] "Biography of Liu Kung-ch'üan" (*Liu Kung-ch'üan chuan*); *T'ang shu,* roll 165.

He was very particular, however, about his inks, brushes, paintings, and calligraphic masterpieces. He locked them inside a vault, and would not let anyone open it except himself.

He died on the sixth year of Hsien-t'ung (A.D. 865) at the age of eighty-eight.

Chao Meng-t'iao [6]

Chao Meng-t'iao, whose courtesy name was Tzu-ang, was a native of Huchow [7] and a descendant of Sung T'ai-tsu.[8] He was born with high intelligence and could memorize a passage after reading it only once. In a moment's notice, he could write classical Chinese of great beauty which never needed to be polished or corrected. He became a government official at the age of fourteen.

In the third year of Chih-ta (1310) Chao Meng-t'iao was summoned to the capital and was subsequently appointed as a reader in the Hanlin Academy. He left the post after he had expressed disagreements with his colleagues in the composition of a sacrificial essay [9] and the naming of a palace. The crown prince had heard about his name for a long time; and, when he ascended the throne as Jen-tsung (r.1312–1320), Chao Meng-t'iao was once again called back to the capital. Chao was appointed as a reader in the Hanlin Academy in the first year of Yüan-yu (1314) and was promoted to the rank of academician two years later. The emperor called him by his courtesy name [10] and compared him with Li Po of the T'ang dynasty and Su Shih of the Sung dynasty. "Tzu-ang is not only virtuous as a gentleman and learned as a scholar but also unsurpassed as a calligrapher and a painter," said the emperor. "He is also proficient in the Buddhist and Taoist ideologies. As I look around, no one has a better claim to fame than he has." Some of the emperor's ministers attempted to slander Chao, but the emperor paid no attention.

Chao Meng-t'iao's writings, in prose as well as in poetry, are characterized by an element of quietness or serenity, so much so that when reading them one feels a strong desire to leave this world and join the monastic ranks. As for calligraphy, he was versatile enough as to be unsurpassed in all of its styles, from ancient to modern and from "block" to "grass." [11] Despite his many talents, it was calligraphy that made him famous both at home and abroad. Indian monks traveled thousands of *li* for the sole purpose of obtaining his calligraphic masterpieces. As for painting, he was particularly good in the painting of landscape, wood and stones, flowers and bamboo, and people and horses. The historian Yang Tsai once said: "Versatile as he was, Chao Meng-t'iao's true talents were overshadowed by his accomplishments in painting and calligraphy. Those who knew his achievement in these two fields tended to forget that he was also a great writer. Those who admired his writings sometimes neglected the fact that he was equally great as a statesman of noble ideas." This is perhaps the most appropriate comment ever made on the career of Chao Meng-t'iao.

[6] "Biography of Chao Meng-t'iao" (*Chao Meng-t'iao chuan); Yüan shih,* roll 172.
[7] Located in modern Chekaing province.
[8] Founder of the Sung dynasty.
[9] To be read by the emperor, or some one on his behalf, during a ceremony offering sacrifices to Heaven or Earth.
[10] This was equivalent to calling a person by his first name in a Western society.
[11] A character written in the "block" style *(li t'i)* looks like a printed character. A character written in the "grass" style *(ts'ao t'i)* has strokes that are supposedly shaped like grass, characterized by sweeping and generally graceful lines.

175 · Fang Hsüan-ling *et al.: Famous Painters*

Ku K'ai-chih [12]

Ku K'ai-chih, whose courtesy name was Ch'ang-k'ang, was a native of Wuhsi.[13] His father Yüeh-chih was at one time the vice president of the executive department [14] of the imperial government. K'ai-chih was as learned as he was talented.

Among K'ai-chih's many achievements the greatest was in the field of painting. Hsieh An [15] spoke of him highly and regarded him as the greatest painter since the beginning of mankind. Whenever he painted a portrait, he always painted the eyes last, and sometimes the eyes were not added until several years had elapsed. Asked the reason for this peculiar habit, he replied: "As far as the body is concerned, the difference between people is comparatively little. What makes one person so distinctly different from others is his eyes which alone reflect his individuality. How can a painter not be careful when he paints the eyes?"

At one time he was interested in a girl in his neighborhood, but the girl was unresponsive to his advances. He painted the girl's portrait on a wall and then pierced her painted heart with a needle. Immediately the girl suffered heart pain as he had expected. He propositioned her again, and this time she agreed. He took the needle away from the portrait, and she was recovered to her normal health.

K'ai-chih could paint a person to his exact likeness, and sometimes the man depicted in the painting looked more like the man than the man looked like himself. When he made a portrait of P'ei K'ai, for instance, he added three strands of hair to his checks, even though the real P'ei K'ai did not have any hair on his checks. The result was much more satisfactory because it caught the spirit as well as the outward likeness of the portrayed subject.

One day he packed some of his most cherished paintings in a carefully sealed box and then sent them to Huan Hsüan for safekeeping. Upon receiving the treasure, Huan Hsüan opened the box at its lower end and took out the paintings; he then lied to the sender that he had never opened the box. Noticing that the seal had not been tampered with even though the box was empty, K'ai-chih did not show the slightest suspicion that the paintings might have been stolen. "All things, when reaching perfection, will ascend to Heaven," he commented calmly. "This is true with man; it is also true with paintings."

People say that Ku K'ai-chih possessed three unusual qualities: unusually bright, unusually artistic, and unusually naive.

Wu Tao-tzu and Li Ssu-hsün [16]

Wu Tao-hsüan, whose courtesy name was Tao-tzu, became a master painter while still in his teens. One day during the T'ien-pao period (742–755) he suddenly thought of the majestic scenery of the Chialing River [17] and decided to journey to Szechuan to take a look at it himself. Returning to the capital, he was

[12] Ku K'ai-chih lived in the fourth century A.D. and died in 410 or thereabouts. Source: "Biography of Ku K'ai-chih" *(Ku K'ai-chih chuan); Tsin shu*, roll 92.
[13] Located in modern Kiangsu province.
[14] *Shang-shu.*
[15] A statesman of the Tsin dynasty.
[16] *Commentaries on the T'ang Paintings (T'ang hua tuan).*
[17] A river that pours into the Yangtze at Chungking.

asked by Emperor Hsüan-tsung (r.713–755) whether he had transcribed his observations to the canvas. "I did not carry my painting materials with me," he replied; "but I have memorized everything I saw." He was ordered by the emperor to project what he saw on the walls of the Tat'ung Palace, and he completed in one day a landscape that covered the entire Chialing River in its three-hundred-*li* tortuous route.

Then Li Ssu-hsün, a landscape painter of equal fame, was also projecting his masterpieces on the walls of the Tat'ung Palace. However, it took him several months to finally complete his work. "Mr. Wu paints quickly while Mr. Li works in a slow pace," the emperor commented, "but each is unsurpassed in his own style."

Tung Ch'i-ch'ang [18]

Tung Ch'i-ch'ang, whose courtesy name was Yüan-tsai, was a native of Sung-kiang.[19] He passed the metropolitan examination and received the *chin-shih* degree in the seventeenth year of Wan-li (1589).

As for his painting, he first followed the style of Mi Fei [20] of the Sung dynasty and then founded a school of his own. His works might be said to have synthesized the good points of all of the Sung-Ming schools without their defects; as a painter, he was known both at home and abroad. He followed his own design whenever he painted; being unconventional, his works were characterized by a natural gracefulness which no other painter could hope to match.

Tung Ch'i-ch'ang was equally famous for seal carving and calligraphy. Hardly did a day pass without someone requesting his work. Even a letter or a brief note of his become a collector's item, and people were willing to pay a high price for it. He was profound and discriminating as a critic—a single word in his own handwriting commanded such attention that a collector would consider it a matter of great prestige to have obtained it.

As a person, he was gentle as well as genteel; he never uttered a vulgar word as far as anybody could recall. He was thoroughly familiar with Buddhist ideology. People often compared him to Mi Fei of the Sung dynasty and Chao Meng-t'iao of the Yüan dynasty.

He died in the ninth year of Ch'ung-chen (1636) at the age of eighty-three.

176 · CHANG TAI: *The Seventh Full Moon in the West Lake* [21]

On the full moon of the seventh month there is not much to be seen in the West Lake [22] except the people who come to see the moon. Of the moon watchers there are five kinds.

[18] "Biography of Tung Ch'i-ch'ang" *(Tung Ch'i-ch'ang chuan); Ming shih,* roll 288.
[19] Located in modern Kiangsu province.
[20] Mi Fei (1051–1107) was famous for landscape painting.
[21] Chang Tai, who lived in the seventeenth century, was a prolific writer of light topics. His best known book was *My Reminiscences (T'ao-an meng-yi)* from which this selection is taken.
[22] The West Lake is a scenic spot and famous tourist attraction located west of Hangchow, Chekiang province. The fifteenth day (full moon) of the seventh month is a day of Buddhist festival and people in Hangchow, then as now, visit the lake in large numbers.

The first kind consists of those who come in large boats equipped with flutes, drums, and other musical instruments. Under the light one can see not only well-dressed hosts and guests but also entertainers and servants. While music wafts through the air, the occupants are enjoying a meal of delicacies. They come to see the moon, but they never see it throughout the evening.

The second group arrives in the same fashion as the first group—large boats with two or three decks. The occupants are the daughters of celebrated families, accompanied by young male slaves. Laughs and cries are mingled; who can tell one from the other? Sometimes they move to the open decks where they sit and turn their eyes from left to right and then from right to left. They are underneath the moon, but they never see it.

The third group comes in boats that are likewise equipped with music. Here the hosts are surrounded by prostitutes of note and monks of leisure. The music is soft, the singing is low, and the occupants, enjoying the atmosphere, sip their wine in the most leisurely manner. Though underneath the moon, they are more interested in seeing others seeing them than in seeing the moon.

The fourth group comes with neither boats nor vehicles. Dressed in the most informal manner, they fill their stomachs with meat and wine the first time they have the opportunity. Then in groups of three or five, they push themselves into wherever there is a crowd. They are in Chaoch'ing and then they are in Tuanch'iao.[23] They make noises wherever they go, singing loudly even though they cannot carry a tune and acting like drunkards even though they are sober. In name they come to see what can be seen: the moon, the moon-watchers, and those who do not watch the moon. Actually they are not interested in seeing anything.

The last group rides in small boats decorated with curtains made of light silk. Inside the boats are small, narrow tables that are crystal clear, plus wine warmers and tea makers that are ready to serve whenever serving is called for. The hosts and their friends, both male and female, sit and watch the moon or, whenever they choose, hide themselves underneath the shadow of a huge tree. Oftentimes they repair to the Inner Lake[24] to escape from the noisy crowd. They come to see the moon, but nobody can see them. In fact, they do not feel that they have missed anything even if they never saw the moon.

The people in Hangchow visit the lake between eleven in the morning and seven in the afternoon, and they avoid the moon as if it were a deadly enemy. Yet, on the evening of the fifteenth day of the seventh month, they go to the lake in large numbers, ostensibly for the purpose of watching the moon. They generously tip the gate keepers,[25] and then go straight to the shore of the lake where the sedan-chair bearers, holding the torches high, help them into the boat. Once in the boat, they order the boatmen to row to Tuanch'iao as fast as possible so that they will not be late for the elaborate Buddhist rituals. Thus before ten

[23] Chaoch'ing is the name of a temple located on the northeastern shore of the lake. Tuanch'iao is the name of a bridge in the northern section of the lake, reportedly built by the T'ang poet Po Chü-yi (772–846) who was then the mayor of Hangchow.

[24] Located in the northern side of the West Lake, separated from the main water by a causeway.

[25] During the Ming dynasty Hangchow, like most cities in China, was surrounded by a wall, and people went into or came from the city via the city gates. Since then the wall has been torn down.

o'clock there is nothing to hear except noise and nothing to see except crowds. All boats, large and small, rush towards the shore at the same time: all one can see is poles [26] clashing against poles, boats bumping into boats, shoulders rubbing against shoulders, and faces meeting faces.

It does not take long before all of these excitements are over. The soldiers cry aloud to pave the way for the officials to return home, soon after the banquets have come to a close. The sedan-chair bearers rush the boatmen to row faster, lest the city gates will be closed before they reach there. Along the roads are lamps and torches that shine like stars; they move in groups that follow one another. Meanwhile those who have spent the evening on the shore are also rushing towards the city gates before they are closed. The crowd becomes thinner and thinner until it eventually disappears.

It is only then that we anchor our boats against the shore of Tuanch'iao. We sit on the stone steps that have begun to feel cool, and we call upon our guests to drink as much as they can. At this time the moon looks like a mirror only recently cleaned; the mountains are more beautiful than ever; and the lake seems to have once again washed her own face. Those who love soft music and leisurely drinking have finally emerged; so do those who until then have hidden themselves under the shadows of the trees. To them we send our invitation; and if they are too modest to accept, we drag them by their hands. Here come the friendly poets and the cultured prostitutes with whom we share our wine and music. The merriment continues until the moonlight becomes feeble and the day is about to dawn. Our guests bid us good-bye; and we, finally, return to our own boat. The boat wanders its way among a sea of lotus flowers, while we sleep soundly in it. The air is full of fragrance: can there be a better environment to induce a beautiful dream?

177 · Ssu-ma Ch'ien: *Drinking* [27]

In a joyful mood, King Wen [28] invited Shun-yü K'un to drink in his palace.

"Sir, how much can you drink before you become intoxicated?" asked the king.

"Your servant may become intoxicated after one goblet or may not become intoxicated after ten goblets," K'un replied.

"If you become intoxicated after one goblet, how can you possibly drink ten goblets? Will you explain this inconsistency for me?"

"Yes, sir," K'un replied. "When I drink before Your Majesty, with prosecution attorneys on my left and right and royal censors behind my back, I tremble with such fear that I can drink comfortably only when I prostrate on the floor. In such a case it will not take one goblet before I become intoxicated. When my parents invite a man of high position as their guest, with my sleeves rolled up, I bend my knees so as to serve them. From time to time they give me the leftovers with which I toast them and pay them my tribute. Several rounds later, I have drunk about two goblets which are more than enough to make me intoxicated. If on the

---

[26] Boat-poles.
[27] "Biographies of Jesters" (*Hua-chi lieh-chuan*); *Shih chi*, roll 126.
[28] King Wen of Ch'i, fourth century B.C.

other hand I encounter by accident an old friend whom I have not seen for a long time and with whom I can exchange affection and reminiscences, I shall not become intoxicated until I have swallowed five or six goblets.

"From time to time there are country gatherings when men and women sit intermingled around the same table and sip their wine unhurriedly and at ease. They can gamble a little if they wish to and play the pitch-pot game [29] whenever they choose. Each seeks his own partner; there is no inhibition against staring at a beautiful woman or holding her hands. The merriment continues until earrings and hairpins leave their owners in quick succession and are scattered all over the place. How much I enjoy this! I can drink eight goblets and still remain sober.

"At dusk, most drinkers are gone and we the remainder, men and women, join our goblets and sit closely together. Our feet are interwoven underneath, and cups and dishes are scattered about in total confusion. The hall is dim, since the candles above it have been put out. Eventually our hostess escorts all the guests out, with me as the only exception. I open her silk blouse, and I loosen her skirt—I smell a faint fragrance. This is the time I am the happiest: I can drink as much as ten goblets. . . ."

"Well said," said the king. He ordered that the all-night drinking which had been previously planned be immediately suspended.

178 · SUN CH'I: *The P'ingk'ang Village* [30]

The three blocks inside the city wall [31] and to the east of the Northern Gate was the P'ingk'ang Village where most of the city's prostitutes lived. The best among them lived in the southern and central blocks, while the less expensive ones lived in the block next to the wall. The last-mentioned group was looked down upon by those who reside further to the south. The houses located in the middle section of the southern block could be reached via the Cross Street. The scholars who had passed the metropolitan examination and had thus secured positions with the government often came here for a visit.

In the middle of each of the two better blocks were three houses that were as elegant as they were expensive. They were quiet and spacious. Each house contained a main hall that had a garden in its front as well as in its rear. The garden was planted with bushes and flowers, interposed by oddly shaped rocks and water pools. Across the hall were the apartments that were beautifully decorated with screens, curtains, cushions, and beds. Each apartment housed one prostitute, and all the furnishings inside the apartment were exclusively hers. Inside the main hall was a many-colored board on which were recorded the death anniversaries of emperors and empresses.[32]

Most of the so-called "mothers" in these brothels were not true mothers; they were aged, retired prostitutes. Some of these prostitutes were bought from beggars when they were very young. Others were former servants employed in low-income households. In the latter case, more often than not they had sexual relations with

[29] An ancient game in which arrows were thrown into a vase placed at a distance.

[30] *A Story of the Northern Villages (Pei-li chi)*, roll 1, by Sun Ch'i who lived in the ninth century.

[31] The city wall of Ch'angan, capital of the T'ang dynasty.

[32] During these anniversary days all business transactions were legally forbidden, including that in the brothels.

bad men before they became prostitutes. Sometimes these servant girls were officially married to men of reputable families who later sold them because for reasons of their own they did not wish to turn down the high price offered by the brothels. Once they were in, these girls could never get out.

The "mothers" first taught the girls how to sing. Since they wanted their investment to yield interest as early as possible, they pushed hard on their training program. If the girls were lazy, reluctant, or slow in learning, their "mothers" would beat them without mercy.

These "mothers" did not have husbands of their own. Those who were comparatively young or attractive were kept by rich men as mistresses. In other cases, they kept lovers of their own choice. These lovers, being supported by their women, did not receive the respect as normally accorded to husbands.

I have also visited brothels in Loyang.[33] The girls in that city were generally superior to the "barmaids"[34] found in the provinces. Yet they still showed shyness when eating with their customers; they were punctiliously correct in their mannerism and were generally unsure of themselves. The girls in the P'ingk'ang Village, on the other hand, were at home with customers of all kinds, whether they be ministers or scholars. Only when a customer's rank was unusually high would they perform the ritual of kowtow. There was little the mayor of the capital could do with regard to these customers. One measure he could have taken was to restrict the movement of their sedan-chair bearers; in such a case, he might have been able to prevent them from visiting this place.

The girls were not allowed to step out from the P'ingk'ang Village, however temporarily. Only on the eighth day of each month when the monks in the Paot'ang Temple in the South Street gave sermons on Buddhist scriptures would they be permitted to leave the village in groups to attend the sermons. Before their departure, however, each of them had to pay her "mother" a permission fee of one hundred standard coins. She could not leave the village otherwise, unless she were invited and escorted by a customer, or had invited a customer as her escort. In either case, she would have to deposit a sizeable sum as security before she was allowed to leave. Since people knew that the girls customarily visited the Paot'ang Temple on the eighth day of each month, they swarmed to that temple in droves on that day, in the hope that they might receive favor from these girls.

There was an old woman from Pienchou[35] who had a rented house in the village, next to the house where a group of musicians lived. Her house was well furnished with fine clothes, utensils, and other household items. She was wealthy and had several girls under her custody. Unlike the prostitutes in other houses, her girls could be summoned to a place preferred by their customers. An invitation to any of these girls for a drink cost eighteen taels of silver. The price would be doubled if the customer wanted her to stay for a longer period, *i.e.*, long enough to burn two consecutive candles.

[33] The second largest city in China during the T'ang dynasty, next only to Ch'angan, the capital.
[34] "Barmaids" or *yin chi* (literally, "drinking prostitutes") who drank with their customers as part of their professional duties.
[35] Modern Kaifeng, Honan province.

179 · CHANG TAI: *River Houses Along the Ch'inhuai River* [36]

The river houses along the Ch'inhuai River [37] can serve any or all of the following purposes: temporary housing, social gathering, and sexual indulgence. Though the rent is high, rarely has been a room vacant for a single day. Pleasure boats, playing music, go to and fro along the river and zigzag around these houses.

Outside each river house is an exposed terrace protected by red railings and enclosed with open silk. To assure privacy, bamboo curtains and silk screens are used to separate one section of the terrace from the other. In summer months the girls sit leisurely on the terrace after their bath; and when a breeze gently lifts up the edge of their skirts, one smells a scent of jasmine, heavenly enchanting. They wear light silk and keep themselves cool with round fans. The hair on the temples is loose, and the curls, casually tied together, are leaning towards one side. They are soft, charming, and irresistible.

On the day of the dragon festival,[38] men and women in the capital [39] swarm to the river houses to see the lantern boat parade. Several hundred small sailboats are linked together, and on the sail of each is hanging a chain of horn-shaped lanterns that looks like a string of pearls from a distance. Sometimes a thousand of such boats are tied together, each boat's bow being chained to the next one's stern. When the whole thing moves, it looks like a dragon made of lanterns or a serpent made of fire. It twists and turns; it coils and then stretches. Lights from the boats and their reflections in the water are madly shooting at one another. From the boats comes a profusion of music, so interwoven and loud that it sounds like water boiling in a pot. Men and women, leaning against the railings on the terraces, talk among themselves and laugh loudly at the sight. There is so much to hear and so much to see; how ardently one wishes that he had been born with more eyes and ears! It is not until midnight that the music slowly vanishes and the lights become scattered. Like stars at dawn, the spectators disappear, one after another.

Chung Pai-ching [40] wrote a *fu* [41] entitled "Lantern Boats in the Ch'inhuai River." It describes the festival in great detail.

180 · TS'AI-HENG-TZU: *Boy Actors in Peking* [42]

A drama troupe in Peking usually has a dozen or so boy actors. Each of these boys learns only two or three dramas and acts in them; the number is deliberately kept small so he can be truly proficient in the role or roles which he plays. What-

[36] Source: *T'ao-an meng-yi.*
[37] A river that passes through the city of Nanking. Beginning in the fifth century A.D. the areas adjacent to the river were widely known for their entertainment facilities, including houses of prostitution.
[38] Celebrated on the fifth day of the fifth lunar month.
[39] Nanking.
[40] Pai-ching was the courtesy name of Chung Hsing who, like the author, lived in the Ming dynasty.
[41] A lengthy form of poetry.
[42] Ts'ai-heng-tzu was the pen name of an anonymous author who lived in the nineteenth century. Source: *The Cry of An Insect (Ch'ung-ming man-lu).*

ever part he has in a play, it is usually accentuated by satire or humor; and it does not take too long before he can make a name for himself. If he has a clean, white complexion and is unusually good-looking, it is safe to assume that he has other skills unknown to outsiders.

The drama troupes buy these boys from faraway places, and most of them come from Soochow, Hangchow, Anhwei, and Chekiang. The troupes deliberately choose those who are unusually attractive; and once chosen, these boys are taught to speak and walk in the most charming manner and to use their eyes with great efficiency. Their owners will not be satisfied until they reach the stage of perfection. Soon after they get up in the morning, they wash their faces with meat broth. They drink nothing except egg soup, and their meal consists of the choicest, tenderest meat. Before they go to bed, their whole bodies are covered with medicine; the only exception is their hands and feet that are not covered so as to make sure that they will not become sick as a result of skin suffocation.

Three or four months after the training program begins, these boys are as delicate and genteel as lovely maidens. One glance from them will create hundreds of charms. Facing them, even a man like Liu Hsia-hui or Lu Nan-tzu [43] would not be able to escape their ensnarement.

Since their natural voice is different, these boys are taught to sing roles most congenial to their endowment.

I saw some of these boy actors in the Sanch'ing drama troupe. All of them were about fourteen or fifteen years old. After they finished their singing, they helped me with my drinks. They wore clothes made of light silk, and their sleeves were narrow and tight. They were so delicate and lovely that one could not but feel a sentiment of endearment.

On the stage these boy actors play all kinds of roles, not necessarily the impersonation of females.

181 · LIU OH: *Lao-ts'an Attends a Theater* [44]

It was about ten o'clock in the morning that Lao-ts'an arrived at the Minghu Theater. There were more than one hundred tables in front of the stage, but practically all of them had already been occupied. Only seven or eight tables remained vacant, each of which was pasted with a slip of red paper indicating that it had been reserved for the governor's office, the circular court, or the department of education. Lao-ts'an wandered around the theater for a long time, but he could not find a seat. Finally he took out two hundred copper coins and handed them over to one of the ushers. The usher came back with a small bench and seated him in the midst of a group of other spectators.

On the stage was a small, rectangular table on which was placed a flat drum. On top of the flat drum was a pair of iron clappers which Lao-ts'an immediately recognized as the often-talked-about "pear clappers." Beside the flat drum was placed a three-stringed guitar. Behind the rectangular table were two chairs that

---

[43] Two legendary figures each of whom was said to have successfully resisted temptation when, in the middle of the night, a lovely woman came to his room, sat on his lap, and begged for his attention. Both of them were praised highly by China's ancient sages.

[44] *The Travels of Lao-ts'an (Lao-ts'an yu-chi),* Chapter 2.

were not yet occupied. These were the only things on the stage. The stage was so large that it looked rather ridiculous since it was so empty.

By eleven o'clock more people began to arrive in carriages and sedan chairs. These were government officials who, accompanied by their servants, were all attired in informal street clothes. By twelve o'clock the seven or eight tables in front of the stage were all occupied. Still there were more people coming in and they, like us common people, were forced to sit on small benches temporarily placed in the midst of a big crowd. These officials saluted one another when they met; they talked and laughed and seemed to thoroughly enjoy themselves. Aside from these officials, most of the audience seemed to be merchants, though here and there one might encounter a few who looked like intellectuals. All of the spectators talked among themselves; since the crowd was so large and the noise so deafening, nobody knew what people outside of his own group were talking about.

Around 12:30 P.M. a man wearing a blue gown emerged from a backstage and stepped forward. He had a long, narrow face which, being completely covered with pimples, looked like the skin of a dry orange and was extremely repulsive to the eyes. However, his demeanor was gentle and dignified. He seated himself in the left chair without a word; then he slowly picked up the three-stringed guitar from the table. He adjusted the strings and played one or two popular melodies, but nobody in the audience seemed to give him much attention. Then he played one of those classical compositions, the name of which, unfortunately, Lao-ts'an could no longer remember. The player rolled over the strings with his right fingers, and the guitar yielded a stream of sound extremely pleasant to the ears. The sound alternated between the high and the low notes in quick succession, so quick that the guitar seemed to have scores of strings and the player hundreds of fingers. The audience responded with repeated "bravos"; and loud as the audience's shoutings were, they could not submerge the music that continued to stream out from the man's instrument. When finally he stopped, a man from the backstage brought him a cup of tea.

Several minutes passed. When again the backstage curtain was pushed aside, a girl emerged before the audience. She looked about sixteen or seventeen and had a delicate face shaped like a duck's egg. Her hair was coiled into a bun, and her earrings were those made of silver. She was dressed in a blue jacket and a pair of blue trousers, both of which were fringed with bands of yellow cloth. Though her clothes did not seem to be those of the finest quality, they looked neat and clean. The girl took the right seat behind the rectangular table, and the guitar player played again.

Following the music, the girl stood up. With her left hand she picked up the clappers and held them between her fingers. The clappers went up and down and yielded a tinkling sound that was repeated to accentuate the music. A moment passed. Then she picked up the drum stick with her right hand while listening attentively to the melody. At a precise moment she suddenly beat the drum and began to sing. Each word she sang was clear and crisp; the whole song was so effectively rendered that it seemed to have come from "a golden oriole flying skyward from a deep gorge" or "a young swallow returning home to join her parents." Each line of her song contained seven syllables,[45] and each passage consisted of

[45] Seven Chinese characters.

ten lines. Sometimes she rushed quickly through the lines and then slowed down; other times she raised her voice to a high pitch, only to drop it to render a low, soft, and melodious tune. The numerous twists and turns were extremely pleasant to the ears and yet totally unpredictable. As far as Lao-ts'an was concerned, this was the best song he had ever heard.

A man sitting next to Lao-ts'an whispered to his neighbor and asked him whether this young singer was the famous Miss White. "No," said his neighbor. "This girl is called Miss Black, the younger sister of Miss White. She learned to sing from her elder sister to whom she is regarded as inferior. A discriminating critic can describe how good Miss Black is, but he will have a difficult time to find words that can do justice to Miss White's performance. Miss Black's style can be imitated, but Miss White's is so unique that nobody has been able to come close to it. For several years many singers have tried to copy her style, including many in the brothels, but all they can hope to achieve is the level of her younger sister. To my knowledge, no singer has been able to reach one-tenth of her perfection." By the time this man finished his comment, Miss Black had already completed her singing and retreated to the backstage.

While waiting for the next number, the audience resumed their laughing and talking. The vendors went to and fro and shouted aloud to sell their wares; roasted watermelon seeds, peanuts, wild nuts, almond nuts, etc. Once again it was noise instead of music that dominated the theater.

While the noise went on, there emerged on the stage another girl who looked about eighteen or nineteen, dressed almost identically to the first girl. She had a white, oval face and was only a little above average insofar as physical attractiveness was concerned. Yet she possessed an element of elegance which seemed to have uplifted her into a different category in which our earthly concept of attractiveness or beauty could no longer apply. Her head bowing slightly, she walked slowly towards the back of the rectangular table where she picked up the two iron clappers. The two clappers, once in her hand, seemed to have suddenly undergone a great transformation; they produced a sound that could have only come from a combination of all of the tuneful instruments in the world. Gently she beat the drum twice, and it was only then that she raised her head for the first time. She cast a glance at the audience, and the audience was enchanted.

How could anyone describe creditably that pair of eyes? They were like water in the fall, cool, tranquil, and crystal clear; they were like two stars in a cold, dark night; they were like a pair of precious pearls inlaid in white mercury of the purest quality. Inside the precious pearls were two black, shining crystals which, moving from left to right and then from right to left, made every spectator in the audience feel that she, the famous singer, was to perform for him, and him alone. Those who sat close to the stage were so enchanted as to be bewitched. There was total silence in the theater as if His Majesty the Emperor had personally appeared. The drop of a pin on the floor would have sounded like a thunderbolt.

Miss White, as this girl was called, opened her mouth and revealed two lines of teeth that were as shining as they were white. She sang a few lines in a gentle, soft voice which, passing through the spectator's ears, soon affected his entire body. It seemed that all of his internal organs were being smoothed by a cool iron and that all of his skin pores had become wide open. About ten lines later, the melody rose higher and higher; and, suddenly, like a steel wire throwing upward into the sky, it reached a crescendo. Nobody uttered a word, but everybody yelled a silent "bravo." Reaching the crescendo, the melody began to whirl around as if it were circling a giant mountain. It orbited around the mountain several times before it rose again to reach a new peak around which it circled again. It climbed one peak after another, and each peak became more precarious than the preceding one. Finally, after it had reached the highest point, it began to drop. Like a flying serpent, it turned around each of the peaks in its descent which it had only recently climbed. Meanwhile her voice became softer and softer until it became totally inaudible.

For two or three minutes the audience held its breath in total silence. Then it heard a barely audible thin voice that seemed to have come from the ground. The voice became stronger and stronger; suddenly and without a warning, it darted straight towards the sky. In the sky it burst into thousands of variations, like a giant firecracker which had been suddenly transformed into millions of shining, sparkling stars, of all colors and of all shapes. All this time the three-stringed guitar escorted the voice in confidence and went with it in harmony in all of its adventurous courses. Sometimes the sound from the guitar was high; other times it was low. Sometimes it was strong; other times it was weak. It could be compared with hundreds of birds chattering in a flower garden in a spring morning; and the chatterings were so mixed and intertwined that no one could tell the exact bird from which a particular sound came.

While the audience was completely carried away in enchantment, both the voice and the guitar stopped. A thunderous applause followed, and wave after wave of "bravos" deafened the ear. When the noise finally subsided, Lao-ts'an heard a young man of about thirty, who had been sitting in the front, make the following comment with a Hunanese accent: [46] "Formerly, whenever I encountered the statement in our ancient books that 'A piece of well-executed music will haunt the stage for three days after the performance,' I was frankly dubious. Now I know how correct this statement is."

182 · LIN SSU-HUAN: *Mimicry* [47]

In the capital [48] there was a mimic who was extremely good in imitating sounds.

At a dinner party I attended, he was invited to entertain. He set up a screen of about eight feet in height in the northeastern corner of the dining hall. Behind the screen were a table on which were placed a fan and a ruler, and a chair where the mimic sat. All the guests sat in a semicircle around the screen.

Moments later, the guests heard a crisp sound made with the ruler behind the screen. Everybody became suddenly quiet; there was not even a murmur from the audience.

The audience first heard a dog bark in a long, narrow valley in the distance. A woman was suddenly waked up by the dog's bark, stretching her arms and yawning. Meanwhile her husband was murmuring in his sleep. A moment later, a baby woke up and began to cry. The woman comforted him by feeding him with

[46] This young man presumably came from Hunan province, South China.
[47] Lin Ssu-huan, a native of Fukien, lived in the seventeenth ventury. A copy of the original can be found in *Ming Ch'ing san-wen hsien*, pp. 131–132.
[48] Peking.

her breast, but the baby was still crying. She gently patted his back and hummed along. By then the elder son also woke up and annoyed his mother with a string of vexatious words, only half intelligible and seemingly endless. Losing her temper, she hit him with her hand. At this moment a multitude of sounds had emerged from behind the screen: the sound that came from the woman's spanking of her elder son, her humming to comfort the baby, the baby's crying while sucking his mother's breast, the elder son's complaints shortly after waking up, and the husband's scolding of the boy. These sounds were so realistic that they seemed to be real.

The guests stretched their necks, looked at one another, and applauded in silence. They had never experienced anything so enjoyable.

A minute later, they heard the husband's snoring, and the woman's patting of the baby became softer and more intermittent until it finally stopped. Then they heard the sizzling sound of a mouse who, apparently in search for food, tipped over an earthenware vessel. The woman coughed while sleeping.

Influenced by what they had heard, the audience also became more restful. They stretched their legs and felt relaxed and comfortable.

Suddenly some one shouted: "Fire!" The husband jumped out from his bed and shouted "Fire," and the wife did the same. The two children cried simultaneously. A moment later, hundreds of people were shouting "Fire," hundreds of children were crying, and hundreds of dogs were barking. In the midst one heard the forcible pulling of the walls and their subsequent collapse. There were also the sounds of explosion, accompanied by the blowing of the wind. Hundreds of people were crying for help, while firemen were attempting to pull down houses. Those whose houses were burning were rushing to and fro, trying to save their belongings. Meanwhile one heard water splashing all over the places.

All the sounds in a fire were clearly there. Even if a man had a hundred hands, each of which in turn had a hundred fingers, he could not point out all the hustle and bustle that were then taking place. Even if he had a hundred mouths, each of which in turn had a hundred tongues, he could not name all of the items involved in this assimilated fire.

The listeners were so astonished that their facial expressions changed, and they were about to leave their seats. Some rolled up their sleeves and exposed their arms as if they were about to fight the fire. Others were trembling with fear, and their legs, still shaking, refused to take them away quickly from their seats.

Suddenly they heard the ruler once again beating against the table, and all sounds from behind the screen disappeared. The screen was pushed aside; there were the man, the table, the chair, the fan, the ruler, and nothing else.

183 · T'AO TSUNG-YI: *Animal Show* [49]

The day when I was at Hangchow,[50] I went to see an animal show. The trainer had seven turtles of different sizes which he placed on a small table. At the sound of a drum, the largest turtle moved to the center of the table and stood

[49] T'ao Tsung-yi, a native of Chekiang and a prolific writer, lived in the fourteenth century. The original appears in *A Little Rest from My Farm Labors (Cho-keng lu).*
[50] Capital of modern Chekiang province.

still. The second largest turtle climbed up to its back and was then followed by the third largest turtle. This process went on until the smallest turtle climbed up and perched on the back of the next smallest turtle. The smallest turtle then stood up on its head as well as its fore legs, and stretched its tail upward. The whole structure looked like a small pagoda. In fact, the trainer called this show "the building of a turtle pagoda."

A moment later, the trainer placed nine frogs and one small mound on the table. The largest of the frogs moved towards the mound and perched on its top, while the eight small frogs lined up in two rows of four, facing each other in front of the mound. When the largest frog made one sound, the small frogs responded by making one sound. When it made several, they responded likewise. Then one after another each of the small frogs walked towards the largest one, nodded its head, made noises, and then retreated. It seemed that each of them had performed an act of homage. The trainer called this show "the king frog holds a court."

In Sungkiang[51] I met a Taoist priest who resided in the T'aiku Temple. Each day he picked up from the temple pond two carps of similar size, one yellow and one black. Using a sharp knife that was coated with medicine, he cut both fish into two pieces right through the middle. Then he joined the front part of one carp with the back part of the other. Two new fish emerged, each of which had a two-tone color. He threw them back into the pond, and both fish swam as lively as ever. A man named Wei Li-chung, who came from the Sungkiang area, took one of these fish home and placed it in a water basin. It lasted fifteen days before it finally died.

184 · LO KUAN-CHUNG: *Borrow Arrows from the Enemy*[52]

After Chou Yü had made up his mind that K'ung-ming[53] would have to be eliminated, he conveyed his decision to Lu Su, one of his chief advisers.

"You cannot kill a man without a justifiable cause," Lu Su protested.

"I shall kill him with a justifiable cause," said Chou Yü. "He will die, but he will not blame me for his impending death."

"How can you invent a justifiable cause when there is none?"

"You will find it out tomorrow," Chou Yü replied.

The next day Chou Yü summonded all of his generals to appear in his commanding tent. Then he invited K'ung-ming to come in to discuss military strategy for the forthcoming battle.[54]

"In our present struggle against Ts'ao Ts'ao," said Chou Yü, "we will have to fight two battles simultaneously, one on land and the other on water. Will you kindly tell me, sir, what weapon is the most important?"

"I should say that bow and arrows are the most important in fighting a river battle," K'ung-ming replied.

"I cannot agree with you more," said Chou Yü. "We are now in great shortage

[51] Located in modern Kiangsu province.

[52] *The Romance of the Three Kingdoms (San-kuo yen-yi)*, Chapter 46.

[53] K'ung-ming was the courtesy name of Chu-ko Liang who later became the prime minister of Shu, one of the Three Kingdoms in the third century A.D.

[54] This was the Battle of Ch'ihpi (modern Anhwei province) in which the southerners, under the leadership of Sun Ch'üan and his prime minister Chou Yü, decisively defeated Ts'ao Ts'ao and prevented the unification of China by the northerners. The battle, fought in A.D. 208, ushered in the period of the Three Kingdoms.

of arrows. I am wondering whether I can bother you with the task of supervising the production of 100,000 arrows. Since this is a matter of great importance, I trust that you will not decline my request."

"How can I decline a request from you, sir? May I know when you need these arrows?"

"Can you deliver them in a period of, say, ten days?"

"Ts'ao Ts'ao's army will arrive at any moment. The delivery would not be of any use if it were to be made in such a long period as ten days."

"When do you think you can deliver them then?"

"I should have them ready at the end of three days."

"How can you make 100,000 arrows in three days? I hope you understand that we do not exchange jokes when discussing military campaigns."

"How dare I joke with you, sir? I am willing to sign a pledge that if I cannot deliver 100,000 arrows at the end of three days, you can punish me as severely as you choose."

Chou Yü was pleased; he asked his secretary immediately to draft a pledge to incorporate what K'ung-ming had promised. He drank a toast to his intended victim and then said that after the battle was over, the latter would be abundantly rewarded.

"It is already late today," said K'ung-ming. "But I shall begin my work tomorrow. At the end of the three days, please send 500 soldiers to collect the arrows on the river bank." He drank a few more cups of wine before he finally left.

"Is this man stupid or is he playing a trick upon us?" asked Lu Su.

"He is requesting his own death sentence," Chou Yü replied. "He certainly cannot blame me since he has voluntarily signed a written pledge in front of all of us, including the generals. However clever he is, he cannot escape from my palm even if he had two wings. I shall order the arrow-makers to go slow with their work; moreover, they will not be adequately supplied with raw materials. I cannot see how he can possibly complete his task in three days. At the end of the three days he will have no defense when I sentence him to death. Pay him a visit and see what he is doing. Then make a report to me in person."

"Please help me," said K'ung-ming to Lu Su who had come to see him. "How can I possibly make 100,000 arrows in three days?"

"You ask for trouble and you get it. There is nothing I can do."

"Yes, there is," said K'ung-ming. "Please lend me twenty ships, each of which is to be covered with curtains of blue cloth and to be tied with a thousand straw bundles on both sides. In each ship please place thirty soldiers. If you help me with this arrangement, I guarantee that there will be 100,000 arrows at the end of three days. Please do not mention this to Chou Yü. If you do, my plan will be ruined."

Lu Su agreed to his request and, true to his words, did not mention the loan of ships to Chou Yü when making his personal report. He only said that K'ung-ming had a peculiar way of making arrows which did not require the usual raw materials such as bamboo, feather, glue, and lacquer. Chou Yü was puzzled. "I shall see what kind of answer he has for me at the end of the three days," he commented.

Meanwhile Lu Su secretly prepared the ships in accordance with K'ung-ming's instructions.

In the first day of the three-day period K'ung-ming did nothing. Nor did he begin to make arrows on the second day. About 2 A.M on the third day he secretly sent a messenger to ask Lu Su to join him in his boat.

"What is the meaning of inviting me in this unholy hour?" Lu Su asked.

"I want you to accompany me to pick up the arrows," K'ung-ming replied.

"Where?"

"No more questions. You will find out soon."

Then K'ung-ming gave the order that the twenty ships be chained together to form a long train and that they be rowed towards the northern bank of the river.[55] The fog was heavy that night and became heavier as the ships moved towards midstream. It was so dense that people a few feet apart could not see each other. K'ung-ming ordered the boatmen to row faster.

About 6 A.M. this train of ships was approaching Ts'ao Ts'ao's water headquarters on the northern bank. Then it was stretched along a west-east direction so that one side of each ship would face the northern direction. K'ung-ming ordered the boatmen to beat their drums and shout aloud as if they were about to launch an attack.

"If Ts'ao Ts'ao's navy moves to attack us in massive numbers, what can we do?" asked Lu Su.

K'ung-ming laughed. "It is my estimation that Ts'ao Ts'ao will not venture to attack us in this heavy fog. Let us enjoy ourselves and have a few drinks. When the fog begins to dissipate, we shall go home."

Meanwhile on the northern bank, Ts'ao Ts'ao's water headquarters had heard the drumming and the shouting from the river. Not knowing what to do, the two admirals in charge, Mao Chiai and Yü Chin, hurried to Ts'ao Ts'ao for instructions. Having heard their report, Ts'ao Ts'ao issued the following order: "The sudden arrival of the enemy in a heavy fog indicates that he intends to induce us to take a rash course. This is a trap, and we should by no means fall into it. All sailors on the river bank are hereby ordered to shoot with arrows towards the direction from which the noise comes." To strengthen his defense, he also ordered Generals Chang Liao and Hsü Huang of the army to rush 3,000 archers to the river bank so as to help the shooting. Meanwhile Admirals Mao and Yü, being fearful that the southerners might attempt to capture their water headquarters, ordered their saliors to commence shooting immediately. By the time the three thousand soldiers arrived, there were altogether ten thousand archers, all shooting towards the river. The shooting was so heavy that it looked like raindrops in a heavy thunderstorm.

After one side of the ships had received enough arrows, they were turned around so the other side could receive the same. When the sun rose higher and the fog was about to dissipate, K'ung-ming gave the order that the ships be speedily turned back towards the southern bank. By then all the straw bundles had been clustered with arrows. "Thank you, prime minister,[56] for your generous gift of arrows," the soldiers shouted towards the northern shore. By the time the northerners had found out about their error and reported it to Ts'ao Ts'ao, the southern ships, moving downstream, were already twenty *li* away. It was impossible to catch them.

On their way home, K'ung-ming said to Lu Su: "Each of our ships must have five or six thousand arrows. Thus, without costing us one penny, we have obtained

---

[55] The Yangtze River.

[56] Ts'ao Ts'ao was then the prime minister of the Han dynasty.

from our enemy 100,000 arrows. Tomorrow we should be able to use them against him with good effect. This is a nice arrangement; is it not?"

"All I can say is that you are a true genius," Lu Su replied. "But how did you know that there would be a heavy fog today?"

"A general who does not know meteorology, geography, cartography, military science, or Dualism [57] cannot be considered a great commander. Three days ago I knew that there would be a heavy fog this morning; that is why I dared to promise the delivery of 100,000 arrows in a three-day period. I also knew that Chou Yü was looking for an excuse to kill me. Fortunately, my life is in the hands of Heaven instead of his." Lu Su saluted to express his respect.

By the time the ships arrived at the southern bank, the 500 soldiers dispatched by Chou Yü were already there. The arrows were counted, and they numbered more than 100,000. Having heard from Lu Su the manner in which K'ung-ming obtained these arrows, Chou Yü was astonished. "This man is superior to me," he sighed.

185 · CHUANG CHOU et al.: Wit and Humor [58]

The Wit of Chuang Chou [59]

There was an old tortoise who, it was said, had lived a miserable life in mud for three thousand years.

The king of Ch'u felt sorry for him and decided to make him an offer. If the poor tortoise simply let himself be killed, he, the king, would honor him by using his body as royal sacrifice and preserve his bones in the imperial temple.

The tortoise, having thought it over, decided to turn down the offer.

       *   *   *   *   *

A beautiful bird rested in the suburb of Lu. The Duke of Lu was so pleased that he wanted to entertain her with his very best. He proposed to serve her a royal banquet, accompanied by the best music played by the court musicians.

The bird, taking a look at all this fuss, uttered a cry of protest and flew away.

       *   *   *   *   *

Yang-tzu went to Sung and stayed in a small inn. The innkeeper had two wives, one very beautiful and the other very plain. Strange as it might seem, the inn-keeper liked the plain one better than the beautiful one. Asked by Yang-tzu the reason for his preference, the innkeeper replied: "The beautiful one thinks so much of her own beauty that I do not see any beauty in her. On the other hand, the plain one thinks so much of her own plainness that I do not see any plainness in her at all."

       *   *   *   *   *

[57] *Yin* and *yang*.

[58] While the theme of each of these parables remains the same as that of the original, it has been rewritten to conform to a more acceptable Western style.

[59] Source: *Book of Chuang-tzu*.

A man wanted to walk as gracefully as many dignitaries. So he went to the most famous posture school in Chao to learn how to walk like a dignitary.

He spent three months in that school; yet he was unable to master the dignitary's steps. In the meantime, he forgot how he had walked before he came. His money was gone and he had to go home. Unable to walk in his newly learned steps and having forgotten how to walk in the old way, he had no choice except to crawl his way home on his hands and knees.

*   *   *   *   *

A man opened a school to teach dragon-killing, advertising it as the newest and the most advanced profession in the world. Chu P'ing-man, looking for a profession, sold his house and traveled thousands of miles to learn this new trade.

He stayed in this school for three years, studying very hard and at the end mastering every detail of dragon-killing. His money was gone, and his master let him graduate. "You are the most skillful dragon-killer in the world," his master commented.

After his graduation, he looked everywhere for dragons to kill to practice his profession. He was bound to be disappointed since there was no such animal as a dragon, as he was later told.

*   *   *   *   *

Hsi Shih, the most beautiful woman in ancient China, once had a heart illness. To relieve the pain, she often crossed her hands over her heart and frowned pitifully.

"How more beautiful she is when she crosses her hands over her heart!" said one.

"How much more beautiful she is when she frowns!" said another.

Having heard the great admiration heaped on her, Tung Shih, her neighbor, decided to do likewise, though her heart was hale and sound. "If a woman can become more beautiful by crossing hands over her heart and by continuing to frown, certainly I can be beautiful too," she said to herself.

So she began to cross her hands over her heart and frowned constantly. To her surprise, everybody began to avoid her, including her former suitors.

*   *   *   *   *

The king of the North was Shu; the king of the South was Fu. They often met each other at the house of Hun T'un, the king of the Middle, who entertained them royally.

To express their appreciation, Shu and Fu invited Hun T'un, so that they could entertain him in the same lavish manner as they themselves had been entertained by him.

However, Hun T'un had no sense organs. How could he be entertained when he had no eyes to see the most beautiful, no ears to hear the most musical, and no mouth to taste the most delicious?

Determined that their friend should enjoy their entertainment, Shu and Fu decided to do something about this. With a hammer and a drill, they started to make eyes, ears, and mouth for him.

Before their work could be completed, they found that their friend was dead.

*   *   *   *   *

Chi Hsiao was training a fighting cock for the king.

After ten days, the king asked him whether the cock was ready for fighting. "The cock has a long way to go," replied Chi. "It is still arrogant."

Ten days later, the king asked the same question. "Not yet," Chi replied. "Though no longer arrogant, it is still proud of itself."

After the cock had been trained for one month, the king asked the trainer again: "How does it look to you now?"

"It is neither arrogant nor proud of itself," the cock trainer replied. "But it still becomes angry whenever it is aroused."

Ten more days passed. The king, anxious to put the cock to a test, again asked Chi about it.

"It is about ready, sir," said the cock trainer. "It looks dumb and stupid as if it were made of wood. It will not become irritated even when it is challenged."

The cock was then put to a test. The other cocks, seeing it, simply ran away. From then on it won every fight in which it was engaged.

The Wit of Lieh-tzu [60]

A man lost his ax. He thought that his neighbor might have stolen it. The more he thought of it, the more suspicious he became. So he decided to visit his neighbor to find out.

Upon seeing his neighbor, he was immediately convinced that the latter had stolen his ax. In his eyes his neighbor walked like a thief, talked like a thief, and behaved in every way like a thief. Even his physical feature could be only that of a thief. "My goodness, why did I not realize this before?" he said to himself.

He came home very depressed, not knowing how to get back his ax.

The second day he found the ax in his own house. It was simply misplaced; it had not been stolen at all.

He paid another visit to his neighbor. To his surprise, his neighbor had totally changed. He did not walk, talk, or behave in the slightest way like a thief. "My goodness," he said to himself, "how on earth could I possibly suspect him? Even his physical appearance can be only that of a gentleman."

*   *   *   *   *

A peasant presented Prince Chien with a live pigeon on New Year's Day. Prince Chien released the pigeon and rewarded the peasant generously. Having been asked why he did this, the prince replied that saving a pigeon's life would put him in good grace with the gods.

Other peasants, hearing of the generous reward and anxious to help their

[60] *Book of Lieh-tzu,* by anonymous author or authors.

prince to be in good grace with the gods, began a mass hunting of the pigeons. They presented their catches to the prince for release and were duly rewarded.

During this process of hunting and releasing, thousands of pigeons died as a result. On the second New Year's Day there was not a single pigeon presented to the prince for release, since all had died and none could be found within the principality.

*   *   *   *   *

During his travels in the east, Confucius saw two children arguing with each other. He asked them what they were arguing about.

"I say that the sun is closer to us when it rises in the morning and is far away from us at noon," said one child.

"But I say that the sun is far away from us when it rises in the morning and is closer to us at noon," said the other child.

"When the sun rises in the morning, it is as large as a carriage's canopy. At noon it is as small as a bowl. Is it not true that a thing is smaller at a distance and larger when close by?" said the first child.

"When the sun rises in the morning, it is cool. At noon it becomes hot. Is it not true that a hot object feels cooler at a distance and warmer when close by?" said the second child.

Confucius hesitated and could not decide which child was right. "Who says that you are a man of knowledge?" the children commented simultaneously.

*   *   *   *   *

Mr. Stubborn was digging at mountains when he was spoken to by a passer-by. "What are you trying to do, Mr. Stubborn?" inquired the passer-by.

"I am trying to remove these two mountains in front of my house," Mr. Stubborn replied. "The sun cannot come to my house as long as they stand there."

"How can you, Mr. Stubborn, remove these two mountains since you are more than ninety years old? It takes years or even decades to remove them."

"It matters not, my friend," said Mr. Stubborn. "If I cannot finish the job, my sons will continue. If my sons cannot finish it, my grandsons will continue. We will not cease our efforts until these two mountains are removed."

While he was saying these words, the Mountain God was listening. Moved by Mr. Stubborn's determination, the Mountain God decided to lend a helping hand. In the second morning when Mr. Stubborn opened the door, he found that both mountains were gone and that the sun was shining brightly in his house.

The Wit of Han Fei [61]

A man was selling spears and shields.

"My shields are so strongly built that no spear in the world can pierce them through," he announced.

So he sold a large number of shields.

After he sold all of his shields, he boasted again: "My spears are so sharp that there are no shields in the world that they cannot pierce."

[61] Source: *Book of Han Fei (Han-Fei-tzu)*.

So he sold a large number of spears.

A passer-by who happened to see the whole procedure asked him: "Supposing that I use your spear to pierce your shield, what will happen?"

The man did not reply.

* * * * *

A poor man in Wei prayed every day. He was hoping that the gods would help him to become wealthy.

He was happy that his wife prayed too.

Out of curiosity, he wanted to find out for what she was praying.

"Dear gods, please help my husband to remain as poor as he is." He clearly heard what she had been saying.

"Why do want me to remain poor?"

"Otherwise you will take a second wife," she replied.

* * * * *

There was a humble man in Sung who mourned sadly after the death of his father. He was so heartbroken that he refused to eat and sleep. By the end of the year he looked almost like a skeleton.

Moved by this true sense of filial piety, the king of Sung decided to reward him and offered him a job with the government.

To the dismay of the king, dozens of his subjects died of mourning the next year.

* * * * *

While working in the fields, a farmer saw a rabbit running against a tree. The rabbit was instantly killed.

He took the rabbit home, cooked it, and found it delicious.

In the second day, he gave up his farming and sat under the same tree, hoping that the same thing would happen again. It never did.

* * * * *

Yang Pu went out in a light-colored coat. Since it had been raining, he changed into a dark raincoat when he came home. While he was approaching his house, the family dog barked at him furiously. He became very angry and was about to hit the dog when he was stopped by his brother.

"How can you blame the dog?" said his brother. "Suppose that the dog went out as a white dog and came home as a black one, would you recognize him?"

* * * * *

King Hsüan of Ch'i liked flute music, and there was an orchestra in the royal court composed of three hundred flute players. When entertaining the king, they always played together.

Mr. Nan-kuo applied to the king as a flute player and was immediately accepted in the orchestra, since the king had always liked flute players.

After King Hsüan died, King Min ascended the throne. Unlike his father, King Min liked to hear flute solo, instead of all flutes playing together.

Mr. Nan-kuo resigned and ran away as fast as he could because, as the king learned later, he could not blow a note with his flute.

*   *   *   *   *

Tzu-wei was present when Confucius paid a visit to the prime minister. After Confucius left, he asked the prime minister what he thought of the visitor. "After I have seen Confucius, people like you look no better than fleas," the prime minister replied. "I am going to recommend him to the king."

Lest Confucius might be appointed in a high position by the king at his expense, Tzu-wei said to the prime minister: "I am afraid that after the king sees Confucius, he will look at you the same way you look at us, namely, as fleas."

This brought the prime minister to serious thinking. He did not recommend Confucius to the king.

*   *   *   *   *

The royal painter of Ch'i was asked by the king what objects were the easiest and what objects were the most difficult to paint.

"It is the most difficult to paint dogs and horses; it is the easiest to paint ghosts," the painter replied.

"Why?" asked the king.

"People know what dogs and horses look like. When I paint them, I have to make them look like dogs and horses, which is rather difficult. But nobody knows what ghosts look like. I can paint them anyway I wish, and yet no one can contradict me. That is why, Your Majesty, I have always preferred to paint ghosts rather than dogs and horses."

The king nodded in agreement.

*   *   *   *   *

The prince of Chou lost his jade and ordered the police to search for it. The police searched over the whole principality for three days consecutively and found no trace of it. So they reported their failure to the prince.

"How useless you are," said the angry prince. "I am going to do the searching myself."

The prince started to search indeed. It did not take him long to find the jade, since it had been merely misplaced underneath his own pillow.

Upon hearing this all the policemen shouted: "How wise our prince is! He is a great genius whatever he does. He can achieve in a few minutes what we, the trained policemen, have not been able to achieve in three days."

Thus the wise reputation of the prince of Chou spread far and wide.

*   *   *   *   *

A hunting dog was chasing a rabbit and finally caught him.

"Do not kill me, please," pleaded the rabbit.

"Why not?" asked the dog.

"Because it is for your sake."

"Why is it for my sake?"

"You are valuable to your master as long as there are rabbits. Once all the rabbits are hunted off, you will be no longer useful to him, and he will kill you."

The dog ignored his advice, killed him, and brought him to his master.

The dog was so efficient that soon all the rabbits in the neighborhood were hunted off.

"There are no more rabbits. To keep the dog has become very expensive indeed," said the master.

"Why do you not kill him?" said his wife.

So the dog was killed and cooked as food.

"This is a very unusual dog," commented the master; "it tastes delicious."

The Wit of Lü Pu-wei [62]

A man went to steal a bell. The bell was so heavy and large that he could not carry it. Finally he decided to break the bell and take home the pieces.

Using a hatchet, he hit the bell with all his energy. The bell, naturally, made a noisy sound.

Being afraid that people might hear the sound and catch him as a thief, he put his ear plugs on. He went on with his work, confident that there was no sound.

When finally caught, he was puzzled about the outcome, since he thought that he had taken good precautions.

* * * * *

A man in Ch'i wanted to have some gold; so he went to a goldsmith.

On display were various shapes of gold which people were admiring. The man grabbed some gold on the table and started to run. He was soon caught by the police.

"Why did you steal when there were so many people around?" asked the police.

"When there was gold, the only thing I could see was gold," the man replied; "I did not see any people."

* * * * *

A man in Ch'u was known for his carefulness. One day he rode a ferryboat across a river and accidentally dropped his sword into the water. Being a careful man, he immediately made a mark on the edge of the boat and announced that this was the place where the sword was dropped and that he should seek the sword from there. Meanwhile the boat kept on moving.

When the boat was finally anchored, he dived into the river from where the mark was made. After a considerable time, he emerged from the water and was puzzled that he could not find his sword at all.

[62] Source: Mr. *Lü's Annals (Lü-shih ch'un-ch'iu).*

Wit and Humor from Chan-kuo Ts'e [63]

A mussel had opened its shell and was sunning itself on the beach when a snipe pecked at its flesh. It quickly closed its shell, and caught and tightly held the snipe's beak. The mussel could not go back to the river; nor could the snipe walk away.

"If it does not rain for two days, soon the mussel will be dead," thought the snipe. "If I keep his beak between my shells for two days, soon there will be a dead snipe," thought the mussel.

While the mussel and the snipe were angry at each other and neither one wished to make any concessions, a fisherman walked by and caught both of them.

*   *   *   *   *

Wang's neighbor had two wives, both of whom were very beautiful. First Wang tried to seduce the elder one who scolded him and turned him down. He gave up and started to seduce the younger one. The younger one was very responsive, and soon they had a merry time.

Not long afterwards, his neighbor died. Wang was free to marry either of the two widows. He chose the elder one and soon married her.

Asked why he married the woman who once scolded him and did not marry the woman who had been so responsive, Wang replied: "As long as a woman is somebody else's wife, I want her to be responsive to me. Once she becomes my wife, I want her to scold everybody else."

*   *   *   *   *

In the family temple of Ch'u, the servants found that the wine which had been used for sacrifice was not adequate for all of them. One suggested that each draw a snake on the ground, and whoever finished first would have the whole pot for himself. All agreed.

One man finished first and took the pot.

While he held the pot in his left hand and was drinking joyfully, he announced that not only could he draw a snake faster than others, he could also make it better by adding legs to it.

While he was busy with the legs, another servant finished his drawing. He went to the first servant and took the pot away from him.

"How can you add legs to a snake when it does not have any?" said the second servant. "What you have drawn is not a snake, while mine is." The rest of the servants agreed to his reasoning. The wine was awarded to him accordingly.

*   *   *   *   *

A hungry tiger was looking for food and captured a fox.

"You cannot kill me," said the fox.

"Why not?"

[63] Source: *Chan-kuo ts'e* or *Documents of the Warring States.*

"Because I am the king of the forest."

"Ha, ha! ho, ho!" the tiger laughed loudly. "You certainly know how to tell a joke. Every animal knows that I am the king of the forest, not you or anybody else."

"If you do not believe me," said the fox, "I can prove it to you."

"How?" asked the tiger.

"If you just follow me, you will believe what I have said. Wherever I go, every animal in the forest will be so frightened that he will flee as fast as he can," said the fox.

So the tiger followed the fox and walked behind him in the forest. The deer, the bear, the wolf, the rabbit, and every other animal, seeing the coming of the tiger, fled as fast as he could.

"Now that you have seen with your own eyes that every animal is afraid of me, are you convinced that I am really the king of the forest?"

The tiger, completely puzzled, agreed with the fox and let him go free.

CHAPTER TWENTY

Education and Technology

Prior to the modern period few peoples in the world emphasized the importance of education more than the Chinese. As Confucius defined it, the purpose of education was not merely the acquirement of knowledge; it was the refinement of moral character that an educator should strive to achieve (Selection 186). Following Confucius' leadership, later scholars repeatedly emphasized the moral aspect of the educational goal (Selection 187). A teacher could not teach unless he was morally sound and was capable of setting an example for his students. It was hoped that through education a moral elite would be created to set examples for the nation as a whole.

One of the earliest essays on education appears in the *Book of Rites* and is entitled *Hsüeh chi* or "On Learning" (Selection 188). It contains ideas which even today may be considered progressive and modern. Beginning in the third century B.C. when China was for the first time unified under an all-powerful, centralized government, the academic independence as envisaged in *Hsüeh chi* became a matter of the past. As time passed and monarchic power continued to grow, schools increasingly became a tool of political indoctrination and a means through which the government exercised its thought control. Insofar as free expression of ideas was concerned, few institutions did more harm than the civil service examination system that was introduced during the Sui-T'ang period, though the system itself may be defended on other grounds (Chapter Nine). From then on, not only were ideas stereotyped, but the forms for expressing these ideas also eventually became standardized. When a child was sent to school, his parents had one primary purpose in mind: to pass the civil service examinations and thus acquire fame and wealth. This corruption of educational ideals was deeply deplored by such men as Huang Tsung-hsi (Selection 189).

In China as well as in other societies each generation produced its fair share of talented men, and the inadequate supply of talent in a given generation reflected the lack of adequate means to train or discover them rather than some inherent deficiency of that particular generation (Selection 190). Moreover, if a society emphasized a certain type of learning, most talented people in that society would choose to develop their talent in that field. Since literature was the most emphasized field in traditional China, a man of talent was almost synonymous with a man of letters. The civil service examination system further strengthened this ancient bias, since the examination from which talented men were chosen was essentially a test on literary ability. Before the twelfth century the examination emphasized poetry, and too often was a man's talent judged in accordance with his ability or the lack of it to write presentable poems (Selection 191). During the Ming-Ch'ing period when writing poetry was no longer required in the examination, many considered this skill a frivolity and the efforts made to improve it a waste of time (Selection 79).

Schools were generally small, and the teacher-student relationship was as close as it was personal (Selection 192). A child of wealthy parents was more likely to be tutored at home, and often his teacher was a disappointed, unsuccessful candidate in the civil service examinations. The teacher taught the fundamentals: reading, writing, and calligraphy (Selection 193). Once a student knew how to read independently, his dependence on his teacher lessened and he was practically on his own. How far he could advance in the academic world depended upon his own interest and effort (Selections 194 and 195).

It is easy to see that the traditional Chinese training was heavily one-sided, and little room was provided for other studies besides ancient classics and literature. Practically all the great technological inventions for which China was known to the outside world were the products of individual geniuses who, more often than not, were not associated with the academic world. Printing, perhaps the greatest technological contribution China has made to the civilized world, was invented by men who, as artisans, were looked down upon by the scholars (Selection 196). Once its value was recognized, however, the government and the academic world were only too happy to use it for their own purposes (Selection 197).

While the usefulness of printing is easily understood, the traditional Chinese medicine was and still is a puzzle to many Westerners. Is it a science, superstition, or something between? After reading Selection 198, the reader may be in a better position to answer his own question.

186 · CONFUCIUS: *Education and Learning* [1]

Confucius says, Is it not a great pleasure to learn and to review constantly what you have learned? Will you not be pleased when a friend comes from afar to see you? Is he not a gentleman indeed who shows no annoyance even though nobody knows his goodness?

Confucius says, A young man should be dutiful towards his parents and respectful towards his elders. He loves all men under Heaven and particularly those who are virtuous. Only after he has done all his duties as a man should he think seriously about the study of literature.

Confucius says, If a man is not serious with himself, he cannot expect respect from others. Moreover, he cannot even be persistent in his studies. A gentleman should constantly uphold the principle of loyalty and faith and should not associate with those who are less virtuous than he is. If he makes a mistake, he is not afraid to correct it.

[1] Source: *Analects of Confucius* or *Lun-yü*.

Confucius says, A gentleman is not concerned with what kind of food he eats or in what kind of place he lives. He is prompt in doing his duty and careful in his speech. If he does not know whether he is doing the right thing, he asks those who know. A gentleman of this nature is one who really loves learning.

Confucius says, A gentleman is not worried whether others understand him; he is worried whether he understand others.

Confucius says, A man who acquires new meanings when reading old books is qualified to be a teacher.

Confucius says, A gentleman does not specialize.

Confucius says, A student who does not think through what he has learned will be confused. On the other hand, his knowledge is unreliable if it is based upon thinking alone.

Confucius says, Yu,[2] do you still remember what I once told you? When you know, say that you know; when you do not know, say that you do not know. This is the secret of knowledge.

Confucius loved to ask questions whenever he entered the Grand Temple.[3] "Who says that the son of Chou [4] knows about rites?" someone remarked. "He asks questions whenever he enters the Grand Temple." Having heard this comment, Confucius said: "To ask about rites is an indication of knowing about the rites."

Confucius says, If a man hears about The Truth in the morning, he should have no regret to die in the evening.

Confucius says, I shall not speak with a man who, saying that he seeks The Truth, is ashamed of the kind of food he eats or the kind of clothes he wears.

Confucius says, When I see a virtuous man, I shall try to be as virtuous as he is. When I see an evil man, I shall ask myself whether I have some of his characteristics.

Confucius says, People of ancient times did not make easy promises because they were afraid that they might not be able to keep them.

Confucius says, A gentleman is clumsy in making speeches but quick in performing righteous deeds.

Confucius says, In as small a village as that of ten households there can be a man as virtuous as I am. But I doubt that he loves learning as much as I do.

Confucius says, A gentleman is broad in learning and conducts his life in accordance with the rule of propriety. He will not violate the principle of ethics.

Confucius says, I relate what I have learned; I do not write or create. I have faith and confidence in the ancients. People compare me to Lao P'eng.[5]

Confucius says, How much I hope that I possess all of the following characteristics: ceaseless learning, tireless teaching, and the ability to retain what I have studied!

Confucius says, If a man brings me some meat, I shall not hesitate to teach him.

Confucius says, I shall be less subject to error if Heaven grants me more years so that I can complete the studying of the *Book of Changes* by the time I reach fifty.

---

[2] Chung Yu, better known as Tzu-lu, a disciple of Confucius.
[3] A temple that was built to honor Duke Chou of the Chou dynasty.
[4] Confucius.
[5] A virtuous minister of the Shang dynasty.

The books Confucius often spoke about were the *Book of Odes,* the *Book of History,* and the *Book of Rites.*

Yeh Kung [6] asked Tzu-lu about Confucius. Tzu-lu did not reply. Hearing this, Confucius said: "Why did you not tell him that Confucius is a man who loves learning so much that he often forgets to eat, enjoys life so much that he does not know such things as worries, and is so content within himself that he does not realize that he is getting old?"

Confucius says, I was not born with knowledge. I love to read ancient books; I am constantly searching for knowledge.

There were four things Confucius did not wish to talk about: miracles, violence, anarchy, and gods and spirits.

Confucius says, Among any three men who walk in the street, there is one who could be my teacher. I shall follow their good traits, while correcting my own weaknesses which I have also found in them.

Confucius emphasized four items in teaching his students: literature, conduct, sincerity, and faith.

Confucius says, There are people who take action without thinking much about it in advance, but fortunately I am not one of them. I learn as much as I can and then choose the best course to follow. A man who learns and experiences a great deal is on his way to wisdom.

Confucius says, He is very rare indeed if, after studying three years, he is not thinking of using his knowledge as a key to officialdom.

Confucius says, Pursuing knowledge is like walking on a long road. No matter how diligent he is, a good student is always afraid that he might not be able to reach his destination in time.

Confucius says, Do I have knowledge? I should say not. However, if an uneducated man chooses to seek information from me, I shall tell him all I know and tell him in such a manner that he will understand.

Confucius says, The future of the young is unlimited. But how do you know that their future will not be the same as mine is today? If a man has not accomplished anything by the time he is forty or fifty, he has become hopeless indeed.

Confucius says, Yen Hui [7] does not help me at all. He is pleased with everything I say.

Chi-k'ang-tzu [8] asked Confucius which student of his loved learning most. "Yen Hui loved learning," Confucius replied, "but unfortunately he has died. Since then I have not met anyone who really loves learning."

Confucius says, If a man cannot serve effectively as either a minister or an ambassador after he has studied the *Book of Odes,* reading is of no use to him, no matter how much he is going to read.

Confucius says, The moment a scholar wishes to live a life of ease, he is no longer a scholar.

Confucius says, How can you say that you love a person without asking him to work hard? How can you say that you are loyal to a person without telling him what you really think of him?

Confucius says, The scholars of ancient times studied to improve themselves; today's scholars study in order to impress others.

[6] An official in the state of Ch'u.
[7] Also known as Yen Yüan, a disciple of Confucius.
[8] A minister in the state of Lu.

Confucius says, I shall teach anyone who wishes to learn.

Confucius says, A good piece of writing is one which the reader can understand.

Confucius says, A superior man is born with knowledge, and a less superior man acquires knowledge through learning. An average man learns when he seeks solutions to his problems, and a less than average man will not learn even when faced with problems.

Confucius says, Human nature is similar; only environment makes it diverse.

Confucius says, The most superior do not need improvement; the most ignorant cannot be improved.

Confucius says, As for you students, I see no better book to read than the *Book of Odes*. It is interesting; it will also help you to understand the customs of different states. It teaches you how to live harmoniously with others, besides serving as an outlet for your own emotions. Moreover, what you learn from this book will help you to serve your father and your king more effectively. You will also learn the names of many kinds of birds, beasts, grass, and trees of which you may never have heard before.

187 · YEN CHIH-T'UI: *The Purpose of Reading* [9]

The purpose of reading is to enable the reader to broaden his mind and to enlighten his experience. The ultimate goal is to make him a better man so that he can live a more virtuous, wholesome life.

He who does not know how to serve his parents may well be advised to read the examples set by the dutiful sons of ancient times who tirelessly waited on their parents without complaint. He may feel ashamed of himself by comparison and decide to do likewise.

He who does not know how to serve his king is urged to read the examples set by the ministers of ancient times who performed their official duties faithfully, sacrificed their lives whenever honor called upon them to do so, and remonstrated fearlessly with their sovereign if they felt that by doing so they were to benefit the nation as a whole. He may ask himself whether he has lived up to the ancient standard and may finally decide to follow their good examples.

He who is vain and extravagant should read the examples of ancient men who were humble and thrifty, abided by the rule of propriety in whatever they did, and adhered to the principle of reverence as the code of personal conduct. He may feel awkward by comparison and may wish to change his arrogant ways.

He who is miserly and parsimonious should read the examples of ancient men who placed the principle of righteousness above that of material gains, were generous with others as they had been thrifty with themselves, and distributed their wealth among the needy and the poor instead of accumulating it for the sake of accumulation. He may feel embarrassed; he may decide to give away his wealth as efficiently as he has accumulated it.

He who is cruel and violent should read the examples of ancient men who valued other people's limbs as well as their own, would not think of retaliation despite provocation, and showed respect for the elderly and the virtuous while

[9] Translated from "The Promotion of Learning" *(Mien hsüeh)* in *Family Instructions for the Yen Clan (Yen-shih chia-hsün)*, Essay No. 8. As for the author, see p. 342, Footnote 7.

learning to get along with the commonplace. He may feel that he, in fact, is really a bully, and a bully is as injurious to others as he is insulting to himself.

He who is timid and cowardly should read the examples of ancient men who kept their promises regardless of the change of circumstances, upheld the principle of justice with steadfastness despite personal risks, and were happy and willing to lay down their lives for the ideas or ideals they believed. He may suddenly become brave and fearless.

We can go on indefinitely in citing the benefits that result from reading books. In short, a learned man is not a person who has accumulated a large amount of information upon which he can elaborate; he is a person who can incorporate what he has learned in the conduct of his daily life.

188 · ANONYMOUS: *On Learning* [10]

A delicacy remains unknown if untasted. Likewise there is no way of knowing the goodness in virtue unless one has learned about it. Only through learning can we become aware of our inadequacies, and only by teaching do we know how difficult teaching is. Knowing our inadequacies, we strive to learn more; realizing how difficult teaching is, we will be motivated to strengthen ourselves further. Learning and teaching go hand in hand; achievement in one is bound to enhance the achievement in the other. . . .

A student is subject to four errors which his teacher must know. He either attempts to learn more than he can digest, or fails to learn to the extent of his capacity. He either finds a subject too easy to maintain his interest or challenge his ability, or stops learning when in fact he should have continued. The causes for each of these errors are different from one student to another; only by finding these causes can a teacher provide remedies. The purpose of teaching, in fact, is to explore and then enhance a student's native ability and to find remedies for whatever inadequacies he might have.

One of the most difficult things in education is to find dedicated teachers. Only when teachers are serious can their students acquire respect for what they teach. Once the students manifest such respect, the people in general will attach great importance to education.

There are two kinds of people from whom even the king cannot exact absolute obedience: people who temporarily play the role of spirits [11] and people who have become teachers. According to an ancient custom, when summoned before the king, a teacher does not have to perform the act of homage. This custom is maintained in order to show the nation's profound respect for teachers.

A good student does not tire his teacher; he learns effortlessly and acquires a great deal in a short space of time. He continues to learn when learning has

[10] Translated from *Hsüeh chi* in the *Book of Rites*.

[11] According to an ancient Chinese custom, after a man died, one of his younger sons would be assigned to personalize his departing spirit to receive worship and sacrifice which was offered by his eldest son, the chief mourner. During the time when he personalized his father's spirit, he was regarded as sacred and inviolable, and even the king could not exact absolute obedience from him. Later, the custom changed when the dead man's painted image replaced a living person as a symbol to receive worship and sacrifice. In this case the dead man's spirit was supposedly to have been incorporated in the image.

ceased to be an exercise of effort. A poor student, on the other hand, tires his teacher needlessly and learns little. He complains because he has learned little.

Like a carpenter who learns to cut softwood first before he tackles with the stronger variety, a good student asks the easiest question first before he proceeds to the more difficult ones. As he accumulates knowledge during each step of his questioning, eventually he becomes a master of the entire topic. A poor student does exactly the opposite.

Like a bell which yields a low sound when hit gently and a loud response when struck more forcibly, a good teacher provides answers in proportion to the questions raised by his students. He does not proceed to answer unless his students have clarified their questions. When he answers, he answers thoroughly and without any reservation. A poor teacher does exactly the opposite.

An accumulator of miscellaneous information is short of being a good teacher; a teacher should be judged according to his power of reasoning. If he can neither ask intelligent questions nor provide sensible answers, he is useless as a teacher, and no harm will be done by dismissing him.

189 · HUANG TSUNG-HSI: *Schools* [12]

According to a popular concept, the purpose of schools is to cultivate scholars. The ancient concept of education, however, goes far beyond this: all institutions that are created for the purpose of running a harmonious society are the proper subjects to be taught in schools. Needless to say, the ancient concept is more adequate than the contemporary one, as far as the goal of education is concerned. Thus a good school not only teaches such subjects as public administration, social welfare, and judicial procedure, it also familiarizes the students with such topics as military science, criminology, and religious rituals. The purpose is to enable the students to acquire a liberal, broad background for every subject worthy of being learned, from that dealing with governmental policies to that concerning the private life of an individual.

Scholars thus trained form independent opinions of their own. They will not say that this is so or not so simply because the emperor has said that this is so or not so. Respecting the integrity of these scholars, even the emperor will not insist that he is right when he is obviously wrong. Whenever a controversial issue arises, the ideal place to settle it is not the court which is controlled by the government but schools where independent scholars judge the issue in accordance with its merit. This is what I mean when I say that the purpose of education should go beyond the cultivation of scholars.

This ideal of schools described above was upheld during the Three Dynasties but has since then completely disappeared. Nowadays only the government decides what is right or wrong. If the emperor says yes, everyone else says yes; if he says no, everyone else says no. Meanwhile all the administrative duties in the government, such as secretarial work, tax collection, and the arraignment and trial of criminals, are carried on by unimaginative bureaucrats in a routine manner, completely independent of popular influence. There are those who believe that students in schools should be taught in such a way as to enable them to meet the

[12] *Ming-yi tai-fang lu,* Essay No. 5.

needs of society upon graduation. But the students, educated along this line of thinking, merely equip themselves with the attributes necessary to compete successfully in the civil service examinations; with nothing else in mind except power and wealth, they distinguish themselves only by their ability to seek the easiest avenue to, and subsequently ally themselves with, whoever happen to be in power. Because of the condition of our schools, the most learned and the truly able are usually self-educated men who have little or no formal education. Though the cultivation of scholars is not the most important goal in education, our schools have deteriorated to such an extent that today they do not even produce scholars.

As for private academies, the government honors them for the same reason that the public criticizes them. On the other hand, if the public likes a certain academy, the government is bound to find something wrong with it and persecute it accordingly. Time and again it takes the initiative to ban the so-called "false learning" or close the non-conforming schools on the ground that they have challenged the established authority. Those scholars who decline the government's invitation to serve as officials run the risk of inviting prosecution against themselves; they are accused of having set a bad example for others to follow or having attempted to lead all scholars to "revolt" against the government. When the government regards schools as its enemies (a development which is recent in origin), schools can no longer perform the function for which they are intended. Not only do they stop nourishing scholarship; they also bring harm to it. For all practical purposes they lose their use as schools.

From time to time there has been a resurgence of our ancient educational ideal. During the East Han dynasty, for instance, the 30,000 students in the Central University expressed their independent opinions, lofty and selfless, and they cared not whether by expressing these opinions they were antagonizing the powerful and the influential in the government. Even the ministers had to behave in such a way as not to become the targets of the students' criticisms. During the Sung dynasty the students in the Central University, in their efforts to influence the government to reinstate the courageous minister Li Kang, marched towards the palace ground and demonstrated.[13] In each of these two cases, if the government had accepted the students' advice and dismissed the evil elements whom it had employed, not only would the king's safety have been secured, the dynasty itself would also have been preserved. Many critics maintain that both incidents were merely phenomena in a declining age and that no great significance should be read into them. They do not realize that once a government starts to close schools and arrest scholars, it is paving the way for its own destruction. No government can blame the scholars for its self-inflicted demise.

After Heaven created men, it entrusted the duty of feeding and educating them to the king. Since the abolition of the land granting system, people have been forced to purchase land to raise crops for their own support. The government, instead of providing them with means of support, taxes them instead. The kind of educational system prevalent in ancient times has also been abolished, and people have not been properly educated since then. Instead of educating the people, the government of today chooses to demoralize them by dangling in front

---

[13] This incident occurred in 1126 when Kaifeng, the capital of the Sung dynasty, was besieged by the invading Nuchens. Li Kang was one of the few ministers who advocated continuous resistance instead of abject surrender.

of their faces the prospect of power and influence.[14] How can it be so heartless and cruel? Who would be naive enough still to regard it as the "father" of all of the people?

190 · HAN YÜ: *On Horses*[15]

Only when there is a Pai-yüeh[16] can there be fleet horses.[17] The problem is this: while fleet horses often occur, a Pai-yüeh appears only once in a long time. Even when there is a fleet horse, it is abused in the hands of ignorant grooms and dies in the stable with ordinary breeds. How can it ever be known as a fleet horse?

A fleet horse will eat one picul of grain per meal; it eats so much because of the fact that it is a fleet horse. If its owner does not understand this fact and chooses to underfeed it, its ability will not be fully developed even though it possesses the potential of being a fleet horse. Inadequately fed and lacking strength, it may not even be able to compete with ordinary horses in performance. Ignorant of the proper way of raising it and oblivious to its cryings for help, we raise our riding-whip and say: "There is not a single good horse in the world." Alas! Is it really true that there are no good horses in the world? The truth is that there are too few people in the world who recognize and understand good horses.

191 · WANG AN-SHIH: *A Precocious Child*[18]

The family of Fang Chung-yung had been farmers in Chinch'i[19] for many generations. Until the age of five Chung-yung had never seen any books or writing equipment. One day he suddenly cried for them; his father, surprised, borrowed some ink and brush from the neighbors, being interested in seeing what the child would do with them. Chung-yung wrote a poem consisting of four lines and even signed his own name. The general idea of the poem was that one should be dutiful towards one's parents and helpful towards one's relatives. A local scholar was reported to have seen this poem.

From then on, one needed only to mention a topic and Chung-yung would compose a poem immediately. In each case the poem was more than merely presentable. Local people were happily surprised at the performance of this young genius and became more and more friendly towards his father. Some even gave money to him. Taking advantage of the situation, his father dragged him along to visit one household after another, while keeping him out of school.

[14] This refers to the civil service examination system.
[15] *Ku-wen kuan-chih,* roll 8.
[16] A famous horse trainer of ancient times who reportedly could tell a horse's capacities by simply looking at it.
[17] The Chinese original is *ch'ien-li ma* or horses which can run 1,000 *li* (or 300 miles) per day.
[18] *Sample Prose of the T'ang-Sung period (T'ang Sung san-wen hsien),* edited by Hu Lun-ch'ing, pp. 204–205. The author was a famous reformer of the Sung dynasty.
[19] Located in modern Kiangsi province, near Linan where Wang An-shih, the author, was born.

I had heard about this young genius for a long time. However, I did not have the opportunity of meeting him until the Ming-tao period (1032–1034) when I returned home with my late father and saw him in my uncle's [20] house. He was then about twelve or thirteen. I asked him to write a poem, but the poem was not so good as those that I had heard about. Seven years later when I again returned home from Yangchow,[21] I heard from my uncle that Chung-yung was as ordinary as any other young man.

"Chung-yung's natural intelligence was provided by Heaven and was infinitely superior to that of an average person," Mr. Wang [22] commented. "The reason that he could not do better was because of the lack of human effort. If a man so richly endowed turns out to be ordinary because of the lack of effort, pity the ordinary person who, without being gifted by Heaven, chooses not to offset his natural deficiency by hard work!"

192 · Han Yü: *On Teachers* [23]

All scholars of ancient times had teachers. The duty of a teacher is to transmit an ancient heritage, diffuse knowledge, and elaborate what cannot be easily understood. Man is not born with knowledge; it is impossible that he can answer all the questions he has in his mind. With questions in mind and yet refusing to seek answers from others, he will remain ignorant throughout his life. A teacher is a person who knows the answers before I do, regardless of whether he is older or younger than I am. He is wherever knowledge is; his age or social standing is immaterial.

Since the true meaning of the word "teacher" has been forgotten for a long time, it is not surprising that we are more confused than ever. The sages of ancient times were richly endowed with native intelligence; yet they were not hesitant to ask their teachers questions. People today are much inferior to the ancient sages; yet they are ashamed of learning from their teachers. As a result, the wise become wiser, and the ignorant become more ignorant. The eagerness to learn or the lack of it is perhaps the reason that some people are wise and others are not.

A man who loves his son selects a good teacher to teach him. Yet he himself is ashamed to learn from those who can be teachers to him. By "teachers" I do not mean those who can teach people how to read or write; I mean those who can transmit our ancient heritage and provide answers for our problems. We are eager to learn to read when illiterate, but somehow we are reluctant to learn when faced with important or difficult problems to solve. It is strange that we should de-emphasize the important while emphasizing the less significant. A magician, physician, musician, or craftsman is not ashamed to have teachers to teach him. Among scholars, however, people begin to laugh when one addresses the other as "teacher" or "student." They would say, since these two persons are of the same age and believe in similar things, why should one be a teacher and the other be a student? They say that to address a man as teacher is disgraceful if his

[20] The brother of his mother.
[21] Located in modern Kiangsu province.
[22] The author refers to himself.
[23] *Ku-wen kuan-chih*, roll 8.

position is inferior, and amounts to adulation or flattery if he is a high official. The truth is, they do not understand the real meaning of the word "teacher." Our scholarly gentlemen look down upon magicians, physicians, musicians, and craftsmen. Is it not strange indeed that in this respect they are inferior to the latter in good judgement?

A sage has a variety of teachers. Confucius' teachers included T'an-tzu, Ch'ang-hung, Shih-hsiang, and Lao-tzu, all of whom were less virtuous than Confucius was.[24] "Among every three men who walk in the street," said Confucius, "one of them is good enough to be my teacher." It is not necessary that a student should know less than his teacher, or a teacher should be more virtuous than his student. A teacher is only a person who knows certain things earlier than others and is more specialized in his own field.

P'an, a son of the Li family, is seventeen and is interested in writing essays of the ancient style. He is thoroughly familiar with the Six Arts and the classics, together with their commentaries. He is free from popular but wrong ideas and wishes to learn from me. Pleased with his desire to learn the old ways, I write this essay "On Teachers" as a gift to him.[25]

193 · TS'AO HSÜEH-CH'IN: *Precious Jade Goes to School*[26]

Early the next morning, Hsi-jen[27] woke up Precious Jade, washed him, combed his hair, and helped him to put on his new clothes. She instructed a female slave to give a message to Pei-ming[28] who should be waiting at the second gate with his master's books and other school equipment. She prodded Precious Jade twice before the latter, reluctantly, emerged from his own room and was ready to go to his father's study. Before he left, however, he sent a servant to find out whether his father was already there. "A man just came here for an answer to his request, and the honorable lord ordered him to wait outside," the servant reported. "The honorable lord is now washing himself." Hearing this, Precious Jade felt much easier.[29] Nevertheless, he walked towards his father's study as fast as he could.

Chia Cheng was about to summon Precious Jade when the latter arrived. He gave his son a few last-minute instructions before escorting him to the carriage. Meanwhile Pei-ming, carrying the books, was walking directly towards the school.

Before Chia Cheng's arrival, one of the servants had already come to the school, reporting to Tai-ju, the teacher, that the honorable lord was coming. Hardly had the teacher had time to prepare himself before Chia Cheng was in. The honorable lord inquired about the teacher's health, and the teacher, holding Chia Cheng's hands, responded with the same. "How is the Grand Dowager?"[30] the teacher added. After this exchange of greetings, Precious Jade stepped forward to pay his respect to the teacher.

---

[24] T'an-tzu was an expert on governmental institutions; Ch'ang-hung and Shih-hsiang were famous musicians; and Lao-tzu was the legendary founder of the Taoist philosophy.

[25] Later, in A.D. 803, Li P'an passed the imperial examination and received the *chin-shih* degree.

[26] *The Dream of the Red Chamber (Hung-lou meng)*, Chapters 81 and 82.

[27] Precious Jade's favorite female slave. See also pp. 377–379.

[28] Precious Jade's male slave.

[29] A son should never let his father wait for him.

[30] Chia Cheng's mother and Precious Jade's grandmother.

Chia Cheng continued to stand until Tai-ju agreed to his request to be seated first.[31] "The reason that I escorted my son to school is because I have a personal request to make," said Chia Cheng after he had taken his seat. "He is not a child any longer, and he should be concerned with his career so as to establish a name for himself. At the moment he is not interested in doing anything except playing with other children at home. Though he understands a little about poetry and composes some, there is nothing remarkable about his work. Even his best poems are those dealing with such topics as 'the wind, the cloud, the moon, and the dew'[32] which, as you know, have nothing to do with his career."

"To me he looks not only presentable but also fairly intelligent," said Tai-ju. "I cannot see any reason why his mind should be wild and why he only wishes to play. There is nothing wrong with poetry, of course; but it would be better not to devote too much time to it until one has established oneself."[33]

"You are right," said Chia Cheng. "From now on he should be ordered to do nothing except to study the ancient classics and to compose themes in prose.[34] If he does not obey your order, I beg you to be very strict with him, so that he will not live his whole life in vain."

After finishing his words, Chia Cheng stood up and saluted Tai-ju again. They exchanged a few casual remarks before Chia Cheng proceeded to leave. Tai-ju escorted him to the front door and then said: "Please give my respect to the Grand Dowager." Chia Cheng said that he would and then stepped into his carriage.

Returning to the school house, Tai-ju saw Precious Jade sitting in front of a small desk in the southeastern corner next to a window. On his right were piled up two sets of old books, and on his left was a thin volume of model compositions.[35] He had already ordered Pei-ming to put in the drawer his paper, brush, ink, and ink stand.

"Precious Jade, I heard that you were sick not long ago," said Tai-ju. "How do you feel now?"

Precious Jade stood up and replied: "I have completely recovered, sir."

"Now that you are in school, you should study very diligently since your father expects so much from you," the teacher continued. "From now on your daily schedule is as follows: review the books you have read early in the morning, practice calligraphy after breakfast, and study ancient classics in the afternoon. Your daily assignment will not be considered satisfactorily completed, however, until you have recited two or three of the model compositions several times."

Precious Jade respectfully replied "yes."

After sitting down, Precious Jade could not help looking around. Some of the Chin Yung[36] group were no longer there; there were a few new youngsters all of whom looked crude, dull, and uninteresting. Suddenly he thought of Ch'in Chung.[37] Now there was not a single boy who could become his true companion and with whom he could speak in an intimate manner! He felt sad and depressed.

[31] Chia Cheng was showing his respect to the teacher.
[32] Poems of light topics such as romance.
[33] That is, after one has passed the civil service examinations.
[34] These skills were the most important in passing the civil service examinations during the Ch'ing dynasty.
[35] These were compositions that could be memorized to great advantage when taking the civil service examinations.
[36] The boy with whom he once had a fight.
[37] His best friend who had since then died.

He dared not to speak out what he felt, however; he tried to bury his melancholy by reading the books.

"This is your first day in school, and I shall let you go home early," said the teacher. "Tomorrow I shall explain the classics to you. On second thought, since you are not stupid by any means, I shall ask you to explain some of the ancient passages to me. That will give me some idea as to how well you have done lately and how far you have progressed." Precious Jade felt that his heart was beating hard.

On the next day Precious Jade did not wake up until the sun was far above in the sky. "I am late; I am in trouble!" he said to himself. Quickly he washed himself and paid respect to his parents before he rushed towards the school. Seeing him, Tai-yü immediately changed his expression. "I do not blame your father for being angry with you and for saying that you are hopeless," he scolded. "This is only your second day in school, and you are lazy already. Why did you come here so late?" Precious Jade replied that he had incurred a minor fever the evening before, and the teacher, having heard his explanation, seemed to be satisfied.

When the afternoon arrived, Tai-ju said to Precious Jade: "Here is a passage; let me see how you explain it." Precious Jade took a look and found that it was entitled "The Future of the Young Is Unlimited." [38] "I am lucky that it is not a passage from the *Great Learning* or *Doctrine of the Mean*," he said to himself. "In what way do you wish me to explain this passage?" he asked his teacher.

"You should explain it sentence by sentence and phrase by phrase, in as much detail as you are able to muster," Tai-ju replied.

Precious Jade read aloud and clearly the entire passage and then said: "The sage [39] wrote this passage to encourage the young to work diligently when there is still time, so that they will not end up as . . . ." He stopped and raised his head to take a look at Tai-ju. The latter noticed his sudden stop, smiled, and then said to him: "You should say whatever you wish to say. There should not be any inhibition when explaining a book's meaning. Does not the *Book of Rites* say that 'one should not shun the truth when interpreting a piece of literature?' Go ahead! As what?"

"As an old man without any accomplishment," Precious Jade replied.[40] "The sage uses the word 'unlimited' in order to stimulate young men's desire for advancement. Later, he uses the word 'hopeless' in order to warn them against failure later in their lives." [41] He looked at Tai-ju after finishing these remarks.

"Not bad," Tai-ju commented. "Now explain this passage sentence by sentence."

"The sage says that when a man is young, his mind is sharp and his energy is supreme. His future is therefore unlimited. Little does he realize that his future will be likely the same as a middle-aged man's future is today. In other words, if he simply fritters away his time, he will soon reach forty and then fifty without securing any advancement for himself. Even though his future was unlimited when he was young, he is hopeless now."

---

[38] *"How-sheng k'o-wei"* that appears in the *Analects of Confucius,* roll 5.

[39] Confucius.

[40] Precious Jade suddenly stopped because he thought that if he said what he was about to say, his teacher, an old man who was now making a meager living by teaching the children, would be offended.

[41] For the text of the entire passage, see p. 445.

"Your explanation is clear enough, but some of the words you used are rather juvenile," said Tai-ju. "The phrase 'has not accomplished anything' does not have anything to do with 'advancement' in officialdom as you seem to have implied that it does. 'Accomplishment' means the ability to recognize what is right and true. This ability may or may not have anything to do with 'advancement' in officialdom. Otherwise, how can we call some of the hermits in ancient times men of great virtues even though they were never employed by the government? Do you understand?"

"Yes, I do," Precious Jade replied.

"There is another passage which I would like you to explain to me," said Tai-ju. He flipped a few more pages and pointed out the place for Precious Jade to see. It was the passage that contained the statement: "I have not met a man who loves virtue more than sex." [42]

Reading this statement, Precious Jade felt as if some one had used a needle to pierce his heart.[43] He said with a smile: "There is not much to say about this statement."

"Nonsense!" Tai-ju rejoined. "If this is the topic for you to write a theme on during the civil service examinations, will you still say that there is not much to write about it?"

Reluctantly Precious Jade explained this statement as follows: "The sage made this statement because he had seen with his own eyes that people preferred sex to virtue. Though both virtue and sex are inherent in our nature as men, people like sex infinitely more than they like virtue. They do not realize, however, that virtue represents Heavenly reason while sex denotes only human desires.[44] Few, if any, love Heavenly reason to the same extent they love human desires. Though this statement of Confucius conveys a feeling of sorrow and regret, its real purpose is to encourage people to change their evil ways. Even those who say that they love virtue do not love it to the same extent they love sex. Only when their love of virtue is as intense as their love of sex can it be truly said that they really love virtue."

"Your elaboration is not bad," Tai-ju commented. "I have a question for you, however. Since you have clearly understood the sage's sayings in both cases, why do you choose to violate them? I know your shortcomings very well even though I do not live inside your house and your father has never said anything about them. Why do you not wish to improve yourself? You are young, when 'the future of the young is unlimited.' It is completely up to you whether you can or cannot accomplish something worth while later in your life. Now I am giving you one-month time to review all the books which you have read. After that you have another month to read the model compositions. Then I shall assign you topics on which you will write your themes. I will not forgive you if you are lazy. As an ancient saying goes, 'Those who are satisfied cannot succeed; those who succeed will never be satisfied.' I hope that you will remember my words." Precious Jade answered "yes."

From then on Precious Jade had no choice except to do his assignments every day. . . .

[42] *Analects of Confucius*, roll 8.

[43] Precious Jade's reputation as a gay blade was known to practically everyone, including his teacher.

[44] Note the strong influence of Chu Hsi's interpretations.

194 · Liu Chih-chi: *My Education* [45]

By the order of my father I was exposed to literature at an early age. I was taught to read the *Book of History* in the ancient text when I was still in my breeches. I found the book extremely difficult to understand, and it was written in such a way that it was not easy to recite the words either. Despite repeated beatings, I failed to master it.

Meanwhile I enjoyed listening to my father when he lectured upon the *Commentaries of Tso* [46] to my elder brothers, while neglecting the work to which I had been assigned. After each lecture, I went to my elder brothers imploring them to explain it to me. "If all books were as interesting as the *Commentaries of Tso*," I said to myself, "I should not be so indifferent to learning as I have been." Happily surprised at my private wishes, my late father decided to teach me the *Commentaries of Tso*. The work was completed in one year; by then I was twelve years old. [47] Though I could not understand everything my father said, I had acquired a general idea of what this book contained. My father wanted me to become especially proficient in this particular classic and ordered me to read all comments and elaborations relating to it.

The *Commentaries of Tso* ended with the capture of the unicorn, [48] and I was anxious to know what followed afterwards. I wished to read more to broaden my knowledge and was advised to read the *Historical Records*, [49] *History of the Han*, [50] and *History of the Three Kingdoms*. [51] Moreover, in my desire to be familiar with the chronological developments of all major events in the past, I systematically read all facts relating to a particular subject. I found that I could acquire great understanding and insight without the help of teachers. I read all the important materials, from those of the regenerated Han [52] to the *Royal Records* [53] of the present dynasty. [54] I was then seventeen years old. [55]

Most of the books which I read were borrowed from other people. Often the volumes were incomplete; sometimes entire chapters were missing. Despite these handicaps, I had no difficulty tracing the broad trend of each event and assessing the main theme of each author. However, I was soon distracted from my favorite pursuit by the necessity of preparing for the civil service examinations. As my attention was diverted to the writing of acceptable compositions in order to pass the examination, I could no longer concentrate my mind on history. At

[45] The original appears as a preface to *The Understanding of History (Shih t'ung),* written by Liu Chih-chi (661–721), one of the greatest historians China has ever produced.

[46] The authorship of the *Commentaries* of *Tso* or *Tso chuan* was attributed to Tso Ch'iu-ming who lived perhaps in the fourth century B.C. It was written to supplement the *Spring and Autumn Annals,* allegedly written by Confucius.

[47] Eleven years old according to the Western custom.

[48] Acording to tradition, Confucius ended the *Spring and Autumn Annals* with the capture of a unicorn (a sacred, propitious animal) in c.481 B.C.

[49] *Shih chi* or *Historical Records* was written by Ssu-ma Ch'ien (second century B.C.).

[50] *Han shu* or *History of the Han* was written by Pan Ku (A.D. 32–92).

[51] *San-kuo chih* or *History of the Three Kingdoms* was written by Ch'en Shou (third century A.D.).

[52] This refers to the Later or East Han dynasty (A.D. 25–220).

[53] *Huang-chia shih-lu.*

[54] T'ang dynasty.

[55] Sixteen years old according to the Western custom.

the age of twenty [56] I passed the examination and acquired a governmental position. Once again I had time to devote myself to what I truly loved.

For many years I worked and traveled between Ch'angan and Loyang.[57] I borrowed books from private as well as public sources, and I indulged myself in reading everything I wished to read. For the history of each dynasty I read several schools of interpretations. I perused all writings pertaining to a particular period, including sketches, short stories, novels, and even mysteries, so as to enhance my own knowledge of the period in question.

I loved good reasoning even when I was a small child. Whatever understanding I had came mostly from my own reasoning process; it was not derived from reading other people's works. I recall that when I read the two Han histories [58] at a tender age, I felt that the *History of the Han* should not contain a chart of important persons throughout the ages and that the *History of the Later Han* should include a royal biography of Keng-shih.[59] Those who heard me scolded me for my impudence, saying that I, then only a little boy, should not criticize the great writers of the past. I was ashamed of myself and did not know how to answer. Later when I read the collective works of Chang Heng [60] and Fan Yeh, I was happy to know that the two Han histories were criticized on the same ground that I had once criticized them. There were numerous cases in which I reached my own conclusions which, I later found, were also shared by the great thinkers of the past. By then I concluded that it was useless to argue with contemporary scholars who only followed clichés, and when differing from others, I kept my opinion to myself.

After I passed thirty, my understanding became more profound, and my findings became even more numerous. To my regret, there were few scholars in the nation who shared my judgements and with whom I could discuss my ideas. The only exception was Hsü Chien of Tunghai [61] whom I met later in my life and with whom I maintained the most cordial relationship. Our friendship was such that it would well match that between Pai-ya and Chung Ch'i [62] or between Kuan Chung and Pao Shu [63] of ancient times. Among others with whom I exchanged ideas and shared interest were Chu Ch'ing-tse of Yungch'eng, Liu Ch'ung-chi of P'eikuo, Hsüeh Ch'ien-kuang of Yihsing, Yüan Hsing-ch'ung of Honan, Wu Ching of Ch'enliu, and Fei Huai-ku of Shuch'un. To these gentlemen I could express my opinions without feeling any restraint or reservation. Though it is true that "a virtue, to be a true virtue, will receive its due response," the people who understood me throughout the years were confined to these few mentioned above. . . .

[56] Nineteen according to the Western custom.
[57] Ch'angan was the cultural as well as political capital of T'ang China. Loyang was another center of culture.
[58] This refers to the *History of the Han* by Pan Ku and the *History of the Later Han* by Fan Yeh (fifth century A.D.).
[59] Keng-shih was the reign title of Liu Hsüan who revolted against the Hsin dynasty headed by Wang Mang early in the first century A.D. Since his regime lasted only a brief period, traditional historians in China debated for centuries as to whether he deserved a royal biography (*pen-chi* as contrary to *lieh-chuan* or biography) in the official dynastic history.
[60] Chang Heng (78–139), a famous poet and scientist of the Later Han dynasty.
[61] A subprefecture located in modern Kiangsu province.
[62] Lü Pai-ya and Chung Tzu-ch'i. See pp. 370–371.
[63] Kuan Chung and Pao Shu-ya. See pp. 369–370.

195 · OU-YANG HSIU: *A Footnote to the Essays of Han Yü* [64]

Hantung, the place where I spent my childhood, was remote from cultural centers and did not have many scholars. My family, being so poor, did not have a library of its own. Fortunately, there was a famous Li family in the southern section of the county whose son, Yao-fu, loved learning; I, as a child, often visited the Li household. During one of my visits I found many old books in a worn-out basket that was stored away inside a wall. Opening the basket, I found six rolls of Han Yü's essays [65] that were not arranged in a proper order, with some of the passages already missing. I borrowed this book from Mr. Li and took it home. Reading it, I found that the words were sincere and its views were broad. Being so young as I was, I did not really understand all of its meanings. I loved it because it had opened a new horizon for me.

In those years the scholars in the nation followed the style of Yang Yi and Liu Yün; [66] writings executed in such a style were called "contemporary writings" which, if mastered, would enable a person successfully to pass the civil service examinations, build a reputation for himself, and boast of his achievements among his contemporaries. To my knowledge, none of these scholars had spoken of Han Yü's essays.

Then I was working towards the *chin-shih* degree and was concentrating my efforts on poetry so as to pass the examination administered by the Ministry of Rites. At the age of seventeen, I took the examination in the provincial capital, but failed to pass. Once again I read my copy of Han Yü's essays, and I said to myself: "These are the very best that a scholar should strive to achieve." I was surprised that people paid no attention to them, though at that time I did not have a spare moment to pursue them either. However, their importance never left my mind even for a single moment; I vowed that once I received the *chin-shih* degree and thus earned a salary to support my parents, I would concentrate my efforts on Han Yü's essays so as to fulfill a personal wish that had been with me for a long time.

Seven years later, I passed the examinations and received the *chin-shih* degree, and subsequently became an official at Loyang.[67] Then people like Yin Shih-lu [68] were still around, and we all decided to write essays in the ancient style. I took out my own copy of Han Yü's essays and edited it, using the old copies from other people's holdings as references. From then on other scholars in the nation began to write essays in the ancient style, and Han Yü's name became gradually known throughout the empire. For more than thirty years, all scholars have learned to write in Han Yü's style. This is a very encouraging situation indeed. . . .

When I first discovered the *Han Yü,* it had been neglected by practically all scholars. I knew that I could not use it to please my contemporaries so as to

---

[64] *T'ang Sung san-wen hsien,* pp. 142–143.

[65] This is the same Han Yü whose writings appear in this chapter as Selections 189 and 191.

[66] Yang Yi and Liu Yün, both of whom lived in the first half of the eleventh century, were noted for their essays written in the "parallel form" *(p'ien t'i),* a highly ornamented style.

[67] Located in modern Honan province.

[68] His real name was Yin Chu, an authority on the *Spring and Autumn Annals.*

acquire power and influence, but I studied it nevertheless. Obviously I did not study it for worldly reasons; I did it merely to satisfy a long-time personal desire. During my career as a government official, I was never excessively jubilant when promoted or fearful when demoted. I attributed my emotional stability to the nature of the subject which I wished to learn and the strong will to pursue such learning despite the vicissitudes of my official life.

My copy of *Han Yü* was published in Shu; [69] the printing is sharp and clear and is of a better quality than that found in many contemporary editions. However, it contains many omissions and numerous typographical errors. For the past thirty years, whenever I heard of a better edition, I requested its owner to let me borrow it so as to make the necessary corrections. The last few rolls in my copy are incomplete, but I have chosen not to make the necessary redress because to do so would make the collection too voluminous.

Nowadays my library consists of ten thousand rolls. With the exception of Han Yü's essays, all of them are new acquisitions. Han Yü's works, as the property of all men, will be transmitted through thousands of generations and will be praised until eternity to come. As far as my copy is concerned, it has become an old friend, and I value it more highly than anything else.

196 · SHEN KUA: *The Invention of Movable Type* [70]

As late as the T'ang dynasty the production of books by block printing was still practiced on a limited scale. It was not until the time of the Later T'ang (923–936) that the government, upon the recommendation of its prime minister Feng Tao, first sponsored the reproduction of the *Five Classics* by block printing. From then on practically all important books were produced by block printing.

During the Ch'ing-li period (1041–1048) a commoner named Pi Sheng first invented the movable type. Each type was made of moistened clay upon which was carved one Chinese character. The portion that formed the character was as thin as the edge of a small coin. The type was then hardened by fire and thus made permanent.

To proceed with the process of printing, a printer smeared an iron plate with a mixture of turpentine, resin, wax, and burned paper ash. Pieces of movable type were then placed on the plate closely together and were arranged in such a way as to reflect the text of a book to be printed. They were confined within the plate by an iron fence fastened tightly to the plate.

The iron plate was then placed on a gentle fire in order to melt the mixture previously described. A wooden board with smooth surface was pressed upon the type so that the heads of all pieces would appear on the same level. The plate was then ready for printing.

The cost would be very high if the printer intended to print only two or three copies of a book. If on the other hand hundreds or thousands of copies were to be printed, the amount of time required to print each copy would be reduced to a minimum. Usually two plates were used when a book was printed. While one plate was in the process of printing, pieces of movable type were arranged and

[69] Modern Szechuan province.
[70] Source: *Meng-hsi Sketches (Meng-hsi pi-t'an)*, roll 18, by Shen Kua who lived in the eleventh century.

set on the other plate. When the required number of copies had been printed by the first plate, the second plate was ready. Thus the two plates changed their role alternately.

For each Chinese character there were several pieces of type. The number reached twenty or more for each of such commonly used characters as *chih* and *yeh*. The availability of a large number of the same piece of type was necessitated by the repeated occurrences of the same Chinese character on the page of a book to be printed. When pieces of type were not in use, they were covered with paper for the purpose of protection, were grouped together according to rhymes, and were stored away in wooden frames. Occasionally there were uncommon Chinese characters that had not been prepared in advance. In such cases the printer had to carve them on the spot, harden them by fire, and make them fit for printing in a minimum amount of time.

The fact that moistened clay, instead of wood, was used as the material to make movable type was because wood was subject to change and tended to distort the Chinese character carved on it. When exposed to moisture, the surface of a piece of wooden type became uneven, and the type itself became thus unusable. Moreover, after it had been glued to the plate by the mixture previously described, it was extremely difficult to detach it when this particular piece of type had to be used somewhere else. The movable type made of clay, on the other hand, encountered no such difficulties. When exposed to a gentle fire which melted the mixture that glued it to the plate, it required only a gentle push by the hand before it easily came loose from the plate.

197 · WANG P'U: *The Printing of the Nine Classics* [71]

In the second month of the third year of Ch'ang-hsing (A.D. 932) the First and Second Secretariats [72] petitioned the emperor for the printing of the *Nine Classics*,[73] the text of which would be based upon stone inscriptions. The Department of Cultural Affairs,[74] ordered by the emperor to be in charge of this undertaking, was to recruit professors and students to collect authentic copies based upon stone inscriptions. Each professor or student was to examine the different versions of a classic in which he specialized, and once the authentic version was determined, duplicate it by hand for as many copies as possible.

The Department of Cultural Affairs was also charged with the responsibility of hiring carvers who would make printing blocks in accordance with the adopted text based upon stone inscriptions. Copies of the *Nine Classics,* once printed, would be distributed throughout the empire. The imperial order made it clear that anyone who wished to copy any or all of the *Nine Classics* for his own use should copy from the authorized version which was now in printed form. He should not be allowed to use any of the unauthorized versions.

---

[71] Source: *The Institutions of the Five Dynasties (Wu-tai hui-yao)* by Wang P'u (d.982).

[72] *Chung-shu Meng-hsia.*

[73] The *Nine Classics* were *Book of Changes, Book of History, Book of Odes, Spring and Autumn Annals, Commentaries of Tso, Book of Rites, Chou Institutions, Book of Filial Piety, Analects of Confucius,* and *Book of Mencius.*

[74] *Kuo-tzu chien.*

In the fourth month of the same year Ma Kao, a tutor of the crown prince, T'ien Min, an official in the executive department,[75] and two professors were appointed by the emperor as overseers of the printing program. The Department of Cultural Affairs then selected the best calligraphers it could find and entrusted them with the duty of copying the text of the Nine Classics in "block" form.[76] The copied text was subsequently sent to the carvers to make printing blocks. The daily load was five sheets for the calligraphers and five printing blocks for the carvers.[77]

In the sixth month of the third year of Kuang-shun (A.D. 953), T'ien Min, the Commissioner of the Department of Cultural Affairs, presented to the emperor two sets of the *Nine Classics* in printed form, each set consisting of 130 volumes.[78]

Ho Ling, a writer of short poems and love songs, had accumulated 100 rolls of his own writings throughout the years. Being so vain as he was, he decided to print them at his own expense. Several hundred copies were printed, and were then distributed among his relatives and friends.[79]

198 · Ts'ao Hsüeh-ch'in: *Dr. Chang* [80]

About noon in the next day the doorkeeper came in and reported that Dr. Chang had arrived. Chia Chen escorted the doctor to the main hall where a servant served tea.

"You, sir, have been recommended to us by His Excellency Feng," said Chia Chen after the tea. "Not only are you upright in conduct and learned in scholarly pursuit but are also masterful in the field of medicine. Let me offer you my admiration and respect."

"On the contrary, sir," Dr. Chang replied. "I am uncultured as a gentleman and superficial as a scholar. Yesterday His Excellency Feng, in his usually generous manner, instructed your humble servant to repair to your honorable household. How dare I disobey His Excellency's order! Unlearned as I am, I am facing my assigned task with great apprehension."

"Do not be so modest, please!" said Chia Chen. "If there is not too much inconvenience, would you kindly go to the inner chamber to see my daughter-in-law? I trust that your ability will relieve me from my worries." After Chia Chen had finished these words, Chia Yung, his son, escorted the doctor to the inner chamber.

Entering the inner chamber, Dr. Chang saw a woman lying in bed. Turning to Chia Yung, he said: "Is she your honorable wife?"

---

[75] *Shang-shu.*

[76] See p. 417, Footnote 11.

[77] Since each printed sheet was equal to two pages in the Western sense, the normal load amounted to ten pages daily. Normally only one side of a sheet of paper was printed.

[78] The reader may notice that the entire project took twenty-one years (932–953) to complete.

[79] Ho Ling, who died in A.D. 955 at the age of fifty-eight, was a distinguished literary figure of his time.

[80] *The Dream of the Red Chamber (Hung-lou meng),* roll 10.

"Yes, sir," Chia Yung replied. "Please be seated. Do you mind if I describe to you her illness before you feel the pulse?"

"In my humble opinion, sir, I should first feel her pulse before I seek information from you about the causes of her illness. This is the first time that I have had the privilege of visiting your honorable household of which I must admit my ignorance. I was instructed to come here by His Excellency Feng whose wishes I consider a great honor to observe. Please let me feel the pulse first and then tell me whether my diagnosis is correct. Only later shall I ask you to describe the symptoms of her illness. We shall then deliberate a prescription most befitting her situation. It is up to you, sir, to decide whether you will use this prescription." [81]

"I have nothing but the highest confidence in you, sir," said Chia Yung. "Feel the pulse, if you please. Then tell us whether my wife can recover her normal health. I would like to relieve my parents from their worries."

The maids placed a huge pillow behind the patient's back and gently pulled her right hand out from the sleeve. The doctor placed his fingers on her wrist to feel the pulse and concentrated for about fifteen minutes. He did the same with her left hand and then said: "Let us go outside."

Outside in the antechamber Chia Yung and the doctor sat side by side in a couch, and a maid again served tea. After the tea the doctor was asked whether the illness was curable.

"Having felt the pulse of your honorable wife," said the doctor, "I would like to venture the following opinions. Her left pulse is heavy and slow, and the beat of her left joint is feeble and concealed. Her right pulse is weak and thin, and the beat of her right joint is spiritless and empty. The heaviness and slowness of her left pulse result from the weakening of her heart which in turn generate the element of 'fire,' and the feeble and concealed beat of her left joint comes as a result of the lack of sufficient blood in her liver. The weak and thin beat of her right pulse can be attributed to the feebleness of her lungs, and the lack of spirit in her right joint results from the fact that the liver, which represents the element of 'wood,' has completely dominated the spleen which represents the element of 'earth.'

"The generation of 'fire' that results from a weakening of the heart affects a woman's menstruation which, consequently, becomes irregular. It also causes sleeplessness at night. The lack of sufficient blood in her liver results in swelling and pain below the ribs, lateness in menstruation, and burning sensation inside the heart. The feebleness of her lungs causes periodical dizziness as if she were sitting in a boat, and also perspiration during the early hours of the morning. When the liver has completely controlled and dominated the spleen, a person does not feel like to drink or eat; she is tired easily; and her four limbs, being limp, have no strength. These should be the symptoms if my diagnosis is correct. I should have nothing to say if people insist that the honorable wife of yours is pregnant."

"How correct you are!" said the nursemaid who had attended the patient during the latter's illness. "You, sir, are like a god who knows everything without us uttering one word. Several doctors have attended our mistress, but none has been able to speak so accurately as you do. Some of them say that she is merely

---

[81] A good Chinese physician was supposedly able to tell the causes and symptoms of an illness by simply feeling the pulse. Chia Yung's suggestion that the doctor should be informed of the symptoms before he felt the pulse had apparently offended the doctor.

pregnant; others say that she is really ill. Some say that everything will be all right; others say that the crucial moment will arrive around the winter solstice. None of them has ever told us the truth."

"The illness of your honorable mistress has been unnecessarily prolonged by these doctors," said Dr. Chang. "If she took the right medicine when the first menstrual irregularity began, she would have been well now. It seems that she has been destined by fate for such long sufferings. As far as I can see, her illness is still 30 percent curable. If she has a good sleep after taking the medicine, her chance of recovery will be increased to 50 percent. From what I can observe by feeling the pulse, your mistress is a very ambitious and highly intelligent person. If a person is too intelligent, she is bound to have more than her fair share of unhappiness. An intelligent person worries often; and worries affect the spleen adversely and make the liver unusually strong and dominant. The net result is the irregularity of her menstruation. The irregularity takes the form of lateness rather than early arrival. Am I correct on this?"

"Yes," said the nursemaid. "Her menstruation always comes too late rather than too early. Sometimes it is overdue by two or three days, and other times by as long as ten days."

"Now we have found the cause of this illness," said the doctor. "If she had taken tranquilizing drugs, her illness would not have deteriorated to such an extent. As far as I can see, this is a clear case of 'strong fire' and 'weak water.' The purpose of my prescription is to reestablish the balance." The doctor wrote down the prescription and then handed it over to Chia Yung. The prescription read as follows:

A Prescription to Nourish the Spleen and the Liver

Ginseng, 0.2 ozs.; *Podophyllum versipelle* (roasted), 0.2 ozs.; "cloudy" fungus, 0.3 ozs.; "cooked earth," 0.4 ozs.; *kuei-shen*, 0.2 ozs.; white peony roots, 0.2 ozs.; *Cnidium officinale* (Szechuanese), 0.15 ozs.; *Astragalus reflexistipulus*, 0.3 ozs.; roasted rice, 0.2 ozs.; *Dioscorea japonica* (Huai), 0.2 ozs.; *chen-a-chiao* (fried with clam powder), 0.2 ozs.; *Bupleurum sachalinense* (sour and roasted), 0.08 ozs.; *Corydalis ambigna* (fried with wine), 0.15 ozs.; *Glyoyrrhiza glabra* (burned), 0.05 ozs.

Catalysts: seven lotus-seeds minus kernals, and two large plums.[82]

Looking over the prescription, Chia Yung said: "This looks very good to me. Please tell me: Is my wife's life really in danger?"

"An intelligent man like you should know that when a person is as sick as your honorable wife is, nobody can forecast the outcome," Dr. Chang replied. "Let her take this prescription first, and we shall see what fate has in store for us. If I were you, I would not expect too much improvement before this winter. We shall place our hope sometime in the spring."

Being so intelligent, Chia Yung did not ask any more questions. He escorted the doctor to the front door and then discussed the prescription with his father.[83]

[82] Some of the herbs used in this prescription cannot be easily identified in the English language.
[83] Despite Dr. Chang's efforts, the patient died shortly afterwards.

APPENDIX ONE

Chinese Dynasties

Hsia, *c*. 2205–c. 1766 B.C.

Shang, *c*. 1766–c. 1122 B.C.

Chou, *c*. 1122–249 B.C.

West Chou, *c*. 1122–771 B.C.
East Chou, 770–249 B.C.
Spring and Autumn period, 722–481 B.C.
Warring States period, 403–221 B.C.

Ch'in, 221–207 B.C.

Han, 202 B.C.–A.D. 220

Former Han, 202 B.C.–A.D. 9
Hsin, A.D. 9–23
Later Han, A.D. 25–220

Three Kingdoms

Wei, 220–265
Shu, 221–265
Wu, 222–280

Tsin, 265–420

West Tsin, 265–317
East Tsin, 317–420

Southern and Northern Dynasties

South

Liu Sung, 420–479
Ch'i, 479–502
Liang, 502–557
Ch'en, 557–589

Southern and Northern Dynasties (Cont.)

North

Later (North) Wei, 386–535
East Wei, 534–550
West Wei, 535–556
North Ch'i, 550–577
North Chou, 557–581

Sui, 590–618

T'ang, 618–906

Five Dynasties, 907–960

Later Liang, 907–923
Later T'ang, 923–936
Later Tsin, 936–947
Later Han, 947–950
Later Chou, 951–960

Sung, 960–1279

North Sung, 960–1126
South Sung, 1127–1279
Liao, 907–1125
West Hsia, 990–1227
Chin, 1115–1234

Yüan, 1260–1368

Ming, 1368–1644

Ch'ing, 1644–1912

Republic, 1912–

People's Republic, 1949–

Transliteration and Pronunciation of Chinese Names

The following rules are generally observed in this book in the transliteration of Chinese names:

1. For names long familiar to Western readers, the standardized forms are used: *Confucius, Mencius, Peking, Nanking,* etc.

2. All other names are romanized according to the Wade-Giles system.

3. Personal names consisting of two Chinese characters are joined by a hyphen: *Tuan-lin, Shou-jen,* etc. This practice is also followed when the name is actually a title: *Wen-ti* (Emperor Wen), *Wu-ti* (Emperor Wu), etc.

4. Geographical names have no hyphens even though they contain two or more Chinese characters: *Ch'angan, Ch'üanchou, Shanhaikuan,* etc. A hyphen will be inserted, however, if a name with two Chinese characters actually represents two distinct geographical entities: *Yun-Kwei* (Yunnan and Kweichow provinces), *Kiang-Huai* (the Yangtze and the Huai River), etc. One might also notice that the first letter of each of the second components is capitalized.

5. All Sinicized foreign names with two or more Chinese characters are romanized with hyphens to separate one Chinese character from the other: *Hsiung-nu, Ta-yüeh-chih, A-mei,* etc. An exception is made in instances when standardized English equivalents have been long in use: *Kublai Khan* instead of *Hu-pi-lieh,* for instance.

In short, the Wade-Giles system is followed unless there are valid reasons for not doing so. Though this system does not provide the exact pronunciation of Chinese words, it will be useful for students to observe the following simple key:

a as in t*a*r	*e* as in *e*ver
i as the first *e* in *e*voke	*o* as in b*o*ne
u as in r*u*ne	*ü* as the German *ü*
ai as the *i* in l*i*ne	*ao* as the *ow* in c*ow*
ou as the *o* in *o*bey	
ch as the *j* in *j*ust	*ch'* as in *ch*ance
k as the *g* in *g*ift	*k'* as in *k*ind
p as the *b* in *b*at	*p'* as in *p*age
t as the *d* in *d*og	*t'* as in *t*op
ts and *tz* as *dz*	*ts'* as in oa*ts*
tz' as in quar*tz*	*hs* as *sh* in *sh*ip
j has no English equivalent but is pronounced more like *r* than like *j*	*ss* is pronounced as *s*

Index